D1068616

Courtesy Marshall DeMotte, Esq.

This hitherto unknown photograph shows the Abraham Lincoln contemporary writers described, but whom the camera seemed never able to portray. Marshall DeMotte of Oakland, California, revealed it to the world in 1949 through the Abraham Lincoln Association. On the back of the original print there appears in the handwriting of Mr. DeMotte's father this notation: *This is one of the last, if not the last, taken of Mr. Lincoln. I got it at Gardner's in Washington a few days before the assassination because of the striking likeness. W. H. DeMotte, Indpl's, Ind., Jan. 10, '94.*

Mr. Marshall DeMotte further explains: "Father told me once that Mr. Nicolay, Mr. Lincoln's secretary, told him he thought it the best of Mr. Lincoln's photographs." William H. DeMotte (1830–1910) served as Military and Sanitary Agent of Indiana during the Civil War by appointment of Governor Oliver Perry Morton. The present owner of the photograph has a long record of public service in California. (Reproduced by special permission.)

# Lincoln and the Press

by ROBERT S. HARPER

E457
H295

UNIVERSITY OF
PITTSBURGH LIBRARY

McGRAW-HILL BOOK COMPANY, INC.

*New York*      *London*      *Toronto*

E 457
H 295
cop. 1

## LINCOLN AND THE PRESS

Copyright, 1951, by Robert S. Harper. All rights in this book are reserved. It may not be used for dramatic, motion-, or talking-picture purposes without written authorization from the holder of these rights. Nor may the book or parts thereof be reproduced in any manner whatsoever without permission in writing, except in the case of brief quotations embodied in critical articles and reviews. For information, address the McGraw-Hill Book Company, Inc., Trade Department, 330 West 42d Street, New York 18, New York.

Published by the McGraw-Hill Book Company, Inc.

PRINTED IN THE UNITED STATES OF AMERICA

*to* LUCY HESS HOLMES, *with love*

4/3/57 local

# A Note of Gratitude

THE KNOWLEDGE, labors, and patience of several persons other than myself have gone into this book. To C. Gibson Scheaffer of the McGraw-Hill Book Company, Inc., I am indebted for guidance until the manuscript became an actuality. For explicit direction, I thank Allan Nevins of Columbia University. F. Lauriston Bullard of Boston tendered helpful advice. Constructive services were extended by Margaret A. Flint, reference librarian of the Illinois State Historical Library. Florence J. Kennedy of the Maryland Historical Society helped me solve the Baltimore chapter. Robert C. Wheeler of the Ohio State Archaeological and Historical Society made valuable newspaper files available. Librarians in Springfield, New York, Chicago, Philadelphia, Baltimore, Indianapolis, Albany, and other cities also helped assemble the newspaper files, and the contribution of the New York Public Library was especially important. The staff of the State Library at Columbus was always helpful in selection of source books. James E. Pollard of Ohio State University aided in solving knotty problems. Roy P. Basler, executive secretary of The Abraham Lincoln Association, stood always ready to assist me. I wish to express my deep appreciation to Marshall DeMotte of Oakland, California, for permission to use his unknown photograph of Abraham Lincoln. The professional services of Josephine Duvall constitute a chapter in the personal history of *Lincoln and the Press*. Carrying a load of drudgery during the years this book was in preparation were Maryellen Johnson, who acted as my secretary; my son Robert, who helped gather the illustrations; and my wife, who read and criticized.

ROBERT S. HARPER

# Preface

ONE MAJOR BOOK on Abraham Lincoln remained to be written: the story of his handling of the press and how the press reacted to him from the day he became a voice in politics until the shot was fired that martyred him. As a newspaperman for many years, a lifelong admirer of Lincoln, and student of the Civil War period, I set myself the task of producing this volume.

Works by earlier writers had hinted at the rich store of information to be explored. After exhausting these sources I went into the yellowing files of the newspapers themselves. There it lay, the whole story of Lincoln and the press. Speaking from those dusty pages were a few editors who saw the contemporary Lincoln as a great man. But speaking in louder tones were those who hated him. Those files—incredible though it may seem today—bared an awesome story.

Freedom of the press, guaranteed by the Constitution of the United States, was established as one of the blessings of democracy. But the molders of the Constitution made no provision for handling a sectional and intensely partisan press in a period of civil strife. Whether the press should remain free when the safety of the nation is paramount raised a question which is still unanswered. Lincoln had no precedent. He set his own.

The struggle between the opposition press and the Federal government—long since forgotten and interred with the bones of Lincoln's contemporaries—was one of the major problems of the great conflict. Deep-lying political currents were brought into the open to plague a harassed president trying to save the Union. The Constitution was strained until it threatened to crack.

From the pages of newspapers of the Civil War period there emerges a new facet to the many-sided Lincoln and there emerges, too, the heretofore untold story of significant events on the home front.

R.S.H.

# Contents

# Lincoln and the Press

# 1 Newspaper Correspondent

ON A JUNE DAY in 1836 a newspaper printer stood before a type case to set a letter to the editor. He held his composing stick in one hand; the other moved back and forth across the case as the deft fingers set four paragraphs in single-column measure. He then picked up eight letters to form the signature. Those eight letters spelled A. Lincoln.

That was the first time Abraham Lincoln, born of Kentucky hill folk in 1809, reared in Indiana wilderness and self-educated, used the newspaper press as a political tool. It was the first outcropping of a predilection for newspaper writing that shaped the course of his life and left its mark on the history of his country.

He was twenty-seven years old, a candidate for reelection to the Illinois state legislature, living in the village of New Salem. He had served as a captain of militia in the Black Hawk War and had been the village postmaster. In a clearing seven miles away, the first summer's grass was growing on the grave of Ann Rutledge, whom Lincoln had loved.

Lincoln wrote the letter to the editor of the *Sangamo Journal*, published at nearby Springfield, dating it June 13, 1836. It appeared in the weekly newspaper on June 18, prominently displayed on page three of the four-page edition. It said:

To the editor of the *Journal:*

In your paper of last Saturday I see a communication over the signature of "Many Voters," in which the candidates who are announced in the *Journal* are called upon to "show their hands." Agreed. Here's mine.

I go for all sharing the privileges of the government who assist in bearing its burdens. Consequently, I go for admitting all whites to the right of suffrage who pay taxes or bear arms (by no means excluding females).

If elected, I shall consider the whole people of Sangamon my constituents, as well those that oppose as those that support me.

While acting as their representative, I shall be governed by their will on all subjects upon which I have the means of knowing what their will is; and upon all others, I shall do what my own judgment teaches me will best advance their interests. Whether elected or not, I go for distributing the proceeds of the sales of the public lands to the several States, to enable our State, in common with others, to dig canals and construct railroads without borrowing money and paying the interest on it. If alive on the first Monday in November, I shall vote for Hugh L. White for President.

Very respectfully,
A. Lincoln.[1]

Seven men were sent to the House by Sangamon County, and Lincoln led the ticket.[2] The legislative sessions were held at Vandalia, then the state capital. One of the first acts of the new legislature was the designation of the *Illinois State Register and Vandalia Republican* as the "official paper" to report the legislative action. The newspaper was launched in 1836 by William Walters, whose editorial assistant was Charles H. Lanphier.[3]

With Lincoln's return to Vandalia, the *Sangamo Journal* gained a news correspondent in the Capital. The editor of that newspaper was Simeon Francis, who established it in 1831. The files of the *Journal* during the period Lincoln was at Vandalia reveal a series of quaintly written articles about the goings-on in the legislative hall, and some authorities are convinced they were written by the tall Sangamon Solon.[4]

The *Journal* of January 6, 1837, carries a satirical letter in which the correspondent pretends he was formerly employed by the *National Intelligencer* at Washington but quit because he could not make a living there.[5] There are many other letters in the *Journal* files during the next few years that bear the unmistakable sign of Lincoln. These are signed "Johnny Blubberhead, Citizen of Sangamon, Conservative, Our Correspondent and Sampson's Ghost." Lincoln later used the pseudonyms Old Settler and Rebecca.

As Whig floor leader, Lincoln was a man of some importance during his second term. Soon the *Sangamo Journal* was publishing Lincoln's speeches at Vandalia, the first appearing January 28, 1837. It was a defense of the state bank at Springfield. Francis exalted the speaker in an accompanying editorial, saying, "Mr. Lincoln's remarks . . . in this paper are quite to the point. Our friend carries the true Kentucky rifle, and when he fires seldom fails of sending the shot home."[6]

The Illinois legislature chose Springfield as the permanent capital in February, 1837, and during that same spring Lincoln moved there from New Salem to practice law. He was admitted to the bar on March 1 by the state supreme court. The new attorney had an office with John T. Stuart, but the dingy room could not compete with the bustling editorial department of the *Sangamo Journal*. He made the newspaper office his loafing place, telling stories and talking politics.[7] The editor and his wife treated Lincoln as one of the family, and a lifelong friendship was formed. William H. Herndon, one of Lincoln's law partners, observed that the attorney practically took over the newspaper, having "undisputed control" for years and that whatever he wrote was published on the editorial page.[8]

Lincoln had lived in Springfield only a few weeks when he got his editor friend in hot water. On behalf of a widow, he filed suit for recovery of land against former Major General James Adams. At the same time, Lincoln began to attack Adams in the *Journal* through a series of anonymous letters signed "Sampson's Ghost." The first appeared on June 24, 1837.[9] Adams was a candidate for probate judge on the Democratic ticket, and he replied to the "ghost" letters through the columns of the *Republican*, Springfield's Democratic newspaper.

A handbill addressed "To The People" appeared in the *Journal* on August 19, making further charges against Adams and ending thusly: "I shall not subscribe my name; but I hereby authorize the editor of the 'Journal' to give it up to any one that may call for it." In an editor's note that followed, Simeon Francis explained that he had been falsely accused of refusing to give the name of the writer and "to save any farther remarks on this subject, I now state that A. Lincoln, Esq., is the author of the hand-bill in question."[10]

Adams won the election, but he and Lincoln continued their newspaper duel. Lincoln wrote at least two more letters, signing them with his own name, and he probably wrote a third, signed "An Old Settler."[11]

The state government finally moved to Springfield in 1839 and brought its "official paper" with it, Walters having been appointed state printer, a well-paying political sop. Walters renamed his newspaper the *Illinois State Register*.[12] At the next session of the legislature, Lincoln went to bat for his friend Francis by bringing about the appointment of a special committee to inquire into "the very large expenditure for public printing." Lyman Trumbull, a Democrat, was named chairman. As soon as the investigation opened, the *Journal* charged Walters was overpaid. Nothing came of the inquiry, and the *Register* crowed in victory, asking why Lincoln, who had served on the committee, did not file a minority report.[13]

The *Register* observed that Lincoln was back in the House, having "recovered from his indisposition," although he attended all meetings of the investigators.[14]

The "indisposition" to which the *Register* referred was a period of melancholy suffered by Lincoln after a breakup of his engagement to Mary Todd, a transplanted Kentucky belle; some say he was to have married her at the home of her sister, Mrs. Ninian Edwards, on January 1, 1841.[15]

Lincoln's state of mind at that time was reflected in a poem which he wrote for the *Journal*. It was called *Suicide*.[16]

The breakup of the romance between Lincoln and Mary Todd worried Mrs. Francis, and she resolved to attempt a reconciliation. She was a leader in Springfield social circles and noted for her entertainments and parties. Determined that Lincoln and Mary should meet again, she invited them to her next affair.[17]

The reunion party was a success; soon Lincoln and Mary Todd were meeting secretly in the Francis parlor. The courtship continued as a secret affair, known to none but the editor and his wife, until Mary's sister heard about it. Mrs. Edwards asked Mary why she was concealing Lincoln's renewed attentions, and she said she thought it best to keep her affairs to herself.[18]

The Illinois state auditor was James Shields, three years older than Lincoln and a native of County Tyrone, Ireland. He was a leader in the Democratic party in Illinois, and the general assembly elected him state auditor in 1839. The choice of Shields was a disappointment to Lincoln, who had written to the Governor four years before in behalf of Levi Davis for auditor. When the choice was left to the assembly in 1839, the Whigs, including Lincoln, voted for Davis. Shields was re-elected in 1841.[19]

Shields, a cultured and educated man, was a friend of Stephen A. Douglas, another young Democrat, who had paid marked attention to Mary Todd.[20] In the summer of 1842, Shields had his troubles; the state bank of Illinois having failed in February, the state issued an order that no longer would the Springfield Bank notes be accepted in payment of taxes. The action caused an economic crisis in the state, and the auditor bore the brunt of the people's wrath.[21] His opponents, who included Lincoln, attacked him from all sides. Lincoln's dislike for Shields, both politically and personally, dated back to December 24, 1836, when he wrote a newsletter from Vandalia that ridiculed the future auditor as "Paddy Shields."[22]

The financial condition of the state and the plight of the taxpayers became the main topic of conversation in Springfield; Lincoln and Mary Todd probably talked of it in their secret meetings at the Francis home. From these gay little evenings emerged the famous "Lost Townships" letters, published in the *Sangamo Journal* in August and September, 1842. The letters ridiculed Shields.

The first letter from the "Lost Townships" was published in the *Sangamo Journal* on August 19, 1842; it was dated August 10, 1842, signed "Rebecca." It occupied the first column on page three. The second, published September 2, was dated August 27 and held the same position. Two more letters appeared, both in the issue of September 9; one on page two, column five, the other on page three.[23]

No explanation is offered for publication of two letters in a single issue, but it is reasonable to suppose the printer ran short of type when he closed page two and reached for the galley as filler. The *Journal*, meanwhile, published a long editorial highly critical of Shields and his bank proclamation, although the order was authorized by the governor and treasurer of Illinois.[24]

Of the two letters published on September 9, one was dated August 27, the other September 8. It was the September 8 letter that left Shields no choice but to challenge the writer to a duel. A portion of this letter reads:

I have long expected to die a widow; but, as Mr. S . . . is rather good looking than otherwise, I must say I don't care if we compromise the matter by—really, Mr. Printer, I can't help blushin'—but I—it must come out—I—but widowed modesty—well, if I must, I must—wouldn't he—maybe sorter let the old grudge drap if I was to consent to be—be—h-i-s w-i-f-e? I know he's a fightin' man, and would rather fight than eat; but isn't marryin' better than fightin', though it does sometimes run into it . . . ? But, after all, maybe I'm countin' my chickins before they are hatched, and dreamin' of matrimonial bliss when the only alternative reserved for me may be a lickin'. Jeff tells me the way these fire-eaters do is to give the challenged party choice of weapons, etc., which bein' the case, I'll tell you in confidence that I never fights with anything but broomsticks or hot water or a shovelful of coals or some such thing; the former of which, being somewhat like a shillalah, may not be very objectionable to him. I will give him choice, however, in one thing, and that is, whether, when we fight, I shall wear breeches or he petticoats, for, I presume that change is sufficient to place us on an equality.

The letter was signed "Rebecca" and carried this postscript: "Jist say to your friend, if he concludes to marry rather than fight, I shall inforce one condition, that is, if he should ever happen to gallant any young gals home of nights from our house, he must not squeeze their hands."[25]

It is generally agreed that this letter was written by Mary Todd and her intimate friend, Julia M. Jayne, to whom the secret of the Lincoln-Todd renewed romance had been divulged.[26] Shields was in Quincy when the letters were published, and he returned to Springfield to read in the *Journal* a verse of eighteen lines, signed "Cathleen," and purporting to show "Rebecca" had won "Erin's son."[27] That, too, is believed to have been written by the Misses Todd and Jayne.

Shields sent a friend, John D. Whiteside, to the editor of the *Journal* to demand the name of the letter writer. Francis reluctantly admitted Lincoln had written the entire "Rebecca" series but did not mention the part the girls had in the affair because Lincoln told him he would assume all responsibility.[28]

Shields challenged Lincoln to a duel, and he accepted, specifying cavalry broadswords as his choice of weapons. They were to face each other across a plank set edgewise in the ground. The site chosen was in Missouri, across the Mississippi from Alton, Ill. Lincoln and Shields removed their coats and were ready to fight when sanity finally prevailed. Shields's seconds took back his challenge note to Lincoln, and the latter's formal apology was read.

In justice to Shields, it should be stated he withdrew his challenge when his friends told him Lincoln accepted to protect the name of Mary Todd.[29]

Lincoln never again wrote anonymous letters to lampoon any person. All his recorded writings and public statements are free of any word of insult. He continued to write on politics for the *Journal*, but nothing like the "Rebecca" correspondence ever appeared again.

For days after the duel affair, the Springfield newspapers carried stories about it, mainly because the men who had acted as seconds fell to quarreling and began to hurl challenges at each other. Editor Francis published all the formal correspondence as both sides rushed into print.[30] The names of neither Mary Todd nor Miss Jayne appeared in the newspaper. No duels were fought except with printer's ink, but the excitement around town must have been intense for days.

The result was that the whole town knew Abraham Lincoln was courting Mary Todd again and that he had offered to fight a duel to save her honor. Late in the afternoon of November 4, 1842, Lincoln said to James H. Matheny, "Jim, I shall have to marry that girl," and asked him to be his best man.[31] That evening, in a hastily arranged ceremony at the Edwards's home, Mary Todd became Mrs. Abraham Lincoln.

# 2 "Out Damned Spot"

IN HIS FIRST BID for election to Congress, Abraham Lincoln was one of three who sought the Whig nomination in the Seventh Illinois District, the others being John J. Hardin and Edward D. Baker. Lincoln had been married six months when the Sangamon County Whigs pledged their delegation to Baker for the Congressional convention at Pekin. This action forced Lincoln out of the race. Hardin was nominated and subsequently elected in August of 1843, a month that also saw the birth of Lincoln's first-born, a son, Robert Todd.[1] Lincoln then looked forward to 1844, but Baker was the choice that time and succeeded Hardin in Washington.

Again Lincoln was forced to bide his time and began to build his political fences for 1846. He finally won the nomination in a Whig convention at Petersburg, May 1, 1846,[2] to face as his opponent Peter Cartwright, a Democrat, Methodist preacher, and circuit rider.[3] He won the nomination after carrying the party fight straight to the Whig newspaper editors of his district.

In the fall of 1845, Lincoln learned Hardin might seek a second nomination, and he wrote to B. F. James, editor of the *Tazewell Whig*, saying he feared the party papers in the district might swing to the former Congressman. He asked nothing appear in the *Whig* that might hurt his own chances.[4]

A week later, Lincoln again wrote to James, calling his attention to a recent article on the same subject in the *Sangamo Journal*. Lincoln said the article for the *Journal* was written without consultation with him, but the editor told him of its contents before publication.[5] Lincoln also wrote to Henry E. Dummer, an attorney, asking him to see Sylvester Emmons, editor of the *Beardstown Gazette*, to make sure he took no stand that would injure him.[6]

Just as Lincoln feared, Hardin announced his candidacy and proposed he and Lincoln submit their names to a limited primary.[7] Lincoln acted quickly. He wrote to James of the *Tazewell Whig* on January 16, 1846, asking him to publish an article in support of the system by which Baker

and Hardin had been nominated.⁸ James followed orders and sent
Lincoln a copy of the article, receiving in return a letter in which
Lincoln told him he had stated the case properly. Lincoln said he
intended to have the article reprinted in the *Sangamo Journal*.⁹ Hardin
withdrew and left Lincoln a clear field for the nomination.

Ten days after Lincoln was nominated, the United States declared
war against Mexico; 50,000 volunteers were called, and 300,000 responded. Hardin enlisted and was made a colonel. Baker came from
Washington and recruited a regiment. James Shields, who held the
office of general land commissioner at Washington, was made a brigadier
general in charge of all Illinois troops. William Walters of the *Illinois
State Register* left his paper for the army, never to return, and Charles
H. Lanphier took full control.

The *Sangamo Journal*, leading Lincoln's campaign, demanded Presi-
dent James K. Polk adopt a sterner policy with Mexico, charging the
United States government had been insulted and the people robbed.¹⁰
The *Journal's* editorial policy was in line with speeches made by
Lincoln during his campaign, both he and Cartwright supporting the
declaration of war.¹¹

About a month after Lincoln won his race for Congress, the Illinois
state legislature elected Congressman Stephen A. Douglas to the United
States Senate, the "Little Giant" being at that time thirty-three years
old.

While waiting to leave for Washington, Lincoln attended a river-
and-harbor convention in Chicago. The convention attracted national
attention and drew 20,000 men. Newspaper correspondents came from
Eastern cities, among them Horace Greeley of the *New York Tribune*
and Thurlow Weed of the *Albany* (N. Y.) *Evening Journal*. Lincoln
got his name in the *New York Tribune* by saying something in reply
to David Dudley Field, a New York attorney. Only Greeley thought
the incident was important. He wrote, "Hon. Abraham Lincoln, a tall
specimen of an Illinoian, just elected to Congress from the only Whig
District in the state, was called out, and spoke briefly and happily in
reply to Mr. Field."¹²

Hardin was killed at Buena Vista. Shields was wounded but survived
to fight in another war. Baker's gallantry made the headlines. The war
had been in progress more than a year and a half and was in its final
stages when Lincoln went to Washington in December of 1847 to
claim his seat in Congress, taking his family with him.¹³

Early enthusiasm for the war had subsided, and the Whigs saw
an opportunity to make political fortune at expense of the Democrats;

the Whig press began to express doubts and dissatisfaction. The situation in Illinois was typical. The *Illinois State Register*, always Democratic, on November 12, 1847, quoted the *Rockford Forum* as saying "it cannot now be doubted" the people want peace. The *Register* retorted: "They desire for mere political effect to make the whole Mexican war a farce." Lincoln's old friend, the *Quincy Whig*, asserted: "The war is already becoming distasteful to the public mind."[14]

On December 13, seven days after Lincoln took his oath of office, he wrote to his young law partner, Herndon, in Springfield, "As you are all so anxious for me to distinguish myself, I have concluded to do so before long."[15] On December 22, when he had sat in Congress only two weeks, Lincoln introduced resolutions in the House in which eight questions were addressed to President Polk, demanding he tell the exact spot where the first blood was shed by Americans at the hands of the Mexicans. He used the word "spot" three times, and his eight interrogatories became known as the "Spot Resolutions."[16]

The Washington correspondent of the *Baltimore Patriot* wrote that the Lincoln resolutions "stick to the *spot* in Mexico, where the first blood of the war was shed, with all the tightness that characterized the fabled shirt of the fabled Nisus. Evidently there is music in that very tall Mr. Lincoln."[17] The *Illinois State Register*, on January 7, 1848, declared the Whig voters in the Seventh District in Illinois, many of them in the army and some dead, had never expected their Congressman to oppose the war.

A resolution of thanks to General Zachary Taylor, a war hero and a Whig, with a rider attached that said the war was "unnecessarily and unconstitutionally" started by Polk, was offered by the Whigs in Congress. The resolution passed by one vote, a strictly party affair, with Lincoln voting for it.[18] Back home at Springfield, the *Illinois State Register* wanted to know what the "gallant heroes" would think of Lincoln.[19]

Lincoln resumed his assault on January 12 with a demand that the President answer his questions, and he called Polk "a bewildered, confounded, and miserably perplexed man."[20]

Fortunately for Lincoln, the press paid scant attention to his political tirade, and it would have passed virtually unnoticed except for the Springfield newspapers. But it was the Springfield newspapers that the voters of the Seventh District read. Both the *Illinois State Register* and the *Illinois Journal*[21] carried the "Spot Resolutions," the *Register* denouncing Lincoln in an editorial headed, "Out Damned Spot."[22]

When Lincoln followed the resolutions with his speech, the *Journal* printed the text and challenged the *Register* to do likewise.[23]

The *Register* published an imaginary reply to Lincoln's speech in Congress which it called, "Speech Not Delivered in the House of Representatives in Reply to Mr. Lincoln of Illinois." This journalistic effusion said Lincoln's speech was an "imbecile" effort and that everybody had read abler ones "in the most obscure" Whig newspapers.[24]

The *Illinois Journal* countered by publishing an article purportedly clipped from the *Missouri Republican* of St. Louis. It said:

Washington, D. C. Jan. 12, 1848.—In the House today, the Hon. Abraham Lincoln . . . defined his position on the war, and took up the question of the right of Texas to all of the territory this side of the Rio Grande. . . . He commanded the attention of the House, which none but a strong man can do . . . the people may well feel proud of such a representative.[25]

Senator Douglas, always backed by the *Illinois State Register,* defended the administration in a speech that delighted Democrats everywhere. The *Register* published it in full and dared the *Journal* to print it.[26] The files of the *Journal* show it remained silent.

The attack on Lincoln had just begun. Under the headline, "Another 'Spot' For Lincoln," on March 10, 1848, the *Register* published resolutions passed in a Morgan County Democratic meeting that declared: "Henceforth will this Benedict Arnold of our district be known here only as the Ranchero Spotty of one term."[27] The *Peoria Democratic Press* called Lincoln "a second Benedict Arnold," and the *Belleville Advocate* said the Whig Congressman's course "in denouncing his country" would be condemned.[28]

The fighting in Mexico had been over for months and the peace treaty signed when Lincoln wrote a letter to Horace Greeley, saying the *New York Tribune* of June 27, 1848, had erred in a statement about the Texas boundary line. He wanted a correction. Enclosing a copy of a speech he made on "this very point," he asked Greeley to read it.[29]

Lincoln did not seek reelection, and the nomination went to his former law partner, Stephen T. Logan, who ran on Lincoln's record and was defeated.[30]

The editor of the *New York Tribune,* whom Lincoln had addressed in his letter as "Friend Greeley," was in the House for three months to fill a vacancy in 1848. He charged members of Congress were abusing their mileage accounts and published a list of submitted claims that was the sensation of the day.[31]

One of the names on the list was Abraham Lincoln, who had collected, charged the *Tribune*, for 1,626 miles and had been paid as reimbursement $1,300.80. This amount, the *Tribune* contended, was $676.80 more than he should have received. Greeley's figures were based on the mail route between Springfield and Washington, 780 miles. Lincoln's account had been figured on the Great Lakes route, popular with those living in the West.[32]

"The usually traveled road" was the route specified by law, the *Tribune* pointed out, adding: "The usually traveled road for a great many members of the last Congress was an exceedingly crooked one, even for politicians."[33]

In June of 1848, the Whigs nominated Taylor for President, and Lincoln began to work for him, even trying to get subscriptions for a campaign paper called *The Battery* in Washington.[34]

The national committee feared Whig prospects in New England were doubtful, and Lincoln was sent there as a field campaigner.[35]

Lincoln made his first speech at Worcester, Mass., on September 12, 1848, before the Whig state convention.[36] The *Boston Advertiser* gave him a long story, remarking: "Mr. Lincoln has a very tall and thin figure, with an intellectual face, showing a searching mind, and a cool judgment."[37] The *Boston Atlas* reported the speech, but the Worcester press gave Lincoln scant space. *The Palladium* noted only that he had spoken, while the *National Aegis* paid him this compliment: "For sound, conclusive reasoning and ready wit it (the Lincoln speech) is unsurpassed in the campaign."[38]

After Lincoln spoke at Lowell, Mass., the *Journal and Courier* said "It would be doing injustice to his speech to endeavor to give a sketch of it. It was replete with good sense, sound reasoning, and irresistible argument, and spoken with that perfect command of manner and matter which so eminently distinguishes the western orators."[39]

Through the recommendation of William Schouler, editor of the *Boston Atlas* and a militant Whig, Lincoln spoke at Dedham, Mass.[40] Lincoln had corresponded with Schouler before he left Washington to inquire about the political situation in Massachusetts.[41] He spoke in Boston on September 22, 1848, but was overshadowed by the orator of the occasion, William H. Seward, former Governor of New York soon to be elected United States Senator.

The next morning, the *Boston Atlas* gave Seward a column and explained it had no space for Lincoln's speech, although his words were "powerful and convincing, and cheered to the echo."[42] Two days later, the *Atlas* said: "In answer to the many applications which we receive daily from different parts of the state for this gentleman (Lincoln)

to speak, we have to say that he left Boston . . . on his way home to
Illinois."[43]

Lincoln stopped in Albany, N. Y., to discuss the political situation
with Thurlow Weed of the *Albany Evening Journal*.[44] On the long
steamer ride from Buffalo to Chicago, Lincoln may have thought of a
remark he made to Seward after hearing him speak in Boston. Years
later, when writing his memoirs, Seward said Lincoln told him in
Boston that the slavery question must be dealt with and more attention
should be paid to it.[45]

Lincoln returned to Washington in December of 1848 for the short
session of Congress and remained there until Taylor was inaugurated.
In the closing weeks of his term, Lincoln vainly sought appointment to
the office of commissioner of the General Land Office.[46] The Taylor
administration offered him, instead, the position of secretary of the
Oregon Territory; he refused the job, his wife making the decision.[47]

Lincoln tried to obtain the Oregon place for Editor Francis of the
*Illinois Journal*, but nothing came of his recommendation.[48] While still
in Washington, he tried to start a boom for Colonel Baker for Secretary
of War, clipping an editorial from the *Journal* and sending it to "Friend
Schouler," in Boston, with a request that it be reprinted in the *Atlas*.[49]

Baker was not appointed. Lincoln went back to his Springfield law
practice and his habit of loafing in the *Journal* office.

# 3  "Somebody Named Lincoln"

AFTER THE WAR with Mexico, the United States, gorged on new territory, lay like a sprawled giant from ocean to ocean. The question of the
extension of slavery came to the territorial feast as the unbidden guest
and refused to leave the banquet hall. It was the political issue that stood
before the nation. Safe in obscure Springfield, Lincoln watched the
controversy destroy the leaders of the day one by one.

He rode the court circuit, pleading cases and entertaining tavern
guests with droll stories, but he followed events as a hound follows the
trail by reading a list of newspapers that presented all sides of the
slavery problem.

He subscribed to the *Chicago Tribune, New York Tribune, Anti-Slavery Standard, The Emancipator,* and the *National Era.* Those newspapers represented the Northern view exclusively. He wanted to read the other side of the question, too, so he subscribed to the *Charleston Mercury* and the *Richmond Enquirer.*[1] He also continued to read the *Congressional Globe,* the newspaper he had known while in Washington, and the *National Intelligencer,* Whig party spokesman.[2]

A parade of national events scurried across the pages of history. President Taylor died in office, and Millard Fillmore succeeded him. In the next national election, Franklin Pierce, a Democrat, defeated the Whigs, represented by the soldier, Winfield Scott. Lincoln kept his political fences intact in the campaign of 1852 as a member of the national Whig committee and spoke a few times for Scott.

In May of 1854, Congress passed the Kansas-Nebraska bill, a measure designed and pushed through both Houses by Senator Douglas to supersede the Missouri Compromise of 1820 and the compromises of 1850, which had permitted California to enter the Union as a free state. The squatter-sovereignty philosophy of Douglas gave the settlers in Kansas and Nebraska the right to make their own decision on slavery. Both Abolitionists and slavery advocates stormed into the new territories, and the result was a collision that shook the nation. Blood was shed, and civil war began years before secession became a fact.

Douglas came home to Illinois, the most highly lauded and at the same time the most roundly cursed man of the times, and Lincoln rose to meet him.

The hour had struck for Abraham Lincoln.

Douglas felt the temper of the people when he arrived in Chicago. He announced he would speak there on the evening of September 1, 1854, and wrote to his friend, Editor Lanphier of the *Register* at Springfield that mob action against him [Douglas] was threatened. He asked Lanphier to publish a notice of the meeting and invited him to come to Chicago and bring "our friends" with him.[3]

A hostile crowd of thousands drowned out Douglas's voice when he tried to speak. He battled the crowd for two hours, then gave up, but not until he charged the *Chicago Tribune* was responsible for public feeling against him. When he mentioned the *Tribune,* the thousands in the public square cheered the name of the newspaper.[4] The Chicago incident made headlines all over the country and centered political attention on Illinois, then in the midst of an election campaign.

Douglas was not a man who could be intimidated; he spoke in the counties around Chicago, and gradually his audiences grew more friendly.[5] His purpose seems to have been to pacify his constituency. His real antagonist was waiting for him at Springfield.

Lincoln had worked all summer to prepare himself. He went through volume after volume at the Illinois State Library; he jotted down his thoughts on the slavery question; he read all the newspapers available. He was a candidate, without his sanction, for the state legislature and did some campaigning in behalf of his party, but he thought only of Douglas and the burning slavery issue.[6] The clash of Lincoln and Douglas in that campaign was a full-dress rehearsal for the debates four years later.

The big test came in Springfield during state-fair week. Douglas spoke in the Statehouse on October 3, 1854, and Lincoln answered him the next day.[7] The Capital's rival newspapers reported these events at length. The *Register* was lost for words, saying it was "impossible to do justice" to Douglas's speech; his argument, thought the *Register*, was "unanswerable." After Lincoln replied, the *Register* said it had not known at first just how "unanswerable" Douglas's speech really was.[8]

A long and dull synopsis of Lincoln's speech was published by the *Journal* on October 5. Herndon did not think the article sufficiently laudatory, and he wrote an editorial published the next day in the *Journal*. The zealous Herndon wrote:

The anti-Nebraska speech of Mr. Lincoln was the profoundest in our opinion that he has made in his whole life. . . . His feelings once or twice swelled within, and came near stifling utterance. He quivered with emotion. The whole house was still as death. . . . At the conclusion of this speech every man and child felt that it was unanswerable. He took the heart captive and broke like a sun over the understanding.[9]

Lincoln and Douglas met by agreement at Peoria on October 16. Douglas spoke in the afternoon, and Lincoln replied at night. The "Peoria Speech," as it has come to be known, gave Lincoln a voice in national politics.[10] Compared with his speeches made in Congress, it reads as though it were written by another man. For the first time in his life, he publicly denounced slavery; yet his plan was only restriction, not abolition.[11]

Twenty-year-old Horace White, a reporter on the *Chicago Journal*, covered the Lincoln speech at Springfield and Peoria. He took special note of the fervor with which Lincoln attacked slavery, saw his hair in disarray, saw the sweat pouring down his face, listened to tumultuous applause.[12]

The pages of the Springfield *Journal* show that both Lincoln and

Editor Francis feared he had gone too far in his statements on slavery. The paper acted at once to dispel in the public mind any thought that Lincoln was an Abolitionist. On October 18, two days after he spoke in Peoria, the *Journal* published an editorial written probably by Lincoln. The editorial said: "This nation is to become a nation of slaves or a nation of freemen," hastily adding, "We are not Abolitionists."[13] To make sure its position was understood, the *Journal* ran another editorial the next day, saying: "Abolition is an odious epithet among us; and we do not believe that there are a dozen men . . . in Sangamon County to whom it can be properly applied."[14]

The *Journal* editorial of October 18 contains the germ of the "House Divided" speech four years later. Herndon lays no claim to having written the editorial; it could hardly have been written by Simeon Francis, nothing like it ever having come from his inkwell.

Before the campaign was over, Lincoln spoke in Chicago, the *Chicago Journal* saying his speech "was as thorough an exposition of the Nebraska iniquity as has ever been made and his eloquence greatly impressed all his hearers." Of far more importance was a "side bar" on Lincoln, a little sketch that told of his humble origin. It was widely reprinted in Illinois newspapers. It follows:

Mr. Lincoln has seen something of life—not in the common acceptation of the phrase but in reality. Born of parents who could only give him faith in rectitude and virtue, he has become what he is through the trials of poverty, and by the sweat of his brow. How he guided a flatboat over the Ohio, or how he afterwards had his last article of property consisting of a chain and compass, sold under the sheriff's hammer, are matters of small interest now. How he became the most powerful speaker and one of the ablest lawyers in the West are of more moment.[15]

The Democrats lost ground in the Illinois election, and Lincoln saw the possibility of a Whig being elected to the United States Senate by the state legislature to succeed James Shields, the Democratic incumbent. Lincoln wanted the office.[16] He had been elected to the state legislature over his protest, and, with the approval of Mrs. Lincoln, he resigned his newly won office to oppose Shields.[17]

Neither Shields nor Lincoln won. As the legislature began to ballot, Lincoln saw he had no chance and threw his strength to Congressman Lyman Trumbull, the man Julia Jayne had married. Trumbull, an anti-Nebraska Democrat and foe of Douglas, was named Senator.[18]

The *New York Tribune* rejoiced, saying: "This . . . is a fitting finale to the repeal of the Missouri Compromise by Douglas &

Co. . . ."[19] The *Washington Sentinel* said a gallant soldier and statesman had been defeated by a "traitorous coalition of Know-Nothings,
Abolitionists and trading politicians."[20] Only in the Springfield newspapers was there any discussion of Lincoln's part in the senatorship
battle.[21] Again Lincoln went back to his law practice, and again he rode
the court circuit.

During the next few years, agitation over the slavery question un-
loosed a cascade of events destined to shape the future of the nation.
Lincoln followed these events closely; he studied the country's press
and made personal contact with editors within his reach who were
sympathetic with the new political movement. Numerous letters to
newspaper men and his recorded comments concerning the press indicate he kept his nose in newspapers constantly.

On February 22, 1856, the Republican party was formally organized
at Pittsburgh, Pa., and in a convention hall at Philadelphia the American
party, also called Know-Nothing, nominated former President Fillmore.
On that same Washington's birthday anniversary, a group of Illinois
newspaper editors who opposed the Kansas-Nebraska Act met in
Decatur to plan a political campaign.[22]

Lincoln helped draw up the platform, a carefully worded instrument
that opposed the extension of slavery. The *Journal* at Springfield saw
the platform as neither Republican nor Know-Nothing and gave it full
approval.[23]

Francis had left the *Journal*, and Edward L. Baker was the new
editor. Herndon was no longer an influential person around the *Journal*
office.[24] Baker (not to be confused with Edward D. Baker) and Lincoln
were friends, both personally and politically, and the newspaper continued to be his strongest supporter. The *Journal* files show Baker vastly
improved it.

On May 22, 1856, the South Carolina Congressman, Preston Smith
Brooks, went into the Senate chamber and caned Senator Charles
Sumner of Massachusetts into a jittery hulk two days after the bitter-
tongued Solon spoke on "The Crime Against Kansas." A week later—
and while the country was still at white-hot heat—at a state convention
in Bloomington, the Republican party came into formal existence in
Illinois.[25] Lincoln attended the convention as a delegate from Sangamon
County and there made the address that was to become known as the
"Lost Speech."

Herndon, who read or heard all the Lincoln utterances, said the
speech was "the grand effort" of Lincoln's life. He sorrowed that no
written or printed record was made.[26] In the audience were the best

newspaper men of the Western country, among them John L. Scripps, editor of the *Chicago Press;* Joseph Medill, of the *Chicago Tribune,* and Dr. Charles H. Ray, his partner and editor.[27] There were many other editors in attendance, including J. O. Cunningham, who traveled from Decatur to Bloomington with Lincoln.[28]

Not one newspaper published Lincoln's speech, although much laudatory comment was printed by that section of the press friendly to the Bloomington convention. Medill admitted later he took no notes on the speech, although it was his duty to cover it for the *Tribune.* He explained he was in a "sort of hypnotic trance," so interested in Lincoln's oratory he forgot what he was doing and joined in the cheering, the hand clapping, and stamping of feet. When he awakened from this "hypnotic trance," he found he had written nothing but a few notes. The other newspaper men were similarly affected, he said.[29]

The press agreed, however, that the convention "went wild" over the speech and that delegates rushed forward to shake Lincoln's hand. The *Illinois Daily State Journal* reprinted from the *Chicago Press* an editorial which said:

Abraham Lincoln of Springfield . . . made *the* speech of the occasion. . . . For an hour and a half he held the assembly spellbound. . . . When he concluded the audience sprang to their feet, and cheer after cheer told how deeply their hearts had been touched, and their souls warmed.[30]

Years later, Henry C. Whitney, who heard the speech as a young admirer of Lincoln, offered a version from yellowed sheets of notes made at Bloomington. Medill read it and termed it remarkably accurate. It revealed Lincoln as having delivered an Abolition talk, a policy he avoided before and after the Bloomington convention.[31]

The explanation is simple. The Bloomington speech was "lost" because Lincoln and the editors wished it to be "lost." The opposition press was not represented at the convention. In a day of purely political editing, it was the custom for editors to ignore what the other party was doing so far as factual reporting was concerned. The Bloomington convention was guided by a radical spirit; Kansas antislavery agitators had been imported for the occasion. Lincoln gave them the talk they wanted to hear.

The editors who covered the convention had the interest of their new party and their spokesman Lincoln foremost in their thoughts. Could it have been that self-imposed censorship, not a "hypnotic trance," kept Lincoln's speech off the printing presses?

The national Democratic convention in June of 1856 nominated James Buchanan for President. That same month, the first national Republican convention nominated John C. Frémont, the Continental explorer and radical Free-Soiler. Leaders of the Illinois delegation, displeased at the selection of Frémont to head the ticket, placed the name of Lincoln in nomination for Vice-President and garnered 110 votes for him on the first ballot, William L. Dayton eventually being named.[32]

*The New York Times* noted on October 11, 1856, that the *Charleston Mercury* insisted the Union would be split if Frémont were elected.[33] Other Southern newspapers, taking their cue from the *Mercury*, advocated secession if the election went against them. Buchanan's election postponed the crisis another four years. Illinois elected a Republican governor, although Buchanan took the state electoral vote.

During the campaign, the Fillmore faction in the Illinois capital was represented by the *Conservative*, a weekly newspaper. Lincoln and Herndon believed the paper was supported by Buchanan money; it was doing more harm to the Republicans than an outright Democratic paper could have done. Herndon clipped from the *Richmond Enquirer* an article that argued slavery was right, and together they planned to plant it in the *Conservative*. The fast-talking Herndon succeeded in having it accepted by the editor. The antislavery people, Lincoln included, then denounced what they termed the endorsement of slavery by an Illinois newspaper.[34]

Lincoln's efforts to propagandize his political sentiments through the press met a stinging rebuke in at least one instance. Writing to Jacob Harding, editor of the *Prairie Beacon* at Paris, Ill., Lincoln said he had received the newspaper three or four years and had paid nothing. He enclosed an order for ten dollars.[35] Later, Lincoln sent a political article to Harding, asking him to publish it. The editor returned the manuscript with the explanation that he himself wrote all the editorials for the *Prairie Beacon*. Lincoln told Herndon that Harding had a true understanding of journalism.[36]

On March 6, 1857, the Supreme Court of the United States delivered a decision in the Dred Scott Case, an opinion that held the Missouri Compromise was void. Congress, said the court, was not empowered to keep slavery out of the territories. Douglas came home when Congress adjourned and spoke in Springfield on June 12, 1857, saying his Kansas-Nebraska Act was vindicated by the Supreme Court decision. Lincoln answered him on June 26. That fall, Senator Douglas broke with the Buchanan administration.

The Illinois Republicans soon were to choose their senatorial candidate, and Lincoln again had his heart set on the prize. When the anti-Democratic press lauded Douglas's break with Buchanan, Lincoln feared the newly hatched Republicans might rush to the hero of the hour. He was perturbed over the attitude of the *New York Tribune*. He wrote to Senator Trumbull in Washington and demanded to know what the *Tribune* meant by expressing admiration for Douglas. He also wanted to know whether the *Tribune* was speaking for Republicans in the Capital and warned that if the *Tribune* continued this policy it would cause many to bolt the new party.[37]

In the privacy of his law office, Lincoln complained to Herndon that Greeley was not treating him right, that he was "taking up" Douglas, who dodged the slavery issue, while he himself was in the thick of it. Lincoln was upset; he put all business aside for the day and left the office. The faithful Herndon went East to see the party leaders in Washington and New York, among them the editor of the *New York Tribune*.[38]

Herndon reported to Lincoln by letter. He talked with Greeley twenty minutes and gained the impression the editor wanted Douglas reelected. Greeley spoke harshly of the Illinois newspapers and called the editors fools.[39]

As the day drew near for the Republican state convention at Springfield, rumors were heard that "Long John" Wentworth, mayor of Chicago and editor of the *Chicago Democrat*, had his eye on the Republican nomination for senator. Wentworth did not hold Lincoln in high political esteem at that time, but Lincoln had a friend in Charles L. Wilson, editor of the *Chicago Journal* and a leader in the powerful Cook County delegation.[40] Wentworth's ambitions were the subject of a little caucus in the Illinois State Library on April 21, 1858. Dr. Ray, editor of the *Chicago Tribune;* William Bross, editor of the Chicago *Democratic Press,* a paper that went Republican in 1856; George T. Brown, editor of the *Alton Courier,* and one or two others, including Norman B. Judd, chairman of the Republican state committee, and Lincoln were present.[41]

They were afraid Wentworth might control enough members of the state legislature to elect him senator if the Republicans won the fall election. He was outwitted by the simple declaration in the Republican platform that the candidate for senator was Abraham Lincoln.[42]

When the convention was held on June 16, 1858, Wilson offered the resolution "that Abraham Lincoln is the first and only choice of the

Republicans of Illinois for the United States Senate, as the successor of Stephen A. Douglas." Lincoln was nominated by acclamation.[43]

The telegraph wires carried the news to Washington, and Senator Douglas said to his leading supporter, John W. Forney, editor of *The Press* at Philadelphia, that he would have his "hands full."[44]

That night Lincoln spoke before the convention and delivered an address on which he had labored for days, the one known today as the "House Divided" speech.[45] As soon as he finished speaking, he turned to twenty-four-year-old Horace White, now working for the *Chicago Tribune*, gave him the manuscript, and requested him to go to the office of the *Illinois State Journal* and read proof on it.

White found the speech already in type. As he finished reading, Lincoln came into the composing room and pored over the revised proofs. Lincoln explained he wanted to see it in the newspaper just as he had written it. Some of his friends, he told White, asked him to leave out the paragraph about "the house divided against itself." Lincoln asserted it was going to stay, no matter what happened.[46] Obviously, Lincoln did not trust Baker, his editor friend, too far. These are the words Lincoln was guarding:

> A house divided against itself cannot stand. I believe that this government cannot endure permanently half slave and half free. I do not expect the Union to be dissolved—I do not expect the house to fall—but I do expect it will cease to be divided.

The speech was printed by the leading Republican newspapers of Illinois while the smaller ones gave excerpts. Orville P. Bassett, editor of the *True Republican* of Sycamore, Ill., published a pocket edition of the speech.[47] The coverage of the *Chicago Tribune* was outstanding, first the news story on June 18 and the text of the address the next day, with an editorial that said it was one of the "most masterly" ever delivered by man.

The speech attracted little press attention beyond the Illinois border, with one singular exception; the *New York Tribune* published the whole address! Greeley also printed editorial words of praise, saying the speech was "compact and forcible."[48]

As was to be expected, the opposition press in Illinois, led by the *Chicago Times* and the *Illinois State Register*, lashed Lincoln unmercifully. Lincoln had used the quotation, "A living dog is better than a dead lion," and added that Douglas, "if not a dead lion for this work, is at least a caged and toothless one." The *Chicago Times* said it was appropriate that Lincoln should call himself a "living dog" and asked

whether he had not won the name of "Spot."[49] The *Register* reprinted
that editorial and added the charge that the speech approached treason
because it meant war.[50]

When the *Chicago Times* continued to assail Lincoln and his Mexican
War record in Congress, the *Chicago Tribune* defended him, saying the
war was fought for Southern politicians. Medill wrote to Lincoln to
obtain the record of his voting on war measures, a record that showed
he voted for all men, money, and materials asked.[51]

Of all the newspaper comment on Lincoln's nomination, the most interesting, viewed in the light of history, was that in the *New Orleans
Delta*, which said:

> Somebody named Lincoln, who in the eyes of his friends is an unshorn
> Samson of the Free Soilers, was the choice for the United States Senate. . . .
> Everywhere in the West, anti-slavery leaders survey the field, raise them-
> selves in their stirrups and swing high the black banner, confident of
> success in the great battle of 1860.[52]

# 4 "Defeat Works Wonders"

DURING THE ILLINOIS election campaign in the summer and fall of 1858,
Lincoln and Douglas spoke more than one hundred times each—this
figure is conservative—in all parts of the state, but it is the seven debates,
when they stood side by side on the platform, that are remembered.
Douglas was the drawing card, the political comet of the day, and
Lincoln shared the national limelight only because he was the "Little
Giant's" opponent.

The campaign was reported by trained newspaper men for both the
Middle Western and the Eastern press. There was, however, only a
smattering of truly objective reporting, and the political chaff must be
blown from the grains of fact to obtain a clear view.

The senatorial campaign opened on July 9, 1858, when Senator
Douglas spoke from the balcony of a Chicago hotel, welcomed home
from Washington by cheering thousands, a reception quite different
from that of two years before when he was shouted down. The *Chicago
Press and Tribune* scored a news beat by publishing the text of Douglas's

speech the next morning, carrying a story almost four columns long on page one. The *Chicago Times*, Douglas's political servant, went to sleep, never dreaming the *Press and Tribune*, Lincoln's chief exponent, would go to such lengths to publicize Douglas.

The *Press and Tribune's* reportorial feat enabled it to present to a greatly enlarged reading audience the news that Lincoln would reply to Douglas that evening from the same hotel balcony.[1] The two newspapers had made special preparations to cover the campaign, each employing shorthand reporters to take down the speeches.

Horace White, assigned by the *Press and Tribune* to stay with Lincoln until the campaign was over, helped perform the news beat.[2] While he was taking notes for his lead on Douglas, twenty-four-year-old Robert Hitt was busy with his shorthand pencil. As soon as the speech was over, Hitt went to the *Press and Tribune* office and transcribed his notes.

The *Chicago Times* had two shorthand men on the job, Henry Binmore and James B. Sheridan, the latter a staff man on John W. Forney's Philadelphia *Press*, who seems to have been lent to either Douglas or the *Times* for the campaign.[3] Forney was a Douglas man, having broken with the Buchanan administration.

Binmore and Sheridan took their notes home with them and went to bed, intending to transcribe them the next day, the *Times* to publish the text of Douglas's speech the second day after delivery. They read it all in the *Press and Tribune* the next morning!

The *New York Tribune* worried the anxious Lincoln managers. After Chicago's tumultuous reception to Douglas, the *Tribune* said "the vast assemblage . . . was a well deserved tribute." It praised Douglas as a man of "profound sagacity" and asserted that if the Democratic party was to be saved, the credit would belong to him.[4]

Norman B. Judd, state Republican chairman of Illinois, was in New York. After reading the *Tribune's* story, he wrote to Senator Lyman Trumbull that some Republican strength had been lost because of Horace Greeley's attitude. Judd asked the Senator to come to New York to "straighten out the newspapers." He also asked him to campaign in Illinois.[5]

Lincoln's reply to Douglas was published by *The New York Times* on July 16, occupying about as much space as that accorded the Senator. The *Chicago Press and Tribune* carried both speeches in its weekly edition and sent it all over Illinois, inviting comparison to show Lincoln's "masterly refutation of Douglas's point."[6] The Chicago agent of the *Associated Press* was accused of bias by the *Press and Tribune*, which charged he filed half a column on the Douglas speech while he gave but five lines to Lincoln.[7]

A few days later, the *Press and Tribune* announced a special subscription price for the duration of the campaign, and downstate Republican newspapers followed suit with the blessing of the party.[8] John G. Nicolay, of Pittsfield, Ill., went out to seek subscriptions for the *Press and Tribune*. He wrote to Senator Trumbull that times were hard and subscriptions few.[9] Nicolay, as editor of the *Pike County Free Press* in 1856, had served the Republicans well by helping to promote the convention of anti-Nebraska editors at Decatur.[10] O. M. Hatch, Illinois secretary of state, found a place for him in the state auditor's office.[11] This is the Nicolay who became President Lincoln's private secretary.

Senator Trumbull, complying with Judd's request, did such a complete job of "straightening out" the New York press that he began to steal headlines from Lincoln when he entered the campaign to help him. It began to appear as though Trumbull, not Lincoln, was Douglas's opponent, and the whole Eastern press was influenced. A headline in the *Boston Traveller* said: "Illinois—Trumbull and Douglas."[12]

Lincoln's strategy in following Douglas from town to town drew ridicule from the opposition press, and his advisers realized he must take the offensive. The *New York Tribune* came close to the debate idea in an editorial, saying: "We trust Messrs. Lincoln and Douglas will speak together at some fifteen or twenty of the most important and widely accessible points throughout the state."[13]

Lincoln's loyal friend, the *Illinois State Journal*, tried to defend him from attacks by the *Chicago Times*, saying: "The *Chicago Times* launches out into a personal attack upon Mr. Lincoln for presuming to be present when Mr. Douglas speaks. One would think from this that Mr. Douglas has a patent right to audiences in Illinois."[14]

The *Times* continued its tirade, saying: ". . . the cringing, crawling creature (Lincoln) is hanging at the outskirts of Douglas's meetings, begging the people to come and hear him. . . . He went yesterday to Monticello in Douglas's train; poor, desperate creature, he wants an audience; poor unhappy mortal. . . ."[15]

The Philadelphia *Press*, in a story out of Peoria by special correspondent, said: "Lincoln, unable to draw a crowd himself, follows up Douglas and attempts to reply; but they are mere statements . . . by the time he is done begging for a seat in the Senate he finds himself minus an audience."[16]

The *Chicago Journal* and the *Chicago Press and Tribune* replied to these attacks in every edition, but still they continued. The *New York Herald* reprinted this article from the *Chicago Times:*

Lincoln was present during delivery of the speech (at Clinton). . . . After Senator Douglas had concluded . . . Mr. Lincoln . . . said that he would not take advantage of Senator Douglas's crowd, but would address "sich" as liked to hear him in the evening at the Court House. Having made this announcement . . . he stood washing his hands with invisible soap in imperceptible water, until his friends, seeing that his mind was wandering, took him in charge, and bundled him off the ground.[17]

To which the *Herald* added this comment: "Mr. Lincoln's course in following Senator Douglas is condemned here even by his friends."[18]

A week or so before the *Herald* took Lincoln to task, he wrote to Douglas to suggest "an arrangement for you and myself to divide time." Douglas replied he would grant the request "as far as it is in my power to do so."[19]

On July 30, just six days after Lincoln wrote to him, Douglas drew up a list of places and dates for the debates. They were to be at Ottawa, Freeport, Jonesboro, Charleston, Galesburg, Quincy, and Alton, the first to be held August 21 and the seventh on October 15. The correspondence between the candidates made a nice story for the newspapers.[20]

The spectacle of formal debate captured the imagination of the country. William Cullen Bryant, editor of the New York *Evening Post,* sent Chester P. Dewey to Illinois. A young German reporter named Henry Villard was assigned to Illinois by the *New York Staats-Zeitung.*[21] White and Hitt, always at Lincoln's elbow for the *Chicago Press and Tribune,* were joined at various times by Medill and Bross, with Ray and Scripps also working at the reporters's table.

The first debate was publicized as though it were a championship prize fight, and perspiring thousands converged on Ottawa that hot August Saturday. Headlines of the two rival Chicago papers were typical of the press throughout Illinois in describing the opening debate. "Dred Scott Champion Pulverized," said the *Press and Tribune.* "Lincoln Breaks Down—Douglas Skins Living Dog," said the *Times.*[22] Not again was the *Times* to be caught napping as it was when Douglas opened in Chicago. It said: "We delayed the issue of our Sunday morning's paper some hours in order that we might publish in full the speeches of Lincoln and Douglas at Ottawa."[23]

No sooner did the two great Chicago newspapers begin to publish

the text of the speeches than a fight started over which was offering
the more faithful reproduction. The *Press and Tribune* charged that
Lincoln's speech had been mangled by the *Times* and that the act was
performed by Douglas and "two Dred Scott lawyers."[24]

The *Times* tartly replied: "Any person who heard at Ottawa the
speech of Abraham, alias Old Abe, alias Abe, alias 'Spot' Lincoln,
must have been astonished at the report of that speech as it appeared
in the *Press and Tribune*. . . ."[25]

After the Galesburg debate, the *Galesburg Democrat* charged the
*Times* altered Lincoln's speech in 180 instances, saying: "There is
scarcely a correctly reported paragraph in the whole speech . . . ! the
whole aim has been to . . . make him talk like a booby, a half-witted
numbskull."[26] The *Times* continued to insist to the end of the debates
that the *Press and Tribune* was "garbling" Senator Douglas.[27] After
Quincy heard the gladiators, the local newspaper, the *Daily Whig*,
said: "Douglas carries around with him a reporter by the name of
Sheridan whose business it is to garble the speeches of Mr. Lincoln
and amend and elaborate those of Douglas for the *Times*."[28]

In his story of the debates, written thirty-two years later, White
explained that Hitt took down the text of the seven joint debates and
that after his notes were transcribed the manuscript went through his
hands before going to the composing room. He asserted that no
changes were made except where there was "some slight hiatus or
evident mistake" in taking the speaker's exact words, owing to the
turmoil about the reporter. He complained there was often confusion
on the platform and that high winds also caused trouble.[29]

Today's reporters will wonder how those on the Lincoln-Douglas
assignment were able to do any kind of a job at all. Neither candidate
spoke from manuscript, and they sometimes paused for asides. The
platforms were jammed with local politicians until the reporters had
scarcely room to work. The shouting of unruly crowds often made it
difficult to hear the speaker. All meetings were held outdoors, regardless
of weather conditions, and when the reporters were not choked with
dust they were wet and muddy. Bands and fireworks added to the confusion; frightened horses ran away, and a fist fight was usually in
progress on the edge of the throng.

Dewey of the New York *Evening Post* wrote from Freeport that
crowds jammed the speaking platforms and "the newspaper gentry
have to fight a hand-to-hand conflict for even the meagerest chance
for standing room."[30] The *Press and Tribune's* Hitt was unable to
make his way to the stand at Freeport. Lincoln stepped forward to

speak when Bross warned him the shorthand reporter was not there.

Far out on the rim of the crowd, Hitt was waving and shouting. Finally, he was picked up and passed over the heads of the packed standees to the platform.[31]

It was at Freeport that Lincoln, acting contrary to the advice of Medill and others members of his party, put this question to Douglas:[32] "Can the people of a United States territory, in any lawful way, against the wish of any citizen of the United States, exclude slavery from its limits prior to the formation of a state constitution?"[33]

Douglas answered in the affirmative.[34] His followers staged a demonstration while the Lincoln entourage was downcast, believing Douglas's answer saved him from defeat in Illinois.[35] Lincoln's advisers did not see that he had compelled Douglas to trip the blade of the political guillotine on his own head.

Between debates, both Lincoln and Douglas gave separate speeches, and Lincoln was scheduled to appear at Clinton after the Freeport meeting. White accompanied him to write a general story, the shorthand reporter not covering these side trips. They left Springfield in the evening en route to Decatur where they were to change trains for Clinton. White was tired and decided to take a nap, telling Lincoln to awaken him when they reached Decatur.

When White awakened, it was daylight and he was in State Line, on the Indiana border. There he waited until the next train back to Decatur, reaching Clinton at six o'clock that evening. The incident became one of Lincoln's favorite yarns.[36]

The nation watched as the day of decision drew near. The *Burlington* (Iowa) *State Gazette* seemed to speak for all newspapers when it said: "What a night next Tuesday will be all over the Union! . . . . No state has ever fought so great a battle as that which Illinois is to fight on that day."[37]

On November 2, a cold rain struck the Illinois prairies, rattled the yellowed cornstalks, and made the black mud roads almost impassable. The streets of Springfield were a quagmire. There were reports of men unable to reach the voting places.[38]

The Republicans polled 125,430 votes to 120,609 for the Douglas Democrats, while 5,071 votes were cast by Buchanan Democrats, giving the Republicans the state ticket and putting Illinois in the Republican column for the first time. But Lincoln was defeated; the apportionment law of the state gave the Democrats the majority in both branches of the state legislature, the body that was to cast the formal vote for senator. Douglas received 54 votes, Lincoln 41.[39]

An editorial in the *Chicago Press and Tribune* said of Lincoln after the votes were counted: "He has created for himself a national reputation that is both envied and deserved. . . . His speeches have become landmarks in political history. . . . Mr. Lincoln at Springfield . . . is more to be envied than Douglas in the Senate. Long live Honest Old Abe!"[40]

Upon Douglas's return to Washington, he was assailed by Senator Jefferson Davis and other powerful Southern men who called his reply to Lincoln's question the "Freeport heresy."[41]

Disappointed Republican newspaper editors, aided by others simply reporting the news, immediately launched a Lincoln-for-President boom whose origin probably never will be solved to the satisfaction of everyone. A newspaper historian says the honor belongs to the *Illinois Gazette* of Lacon, which "nominated" Lincoln on November 4, 1858.[42] On November 6, 1858, the *Commercial Register* of Sandusky, Ohio, falsely reported a Lincoln-for-President meeting was held the night before in the neighboring town of Mansfield. The *Illinois State Journal* at Springfield reprinted the story on November 13.

Someone wrote a letter to the *Cincinnati* (Ohio) *Gazette* to suggest Lincoln for President, and this was published on November 10. The *New York Herald* came forth with this paragraph: "The following ticket has just been brought out at Cincinnati: For President, Abraham Lincoln, of Illinois; for Vice-President, John B. Kennedy, of Maryland —with a platform embracing . . . opposition to the extension of slavery by free emigration into the territories." The *Journal* at Springfield also reprinted that story.[43]

The *Peoria Daily Message* said:

Defeat works wonders with some men. It has made a hero of Abraham Lincoln. Two or three Republican journals in different sections of the Union are beginning to talk of him for Vice-President, with Seward for President; and a Republican meeting just held in Mansfield, Ohio, raises him a notch higher, by announcing him as its candidate for President.[44]

Wentworth's *Chicago Democrat* said in an editorial on November 11 that Lincoln was "fully competent to fill any post within the gift of the people of this Union" and that Illinois should present his name for President.[45] A week later, the *Olney* (Ill.) *Times* came out for Lincoln for President.[46]

The *Chicago Press and Tribune* noted that *The New York Times* was "out" for Senator Douglas for President while the *New York Herald* favored the renomination of Buchanan. It said the New York

*Evening Post* liked Governor Salmon P. Chase of Ohio and that the *New York Tribune* was noncommittal. It offered this advice:

The *Press and Tribune* thinks it premature to name the Presidential candidate, as it is impossible to tell what the year may bring forth, and it is nearly two years yet before the campaign of 1860. Wait patiently until the signs come right.[47]

And yet a month later, the *Press and Tribune*, noting the Lincoln boom "in various parts of the country," was of the belief that Lincoln could be made the candidate for 1860 if his supporters presented an unbroken front.[48]

Even the *Illinois State Register*, Lincoln's Springfield enemy, finally had to take recognition of the presidential boom. In an editorial on December 1, 1858, it said: "If the Illinois Republican journals are to be taken as an index, Mr. Lincoln is to be made a presidential candidate upon the creed which he enunciated here in his June convention speech. . . . Whether this extreme ground will be adopted by the Republicans generally, in a party platform, is a matter of doubt."

Lincoln himself had high hopes, it is revealed in a letter he wrote to Ray of the *Press and Tribune* a couple of weeks after the election. Telling Ray he heard the newspaper man was "feeling like hell," he said another chance would come. He requested Ray to send him a complete set of the debates as published in his newspaper.[49]

Editors of two small Illinois newspapers kept the Lincoln boom alive during the next year. Thomas J. Pickett, editor of the *Weekly Register* at Rock Island, notified Lincoln he was boosting him for the Presidency, and Lincoln replied on March 5, 1859, that he did not think he was "fit."[50] Pickett wrote to him again on April 13, saying he planned to propose that all Illinois Republican editors make a simultaneous announcement of Lincoln for President. Lincoln's reply on April 16 said he was flattered but that he must say again he did not believe himself adequate.[51]

The forty-year-old Pickett was a man of some importance, a state senator for two terms, a regent of the Illinois State Normal University, and president of the Illinois Editorial Association. He was a delegate to the national Republican convention in 1856. He boosted Lincoln for governor in 1856 and always claimed he proposed Lincoln for President more than two years before the nomination.[52]

William Osborn Stoddard, twenty-four years old and just out of the University of Rochester, wrote a Lincoln-for-President editorial for his *Central Illinois Gazette* at Champaign and mailed copies to newspapers all over the country in May of 1859. The editorial said: ". . . we need not fear that fanaticism on the one side, or servility on the other will lead him to the betrayal of any trust."[53]

Stoddard said hundreds of the newspapers to which he mailed the editorial reprinted it in whole or part. He acted alone, he said, and no one suggested the idea to him.[54]

Both Stoddard and Pickett were rewarded after Lincoln became President. He took Stoddard with him to Washington as a private secretary and later appointed him United States marshal for Arkansas.[55] Pickett became custodian of the army quartermaster depot at Rock Island.[56]

In 1864, Pickett was suspended on a charge of having sold, for his own benefit, stone and lumber from the land on which the depot stood. President Lincoln went to his rescue, ordering that all testimony at the hearing of his "old friend" should be sent to him.[57]

The Pickett and Stoddard boom for Lincoln brought it into the summer of 1859 and prevented a slump in his political fortunes that might have followed the general outburst in the wake of the senatorial election. The *Chicago Press and Tribune* sounded a note of caution on March 29, 1859, saying: "The day for the nomination of the Republican candidate has not yet arrived. There is harm in premature discussion. The hour and the man will come together."[58]

Leaders of the Republican party in Illinois discussed the Lincoln candidacy in a conference in the *Press and Tribune* office about the time the "hour and the man" editorial was published.[59] They agreed it was best not to push Lincoln too hard but to keep him in the background until the logical time.[60]

There is evidence that Medill was playing some sort of a game with the ambitious Chase of Ohio, who had been close to him in politics when the Chicago editor was publishing a newspaper in Cleveland a few years before. In a letter dated June 8, 1859, Medill told the Ohio Governor he thought the time not ripe to commit the *Press and Tribune* in print in behalf of any candidate and that it was better to work secretly for him and in the open for a Westerner. In August, Medill told Chase that if Edward Bates, the Missouri Whig, lent a hand, Chase could count on the nomination.

A month later, Medill informed Chase that Lincoln was making strides in Illinois and Indiana.[61] The Chicago editor was simply telling Chase he had decided Lincoln was his man.

That Lincoln was attempting to further his presidential ambitions is attested by his proposition to Johnson & Bradford, a printing firm at

Springfield, to publish the debates. They turned him down in a letter dated "March 21, 1859."[62] The publisher was cold to the idea, contending there was no market for such a book.[63]

An Ohioan, George M. Parsons, acting as an agent for Lincoln, negotiated with a Columbus publisher, Follett, Foster & Co. Lincoln forwarded copies of the speeches, his own from the *Chicago Press and Tribune,* those of Douglas from the *Chicago Times.* The book was whipped into shape and was soon a best seller.[64] After the book had run into many editions, Lincoln sent a copy to the Springfield publisher with "Compliments of A. Lincoln" written on the flyleaf.[65]

# 5 "On the Wings of Rosy Dawn"

THE FALSE REPORT of a Lincoln-for-President meeting at Mansfield, Ohio, published by the *Daily Commercial Register* of nearby Sandusky on Saturday morning, November 6, 1858, created a tempest in a teapot, was forgotten for half a century, then bobbed up as another mystery in the Lincoln story.

Disguised as a telegraph dispatch and bearing earmarks of having been nursed by the editor, Henry D. Cooke, the false story occupied a position at the top of the lead column on the editorial page. This is the story exactly as it was published:

### LINCOLN FOR PRESIDENT

We are indebted to a friend at Mansfield for the following special despatch:

Mansfield, Nov. 5th, 1858

Editor *Sandusky Register:*—An enthusiastic meeting is in progress here to-night in favor of Lincoln for the next Republican candidate for President.

Reporter.

That was the story, no explanation, no comment. Below it was an editorial that discussed the election result in Michigan. On the opposite page, where the night's run of wire news appeared, were follow-ups on the Illinois election of November 2, giving final figures on the voting.

The little lake port of Sandusky may not have been rocked by the report of a Lincoln meeting only 45 miles away in Richland County, but it was certainly big news in Mansfield, whose 3,000 inhabitants had yet to learn about it. The story in the Sandusky *Register* was especially disconcerting to the editors of the two Mansfield newspapers.

The Mansfield *Shield and Banner*, edited by John Y. Glessner, was a Douglas newspaper, and its files today reveal no mention of a Lincoln meeting in Mansfield, nor is there any reference to the Sandusky *Register* story.[1]

The other newspaper in Mansfield, the *Herald*, edited by Roeliff Brinkerhoff, an admirer of Salmon P. Chase, was indignant. Brinkerhoff flatly declared in his paper on November 10, 1858, that the report of a Lincoln meeting in Mansfield was a hoax. He reprinted the Lincoln story as published in Sandusky and asserted:

"To learn the news of the town, go to the country," is an old saying which, with a slight alteration, would read, "to learn the news of Mansfield go to Sandusky." Mansfield we know is a large city, and a great many occurrences doubtless take place in it which we never hear of, yet we are inclined to think that a "large and enthusiastic" political meeting would be likely to come to our knowledge. Under these circumstances we are rather disposed to consider the *Register's* Lincoln demonstration somewhat imaginary. The truth is, the *Register* has been hoaxed.[2]

This positive refutation was not heard beyond the limits of Richland County, owing to the local circulation of the *Mansfield Herald* and the fact that the perpetrator of the hoax paid no attention to the denial. Meanwhile, the *Register's* false dispatch was reprinted by several Middle Western Republican newspapers.

At the time he published the Lincoln meeting story, Cooke and some others were negotiating for the purchase of the *Ohio State Journal* at Columbus, the transaction being announced on November 19, 1858.[3] Editor Cooke was an outstanding journalist, and his ability was destined to carry him far. He took over the *Ohio State Journal* when it was tottering, put it on its feet, and went on to Washington to join his brother, Jay Cooke, in floating the government loans that financed the Civil War for Lincoln.[4]

Cooke, working at his Sandusky desk, had heard that a strong Douglas movement was growing in northeastern Ohio. A new paper that called itself the *Herald* was launched in the neighboring city of Toledo on that same November 6, 1858, "ardent in the support of Mr. Douglas."[5] Cooke was a strong Lincoln man, it was revealed as soon as he took hold of the *Journal*, the paper recognized as the spokesman for the Republican party in Ohio at that time.

The years rolled on. Those who wrote of Lincoln found the little story about the Mansfield meeting in the files of the Sandusky *Register*. They seized upon it as a rich discovery, a milestone in the mysterious path that Lincoln trod to the White House.

When Ida M. Tarbell wrote *In the Footsteps of the Lincolns* in 1924, she reproduced the Mansfield dispatch in her book. Her treatment indicates she accepted the story as true, and her main concern was with the identity of the "reporter" who filed it.

Miss Tarbell wrote that she had "always supposed" the "reporter" to have been David R. Locke, later famous as the humorist, Petroleum V. Nasby. She said that at the time the story appeared Locke was the editor of the *Mansfield Herald*. Locke, she pointed out, was an early admirer of Lincoln and had heard him debate with Douglas at Quincy. She therefore reasoned that Locke "engineered" the demonstration at Mansfield.[6] She was completely in error.

Miss Tarbell's book had an immediate effect on Mansfield's civic pride. On September 22, 1925, a dignified monument bearing a bronze plaque was set up in the public square at Mansfield with imposing ceremonies. The plaque bore a likeness of Abraham Lincoln and these words:

> The first public and official endorsement of Abraham Lincoln as a candidate for President of the United States was given him in Mansfield at a county convention held November 5, 1858. Erected by the Richland County Lincoln Association.

The speaker for the dedication ceremony was Charles H. Workman. He proclaimed, "May it be known from this day, henceforth, and throughout the land, that on November 5, 1858, in this city, began the organized movement which resulted in the election of Abraham Lincoln to the office of President of the United States." Then, to Workman's credit, he began to dismantle, word by word, the statement he had just made by confessing he had serious doubts of the authenticity of the legend on the plaque.

Workman told the assemblage he could find no account of a Lincoln meeting in any history and that he had gone to the files of the old newspapers. There he discovered, he said, that the "Lincoln men of Mansfield" had no newspaper to represent them in 1858. Messages of the "Lincoln men," he poetically explained, "were carried by post, or messenger, or on the wings of rosy dawn, the wings of morning, and this explains why the dispatch . . . found publication in the Sandusky *Daily Register*."

He went further, telling of Brinkerhoff's denial in the *Mansfield Herald* and saying he examined the files of the Sandusky *Register* from November 5 to December 15, 1858, but could find no refutation, while the story was reprinted in all points of the compass.

With his own conscience satisfied, Workman fell again into the spirit of the occasion and said the effect of the little story—no matter what its origin—on the career of Abraham Lincoln could not be discounted. The fact remained, he said, that out of Mansfield had come the first announcement of organized men to make Lincoln President.[7]

Now as for Miss Tarbell, her statement that she "supposed" Locke sent the telegram to the Sandusky *Register* because he was editor of the *Mansfield Herald* is a groundless assumption. The fact is that Locke was not editor of the Mansfield newspaper but was editor of the *Journal* at Bucyrus, Ohio, and was living there.

Had Miss Tarbell turned a few more pages in the files of the Sandusky *Register*, she would have found in the issue of November 20, 1858, a story about Locke that would have set her straight. The story said:

David R. Locke, Esq., senior editor of the *Bucyrus Journal*, died on Thursday of last week, aged about thirty years. A short time ago he was thrown from a buggy and received an injury that caused an enlargement of the liver, which was the immediate cause of his death. . . . He was an industrious and competent editor, a warm-hearted and honest man. He leaves a wife and one child.

Those shedding a bitter tear for David Locke put their handkerchiefs away two days later when the *Register* rushed into print to correct a slight error, saying: "We learn . . . we were mistaken in . . . stating that D. R. Locke, of the *Bucyrus Journal*, was dead. It is his brother, D. W. Locke, of Plymouth, who deceased at the time mentioned."[8]

When Edwin Erle Sparks, president of Pennsylvania State College, compiled the work known as "Debates" for the Illinois State Historical Library in 1908, one of the striking illustrations was a full-page photograph of the Sandusky *Register's* Mansfield story. The cut line said the story "probably" was the first public announcement of Lincoln's name as a presidential candidate.[9]

A study of the complexities of editing and publishing a daily newspaper should be taken into consideration when the story of the Lincoln meeting as it appeared in the Sandusky *Register* is examined. The editorial page is, and always has been, the most closely supervised in the newspaper. It is significant that Editor Cooke placed a news story about Lincoln at the very top of his editorial column.

Other news received by wire that night was used in its regular place on the opposite page. Those brief news flashes ran up to a late hour, proving that page was kept open till just before the *Register* went to press sometime after midnight. The editorial page of any newspaper is always closed early.

It is apparent the *Register's* editorial page was made up that night to include the "telegram" from Mansfield. Had the story appeared in the *Register's* office in the regular routine of publishing the paper, it would have, of course, been placed with the other telegraph news.

Cooke was ready to leave Sandusky; only a few more days and he would be in Columbus, editing the *Ohio State Journal*, mixing with all the bigwigs of the Republican party. Why not have a little fun?

He might have arranged to have the "telegram" sent from Mansfield. Or, he himself might have written it, right there at his desk.

# 6  1859: Abram C. Lincoln

OHIO WAS THE key state in the fall elections of 1859, and the situation there presented a challenge to both the Democratic and the newly organized Republican parties. The issue was clear. There was little to choose between the candidates for governor, Rufus P. Ranney, the Democrat, and William Dennison, the Republican. It was a matter of purely political texture, whether the pivotal state was to go Democratic or Republican.[1] The outgoing Governor was Salmon P. Chase, a former leader of the Liberal party who had joined the radical wing of the Republicans. Always an Abolitionist, six years in the United States Senate and two terms in the Governor's chair, he was looked upon in 1859 as Ohio's "favorite son" for the next presidential nomination.

The Democratic party, sensing the importance of the result in Ohio for the national elections in 1860, sent Senator Stephen A. Douglas into the state as a stump speaker. He drew huge crowds, and the Republicans, alarmed at his personal popularity, decided something must be

done to counteract his influence. They called on Abraham Lincoln of
Illinois.

Senator Douglas spoke in Columbus on September 7, and *The New
York Times* had his entire speech of more than seven thousand words
telegraphed from Columbus. This journalistic enterprise was the talk
of newspaper circles and the cost, $497, the subject of much comment.

The Columbus *Ohio State Journal,* Republican voice in the Capital,
reported the Douglas speech the next day, saying: "The whole of the
first half was a direct and palpable violation of the copyright of his
article in *Harper's Magazine,* for which those publishers should prosecute him and recover back the price." The article to which the paper
referred was a political sensation, written by Senator Douglas. It was
called "The Dividing Line Between Federal and Local Authority" and
was a discussion of his theory of popular sovereignty.

The *Journal's* story ended with this snapper: "He closed by exalting
Democratic obedience to law and the Constitution, as expounded by the
Supreme Court, and thus brought himself around to the Dred Scott hole
which he always keeps ready lubricated."

On the following day, the *Journal* broke the story that Lincoln was
coming into the state, headlined "The Hunters On His Track." It said
in part:

We take very great pleasure in announcing to the people of Ohio that a
dispatch just received by the Secretary of the State Central Committee,
announces that HON. AB. LINCOLN, OF ILLINOIS, will address the
people, at Columbus, on Friday afternoon the 16th inst., and at Cincinnati
on Saturday, the 17th inst.

The great renown and national reputation of Mr. Lincoln, as speaker,
cannot fail to attract an immense assemblage. His famous series of debates
last year with Mr. Douglas, in which the little rebel was thoroughly
worsted, and by reason of which the Republicans carried the State of
Illinois by several thousand majority, all conspire to give great interest to
this contemplated visit. He follows on the track of Douglas, and will not
leave a shred of his miserable logic unravelled and exposed. . . .[2]

Although the *Journal* spoke of the "great renown and national reputation" of Lincoln, a survey of the Ohio press shows that, despite all
the publicity he had received in the debates, the editors did not know
his right name. He was advertised as Abram Lincoln, Ab'm Lincoln,
Ab. Lincoln, Abe Lincoln and Abr'm Lincoln. Most newspapers settled
for just plain A. Lincoln. The usually well-informed *Cincinnati Enquirer* called him Abram C. Lincoln.

The *Journal* was carrying an advertisement for a bookstore that offered a volume of biographical sketches of "all the prominent candidates for the presidency in 1860." The advertisement said the men sketched were Seward, Douglas, Chase, Bates, Dickinson, Bell, Hale, Stephens, Banks, Lane, McLean, Wise, Hunter, Wilson, Davis, Orr, Botts, Hammond, Cobb, Breckinridge, and Frémont. Lincoln's name was not listed.

The *National Democrat,* a Buchanan newspaper published at Cleveland, Ohio, printed a little story about Douglas that was eagerly copied by the *Journal.* It said:

> Mr. Douglas has written a long article for *Harper's Magazine,* on Squatter Sovereignty, which is highly eulogized by a correspondent of Forney's *Press,* who concluded his eulogy on the article thus:
>
> "I am happy to say that Mrs. Douglas continues in excellent health."
>
> From this it is to be inferred that Mrs. Douglas never read her husband's article.[3]

The *Journal* had help from the *Louisville* (Ky.) *Journal,* edited by George D. Prentice. The *Journal* said of Douglas: "A rumor prevailed in the street yesterday that the little giant was to speak from the tall tower over the artesian well in the State House yard." Prentice picked up the sentence and added this comment: "If he had done so, would the greater bore have been at the bottom or top of the tower?"[4]

Speaking on the east terrace of the Ohio capitol, Lincoln began his address with an attack on the *Daily Ohio Statesman,* of Columbus, saying:

> Appearing here for the first time in my life, I have been somewhat embarrassed for a topic by way of introduction to my speech; but I have been relieved from that embarrassment by an introduction which the *Ohio Statesman* newspaper gave me this morning. In this paper I read an article in which, among other statements, I find the following:
>
> "In debating with Senator Douglas during the memorable contest last fall, Mr. Lincoln declared in favor of negro suffrage, and attempted to defend that vile conception against the Little Giant."
>
> I mention this now, at the opening of my remarks, for the purpose of making three comments upon it. The first I have already announced—it furnished me with an introductory topic; the second is to show that the gentleman is mistaken; thirdly, to give him an opportunity to correct it.
>
> In the first place, in regard to this matter being a mistake. I have found that it is not entirely safe, when one is misrepresented under his

very nose, to allow the misrepresentation to go uncontradicted. I therefore propose, here at the outset, not only to say that this is a misrepresentation, but to show conclusively that it is so. . . .

He then read the exact language he used in his speech at Ottawa, declaring he had never stated he was in favor of Negro suffrage but had twice stood against it. He demanded the *Daily Ohio Statesman* publish a retraction, saying:

I presume the editor of that paper is an honest and truth-loving man and that he will be greatly obliged to me for furnishing him thus early an opportunity to correct the misrepresentation he has made, before it has run so long that malicious people can call him a liar.[5]

The *Daily Ohio Statesman*, as was to be expected, did not publish Lincoln's speech but took advantage of the occasion to ridicule him. It ignored Lincoln's charge that he had caught it lying and said:

The Young Men's Republican Club must have been mortified at the very meagre audience in attendance at the Lincoln meeting held yesterday afternoon. . . . The meeting was indeed a "beggarly account of empty boxes," and the speaker disappointed all who heard him. . . . He is not an orator. He can hardly be classed as a third rate debater. . . .

We think Mr. Lincoln will never be invited here again, and that was perhaps his opinion, as he had his daguerrotype taken in the forenoon, with a view of leaving it, we suppose, as a remembrancer for his Columbus friends.[6]

The accounts of the reception accorded Lincoln are so at variance it is impossible to ascertain just what took place that September afternoon. The *Ohio State Journal's* version was exactly opposite to the *Statesman's*. The *Journal* gave Lincoln half a column of laudatory comment, followed by text of his speech. The reporter wrote:

Mr. Lincoln was enthusiastically received, and held the attention of the audience for two hours, his clear and irresistible points eliciting frequent marks of approbation. . . . The two Illinois champions are in themselves fair illustrations of the features of Democracy and Republicanism; Lincoln candid, logical and clear-headed, planting himself on principles that no one can controvert and winning the entire confidence of the audience; Douglas aiming at nothing higher than a political dodge. . . .[7]

Lincoln boarded a train the next morning for Cincinnati. The first stop was Xenia. One of the town's two weekly newspapers, the *Xenia Torch-Light*, said in its next issue:

A large crowd gathered last Saturday morning at the Lower Depot to get a good look at HON. ABRAM LINCOLN OF ILLINOIS. A Cincinnati contemporary draws his portrait very accurately thus: Abram Lincoln is a dark complexioned man, of very tall figure, and so exceedingly "well preserved" that he would not be taken for more than thirty-eight, though he is rising fifty years of age. His countenance should be called a very good one; his features are strongly marked. . . . We don't know his lineage, but he is evidently of the Kentucky "race" of men, and a fine type of that race.[8]

A young man led cheers for Lincoln at the station. He was twenty-one-year-old Whitelaw Reid, just out of Miami University, editor of the *Xenia News*, a struggling weekly that was preaching Republicanism and hatred of slavery.[9] Reid heard Douglas speak at Columbus and wrote for his little newspaper that the Senator's face "is essentially vulgar—a compound of low cunning and sensuality."[10]

When Reid heard Lincoln was coming to Ohio, he told his readers, "Abe Lincoln, of Illinois, the great antagonist of Douglas, who came off from the contest last fall defeated, but with the sympathies and high esteem of the entire north, is to administer an antidote to Douglas's last Squatter Sovereignty effort."[11]

He organized a delegation to go to Columbus. His enthusiasm for Lincoln approaching evangelistic proportions, he followed him to Cincinnati with another delegation.[12] Reid's report of the two speeches filled three columns in the *Xenia News*. He wrote that the man from Illinois offered "the calmest, most convincing and most complete refutation of the humbug of Squatter Sovereignty that had yet been given to the public of Ohio."[13]

The train carrying Lincoln and his party went on to Dayton, where he had to wait several hours for the Cincinnati train. Dayton Republicans met him at the station and escorted him to the courthouse where he gave a speech, holding his listeners for nearly two hours "with utmost attention."[14]

The *Dayton Daily Journal*, a Republican organ, said Lincoln spoke before a large crowd, a statement denied by the *Dayton Daily Empire*, the Democratic newspaper. The *Empire* said:

. . . instead of tens of thousands of persons being assembled in our city, and the streets being deluged with people . . . a meagre crowd, numbering scarcely two hundred, was all that could be drummed up, and they were half Democrats, who attended from mere curiosity.

Mr. Lincoln is a very seductive reasoner, and his address, although a network of fallacies and false assumptions throughout, was calculated to deceive any man, who would not pay very close attention to the subject and keep continually on the guard.[15]

After Lincoln had gone on to Cincinnati, Dayton Republicans held a rally that night. Robert C. Schenck, a former Congressman and a former minister to Brazil, was the main speaker. He declared Lincoln was the "proper man" for the Republican presidential nomination.[16]

Upon Lincoln's arrival in Cincinnati, he was hailed by a "large concourse of persons who had assembled to greet the Champion of Freedom in the Sucker State. Guns thundered welcome, music greeted, and the people cheered at each place of stopping."[17]

The *Cincinnati Enquirer* paid little attention to Lincoln until he spoke. While he was in Columbus, it reprinted from *The New York Times* an editorial which said: "Mr. Seward . . . stands clearly and unmistakably at the head of the Republican party, and will be entitled to their nomination."[18]

The *Enquirer* carried a brief article on Lincoln, referring to him as "the Black Republican Senator of Illinois, who is invited here by his political brethren to make them a speech in opposition to that lately given us by the little giant." It said that when "Abe" was asked how he felt after his defeat by Douglas in Illinois, he replied, "Well, I feel just like the little boy who stubbed his toe—*too damn badly hurt to laugh and too damn proud to cry!*"

The *Enquirer* added this warning: "Abe will stub his toe here if he comes."[19]

On Saturday morning, September 17, with Lincoln on his way to Cincinnati, the *Enquirer* carried a long account of a speech made the day before by Douglas at Wooster, Ohio, reporting 15,000 persons heard him. Under the label, "From Columbus," this is what it said about Lincoln:

Columbus, Friday, Sept. 16.—Hon. Abram C. Lincoln of Illinois addressed a large crowd in Capitol Square this afternoon.

The Democratic *Enquirer* may have been slow to herald the approach of Lincoln, but it had plenty to say after he left town. His speech featured the Sunday morning edition. The full coverage may have been due to the fact that none of the Republican dailies had Sunday editions, and it was journalistic enterprise to be first with the Lincoln story. It gave a fair account of the address but did not print the text.

"He was, he said," wrote the *Enquirer* reporter, "what was termed a Black Republican—thinking slavery wrong, morally, socially and politically; and he should feel no regret if it should be terminated altogether. This he said for himself, independent of his party."

A separate story was given to "Mr. Lincoln's Appearance and Manner." He was thus described:

Hon. Mr. Lincoln is a tall, dark-visaged, angular, awkward, positive-looking sort of individual, with character written in his face and energy expressed in his every movement. He has the appearance of what is called in the North-east a Western man—one who, without education or early advantages, has risen by his own exertions from an humble origin. Indeed, in this respect he resembles Douglas, to whom, however, in largeness of thought, profundity of penetration and excellence of judgment, he is greatly inferior.

Mr. Lincoln . . . makes no pretension to oratory or the graces of diction. . . . With orthoëpy he evidently has little acquaintance, pronouncing words in a manner that puzzles the ear sometimes to determine whether he is speaking his own or a foreign tongue.[20]

Two days later, the *Enquirer* reviewed the speech in an editorial a full column long. After admitting Lincoln drew a "large and respectable audience," the editor observed that the "enterprising *Gazette*" had published the text of the speech but he had merely "glanced over it." Then he wrote:

It is, in a single expressive word, trash—trash from beginning to end; trash without one solitary oasis to relieve the dreary waste that begins with its nearest and ends with its furthest boundary.

Among public addresses from the stump the speech of Mr. Lincoln belongs to the lowest order. It is not the speech of a statesman; it is not the speech of a politician; it is not even the speech of a fair partisan. It is the speech of a pettifogging demagogue. . . .[21]

The "enterprising *Gazette*" to which the *Enquirer* referred was the *Cincinnati Daily Gazette,* whose editor was Richard Smith, called "Deacon" because he offered the rare spectacle of a newspaper man who attended church. Smith, a radical Republican, covered Lincoln from the time he crossed the Ohio border. On September 17, the *Gazette* told its readers, "Much of our space is occupied this morning with a report of the Hon. A. Lincoln's speech at Columbus yesterday. He scored Mr. Douglas right and left . . . and the remainder of the . . . humbug he may be expected to scatter . . . this evening."[22]

The *Gazette* could not report the Cincinnati speech until Monday when it said Lincoln "is deficient in claptrap, but excels in logic and honesty and herein he differs from Judge Douglas."[23] The *Cincinnati Commercial*, whose "big man" on the staff was Murat Halstead, followed the *Gazette's* procedure. The story on Lincoln was not signed, but it was written in Halstead's style. It said in part:

The crowd was not as great as that drawn by Senator Douglas . . . but was three or four thousand strong. Among the appliances to bring out a crowd were a band of music, a cannon and rockets. The cannon was evidently fired without regard to economy in powder, for after every discharge there was a shrill jingle of falling glass. . . .

It is not wonderful that he is called "Old Abe," for his personal appearance is odd enough, and eminently suggestive of kindly nick-names.

The *Gazette* took issue with the *Enquirer's* statement that Lincoln spoke "in a manner that puzzles the ear," saying that he had a "singular clearness of enunciation . . . duly punctuating every sentence as he uttered it."[24]

The *Chicago Press and Tribune* sent shorthand reporter Robert Hitt to Ohio for Lincoln's speeches.[25] The *Cleveland Plain Dealer*, boosting Douglas, ignored Lincoln's Ohio visit until after he had spoken at Cincinnati, when it gave him 200 words under the head, "Lincoln At Cincinnati—A Great Fuss And A Great Fizzle." The story said Lincoln was not "a very pleasing or impressive speaker."[26]

Writing headlines for the *Plain Dealer* was Charles F. Browne, associate editor, soon to achieve fame as the humorist, "Artemus Ward," later editor of *Vanity Fair*.

While *The New York Times* was stealing the spotlight with its use of the "magnetic telegraph" to cover the Ohio campaign, the *New York Tribune* was giving it only routine attention. Editor Horace Greeley was on a trip to California, the *Mariposa* (Calif.) *Star* noting that he was a man of many peculiarities and "in a devil of a hurry to get back to New York."[27]

The *Tribune* printed Douglas's Wooster speech of September 16 on September 21, giving him more than half a column of unleaded type while Lincoln, speaking in Columbus, got but two inches. A week elapsed.

The *Tribune* on September 28 carried on page seven almost a full column under the heading, "Speech of the Hon. A. Lincoln of Illinois." An explanatory paragraph said: "We find in the Chicago *Press and Tribune* a phonographic report of a speech delivered by Mr. Lincoln of Illinois at Columbus, Ohio, on Friday, the 16th. We make a few extracts."[28]

There is only one explanation of the fact that the *Tribune* turned back to make a new coverage of Lincoln in Columbus. Greeley's editorial page contained a paragraph the day before that noted his return from California. It is wholly logical to presume that Greeley, looking over the file of papers published in his absence, noted his *Tribune* had not taken sufficient notice of Lincoln; he must have ordered the complete version published belatedly to cover up.

The *Daily Ohio Statesman* waited until Lincoln was home in Springfield before it published the correction he demanded. In a well-buried item, the *Statesman* begrudgingly said:

This gentleman took occasion in his speech in this city to say that he had never been in favor of granting the elective franchise to the negro, which we had stated to be his position. We give Mr. Lincoln the benefit of this denial and yet we are not satisfied but he did in some parts of Illinois preach that doctrine in the campaign of 1858. He, however, says he did not, and we make the correction so far as he is concerned. . . .[29]

The Ohio voters went to the polls on the second Tuesday in October. The result was a sweeping Republican victory.

It remained for an unpretentious weekly, the *Columbus* (Ohio) *Gazette*, to publish an editorial on the election that, for clarity of thought and power of prophecy, had no equal in any contemporary newspaper. Although the editor, John Greiner, could not find room to print a word about Lincoln's address in Columbus—all his space that week going to the list of prize winners at the Franklin County Fair—he wrote a remarkable editorial after the election. He said:

The recent results in Pennsylvania, Ohio, Indiana, Iowa and Minnesota seem to leave no doubt of the power of the opposition to carry the next Presidential election if proper wisdom and discretion are used in the selection of candidates. The united forces of the two wings of the Democracy, those who follow the lead of Douglas and talk of Squatter Sovereignty, and those who follow the President and join with him and his cabinet in their war upon the Douglas heresy, were not strong enough to save them from a complete rout in Ohio. What can they hope for in the coming struggle when these two elements, from their very nature, must be arraigned against each other?[30]

An event far more startling to the nation than the Ohio election occurred on October 16. John Brown, a fiery Abolitionist, spurred by guns and gold supplied by fanatical Northern men, seized the United States arsenal at Harpers Ferry, Va. His action was believed motivated by ambition to arouse the country and attract recruits before setting out to wrest slaves from their owners and free them.

Brown and twenty-two followers were trapped in the arsenal, and six, including their leader, were taken alive. Before Brown died on the scaffold on December 2, 1859, he said, "I am now quite certain that the crimes of this guilty land will never be purged away but with blood."[31]

During the first week in December, when the newspapers were filled with accounts of Brown's hanging, Lincoln made five speeches in Kansas at the request of Republicans.[32] In one of his speeches, he said neither he nor Seward was the first to express belief the government could not endure half slave and half free. He attributed it to the *Richmond* (Va.) *Enquirer*, edited by Roger A. Pryor, in 1856.[33] Actually, the quoted editorial was written by George Fitzhugh, who believed slavery was a rightful condition of society, for the *Enquirer*.

Upon his return to Springfield, Lincoln wrote for Jesse W. Fell, a Bloomington, Ill., businessman, a thumbnail sketch of his life.[34] Fell, long a friend of Lincoln, often wrote articles for the *Pantagraph*, his home-town newspaper. He had been in the Eastern states where he was struck by the number of inquiries about Lincoln. He conceived the idea of sending a brief biographical sketch of Lincoln to Eastern editors.[35]

Lincoln wrote for him the miniature biography which says, "I was raised to farm work . . . coarse black hair and gray eyes. No other marks or brands recollected."[36]

Probably to make it appear that the Eastern press was discussing Lincoln, the *Chicago Press and Tribune* published the sketch as a reprint from the *Chester County* (Pa.) *Times*.[37]

# 7 "That Thing of Mine in the Cooper Institute"

AFTER LINCOLN HELPED rout the Douglas led Democrats in Ohio, he found himself in demand as a speaker throughout the Midwest.[1] Without benefit of public office, he had become a big man west of the Alleghenies.

Among invitations to speak received by Lincoln was one that came by telegraph from New York on October 12, 1859. It was from James A. Briggs, offering him two hundred dollars to appear in "Mr. Beechers Church Brooklyn" on November 29.[2] By this Briggs meant Plymouth Church, where Henry Ward Beecher, Abolitionist and most famous preacher of his day, occupied the pulpit.

Lincoln and Briggs exchanged letters, with Lincoln insisting he make a political speech.[3] Because of financial or some other difficulty, Lincoln's engagement was taken over by the Young Men's Central Republican Union of New York.[4] In a letter dated "February 9, 1860," written from 69 Wall Street, Charles C. Nott, representing the Union, told him the lecture had been set for the "ensuing month."[5] Obviously, Nott was not aware of Lincoln's correct name, addressing him as "Abram Lincoln." The date was finally set: February 27.

On February 23, 1860, the *Illinois State Register* at Springfield, published this little item:

The Hon. Abraham Lincoln departs today for Brooklyn under an engagement to deliver a lecture before the Young Men's Association of that city in Beecher's church. Subject, not known. Consideration, $200 and expenses. Object, presidential capital. Effect, disappointment.[6]

The first leg of Lincoln's journey carried him to Chicago where he went to the office of the *Press and Tribune* and saw his friends, Joseph Medill and Dr. Charles H. Ray. He showed them the manuscript of his speech, telling them to look it over and to feel free to offer suggestions. He told them to make notes but to bear in mind he wanted the speech to stand so far as his arguments were concerned.[7]

The two newspaper men were eager to get their hands on the manuscript. They did not want their candidate for President to stub his toe in New York. Only a few days before, the *Press and Tribune* had published an editorial which said:

We have no hesitancy in saying that . . . Abraham Lincoln of Illinois is the peer of any man yet mentioned in connection with the Republican nomination, while as regards availability we believe him more certain to carry Illinois and Indiana than anyone else and his political antecedents are such as to commend him heartily to the support of Pennsylvania and New Jersey.[8]

Lincoln said he would return later to pick up the manuscript. Medill and Ray went to work; one read the speech aloud while the other listened. They made many notes for suggested changes, marking the proof for inserts and revisions. When he returned, he looked over their notes casually, telling them a funny story as he fumbled with the sheets, thanked them for their trouble, rolled up the manuscript, and left the office.[9]

When Lincoln arrived in New York, he learned for the first time that he was to speak in the Cooper Institute in New York, not in Plymouth Church across the river as he had supposed.[10] That was on February 25, a Saturday, and he could have read in the *New York Tribune* a story telling the people that Abraham Lincoln of Illinois was "a man of the people, a champion of free labor, of diversified and prosperous industry."[11]

Monday morning came and with it a last reminder to *Tribune* readers that Lincoln was to talk that night. At the top of the editorial page, Horace Greeley published this notice:

Remember Abraham Lincoln's address at the Cooper Institute tonight and ask your friends who are not Republicans to accompany you to hear it. It is not probable that Mr. Lincoln will be heard again in our city this year, if ever. Let us improve the present opportunity.[12]

Lincoln probably read on Saturday afternoon the New York *Evening Post*, edited by a man he was much interested in meeting, William Cullen Bryant, the noted poet. The *Post* made special mention of Lincoln's arrival in town and forecast he would make "a powerful assault upon the policy and principles of the pro-slavery party, and an able vindication of the Republican creed."[13]

The gray-bearded poet-editor of the *Evening Post* introduced Lincoln to the Cooper Institute audience Monday night. Greeley was seated on the stage, ready to say a few words after Lincoln finished. When Lincoln walked to the front of the stage, he looked down on men busy with pads and pencils in the first row. They were the reporters for the leading New York newspapers.

After the meeting, two members of the Republican Union took Lincoln to supper at the Athenaeum Club. Five or six other members joined them at the table. Nott, head of the lecture committee, offered to show Lincoln the way to the Astor House, where he was registered. They boarded a streetcar together, but Nott could only ride part way and Lincoln went on alone, the sole occupant of the horse-drawn vehicle.[14]

Later in the evening, Lincoln appeared in the office of the *New York Tribune*, going there at the invitation of Greeley to look over the proofs of his speech. He had been told upon arrival in New York that if he gave one newspaper the text, it would be set up and corrected proofs passed around to the others.

Amos J. Cummings, an eighteen-year-old proofreader, had just received the galley proofs, still damp with ink, when Lincoln entered the office. Cummings told Lincoln to draw up a chair to the table where he worked. Lincoln took the proofs, put on his glasses, and read each word carefully. Cummings suggested that Lincoln also read the revised proof but said he would have to wait until the corrections were made in the composing room. Lincoln appeared to be much interested in what was going on about him and made some remark to Cummings of the midnight life in a great newspaper office.

After Lincoln read the revised proof, he thanked Cummings and said good night to him. According to Cummings, Lincoln left the original manuscript of his speech lying on the table, and it was tossed into the wastepaper bin.[15]

Cummings was a man to be believed. He later fought as a Union volunteer in the army at Fredericksburg and Chancellorsville, returning after the war to the *Tribune*, where he became city editor and later was elected to Congress.[16]

The next morning, Lincoln left for Providence, R. I., where he was to speak that night. If he saw *The New York Times* before he left, he read:

There was a very large meeting of Republicans at Cooper Institute last night to listen to that noted political exhorter and prairie orator, Abe Lincoln. The speaker, as soon as he appeared on the platform, was vehemently cheered, and during the delivery of his address frequently applauded.[17]

That was all the *Times* had to say. The *New York Tribune* published the text under the dignified heading of "National Politics," with a deck beneath it that said, "A Speech Delivered At The Cooper Institute Last Evening By Abraham Lincoln Of Illinois." A separate story on the editorial page said:

The speech of Abraham Lincoln at the Cooper Institute last evening was one of the happiest and most convincing political arguments ever made in this city, and was addressed to a crowded and appreciating audience. Since the days of Clay and Webster, no man has spoken to a larger assemblage of the intellect and mental culture of our city. Mr. Lincoln is one of nature's orators, using his rare powers solely and effectively to convince, though their inevitable effect is to delight and electrify as well. We present herewith a very full and accurate report of the speech; yet the tones, the gestures, the kindling eye and the mirth-provoking look defy the reporter's skill. The vast assemblage frequently rang with cheers and shouts of applause, which were prolonged and intensified at the close. No man ever before made such an impression on his first appeal to a New York audience.

The editorial also said the *Tribune* planned to issue the speech in pamphlet form "for cheap circulation."[18]

The coverage of Bryant's *Evening Post* was similar to that of the *Tribune's*, with the text of the speech and a laudatory editorial. The *Post* wished its columns were "indefinitely elastic" for such an address. It reported that after Lincoln had finished the audience rose almost to a man, cheering, waving hats, and applauding.[19]

The *Evening Post*, appearing in the afternoon, was not on the streets when Lincoln left for Providence. Upon his return to New York en route to Springfield, he told Briggs he had seen what all the New York papers said "about that thing of mine in the Cooper Institute" with the exception of the *Evening Post* and that he was curious to know what Bryant thought of it. Briggs obtained a copy of the issue of February 28, 1860, for him.[20]

Lincoln's New England swing, starting at Providence, brought him eight platform appearances. The reaction of the press was generally favorable, some newspapers even enthusiastic.[21]

At Hartford, Conn., Lincoln found the man destined to be his Secretary of the Navy, Gideon Welles, editorial writer for the *Hartford Press*, a Republican newspaper founded by public subscription to offset influence of the conservative Democratic *Hartford Times*. Welles was formerly associated with the *Times*.[22] Joseph R. Hawley held the title of editor of the *Evening Press*.

Welles, defeated for governor as the first Republican nominee in Connecticut in 1856, also wrote political leads for the New York *Evening Post* and the *National Era* at Washington. He was a member of the Republican National Committee.

Greeted at the Hartford station by enthusiastic Republicans and the Hartford Cornet Band, travel-stained Lincoln climbed off the train and went directly to the speaking hall without changing into fresh linen. A keen-eyed reporter for the hostile *Hartford Times* noted the visitor wore a "dirty shirt" and later upbraided him for this social error.[23]

Lincoln called on Welles at the *Press* office before he left Hartford. After their meeting, Welles wrote for his newspaper, "He is an effective speaker and clear as crystal in his logic."[24]

The coolness of *The New York Times* to Lincoln after his address
at Cooper Institute has an explanation that lies deep in the marrow of
politics. Henry J. Raymond, editor of the *Times* and a canny politician,
had thrown all his strength into the effort to make Seward the outstanding candidate for the Republican presidential nomination in 1860.
He knew that a Western group, headed by Medill of the *Chicago Press
and Tribune*, was grooming Lincoln as the dark horse to defeat Seward.

On the very day Lincoln spoke in Cooper Institute, Medill's newspaper published a "Washington letter" aimed directly at Seward. The
"letter" was signed "Chicago," written by Medill, who had recently
been in the national capital. It was a follow-up to Medill's editorial of
February 16 that boomed Lincoln for the nomination.

The *Press and Tribune* called special attention to the "Washington
letter" with a blurb which said:

Our Washington letter, printed herewith, points out with great clearness
the path in which both principle and expediency demand that the Republican party should go. Avoiding, on the one hand, the radicalism which the
popular belief, rightfully or wrongfully, attributes to Mr. Seward, and the
politicians of his school; and on the other hand, the profound conservatism
of Mr. Bates and gentlemen of this belief, it leads, through a fearfully fought
field, straight to victory.

The "letter" was a 1,500-word analysis of the political situation as
Medill observed it in Washington. It pointed out in carefully phrased
sentences that Seward, as a radical, would alienate the more conservative Republicans, while of Bates the opposite was true. It asked: "Does
not common sense whisper in every man's ear that the middle ground
is the ground of safety?" It concluded:

I hear the name of Lincoln mentioned for President in Washington circles
ten times as often as it was one month ago. The more politicians look over
the field in search of candidates, the more they are convinced that "Old
Abe" is the man to win the race with. If the states of the Northwest shall
unite behind him, and present his name to the Chicago convention, there is
a strong possibility that he will receive the nomination, and as certain as he
is nominated that he will be President.[25]

Medill and Ray eagerly awaited the mail from the East to bring them
the *New York Tribune* of February 28. They wished to clip and reprint Lincoln's speech. They had still another interest in it; they wanted
to see how he used the changes they suggested. Lincoln used none of
them. Ray said "Abe" must have lost the notes out the car window.[26]

# 8 "Purely an Accident"

NOMINATION OF ABRAHAM LINCOLN by the Illinois Republicans as their choice for President—actually the pledging of the delegation—was a formality at the state convention at Decatur, May 9 and 10, 1860. While the convention merely went through the motions for their "favorite son," it provided the incident that gave Lincoln the name of "the rail splitter." It was the greatest publicity stunt ever staged for a political candidate.

The designation of Lincoln as "the rail splitter," at exactly the right time, caught the immediate fancy of the country. The very mention of the name caused people to forget he was a lifelong politician and lately a corporation lawyer. It put Lincoln back among the common people, placed his feet in the soil he once had tilled, garbed him in a raccoon-skin cap. It put an ax and a maul in his hands.

As the cheers were subsiding after Lincoln appeared on the platform at Decatur, the chairman announced to the delegates that an old Democrat of Macon County, "who had grown gray in the service of his party," desired to make a contribution to the convention.

John Hanks, Lincoln's cousin, came down the aisle carrying two old fence rails, decorated with flags and streamers of ribbon. Slowly he worked his way to the platform, taking his time so that all might read the placard attached to the rails. It said:

---

The Rail Candidate

For President in 1860

Two rails from a lot of 3,000 made in 1830 by Thos. Hanks and Abe Lincoln, whose father was the first pioneer of Macon County.

---

As soon as he could make himself heard, Lincoln explained that some thirty years before, while emigrating to Illinois, he stopped with his "mother's family" for one season in what is now Macon County; they built a cabin, split rails, and farmed "down on the Sangamon" six or eight miles from Decatur. Those rails, he said, pointing to the two held by Hanks, were taken from a fence built on that farm; but, whether they were or not, he had mauled many and better ones since he had grown to manhood.[1]

The story of the Decatur convention received only passing notice in the press. A dispatch out of St. Louis covered the meeting for the *New York Tribune,* and Lincoln's name was carried as "Abram." To add insult to injury, a *Tribune* editorial in the same edition also failed to give his right name.[2] A few days later, the fence-rail story began to circulate and was taken up by editors of Republican newspapers in all parts of the North. The widely read *Tribune* carried a feature story on the rails, and from that time on Lincoln was the "Rail Splitter."[3]

The Republican National Convention opened on May 16 in a huge, barn-like structure called the Wigwam in Chicago. Early arriving delegates read in the *Chicago Press and Tribune* an editorial a column long, entitled, "Abraham Lincoln, the Winning Man," offering eight itemized points why Lincoln should be supported for the nomination. The editorial was reprinted the next day.[4]

Representatives of the nation's press poured into Chicago. Early on the scene was the pilgarlic Horace Greeley of the *New York Tribune,* wearing his trade-mark, a duster, a sloppy coat of lightweight cloth that fell below his knees. Behind his spectacles, there was a gleam in his milk-blue eyes. Henry J. Raymond represented his own *New York Times* and was usually seen in the company of Thurlow Weed, editor of the *Albany Evening Journal* and manager of the forces behind the candidacy of Senator William H. Seward. Working in the press gallery was Murat Halstead, of the *Cincinnati Commercial,* outstanding political reporter of the day.

In addition to his notebook and pencil, Greeley carried the credentials of a delegate from Oregon pledged to Edward Bates of Missouri. He brought a staff of reporters with him from New York, but he was the busiest man in town, seen at all sessions in the Wigwam, in the smoke-filled hotel rooms, in the lobbies, and on the street corners.

Greeley's national reputation made him a news item, and even his rival, *The New York Times,* carried a story about him, saying:

Mr. Greeley made a great sensation here. He is surrounded by a crowd wherever he goes, who besiege him for a speech, and failing in that seduce him into conversation, which inevitably becomes a speech ere he closes.

Some foolish wag pinned to his coat tail a paper bearing an inscription, "For Wm. H. Seward," and for several hours he unconsciously carried the irrepressible badge with him. . . .

The New York delegation gave a dinner . . . this afternoon. . . . In response to several speeches about Mr. G., who was not present, Mr. Raymond defended Mr. G. from the imputation of selfishness, and vindicated his right to act as the best interests of the Republican Party seem to require.[5]

The day before the convention opened, the *New York Tribune* published a lead editorial in which the chances of all candidates for the nomination were discussed. Buried near the end was this one mention of Lincoln: "Mr. Lincoln of Illinois, however, is rising in prominence."[6]

After the first day's session, Greeley filed a special dispatch, signed with his initials, that led all the convention coverage by the *Tribune* staff. A sort of bulletin, it said:

Chicago, Wednesday, May 16—10:40 P.M. As to the Presidency, I can only say that the advocates of Gov. Seward's nomination, who were much depressed last night, are now quite confident of his success. . . . I should say that the chances of his nomination are now about even. Mr. Lincoln now appears to have the next best look.[7]

The convention approached the climax of balloting the next day, and Greeley waited until near midnight to file his final dispatch for the next morning's *Tribune*. Under the headline, "Gov. Seward Will Be Nominated," the dispatch, signed "H. G.," said:

Chicago, Thursday, May 17—11:40 P.M. My conclusion, from all that I can gather, tonight, is that the opposition to Gov. Seward cannot concentrate on any candidate, and that he will be nominated.[8]

Halstead was of the same opinion, and he wired his newspaper that "the indications now are that Seward will be nominated tomorrow. . . . The Seward men are greatly elated, and champagne flows abundantly at their headquarters. It is reported that three hundred bottles were cracked tonight. . . ."[9]

The Lincoln managers packed the spectators's seats with their friends when the Wigwam opened the next day. Not a seat was available in the great hall an hour before the session began. An angry Pennsylvania delegate called out to the chairman that seats in his section were occupied by outsiders, and a voice from the Ohio delegation roared, "Same here!"[10]

There were no nominating speeches. William M. Evarts rose to present Seward's name and received thunderous applause. Other names,

favorite sons, were presented. Norman B. Judd offered the name of
Abraham Lincoln in behalf of the Illinois delegation. The demonstration
that followed was thusly described by Halstead:

Imagine all the hogs ever slaughtered in Cincinnati giving their death
squeals together. . . . I thought the Seward yell could not be surpassed;
but the Lincoln boys . . . made every plank and pillar in the building
quiver. The New York, Michigan, and Wisconsin delegations sat . . . very
quiet. Many . . . faces whitened. . . .[11]

An Ohioan with the unusual name of Columbus Delano was
recognized by the chair and said, "I arise on behalf of a portion of the
delegation from Ohio to put in nomination the man who can split
rails and maul Democrats." At the time, the press gallery believed
Delano was seconding the Lincoln nomination, and it was so reported
in many newspapers.[12]

At last all entries were made, and the roll of states was called for the
first ballot. Seward led, as his supporters had anticipated, with 172½
votes; Lincoln, 102; Cameron, 50½; Bates, 28; Chase, 49. Other votes
were scattered. Lincoln jumped to 181 on the second roll call, Seward
to 184½. Chase had 42½, Bates had 35, and others were again scattered.
The number of votes in the convention was 465, with 233 needed to
nominate.

A third roll was called. Lincoln went to 231½; Seward dropped to
180. Lincoln needed only a vote and a half to win.[13] Halstead, in the
press gallery with poised pencil, tabulated the vote as it was called and
knew what to expect.

I looked up to see who would be the man to give the decisive vote. . . .
In about ten ticks of a watch, Cartter, of Ohio, was up . . . and everybody
who understood the matter at all knew what he was about to do. He is a
large man with rather striking features and . . . has an impediment in his
speech, which amounts to a stutter; and his selection as chairman of the
Ohio delegation was . . . altogether appropriate. He had been quite noisy
during the sessions of the convention, but had never commanded, when
mounting his chair, such attention as now. He said, "I rise (eh) Mr. Chairman (eh) to announce the change of four votes of Ohio from Mr. Chase to
Mr. Lincoln." The deed was done.[14]

That was fine surface reporting, but it did not tell the whole story.
Halstead did not know—at least he said nothing about it—that Joseph
Medill of the *Chicago Press and Tribune* had wedged himself into the
Ohio delegation and was the principal actor in the little drama that

preceded Cartter's momentous announcement. Thirty years later, Medill revealed the details.

The Ohio delegation went to Chicago with eight of their number pledged to Lincoln. The rest of the delegation was bound to Chase. As part of the Lincoln strategy, Medill sat with the Ohioans, many of whom he knew as friends of his Buckeye publishing days. Delano spoke only for the eight Lincoln pledges.

When the second ballot revealed Lincoln's growing strength, Medill whispered to David Kellogg Cartter, a Massillon attorney, that Chase could have "anything he wants" if the Ohio delegation went over to Lincoln. Cartter had the four votes ready before the third roll call was tabulated.[15] Hannibal Hamlin was nominated for Vice-President.

After the convention, there was some newspaper comment as to the identity of the four Chase delegates who turned to Lincoln at Cartter's bidding. Halstead wrote that it mattered little, that the part Cartter played was overdrawn in the press. He pointed out that chairmen of other delegations were waving for recognition, with at least fifty votes ready for delivery to Lincoln. But the eye of Chairman George Ashmun had fallen on the blustery Cartter, and to him went the honor of the convention.[16]

Cartter was rewarded by appointment as Minister to Bolivia, a post he resigned after a year. In 1863, President Lincoln named him chief justice of the supreme court of the District of Columbia.[17]

Halstead's narrative continued:

I left the city on the night train. . . . At every station where there was a village, until two o'clock there were tar barrels burning, drums beating, boys carrying rails; and guns, great and small banging away. The weary passengers were allowed no rest, but plagued by the thundering jar of cannon, the clamor of drums, the glare of bonfires, and the wild whooping of the boys, who were delighted with the idea of a candidate for the Presidency who thirty years ago had split rails on the Sangamon River—classic stream now and forever more—and whose neighbors named him "honest."[18]

"Perhaps some reader," said the *Chicago Journal*, "will be curious to know how 'Honest Old Abe' received the news of his nomination." It related that Lincoln was waiting in Springfield with a group of friends, all of them hanging over the telegraph wire as the operator took down the vote state by state. It continued:

Mr. Lincoln walked over to the *State Journal* office. He was sitting there conversing while the third ballot was being taken. When Cartter, of Ohio, announced the change of four votes, giving Lincoln a majority . . . it was telegraphed to Springfield. Mr. Wilson, the Telegraphic Superintendent, who was in the office, instantly wrote on a scrap of paper, "Mr. Lincoln, you are nominated on the third ballot," and gave it to a boy who ran with it to Mr. Lincoln. He took the paper in his hand and looked at it long and silently, not heeding the noisy exultation of all around him, and then rising and putting the note in his vest pocket, he quietly remarked, "There's a little woman down at our house would like to hear this. I'll go down and tell her."[19]

The day after the nomination, Ashmun headed a committee that went to Springfield to officially notify Lincoln that he was the Republican candidate for President. The press also sent a delegation, one of its number being Raymond of *The New York Times*.

Of the occasion, the *Times* said:

No one doubts that he has all the intellectual ability, the honesty of purpose, and the fixedness of political principle essential to the high position for which he is in nomination. The only apprehension which any of his friends entertain is that he may lack the iron firmness of will and the practical experience of men of factions, which the passing crisis will render indispensable in a Republican President.

Another sentence paid high compliment to the future First Lady, saying: "Mrs. Lincoln is apparently fifteen years younger than Mr. Lincoln."[20]

Greeley's *New York Tribune* said in an editorial that the Republican nominee was probably of the race of Massachusetts Lincolns and that his father died when he was six years old.[21] The *Tribune* was not alone in its amazing ignorance. Many leading newspapers still did not know Lincoln's first name. Even the *Peoria* (Ill.) *Transcript* was befuddled and published an appeal to be enlightened, saying: ". . . is it Abraham or is it the shorter name of Abram? We want the sign manual of Old Abe on his letter of acceptance to settle the question."[22]

The case of the *Toledo* (Ohio) *Blade* stands out. After the nomination, the *Blade* lauded Lincoln and asserted he was "no new man," then proceeded to call him Abram twice in the same column.[23]

Weed, whose best efforts for Seward were beaten, was a hard fighter but a good loser, saying in his *Albany Evening Journal:*

It would be idle to attempt to disguise the disappointment which the people of this State feel at the failure of the Chicago Convention to place in nomination for President the candidate of their own State. But there can be no doubt that the nomination which was made is regarded as the very next choice of the Republicans of New York. No other man, beside their own favorite, so well represents the party in the great struggle now going on as Abraham Lincoln.[24]

The nomination of Lincoln, wholly unexpected, was a profound sensation for the press, both Republican and Democratic, throughout the Northern states. Following are excerpts from representative Republican newspapers in the Eastern states:

New York *Evening Post:* "It is written on the tablet of destiny that Lincoln is to be next President of the United States."

New York *Commercial Advertiser:* ". . . in some respects Abraham Lincoln is as truly a representative man as William H. Seward."

*Buffalo* (N. Y.) *Express:* "Next to William H. Seward we believe that no man before the Convention could have been chosen so generally satisfactory to the Republicans of this State as Abraham Lincoln."

*Syracuse* (N. Y.) *Standard:* "In his hands the executive office will be disgraced by no chicanery or corruption."

*Troy* (N. Y.) *Daily Times:* "Mr. Lincoln is a representative Western man; one who owes what he is to his own exertions, and who comes fresh from the ranks of the people."

*New Haven* (Conn.) *Palladium:* " 'Honest Abe Lincoln,' as everybody calls him where he is best known, is just the man that this sorely swindled and disgraced nation needs for President."

*Hartford* (Conn.) *Press:* ". . . just the man the crisis demands."

*Hartford* (Conn.) *Courant:* ". . . the intellectual power of a giant with the simple habits of a backwoods farmer."

*Springfield* (Mass.) *Republican:* "In ways which it is useless to mention now, we are, of course, disappointed."

*Boston Advertiser:* "The next President of the United States will be Abraham Lincoln."

*Boston Journal:* "Mr. Lincoln has that simple integrity of character, that broad and genial nature, to which the masses of our people are ever attracted."

*Boston Atlas and Bee:* "Mr. Lincoln is all that could be desired."

*Newark* (N. J.) *Daily Advertiser:* "Mr. Lincoln deserves and will have the support of the common people for he is one of them."

*Philadelphia Inquirer:* ". . . a true type of the sturdy pioneers who settled the Western wilderness and made it blossom like a rose."

*Pittsburgh Journal:* "He is the idol of the Northwest, and will nowhere encounter any prejudice."

*Detroit* (Mich.) *Daily Advertiser:* "The heart of Michigan was set on her beloved Seward and she had warmly hoped . . . he would be the choice."

*Albany* (N. Y.) *Daily Union:* ". . . we are entirely satisfied with the nominee, and shall go into the canvass with the utmost confidence."[25]

Some editors of Democratic newspapers indulged in ridicule while others, foreseeing the defeat of their party, wrote words of warning. The following are fair samples:

*New York Herald:* "The conduct of the Republican party in this nomination is a remarkable indication of small intellect, growing smaller. They pass over Seward, Chase and Bates, who are statesmen and able men, and they take up a fourth-rate lecturer, who cannot speak good grammar, and who, to raise the wind, delivers his hackneyed, illiterate compositions at $200 apiece. Our readers will recollect that this peripatetic politician visited New York two or three months ago on his financial tour, when, in return for the most unmitigated trash, interlarded with coarse and clumsy jokes, he filled his empty pockets with dollars coined out of Republican fanaticism. If, after he becomes President of the United States, the public finances should fail, he can set out on a lecturing mission through the country, taking Horace Greeley along with him."

New York *Journal of Commerce:* "While we have no desire to detract from Mr. Lincoln's position as a respectable citizen of Illinois, we are not aware that he possesses, in any considerable degree, the qualifications demanded for so elevated a position as that of Chief Magistrate of the United States. Probably an attempt will be made to . . . present him as . . . the candidate who can 'split rails and maul the Democrats.' "

*New York Day Book:* "The nomination of Lincoln . . . is a formidable one, probably more so than would be that of any other man who has been named in connection with it."

New York *Sun:* "Lincoln's nomination is considered a challenge to the Democrats to nominate Douglas when their convention resumes at Baltimore."

Albany, N. Y., *Atlas and Argus:* "He . . . is not known except as a slang-whanging stump speaker . . . of which all parties are ashamed."

Trenton, N. J., *True American:* "By what process this selection was made it is hard to understand."

Philadelphia *Press:* "It is now quite certain that if Mr. Douglas be rejected by the Democratic Convention of Baltimore, Mr. Lincoln will sweep Illinois, Indiana, and the whole North-West, and his election by the people becomes, perhaps, a foregone conclusion."

*Boston Post:* "The Chicago sectional Convention—a thorough geographical body—has crowned its work by nominating a mere local politician. . . . When and how has Abraham Lincoln shown ability to warrant this distinction over his competitors?"

*Boston Herald:* "The nomination in many respects is a strong one, and will be difficult to defeat."

*Rochester* (N. Y.) *Advertiser:* "Lincoln is a man not to be despised. He is a man of fair talents, a self-made man, a tall, swarthy, rather cadaverous-looking Kentuckian, a good stump talker, and possesses the qualities which make men popular with 'the boys.' "[26]

Millions upon millions of words were printed, with the Democratic attack reinforced by disgruntled Republican editors. Many newspapers that had been on the political fence were forced to make a decision. Here are editorial excerpts picked at random from the Northern press:

*Boston Traveller:* "Mr. Lincoln is well known to be a man of chivalrous courage, and frank and open as light itself, qualities that ever tell with the people."

*Boston Transcript:* ". . . he seems to combine in a rare degree shrewdness with enthusiasm and practical sagacity with passionate devotion to principle."

Washington *National Intelligencer:* "Mr. Lincoln . . . has not until recently occupied a prominent place in the list of distinguished citizens from which it was supposed the Republicans would make a selection."

Philadelphia *Evening Journal:* "To expose Mr. Lincoln and to cover with shame the party that nominated him, we need only to quote from these harangues (the house divided speech and others)."

*Troy* (N. Y.) *Whig:* "The nomination . . . will disappoint the country."

*New York Evening Express:* "Mr. Lincoln is a very respectable lawyer in
Illinois, but with not the twentieth part of the education or talent that
Mr. Seward has."

*Detroit* (Mich.) *Free Press:* "The Black Republican convention . . . nominated Lincoln for President . . . the man whom Douglas beat two years
ago. That is all the reputation he has . . . and this reputation will not
desert him this year."

*Buffalo* (N. Y.) *Daily Courier:* "He is a man of nerve, independence, and
perseverance, but is lacking in culture. . . . Hannibal Hamlin . . . is a
man of much higher order of ability than Mr. Lincoln."[27]

The flood of newspaper comment had begun to subside when Horace
Greeley decided to share the secrets of the Chicago convention and to
indulge in "personal reminiscences" for the enjoyment of *New York
Tribune* readers. On Tuesday morning, May 22, 1860, he published on
the editorial page a story signed with his initials, under the heading,
"Last Week At Chicago." The pronoun "I" was used, instead of the
editorial "we," an unusual procedure for even such an egotist as
Greeley. The story said in part:

The history of the late Republican National Convention is already before
the public; but some personal reminiscences of that struggle may still pos-
sess a shade of interest; so I shall brave the charge of egotism by narrating
them.

My mind had been long before deliberately made up that the nomination of Gov. Seward for President was unadvisable and unsafe. . . .

I went to Chicago to do my best to nominate Judge Bates, unless facts
there developed should clearly render another choice advisable. . . . I think
Judge Bates, to whom I never spoke nor wrote, would have been the wiser
choice. . . .

There is no truer, more faithful, more deserving Republican than Abraham Lincoln; probably no nomination could have been made more condu-
cive to a certain triumph; and yet I feel that the selection of Edward Bates
would have been more far-sighted, more courageous, more magnanimous. . . .

Raymond of *The New York Times* was with Seward at his home in
Auburn, N. Y., when Greeley's "reminiscence" appeared in the
*Tribune.* Writing under date of May 22, Raymond answered Greeley
in a long letter published in the *Times,* saying in part:

I observe that today's *Tribune* contains a long personal explanation from Mr. Greeley of the part which he took in the action of the Chicago Convention. It is never easy for a public man to be the historian of his own exploits. . . . With the generosity which belongs to his nature . . . he awards to others the credit which belongs transcendently to himself.

The main work of the Chicago Convention was the defeat of Gov. Seward; that was the only specific and distinct object toward which its conscious efforts were directed. The nomination which it finally made was purely an accident. . . .

He (Greeley) had special qualifications as well as a special love for the task. . . . For twenty years he had been sustaining the political principles and vindicating the political conduct of Mr. Seward through the columns of the most influential political newspaper in the country. . . .

Mr. Greeley was largely indebted to the forbearance of those upon whom he was waging this warfare, for the means of making it effectual. While it was known to some of them that, nearly six years ago—in November, 1854 —he had privately, but distinctly, repudiated all further political friendship for and alliance with Gov. Seward . . . for the avowed reason that Gov. Seward had never aided or advised his elevation to office. . . .

. . . no use was made of this knowledge in quarters where it would have disarmed the deadly effect of his pretended friendship. . . .

Raymond further charged that Greeley was in Chicago several days before the convention opened, laying plans for the defeat of Seward. He said Greeley approached the delegations from Vermont, New Hampshire, Ohio, Indiana, and other states "in favor of Seward" with a story to this effect: He favored Governor Seward through long personal and political friendship, but the Republican party could not win with him.[28]

The exchange of letters between the two leading Republican editors became the talk of the country overnight. The press, both Republican and Democratic, reprinted them. Never before was there such a public laundering of dirty political linen.

In an immediate reply to Raymond, Greeley called the Auburn letter "a carefully drawn indictment" and said it contained "a very artful mixture of truth and misrepresentation." This was his sarcastic beginning:

The Hon. Henry J. Raymond, of *The* N. Y. *Times,* has returned from the Chicago Convention to New York, and with his constitutional addiction to crooked ways, appears to have taken both Springfield, Illinois, and Auburn, N. Y., on his homeward route, paying court alike to the rising and the setting sun. A narrative of his observations and gleanings at the residences respectively of Gov. Seward and Mr. Lincoln appears in *The* N. Y. *Times* of yesterday, having for its undisguised *animus* the bitterest hostility to myself.[29]

Greeley reprinted Raymond's letter exactly as it appeared in the *Times* and hurled this challenge: "I therefore call on him for the private letter which I *did* write him in November, 1854, that I may print it *verbatim* in THE TRIBUNE, and let every reader judge how far it sustains the charges which his mouth-piece bases thereon."[30]

There was a story behind the letter. Greeley for years had considered himself a member of the self-styled "political firm" of Seward, Weed, and Greeley, his association with the two politicians dating back to his early days when he edited the Whig campaign organ. With public offices handed out at the wave of a Seward or Weed hand, Greeley finally became aware he was not sharing in the spoils and in 1854 asked Weed for the nomination as governor. The Albany editor knew Greeley, at that time a leading prohibitionist, could not win, and he refused the request. Greeley went back to Albany with his hat in his hand and asked Weed to have him nominated for lieutenant governor. Again the answer was no.

When the New York Whigs held their state convention, Raymond was nominated for lieutenant governor.[31] He was swept into office by the Whig victory. Greeley saw he had been supplanted as junior partner in the "political firm" by Raymond, and on November 11, 1854, he wrote the letter in question to Seward, not to Raymond. He began, "It seems to me a fitting time to announce to you the dissolution of the political firm of Seward, Weed, and Greeley, by the withdrawal of the junior partner, said withdrawal to take effect on the morning of the first Tuesday in February next."

The date Greeley set for "dissolution" was the day Seward was slated to be elected United States Senator by the New York assembly.

He closed the letter with this statement: "All I ask is that we shall be counted even on the morning after the first Tuesday in February, as aforesaid, as seems best without reference to the past."[32]

Seward and Raymond called Greeley's hand by sending the letter to him for publication. It was printed in the *Tribune*, a full column on the editorial page, a couple of weeks later. In a signed editorial that accompanied the letter, Greeley said:

I am indebted to Senator Seward through Mr. Thurlow Weed for the manuscript of my private letter to Gov. Seward, written soon after the conclusion of the canvass of 1854. . . . If ever in my life I discharged a public duty in utter disregard of personal considerations, I did so at Chicago last month.[33]

Weed acted as though Greeley's letter to Seward was all news to him and said in the *Albany Evening Journal* that, having existed for six years in "blissful ignorance of its content, we should much prefer to have ever remained so." He added tenderly that the letter "jars harshly upon cherished memories."[34]

A year later, Weed and Seward got their revenge. Greeley sought the office of United States Senator and seemed to have a good chance of winning. His only close rival was William M. Evarts, a favorite of Weed and Seward.

When the balloting started at Albany, Weed was behind the scenes for Evarts. Greeley showed much strength, and Weed saw the fight for Evarts was hopeless. The Albany magician suddenly presented the name of Ira Harris to the assembly and went on to victory with him. Harris, a judge on the state supreme court bench, had not been seriously considered until Weed touched him with his magic wand.[35]

The fight between Greeley and Raymond, coming at a time when a united party front was essential to the welfare of the Union, left political sores that ran all during Lincoln's administrations.

# 9 "Secession Becomes the Glory"

THE REPUBLICAN NATIONAL CONVENTION that nominated Lincoln was the third held in that summer of 1860. The Democrats had met in Charleston, S. C., in April, splitting wide open on the slavery issue. The slave-state delegates demanded a platform that held slavery existed in the territories by right of the Constitution. Free-state delegates pushed across a platform which left the issue to the people of the territories, whereupon Alabama, South Carolina, Mississippi, Louisiana, Arkansas, Florida, and Texas withdrew. The convention adjourned to meet at Baltimore, Md.

The eight slave states that refused to walk out with the "cotton states" were Georgia, North Carolina, Virginia, Tennessee, Missouri, Maryland, Delaware, and Kentucky. This meant slavery no longer owned the Democratic party lock, stock, and barrel.

The Democratic party continued to divide. Delegates from both slave and free states, calling themselves the Constitutional Union party, nominated John Bell, a Tennessee slaveholder, for President, with Edward Everett, former president of Harvard College, as his running mate. Then came nomination of the unknown Lincoln at Chicago on May 16 by the Republicans.

The adjourned Democratic convention met in June and, after a row over delegates who had walked out at Charleston, nominated Senator Stephen A. Douglas for President and Herschel V. Johnson, of Georgia, for Vice-President. In the fight over delegates, the Virginians withdrew, followed by representatives of other slave states and some from states where slavery did not exist. The seceding group chose their own candidates, John C. Breckinridge of Kentucky and Joseph Lane of Oregon.[1]

The handwriting on the wall was clear to unbiased political observers. With the Democrats split three ways, nothing stood between the Republicans and the White House except the intervening months.

An old story told about James K. Polk in 1845 was revived, making Lincoln the central figure, after the Republican convention. The captain of a sailing vessel, homeward bound from China, hailed an outbound ship off Sandy Hook and called, "Who is President of the United States?" The answer came back, "James K. Polk." The captain had a second question: "Who in the hell is James K. Polk?" Fifteen years later, the people were asking: "Who in the hell is Abraham Lincoln?"[2]

Follett, Foster & Co. of Columbus, Ohio, publisher of the Lincoln-Douglas debates, thought it good business to answer that question. They planned a book on the life of Lincoln and assigned to the task of writing it a newly hired manuscript reader named William Dean Howells, twenty-three-year-old former news editor of the *Ohio State Journal* of Columbus. Howells had been released by the *Journal* in an economy wave that overlooked two hundred dollars due him in back pay.[3]

Follett wanted Howells to go to Springfield and obtain from Lincoln the facts on which to base the story. Howells refused to go, explaining the interview was "distasteful" to him, and Follett found a young law student to make the trip. James Quay Howard accepted the assignment and brought back to Columbus a stack of notes from which Howells wrote *Lives and Speeches of Abraham Lincoln and Hannibal Hamlin.*[4]

The book was padded with campaign oratory of both Lincoln and Hamlin. It carried a page-size engraving of the beardless Lincoln, from a photograph by Brady at the time of the Cooper Institute address. On page 94, Howells wrote: "The biographer's task ends here. . . . He prefers to leave the future of Abraham Lincoln to Providence and to the people, who often make history without the slightest respect to the arrangements of sagacious writers."

Others wrote campaign lives of Lincoln, but it is Howells's book that is remembered because he became a literary lion, renowned in America and Europe.

When the Robert Todd Lincoln Collection of the Papers of Abraham Lincoln was opened in the summer of 1947, the sheaf of notes made by Howard came to light. No one knows how the notes came into Robert Lincoln's hands, but several explanations have been offered. Howells gave them back to Howard, who may have handed them to Robert. Or, John G. Nicolay and John Hay, the President's private secretaries, may have obtained them from Howard and passed them on to the son. Only an initialed "H" appears in the notes as the clue to the writer, but the contents stamp them as Howard's work. It was at first believed the "H" stood for John Hay.[5]

The notes reveal Lincoln was concerned over the public's ignorance of his correct name. Howard wrote, "Lincoln says my name should be written '*Abraham* Lincoln.' "[6]

Editor William Cullen Bryant of the New York *Evening Post* wrote to Lincoln on June 16, 1860, a long letter full of sage advice on the proper conduct of a campaign. Referring to himself as "an old campaigner," Bryant told Lincoln he should make no speeches and write no letters.[7] Lincoln thanked him.[8]

A letter to Lincoln from Joseph Medill of the *Chicago Press and Tribune,* dated June 18, was of far more importance. Medill said he was leaving for New York to attempt to obtain support of the *New York Herald* in the presidential campaign. An intermediary had sounded out Publisher James Gordon Bennett and had found him willing to "dicker," Medill said. Bennett's ambition, wrote Medill, was to be a guest with his wife and son at the White House, being "too rich" to desire money. Medill thought it best that the *Herald* should maintain a policy of neutrality, explaining that Bennett's active support would be of little moment, but he could cause a great deal of trouble unless his guns were spiked. Medill promised to see his "Satanic Majesty" and find out what he wanted.[9]

Lincoln was corresponding with other important newspaper editors, among them Weed, Raymond, and George G. Fogg, the editor of the *Independent Democrat*, Concord, N. H. Fogg, a member of the Republican National Committee, told Lincoln not to accept an invitation to speak in Springfield, Mass., but to maintain his "retirement."[10]

Correspondence conducted by Lincoln with Samuel Haycraft, living at Elizabethtown, Ky., who had written to him to ask about his place of birth and his family, resulted in the *New York Herald* publishing a damaging story about the Republican nominee. Haycraft suggested Lincoln might like to visit his birthplace, and he answered in a playful moment, asking whether it would be safe and whether the people might not lynch him. Although Lincoln marked his letter "Private," Haycraft displayed it to his friends.

A few weeks later, Lincoln took Haycraft to task, complaining that the *Herald* reported Lincoln had been invited to Kentucky but that the candidate feared "violence" if he went there. Haycraft denied any knowledge of the *Herald* story and offered to write a correction.[11]

Ohio, Indiana, and Pennsylvania held state elections on October 9, 1860, and the Republican victory foretold what was to happen when the nation cast its vote on November 6. Henry S. Lane was elected Governor of Indiana; Andrew G. Curtin won the Pennsylvania governorship; Ohio went Republican by more than twenty thousand in the Congressional contests, assuring the state for Lincoln, but in the Third District, Clement L. Vallandigham, a Democrat, won his race for re-election.[12]

The South was in ferment. Many newspapers there said election of Lincoln would mean dismemberment of the Union. A New York printer went to Charleston, S. C., to take a job on the *Mercury* and was jailed as an "Abolition emissary." He was freed on his promise to leave the state in twenty-four hours. The alternative was a public flogging, bread and water, and thirty days in jail.[13]

The *Charleston Mercury* was widely reprinted in the Northern press, and the *New York Tribune* ran a feature story from a Charleston correspondent about the fiery Southern publication. The owner of the *Mercury*, said the correspondent, was R. Barnwell Rhett, "a well-known wealthy agitator," whose slogan was, "I'd rather rule in Hell than serve in Heaven." The circulation of the *Mercury* was estimated to be only five hundred and fifty daily, half of which went out as exchanges. Rhett, the story said, lost about eight thousand dollars annually in his newspaper.[14]

On the day before election, Governor William H. Gist of South Carolina recommended to his state legislature that it vote to secede

from the Union "in event of Abraham Lincoln's election to the Presidency."[15]

Lincoln went to the polls at Springfield on the afternoon of November 6 but refused to vote for himself, cutting his name from the top of
the ticket.[16] About nine o'clock that evening he went to the telegraph
office where, stretched at full length on a sofa, he heard the returns
read to him by excited operators. Near midnight, he went out for a bite
to eat. A special correspondent of the *New York Tribune*, covering
events in Springfield that night, scratched this paragraph and filed it to
his newspaper:

The ladies of Springfield have prepared an entertainment for their voting
brethren, at which all the convivialities of coffee, fine chorus singing, and
the like are offered. Mr. Lincoln has gone over for awhile to share the
merriment, and his reception was the wildest climax of feminine ecstacy.
Mrs. Lincoln was also present, an honored guest.[17]

All night the *Tribune* correspondent watched Lincoln. His last
bulletin, dated 4:45 A.M., said: "Mr. Lincoln has just bid good night
to the telegraph office and gone home."[18]

The Lincoln seen by the *Tribune* writer was a beardless man in the
prime of life, a man who laughed easily. His story said: "Mr. Lincoln's
age, I believe, is fifty-one, but he certainly has no appearance of being
so old. His hair is black, hardly touched with gray, and his eye is
brighter than that of many of his juniors."[19]

There is a possibility the *New York Tribune*'s reporter that night was
John G. Nicolay, who became Lincoln's secretary after the election.
Just two years before, November 8, 1858, Lincoln wrote to Horace
Greeley, recommending Nicolay as a correspondent.[20]

The day after the election, the *Tribune* representative sent another
story that showed an intimate knowledge of Lincoln's affairs. It would
seem the correspondent visited the Statehouse, where the President-elect
was receiving visitors. He wrote:

One table is covered with law books, and another is littered with newspapers enough to supply a country journalist with items for a year. Heaps
and hills of newspapers, a few opened, the greater part still unfolded. If
you take the wrappers from a few of these neglected sheets, you will find,
within, whole columns of fervid eloquence, sonorous with big capitals, and
bursting with hot Republican sentiment, all carefully marked and under-
lined, the sooner to catch the eye of the great chief. Alas for the little
ambitions of village editors. They have sent the cherished begettings of

their brains to an oblivion too deep and too crowded for any chance of rescuing.[21]

The story cries aloud that it was written by Nicolay. He himself had been one of the "village editors," writing of the Republican party with "fervid eloquence."

On his editorial page in the *New York Tribune*, Greeley served soothing syrup to an agitated country. The editorial said: "It is not to be supposed that the election of Abraham Lincoln as President of these United States—conspicuous and glorious triumph as it is—will at once restore the country to political harmony and quiet, though we are convinced that the agitation raised in the South will gradually and surely subside into peace."[22]

The words "irrepressible conflict" were on everybody's tongue. Merchants recognized the thought of the day in advertising. A Broadway hat store published this notice: "The IRREPRESSIBLE CONFLICT is not a circumstance to the irrepressible Knox who still remains stubbornly obstinate in his course, and will insist on selling the best, the neatest and most stylish HATS and CAPS in the city at the very lowest prices . . . !"[23]

Bennett's *New York Herald* reported in a dispatch from Washington how the Capital received the news of Lincoln's election, saying:

The effect . . . upon the people of this District can be more easily imagined than described. There is no place in the United States where the officeholders, for nearly everybody has an office—feel it more disastrously. The defeat of Lincoln was a matter of life and death with them, and when it was announced that he was elected, curses loud and deep went up from these infuriated individuals. They were for forming a Southern Confederacy at once, and some of the more resolute and determined donned the cockade, and indicated their willingness to shoulder their musket and resist the inauguration of Lincoln.[24]

The *New Orleans Delta* reported a shipment of *Harper's Weekly* was fired back to New York by the dealer because there was a picture of Abraham Lincoln in it.[25] Rhett of the *Charleston Mercury* spoke before an indignation meeting in Charleston. "They have elected a Southern renegade—spewed out of the bosom of Kentucky into Illinois—and a Northern white-washed octoroon mulatto, to be President and Vice-President of the United States," he said.[26]

The Southern press fairly boiled. Almost every newspaper published in the slave states had some insult or a word of warning for Lincoln. These editorial excerpts are typical:

Baltimore, Md., *Daily Republican:* "Abraham Lincoln has been voted for by the North and East. . . . But it is very doubtful . . . he will ever be President of the *United* States."

*Richmond* (Va.) *Enquirer:* "From the beginning to the end this has been a sectional contest."

*Richmond* (Va.) *Dispatch:* "The election of Abraham Lincoln has indeed put the country in peril."

*Alexandria* (Va.) *Sentinel:* "We of the South have thus imposed upon us a government outside of ourselves, and founded on a sentiment hostile to our social system."

*Raleigh* (N. C.) *Press:* "The die is cast."

*Wilmington* (N. C.) *Herald:* "We will have trouble."

*Wilmington* (N. C.) *Journal:* "The election of Lincoln . . . means all the insult . . . that such an act can do."

*Charleston* (S. C.) *Courier:* "The memorable event of the 6th November, 1860 . . . determined the failure of the great American experiment of self-government."

*Charleston* (S. C.) *Mercury:* "In the spirit and temper of the times, a convention of the people of South Carolina, to be held within four weeks, to pronounce upon her remedies in the crisis which is at hand, means disunion—means the separation of South Carolina, whether alone or with others, from the Union which can only be a badge of infamy to her!"

*Savannah* (Ga.) *Republican:* "The responsibilities are fearful, for the future is unknown."

*Augusta* (Ga.) *Sentinel:* "The times require that we should be perfectly cool, or as cool as we can be."

*Atlanta* (Ga.) *Intelligencer:* "Secession becomes the glory and prosperity of the South."

*Montgomery* (Ala.) *Advertiser:* "You (men of the South) are the greatest power on earth, and you can dictate to Christendom as a separate Confederacy; you can only sink to the condition of Ireland as members of this Union."

Raleigh, N. C., *Standard:* "We will never permit Mr. Lincoln or his party to touch the institution of domestic Slavery."

*New Bern* (N. C.) *Progress:* "If Lincoln violates his oath, let us dethrone him."

*Savannah* (Ga.) *News:* "The result and its inevitable consequences have been anticipated by all thoughtful men."

St. Louis *Missouri Republican:* "Let there be peace between the North and the South until Lincoln is guilty of some act of oppression justifying revolution."

*Augusta* (Ga.) *Constitutionalist:* "The South should arm at once."

*New Orleans* (La.) *Delta:* "For ourselves, we are not unprepared for this result, nor for the remedy for its consequences."

*New Orleans* (La.) *Picayune:* "There need be no doubt of the position of our whole people if an attempt is made to reduce the doctrines of Republicanism to practice."

*Gallatin* (Tenn.) *Courier and Enquirer:* "We trust that the counsel of wiser and better men will prevail."

*Winchester* (Ky.) *National Union:* "As we have survived the reign of James Buchanan, we can live through the administration of Abraham Lincoln."

*Vicksburg* (Miss.) *Whig:* "We do not mean to rebel against the Government because an obnoxious man has been made President."

*Atlanta* (Ga.) *Confederacy:* "Every member of Congress representing a Southern constituency should resign at once."

*Selma* (Ala.) *Sentinel:* "Let our young men . . . who are urging South Carolina to go out of the Union by herself, consider well what they are doing."

*New Orleans* (La.) *Crescent:* "The Northern people, in electing Mr. Lincoln, have perpetrated a deliberate, cold-blooded insult and outrage on the people of the slaveholding states."

*Memphis* (Tenn.) *Appeal:* ". . . our banks . . . will not buy sight drafts on cotton because Lincoln is elected President."

*Oxford* (Miss.) *Mercury:* "Devotion to the Union is treason to the South."

*Mobile* (Ala.) *Tribune:* "Abe Lincoln would not have been elected if there had been an apprehension among his voters that we mean what we have so repeatedly said."

*Houston* (Tex.) *Telegraph:* "If she (Texas) does go out, we may perhaps look for hard times for a year or two, but nothing too serious to be borne . . . this state will become . . . the harbor of wealth attached to Slavery on this continent."

The *Richmond* (Va.) *Whig* thought the South had only itself to blame, saying: "To the Breckinridgers, led on by Yancey, and to the corruptions of the Buchanan administration, we attribute the election of Lincoln." The *Washington Constitution*, published in the heart of the nation's capital, cautiously voiced secession sentiment. It said: "We may be very treasonable, or very foolish, because we cannot entertain the opinion that Southern men are likely to accept Mr. Lincoln's election without murmur, complaint, or remonstrance, yet we confess that we cannot do so, and we believe, further, that we are not singular in our opinion."

From Tennessee came protests against plans to secede. The *Memphis Enquirer* boldly stated: "Let every man put his foot down on disunion; it is no remedy for Southern wrongs; or it is only the mad man's remedy." The *Knoxville Whig*, spokesman for east Tennessee, a stronghold of Republicanism, warned Union men to be on their guard. It said it knew cotton was an article of commerce but that "Kentucky and Missouri hemp, as a necklace for traitors, is an article of still greater value for home consumption."

A segment of the press in the four so-called border slave states gave quick expression of Union ties that prevented Missouri, Kentucky, Maryland, and Delaware from seceding. The St. Louis *Missouri Democrat*, a Republican newspaper, said: "Throughout the campaign . . . (Lincoln) has been portrayed by most of the newspapers as an Abolitionist; a fanatic of the John Brown type. Never was a public man so outrageously misrepresented."

In Kentucky, the *Frankfort Commonwealth* said that if the people of South Carolina and other Southern states wanted to secede and enclose themselves behind a Chinese wall, "here is one who will contribute his mite toward furnishing the requisite rocks." The *Louisville Journal* told its readers: "We must curb Yancey and Rhett at the same time we check Lincoln and Seward. The Union and the Constitution must be preserved."

*The Clipper*, published at Baltimore, voiced a common conclusion in Maryland by saying: "He (Lincoln) cannot do worse than the Democratic administration that is now drawing to an ignoble and despised conclusion."

The situation in Delaware was correctly plumbed by the *Wilmington Journal and Statesman*. It said: "We of Delaware live in the South. It is a Slave State; and yet there is no man within her boundaries who dares utter seriously the word *secession*. We are all for the Union."[27]

On November 19, 1860, the *Richmond Enquirer*, destined to be the voice of secession, said in a lead editorial:

The significant fact which menaces the South is not that Abraham Lincoln is elected President, but that the Northern people, by a sectional vote, have elected a President for the avowed purpose of aggression on Southern rights. The purpose of aggression has been declared. This is a *declaration of war*.[28]

The *Enquirer's* statement that Lincoln had won with a "sectional vote," a charge that was bound to be popular in the Southern states, was used throughout his administration by unfriendly Democratic editors. The popular vote was: Lincoln, 1,857,610; Douglas, 1,365,976; Breckinridge, 857,953; Bell, 590,631. In the electoral college, Lincoln had 180; Breckinridge, 72; Bell, 39; Douglas, 12.[29]

Events moved swiftly. Congress assembled at Washington on December 3, and President Buchanan delivered his message the next day, a paper in which he denied a state had the right to break up the government, at the same time contending that neither Congress nor the President had the power to coerce a state.

On December 18, Senator John J. Crittenden of Kentucky, violently opposed to secession, proposed a "Peace Congress," and his plan to avert disunion became known as the Crittenden Compromise. Each state was invited to send commissioners to Washington. South Carolina, heedless of all proposed compromises, went out of the Union on December 20 when a state convention passed an ordinance of secession by a unanimous vote at Charleston.[30]

Within a few weeks, South Carolina was followed by Mississippi, Florida, Alabama, Georgia, Louisiana, and Texas. The country sensed that hostilities, if they were to occur, would break out at Charleston where South Carolina troops had batteries trained on the United States forts. During the evening of the day after Christmas, Major Robert Anderson moved his little garrison from Fort Moultrie into Fort Sumter. A supply ship, the *Star of the West*, carrying reenforcements to Anderson, was fired on by the South Carolina batteries and was compelled to turn back on January 9, 1861.

In Galveston, Tex., the editor of a German language newspaper, *Die Union*, dared to print an editorial against secession. He was a slaveholder and had lived in Texas for nineteen years. On January 3, 1861, his office was wrecked by a mob.[31]

# 10 "An Affectionate Farewell"

THE SECEDED STATES seized all national forts, arsenals, ships, mints, and customhouses within reach. They sent representatives to Montgomery, Ala., where, on February 4, 1861, they formed the Confederate States of America, adopted a constitution, and organized a provisional government. Jefferson Davis of Mississippi, former United States senator, was appointed President and Alexander H. Stephens, a Georgian, who had served with Abraham Lincoln in Congress, became Vice-President.[1] On that same February 4, the "Peace Congress" that had been proposed by Senator Crittenden, assembled in Washington. In just one month, Abraham Lincoln would be inaugurated President of the United States.

The troublesome *Charleston Mercury* threw oil on the fire by perpetrating a newspaper hoax on Lincoln. On January 30, the *Mercury* published what was purported to be correspondence between a Wheeling, Va., man and the President-elect. The *Mercury* referred to the correspondence as "The Letter From The Abolition President." Here are the letters as reprinted in the North:

Wheeling, Va., Jan. 12, 1861.

To the editor of the *Charleston Mercury:* Enclosed I send a copy of a letter of mine to the President elect and his reply. You are at liberty to make any disposition of them you may deem proper.

Yours, etc.

J. A. Spencer.

Wheeling, Va., December 24, 1860.

Hon. A. Lincoln—Dear Sir: I hope you will not deem it presumptuous in me, in thus demanding from you a plain reply to the following interrogations, and moreover that you will give me permission to give publication to your answer, should I desire to do so.

1st. Had the jurisdiction of the crime committed by John Brown and als. (sic) been surrendered to the federal government and judgment delayed to the fourth of March next, would you have exercised the pardoning power?

2nd. Do you regard the Dred Scott decision as binding on the people of the North?

Hoping to hear from you soon, I remain, yours truly, etc.,

J. A. Spencer.

The reply alleged to have been made by Lincoln was this plain forgery:

Springfield, Jan. 2, 1861.

J. A. Spencer, esq.—Sir:—I have resolved in my mind to reply to no letters addressed to me from any one, concerning the manifold questions that have of late gained a footing in our distracted country. But as I have frequently had the same interrogatories propounded to me by others, and as your letter seems to be dictated in a spirit of kindness, seeking information only, I have concluded for the present to waive my resolve and reply, giving you permission to dispose of my views as you see fit.

You ask: "Had the jurisdiction of the crime committed by Brown and others been surrendered to the Federal Government, and judgment thereon delayed until the 4th of March next, would you (1) have exercised the pardoning power?" I answer: I have carefully reviewed the testimony in said case, and in my opinion Brown committed no offense against the General Government meriting such severe punishment as he received. The most he committed against the Federal Government was a gross misdemeanor. Had I been governor of your State, I might have pursued the course he did. Yet even then there were strong mitigating circumstances. Brown was no doubt a monomaniac on the subject of negro slavery, and as such close confinement would have been more in accordance with the dictates of justice.

To your second, I reply in the negative for this reason: said decision is hostile to the advancement of Republican principles, and therefore attended with danger in a government like ours.

Hoping the above will prove satisfactory, I am sir, your obed't servant,

A. Lincoln[2]

The *Mercury*, with an exchange list of hundreds, spread the propaganda letter over the country. The *Illinois Daily State Journal* at Springfield promptly identified the *Mercury* "correspondence" as a hoax and remarked: "It is hardly necessary, we presume, to state that the whole is a gross forgery."[3]

*The Crisis*, a newly launched anti-Lincoln newspaper at Columbus, Ohio, reprinted the forgery on February 7, Editor Samuel Medary explaining he could hardly believe the President-elect had written the letter, but that he accepted it as true because he found it in "a Lincoln paper."[4]

Only one editor was sufficiently curious to make an investigation of the identity of "J. A. Spencer." That was the editor of the *Wheeling Intelligencer*, who looked about for his distinguished fellow townsman and discovered no such person existed![5] *The Crisis* printed a retraction only after the *Ohio State Journal* of Columbus demanded it. Medary, who was treading softly in his role of Southern propagandist, said in his retraction that "the whole press of the country should combine against these wicked falsehoods and forgeries that float like mist from the bogs of miasma over the whole country."[6]

The long nose for news possessed by Bennett of the *New York Herald* told him the man packing his trunks at Springfield was the headline of the day. He sent Henry Villard, a twenty-five-year-old German immigrant, to cover Lincoln. It was one of the most important assignments ever made by an American newspaper; Villard's excellent Springfield correspondence was to become a link in the chain of history.

Villard, who landed in New York only a few years before unable to speak or write a word of English, had so completely mastered the language that he could write reportorial prose marked by clarity and dignity. Fresh from Europe, he looked upon Lincoln with a purely objective eye.

His first important newspaper assignment was to cover the Lincoln-Douglas debates for the *New York Staats-Zeitung*. During that campaign, he contributed to *The Press* of Philadelphia.[7] A year later, he covered the gold stampede at Cherry Creek, Colo., for the *Cincinnati Commercial* at the request of Murat Halstead. He met Horace Greeley in Denver and upon his return to Ohio acted as a Middle Western political correspondent for the *New York Tribune*. He also did special assignments for B. Gratz Brown, editor of the St. Louis *Missouri Democrat*.[8] Trying to sell a feature story to Frederic Hudson, managing editor, Villard made the contact with the *New York Herald* that resulted in his Springfield assignment.[9]

On his way to the Illinois capital, Villard remembered how, during the debates, he and Lincoln waited in a boxcar on a siding for a train at a flag stop twenty miles from Springfield. Lincoln told him he did not hope to win the race for senator, adding with a laugh that Mrs. Lincoln insisted he was going to be President of the United States.[10] Villard saw Lincoln again in Kansas in 1859; the reporter was on his way from Cherry Creek, Lincoln on a speaking tour.[11]

Villard found Springfield a city of 9,000, without a paved street and with but one respectable hotel. Lincoln welcomed him as an old friend and introduced him to his new private secretary, John G.

Nicolay. He also introduced him to John Hay, twenty-two-year-old correspondent of the *Missouri Democrat,* who was to become an assistant secretary.[12]

Villard's first move was to study Lincoln's daily schedule. The President-elect held open house every day until noon in a room set aside for him in the state capitol. In the evening, he either stayed at home or loafed in the city room of the *State Journal.* He rarely visited his law office. Villard was amazed to hear rough-looking farmers address the future President as "Abe." He was impressed by Lincoln's inexhaustible supply of stories and noted that some were "coarse or even outright nasty."[13]

Soon after Villard's correspondence from Springfield began to appear, the *New York Herald* said:

As we have had important and exclusive news from Springfield, our contemporaries . . . seem to fear that we intend to monopolize the ancient rail-splitter, and that we are ambitious to reign in the kitchen and parlor of the President's house. You need have no fears, gentlemen; our tastes do not tend in that direction. We are only endeavoring to give accurate news about Lincoln, no matter how far we disagree with him politically, as part of our duty to the public as a journalist.[14]

Villard saw a parade of visitors beat a path to Lincoln's door. In that parade were office seekers, cabinetmakers, would-be ministers, and the rank and file of political meddlers. Every one wanted to give advice to the President-elect. Big names called for a declaration of policy. Mail poured in from Northern and Southern states; cranks threatened to kill him; obscure persons warned him he would never reach Washington alive; friends in Washington wrote him of the latest developments of secession, some of them fearful a rebel army might seize the Capital at any moment.[15]

The young *Herald* correspondent chose Thurlow Weed as the most interesting figure who came to Springfield. Gradually, Villard grew to know Lincoln, recognized the patience and shrewdness with which he handled the political mob. The President-elect's harassed appearance and his careworn look aroused the reporter's sympathy.[16]

Lincoln confided to Raymond of *The New York Times* why he refused to break the silence at Springfield. He pointed out that a speech made by Senator Lyman Trumbull of Illinois had not been used by a single newspaper with the aim of quieting public anxiety, but, on the contrary, the *Boston Courier* and others of its "class" blamed Lincoln for the sentiments expressed and read into it "an abandonment" of his party principles. Lincoln further wrote that the *Washington Constitution* and similar newspapers said the speech was a declaration of war against the South.[17]

The editor of *The New York Times* was worried because he received a letter from a Mississippi colonel who said a story was afloat in the South that Lincoln had made an address for the occasion when a group of "Free Negroes" presented a silver pitcher to Salmon P. Chase. Raymond remembered something to that effect in the *New York Herald* and at that time put it down as a forgery. He wanted a denial from Lincoln.[18]

Lincoln replied he had never seen Chase, never attended a meeting of Negroes in his life, and never saw a pitcher presented to anybody.[19]

Bryant of the New York *Evening Post* tried to dictate Lincoln's Cabinet appointments. He wrote to the President-elect on January 4, 1861, when he heard Simon Cameron of Pennsylvania was to be honored. He said in about four hundred words that Cameron was a crook, insisting it was an effort for him to break his "usual reserve" to write such a letter. Then on January 22, Bryant said he risked being "somewhat troublesome" to take a hand in Cabinet selections. This time he asked that Chase be made Secretary of the Treasury.[20]

Thurlow Weed, always brief and straight to the point, pleased because Seward was to be Secretary of State, wrote to Lincoln that the "Border States" must be held in the Union by conciliation, a policy which Lincoln followed to the letter.[21]

Edward Bates came from Missouri to be told by Lincoln he was to serve in the Cabinet. Upon his return to St. Louis, Bates told Lincoln in a letter that it might be good policy to let the border slave states know he was to have a hand in the government. He wanted to know how he could break the news to the public.[22]

Lincoln had the answer at his finger tips. He told Bates to "let a little editorial appear" in the *Missouri Democrat*, stating the newspaper had permission to say Bates had been offered and would accept a place in the new Cabinet, the department to be assigned later.[23]

About the time Bates was in Springfield to confer with Lincoln on his appointment, the President-elect took note of talk of a coalition Cabinet by writing this editorial for the *Illinois State Journal:*

We hear such frequent allusions to a supposed purpose on the part of Mr. Lincoln to call into his cabinet two or three Southern gentlemen from the parties opposed to him politically, that we are prompted to ask a few questions.

*First.* Is it known that any such gentlemen of character would accept a place in the cabinet?

*Second.* If yea, on what terms does he surrender to Mr. Lincoln, or Mr. Lincoln to him, on the political differences between them; or do they enter upon the administration in open opposition to each other?[24]

Bates was a slaveholder, but he was a Republican and devoted to preservation of the Union.

Newspaper editors and correspondents who had supported Lincoln in the presidential campaign were among the thousands clamoring for public office. Lincoln had to think about them. He arranged these appointments:

Charles Wilson, *Chicago Journal,* Secretary of Legation to London; J. S. Pike, *New York Tribune,* Minister to The Hague; W. S. Thayer, New York *Evening Post,* Consul to Alexandria; George G. Fogg, *New Hampshire Democrat,* Minister to Switzerland; W. H. Fry, *New York Tribune,* Secretary of Legation to Sardinia; Rufus King, *Milwaukee Sentinel,* Minister to Rome; J. E. Harvey, *North American* and *New York Tribune,* Minister to Portugal; Rufus Hosmer, *Michigan Republican,* Consul to Frankfort; James Watson Webb, New York *Courier and Enquirer,* Minister to Turkey; Richard Hildreth, *New York Tribune,* Consul to Tripoli.

Others, editors and publishers, were to get postmasterships. They included: George Dawson, *Albany* (N. Y.) *Evening Journal;* A. M. Clapp, *Buffalo* (N. Y.) *Express;* E. Cowles, *Cleveland* (Ohio) *Leader;* W. F. Comly, *Dayton* (Ohio) *Daily Journal;* A. P. Miller, *Chillicothe* (Ohio) *Scioto Gazette;* A. W. Campbell, *Wheeling* (Va.) *Intelligencer;* John L. Scripps, *Chicago Tribune;* Peter L. Foy, St. Louis *Missouri Democrat.*

Still others were to be rewarded. They were: Thomas McElrath, *New York Tribune,* appraiser for New York customhouse; D. P. Holloway, *Richmond* (Ind.) *Palladium,* commissioner of patents; John D. Defrees, *Indianapolis* (Ind.) *Atlas,* superintendent of public printing.[25]

Murat Halstead branded these appointments a "disgrace to journalism" and declared, "The public has a right to suspect the qualifications of men who are continually eager to forsake their legitimate and chosen profession for an office."[26]

Lincoln had still another little piece of business that concerned a newspaper before he could close his books in Springfield. Since May 30, 1859, according to the date of contract, Lincoln had secretly owned the *Illinois Staats-Anzeiger,* an obscure, weekly German language publication. The paper was edited by Theodore Canisius, who moved the office equipment from Alton, Ill., where he had operated at a loss. The paper appeared in Springfield in June of 1859, soon after the contract was signed. It was stipulated in the contract that Canisius was to continue as editor, that he was to maintain a Republican policy and publish articles in both German and English. If the paper did not operate as a Republican organ, Lincoln was to take over for Canisius. The document of ownership gave the price as four hundred dollars.[27]

Now that he had been elected President, Lincoln made a deal with Canisius that transferred ownership back to the editor.[28] The post of American Consul at Vienna went to Canisius later that year.[29]

As early as December 31, 1860, Medill of the *Chicago Tribune* wrote to Lincoln from Washington as a "volunteer sentinel on the walls" that the disunionists planned to seize the city with an army and that the President-elect should grab his "carpet sack" and come on down.[30]

Lincoln decided to leave Springfield on February 11. Arrangements were made for a special train. It was to pass through Indianapolis, Cincinnati, Columbus, Pittsburgh, Cleveland, Buffalo, Albany, New York, Philadelphia, Harrisburg, Baltimore, thence to Washington.

The announced route caused *The Crisis* at Columbus to exclaim:

Mr. Lincoln has consented to pass through Indianapolis, Columbus, Albany, and Harrisburgh, to Washington, and of course other towns on the road. So we shall have an "ovation" before he reaches the capital of the nation. . . . all this is in extremely bad taste at this time. How little he seems to estimate the troubled times, the importance of his position, or the true theory of our system.[31]

Horace Greeley arrived in Springfield on February 5 to give a lecture that evening. He registered at a hotel, and Lincoln called on him in the afternoon. They talked for hours, and, according to a story published the next day in Greeley's *New York Tribune*, he did most of the talking. This dispatch appeared in the *Tribune* on the morning of February 6:

Springfield, Ill. Tues., Feb. 5, 1861. Horace Greeley returned from the West this morning. This afternoon he was called upon at his hotel by Mr. Lincoln. The interview lasted several hours. Greeley urged a strict adherence to an anti-compromise policy, and is said to have received gratifying assurances. His opinion as to the Cabinet and other appointments was freely solicited and given. He is known to be strongly opposed to Cameron, and very much interested in the appointment of Chase and Colfax. Col. Fremont, he thinks, should have the mission to France. Although just defeated in Albany, he did not ask anything either for himself or friends.

The dispatch was, in all probability, written by Greeley himself; it sounds exactly like him. The denial that he was seeking any political favor was Greeley's theme song.

The Northern press, both Republican and Democratic, continued its incessant call for an expression of policy from the President-elect. They wanted to know how he felt about a compromise with the seceded states and what steps he intended to take if they were to be disciplined. He gave them the answers in editorials published by the *Illinois State Journal*. On February 6, under the heading, "Compromise Not To Be Thought Of," the *Journal* said:

We want concession. We want the southern states which are clamoring about concession and compromise to concede that ours is a government proper, and not a compact between the states. We want them to concede that a state cannot dissolve its connection with the Union at will. We want them to concede that this government has a right to enforce its laws and protect its property, even if it becomes necessary to hang or shoot every traitor in the United States to do it. . . . We want them to concede that Abraham Lincoln, having been constitutionally elected President of the United States of America, has a right to take his seat without any opposition from any quarter whatever. . . . We want them to concede that the seceding states have violated the Constitution—that they are in rebellion against the federal government and that it is the duty of this government to put down rebellion.

. . . we do not ask the South to concede a single thing that is not demanded by the Constitution of the United States.

A separate editorial was headed, "The Forts Must Be Retaken—The Revolution Must Be Checked." It revealed that Lincoln would use all the military might at his command to save the Union. It also warned the Confederacy not to fire on Fort Sumter, saying:

It is the duty of the government to retake its stolen forts and other property wrongfully withheld. . . . If individuals attack the government in its discharge of its duty, and lose their lives thereby, can it be charged that the government has wantonly shed "fraternal blood" . . . ? If treason and rebellion make it necessary to use force to execute the laws, is he (the President) not justified in using it? Is it coercing South Carolina to defend Fort Sumter against the attack of a mob collected from South Carolina, Georgia and other states . . . ?

Coercion of a state! He who invented the expression did a good work for traitors.[32]

There it was—the Lincoln policy—for all the world to see. Only a few editors were quick enough to grasp the story, the biggest news break that ever came out of Springfield. Although Henry Villard had written in the *New York Herald* that Lincoln was spending his evenings in the Springfield *Journal* office, not many newspaper men knew the close connection between the President-elect and Editor Edward L. Baker. Not until the February 6 issue of the *Journal* reached New York was there reaction.

On February 11, the *New York Evening Express* reprinted the *Journal* editorials and announced it had discovered the Springfield newspaper was the "official mouthpiece" of Abraham Lincoln. It pointed out that Baker, the editor, was a member of the Lincoln party aboard the special train en route to Washington. The *Express* told its readers to study the editorials and to judge for themselves whether the *Journal* was "the confidential organ of Mr. Lincoln."[33]

Two days later, on February 13, the *New York Tribune* editorial page said Lincoln had revealed his policy in "two remarkable articles in the Springfield *Journal*." The articles, said the *Tribune*, "were obviously inspired by him, if not actually written by his own hand."[34]

With only four days remaining until Lincoln's momentous journey was to begin, the *Journal* published this little item: "The present week being the last that Mr. Lincoln remains at Springfield, and it being indispensable that he should have a portion of his time to himself, he will see visitors, only at his office, No. 4 Johnson's building, from 3½ to 5 o'clock, P.M. each day."[35]

The day of departure arrived. Under the heading, "President Lincoln," the *Journal* said on that Monday morning, February 11, 1861:

Mr. Lincoln leaves for Washington, this morning, for the purpose of assuming the position of President of the United States, to which he has been elected by votes of the American people. He is about to take the reins of the government at a time when discord and treason are intent upon tearing the Union into dismembered fragments; in the midst of a political crisis when the stoutest hearts are beginning to despair of the Republic. No President was ever inaugurated under circumstances more trying to the patriot and the lover of his country. . . . We believe Mr. Lincoln has the courage, the nerve, and the undaunted intrepidity to do his duty. . . .

The *Daily Illinois State Register*, pro-Southern in its sympathies, was compelled to say something. In contrast to the column-long story

in the *Journal,* the *Register* published a single paragraph which said,
"The President elect leaves town this morning at 11 o'clock, for
Washington by special train. He is to be accompanied by a select
number of friends. None but the presidential party will go upon the
train." It then listed the cities through which Lincoln would pass.[36]

Down at Charleston, an editorial writer for the *Courier* was preparing to say in the next day's edition that the struggle was as good as over.
He wrote: "The South *might* . . . treat the disorganized and de-
moralized Northern states as *insurgents,* and deny them recognition.
But if peaceful division ensues, the South, after taking the federal capital
and archives, and being recognized by all foreign powers . . . can, if
they see proper, recognize the Northern confederacy or confederacies,
and enter into treaty stipulations with them."[37]

The Springfield newspapers on Tuesday morning, February 12, described Lincoln's departure. The *Journal's* report said in part:

Long before the hour appointed for the departure of the special train
. . . hundreds of his friends and fellow-citizens, without distinction of
party, had assembled at the station of the Great Western Railway. . . . All
seemed to feel that they were about to witness an event which, in its relations to the future, was of no ordinary interest.

At precisely five minutes before eight o'clock, Mr. Lincoln, preceded
by Mr. Wood, of New York, slowly made his way from his room in the
station, through the expectant masses which respectfully parted right and
left at approach to the car provided for his use. At each step of his progress
toward the car, friendly hands were extended for a last greeting. On reaching the platform of the car, Mr. Lincoln turned toward the people, removed
his hat, paused for several seconds, till he could control his emotions, and
then slowly, impressively, and with profound emotion, uttered the following words:

"Friends, no one who has never been placed in a like position, can understand my feelings at this hour, nor the oppressive sadness I feel at this
parting. For more than a quarter of a century I have lived among you,
and during all that time I have received nothing but kindness at your
hands. Here I have lived from my youth until now I am an old man.
Here the most sacred ties of earth were assumed; here all my children
were born; and here one of them lies buried. To you, dear friends, I
owe all that I have, all that I am. All the strange, chequered past seems
to crowd upon my mind. Today I leave you; I go to assume a task more
difficult than that which devolved upon General Washington. Unless the
great God who assisted him, shall be with me and aid me, I must fail. But

if the same omniscient mind, and the same Almighty arm that directed and protected him shall guide and support me, I shall not fail. I shall succeed. Let us all pray that the God of our fathers may not forsake us now. To Him I commend you all—permit me to ask that with equal security and faith, you all will invoke His wisdom and guidance for me. With these last few words I must leave you—for how long I know not. Friends, one and all, I must now bid you an affectionate farewell."

"It was a most impressive scene," said the *Journal*. "We have known Mr. Lincoln for many years; we have heard him speak upon a hundred different occasions; but we never saw him so profoundly affected, nor did he ever utter an address which seemed to us as full of simple and touching eloquence, so exactly adapted to the occasion, so worthy of the man and the hour. Although it was raining fast when he began to speak, every hat was lifted, and every head bent forward to catch the last words of the departing chief. . . .

"At precisely eight o'clock, city time, the train moved off, bearing our honored townsman, our noble chief, ABRAHAM LINCOLN, to the scenes of his future labors, and we firmly believe, of his glorious triumph. God bless ABRAHAM LINCOLN."[38]

The Democratic *Register* described the farewell in this fat paragraph:

The President-elect and his suite left this city at 8 o'clock yesterday morning, by a special train, for Indianapolis. A large crowd of his personal and political admirers assembled at the depot to bid him God-speed on his journey to the seat of government. As he entered the car he was greeted with three cheers, which he acknowledged in a few appropriate remarks that were made inaudible to a large portion of the crowd by the incorrigible hissing of the locomotive. The iron horse was then let loose, and darting off with electric speed, soon became lost to sight in the distance.[39]

# 11 "The Outrageous Romance"

HENRY VILLARD WAS the only metropolitan newspaper correspondent aboard the Lincoln special as it pulled out of Springfield.[1] He was granted permission to make the trip by W. S. Wood, railroad superintendent in charge of the train, after Lincoln interceded for him.

Villard's news sense told him he had missed a story by failing to take down the President-elect's remarks from the rear platform. Knowing Lincoln had spoken extemporaneously, Villard went to him and requested he repeat what he had just said to the crowd. Taking the correspondent's pad and pencil, Lincoln wrote for him a slightly different, more polished version than the *Illinois State Journal* reporter heard at Springfield. It said:

My Friends: No one not in my position can appreciate the sadness I feel at this parting. To this people I owe all that I am. Here I have lived more than a quarter of a century; here my children were born, and here one of them lies buried. I know not how soon I shall see you again. A duty devolves upon me which is, perhaps, greater than that which has evolved upon any other man since the days of Washington. He never would have succeeded except for the aid of Divine Providence, upon which he at all times relied. I feel that I cannot succeed without the same Divine aid which sustained him, and in the same Almighty Being I place my reliance for support, and I hope you, my friends, will all pray that I may receive that Divine assistance, without which I cannot succeed, but with which success is certain. Again I bid you all an affectionate farewell.[2]

Villard incorporated the text of the "farewell" in his lead and wrote this fine descriptive passage:

Toward the conclusion of his remarks himself and audience were moved to tears. His exhortation to pray elicited choked exclamations of "We will do it; we will do it." As he turned to enter the cars three cheers were given and a few seconds afterward the train moved slowly out of the sight of the silent gathering.[3]

The correspondent filed his story to the *New York Herald* at the first telegraph station. He placed the copy Lincoln had written for him in his pocket to keep as a souvenir. It was in a knapsack he lost while covering one of the battles during the war.[4]

Villard added to his "lead" as the train sped eastward, writing a running story of the journey. He moved through the three coaches and took note of the personages who made up the presidential party. He saw Colonel Edwin V. Sumner, Major David Hunter, Captain John Pope, and Captain George W. Hazzard, all of the United States Army. He saw Colonel E. E. Ellsworth, leader of a famous Chicago drill company, and Ward Hill Lamon, the Bloomington lawyer and close friend of Lincoln, carrying his banjo and singing Negro comic songs.[5]

Villard filed these paragraphs at stations along the way to Indianapolis:

The turnout of the yeomanry increases as the train progresses eastward.
Most of the stations are handsomely decorated with flags.

The Yankee Prince of Wales, Bob Lincoln, the heir apparent to the
President elect, adheres closely to the refreshment saloon, the gayest of
the gay. . . .

The President elect continues reserved and thoughtful and stays most
of the time alone in the private saloon prepared for his special use.[6]

Only in the *New York Herald* did the story appear as "reserved and
thoughtful." In other newspapers that obtained the dispatch through
the *Associated Press*, such as the *New York Tribune*, it read "prone and
thoughtful."[7] The story may have been garbled in transmission, but
it is likely that Villard, in groping for the English expression, may
have used the word "prone" and it was made to read correctly by the
*Herald* copy desk.

The first day's journey ended at Indianapolis where Lincoln remained
all night. He spoke to the Indiana legislature the next day, February 12,
his fifty-second birthday anniversary. Mrs. Lincoln and the two younger
sons joined him at Indianapolis, and they continued on to Cincinnati
for another overnight stop. While Lincoln was receiving visitors in
his hotel suite at Cincinnati, an incident occurred in Albany, N. Y.,
that was worth a paragraph in the newspapers. The *New York Tribune*
said:

Albany, Tuesday, Feb. 12, 1861. J. Wilkes Booth, a tragedian, met with
an accident at the Gayety Theater this evening by falling on his dagger,
and inflicting a muscular wound under his right arm between one and two
inches in depth. It is not serious in character, however.

Columbus, Ohio, was the next stop. Big news awaited Lincoln there.
He was told the certificates of election from all the states of the Union
had been opened and read before a joint session of the Senate and the
House of Representatives in Washington and that Vice-President John
C. Breckinridge had declared Abraham Lincoln and Hannibal Hamlin
duly elected President and Vice-President, respectively, of the United
States for the term beginning March 4, 1861.[8]

The Lincoln party was given a royal welcome to Columbus by
Governor Dennison. There was a big reception in the Statehouse and
many private parties. William Dean Howells, rehired by the *Ohio
State Journal* in a wave of prosperity brought to it by its new editor,

Henry D. Cooke, walked across the public square to the capitol and saw the President-elect shaking hands with a "never-ending crowd." He looked on the scene for a time, then went home without pressing forward to meet the man whose biography he had written.[9]

After Lincoln's victory at the polls, Howells applied for appointment to a consulate, holding the President-elect should reward him for his campaign book as Franklin Pierce had done for Nathaniel Hawthorne under similar circumstances.[10] He wanted to see Nicolay and Hay to inquire about his application but was not among the guests invited to a party where they were entertained. Since rejoining the *Journal* staff, Howells devoted his evenings to writing and rejected so many party invitations that he had been forgotten socially by Kate Chase, leader and dictator of the younger set in Columbus. He walked the streets all evening. His disappointment was even keener the next day when he was told Nicolay and Hay asked about him and spoke of his recent work in the *Atlantic Monthly*.[11]

The Lincoln train left Columbus on the morning of February 14, pausing at Steubenville en route to Pittsburgh, then back into Ohio to Cleveland, arriving there February 15. Newspaper correspondents, who began to join the party at Cincinnati, increased in number until they occupied an entire car. On the way from Cleveland to Buffalo, they ran into a little feature story that made good copy. This is the story as told by the correspondent of the New York *World:*

> At Girard, a station near Erie, a profound sensation was created by the sudden appearance of Mr. Horace Greeley. He wore that mysteriously durable garment, the white coat, and carried in his hand a yellow bag, labelled with his name and address in characters which might be read across Lake Erie. He had, it was said, mistaken the special for the general train, and was a great deal embarrassed on finding himself suddenly cheek by jowl with the chief of the great and triumphant party which he had so large a hand in establishing, and of which he is one of the most powerful and least judicious supporters. He at first made an incursion into the reporters' car, where he was captured, and marched off in triumph, by Mr. Secretary Nicolay, to the President's car. Here he was introduced for the first time to Mrs. Lincoln. At the next stopping place, Greeley suddenly disappeared. His arrival and departure were altogether so unexpected, so mysterious, so comical, that they supplied an amusing topic of conversation during the rest of the journey.[12]

Lincoln was looking for a friend when he reached Westfield, N. Y. Shortly before the election, Lincoln received a letter written on

October 15, 1860, from a little girl, Grace G. Bedell of Westfield, telling him he would be much better looking if he would "cultivate his whiskers." Lincoln replied to her on October 19, asking whether she did not think people might call him affected if he wore a beard.[13]

The bearded Lincoln appeared on the rear platform of the train as it ground to a halt and called for Grace. An old man came through the crowd, holding the little girl by the hand. Lincoln greeted her with a kiss. The New York *World* correspondent wrote:

Her advice has not been thrown away upon the rugged chieftain. A beard of several months' growth covers (perhaps adorns) the lower part of his face. The young girl's peachy cheek must have been tickled with a stiff whisker, for the growth of which she was herself responsible.[14]

All the correspondents wrote a story about Grace and Lincoln's new beard. The story grew in importance with the passing years, with Grace receiving full credit for the transformation in Lincoln's appearance. When the Robert Todd Lincoln Collection of the Papers of Abraham Lincoln was opened in 1947, some of the glory was taken from Grace Bedell. A letter dated "October 12, 1860," signed by "True Republicans" of New York, revealed their desire for a bewhiskered candidate.[15]

The President-elect's party rested over Sunday in Buffalo. When he left Monday morning, Lincoln was riding in a palatial car used a few months previously by the Prince of Wales on a tour of the country. The correspondents, Villard included, were glad they would soon be back in New York. They had been shoved and pushed around by crowds at every station until their bodies were sore. Villard was still talking of the "miserable dinner" for which they had been charged a dollar apiece at Danville Station, the first meal out of Springfield. In a special story he filed for the *Illinois State Journal* at Editor Baker's request, Villard said the dinner wasn't worth fifty cents. The *Journal* had to publish an apology to the citizens of Danville Station.[16]

The train raced across New York State, sometimes reaching a speed of more than a mile a minute. Towns and cities flew past, a confusion of names and crowds—Rochester, Syracuse, Utica, Schenectady, and then Albany, on February 18, the day Jefferson Davis was inaugurated provisional President of the Confederate States of America at Montgomery, Ala., in the "grandest pageant ever witnessed in the South."[17]

Lincoln made a speech to the legislature at Albany and went on to New York on February 19. Mayor Fernando Wood welcomed the President-elect in a coldly worded statement at City Hall. Barnum's Museum advertised in the newspapers that Lincoln would stop to gaze upon its wonders. The President-elect did not appear at the museum, but Robert, his son, did.[18]

Now called the "Prince of Rails" by a press with which he had grown intimate, Robert was found to be interesting copy by New York reporters. The *New York Tribune* said:

Robert T. Lincoln, the eldest son of the President elect, and who is accompanying him to Washington, is a student at Harvard, and will shortly return to his class. He is a young man of fine abilities and much dignity of character. The reports in various papers intimating that his course of life is what is popularly denominated "fast," are strictly erroneous, and no less painful to him than to his excellent parents, to whom he has ever been a dutiful and affectionate son.[19]

Correspondent Villard had grown so weary of the "traveling show," that he went to the *Herald* office and asked to be released from the assignment as soon as the train reached New York.[20] Thus unwittingly he turned his back on a big news story yet to break, the only one to come out of Lincoln's long ride to Washington.

On February 21, Lincoln spoke to the New Jersey legislature and went on to Philadelphia where he was received by the Mayor. That night, all the wild rumors he had been hearing about a plot to assassinate him came to a head. Just before he left Springfield, Lincoln received a private report from Captain Hazzard on the situation in Baltimore. Hazzard said the Baltimore *Sun* was "the vilest secession sheet in the U.S." and some of the most prominent citizens were disunionists. He suggested Lincoln wear a disguise and pass through the city at night incognito if he went through at all.[21]

Congressman Elihu B. Washburne wrote to Lincoln from Washington on February 3 to inform him that the head of the army, General Winfield Scott, had uncovered evidence of a conspiracy to seize the capitol.[22]

Frederick H. Seward, son of the man Lincoln had chosen for his Secretary of State, met the President-elect in Philadelphia, bearing a note from his father. He handed Lincoln a report, made by Seward's detective to General Scott, revealing a plot to kill him in Baltimore.[23] Lincoln's advisers decided he should leave the party at Harrisburg and slip through Baltimore under cover of night.

Lincoln carried out his part of the Philadelphia program, raising a flag at Independence Hall the next morning at sunup. He made a brief, impromptu talk that revealed he was thinking of what might lie ahead for him in Baltimore. Before surrendering the principles in the Declaration of Independence, he "would rather be assassinated on this spot."[24]

He left Philadelphia by train in midmorning, reached Harrisburg at two in the afternoon, and spoke before the Pennsylvania legislature. The Lincolns were to hold a reception at a hotel in the evening, but this was called off on the plea of travel weariness and Harrisburg went to bed in the belief the President-elect was resting in his suite.

Baltimore seethed with excitement that night; the visit on the morrow of the Republican President-elect was on everyone's tongue. The *Daily Republican* published an article regarded as highly inflammatory by Unionists, who were fearful it was intended to incite an attack on Lincoln. The marshal of the city police placed extra men under orders.[25]

The whole country was stirred the next day when word came from Washington that Lincoln had arrived there in the early morning after a secret night passage through Baltimore, via Philadelphia, and that Mrs. Lincoln and the official party were to follow on the regularly scheduled train. Wire-service stories out of Harrisburg, published in the afternoon papers of February 23, said "the people awakened to find Lincoln had left during the night." An *Associated Press* story from Baltimore said Lincoln went through there "incognito."

The President-elect rode into Washington about six o'clock in the morning, accompanied by two men, Allen Pinkerton, a chief of railroad detectives, and Ward Hill Lamon. Congressman Washburne, hiding behind a pillar in the old depot, formed the welcoming committee. He noted that Lincoln wore "a soft low-crowned hat" and a "bob-tailed overcoat," with a muffler around his neck. To Washburne, Lincoln looked more like a well-to-do farmer than the President-elect of the United States. The four entered a waiting carriage and were driven to Willard's Hotel, arriving there just as daylight broke over the city.[26]

Seward was waiting in the lobby for Lincoln; he had planned to be at the station but overslept.[27] The Washington press corps got the first hint that something unusual was afoot when they learned Seward had been seen pacing the lobby of the Willard, nervously puffing on his cigar long before his customary hour of arising. Employees of the hotel recognized Lincoln's tall form, and soon the rumor was flying around Washington that the President-elect, not due until half-past four that afternoon, was in town.

Reporters for the Washington newspapers hastened to the hotel to obtain verification of the rumor and were told it was true but refused to believe it until they were shown the register with the signature, "A. Lincoln, Illinois." Lincoln, resting in his room, was not disturbed.

Seward took Lincoln to the White House at ten o'clock where President Buchanan was in session with the Cabinet, and there were introductions all around. In late afternoon, Mrs. Lincoln and the official party came into Washington on the train the President-elect was to have ridden. Seward met Mrs. Lincoln and escorted her to the Willard.[28]

Mrs. Lincoln and her party had gone through a nightmare in Baltimore. Although the newspapers posted bulletins that Lincoln was in Washington, thousands refused to believe the report and waited for the special train at the Calvert Street station. The crowd cheered for the Confederacy and for "gallant Jeff Davis." The Baltimore *Sun* described the scene: "As soon as the train stopped the crowd leaped upon the platforms and mounted the tops of the cars like so many monkeys, until, like a hive of bees, they swarmed upon them, shouting, hallooing, and making all manner of noises."[29]

Other newspapers told how "plug-uglies" hurled epithets at Mrs. Lincoln and said unprintable things to her. Secretary Hay slammed a door in the face of a man who tried to gain entrance to her coach. A rough pressed his face against a window, leered at Robert Lincoln, and asked, "How's your old man?" Robert was nonchalantly smoking a cigar.

The newspaper presses began to roll. For the next few days, they printed countless thousands of words of Lincoln's trip and the controversy that it stirred. The pro-Southern press pointed to Mrs. Lincoln's reception in Baltimore as proof that nothing would have happened to the President-elect had he been aboard the train. The Republican newspapers said it merely proved he would have been killed. The *New York Tribune* said guardedly, reprinting the story in *The Sun,* that "the spectacle, even as described by the Baltimore papers, tends very much to abate the condemnation which many were at first inclined to bestow upon Mr. Lincoln's advisers for changing his original programme."[30]

The factual reporting of the *New York Herald's* Washington correspondent gave his newspaper a truthful account of the decision that sent Lincoln on the night ride, saying:

Senator Seward received official intelligence on Thursday evening, from reliable sources, that a most diabolical plot had been successfully arranged, on the part of a secret organization in Baltimore, to assassinate the President elect on his arrival in that city. Mr. Seward communicated this intelligence to a few private friends, and it was determined to dispatch a messenger at once to Philadelphia, informing him of the fact, and urging him to take an earlier train, which would bring him through in the night. Mr.

Lincoln said he had received intelligence from Baltimore of a similar nature. A special train was accordingly arranged, and he departed at once for Washington.[31]

The special train on which Lincoln secretly left Harrisburg took him only as far as Philadelphia where he changed to the regular New York–Washington sleeper. The telegraph wires were cut, the wire and railroad officials cooperating.

During the first few hours after the story of the ride broke, it was treated seriously by both the Republican and the pro-Southern press. Then the country learned what *The New York Times* said, and it rocked with laughter, bringing abuse and ridicule down on Lincoln. Joseph Howard, Jr., a well-known newspaper man, was covering Lincoln for the *Times*. Upon awakening Saturday morning, February 23, in Harrisburg to find Lincoln gone, he wrote a fantastic story that was played on page one by the *Times* and given further circulation when reprinted by other newspapers, including the *New York Tribune*.

Howard's story said "statesmen laid the plan, bankers indorsed it, and adventurers were to carry it into effect." He wrote that Lincoln did not want to go and that Colonel Sumner "actually cried with indignation," but that Mrs. Lincoln, "seconded by Mr. Judd and Mr. Lincoln's original informant," insisted upon it. The next sentence did the damage:

He wore a Scotch plaid cap and a very long military cloak, so that he was entirely unrecognizable.[32]

*The Sun* at Baltimore pounced upon the story, reprinting it word for word, with an accompanying editorial which said:

Had we any respect for Mr. Lincoln, official or personal, as a man, or as President elect of the United States . . . the final escapade by which he reached the capital would have utterly demolished it. . . . He might have entered Willard's Hotel with a "head-spring" and a "summersault," and the clown's merry greeting to Gen. Scott, "Here we are!" and we should care nothing about it, personally. We do not believe the Presidency can ever be more degraded by any of his successors than it has by him, even before his inauguration. . . . But *The New York Times* . . . furnishes the wondering world with ample details of the Lincoln hegira. We are not disposed to deprive our readers of one jot or tittle of the outrageous romance with which the *Times* entertains its own.[33]

All over the country people were saying, "He wore a Scotch plaid cap and a very long military cloak." In the midst of the greatest internal crisis it ever faced, the country burst into merriment at the thought of

Lincoln in a Scotch cap. Because it was published in *The New York Times*, a solidly Republican paper, the man in the street accepted Howard's story as gospel truth. In no other newspaper could it have caused so much damage to Lincoln and the cause he represented.

Delegates to the Peace Congress began to slip out of Washington, their efforts in vain, but "the great Lincoln escapade" still held the center of the stage. Poems were written about the night ride, and a cartoonist for *Vanity Fair* put Lincoln in kilts.

The *New York Tribune* tried to be funny, saying, "Mr. Lincoln may live a hundred years without having so good a chance to die." To which the *New York Herald* added: "What a misfortune to Abraham Lincoln and the Republican cause. We have no doubt the *Tribune* is sincerely sorry at his escape from martyrdom. Mr. Lincoln, with a most obtuse perception to the glory that awaited him, did not 'take fortune at the flood.' "[34]

Halfhearted attempts were made by the press friendly to Lincoln to deny the story of the Scotch cap. Buried on the back page, in the last column, of the *New York Tribune* on February 27 appeared "a statement of the facts which are said to have led to the alteration of the programme of Mr. Lincoln's journey to Washington." Hidden in the story was this sentence: "It should be said that no disguise of any sort was adopted by Mr. Lincoln, all reports to that effect being entirely false."

Murat Halstead's *Cincinnati Commercial* was not surprised that a plot against Lincoln's life was reported in Baltimore. It recalled that, just four years before, President-elect Buchanan was insulted by "the plug-uglies" of that city, stones were thrown at his carriage and he was compelled to leave a hotel by a rear door to avoid a hostile crowd.[35]

A defense of Lincoln came from an unexpected quarter. *The Press*, Douglas-Democrat paper at Philadelphia, in a story written by Editor John W. Forney, denied the cap-and-cloak slur. Forney's article was reprinted by *The World*.[36]

Belated reports came from smaller newspapers of attempts on Lincoln's life along the route. The *Lafayette* (Ind.) *Journal* reported an obstruction was placed on the track in front of the train.[37] The *Syracuse* (N. Y.) *Journal* told of a bomb found in Lincoln's private car.

We have been informed . . . there were several attempts to take his life made during the journey through Indiana and Ohio. The one which threatened the most serious consequences took place on the presidential train leaving Cincinnati, when a grenade . . . was discovered in the car occupied by Mr. Lincoln. . . . It was found in a small carpet bag, which had been deposited in a seat of the car by some unknown person. Attention was drawn to it from the fact that no baggage was allowed in the cars . . . Within fifteen minutes it would have exploded. . . . Of course, the "infernal machine" was . . . disposed of.[38]

But denials were a waste of printer's ink. The public had its story and refused to give it up. The *Louisville* (Ky.) *Courier* said Lincoln traded clothing with his wife at Harrisburg and rode through Baltimore in skirts, not a kilt.[39]

Among the poems written of the midnight ride was one of thirteen stanzas called *Air—Yankee Doodle*, reprinted by Democratic newspapers North and South. Two verses and the chorus read:

> Uncle Abe had gone to bed,
> The night was dark and rainy—
> A laurelled night-cap on his head,
> 'Way down in Pennsylvany.

> They went and got a special train
> At midnight's solemn hour,
> And in a cloak and Scotch plaid shawl,
> He dodged from the Slave-Power.

> *Refrain:*
> Lanky Lincoln came to town
> In night and wind, and rain, sir
> Wrapped in a military cloak,
> Upon a special train, sir.[40]

One of President Lincoln's first official acts after he took office on March 4 was to order an expedition for the relief of Fort Sumter. Washington formally notified the Governor of South Carolina of its intentions. A demand that Anderson evacuate Sumter was the Confederacy's reply. About half-past four o'clock on the morning of April 12, 1861, a mortar shell from a Confederate battery arched across the sky and burst directly over Sumter. The Civil War was begun.

For thirty-six hours, Anderson and his eighty men took a pounding from guns manned by 7,000 ashore before he marched out with colors still flying and without the loss of a man in combat. He was permitted to return to New York.[41]

Noted men of the South gathered in Charleston to see the first shot fired, among them Roger A. Pryor, distinguished Richmond newspaper man. He was in a deputation sent to Sumter under a flag of truce to arrange terms of the evacuation with Anderson. Loaded down with side arms, he strode into Anderson's headquarters where he saw what appeared to be a glass of brandy on a table. He grabbed it and drank it.

The post surgeon saw the editor snatch the drink and quickly informed him that what he had thought was brandy was iodide of potassium, a deadly poison. Pryor, in a state of collapse, permitted himself to be subjected to pumping and purgation, believing the surgeon was saving his life.[42]

On April 15, President Lincoln called for 75,000 troops to put down the rebellion. The response was 300,000. Four more states left the Union: Virginia, Arkansas, North Carolina, and Tennessee. Four slave states were to remain loyal; Delaware, Maryland, Kentucky, and Missouri. The western part of Virginia was to be saved for the Union cause.

The Confederate government moved from Montgomery to Richmond. The press of the new capital of the Confederacy rose to the occasion. The *Richmond Examiner* called for the capture of Washington, where lived "Lincoln the beast" and "the Illinois ape."[43] The *Richmond Whig* vowed "vengeance on the tyrants who pollute the capital of the Republic." It prophesied Jefferson Davis would soon dine in the White House and warned Lincoln he could save himself some trouble if he were "in readiness to dislodge at a moment's notice!"[44]

# 12 Lincoln in Washington

WHEN THE TALL lawyer from Illinois took up his duties in the White House, he was both the man of the hour and the question mark. He was put under a microscope by an inquisitive press. He lived in a glass mansion, his every movement news. His personal appearance was intriguing; he did not even look like any of his predecessors in the lofty office.

A writer for an English magazine gave Great Britain this description of the new American President:

To say he is ugly is nothing; to add that his figure is grotesque is to convey no adequate impression. Fancy a man almost six feet high, and thin in proportion, with long bony arms and legs which somehow always seem to be in the way; with great rugged furrowed hands, which grasp you like a vise when shaking yours; with a long, scraggly neck, and a chest too narrow for the great arms at his side. Add to this figure a head, cocanut shaped, and somewhat too small for such a stature, covered with rough, uncombed hair, that stands out in every direction at once; a face furrowed, wrinkled, and indented as though it had been scarred by vitriol; a high, narrow forehead, sunk beneath bushy eyebrows; two bright, somewhat dreamy eyes that seem to gaze through you without looking at you; . . . a close-set, thin-lipped stern mouth, with two rows of large white teeth, and a nose and ears which have been taken by mistake from a head twice the size. Clothe this figure then in a long, tight, badly-fitting suit of black. . . . Add to all this an air of strength, physical as well as moral, and a strange look of dignity . . . and you have the impression left on me by Abraham Lincoln.[1]

In the eyes of the smart New York crowd, Lincoln was a dismal failure socially, always wearing the wrong clothes and saying the wrong thing. A reporter for the New York *Commercial Advertiser*, writing under the name of "Arabella Smith," dashed this off after an evening at the Executive Mansion:

I don't believe first class people in Washington go to President Lincoln's levees. Why, I've seen more intelligence in a small drawing room in New York than I could see in the reception and ante-rooms together that evening at the White House. Mr. Lincoln is a good man, I am sure; and a modest man. Between ourselves, if he were my husband and President, too, I shouldn't like him to be so good-natured and free-and-easy in his manners. I should want him to look and act the Chief Magistrate a little more. . . .

I'll tell you what I think. The President is Abraham Lincoln, as honest and upright a man as the world ever saw. But Abraham Lincoln, in one respect, is not yet a President. His speech, his bearing, and the society he seems most at home with show him to be still Mr. Lincoln only. He has not yet appreciated, socially, the position he has been called to occupy. . . .

I saw Mrs. Lincoln and I don't think if I had been the President's wife I should dress exactly as she did. . . . And I wouldn't have talked quite so freely in a promiscuous crowd about my husband's affairs. Madam is a smart woman, however, with an indomitable spirit lurking behind her bright eyes, and will not live four years in the White House without making her influence felt. . . .[2]

Mary Clemmer Ames, a Washington correspondent for the *Springfield* (Mass.) *Republican*, wrote an equally unflattering picture of the new pair in the White House, saying, "Abraham Lincoln looks very awkward in white kid gloves and feels uncomfortable in new boots. Mrs. Lincoln is very dumpy and very good-natured and very gorgeous; she stuns me with her low-necked dresses and the flower beds which she carries on the top of her head."[3]

The Washington correspondent of the *New York Evening Express*, a Democratic newspaper, wrote of the First Lady, "How unbecoming does it seem for Mrs. Lincoln to be daily dashing through the lines of soldiers upon the avenue, with her driver and postillion in livery, in a glaringly labelled carriage to denote who is the passer."[4] When Mrs. Lincoln went shopping in New York in May of 1861, the Philadelphia *Sunday Dispatch* printed this story from its New York correspondent:

"Mrs. President Lincoln," as the ladies call her, was shopping to a considerable extent in this city in the early part of the week. She evidently has no apprehension that Jeff. Davis will make good his threat to occupy the White House in July, for she is expending thousands of dollars for articles of luxurious taste in the household way that it would be very preposterous for her to use out in her rural home in Illinois. . . .

Mrs. Lincoln looked paler than she did when I saw her in February last. Gossip insists, too, that she is a warm secessionist.[5]

The older Washington correspondents remembered Lincoln as a Whig Congressman who sat at a desk in the outer row and told droll stories in the cloakrooms. They knew his anecdotes of the Black Hawk War and recalled that he told them his company was mustered into service by a West Point second lieutenant named Jefferson Davis.[6]

Some of Lincoln's old stories were still in circulation in Washington when he arrived to take the oath, and his newspaper friends of other days found it hard to agree with Edwin M. Stanton, soon to be Secretary of War, who said he had known Lincoln at the bar and that he found him to be "a low, cunning clown."[7]

Benjamin Perley Poore, correspondent for Boston newspapers, called on the President-elect at Willard's Hotel and sought to obtain from him a copy of the inaugural address he had prepared for delivery. Lincoln showed it to him after making him promise he would not divulge the contents. Four copies had been printed for him at the newspaper office back in Springfield. A few days later, Poore obtained one of the copies for publication only after delivery.[8]

The White House became the news center of the country, but nothing in the form of a press conference existed and the correspondents obtained their stories in haphazard manner. Lincoln was always willing to talk to reporters who had gained his confidence. The reporters's main difficulty was to find him when he had time to talk to them. If they found him engaged, they sent in their cards, stating in writing what they wanted to know. If the subject was of great interest to Lincoln, he would call the reporter into his office or go to the anteroom and explain the question in detail.[9]

One of the newspaper men at the White House was William Dean Howells, pressing his claim for a consulate in Venice. He saw the President in a corridor but did not make himself known and presented his case to the secretaries. Informed the appointment had been granted, Howells left without thanking his benefactor. He was abroad five years. One of the regrets of his life was his failure to grasp Lincoln's hand.[10]

Among foreign correspondents living in Washington were Edward Dye, George A. Sala, Frank Vizetelly, also noted for his pencil sketches, Anthony Trollope, of London, and Dr. W. H. Russell, writing for the *London Times*.

Russell's fine objective reporting of the first major engagement of the war made him so unpopular in Washington that he was ever after known as "Bull Run" Russell, and it ended his journalistic career in America. He was denied an army pass and transportation by the War Department to cover later campaigns; Lord Lyons, the British Minister, pleaded Russell's case with Secretary Stanton to no avail. Lincoln refused to interfere, and Russell soon returned to London.[11]

Capital news writers were on the prowl for what they called "sensations," and Lincoln was the subject of one of them soon after he took office. Besieged by an army of office seekers who gave him no rest, Lincoln was sick at heart at their greed even in a time of crisis, and his temper was worn thin.

A delegation of Republicans from California went to the White House with a slate of names for Federal patronage on the Pacific Coast. Their selections were at variance with a list previously submitted by Senator Edward D. Baker, who had been elected in Oregon in 1860 by a coalition vote of Republicans and Douglas Democrats. Baker was Lincoln's old friend of Springfield days; he named his second son Edward Baker Lincoln for him. That child died in infancy. After having commanded a brigade in the Mexican War, Baker left Illinois about 1850.

One of the leaders of the protesting delegation was James W. Simonton, editor of the *Evening Bulletin* of San Francisco, a former New Yorker and at one time a stockholder in *The New York Times*. The handling of the story by the *Cincinnati Commercial*, a solidly

Republican paper, is typical of the way it was treated. Under the heading, "Extraordinary Scene in the White House," it said:

A highly exciting scene occured at the White House yesterday morning.
About a hundred citizens of California, including many leading Republicans,
called on the President to protest against the interference of Senator Baker,
of Oregon, with appointments in their state, and his attempt, as they claim,
to foist corrupt and broken-down politicians of doubtful antecedents upon
the administration and the people of the Golden State.

The President had arranged, whether from love of fun or a sense of
justice has not yet appeared, that Senator Baker should be present, without
the knowledge of the protestants. They were surprised to be face to face
with him, but nothing daunted, their spokesman, Mr. Joseph A. Nunes,
read a solemn protest and accompanied it with an emphatic, but respectful
extempore speech.

After him, Mr. Simonton, of the San Francisco *Bulletin*, stepped forward
and read a statement in which he denounced Col. Baker, and the politicians
he intended to saddle upon California as Federal office holders, in un-
measured terms.

The President listened to it quietly, but after its delivery, walked up
towards Messrs. Nunes and Simonton, took hold of their respective documents, and remarked in substance: "This protest deserves to be considered,
but as to your speech," turning to Simonton, "it is disrespectful to myself
and Mr. Baker, and I can make no other disportion of it than this," thrust-
ing it, with the last word, into the fire.

An intense consternation prevailed for some time after this most unlooked
for proceeding. . . .

The story continued that Simonton, who looked as though "he had
been struck with a thunderbolt," finally recovered sufficiently to say,
"I have simply done my duty. I have nothing to expect from the Executive, and in doing what I did, I merely meant to protect the interests
of my state." After some further argument, the President agreed to
confer with committees representing both factions. "The affair created
much excitement in political circles," said the *Commercial*. "The prompt
and decisive action of the President is praised by many as a symptom of
Jacksonism."[12]

Much has been written but nothing has been proved conclusively
about President Lincoln as a newspaper reader. One comes to the belief
he gave as much time to newspaper reading as a busy and harassed executive in the midst of a terrible civil war could find. That was not very
much, but he could always depend on the bright young men who

served him as secretaries to point out anything of personal interest in the public print.

On a table in the President's study there were usually three Washington daily newspapers: the *Daily Morning Chronicle,* the *National Republican,* and the *Evening Star.* He glanced over the telegraphic reports in them.[13]

Nicolay and Hay read many newspapers, among them *The Press* and the *North American* of Philadelphia; the *American* and *The Sun* from Baltimore; the *Tribune,* the *Evening Post, The Independent,* the *Times,* the *Herald, The World,* all of New York; the *Evening Journal* from Albany, N. Y.; the *Transcript,* the *Advertiser,* and the *Journal* from Boston; the *Tribune* and the *Journal* from Chicago; the *Republican* and the *Democrat* from St. Louis, and the *Gazette* and the *Commercial* from Cincinnati.[14]

Editors all over the North sent their newspapers to the White House in the hope the presidential eye might see their carefully prepared editorials, but they rarely reached the man for whom they were intended, being appropriated by members of the presidential staff or the servants.[15]

When talking about newspaper editors, Lincoln liked to tell the story of the man lost in the forest at night during a thunderstorm. Lincoln said the editors should pray as did the man in the woods when he went down on his knees and called out, "O Lord, if it is all the same to you, give us a little more light and a little less noise!"[16] The President told another story, aimed at newspaper editors. This was about two Irish immigrants en route west when darkness overtook them. Hearing the calls of bullfrogs in a pond, they were astonished and frightened, never having heard that sound before. They strained their eyes in the darkness but could see nothing. One of the men finally explained to the other, "It's nothing but noise."

Invited by a committee to examine a newly invented repeating gun, the feature of which was a device to prevent the escape of gas, the President remarked, "Well, I do believe this really does what it is represented to do. Now have any of you heard of any machine, or invention, for preventing the escape of gas from newspaper offices?"

An artist was working on a painting at the White House when Mrs. Gideon Welles, wife of the Secretary of the Navy, dropped in. She said she had read in the newspapers that the work was nearly finished. The artist, pointing out that the canvas was not ready, said the newspapers were not always "reliable." The President broke in, "That is to say, Mrs. Welles, that they lie and then they relie."[17]

Upon entering the White House, Lincoln for the first time in his life came under the observation of the foreign press. British editors and writers had no understanding of the man at all, if one is to judge from their product; they were baffled by his motives and openly took sides with the South. An economic recession in England resulting from the cotton blockade may have been to blame for shortsightedness.

Editors of American opposition newspapers, always eager to reprint articles that belittled Lincoln, found the London press a never-failing source. The Democratic peace faction used comment on conduct of the war as viewed on the other side of the Atlantic, apparently believing it carried great weight with the American reading public.

The President wrote a letter to James C. Conkling to be read before a Union rally at Springfield, Ill., in lieu of a personal appearance. It was really a stump speech, unusual even for Lincoln. While in some aspects it was a state paper, it also indulged in colorful rhetoric and in some places approached blank verse. The President spoke of the Mississippi River as the "Father of Waters" and made mention of the navy as "Uncle Sam's web-feet." He expressed high hopes for peace but cautioned against overconfidence, adding, "Let us be quite sober."[18]

When copies of the New York newspapers carrying the President's letter reached London a fortnight later, the *London Times* said it could hardly believe he had penned "so grotesque a production" and wondered "that such a man should have been called upon to guide the destinies of a mighty nation during a grand historical crisis."

"The early part," the *Times* admitted, "though by no means free from faults of grammar, or compatible with our literary dignity, is not devoid of a certain rough honesty and force. It is this, tempered by a lawyer like smartness, that secures for Mr. Lincoln, in spite of his arbitrary weakness, a certain popularity among people who enjoy a joke, even when it is practiced at the expense of themselves or the dearest interests of their country."

The *Times* could find only one solution for the style of the letter. It concluded Lincoln was drunk when he wrote it, saying:

One is really tempted to think that Mr. Lincoln cannot have been himself. . . . Herodotus tells us that the ancient Persian deliberated drunk as well as sober on important affairs of state; but we may be sure that the conclusion of a debate was conducted in the latter condition. It is difficult to believe that the American President can have observed this precaution, though he winds up with the timely injunction, "Let us be quite sober," and solemnly warns his readers not to be over sanguine of a speedy triumph. . . .[19]

In the month that followed, the *Times* editorial was read by thousands of Americans whose family newspaper clipped and reprinted it.

President Lincoln was often the theme of editorials in the *London Morning Post*. For example:

Mr. Lincoln will go down to posterity as the man who could not read the signs of the times, nor understand the circumstances and interests of his country; who could not calculate his own recourses nor appreciate those of his enemy; who had no political aptitude; who plunged his country into a great war without a plan; who failed without excuse, and fell without a friend.[20]

In the midst of the war, Lincoln issued a "Proclamation of Thanksgiving" for the achievements of the army and navy.[21] The *Post* chirped: "Mr. Lincoln may set apart days of thanksgiving for what he regards as special mercies, but he cannot conceal from his fellow citizens that all efforts made by his Government to crush the rebellion have ended in failure."[22]

Lincoln early took note of the hostile attitude of the foreign press. George Schneider, editor of the *Illinois Staats Zeitung*, published at Chicago, called his attention to feeling against the Union created in northern Europe by the *London Times*. Schneider was a Bavarian revolutionist who fled to America in 1849. His newspaper, printed in German, was a factor recognized by Lincoln in the election of 1860.

The President chose Schneider as Consul to Denmark, but he was actually a propagandist for the Federal government. He visited Hamburg, Bremen, and Copenhagen. The most widely read newspaper in Copenhagen was the *Dag Bladet*, which leaned toward the Confederacy. The paper changed its policy after Schneider visited the editor.[23]

Happily for the Union, there also were newspapers in London that strongly advocated the cause of the North and upheld Lincoln's policies. The *London Daily News*, the *London Spectator*, and the *London Star* were in this category.

When the *London Times* said, "People of the southern states may be wrong, but they are ten millions," the *London Daily News* replied, "The Confederate States may be ten millions, but they are wrong, notoriously, flagrantly wrong."[24]

*Punch*, published in London, at first supported the Union but later turned against it, ridiculing Lincoln in words and pictures. Its chief artist was John Tenniel, whose first cartoons of Lincoln showed him beardless. *Punch* described the bombardment of Fort Sumter with a poem entitled *Ink, Blood and Tears*.[25]

The London *Fun* always portrayed Lincoln as leader of a lost cause, head of a losing state. Its artists made him appear vicious and coarse. *Fun's* chief cartoonist was Matthew Somerville Morgan, known as Matt Morgan.[26]

# 13 "In the Depth of Bitterness"

PRESIDENT LINCOLN RECEIVED his baptism of fire from the "newspaper generals" of New York—Greeley, Raymond, and Bryant—in a demand for action after Sumter fell.

Both sides massed thousands of raw troops around their capitals, the untried armies glaring at each other across the miles between Washington and Richmond. In a few weeks, both said, the war would be over. One major engagement, they thought, could turn the trick.

The imagination of the editors was captured by the vast array of arms. They seem to have overlooked the importance of the struggle that was going on for control of the border slave states and the Western part of Virginia.

Greeley, self-appointed chief of staff of the armchair strategists, saw his *Tribune* demand a grand advance, and, soon, "Forward to Richmond!" became the slogan of the hour.

Raymond's *New York Times* charged President Lincoln with vacillation in an editorial headed, "Wanted—A Policy." It laid to the Lincoln administration "a blindness and a stolidity without parallel in the history of intelligent statesmanship." Of Lincoln, it said: "He must go up to a higher level than he has yet reached, before he can see and realize the high duties to which he has been called."[1]

Greeley went to Washington to see the President. He reported that he found an "obstinate calmness" in Lincoln's manner, that he was not perturbed in the slightest over secession and did not appear to realize that he might have to fight to hold the Presidency.[2] Bryant of the *Evening Post* wrote to Lincoln not to let Greeley worry him, that the editor of the *Tribune* was moved by "vagaries."[3]

Lincoln could look for no help from James Gorden Bennett, whose *Herald* had called loudly for compromise when Sumter was threatened,

saying: ". . . our only hope now against civil war of indefinite duration seems to lie in the overthrow of the demoralizing, disorganizing,
and destructive sectional party of which 'Honest Abe Lincoln' is the
pliant instrument."[4]

Bryant, while telling Lincoln to pay no attention to Greeley, was
informing his *Evening Post* readers that "The whole administration has
been marked by a certain tone of languor." And again: "We have been
sluggish in our preparation and timid in our execution."[5] Bryant sorrowed over "Mr. Lincoln's want of decision and purpose."[6]

Greeley's call for action in the *New York Tribune*, reprinted by
newspapers in all the loyal states, was read by millions. The *Tribune*
was the newspaper Bible of the country in the decade that preceded
the Civil War. While the daily edition was popular in the city of New
York, the weekly edition was mailed into practically every community
in the Midwest. The combined circulation of the Greeley papers was
probably in excess of 300,000 in 1860, the weekly alone boasting a paid-
up circulation of 214,000.[7]

From the pulpit he called the *Tribune*, Greeley preached to an estimated million readers. It has been said he exceeded many Presidents in
the influence he exerted through his columns.[8] He was self-educated and
possessed of a certain brilliance and natural talent that made him a good
journalist, but he lacked a sense of true understanding and had no depth
of wisdom. Lincoln might have said that Greeley had no horse sense.
A freethinker, he was a follower of fads and isms. He toyed with
spiritualism under the guise of investigating it; he followed the health
doctrines of Sylvester Graham and lectured on Fourierism.

Men gathered around the cracker barrels of grocery stores at thousands of crossroads every day to discuss what "Uncle Horace" said in
the *Tribune*. When 1860 dawned, history set a stage for Horace Greeley
on which he might have played the greatest part ever offered to an
editor. He failed, utterly and miserably.

Greeley came up to the place where he demanded military action by
a devious route. Only three days after Lincoln's election, a *Tribune*
editorial said:

If the cotton states shall become satisfied that they can do better out of
the Union than in it, we insist on letting them go in peace. . . . The right
to secede may be a revolutionary one, but it exists nevertheless. . . . We
never hope to live in a republic whereof one section is pinned to another
by bayonets.[9]

Three days before South Carolina seceded, the *Tribune* said:

If it (the Declaration of Independence) justified secession from the British Empire of three million of colonists in 1776, we do not see why it would not justify the secession of five million of southerners from the Federal Union in 1861.[10]

A strange and weird doctrine! Greeley, the Abolitionist, was willing to see his country broken up, was willing to see a great slave empire take form on the American Continent!

On December 22, 1860, Greeley wrote to Lincoln a long letter of advice, listing his views in six numbered statements. "Let the Union slide," he wrote, "let Presidents be assassinated—we can elect more." And then he counseled against "another nasty compromise."[11]

Greeley did not think of himself as a secessionist. On January 22, 1861, he made a vicious attack on James Brooks, editor of the *New York Evening Express*, charging that "for months he has been engaged with all his little might in cheering on the traitors." At that time, the *Tribune* was carrying on the editorial page a statement attributed to Lincoln: "I will suffer death before I will consent or advise my friends to consent to any concession or compromise which looks like buying the privilege of taking possession of the Government to which we have a Constitutional right."

On the morning of February 23, the day Lincoln arrived in Washington, the *Tribune* declared that "if the Slave States, the Cotton States, or the Gulf States only choose to form an independent nation, they have a clear moral right to do so. Whenever it shall be clear that the great body of Southern people have become conclusively alienated from the Union and anxious to escape from it, we shall do our best to forward their views."[12]

The thunder of the batteries that fired on Fort Sumter shook the *Tribune* office and set Greeley to quaking with newly found love of the Union. When Anderson evacuated Sumter, the *Tribune* told the people: "Fort Sumter is temporarily lost, but the country is saved. Long live the Republic!" Although not a life was lost, the *Tribune* eulogized "those who gave their lives to defend it." Greeley might have been speaking of his own newspaper when he added:

It seems but yesterday that at least two-thirds of all the journals of this city were the virtual allies of the secessionists, their apologists, their champions. . . .

Most of our Journals lately parading the pranks of the secessionists with scarcely disguised exultation, have been suddenly sobered by the culmination of the slaveholding conspiracy.[13]

A week later, the suddenly belligerent *Tribune* said:

If good Uncle Abe wants to read the secessionists another essay proving that he never meant them any harm, or Gov. Seward has another oration to deliver to them on the glories and blessings of the Union, let the performances come off by all means, but this will have to be before Jeff. Davis and Wise capture Washington.[14]

Greeley now became a military strategist and demanded action, failing to take into consideration that wars are fought with armies and that armies do not spring up overnight. The Confederate Congress had been called to meet at Richmond on July 20, 1861. Why not capture Richmond and prevent the meeting? At the top of the editorial page of the *Tribune* on June 26 appeared this item:

## THE NATION'S WAR-CRY

Forward to Richmond! Forward to Richmond! The Rebel Congress must not be allowed to meet there on the 20th of July! BY THAT DATE THE PLACE MUST BE HELD BY THE NATIONAL ARMY!

The article remained standing on the page for a week. Many kind explanations have been offered in an effort to prove Greeley was not responsible. The truth is he was not in town. Charles Dana, the managing editor, was in charge, and it has been said that he, sensing the fact that the newspaper was lagging behind public opinion, published the slogan to offset Greeley's former peace policy. The slogan was written by the *Tribune's* Washington correspondent, Fitz-Henry Warren.[15]

But no explanation can excuse Greeley from the responsibility. As the captain is master of his ship, so is the editor of a newspaper the person who must answer for everything published. Had this slogan appeared only once or perhaps twice, Greeley might be pardoned, but a newspaper man of Greeley's avidity surely tried to see his paper, even though he might be away from his desk.

Northern newspapers picked up the *Tribune* slogan until the cry, "Forward to Richmond," became the war cry of the Union. The Battle of Bull Run followed on July 21, a complete rout for the Federal forces. Major General Irvin McDowell, in response to the public demand, led about thirty thousand men, of whom about only eight hundred were regulars, attacked the Confederates, commanded by Generals Joseph E. Johnston and G. T. Beauregard, at Manassas Junction. The panic-stricken Union army fled back to Washington with the loss of about three thousand men. The Confederates lost less than two thousand.[16] As result of the defeat, Major General George B. McClellan took over the chief command.

The North was aghast. While five hundred men had been killed and about one thousand wounded, the Union losses were exaggerated by wild reports that literally thousands of dead were left in heaps on the field.

Greeley's enemies charged his powerful newspaper had forced the battle. Bennett's *Herald* had a field day at Greeley's expense. Whether or not the *Tribune's* influence had much to do with the Union advance is debatable; after all, the paper was only repeating what millions in the North were thinking. Again, generals are not supposed to find their orders in the public prints or plan their campaigns on editorial pages. But Greeley, the supreme egotist, took for granted that he himself had sent the army forward, with resultant disaster.

He tried to clear his name with a long explanation to the public in an editorial entitled "Just Once." He said in part:

I wish to evade no responsibility, but to repel a personal aspersion. . . . I wish to be distinctly understood as not seeking to be relieved of any responsibility for urging the advance of the Union grand army into Virginia, though the precise phrase, "Forward To Richmond!" is not mine, and I would have preferred not to iterate it. . . .

If I am needed as a scapegoat for all the military blunders of the last month, so be it. Individuals must die that the nation may live. If I can serve her best in that capacity, I do not shrink from the ordeal.[17]

After having pictured himself as the martyr who must bear all his country's sorrows, Greeley figuratively turned in his newspaper general uniform, saying: "Henceforth I bar all criticism in these columns on army movements, past or future. . . . Correspondents and reporters may state facts, but must forbear comments. . . . Henceforth it shall be the *Tribune's* sole vocation to rouse and animate the American people for the terrible ordeal which has befallen them."[18]

To make sure *Tribune* readers knew the great Greeley himself was speaking, he signed the editorial.

If Lincoln still harbored hope that Greeley was to be of any use to him, it probably vanished when the President opened a letter the editor wrote to him on Monday night, July 29, a week after Bull Run. So that the President might know of the vigil Greeley was keeping, he gave the hour of his writing as "Midnight." In his almost illegible hand, Greeley wrote:

This is my seventh sleepless night—yours, too, doubtless—yet I think I shall not die, because I have no right to die. I must struggle to live, however bitterly. But to business. You are not considered a great man, and I am a hopelessly broken one. You are now undergoing a terrible ordeal, and God has thrown the gravest responsibility upon you. Do not fear to meet them. Can the rebels be beaten after all that has occurred, and in view of the actual state of feeling caused by our awful late disaster? If they can—write me that such is your judgment, so that I may know and do my duty. . . .

If the Union is irrevocably gone, an armistice for thirty, sixty, ninety, one hundred and twenty days—better still for a year—ought at once to be proposed with a view to peaceful adjustment. . . . The gloom in this city is funereal—for our dead at Bull Run were many, and they lie unburied yet. . . .

This letter is written in the strictest confidence, and it is for your eye alone. But you are at liberty to say to members of your Cabinet that you know I will second any movement you may see fit to make. But do nothing timidly nor by halves. Send me word what to do. I will live till I can hear it, at all events. If it is best for the country and for mankind that we make peace with the rebels at once, and on their own terms, do not shrink even from that. But bear in mind the greatest truth; "Whoso would lose his life for My sake shall save it." Do the thing that is the highest right and tell me how I am to second you.

The letter was signed, "Yours, in the depth of bitterness."[19]

Lincoln told no one about the letter, not even his secretaries, Nicolay and Hay. He wrapped a piece of red tape around it and hid it with other confidential papers in his desk. There it lay until April 30, 1864, along toward midnight.

The President and his secretaries were in his study talking about Greeley's opposition to Lincoln's renomination. Lincoln went to his desk, pulled out the bundle of papers tied with a red tape, and extracted Greeley's letter from it. He handed it to Hay with a challenge to "decipher" it. Hay read aloud, stumbling along. Nicolay said Bennett would pay ten thousand dollars for it. After all had a good laugh, Lincoln replaced the letter in the file.[20]

A few months after Bull Run, Greeley was again annoying Lincoln. After the *New York Tribune* abused Ward Hill Lamon, Lincoln's devoted friend whom he had appointed United States marshal for the District of Columbia, a Federal grand jury at Washington indicted Greeley for "malicious libel of public officers," on April 4, 1862.[21]

The next day, the *New York Herald* said:

H. G. is beginning to reap the reward of his labors. He finds that impudent and unwarranted assaults upon honest officials for partisan purposes may not always escape punishment. He will probably ere long pay a compulsory visit to the District, if he should not . . . fly the country.[22]

The Greeley attack on Lamon came because he had held some purported slaves in the district jail, to be claimed by their owners. Lamon's action had long been the practice in the national capital.

The case never came to trial. It was nol-prossed the following December when President Lincoln interceded on behalf of the publisher. On January 6, 1863, Greeley wrote to Lincoln from New York, saying: "I thank you heartily for your interposition in the libel case. . . . I can't spare the time and money required for such a trial in Washington. . . . I have thus kept away from Washington a full year, and feel morally and every way the better therefor. And though I don't want to (be?) under indictment, I am puzzled for so good an excuse for keeping away hereafter."[23]

# 14 Of Brotherly Love

WHILE THE NEW YORK Republican editors were playing into the hands of the Democratic opposition by criticizing the Lincoln administration at every turn, the President had staunch friends in Philadelphia who put their trust in him and never wavered. The "City of Brotherly Love" had been educated to Union loyalty by the well-edited newspapers of the Hardings, the Peacocks, and the Forneys, and other publishers of lesser note.

The outstanding newspapers of Philadelphia were *The Press*, *Philadelphia Inquirer*, *Daily Evening Bulletin*, *Public Ledger*, *Evening Journal*, and the *North American and United States Gazette*. All were Republican with exception of the *Evening Journal*. The *Inquirer*, with a circulation of 60,000, bowed in political influence only to *The Press*, published by the adroit John W. Forney.

Publisher of the *Inquirer* was Jesper Harding, to whom Lincoln was not unknown. His son, George, an attorney, was associated with Lincoln in the famous McCormick reaper case. Jesper had another son, William W., who took over management of the newspaper when the father was appointed collector of internal revenue in Philadelphia by President Lincoln.[1]

The *Public Ledger* spoke for Lincoln and the Union cause, but it was a weak instrument until sold in December of 1864 to George W. Childs and the banking firm of Drexel and Company.[2] There were other newspapers that helped the Union cause, although of limited circulation. They included *The Item*, published by Thomas Fitzgerald, a playwright, and the *Daily News*, a stout party organ.[3] The lofty *North American and United States Gazette* had a large following of Republican readers. Thomas Hawksworth, editor of the *Sunday Transcript*, died fighting for the Union as a soldier.[4]

The *Inquirer* had little respect for the "armchair generals" of the New York press, although Harding himself wrote long editorials boosting McClellan for commander of the Union armies long before Bull Run. Of the New York press, the *Inquirer* said:

The efforts of certain journals in New York to read the Administration out of the Republican party are absolutely ludicrous and when we find the *New York Herald* defending the President against the *New York Times*, the absurdity is heightened.

It is to the last degree unpatriotic that a journal should permit the pique arising from disappointed expectations to overpower the real convictions. That the *New York Tribune*, also, should adopt this tone, will surprise no one, although the liberal share of public office given to its adherents should satisfy it.[5]

While Greeley's *New York Tribune* was crying, "On to Richmond," and the Northern press in general was charging the administration with procrastination, the *Inquirer* was content to let President Lincoln run the war. On July 13, 1861, the *Inquirer* said:

It is three months today since the people of the Free States were electrified by the news of the bombardment of Sumter; yet in that brief space, what wonders have been achieved . . . ! All this has been done by President Lincoln throwing himself upon the patriotism of the people and boldly taking "the responsibility."

The editorial pointed out that Maryland had been saved from secession, western Virginia had been kept within the North, and the enemy had been routed in the struggle for Missouri.

After the Bull Run disaster, the *Inquirer* offered no criticism of the administration or the Union generals but charged that history would say part of the blame could be laid to the "wild and fanatical clamor of the *Tribune* and its allies for an *unseasonable advance*."[6]

"A mischief-maker by instinct" was the name applied to the *New York Herald* by the *Inquirer*, saying Bennett might do "mischief" in Europe, where his newspaper was not understood.[7]

The attitude of the British press worried the *Inquirer*, and it was especially distrustful of the *London Times*, which it said was "stored and vitalized with malignity towards the U.S." It called on President Lincoln to take some action against the "organs of treason" in his own country, saying:

> If there be a point when patience ceases to be a virtue, the Federal Government has reached that point, in the toleration of treasonable presses existing north of the Potomac. . . . Shall we hesitate in such a crisis, and split hairs, about possible abuses of authority when all authority is threatened with annihilation?[8]

Four days before it advocated seizure of "treasonable presses," the *Inquirer* said it heard that "Ben. Wood, editor of the *Daily News*, exultingly paid the expenses to New York of a number of deserters from the regiment of the Fire Zouaves."

Soundly Republican and firm in its support of the Union, the *Daily Evening Bulletin* was edited by Gibson Peacock, who possessed a sense of humor. When Mayor Wood proposed that his city withdraw and become a separate nation, the *Bulletin* rocked with mirth, saying:

> It would be an advantage to the nation, morally and intellectually, to have New York City set off in an isolated position, denaturalized and made a foreign city. . . . We might have restrictions upon New York people coming into the United States. . . . So out with her![9]

The *Bulletin* knew the South would attempt to place the blame on Lincoln for starting hostilities, and it cried in ringing tones when Sumter was under fire:

> He (Lincoln) sought to defend the property he was sworn to defend; and before the supplies and reinforcements he was sending reached their destination, the southern army began to bombard Fort Sumter. Let this be borne in mind; for it will be a capital fact in the history of the momentous struggle begun yesterday.[10]

The *Bulletin* watched with questioning eyes attempts of the Republican newspapers in New York to direct conduct of the war. "Certain journalists in New York," said the *Bulletin*, "which have distinguished themselves in times past by the mode in which they conducted the Crimean and Italian campaigns, are especially eager to criticize and condemn." It was of Greeley the *Bulletin* was speaking when it declared "a certain paper is taking our domestic war in hand."[11]

Popular opinion crushed the small voices of pro-Southern sympathy that tried to make themselves heard. Early in 1861, *The Palmetto Flag*, a slavery newspaper, was established in Philadelphia. On April 15, 1861, it published an editorial in which it attempted to justify the assault on Sumter. An angry crowd gathered at 337 Chestnut Street, where the newspaper was published.

The editorial offices were on the third floor, and the crowd, yelling for a display of the American flag, rushed the stairway but was blocked by police. Mayor Henry Alexander tried to restore order. A flag was finally procured and waved from the window. The crowd went home. The newspaper went out of business.[12]

Soon after *The Palmetto Flag* ceased to wave, the *Evening Argus*, a newspaper of Southern sympathies, suspended publication. The *Bulletin* noted its passing, saying: "The list of killed and wounded among the Democratic newspapers is continually swelling."[13] The Philadelphia *Daily Record* quit later at the age of two years, but politics probably was no factor in its demise.[14]

The first case of a newspaper suppression by the Federal government in Philadelphia came in August of 1861 when the *Christian Observer* was seized by a United States marshal. This paper, a weekly, professed to be the organ of the "New School of Presbyterian Church," but the *American Presbyterian*, long-established, repudiated it. The Reverend Amasa Converse, editor of the *Observer*, published what were purported to be letters from a Virginian. They had a decidedly bogus appearance. This one is typical:

Reunion is an utter impossibility. The gross, brutal, fiendish, demoniac outrages perpetrated by the chicken stealers sent here to ravage the country, pillage the houses and burn them, outrage the women, and shoot down for amusement peaceable citizens, and even children, on the streets, have greatly exasperated the people.[15]

Federal officers went to the office of the *Observer* at 48 South Fourth Street and seized the type. The editor had flown, having previously written in the *Observer* that "the next issue will be the last." That same day the district attorney ordered that copies be seized of several New York Copperhead newspapers, and his order included the latest issue of the *Observer*. This seizure was made under an act of Congress authorizing the President to stop transportation of aid and comfort to those in rebellion.[16] Converse, a native Virginian, reestablished his paper in Richmond.[17]

The link between Lincoln and Forney, who published *The Press* in Philadelphia and the *Chronicle*, a weekly, in Washington, was forged before the President-elect went to the Capital. Lincoln simply reached out from Springfield and put his finger on a disgruntled Democrat. Forney always claimed Lincoln wrote to him after the election, thanking him for having opposed the Buchanan administration. The editor said he replied with a suggestion that Lincoln place Greeley in the Cabinet as postmaster general.[18]

Forney, a career newspaper man and lifelong Democrat, founded *The Press* as a poverty-stricken little sheet on August 1, 1857. He had served four years as clerk of the House of Representatives and in 1856 was named chairman of the Pennsylvania Democratic state committee. As the Democratic candidate for United States senator, he was defeated by Simon Cameron in 1857. When he launched *The Press*, flat broke as a result of his political campaigning, he purchased type on credit and hired the pressroom of the *Sunday Dispatch* to print his paper.

During the war, *The Press* became one of the leading dailies of the country, with a special edition for California and one for the army, and it overshadowed the Philadelphia newspaper scene.

Forney himself gave this explanation for founding *The Press*:

Mr. Buchanan had been elected President in the year previous on a clear understanding that he would not allow the slaveholders to make Kansas a slave state by violent means and *The Press* was started to hold him to that pledge. The message of the President of February 2, 1858, recommending admission of Kansas under the Lecompton constitution, caused that disruption of the Democratic party which two years afterward resulted in its defeat and the election of Mr. Lincoln.[19]

In the presidential campaign of 1860, Forney supported Douglas, but when Lincoln was elected, *The Press* showed an inclination to get behind the incoming administration.[20] When, in December of 1860, *The Press* endorsed John Hickman, a former slavery-advocating Democrat turned Republican, to fill a vacancy in the United States Senate, it was open admission that Forney had joined the new party.[21]

When Lincoln took office, *The Press* made a public announcement of adherence to his administration by lauding the inaugural address and giving its editorial word "to strengthen Mr. Lincoln in all honorable endeavors to promote the general welfare."[22] After Fort Sumter, *The Press* called the secessionists "envenomed and implacable enemies" and praised preparations for war made by the Union.

The President was soon in a position to repay his new friend. Forney sought the place of clerk of the House when the Thirty-seventh Congress met in July of 1861. He failed to get it, but Lincoln used his personal influence to have him chosen secretary of the Senate. The position carried a fair salary and gave Forney an unequaled listening post in Washington.[23] Philip R. Forney, eldest of the editor's three sons, was appointed a lieutenant in the army, and James, another son, received a commission in the Marines, although only eighteen years old.[24]

One of the features carried by *The Press* was a column of political gossip out of Washington, signed "Occasional." This column was usually written by Forney, closely watched by the Republican and Democratic press as a news pipe line from the White House. Lincoln tried his hand at writing this column in at least one instance. On August 16, 1861, Forney sent a clipping of the "President's article" to Simon Cameron, then Secretary of War, so he would be sure to see it.[25]

Forney was one of the first newspaper editors to realize the value of printed propaganda as a weapon in the Civil War. On October 17, 1861, he published an editorial about "The Romance of War" and several times during the conflict charged atrocities had been perpetrated by the "incarnate devils in Confederate gray." *The Press* stressed lack of food, clothing, and war supplies in the South, while belittling defeats suffered by Union arms.

Forney called for "a universal confidence in the administration" when Lincoln was charged with violating civil liberties by arbitrary arrests. He preached a union of parties, a role for which he was ideally fitted because of his former Democratic faith. *The Press* wanted to know what it mattered whether a man was a Democrat or a Republican when the nation was fighting for its life.[26]

During these months radical Republicans and Abolitionists urged upon the President some drastic and abrupt action to terminate slavery. Forney, although a friend of such extremists as Salmon P. Chase, Charles Sumner, Benjamin F. Wade, and others, held *The Press* to a conservative course, following "the lead of Mr. Lincoln."[27]

When the time came and Lincoln was ready to change his slavery policy, *The Press* switched overnight, saying on July 30, 1862: "A million able-bodied men await but our word to ally themselves with us bodily, as they are with us in heart. A magnificent black blister as a counter irritant!" Forney was not in the habit of writing in language so colorful. The words "magnificent black blister" sound more like Abraham Lincoln.

The opposition press in the North called Forney "Lincoln's dog." As long as Lincoln lived, but no longer, Forney was a great editor, with vision and daring and speaking always at the right moment.

In the Philadelphia borough of West Chester, *The Jeffersonian*, an outright antiwar weekly published by John Hodgson, was wrecked by "unidentified persons" on the night of August 19, 1861.[28] After Lincoln's election, it pictured him as drinking beer and smoking cigars while the country was on the verge of ruin; it continued these attacks after inauguration.[29]

Four days after the night raid, two deputy United States marshals, who said they acted "upon the authority of the President," seized *The Jeffersonian*.[30] Hodgson demanded his newspaper be returned to him and was told by the district attorney he could have it if he signed a statement in which he must say that "the only way to put down rebellion and restore the Union is by war." Hodgson flatly refused.

The case went into the United States circuit court in Philadelphia where it was heard on October 7, 1861, with Hodgson represented by attorneys George Biddle and William B. Reed. After several days of wrangling, the court decided *The Jeffersonian* had not been used "to aid and abet insurrection," and it was handed back to Hodgson. When he resumed publication, Hodgson was notified his newspaper was barred from the mails by order of Postmaster General Montgomery Blair, an order that stood until January 18, 1862.[31]

Hodgson retaliated by bringing a suit for damages against the deputy marshals who seized his newspaper. The case was tried before Chief Justice Walter Hoge Lowrie of the supreme court of Pennsylvania. The defense maintained the order for suspension was authorized by President Lincoln, but the jurist could not find "sufficient evidence" that the Chief Executive had acted. The jury awarded damages of five hundred and twelve dollars to Hodgson. The case was retried on a technicality, and this time the jury decided the amount due Hodgson was $504.33.[32]

The case attracted national attention, and when the verdict was announced, the Copperhead press was jubilant. The New York *World* said the jury had "unbarred a gate of light upon a long darkened community."[33]

During the summer of 1861, the word Copperhead, with a capital C, came into use to describe a Northern newspaper whose sympathies lay with the South. It also was applied to individuals. The copperhead is a not uncommon variety of poisonous snake that strikes without warning. The word entered the Civil War language in the Middle West and gradually spread over the country. Peace factionists called Copperheads tried to turn the tables by wearing pins made from copper pennies in their lapels.

The Columbus *Ohio State Journal* said as early as February 13, 1857, in speaking of the *Cadiz* (Ohio) *Sentinel:* "This paper is locofocoish of the most intensified copper-head stripe." After the war was begun, the *Detroit Free Press* suggested the "neutral newspapers" be called Copperheads. That was on May 5, 1861. *The Cincinnati Commercial* used the term on August 17, 1861, and gradually it became common.

*The New York Times* recognized the word in an editorial on February 13, 1863, "The Western Copperheads."[34]

# 15 "The Present Unholy War"

ROUT OF THE Union army at Bull Run hushed the shouting of the loyal Republican press for a quick, decisive battle, but it gave the Peace Democratic newspapers—and they flourished in every state in the North —new incentive to attack President Lincoln. The Democratic editors, almost to a man, demanded the "effusion of blood" be halted with compromise, even recognition of the Confederacy.

By late summer of 1861, the struggle for the border slave state of Missouri was in full swing, and Kentucky was wavering between adherence to the Union and secession. A Union army under Brigadier General Nathaniel Lyon was routed at Wilson's Creek in Missouri by Confederates under Major General Sterling Price, who then attacked Lexington, Mo., and took 3,000 prisoners. The Democratic radicals again demanded peace.

All over the North, Union people, armed with the sympathy of the Lincoln administration, tried to stop the flood of Southern propaganda by wrecking disloyal newspapers. Only in the New York metropolitan area and in New Jersey did the people turn to the courts for relief.

On August 16, 1861, the grand jury for the circuit court of the United States for the Southern District of New York drew up a peculiar document that asked whether certain newspapers could be indicted for their utterances against the Federal government and the war. The jury, whose foreman was Charles Gould, stated the facts at hand in the form of a "presentment" and asked the court for "advice." The "presentment" said:

There are certain newspapers within this district which are in the frequent practice of encouraging the rebels now in arms against the Federal government by expressing sympathy and agreement with them, the duty of acceding to their demands, and dissatisfaction with the employment of force to overcome them. These papers are the New York daily and weekly *Journal of Commerce*, the daily and weekly *News*, the daily and weekly *Day Book*, the *Freeman's Journal*, all published in the city of New York, and the daily and weekly *Eagle*, published in the city of Brooklyn. The first-named of these has just published a list of newspapers in the Free States opposed to what it calls "the present unholy war"—a war in defense of our country and its institutions, and our most sacred rights, and carried on solely for the restoration of the authority of the Government.

The Grand Jury are aware that free governments allow liberty of speech and of the press to their utmost limit, but there is, nevertheless, a limit. If a person in a fortress or an army were to preach to the soldiers submission to the enemy, he would be treated as an offender. Would he be more culpable than the citizen who, in the midst of the most formidable conspiracy and rebellion, tells the conspirators and rebels that they are right, encourages them to persevere in resistance and condemns the effort of loyal citizens to overcome and punish them as an "unholy war"? If the utterance of such language in the streets or through the press is not a crime, then there is a great defect in our laws, or they were not made for such an emergency.

The conduct of these disloyal presses is, of course, condemned and abhorred by all loyal men; but the Grand Jury will be glad to learn from the Court that it is also subject to indictment and condign punishment.[1]

In the excitement of the public mind over the issue of press control, the paper handed to the judge by the grand jury was universally regarded as an indictment, although its wording as a query on the authority of the court was clear. Federal officials were quick to seize upon the action of the jury, and on August 22 an order was issued against the newspapers named by the Post Office Department at Washington. The order, directed to the postmaster of New York, said:

The Postmaster-General directs that from and after your receipt of this letter none of the newspapers published in New York City, which were lately presented by the Grand Jury as dangerous for their disloyalty, shall be forwarded in the mails.[2]

NEW SALEM, June 13, 1836.

To the Editor of the Journal:

In your paper of last Saturday, I see a communication over the signature of "Many Voters," in which the candidates who are announced in the Journal, are called upon to "show their hands." Agreed. Here's mine!

I go for all sharing the privileges of the government, who assist in bearing its burthens. Consequently I go for admitting all whites to the right of suffrage, who pay taxes or bear arms, (by no means excluding females.)

If elected, I shall consider the whole people of Sangamon my constituents, as well those that oppose, as those that support me.

While acting as their representative, I shall be governed by their will, on all subjects upon which I have the means of knowing what their will is ; and upon all others, I shall do what my own judgment teaches me will best advance their interests. Whether elected or not, I go for distributing the proceeds of the sales of the public lands to the several states, to enable our state, in common with others, to dig canals and construct rail roads, without borrowing money and paying interest on it.

If alive on the first Monday in November, I shall vote for Hugh L. White for President. Very respectfully,

A. LINCOLN.

Courtesy Illinois State Historical Library

Lincoln's "show of hands" letter in *Sangamo Journal*, June 18, 1836. His first recorded instance of writing for the public press.

Courtesy Illinois State Historical Library

Charles H. Lanphier, editor of the *Illinois State Register* at Springfield.

Courtesy Ohio State Archaeological and Historical Society

Whitelaw Reid, editor of *Xenia* (Ohio) *News;* later a Washington correspondent.

Courtesy Illinois State Historical Library

Edward L. Baker, editor of the *Illinois State Journal* at Springfield.

Courtesy of the *Chicago Tribune*

Joseph Medill, publisher of the *Chicago Tribune.*

A grand jury at Westchester drew up a "presentment" against two German language newspapers, the *Staats-Zeitung* and the *National-Zeitung*, as "disseminators of treason." A petition for signatures was passed against the *Courier des États-Unis*, a French language newspaper published in New York.[3]

On the same day the Post Office Department barred the five New York newspapers from the mails, the United States marshal in Philadelphia seized all copies of them as they arrived by train. Four days later, the War Department issued General Order No. 67, which said:

By the 57th article of the Act of Congress, entitled "An Act for establishing rules and regulations for the government of the armies of the United States," approved April 10, 1806, holding correspondence with or giving intelligence to the enemy, either directly or indirectly, is made punishable by death, or such punishment as shall be ordered by the sentence of a court-martial.

The public safety requires a strict enforcement of this article. It is therefore ordered that all correspondence and communications verbally, or by writing, printing or telegraphing, respecting the operations of the army, or military movements on land or water, or respecting the troops, camps, arsenals, intrenchments, or military affairs within the several military districts, by which intelligence shall be directly or indirectly given to the enemy, without the authority or sanction of the general in command, be and the same are absolutely prohibited, and from and after the date of this order, persons violating the same will be proceeded against under the 57th article of war.[4]

The names of 154 newspapers appeared in the list opposed to "the present unholy war." It was first published in the *New York Daily News* on August 12 and appeared the next day in the *Journal of Commerce*. The *New York Day Book* picked it up on August 14. Placards then appeared in public places, saying: "The freedom of the press is subordinate to the interests of a nation. Let the three southern organs issued in this city beware!"[5]

The action of the New York grand jury never went beyond the drawing of the "presentment." Judge Samuel R. Betts, who placed the newspaper case before the jury, turned the "presentment" over to the October term of court when it was dismissed or, rather, ignored.[6] Washington took no official notice. The administration was ready to move with other measures.

James A. McMaster, editor of *Freeman's Journal*, was arrested by order of Secretary of State Seward, charged with treason because of statements made in his newspaper, and imprisoned in Fort Lafayette. He was held eleven weeks and released without having been brought to trial.[7]

McMaster, forty years old, did not submit to arrest without a struggle. He was in his office when a United States marshal entered and told him he had an order from Seward for his arrest. The editor demanded to see the warrant, and the marshal, whose name was Murray, replied, "Our presence here is enough warrant."

McMaster lunged at him but was subdued after a tussle. He raved and stormed and declared he would shoot Seward and any one else who had a hand in his arrest. When the marshal made no effort to apply handcuffs, McMaster demanded they be placed on him. After he had cooled off, McMaster asked permission to write a letter to his wife, and the manacle was taken from his right hand. He insisted on wearing the one on the left, exclaiming, "I want it there! I want to keep it on!"

While McMaster was writing the letter, his editorial assistant ran to him with the promise the newspaper would continue "not a bit abated in severity." Murray, who stood waiting, warned that the assistant would, if he persisted in this policy, soon have the opportunity to join McMaster in Fort Lafayette.

McMaster finished the letter, stood up, and announced he was ready to go. The manacle was restored to his right hand. The marshal had a carriage waiting in the street. As the editor was seated in the carriage, he thrust his manacled hands from the open window and called upon spectators to witness what had been done to him. A contemporary journalist wrote, "Getting no reply, he drew in his hands and, threatening vengeance, sat moodily back and in a short time became an inmate of Fort Lafayette."[8]

While the detailed charge of treason was never revealed, McMaster's biographer says he was arrested for his "uncompromising strictures" on President Lincoln's war policies.[9] Newspapers friendly to McMaster insisted the charge of treason was never formally filed.

Following his release from prison, McMaster resumed publication of his newspaper the next April. Arrest and imprisonment did nothing to change his political doctrines, although his newspaper editorials were less bombastic. He worked harder than ever against Lincoln, but his efforts took new form. Talented as a speaker, he campaigned for radical Democrats in the state elections of 1863.

The New York Daily News was purchased in 1861 by the Democratic Congressman, Benjamin Wood, who made it the organ of the

Tammany forces and filled its pages with legal advertising obtained, ostensibly, through his brother, Fernando Wood, mayor of New York.

While Fernando was proposing that New York City secede from the Union with the cotton states, Benjamin laid down a bitter attack on Lincoln, combining a defense of the slavery system with denunciation of the President.[10]

After the New York postmaster refused to accept the *Daily News* for mailing, on orders from Washington on August 22, 1861, Wood shipped his newspaper to other cities by railway express. This system worked for a few days until the government got wind of what was going on and placed detectives on express trains out of New York.[11] The *Daily News* then suspended publication. Eighteen months later, it resumed as an evening paper.[12]

The new *Daily News* made the original seem mild in comparison in its attitude toward the Lincoln administration. An editorial published just before the Battle of Gettysburg helped fan the flames of dissension that brought about the terrible draft riots in New York.[13]

Lincoln's bid for a second term brought this insult from the *Daily News:* "No influence except compulsion can induce any respectable proportion of the people to cast their votes for that compound of cunning, heartlessness, and folly that they now execrate in the person of their chief magistrate."[14]

Insidious peace propaganda was one of Wood's weapons. He used it more and more as it became apparent the South could not win. This is a typical "peace" editorial:

> It is our solemn conviction that no man of ordinary perceptive faculties honestly believes today that further bloodshed will secure a political result more desirable than such, whatever it may be, than can be secured by negotiation. Why do we persist in dealing death-blows that vindicate no principle . . . ?[15]

The *Daily News* specialized in anti-Lincoln rhymes. One of the most widely copied was "A Federal Nursery Rhyme." It follows:

I

Sing a song of Green Backs,
A pocket full of trash,
Over head and ears in debt,
And out of ready cash;
Heaps of tax collectors,
As busy as a bee;

Ain't we in a pretty fix
       With gold at fifty-three?

## II

Abe in the White House
       Proclamations writing;
Meade on the Rapidan
       Afraid to do the fighting;
Seward in the Cabinet
       Surrounded by his spies;
Halleck with the telegraph
       Busy forging lies;

## III

Chase in the treasury
       Making worthless notes
Curtin at Harrisburg
       Making shoddy coats;
Gillmore at Charleston
       Lost in a fog;
Forney under Abe's chair
       Barking like a dog;

## IV

Schenck down at Baltimore
       Doing dirty work
Butler at Norfolk
       As savage as a Turk;
Sprague at Rhode Island
       Eating apple sass;
Everett at Gettysburg
       Talking like an ass;

## V

Banks out in Texas
       Trying to cut a figure;
Beecher in Brooklyn
       Howling for the nigger;
Lots of Abolitionists
       Kicking up a yell;
In comes Parson Brownlow
       And sends all to hell;

## VI

Burnside at Knoxville
In a kind of fix;
Dahlgren at Sumter
Pounding at the bricks;
Grant at Chattanooga
Trying Bragg to thrash;
Is it any wonder
The Union's gone to smash?[16]

The "nursery rhyme" was picked up by Democratic newspapers all over the North. The weekly *Union* at Somerset, Ohio, published the rhyme and came close to being mobbed on account of it. After the paper appeared, about twenty Union soldiers home on furlough went to *The Union* office and demanded the editor write an apology and issue it in an extra. An assistant told the soldiers the editor had left town "on some legal business." The soldiers replied they were going to wreck the plant unless the apology was published immediately.

The Mayor of Somerset tried to restore order and found his own soldier son in the newspaper office. He called out the home guards and posted them around the building until the excitement subsided. In his regular edition the week following, the editor charged the soldiers were "under the influence of liquor" and that their action was "instigated by Abolition fanatics."[17]

As a newspaper editor, Wood poured out his propaganda unmolested, but as a member of Congress his course was not so serene. Charges were brought against him for disloyal sentiments expressed on the floor of the House. The committee to which the charges were referred put them in a pigeonhole and took no action.[18]

In midsummer of 1864, the *Daily News* published *The Walpurgis Dance At Washington*, seven ghastly verses that scored again with the anti-Lincoln press in the North. Here are two:

The night was heavy and murk, the moon shone dusky and red.
The air had an odor of sulphurous smoke and of corpses newly dead.
And I saw in fact or a dream, or both confused in one,
A dance and a revel and a maniac rout too hideous for the sun;
And out of it came a cry:
BLOOD! BLOOD! BLOOD! Let the witches' cauldron boil with a
nation's tears for water!
BLOOD! BLOOD! BLOOD! Slabby and thick as mud, to sprinkle the
hungry soil for the carnival of slaughter!

One, tall, and bony and lank, stood forward from the rest,
And told a ribald story with a leer to give it zest,
And said: "Our fire burns feebly, we must pile it up anew;
Tell me the fuel to feed it with ye friends and comrades true!"
And they shouted with mad rejoicing:
(repeat chorus)[19]

Until the last gun was fired, the *Daily News* scoffed at all reports of
Union victories and insisted the South never could be conquered.[20]

Established in 1848 as an organ of the slavery interests in New York,
the *Day Book,* owned by N. R. Stimson, was in full blast against the
enemies of the South when the Civil War started. A daily evening
newspaper, it claimed to be "saucy, racy and spicy" and lived up to that
boast.[21]

The *Day Book* contended the North was responsible for secession
and quoted speeches of leading Republicans and Republican newspapers
to prove its point. The press of the *Day Book* was fed after Lincoln's
inauguration by attacks made on him by *The New York Times* and the
*New York Tribune.* On April 2, 1861, the *Day Book* told its readers:
"The *Tribune* and the *Times* this morning have strong articles condemning the present 'no policy' course of Lincoln."

The next day, it asked this question: "Has not the election of Lincoln
ruined and broken up the country? What Republican editor will dare
answer that question?" On April 5, the *Day Book* said: "The *Times*
and *Tribune* are pitching into Old Abe because he doesn't pitch into the
South."

The *Day Book* could not repress its joy when it noted that "the
*Richmond Whig,* the ablest paper in the South, which has hitherto
opposed secession, has hauled down its Union flag, and goes for the new
Confederacy. There can be no doubt but the cause of secession is all
the time progressing with a sure step in Virginia."[22] Small wonder that
the *New York Day Book* was the only newspaper in the city that refused to fly the American flag as Lincoln rode to his hotel before a
quarter of a million people in his appearance there en route to Washington.[23]

Lincoln was insulted, lied about, and ridiculed by many newspapers,
but only the *New York Day Book* tried to involve him in an incident
with a sex angle. In the dark days just before Sumter, it said:

Some of the newspapers mention with agreeable surprise the fact that the
President has appointed a young man keeper of some light house on the
sole recommendation of his sweetheart. Old Abe has an eye for a pretty

girl, and why should he not have an ear, too? Did he not refuse, while at City Hall in this city, to shake hands with a young man, but said, "If your sister was here, I would shake hands with her."[24]

The editor of the *Day Book* had imagination, although its expression took unusual form. On Saturday, April 13, 1861, the newspaper appeared in mourning dress. All the column rules had been turned as if marking the death of some national figure. It explained: "With sad hearts we send forth our paper today in mourning—mourning for the fate of our once happy and glorious country, now plunging into the abyss of war, under the black and piratical lead of Abolitionism." The headline over the Fort Sumter story said: "The Abolition Crusade!! Civil War Begun!"

For his editorial comment that day, the *Day Book* editor merely clipped from William Cullen Bryant's *Evening Post* of April 12. He quoted the Republican Abolitionist as saying:

This is a government of the people. There is no doubt that when a majority of the people of this country decide to break up the government, their decision is final; and no sensible man doubts that if, by a fair and unobstructed vote, the majority of the people of the seceded states declared their position and earnest desire to leave the Union, they would not find the remaining states unreasonable.[25]

Editor Stimson added: "Now, after civil war has been inaugurated . . . these very foolish journals that have goaded the rash and foolish Lincoln into a coercive policy, come out and virtually declare in favor of all the southern states have demanded! If this does not look like a deliberate attempt to destroy this Union, and to seal its destruction in blood, then we do not know what does."[26]

On August 22, the day it was denied mailing privileges, the *Day Book* called attention to Horace Greeley's faultfinding, quoting the *New York Tribune* of July 24, 1861, as saying: "A decimated and indignant people will demand the immediate retirement of the present cabinet from the high places of power, which, for one reason or another, they have shown themselves incompetent to fill." It made the *Tribune* look ridiculous by quoting it as having said five days later: ". . . we pray the President to dismiss no one of his Constitutional advisers."

Bennett's *New York Herald* had fun with the story of the barred newspapers by suggesting that the list should include the *New York Tribune*. The *Herald* recalled that the *Tribune*, during the previous October and November and "many times since," had advocated the

right of the Southern states to secede on the principles of "the Revolution and of human liberty." It went on to say:

> The *Tribune*, therefore, ought to be suppressed with the other secession
> sheets, and likewise the New York *Independent* and Garrison's *Liberator*,
> which pronounces the Union "a covenant with death and an agreement with
> Hell."[27]

The *Day Book* reprinted the *Herald* editorial, of course. On August
26, it published without comment the notice it received from the
postmaster on denial of mailing privileges.

Editor Stimson either was a believer in objective reporting or he had
an unusual sense of humor. On August 27, the *Day Book* carried this
story under an Allentown, Pa., date line:

> Wm. Halsey, hailing from Ithaca, was waited on by a party of citizens
> at his hotel yesterday and requested to leave the town, or accept the alterna-
> tive of riding out of town on a rail. He had given provocation beyond en-
> durance by endeavoring to induce parties to take the *New York Day Book*
> and by uttering the rankest treason. He left precipitately.[28]

The daily edition of the *Day Book* ceased on August 29 with a farewell editorial in which it told President Lincoln he was making a mistake in permitting it to be suppressed. It added: "An attempt is now
being made to suppress all the organs of opinion in the North that
differ with the will of the party temporarily in possession of the
Federal Government."

Stimson published a weekly edition called the *Weekly Day Book*,
and this he renamed *The Caucasian*. The action amounted to a bold eva-
sion of the post-office order. After hiding behind the new name for
two years, it resumed its old title of *Weekly Day Book*.[29]

One of McMaster's fellow prisoners in Fort Lafayette was Henry
A. Reeve, editor of the *Watchman*, published at Green Point, L. I. He
was taken into custody by detectives as he was boarding a Hudson
River Railroad train, placed on a boat, and taken down the bay.[30]

Files of the *Brooklyn Daily Eagle* reveal it to have been the least
obnoxious to the government of the five papers named by the grand
jury. At the outbreak of war, the *Eagle* claimed the largest circulation
of any evening paper in the United States. Through the direction of its
talented editor, twenty-nine-year-old Thomas Kinsella, it was a lively
sheet, dressed in attractive type and filled with well-written stories.

In the first few months of conflict, the *Eagle* displayed a pro-Southern attitude, then righted itself into a loyal Union organ, although al-

ways opposed to Lincoln and the party that put him in power. The Eagle always spoke for the Democratic party. It was a constant critic of Lincoln and all his acts, taking the stand that a Republican President could not possibly do the job. It belabored the Lincoln administration on the ground that the people were being robbed of the right of free speech and a free press and contended that all personal liberties were in danger. The always controversial issue of "arbitrary arrests" caused the *Eagle* to say:

The government manages things at Fort Lafayette much as the circus elephant did the fifty cent piece and the money box. The intelligent animal could put the money in easily enough, but didn't know how to get it out. Men are arrested on the impulse of the War Department and sent to Fort Lafayette. After they have been arrested, it is generally found that the prisoners have violated no law, they can't be tried before any tribunal, and the authorities can't let them go without stultifying their previous acts. So the poor devils are kept in limbo for months, until the public has forgotten all about them, when they are quietly released "on parole," which of course is the last heard about the case.[31]

The *Spirit of the Times*, published by George Wilkes, a rabid Abolitionist, was a New York newspaper that, judged by the frequency with which it was quoted by the Copperhead press, did extreme damage to Lincoln and the Union cause. The editor was a strong personality, and his newspaper was popularly known as *Wilkes' Spirit*.

The *Spirit* supported Lincoln until he sought renomination. It venomously charged Lincoln had been manipulated by Seward and Weed from conservatism to Jacobism until he was almost ready to proclaim himself a despot and change the Republic into an empire. It further said:

All this has been brought about . . . by the corrupting temptations of a double term; and we may judge somewhat further of the dreadful rigor of that demoralizing influence by the fact that the patronage of the government is not only being squandered at this moment to debauch the legislators into an illicit nomination of Mr. Lincoln, but he has actually been engaged, of late, in granting pardons to military rebels, who are above the high-water mark of amnesty proclamation in order that they may come within our lines and electioneer to carry out his personal purposes.[32]

Few newspapers of the opposition, no matter how deeply anti-Lincoln in their policy, would have published such an editorial. All they had to do was reprint it, giving full credit to the source, to cause more havoc than if they themselves had written it. That clearinghouse of all Southern propaganda, *The Crisis*, watched the *Spirit* like a hawk and saw that Wilkes never begged for a vast and appreciative audience.

As Wilkes ground out his editorials charging Lincoln plotted a dictatorship, Editor Medary of *The Crisis* observed: ". . . the bitterness with which that paper arraigns Mr. Lincoln for his attempts at despotism is quite refreshing. . . . *Wilkes' Spirit* uses all its power of words to attract the people to the dangers of Lincoln's usurpations."[33]

Just before Lincoln was renominated, the *Spirit* said: "The nation cannot live with Abraham Lincoln and Seward at its head during the next terrible four years. Even if honest, they are unequal to the task."[34]

The *True American*, published at Trenton, N. J., was among the newspapers regarded as "dangerous from their disloyalty" by the Post Office Department. Barred from the mails in early August of 1861, it suspended publication on August 24, charging that the government "has virtually interdicted the publication of every paper that does not support the administration."[35] According to the *New York Tribune*, the *American* "succumbed to popular opinion" when barred in the mails.[36]

A citizen critic of Postmaster General Montgomery Blair's attitude toward the opposition press soon found himself a prisoner for two weeks in overcrowded Fort Lafayette. James W. Wall, of Burlington, was a member of a prominent New Jersey family and an inveterate writer of letters to newspaper editors. Deeply concerned by the government's action, he wrote a letter to Blair, lashing him for his "recent high-handed, unconstitutional act in stopping certain newspapers from being circulated through the mails."

Wall was the son of the late Senator Garritt D. Wall and Blair was the son of Francis P. Blair, Sr., editor of the *Washington Globe* in the days of President Andrew Jackson. In his letter to the Postmaster General, Wall recalled that their fathers had been close friends. Blair replied he was surprised that the son of Garritt Wall, "the friend of Jackson, should have become a disciple of Calhounry in its worse phase."[37]

The next thing Wall knew, he was on his way to Fort Lafayette. He was in a cell from September 11 to September 24, 1861, with no charge filed against him, so far as he was informed.[38] The next episode in this little drama was told in the following news story:

Burlington, N. J. Sept. 25, 1861—Colonel J. W. Wall returned home from Fort Lafayette last evening, receiving quite an ovation. He was escorted home by a band of music and a torch light procession. In a short speech, he said he would endeavor to ascertain his accusers and bring them to justice.[39]

The town of Burlington and the county in which it is situated had given Lincoln a majority of 1,833 votes in the election of 1860; in the fall elections of 1861, Burlington went heavily Democratic.[40]

About a month after a New York grand jury drew up the "presentment" against five newspapers, a grand jury of the United States District Court at Trenton handed down a paper that was even more peculiarly worded. The Trenton jury named five New Jersey newspapers, denouncing them for their disloyalty to the Union cause, and asked the public not to support them.

The papers named were the *Hunterdon Democrat*, the *Plainfield Gazette*, the *New Brunswick Times*, the *Warren Journal*, and the *Evening Journal*, published at Newark. The "presentment" stated that copies of these newspapers covering a period of months were examined by the jurors. The finding of the jury emphasized the criticism against President Lincoln and other Union leaders and said in part:

. . . during the most critical period, while the capital of the nation has been besieged by armed insurgents; while eleven states in actual rebellion, having been striving by invasion and treachery to plunge other states still remaining loyal into open opposition to the National Government, these newspapers have been, up to within a very recent period, persistently denouncing and libelling those to whom this great duty of national defense is necessarily entrusted, in thwarting their efforts for self-preservation, and fomenting rebellion by discouraging, and opposing the only means by which it can be put down. While they (the grand jury) cherish a due regard for freedom of speech, they feel it is their duty to repudiate and denounce the conduct of these journals; that while the press may freely criticize public men and measures in the peaceful contests of party, yet in a war for the life of a nation the press, as well as individuals, should uphold the existing government, or be treated as its enemies. They consider their duty freely discharged in reference to these newspapers by this presentment, leaving them to the wholesome action of public opinion. They recommend all loyal citizens, all public officers, all municipal corporations, rigorously to withhold all patronage from such newspapers as do not hereafter give their unqualified support to the National Government.[41]

The largest paper of the five named was the Newark *Evening Journal*, owned by a stock company and edited by E. N. Fuller. When

Clement L. Vallandigham, the Peace Democrat Congressman from Ohio, began his assault on the Union war policy soon after Fort Sumter, the *Evening Journal* lauded him to the skies, saying: "Mr. V. is on the right track to an immortality of fame, and if we mistake not, his name will hereafter rank high in the future of America."[42]

The action of the Trenton grand jury did not soften the *Evening Journal's* antiwar policy. It continued to belittle Lincoln and all his measures until, on July 21, 1864, military officials tried to put a damper on it.

Major General John A. Dix directed the United States district attorney, A. Q. Keasbey of Newark, to arrest and prosecute the editor of the *Evening Journal* on the grounds that he had published an editorial damaging to the army draft. The arrest was made under the twenty-fifth section of an act of March 3, 1863, entitled, "An act for enrolling and calling out the national forces, and for other purposes." The day after the order was issued, Fuller was taken into custody on two warrants, one for inciting to insurrection, the other for discouraging enlistments.[43]

The prosecution of Fuller was singular in that the action was civil, not military. In many other cases of a similar nature, the editors had been arrested and taken off to a Federal prison on orders from Washington, but at Newark every due process of law was invoked.

The editorial on which the charges were based said in part:

It will be seen that Mr. Lincoln has called for another half million of men. Those who wish to be butchered will please step forward. All others will please stay at home and defy Old Abe and his minions to drag them from their families. We hope that the people of New Jersey will at once put their feet down and insist that not a man shall be forced out of the state to engage in the Abolition butchery, and swear to die at their own doors rather than march one step to fulfill the dictates of the mad, revolutionary fanaticism which has destroyed the best government the world ever saw, and now would butcher its remaining inhabitants to carry out a more fanatical sentiment. This has gone far enough and must be stopped. Let the people rise as one man and demand that this wholesale murder shall cease.[44]

Fuller was indicted in the United States District Court, was convicted and sentenced to pay a fine. The offending editorial was too hot for other Peace Democrat newspapers to reprint. Even *The Crisis* ignored it. Lincoln's old friend, the *Illinois Daily State Journal* at Springfield, reproduced it in reporting the progress of the case, but a Democratic editor reprinted it with disastrous results. O. C. Cone, of the *Messenger*, at Somerville, N. J., was arrested on August 10, 1864, convicted, and fined.[45]

The conviction of Fuller made him more bitter than ever, and he returned to his desk after the trial to write an editorial in which he charged the courts of New Jersey were "controlled" by the Lincoln administration. He paid his respects to the President in these words:

We have no honeyed words for such a ruler as Abraham Lincoln who, if we read, is a perjured traitor, who has betrayed his country and caused the butchery of hundreds of thousands of the people of the United States in order to accomplish either his own selfish purpose, or to put in force a fanatical, impracticable idea.[46]

The New Jersey cases drew the attention of the *New York Tribune*, which remarked: "The Copperhead journals are never so happy as when they are miserable. An act of the military power which affords grounds of complaint is a boon to them. Arbitrary arrests never fail to cause spasms of delight. A good case of newspaper suppression is food for a fortnight of miserable exultation."[47]

A few weeks after Fuller and Cone were convicted, the military took over the case of a New York editor who had expressed opposition to conscription. On August 18, 1864, John Mullaly, editor of the *Metropolitan Record*, was arrested and taken before a United States commissioner on a charge of opposing and counseling resistance to the draft.

The charge was filed by District Attorney E. Delafield Smith, who took copies of the *Record* to the commissioner and demanded a warrant for Mullaly. Before the warrant was issued, the district attorney was asked to make his complaint in writing. The editor was brought into court and posted bond of $2,500 for his appearance later.[48]

Mullaly was tried by a military commission and acquitted. It was reported that the proceedings were reviewed and approved by President Lincoln.[49]

Daniel Flanagan, editor of the *Mason* (Ohio) *Democrat*, reprinted the antidraft editorial from the *Metropolitan Record* and was immediately arrested by army officials. He was tried by a military commission at Cincinnati, was found guilty and sentenced to six months' imprisonment in Fort Delaware in March of 1865. Flanagan's defense was that the article which caused his arrest was a reprint from the *Metropolitan Record*.[50] The conviction of Flanagan after Mullaly had gone free set the Democratic press to howling, and it charged the Ohioan had been treated unfairly in view of the precedent set in New York. *The Crisis* charged the principal reason why Flanagan went to prison was that the government thought it was necessary "to make an example of somebody."[51]

The ranting of the Democratic newspapers in the North got under the hide of William Cullen Bryant, and he sarcastically told the disgruntled editors how to publish "a sound conservative Union paper." The *Evening Post* of May 20, 1863, carried a long editorial in which eight rules were laid down for the guidance of the Democratic press. It follows in part:

All military successes of the rebel armies should be magnified . . . while those of the North should be depreciated.

War reports of the Southern papers should be paraded at great length, especially those . . . which extoll the exploits of their generals.

The efficient and energetic generals in the loyal service should be calumniated in every plausible way; insist . . . they are plunderers and thieves.

Whenever the Union army achieves a signal victory say very little about it.

The finances of the government may be made a fruitful topic of suggestion . . . talk sneeringly of "greenbacks."

In the abuse of Mr. Lincoln and his cabinet . . . Pronounce them all weak, timid, vacillating, and utterly incapable . . . accuse them of tyranny, despotism, excessive rigor, and a determination to trample the rights of the masses into the dust.

By pursuing these rules, and others which we may hereafter prescribe, an excellent conservative journal may be published, orthodox in every respect in the North, and highly popular in the South.[52]

Loyal editors stood firmly against the utterances of anti-Lincoln newspapers, but no more firmly than did a citizen of Catskill, N. Y., who fought a brave but losing battle singlehandedly. Howard Selick resented the attacks made on the Lincoln administration by the *Democrat and Recorder*, published at Catskill. He told the editor that if the attacks did not cease, he would stone the newspaper office windows. When the next issue of the *Democrat and Recorder* appeared, Selick saw his warning had gone unheeded.

He prepared to carry out his threat and was in the act of picking up a rock when a shotgun blast from inside the newspaper building struck him. Carried to a doctor's office, seventeen slugs were removed from his body. Near death for weeks, he finally recovered.[53]

Among editors in New York State who were given a ride down the bay to cool off in Fort Lafayette were J. R. Flanders and J. D. Flanders, coeditors of the *Franklin County Gazette,* published at Malone. They made the trip on October 22, 1861.[54]

According to *The New York Times* of March 25, 1862, the editors of the New York *Journal of Commerce* and the *Sunday Mercury* were ordered to Washington to be tried by a court-martial for disloyal utterances. The editor of the *Boston Journal* was included in the order, which was issued by the Secretary of War, the *Times* said. Somewhere along the line the order was countermanded, and no arrests were made.[55]

# 16   The Battle of Censorship

CENSORSHIP OF NEWS dispatches filed in Washington began during the dark days of April in 1861 when the government assumed control of the telegraph wires leading from the city. It became a football, kicked around among the departments, a new and baffling problem for Federal officials. Control of censorship was first placed under the Treasury Department, then transferred to the War Department, then to the State Department and then back to the War Department, under whose authority it lodged on February 25, 1862.

Capital correspondents, unused to any form of censorship, complained continually; they charged the censors were stupid and ignorant and that they were usually in a nearby saloon when their services were needed. They found it easier to send their news stories by mail, a system that circumvented the censors but wasted a lot of time. The government at no time peeked into letters mailed from any military district to an address on loyal soil.

The controversy over censorship was in full swing when the Federal forces were repulsed and suffered heavy losses in the battle of Ball's Bluff, Va., on October 21, 1861.[1] President Lincoln's friend, Edward D. Baker, who resigned as Oregon senator to recruit and command the 1st California Regiment, was killed.[2]

Charles C. Coffin, correspondent for the *Boston Journal,* was in the War Department building when news of the Ball's Bluff disaster came in. He saw the President and General McClellan in the telegraph room and heard them in low conversation. After about five minutes, Lincoln came from the room alone, tears running down his pale face, his hands pressed over his heart. He almost fell as he reached the door to the street. Coffin leaped from a chair to help him, but the President went on with unseeing eyes, failing to return the salute of the snappy sentinel in the yard.[3]

No two newspaper accounts of the battle agreed, and the censorship squabble was given fresh impetus. Prodded by unceasing complaints of their Washington writers, editors succeeded in bringing about a Congressional investigation of the telegraph censorship.

On December 5, 1861, the House passed a resolution that authorized the Judiciary Committee "to inquire if a telegraphic censorship of the press has been established in this city; if so, by whose authority and by whom it is controlled; to report if such censorship has not been used to restrain wholesome political criticism and discussion, while its professed and laudable object has been to withhold from the enemy information and reference to the movements of the army."

Lincoln, too, had a complaint, but not with the censorship. It was "the faultfinding of the press" against the government. The newspapers, he said, were too impatient. His charge aroused some comment, and the *Cincinnati Enquirer* said he had much reason to protest the "faultfinding spirit" of such leading Republican newspapers as the *New York Tribune, New York Times, Chicago Tribune,* and the *Cincinnati Gazette.*[4] Lincoln made no word of reply to the avalanche of personal criticism against him. He hoped, however, that the Union press could be guided by a spirit of "patriotism and fairness."[5]

During the House investigation, Washington correspondents were called as witnesses before the committee. They testified that soon after General McClellan took command of the Army of the Potomac, he called together the Washington representatives of the press to obtain their cooperation in keeping secret military movements. That conference was held August 2, 1861, and a set of resolutions was passed in which it was agreed not to publish either in editorial form or in correspondence of any description, any information giving aid and comfort to the enemy; the government was in turn to afford the correspondents every facility for transmitting all information suitable for publication, particularly news that concerned engagements with the enemy.

The resolutions were approved and signed by McClellan and the following correspondents: W. D. Shaw, *New York Herald;* W. W. Harding, *Philadelphia Inquirer;* J. A. Paliston, Philadelphia *North Amer-*

*ican;* M. D. Wallach, *Washington Star;* Adam S. Hill, *New York Trib-
une;* George W. Adams, *Cincinnati Gazette* and Philadelphia *Bulletin;*
C. C. Coffin, *Boston Journal;* A. B. Spofford, *Cincinnati Commercial;*
D. W. Bartlett, New York *Evening Post;* L. A. Gobright, representing
the New York *Associated Press;* E. C. Stedman, New York *World;*
U. H. Painter, *Philadelphia Inquirer.*

The correspondents gave their side of the case to the investigators.
For the most part, they testified there was more ground for complaint
after the resolutions were drawn with McClellan than before.[6]

The Judiciary Committee filed a formal report on March 20, 1862. It
stated it had come to the following conclusions:

First. A telegraphic censorship has been established in this city.

Second. The censorship existing at the time the investigation was directed
by the House, was originally established upon the basis of the agreement
between the representatives of the press and Gen. McClellan, but was enlarged in its scope by the Secretary of State.

Third. At the time the inquiry was directed by the House, and for some
months prior to that time, and until the 25th of February last, the censorship was controlled by the Secretary of State.

Fourth. The original design was to prevent the publication of military
information which might be of advantage to the rebel authorities.

Fifth. Despatches, almost numberless, of a political, personal, and general
character, have been suppressed by the censor, and correspondents have
been deterred from preparing others because they knew they could not
send them to their papers by telegraph.

The telegraph has become a most important auxiliary to the press of the
country, and should be left as free from government interference as may
be consistent with the necessities of the government in time of war. These
necessities cannot extend beyond what may be legitimately connected with
the military or naval affairs of the nation, and to these should the government interference with the transmission of intelligence be confined, for it
is this character of information alone which can be of importance to the
enemy, and which may be properly withheld from the press and the public
in order that it may not reach the enemy. The committee, therefore, recom-
mends the adoption of the following resolution by the House:

Resolved, That the government shall not interfere with free transmission
of intelligence by telegraph, when the same will not aid the enemy in his
military or naval operations, or give him information concerning such
operations on the part of the government, except when it may become
necessary for the government, under the authority of Congress, to assume

exclusive control of the telegraph for its own legitimate purpose, or to assert the right of priority in the transmission of its own despatches.[7]

The House agreed with the committee, but in the meantime a newspaper man was the cause of an incident pertaining to war secrecy that set the Capital buzzing. Secretary of War Stanton ordered the arrest as a spy of a *New York Herald* reporter known as Dr. Malcolm Ives, whose brother had resigned from the United States military service to enter the Confederate army as an officer.

Stanton charged that Ives came without invitation to a conference the Secretary of War was holding with several members of Congress in the War Department offices on February 8, 1862. He claimed Ives was there "for the purpose of spying and obtaining war news and intelligence in regard to Cabinet consultations, telegraphs, etc. for publication, which he knew was not authorized to be published."

When told to leave by Assistant Secretary of War Peter H. Watson, the *Herald* reporter blurted out that the full power of the Bennett newspaper would be turned against the Lincoln administration unless he got the story. Ives was arrested and taken off to a cell in Fort McHenry.

In a special report of the case made by Secretary Stanton two days later, he delivered a sermon on conduct of the press in wartime, saying:

Newspapers are valuable organs of public intelligence and instruction, and every proper facility will be afforded to all loyal persons to procure, on equal terms, information of such public facts as may be properly made known in time of rebellion. But no matter how useful or powerful the press may be, like everything else, it is subordinate to the national safety. The fate of an army or the destiny of the nation may be imperilled by a spy in the garb of a newspaper agent. The nation is in conflict with treason and rebellion—may be threatened by foreign foes. . . .

The duties of the President and his Secretary, of every officer in the government, especially in the War Department and military service, are at this moment urgent and solemn—the most urgent and solemn that ever fell upon men. No news gatherer, nor any other person, for sordid or treasonable purposes, can be suffered to intrude upon them at such a time to procure news by threats, or spy out official acts which the safety of the nation requires not to be disclosed.

The *Herald* had assigned Ives to set up a news bureau in Washington. The reporter was not released by Stanton until the following June, although no charges were filed against him. The *Herald* did nothing to defend him during his imprisonment, and his connection with the newspaper was severed. Stanton promised similar treatment if others offended.[8]

President Lincoln tried to remain aloof from squabbles between correspondents and heads of departments. Irate reporters sometimes appealed to him, but he would tell them he did not know much about censorship and coax them into good humor with one of his anecdotes.[9] But the stories the reporters wrote out of Washington were not always passed over so lightly by the Chief Executive. One day he entered the office of L. E. Chittenden, Treasurer of the United States, visibly angry and waving a newspaper clipping. A New York newspaper, making a personal attack on him, said he took his pay in gold while Union soldiers were paid in greenbacks worth only fifty cents on the dollar. As a further insult to Lincoln, the story said Jefferson Davis drew his twenty-five thousand dollars per year in Confederate money, then worth about one-fourth its face value. The story was a lie from start to finish. Lincoln told Chittenden he hoped the scoundrel who wrote the story would "boil hereafter."[10]

Try as hard as it might, the government never succeeded in enforcing the Washington censorship to the letter. The press, both Republican and Democratic, took the position that any news of troop movements could be handled if it came from some source other than the Capital. A flagrant violation involved Bryant's New York *Evening Post*. A heavy movement of troops westward was ordered, the 11th and the 12th Corps of the Army of the Potomac being sent to reinforce Major General W. S. Rosecrans, who had suffered heavy losses in the Battle of Chickamauga. The Washington correspondents were personally requested by President Lincoln and Secretary Stanton not to divulge the information. They gave their word and even notified their respective newspapers that, if the information reached them through other channels, they should not mention it.

On Saturday night, September 26, 1863, Washington learned the *Evening Post* had broken the news in New York. Lincoln was "exceedingly angry," and Stanton roared. The *Evening Post* cleared its Washington correspondent of blame and said others had imposed upon it by bringing "rumors" into the office.

One of the Philadelphia newspapers made the suggestion that Editor Bryant and his staff should take Sunday morning breakfast in Fort Lafayette.[11] The suggestion, had it been carried out, would have produced a result highly popular with editors of some opposition newspapers who found themselves in the grim fortress for lesser violations.

Lincoln had reason to be "exceedingly angry" with Bryant. Just a year before, the *Evening Post* so flagrantly ignored the rules of censorship that it drew a reprimand from H. W. Halleck, General in Chief. The army issued a circular over Halleck's signature, which said:

Major General Foster, commanding the Department of North Carolina, has called attention to an article in the New York *Evening Post* of the (Sept.) 7th, in which is published the numbers and positions of his troops. He remarks that the New York papers always reach the enemy in a few days after publication, and that such information from our friends is more injurious than that gained by rebel spies. The newspaper press is earnestly requested to make no publication in regard to the number and movements of our troops. No information could be more desirable to the enemy than this. Such publications have done immense injury to our cause.[12]

In September of 1863, Lincoln wrote a letter to James C. Conkling to be read at a meeting of Union men in Springfield, Ill. That was the letter in which he poetically described the opening of the Mississippi River by Federal forces by saying, ". . . the Father of Waters again goes unvexed to the sea."[13] The Springfield rally was most important because it was intended to answer a meeting of dissatisfied Democrats and others held there on the previous June 17 when the idea of forming a Northwestern Confederacy was proposed. Lincoln himself thought he had written a "rather good letter."[14]

When word got around Washington that the President had prepared a special paper, the correspondents sought to obtain copies. All, including the *Associated Press* man, were turned down. Lincoln explained he had found it a source of mischief to give advance copies of anything to the press and that he had learned he could not depend on promises of secrecy.

A couple of days before the letter was to be read at Springfield, it appeared word for word in the New York *Evening Post* and was telegraphed back to the Washington newspapers. The meeting was set for September 3; Lincoln saw his letter that day as he looked over the morning newspapers.

The President was so mad he could have cried.[15] He fired a telegram to Conkling, demanding an explanation.[16]

The *Evening Post* never told how it scored the beat. Inasmuch as the matter concerned was political and not military, nothing could be done about it.

Generals Ulysses S. Grant and William T. Sherman complained from time to time that military secrets were revealed in newspapers. Grant distrusted the press and because he would not talk for publication found himself denounced as incompetent and intemperate while lesser generals with larger mouths were praised as peerless leaders. After the Battle of Shiloh in Tennessee, April 6 to 7, 1862, Sherman was the forgotten man while Major General John A. McClernand, a former attorney, and Major General Lewis Wallace were the men of the hour.[17]

Newspaper publishers of the New York metropolitan area called a meeting on June 8, 1863, to protest what they charged were infringements of freedom of the press by the Federal government. With a few notable exceptions, the editors of the important newspapers failed to appear. Horace Greeley of the *New York Tribune* was one of the moving spirits and presided as chairman of the meeting. The editors present were: James Brooks, *New York Evening Express;* John Clancy, *The Leader;* Anson Herrick, *Atlas;* Theodore Tilton, *The Independent;* William C. Prime, *Journal of Commerce;* Oswald Ottendorfer, *Staats-Zeitung;* J. Beach, *The Sun;* William Cauldwell and H. P. Whitney, *Sunday Mercury;* Elon Comstock, *Argus;* C. Mathews, *New Yorker;* P. J. Meehan, *Irish American;* M. S. Isaacs, *Jewish Messenger,* and R. McFarlane, *Scientific American.*

Greeley went to the meeting armed with a set of resolutions he himself had drawn up and which he offered to the committee. The wording of the resolutions was too strong for even that group of malcontents, who toned them down before putting them to a vote. After much debate, four declarations were approved, one of them saying:

While we . . . emphatically disclaim and deny any right as adhering in journalists or others to incite, advocate, abet, uphold, or justify treason or rebellion, we respectfully but firmly assert and maintain the right of the press to criticize firmly and fearlessly the acts of those charged with the administration of the government, also those of all their civil and military subordinates, whether with intent directly to secure greater energy, efficiency, and fidelity to the public service, or in order to achieve the same ends more remotely through the substitution of other persons for those in power.

Another declaration said that the editors denied "the right of any military officer to suppress the issues or forbid the general circulation of journals printed hundreds of miles from the seat of war."[18]

The *New York Daily News* published a story on July 2, 1864, with the date line, "Near Petersburg," that revealed Grant had been reinforced by Major General George G. Meade and described a conference of generals at Major General Ambrose E. Burnside's headquarters. This information fell into the hands of General Robert E. Lee and was useful because it told him Burnside was with Grant.[19]

Lee and his Confederate generals read the Northern newspapers closely and were kept fairly well informed of movements of the Army of the Potomac.[20] Even the strictly loyal *Philadelphia Inquirer* in the early days of the war tipped off Lee so clearly on McClellan's maneuvers that he was able to withdraw troops from the defense of Richmond and put them in the line.[21]

*The New York Times* of November 10, 1864, published a story that revealed the exact strength of Sherman's army and his campaign plan. A protest was lodged with Secretary Stanton by Grant, but nothing seems to have come of it. When Sherman was campaigning in Georgia, the *Indianapolis* (Ind.) *Daily Journal* reported his disposition of troops.[22]

In that same campaign, Sherman was forced into a battle he had hoped to avoid because of a story that appeared in the *New York Tribune*. Sherman was headed for the coast, trying to keep his objective secret from the rebel General Hardee with a series of feints. Hardee was completely in the dark until he got hold of a copy of the *Tribune*. There he read that Sherman's supply ships were gathering at Morehead City. That meant Sherman would effect a rendezvous with the fleet. A heavy loss of men followed in the Carolina campaign. Sherman blamed Greeley, later refused an introduction to him.[23]

Wilmington, N. C., a great Confederate base, was the objective of a combined land and sea force that set out from Hampton Roads in December of 1864 with greatest possible secrecy. *The New York Times* teased the public by telling of the start of the amphibious force and wondering where it was bound.

The *New York Tribune* the next day asked in an editorial whether the *Times* would be suppressed for publishing contraband news. The *Times* paid no attention. On December 19, it reported the fleet was seen off New Inlet, N. C., and named all the vessels in the force!

The *New York Daily News* was not to be outdone. On December 20, it bluntly announced that the fleet was to attack the base at Wilmington and revealed the officers in command as Admiral William D. Porter and Major General Benjamin F. Butler. When the attack was made the day before Christmas, no one was surprised, least of all the defenders of the base. The attack was repulsed.[24]

Secretary of the Navy Welles investigated the publicity that attended the Wilmington expedition and charged a correspondent by the name of "Osborn" was the guilty man. He turned over all the information he had to Secretary Stanton, who promised to make an arrest.

The accused correspondent probably was B. S. Osbon, one of the most distinguished Civil War reporters, writer and artist. He was with Admiral David G. Farragut at Mobile Bay and gave to the world the story of the dauntless old sea dog directing the battle while tied in the rigging of his ship.[25] The case against the correspondent, who was a free-lance writer, was considered in a Cabinet meeting, but the heads of the War and the Navy Departments could not agree on the course to pursue.[26]

Writers who have explored this incident are of the opinion no action was taken against the correspondent, but a one-paragraph item in *The Crisis* at Columbus, Ohio, on July 12, 1865, may furnish the sequel. It said: "B. S. Osborn, the naval reporter who has been so long in the hands of the government without being tried, charged with publishing contraband news, was last week released on parole."

Note again that the name was spelled Osborn. This, however, was a frequent error when the correspondent's name appeared in newspapers. Many news men were arrested during the war with no written charge ever filed against them. This may have been so in Osbon's case. It is of singular interest that the officials in Washington should have vented their wrath on the correspondent, instead of the newspaper that published his stories.

Henry E. Wing, of the *New York Tribune*, cracked the censorship that surrounded Grant's campaign in the Wilderness in May of 1864 and was rewarded with a kiss by President Lincoln. After the first day's fighting, the war correspondents held a conference and decided to attempt to get one man to a telegraph wire with a "pool" story. Wing was chosen to make the attempt, a dangerous undertaking because of stragglers roving the countryside behind the army. Grant gave Wing permission to leave and told him to tell Lincoln there would be no turning back.

The correspondent started on horseback but had to abandon the animal when he was fired on. He walked and ran the last six miles on the railroad ties, finally reaching Manassas Junction late at night. He tried to file his story to the *Tribune* but was refused use of the wire. He knew a message addressed to Assistant Secretary of War Charles A. Dana could not be rejected; Dana was a former managing editor of the *Tribune*, and Wing knew him personally.

Back came three words: "Where is Grant?" Wing knew then for

certain that he alone was in possession of the greatest story of the war and could make his own bargain.

He said he would tell the War Department all he knew if he were permitted to file 100 words for the *Tribune*. Secretary Stanton came on the wire and threatened Wing with arrest. President Lincoln, who haunted the telegraph room of the War Department awaiting word from Grant, took charge and told Wing to send along his *Tribune* story. The correspondent stood beside the army telegraph operator and dictated the short story that appeared in the *Tribune* the next morning, May 7.

While Wing was dictating, Stanton ordered a locomotive sent down the single line of track to bring him to Washington. He found the President waiting for him when he reached the White House at two o'clock in the morning. When he delivered Grant's message, Lincoln threw his arms around him and kissed him on the forehead.[27]

A regular exchange of newspapers kept both the North and South fully informed of current news events on either side of the lines. The Washington correspondent of the *Springfield* (Mass.) *Republican* wrote this revealing account:

The manner in which the regular files of Richmond papers are obtained would astonish some of the slow people of the country if they understood it. The government is generally indebted to the newspaper press of the country for its first copies of the leading rebel newspapers. Two days after Jeff. Davis's message was printed in Richmond, a newspaper man here, a Washington correspondent, presented Mr. Lincoln with an advance copy. U. H. Painter, indefatigable correspondent of the *Philadelphia Inquirer*, presented Mr. Fessenden with a copy of the report of the rebel Secretary of the Treasury, when it was but two days old. On Saturday last, at ten o'clock in the morning, I sat down to a table whereon lay copies of all the Richmond dailies of the previous Thursday. A large proportion of these journals come direct through the lines at Petersburg, but some come direct across the country to Alexandria. Blockade-runners bring them—pickets make exchanges for the New York journals, and in different ways the files are kept perfect.[28]

Soldiers of the rival armies passed newspapers back and forth, a practice strictly forbidden but general. The troops had their own code when trading papers, with a violation of the honor system certain to bring retaliation. The North took a celebrated prisoner in an incident where the honor code failed to work. A dispatch out of Washington, November 29, 1864, said:

The rebel ex-Gen. Roger A. Pryor, serving as a private soldier in the Confederate army, was captured last Friday by our pickets while attempting to exchange papers. This was done in retaliation for the recent capture of Capt. Burbridge on Saturday, and Pryor will probably be returned as soon as Burbridge arrives.

Since Pryor's capture, Burbridge has been dismissed from the army for disobeying the order forbidding the exchange of papers or holding interviews with the enemy under any pretext.[29]

Pryor was one of the best-known newspaper men in the country at the outbreak of the war. He was on the staff of the *Washington Union* and was later editor of the *Richmond Enquirer*. He was sent to Congress from Virginia in 1859 to fill a vacancy, was elected in 1860 but did not take his seat. During his brief term in the House, he engaged in a bitter debate over slavery with Congressman John F. Potter of Wisconsin. Pryor challenged Potter to a duel, but the Northern man chose bowie knives for weapons, and there the matter dropped, not, however, before the affair had been widely discussed in the press.

After he made a sorry spectacle of himself in Sumter, he entered the Confederate army as a colonel and was promoted to a brigadier general, whereupon he resigned and enlisted to serve as a private.[30]

The reporters were wrong in thinking Pryor would be exchanged. The day after he was reported captured, a news dispatch out of New York said: "Roger A. Pryor arrived here this morning and was taken to Fort Lafayette. . . . He says Sherman is the ablest officer in our army and that the South has more to fear from his movements than those in progress elsewhere."[31]

He was transferred to Fort Warren, in Boston Harbor, where he remained until February 18, 1865, when he was paroled as a prisoner of war.[32] The events that brought about his release were not fully known until the Robert Todd Lincoln Collection of the Papers of Abraham Lincoln were opened in 1947.

Found in the collection was a letter written by Horace Greeley to President Lincoln on *New York Tribune* stationery, dated "February 6, 1865," which said: "Roger A. Pryor, now a prisoner of war in Fort Lafayette, was captured under circumstances which seem to give him special claims to exchange. My friend, Mr. W. McLean of Cincinnati is authorized to offer any reasonable exchange for Mr. Pryor, and I hope it may be effected."

The collection also yielded a telegram signed, "U. S. Grant Lt Gen," dated "City Point, Va., 11:30 A.M., February 7, 1865," and addressed to

"Col. Wm. Hoffman, Commanding General prisoners," in which it was stated: "I think Pryor, and a sergeant from Waterbury, now at Point Lookout, should not be exchanged as long as we have a prisoner."

Washington McLean of the *Cincinnati Enquirer* also interceded for Pryor. He took John W. Forney with him to the White House, and Lincoln released the Virginian into Forney's custody.[33]

A newspaper man ordered shot by General Burnside was saved by Grant in the Wilderness campaign. He was William Swinton, who accompanied Congressman Washburne to Grant's headquarters at Spotsylvania. Swinton was presented to Grant as a "literary gentleman," who planned to write a history of the war. Washburne gave the General his word Swinton was not acting as a correspondent but was merely an observer. Grant agreed to the arrangement, although preferring to have Swinton accredited as a correspondent and thus restrict the information he obtained.

Grant soon discovered Swinton was acting as a correspondent and became suspicious of his sincerity. The General, whose Richmond papers were delivered to him as regularly as though he were a paid subscriber, found in one of them a few days later a full account of instructions issued to one of his officers. He thought Swinton was guilty. A few nights later, a staff meeting at Grant's headquarters was disturbed when a colonel found a man listening behind a stump. He grabbed him by the shoulder and came up with Swinton. For that offense, Swinton received a dressing down.

The next time Grant heard of Swinton he was at Cold Harbor, where he learned Burnside had arrested him and ordered him shot that very afternoon. Grant quickly interceded to save the correspondent's life but expelled him from the front with a warning never to return.[34]

When the General wrote his memoirs twenty years later, his experience with Swinton still rankled within him. While he dismissed some battles with a paragraph, some even with a sentence, he wrote three pages about Swinton.

Swinton's brother, John, was managing editor of *The New York Times* during the Civil War. William became a correspondent for the *Times* in 1862 and attracted attention for his articles on tactical military movements. He was especially critical of Burnside. As author of a series of historical works during the war, he won further recognition.[35]

Grant always claimed he had forgotten the name of the newspaper for which he suspected Swinton was writing on his observation tour. He stressed his assertion that Swinton gave "great offense" to Burnside.[36]

# 17 "Spare Me the Trouble"

THE BITTER STRUGGLE for the border state of Missouri was as personal as a back-yard quarrel, with a divided press shouting above the clash of arms. Newspaper relations, owing to a split in the Union faction, were most complicated and presented a problem that taxed the ingenuity of Union generals trying to follow President Lincoln's middle-of-the-road course. Exasperated, he finally had to take a hand in the situation.

Northern sentiment centered in St. Louis where a strong group of Union men refused to let the state slide down the river at the flood tide of secession.

Of the several newspapers in St. Louis, only two had significant political influence, the *Missouri Democrat* and the *Missouri Republican*. Their names and their political affiliations were as confusing as the times they represented. The *Democrat* was Republican, and the *Republican* was Democratic!

The *Democrat* was founded by Francis Preston Blair, Jr., a scion of the famous Blair clan, in 1852 to boost Thomas Hart Benton in his campaign for Congress. The *Democrat* followed the Blair family into the Republican party in 1856.[1]

Blair and Benjamin Gratz Brown, editor of the *Democrat*, spoke at Alton, Ill., in Lincoln's behalf when he ran for senator in 1858 against Douglas.[2] In the Chicago convention, Blair placed in nomination the name of Edward Bates of Missouri, but the *Democrat* got behind Lincoln for President the moment he was nominated.[3] Bates was taken into Lincoln's Cabinet as Attorney General.

When Major General John C. Frémont was appointed commander of the Department of the West in July of 1861, the *Democrat* applauded the move and was enthusiastic when he issued a proclamation announcing he would emancipate the slaves owned by all persons bearing arms against the United States in Missouri.[4] Frémont placed the state under martial law, and this was approved by the President, but he asked the General to withdraw the emancipation clause, which Frémont refused to do. Lincoln then annulled the proclamation in a public order.[5]

The President acted on grounds that an emancipation policy in Missouri would hurt the Union cause in Kentucky, then teetering on the rim of secession.[6]

Both Blair and Brown were in the Missouri military service, Blair a brigadier general under Frémont's command, Brown a colonel of state volunteers. They were cousins, but family ties and business association were not strong enough to make them see eye to eye in the controversy over Frémont's emancipation policy. Blair was a brother of Montgomery Blair, Lincoln's Postmaster General.

In September of 1861, Blair complained to his brother by letter that Frémont was not fighting. The Cabinet member showed the letter to President Lincoln, and in some way Frémont heard about it.

Frémont placed Blair under arrest, charging him with conduct unbecoming an officer, insubordination, and other military offenses. Blair was soon released, but he and Brown went their separate ways. The *Democrat* gave Blair no support and sided with Frémont.[7] The Democratic *Missouri Republican* of August 15, 1862, was of the opinion that jealousy among members of the editorial staff of the *Democrat* caused it to back Frémont in the Blair case. The truth is they split on conduct of the war policy; Brown favored immediate emancipation at whatever cost, while Blair was of the Lincoln conservative school.

In Washington, a military appointment of vast importance was made by President Lincoln on November 1, 1861, McClellan, a War Democrat in political inclination, taking over as commander in chief of the armies to succeed Scott.[8] Blair had powerful friends in the Capital, headed by his brother, Montgomery. One of McClellan's first acts removed General Frémont from the Missouri command.[9]

Frémont left behind him the imprint of a mailed fist on the Missouri press. His crusade to crush printed opposition began with his proclamation of martial law when he suppressed two newspapers "shamelessly devoted to the publication of transparently false statements respecting military movements in Missouri." These were the *War Bulletin* and the *Missourian*. A few days later, on August 24, Reverend David R. McAnally, editor of the St. Louis *Christian Advocate*, wrote to Major J. McKinstry, the provost marshal, saying he had heard his paper was to be suppressed and asking for a definition of policy. The marshal replied: "Let your journal be a religious paper, as it professes to be, and it will never come under the discipline of this department."[10]

Frémont then barred from Missouri the five New York newspapers named in the grand jury "presentment" as being disloyal.[11] The *Louisville* (Ky.) *Courier* also was barred.[12]

The *St. Louis Morning Herald*, "a half-starved secession bantam," was put out of business by the military. A wire story filed in St. Louis said the paper had turned "secesh" so that it would be suppressed to avoid forfeiture of bond money on a city printing contract it had failed to fulfill. That story also said the *Missouri Republican* had turned loyal to the Union since the martial-law proclamation and that the *Democrat* was guarded by police while the printers were setting editorials calling for support of the war against the Confederacy.[13]

The St. Louis newspapers—those that survived Frémont's purge—were close-lipped in their comment on the General's emancipation order. The *Democrat* said: "General Frémont strikes boldly and fearlessly. The consolidated patriotism and the boundless resources of the great Northwest are at his back."[14] The *St. Louis News* said: "The proclamation marks the commencement of a new regime in Missouri—a new policy for the conduct of the war in the West. It will appear severe to many."[15] The *Missouri Republican* said guardedly: "Proclamation of martial law did not take us by surprise."[16]

The press in all the Union states was filled with opinions on the slavery issue raised by Frémont. The *Louisville* (Ky.) *Journal* roundly condemned him,[17] while Joseph Medill's *Chicago Tribune*, which was beginning to learn that Lincoln had a mind of his own, was angry because the President annulled the proclamation. The *Cincinnati Gazette* reported the *Tribune* printed "a severe article" on Lincoln's letter to Frémont, saying the President took away the penalty of rebellion and left the war "a mere scheme for mutual assassination."[18]

General Frémont was displeased with the manner in which the *St. Louis News* handled the Union defeat at Lexington, Mo., on September 20, 1861. It held that Frémont had not supported Colonel James A. Mulligan and his Irish brigade, saying: ". . . the heroic officer calculated too largely on the cooperation of the authorities at St. Louis."[19]

Charles G. Ramsey, editor of the *News*, and his assistant, D. M. Grissom, who wrote the editorial, were arrested and charged with having criticized Frémont's military strategy. Soldiers took possession of the newspaper office, and all copies of the edition carrying the offensive article were seized and destroyed.

Frémont released the editors on their promise not to publish any further articles "injurious to the government," and they resumed publication. The *News* was recognized as a strong Union organ, and Frémont's action against it was widely regretted in St. Louis by loyal men.[20]

The Reverend Mr. McAnally, editor of the *Christian Advocate*, forgot for the moment the advice he received from the provost marshal and spoke sarcastically of the capture of Camp Jackson, where Missouri militia officered by a disloyal staff were taken prisoner early in the war by other home-guard soldiers commanded by Union officers. Arrested and taken before the provost marshal, he pleaded that ill health would not permit his imprisonment and was released, his friends promising there would be no more violations.[21]

A St. Louis editor of pro-Southern sympathies was charged with treason. Joseph W. Tucker, of the *State Journal*, was accused of aiding and abetting the enemy in an affidavit filed against him by John D. Stephenson, a Republican member of the Missouri house of representatives from St. Louis County. He was taken into custody on June 14, 1861, by a United States marshal. The *State Journal* was seized by troops.[22]

The treason charge against Tucker does not seem to have stood up, but he took no chances and was reported to have "vanished." The Republican newspapers said he fled in terror, while the Democratic press explained he was out of the city making speeches in behalf of his party.[23]

After Frémont's recall, Blair went on to military glory. The *Democrat*, now a confirmed radical on slavery, pleaded the cause of emancipation.[24] Brown, a Yale graduate of the class of 1847, led the Radicals in the Missouri state election of 1862, an effort that paid off when the state legislature sent him to the United States Senate to serve the unexpired term of W. P. Johnson, expelled as a secessionist.[25]

Major General Henry W. Halleck took charge in Missouri on November 18, 1861, and proceeded to clean up the mess left by Frémont. He soon pushed the Confederates into Arkansas and turned his attention to the opening of the Mississippi River. Three months later, Fort Henry and Fort Donelson fell before a land and water attack.[26]

General Halleck moved on to larger fields, and Major General Samuel R. Curtis ruled Missouri until May of 1863 when the problem was suddenly placed in the hands of Major General John M. Schofield. President Lincoln wrote a letter to Schofield on May 27, 1863, in which he explained why he had removed Curtis and placed Schofield in the top Missouri command. The President told him to "do right for the public interest," that there were two Union factions in Missouri and that he faced a difficult job. He warned the General to avoid being attacked by one faction while lauded by the other.[27]

On June 27, 1863, the *Missouri Democrat* published Lincoln's letter to Schofield, setting off a political explosion whose echoes finally wore down the patient and understanding Lincoln. William McKee was now editor and senior proprietor of the *Democrat*. He was summoned to General Schofield's headquarters to explain how he came into possession of the letter and why he published it. The editor ignored the summons, and General Schofield ordered the provost marshal to arrest him July 10.[28]

Taken before General Schofield, McKee assumed entire responsibility for publication of the letter, saying he did this to exonerate all members of Schofield's staff. The next day, his newspaper said: "We have only at present to say, under the circumstances, we regard this (the arrest) as a foolish and unwarranted proceeding."[29]

The General released McKee on parole for ten days with the understanding that at the expiration of the period he was to present a written explanation.[30] The editor appeared on the date specified with explanation in his hand and was informed he was unconditionally released. He was presented with a copy of "Special Order No. 42," dated "Headquarters, Department of the Missouri, July 20, 1863," and signed by Major General Schofield. The order read:

William McKee, proprietor of the *Missouri Democrat*, having made satisfactory explanation and apology for failure to obey the summons to appear at headquarters of the commanding general to make explanation of a military offense committed by him, will, in consideration of the facts stated by him in regard to the source from which he obtained the President's letter, and the expressed willingness of the President to overlook the offense committed in the publication of said letter, be excused from giving further testimony in the matter, and will be released from his parole to report at department headquarters.[31]

That was the story as it appeared in the newspapers, but it was not the whole story. This is what happened: On July 13, 1863, President Lincoln sent a telegram to General Schofield, saying he regretted to learn that the editor of the *Democrat* had been arrested. He feared Schofield's action would cost him the "middle position" he wanted the General to hold. The President asked the general to "please spare me the trouble" that the arrest might cause.[32]

In his reply to the President, dated "July 14," General Schofield suggested he drop all action against McKee. Lincoln told him, under date of July 20, to go ahead.[33]

When Lincoln sought renomination in 1864, the *Democrat* was none too friendly to him and quickly came out in opposition to a proposal that the legislatures stamp him as their choice for White House incumbent. The *Democrat* said the proposal was a "trick" and demanded that Lincoln take his chances with other Republican candidates.[34]

The *Missouri Republican* saw its rival's stand as evidence of hostility to the Federal government and charged the *Democrat* was "working body and mind to defeat Mr. Lincoln with either Frémont or Chase."[35] On June 10, 1864, with Lincoln renominated, the *Democrat* declared itself ready to stand by him, but admitted it preferred Grant, Frémont, Butler, or Chase.[36]

Major General William S. Rosecrans succeeded Schofield in the Department of the Missouri in January of 1864. On March 26, 1864, he barred the *Metropolitan Record* of New York. The General described the newspaper as a "Catholic family" journal. It is likely he had the backing of Missouri Catholics in taking this step, inasmuch as he charged articles printed in the *Record* were a libel on the Catholics, whom he described as "loyal and national."[37] The General's brother, Sylvester, was the Catholic bishop of Columbus, Ohio, and edited the *Catholic Telegraph.*[38]

Other newspapers had fallen under the ban to keep published matter unfriendly to the Union cause out of Missouri. In April of 1863, the *Chicago Times* noted that the provost marshal of St. Louis had forbidden circulation there of the New York *Independent*, the New York *World*, the New York *Journal of Commerce*, the *Catholic Register*, the New York *Caucasian*, *The Crisis* of Columbus, and the *Times.*[39]

*The Crisis* carried this story, of doubtful origin, on April 29, 1863:

Louisiana, Mo. April 11 (1863)—*The Crisis, Cincinnati Enquirer, Chicago Times—et id omne genus*—the constitutional beacon lights of the country, have been extinguished in our midst.

Just think of it! A new-fledged political huckster, a hair-brained sycophant, speculating in the sweat and blood of his fellow citizens, lording it over the sovereigns of the land (those once sovereign but now slaves), dictating that you shall not read this nor that, holding the liberties of the people in the hollow of his hand!

On April 27, 1863, the office of the assistant provost marshal at Fulton, Mo., ordered the postmaster to turn over to his headquarters all copies of four newspapers that might come to him for distribution to subscribers. He named them as the New York *Caucasian*, the *Chicago Times*, the *Cincinnati Enquirer*, and *The Crisis*. The order read: ". . . while professing to be loyal to the government, the doctrines promulgated by these sheets are of a character only tending to give aid

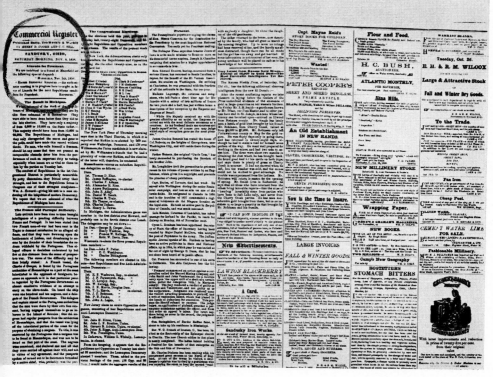

Courtesy Ohio State Archaeological and Historical Society

# Commercial Register

**Published Daily, Tri-Weekly & Weekly**
BY HENRY D. COOKE AND C. C. BILL.

## SANDUSKY, OHIO,
SATURDAY MORNING, NOV. 6, 1858.

### Lincoln for President.

We are indebted to a friend at Mansfield for the following special dispatch :

"MANSFIELD, Nov. 5th, 1858.
"EDITOR SANDUSKY REGISTER :—An enthusiastic meeting is in progress here to-night in favor of Lincoln for the next Republican candidate for President. REPORTER."

How false story on Lincoln meeting was played in Sandusky, Ohio, daily. Top half of editorial page shows position and (*inset*) the purported telegram.

Cartoon (*above*), "The Inside Track," published by *Vanity Fair*, New York, March 2, 1861. Thurlow Weed (left in high hat), editor of the *Albany Evening Journal*, and William H. Seward talk to Lincoln, while Horace Greeley, editor of the *New York Tribune*, carrying a copy of the Chicago platform, tries to get his foot in the door. On the wall is a slate on which is written, "T. Weed. His slate."

"The MacLincoln Harrisburg Highland Fling." Caricature published in *Vanity Fair*, New York, March 9, 1861.

and comfort to the rebels . . . and to stir up a spirit of discord and opposition. . . ."[40]

The unfriendly Canadian press was watched by St. Louis military authorities. George J. Jones, a newspaper dealer, was arrested and imprisoned by order of Brigadier General J. W. Davidson, of the St. Louis district, for selling the *Montreal Commercial Advertiser* in violation of his orders.

General Davidson barred this newspaper in Special Order No. 89, November 1, 1862, which said:

The circulation of a treasonable sheet called the *Montreal Commercial Advertiser*, published at Montreal, Canada, is prohibited in this district from date. All persons purchasing, selling, or in any manner dealing in such a paper, or receiving the same through the mails, or otherwise, will be arrested and committed to prison as aiders and abettors of the rebellion.[41]

The *Missouri Democrat* reported the arrest of Howard S. Harbough, editor of the *Chillicothe* (Mo.) *Constitution*, by Brigadier General Odon Guitar's soldiers. According to the *Democrat*, Harbough was stopped in the street and told to give his name, whereupon the officer in command told him he was under arrest and would be shot if he resisted. Spectators were warned not to interfere, but the Reverend T. B. Bratton, a Methodist pastor and editor of the Kansas City *Journal of Commerce*, refused to be intimidated and demanded to know why Harbough had been seized. Bratton was arrested on the spot. An army captain, R. S. Moore, tried to have the editors paroled, and he, too, was arrested.

A group of women, members of the "Ladies Union Encampment" of Utica, Mo., went to military headquarters at Chillicothe to plead for the editors. They were told to "pull off those badges, roll up that flag, go home and mind your own business."

The charges against the editors, while not specifically defined in news reports of the day, seem to have been their reference to the new order of things in Missouri as the "provisional government." Both were eventually released.

Harbough's state of mind over the treatment accorded him is not a matter of record, but he could have asked himself some serious questions about the rewards of journalism. In 1860, he was publishing a newspaper at Lexington, Mo. Being a Republican, he placed the names of Lincoln and Hamlin on his editorial page. A mob of Democrats destroyed his office and equipment, and he and his family were given twenty minutes to get out of town.

Fleeing to St. Louis, Harbough enlisted as a private in the Union forces and served thirteen months. The Reverend Mr. Bratton also had served in the Union army and was credited with having recruited the 35th Regiment of Missouri Volunteers.[42]

The *Observer*, a Democratic paper published at Booneville, Mo., was wrecked by soldiers on June 18, 1861, and the life of the editor threatened. At Louisiana, Mo., the *Union*, described as a "conservative Republican paper," was destroyed by a mob on June 10, 1864.[43]

The Missouri military suppressed the *Boone County Standard*, published at Columbia, Mo., on April 2, 1862, and the editor, Edmund J. Ellis, tried by a military commission, was sent into the Confederate lines.[44] The *Platte City Conservator* was suspended and the editor placed under arrest by the military on May 25, 1863, because his editorials criticized the Emancipation Proclamation. The conduct of the *St. Joseph Tribune* brought the editor into conflict with the military authorities, resulting in his arrest on October 30, 1863.[45]

On a charge of publishing "treasonable matter," the office of the *Plaindealer*, of Sainte Genevieve, Mo., was seized by the provost marshal of Missouri in August of 1862. The newspaper was suppressed.[46]

Iowa, with the honor of never having to resort to a draft to fill its army quota, was not bothered to any great extent by a press out of sympathy with its strong Union population. It did, however, furnish one of the outstanding cases of Federal action against a Copperhead newspaper editor.

Dennis A. Mahony, editor of the *Herald*, at Dubuque, spokesman for a small Democratic antiwar faction, made the longest trip to a Federal prison of any newspaper man during the conflict. He spent two months in Old Capitol at Washington.

Mahony and his wife were asleep in their home when Mrs. Mahony heard someone knocking at the door about half-past three in the morning of August 14, 1862. A man in the yard called out that he was "Mr. Gregory" of Cedar Falls and that he wanted to see the editor on urgent business.

Mahony, awakened by his wife, peered from the window and saw several armed men. His first impression was that a mob had formed, threats of citizen action against him having been in circulation for some time. His neighbors had promised to help him if threatened by a mob, and he began to yell.

P. H. Conger, a deputy United States marshal, identified himself and told Mahony they had come to arrest him. United States Marshal H. M. Hoxie entered the house with soldiers and told the editor to put on his clothing and come along. Mahony demanded to know by whose authority the arrest was made, and Hoxie, who knew the editor personally, told him it was by order of the Secretary of War. Mahony then asked that he be permitted to see the order, but the marshal refused.

He was marched off to the levee and placed aboard a steamboat that was to sail for Davenport at noon to pick up more political prisoners. At daybreak, news of the arrest got around town and several of Mahony's friends went aboard to bid him farewell.[47]

The next day, Mahony's *Herald*, still operating, published the story of his arrest, saying: "Mr. Mahony was perfectly resigned to his fate and assured us that not one word of that which he had written or spoken could he be induced to retract. He was not guilty, and consoled himself with that."[48]

Upon his arrival in Davenport, Mahony sought an audience with Governor Samuel J. Kirkwood. The reply was a curt note that said the Governor had no desire to grant an interview to a man charged with disloyalty.[49]

Mahony was taken on to Burlington where he was introduced to the man with whom he was to share a prison cell, David Sheward, editor of the *Constitution and Union,* Fairfield, Iowa. Sheward was arrested on Sunday, August 17, and taken to Burlington on a locomotive engaged solely for that purpose.[50] Senator James W. Grimes of Iowa went to the hotel room where Mahony was held and promised to ask the Secretary of War that the editor be granted a speedy trial. Marshal Hoxie made his headquarters over the week end in the office of the *Burlington Hawkeye,* a Union newspaper.[51]

Mahony and Sheward were started for Washington on Monday morning. Mahony had only the clothing on his back. Sheward's wife arrived just in time with clothing and money.[52]

The *Burlington Argus* quaintly reported the editors's departure in this story:

D. A. Mahony and D. Sheward, editors of Democratic papers in the state of Iowa, who were arrested on a charge of disloyalty and left Burlington, Iowa, on the 18th instant, in charge of government officers, bound for some point they know not of, and when enroute to that house from which no traveler returns, save at his own expense, while at a place on the railroad where they had to change and wait an hour, were taken to a hotel. . . .

Mr. Mahony registered his name D. A. Mahony, Dubuque, Iowa; D. Sheward, Fairfield, Iowa. The officer in charge, seemingly to torment his prisoners, remarked to the landlord, "Make these men register their destination." The landlord gave the order and Mr. Mahony stepped forward and added:

"Bound for Hell, sent there by the Devil in charge of some of his angels for speaking the truth!"

Mr. Sheward came forward and added: "Bound for the same place, for the same reason."[53]

Back in Fairfield, Editor Sheward's wife "took up the fallen pen" and announced she would publish the *Constitution and Union* while he was in prison. She ran this notice "To The Public":

My husband having been arrested and conveyed to Washington or some other point, it developed on me, his wife, to conduct the paper in his absence. I ask his friends and the friends of "free speech" and "free press," the Constitution as it is and the Union as it was, and the government as it should be, to give me their aid in this emergency.[54]

The *Dubuque Herald* later made this report on Mahony:

D. A. Mahony has now been incarcerated ten weeks and has not yet been made acquainted with the charges against him or confronted by his accusers. And still we are told that we must sustain the administration. Well, if we must, we must. "Long live Abraham Lincoln, who gives us more liberty than we know what to do with."[55]

While he was in Old Capitol prison, Mahony was visited by Franc B. Wilkie, a correspondent of the *Chicago Times*, formerly employed by the *Dubuque Herald*. He carried to Mahony the word he had been nominated for Congress by the Democrats in his Iowa District.[56]

Mahony and Sheward remained in prison until November 11, 1862, when they took the oath of allegiance and were "honorably discharged."[57] They went home to be lionized by their friends. Each was met in his home town by bands and torchlight processions and hailed as a conquering hero.[58]

Mahony was defeated for Congress. Wilkie later wrote that Mahony was sent to prison on a charge of treasonable utterances, but actually to prevent him from being elected to Congress, having been nominated by the Copperhead faction of his party. He hinted that the War Democrats engineered the editor's removal to prison.[59]

Mahony's ordeal in Old Capitol did not swerve him from his convictions about the war. He began a new attack on the administration by saying:

Are you, as soldiers, bound by patriotism, duty or loyalty to fight in such a cause . . . ? The people are fools to content themselves with assailing tyrants who have deprived them of their liberties. There is but one way to deal with arbitrary power, and that is to treat it precisely as one would do, if he had the power, with a highwayman who might undertake to rob him of his money.[60]

And still later, in a *Herald* editorial, Mahony said, "Permit us to say as a matter of record that we consider separation and the acknowledgement of the Southern Confederacy as a fixed thing. . . . The South will gain its independence—we have always believed so and said so."[61]

That the Union Democrats, as Wilkie said, may have caused the arrest of Mahony was borne out by a story published by *The Crisis* when it announced on August 26, 1863, that Mahony was no longer connected with the *Dubuque Herald. The Crisis* said: "We regret to see Mr. Mahony's announcement of his temporary withdrawal from the editorship of the *Herald.* But under the circumstances in which the party has been placed in Iowa by professed Democrats, we can't say we are surprised."

The *Burlington Hawkeye* reflected public opinion when it said: "It may be as well, perhaps, to come to a definite understanding. . . . But we only give expression to the general feeling when we say that no man's personal safety can be assured for one moment after the conclusion shall have been clearly arrived at that he is a traitor."[62]

Sheward, too, continued to oppose the war and berate President Lincoln. Soldiers of Company C, 2d Iowa Regiment, mobbed the office of the *Constitution and Union* on February 8, 1864. The type was scattered in the street, newsprint destroyed, and subscription books torn to pieces.[63]

About seventy-five convalescent soldiers marched from an army hospital at Keokuk, Iowa, on February 19, 1863, and wrecked the office of the *Daily Constitution,* a newspaper they believed to be disloyal to the Union cause. They left the hospital in the middle of the afternoon, led by four carrying sledge hammers.[64]

Kansas shed so much blood in the years prior to the Civil War that outbreak of formal hostilities was just another phase of the fighting. Editors permitted no long words to confuse their readers. An example was the Democratic *Daily Press* of Kansas City, which described the fall election of 1862 as "a contest between the white and black races for supremacy." It continued: "President Lincoln and the Abolitionists have made it so. The white race is represented by the Democratic party—the black race by the Abolition Republican party. The simple question to be decided is, whether the white man shall maintain his status of superiority or be sunk to the level of the negro."[65]

When Union soldiers poured into Kansas in 1862, they inaugurated a campaign of violence against dissenting editors that silenced all but the hardiest. George E. Dummer, Democratic editor of the *Kansas Frontier* at Junction City, espoused the cause of the South. At midnight on March 10, 1862, about forty soldiers from Fort Riley assembled in front of the *Frontier* office. Dummer, who slept in a room on the second floor of the building, was told to leave town in twenty-four hours or be hanged.

To give emphasis to their warning, the soldiers broke up the office furniture with axes but left the press intact. Others stood guard with drawn pistols to prevent interference by the editor's friends. When they had finished their job, the soldiers fell into formation, called the roll, and marched off as though on parade.

Dummer remained in town. He organized a committee of citizens to call on Captain Graham, in command at Fort Riley, and lay before him a full report of the newspaper mobbing. Graham mustered the entire personnel of his command on the parade ground, called the men to attention, and told the members of the committee to pick out the guilty parties. They looked long and hard, but said they failed to recognize anyone.

Dummer and his committee went back to Junction City and called a public meeting to show that "all honest men condemned the outrage." The Fort Riley soldiers packed the hall. When resolutions of censure were offered, the soldiers voted against them, but the tabulation showed that, in some manner, they passed by a narrow margin. These resolutions were sent to Major General David Hunter, commander of the Department of Kansas, at Leavenworth.

The soldiers paid a return visit to town that night. They riddled the office of the *Frontier* with gunfire, centering on the room where Dummer usually slept. Then they entered the building and smashed the press. A citizen was wounded by a stray bullet.[66]

On the night of August 27, 1863, the office of the *Western Sentinel* at Leavenworth was mobbed by soldiers from the 3d Regiment of Missouri state militia. The troops broke all the windows in the building, knocked the press apart, and threw the type and other mechanical equipment into the street. They were said to have resented *Sentinel* articles critical of their colonel. The *Leavenworth Times* remarked: "Said office is now completely *non est*."[67]

The editor of the *Leavenworth Times* had learned his lesson only a few weeks previously. Because of an editorial that criticized Major General Joseph Hooker's strategy at the Battle of Chancellorsville, Va., in May of 1863, the *Times* man was arrested by Mayor Anthony of Leavenworth. Fined twenty dollars and costs, he refused to pay and went to jail. He obtained his release through a writ of habeas corpus.[68]

Editors of newspapers of opposite political faith sometimes settled their differences without the aid of courts or the military. Under the heading, "Fatal Editorial Collision," the *Cincinnati Gazette* on June 24, 1861, published this story:

D. L. Anthony, editor of the *Daily Conservative*, a Republican paper of Leavenworth, Kansas, and R. C. Satterlee, editor of the *Daily Herald*, Democratic paper of the same city, staged a gun fight in the streets, each man firing several times. Satterlee was wounded in the right side and died in twenty minutes. A Mr. Hamer, innocent bystander, was dangerously wounded.[69]

The *Inquirer*, at Leavenworth, was wrecked by a mob of Union men on February 11, 1863. The *Constitutional Gazeteer*, published at Marysville, was wrecked on August 20, 1863.[70]

Major General James G. Blunt, commander of the Department of Kansas, excluded the New York *Caucasian*, the New York *World*, *Chicago Times*, *The Crisis*, and the *Cincinnati Enquirer* on June 11, 1863, branding them as "incendiary publications" that had "created discord in loyal states and discouraged troops in the field." The order said:

"Postmasters within this district, on receipt of the above named papers, will not deliver them to subscribers, but will destroy them without delay, and in failing to do so, they will be held accountable for violation of military orders."

Postmaster Anthony of Leavenworth read the order, gathered a stack of barred papers in his arms, and rushed into the street where a crowd was listening to an army band. He made a speech, explaining why he was going to destroy the papers. He then burned them.

Said the *Leavenworth Times*: "Thus *The World* passed away with a great noise and fervent heat."[71]

# 18 Maryland, My Maryland

IN BALTIMORE, SEETHING with secession, the Lincoln administration arrested and placed in military prison the only real newspaper friend it had in the city, Charles C. Fulton, editor of the *Baltimore American*, on July 29, 1862. It was a case of misunderstanding all around, but it injured the President and it caused Secretary of War Stanton to get a raking from the opposition press.

The *American* presented the anomaly of a "Union-screamer" in the midst of a pro-Southern journalistic mob, and its editor was a man of courage, moral and physical. It was in Baltimore that a mob attacked the 6th Massachusetts Regiment on its way to the relief of Washington on April 19, 1861. Four soldiers were killed and many wounded in fierce street fighting; twelve civilians were killed.[1]

Mobs in Northern cities compelled Democratic editors to display the American flag, but in Baltimore, the reverse was true. The day after the riot, a mob went to the office of the *Wecker*, a German language Abolition newspaper, and compelled the editor, under threat of death, to hang out a Confederate flag. That night, the mob wrecked the building, and the editor and his staff hid in the homes of friends.[2] A month later, Federal troops moved into Baltimore, and it became an occupied city, but the problem of the bitterly hostile press continued.

During the war, nine Baltimore newspapers were suppressed, either temporarily or permanently, and two were forced to stop publication because of the arrest of their editors. There were twelve separate actions of suppression on the part of the Federal government, and eight of these were permanent.[3]

Fulton's editorials in the *American* in 1860 show him to have been a Bell man and a foe of the Buchanan administration, to which he referred as "the leeches who had fastened themselves to the body politic."[4] He was utterly disgusted by the nomination of Lincoln, calling him a "third rate district politician" whose selection was "an insult" to the great exponents of the Republican party. He thought the nomination of Hannibal Hamlin for second place on the ticket a "much more respectable" choice.[5]

The nomination of Breckinridge by Southern Democrats convinced Fulton that "the election of the Republican candidate is a fore-ordained certainty."[6] Nevertheless, he worked against Lincoln, saying, "The question to be decided . . . is whether the Union shall be preserved. . . . There is one sure way to prevent this calamity, by the defeat of Mr. Lincoln."[7] On November 8, 1860, Fulton softened the blow for his readers by declaring the new administration would be powerless, with both houses of Congress "undoubtedly anti-Republican," and he took a firm stand against secession by saying, "While we are in the Union, we are Mr. Lincoln's master."

When a South Carolina politician spoke of "an accursed Union," Fulton made the stand of the *American* clear by replying, "He overrates, we think, the capacity of South Carolina in supposing that she has only to twine her arms around the pillars of such a fabric as the United States government to bring it down in one common ruin."[8] While the Baltimore press belabored Lincoln for his inaugural statements, the *American* offered but one criticism, one easily understood by newspaper men of both parties. It said:

The President would not permit the copy of his inaugural address to get out of his possession until after delivery, and the feature of previous inaugurations, at which the newsboys screamed about the city, selling copies of the address as soon as it was delivered, was omitted.[9]

Fulton saw the Federal defeat at Bull Run as the answer to a public demand for action, voiced chiefly by the New York press, and he wrote with a stinging pen:

The terrible defeat experienced by the Federal army at Manassas Junction will doubtless now satisfy, to the full, those newspaper generals in New York, and elsewhere in that latitude, who have been so long vociferating for an "advance" and have been so eagerly clamoring for a "battle."[10]

By that time, the *American* was recognized as the leader of "loyal public opinion" in Maryland. Fulton raised public funds for the relief of Union soldiers in Southern prisons and helped his Baltimore friends send aid to sons who had "gone South" and were prisoners in the North. For this work, he was commended by the Maryland state legislature.[11]

Only *The Clipper*, a smartly edited daily of four pages with little political significance, showed an inclination to follow Fulton's example. It set its course in an editorial on May 14, 1861: "The cause of the

Union is strongly on the increase, and those few who would madly ruin our people through the medium of secession are keeping remarkably shady."

*The Sun*, although it hated Lincoln and called him a lunatic, was able to go through the war untouched by military hands because it avoided an overt act while still retaining Southern flavor. Although spitting venom in *Charleston Mercury* style, it suddenly sobered and adopted a conservative policy on May 13, 1861, when Major General Benjamin F. Butler entered Baltimore with a thousand well-trained soldiers to occupy the city.[12]

After two days of rioting between Unionists and pro-Southern men, May 25 to 26, 1862, a mob that called itself a "committee on flag displays" formed in front of the *American* office. It visited the offices of *The Sun*, *Maryland News Sheet*, *German Correspondent*, and the *Daily Republican*, compelling all of them to show the Stars and Stripes.[13]

Although in his middle forties, with a son serving on the flagship *Hartford*, Fulton often went into the field as a war correspondent for his *American*. He also was Baltimore agent for the *Associated Press*, a position retained since he was managing editor of *The Sun*, long before he took over the *American*.[14]

In June of 1862, Fulton obtained a special pass from the War Department to observe the army in Virginia. On a four-day tour of the front, he covered the action at the White House, the fighting before Richmond and made a general survey on the Peninsula. The information he gathered was eagerly awaited by President Lincoln, and a special train was sent to return Fulton to Washington. After reporting to the President, Fulton went home to Baltimore.

He set to work at once on the story he had obtained. As the agent of the *Associated Press*, he thought of it as well as his own paper. He telegraphed the New York office to ask whether his story was wanted. This was his query:

Baltimore, Sunday, June 29th (9 P.M.)

I am writing for the *American* a detailed account of events at White House, before Richmond and on the Peninsula, during the last four days, including facts obtained from Washington, having been sent for by special train to communicate with the President. If you desire it I will send it to you. It will make four or five thousand words. We have the grandest military triumph over the enemy, and Richmond must fall.

C. C. Fulton.[15]

Fulton later wired the *Associated Press* that he had been prevented from filing his story, saying:

The Secretary of War decides that nothing can be telegraphed relative to affairs on the Peninsula. Have tried our best to get it off.

Then an army officer came to the *American* and told the amazed Fulton he was under arrest by order of Secretary of War Stanton and that he was to be taken immediately to a cell in Fort McHenry. Fulton asked permission to send a telegram. He dispatched this plea to President Lincoln:

To the President of the United States:
Sir:—I find myself under arrest and on my way to Fort McHenry. I appeal to you for a hearing and prompt release, in behalf of my family, who will be in great distress at the execution of this inexplicable order. The Secretary of War authorized me to publish my statement.

Respectfully, C. C. Fulton.

Fulton, locked up in Fort McHenry, had not long to wait for a reply. The answer did not come from the President, but it plainly stated Fulton had been arrested with his approval. The wire, signed by E. S. Sanford, superintendent of the Military Telegraph, was as follows:

Washington, June 30th, 1862.
To C. C. Fulton, Fort McHenry:
I am authorized to say to you that your arrest was not made for publishing the statement, but upon your statement that you were preparing a detailed account, including facts obtained from Washington, having been sent by special train to communicate with the President. This is regarded by the President and the War Department as a flagrant and outrageous violation of the confidence with which you were treated. The publication of facts obtained from Washington under such circumstances is a high military crime.

Fulton's surprise at arrest had now changed to anger, and he minced no words when he got off this reply to Sanford:

Col. Sanford—Sir:—The dispatch I sent to New York was a private one, addressed to Mr. Craig, for his information as to whether he desired to receive the report I was preparing for the press. It was not intended for publication, and would not have been published if my report had been permitted to go through by telegraph. I never dreamed of its being published. To find myself in Fort McHenry, the depot for traitors, is a mortification I cannot express. Having risked both life and property in defending the

Union cause when our city was in the possession of traitors, and rendered services as editor and proprietor of the *Baltimore American* to the government in sustaining the laws which no one has excelled, I ask, in common justice, that I should at least be released on my parole. Respectfully yours,

Chas. C. Fulton.

The news that Fulton had been carted off to a Federal bastille was the big story of the day in Baltimore, although it had to compete with a false alarm that the rebel army was marching on the city. One has only to imagine the smiles on the faces of the editors of the other Baltimore newspapers, most of whom were Southern sympathizers. They wondered what brought about Fulton's arrest and the circumstances surrounding it. Fulton himself answered these questions when his *American* published all the correspondence in the case the morning of July 1, 1862. That was on a Tuesday, following the Sunday night episode, and Fulton was still in prison.

This is what had happened. Fulton's telegram of inquiry to D. H. Craig of the *Associated Press* was published in New York and other cities using the news service. The *Associated Press* permitted the Fulton telegram to get into the regular news report. The statements that the country had gained "the grandest military triumph" and "Richmond must fall" were too exciting to be ignored. When Washington refused permission to Fulton to file his story, the query telegram was made into a news item at the New York end of the wire. Fulton was the goat.

At the bottom of page one of the *Baltimore American* on Wednesday morning, July 2, was a tiny three-line item with a one-word headline, "Released." The story said: "Mr. C. C. Fulton, of the *American*, was unconditionally released from Fort McHenry last night by order of the War Department."

Washington's treatment of its only journalistic defender in Baltimore made good copy for the opposition press. The New York *World* made a fuss over Fulton, a man it ordinarily would not have lifted a finger to defend. Describing him as editor and proprietor of "the staunchest and most able of the Baltimore newspapers," it said:

We desire our readers to read attentively the correspondence between Mr. Fulton and Col. Sanford. No argument of ours will then be needed to convince them that this incarceration of a man who has been a brave and loyal Baltimore Unionist—when to be a Unionist was to peril life and property—his imprisonment in a depot for traitors—is the most egregious, not to say the most despotic, blunder of which Secretary Stanton has been guilty since he first undertook a censorship of the telegraph and the press.[16]

Secretary Stanton held a far different view of the results of the Peninsular campaign than Fulton gathered on his quick swing around the front. Obviously, Fulton talked with General McClellan, commanding the Army of the Potomac. His assertion that "Richmond must fall" indicates as much. McClellan wired Stanton on June 28 that he could have taken Richmond the next day if only the administration had sent him 10,000 more men, one of the General's common complaints. Then admitting his drive had bogged down and that the army must be extricated from a dangerous position, he said, "If I save this army now, I tell you plainly that I owe no thanks to you, or to any other persons in Washington." The grand retreat started on June 28.[17] Fulton was silenced the next day.

Fulton, again at his desk in the *American,* looked over the exchanges and found *The World's* account of his misfortune. He reprinted it on page one. Although pilloried in front of his enemies, he never swerved from the administration ranks.

None of the other newspapers in Baltimore made even a pretense of advocating the Union cause. The *Daily Exchange* declared the war "a wicked crusade."[18] *The South,* one of those newspapers that sprung up with the war to fight Lincoln and advocate slavery, began publication April 22, 1861, with the announced purpose "to further the Confederate cause in Maryland and to secure the secession of that state from the Union." The editors said they were rebels, and if that were treason they could be called traitors.[19]

The *Republican,* for years the strongest Democratic paper in Baltimore, attacked the administration in an editorial on July 31, 1861, calling it, "The Despotism of Lincoln and Co." It said: "Our citizens have been imprisoned by the arbitrary mandate of the despot who is laboring to subjugate other states to the same condition of vassalage."

Washington agreed something should be done but could not determine who should order action against the three newspapers. Major General John A. Dix, in command of the Department of Maryland, with headquarters in Baltimore, refused to suppress them of his own volition on grounds that "a measure of so much gravity should carry with it the whole weight of influence and authority of government." Finally, on September 10, 1861, Montgomery Blair, Postmaster General, barred them from the mails.[20]

The dailies denounced the government anew, urging dissolution of the Union and overthrow of the Constitution, at the same time insisting on "Constitutional rights of free speech." The *Exchange* boasted: ". . . we can afford to despise Mr. Lincoln's warnings and menaces."[21]

The government then took into custody Frank Key Howard, editor of the *Exchange*, and Thomas W. Hall, editor of *The South*, and sent them to Fort McHenry. These arrests were made by order of the Secretary of War as a "military precautionary measure" to stop the spread of secession sentiment. The actual arrests were made by Allan Pinkerton, agent of the State Department.

The editor of the *Republican*, less bombastic, escaped arrest, but his newspaper ceased to print its own secession propaganda and adopted the indirect method, reprinting articles from other Copperhead journals.[22]

The *Exchange* appeared on September 14, the day after Howard's arrest, with a blistering attack on the government and a declaration of intention to continue to support the Southern cause. That night, W. W. Glenn, publisher of the newspaper, was arrested on a charge of uttering "treasonable expressions" and joined Howard in Fort McHenry.[23] Glenn was released on December 2 on condition he would not resume publication of the *Exchange* or any newspaper opposed to the administration while the Baltimore censorship was in effect.

Howard and Hall made a round of military prisons, sent from McHenry to Fort Monroe, then to Fort Lafayette and finally to Fort Warren. Hall presumably was released at Fort Warren. Howard refused to admit the government had any authority in his case and wrote many letters of protest to the Secretary of War. After thirteen months in prison, Howard was released on November 27, 1862.[24]

*The South*, promising to report the news without editorial opinion, was permitted to continue. But it grew bolder, and December 3, 1861, found it asking whether the South could be subdued "by a warfare conducted on the principles of Attila and Tamerlane."

By offering for sale pro-Southern pamphlets, *The South* did a little side-line business. The patience of even General Dix was worn thin by this time, and he suggested to the Secretary of War that the newspaper had gone far enough. On the night of February 17, 1862, a squad from the provost marshal's office arrested Samuel S. Mills, one of the proprietors, and Thomas S. Piggott, editor of *The South*. They were sent to Fort McHenry. A few days later, John Mills, publisher of *The South*, became their cell mate.[25] The newspaper never appeared again.

The Federal government now was in a mood to take even further steps to bring the Baltimore press into line. The commanding general was, on specific orders from the Secretary of War on February 18, 1862, placed in the position of a press dictator, with full authority to arrest editors, publishers and to suppress newspapers.[26] Major General John E. Wool succeeded General Dix as commander of the Middle Department on June 18.[27]

First action taken against the anti-Union press by General Wool occurred on August 14 when he permanently suppressed the *Maryland News Sheet* and arrested the two editors, William H. Carpenter and Thomas D. Sultzer, and the proprietor, William H. Neilson, all of whom were sent to Fort McHenry. Wool did not bother to explain his order. Sultzer and Neilson were held only a few days, but Carpenter was imprisoned a month.[28] Neilson and Carpenter reentered the newspaper field in October, publishing the *Daily Gazette*.

Troops entered the office of the *Republican* on September 11, 1863, on orders of Major General Robert C. Schenck, who had succeeded General Wool as Middle Department commander. Publication was halted, and Beale H. Richardson, editor, his son Francis, and Stephen J. Joyce, associate editors, were arrested. The General's wrath was aroused by publication of a parody on *The Star-Spangled Banner*, entitled *The Southern Cross*.[29]

The three editors were banished to the South at the General's direction, entering the enemy's lines at Harpers Ferry, with a warning not to return under penalty of being tried as spies.[30] Francis Richardson and Joyce tried to sneak back into the North in February of 1864 and were arrested in New York, having arrived there via Nassau. They were returned to Baltimore and to jail.[31]

About a year after Neilson and Carpenter established their new *Gazette*, they reported affairs in the North as "desperate." General Schenck sent his men to the newspaper office on September 29, 1863, with orders to arrest the editors, but both had flown. Edward F. Carter, described as one of the proprietors, and four printers were taken into custody as witnesses. All were released four days later, and Carter, as sole owner, was permitted to resume publication.[32]

On September 29, 1863, the same day the *Gazette* was suppressed, the publishers of the *Catholic Mirror* were arrested on charges of having issued a pamphlet called "Fourteen Months in American Bastiles," written by Frank Key Howard, former editor of the *Exchange*. The pamphlet carried a vituperative attack on President Lincoln. Michael J. Kelly, P. J. Hedian, and John B. Piet, the publishers, protested their loyalty and were released after five days in custody. The order under which they were arrested was not aimed at their newspaper but at their bookstore, operated as a side line.

Kelly and Piet spent a few days in Fort McHenry the following summer when they were accused of selling pictures of rebel generals, writing paper with Confederate colors stamped on it, and other articles of similar nature in their bookstore. They promised not to do it again and were released under bond. The *Catholic Mirror*, still free of charges, was suspended for seven days in that instance because the bookstore was padlocked and the editorial offices were in the same building.[33]

Neilson of *News Sheet* and *Gazette* fame started the *Evening Transcript* in October of 1863.[34] General Schenck soon suppressed it for four days while the loyal *Baltimore American* cried that Neilson should be permanently barred. But Schenck lifted the ban, and the *Transcript* continued until May 18, 1864, when still another general suspended it forever. Major General Lewis Wallace, Schenck's successor, was the executioner.[35]

General Wallace charged the *Transcript* printed an exaggerated account of Union losses in the Battle of Spotsylvania Courthouse. He insisted this was not an error but an obvious attempt to show the Federal army had suffered a severe setback. The *Transcript* accredited the story to the *Associated Press*. Wallace proved the dispatch was not from the *Associated Press* but that it had been presented as such to give the story the appearance of accuracy.[36]

A new Baltimore paper called the *Evening Bulletin* was started, only to be put out of business almost before it appeared by Wallace, who did not state his reasons. He may have thought the owners were disloyal.[37] The *Evening Post* was suppressed by Wallace on September 30, 1864, for "the publication of articles deemed offensive to loyal citizens."[38]

An order of permanent suspension was issued by Wallace against the *Evening Loyalist* on November 1, 1864.[39] The *Loyalist* falsely published that the Secretary of War had ordered a fresh draft of 300,000 men and that the hired-substitute plan had been abolished.[40]

A singular case of Maryland newspaper censorship had its origin in the House of Representatives on April 8, 1864, when Congressman Benjamin G. Harris of the Fifth Maryland District made an impassioned plea for the South during debate. He said, "The South asked you to let her go in peace. But no; you said that you would bring them into subjugation. That is not done yet and God Almighty grant that it may never be. I hope that you never subjugate the South."

General Schenck, now resigned from the army and serving in Congress from Ohio, offered a resolution declaring Harris an "unworthy member of the House." It passed, ninety-two to eighteen.

If Harris expected his constituency to read his speech, he was disappointed. The editor of the *St. Mary's Gazette* at Leonardtown was informed by the military he must not publish anything Harris said on that occasion.[41]

Daniel Decker, editor of the *Hagerstown Mail*, was held for a time in Fort McHenry in August of 1861, charged with publishing a "secession paper."[42] Publication of the *Democrat* at Cambridge, Md., was stopped on September 9, 1864, by Brigadier General Henry H. Lockwood, in command of the Middle Department. L. E. Barrett, editor, was accused of having published articles that gave "aid and comfort" to the enemy.[43]

John W. Baughman, editor of the *Republican Citizen* of Frederick, was arrested by Federal officials in 1862 and placed in Old Capitol prison in Washington. Powerful friends in Baltimore interceded for him, and he was released. In 1863, the newspaper was barred from the mails. Major General David Hunter suppressed the newspaper in 1864, confiscated the property, and sent Baughman and his family beyond the Federal lines. The exiled editor obtained a government-bureau job in Richmond. His son Louis joined the Confederate army and was captured. Baughman resumed publication after the war.[44]

The *Maryland Union* of Frederick, published by Bradley T. Johnson and Charles Cole, faced the actual situation of "a house divided" at the start of the war. During the campaign of 1860, Johnson was for Breckinridge, and Cole was a Douglas man. As a result of this disagreement, Johnson left the paper and enlisted in the Confederate army, rising to the rank of brigadier general. He was succeeded as associate editor of the *Union* by John T. Smith. That partnership ended when Smith disagreed with Cole over the policy of the newspaper and enlisted in the Union army.

Cole gave his Southern passion full play in type, and Hunter banished him to the South. Cole's friends went screaming to Washington where the case was brought to the attention of President Lincoln. The President rescinded Hunter's order, and Cole resumed publication of the *Union*. John Smith, who gave up his pen for a musket, was among the dead at Gettysburg.[45]

At least four other Maryland newspapers were taken in hand by the Federal government during the war. The *Marlborough Gazette's* proprietors spent some time in Old Capitol in the fall of 1862. The editor of the *Free Press* at Hagerstown was banished to the South in March of 1863 and his newspaper suppressed. At Chestertown, the editor of the *Conservator* was arrested on April 27, 1863, and held for a time.

A few days later, on May 7, 1863, the editor of the *Leonardtown Beacon* was the object of similar action.[46]

The people of Maryland's neighboring state of Delaware were proud of the 1st Delaware Regiment, a volunteer outfit that answered Lincoln's first call, and they resented "a course of unjust strictures" published about it by the *Delaware Gazette* at Wilmington. The newspaper was out of sympathy with the Lincoln administration and had been, according to the *New York Tribune*, "long detractive of the government."

On Saturday evening, August 24, 1861, a shouting mob formed in the streets, determined to destroy the *Gazette* office. The Mayor pleaded with the mob, and it melted.[47]

# 19  "Until Hell Freezes Over"

PRESIDENT LINCOLN DELIVERED a message to Congress on March 6, 1862, recommending a program of compensated emancipation and proposing the government assist any state willing to adopt gradual abolishment of slavery. The press discussed the proposal at great length, and much of the comment was favorable. Among the dissenters was *The New York Times*, a situation that nettled Lincoln considerably and occasioned one of his many letters to Editor Raymond. The *Times* thought the plan too expensive, but Lincoln pointed out it was trivial compared to the cost of war and suggested the newspaper print another "article."[1]

While editorial writers were discussing the President's novel proposal, the Union's *Monitor* and the South's *Merrimac* fought a naval engagement in Hampton Roads that made the world's navies obsolete.

With such big news to be published, the newspaper columns were filled with comment for several days, but the editors found room for this little item:

> Nashville, March 17, 1862—Parson Brownlow and son arrived at Nashville. Said he was held in a damp room at Knoxville, Dec. 6, 1861; had typhoid fever and was taken home for six weeks under guard. Got pass, but was detained by Gen. Hardee ten days and finally reached the Union lines this A.M. He declines to start a paper in Nashville. He will proceed north to publish the story of his martyrdom.[2]

The information was meager, but it was news the people had been waiting for. Every newspaper reader in the country, both North and South, knew Parson Brownlow was William Gannaway Brownlow, editor of the *Knoxville* (Tenn.) *Whig*, a fabulous character who risked his life to fight secession and became one of the popular heroes of the day. The Brownlow story had been building up to a climax for months. The editor became news when he announced his allegiance to Abraham Lincoln as soon as he was elected. His was a small voice crying in the wilderness of secession, but he made himself heard all over the land.

Until his sense of humor became warped in prison, Brownlow's mirth-provoking stories of conditions below the Mason and Dixon's line made Northern editors chuckle, and he was often quoted. The *Philadelphia Inquirer* said Brownlow told the story of the Tennessee rebel who refused to let his children attend Sunday School because they were taught from books published by the American Sunday School *Union*. Another favorite Brownlow story was his account of a scene in a church in Tennessee when a sign that said *"Union* Prayer Meeting Room" was pulled down.[3]

Born in Virginia in 1805, Brownlow became known as "Parson" during ten years in the Methodist ministry in South Carolina. He entered newspaper work as editor of the *Knoxville Whig* in 1838.

Just before the election in 1860, Brownlow spoke in Knoxville to the Bell-And-Everett Club, saying he was opposed to Breckinridge because of his antislavery record. He pointed out that Bell owned 166 slaves and was "sound" on the slavery question. Brownlow himself owned slaves. At the conclusion of his talk, Brownlow said:

> Candor requires me to admit that the chances are that Mr. Lincoln will be elected. If I am living—and I hope I may be—I shall stand by the Union as long as there are five states that adhere to it. . . . I will sustain Lincoln if he will go to work to put down the great southern mob that leads off in such a rebellion. . . . I expect to stand by this Union, and battle to sustain it, though Whiggery and Democracy, Slavery and Abolitionism, Southern rights and Northern wrongs, are all blown to the devil![4]

Brownlow opened his campaign against secession in the *Whig* on January 12, 1861, with an article that ridiculed the claims to patriotism voiced so loudly by South Carolina revolters, loudest of whom was Robert Barnwell Rhett, publisher of the *Charleston Mercury*.

He published a list of 226 names, representing almost every prominent family in South Carolina, and charged they were Tories in the Revolutionary War. He offered evidence that they had signed a letter of supplication to the British commanders on June 4, 1780, at Charleston, in which they offered congratulations on the "restoration of this capital and province to their political connection to the crown." The supplication was addressed, said Brownlow, to Sir Henry Clinton and Vice Admiral Arbuthnot.

More family names had been changed since the Revolution, by act of the general assembly, in South Carolina than in any other state, Brownlow charged. He asked, "And did not a man named R. Barnwell Smith have the name changed to that of Rhett?"[5]

Brownlow knew what he was talking about. The publisher of the *Mercury* was born Robert Barnwell Smith, the son of James Smith, and in 1837 adopted the name Rhett.[6]

Southern blood boiled, and letters poured in on Brownlow, some threatening his life. Many persons thought Brownlow was a Northern man, and he set the record straight with a sketch of his life in the *Whig*, pointing out he was born in Virginia and his parents also were natives of that state. He added this final word, "Although I am now fifty-five years of age, I walk erect, have but few gray hairs and look to be younger than any whisky-drinking, tobacco-chewing, profane-swearing Secessionist in any of the cotton states of forty years."[7]

When Virginia seceded, Brownlow wrote in his *Whig*, "Virginia, I am sorry to say, is like a hill of potatoes—the best part under ground."[8] That was his way of saying that Washington, Jefferson, and Monroe were resting in the soil of the Old Dominion.

Not until June 8, 1861, did Tennessee leave the Union, the last of the "erring sisters" to depart. The hesitancy in joining the Confederacy was due partly to pro-Union strength massed in its eastern section, an island of loyalty to the Federal government. Out of that situation grew the phrase "East Tennessee Republican," words that were an epithet when used by a rebel. Brownlow was the spokesman for "East Tennessee."

Brownlow and Bell were friends for a quarter of a century; the editor named his son for him. When the former candidate for President told Brownlow he was "going South," they parted in tears. Thus Bell deserted the Union cause, said Brownlow, "leaving the noble Everett and my humble self to battle on beneath the folds of the Star Spangled Banner as the only sacred shield of a common nationality."[9]

Brownlow did not dream that civil war meant the end of slavery. On May 18, 1861, while the country still shook with the roar of Fort Sumter's guns, the *Whig* said there would not be a Union man in the border slave states if they thought the Lincoln administration contemplated the "abolishing of slavery." It added: "We would fight you to the death."[10]

Southern newspapers's accounts of the first fighting were read by Brownlow with disgust, and he labeled them a fabrication in an editorial, saying:

We find in Secession papers some of the most notorious false dispatches ever published in the world. These appear frequently, under sensation heads, displayed in large capitals, and with exclamation points . . . they do not contain a word of truth. Usually, they carry the lie upon their faces, representing a few hundred southern troops as whipping several thousand Yankees, killing and wounding so many, while nobody is hurt on the Confederate side. . . . One would suppose that a regiment of Yankees will take to flight upon seeing one southern man in uniform.[11]

All during the summer of 1861, Brownlow continued his attack on the Confederacy while the Northern press watched, wondering how long the Richmond government would permit his newspaper to be published. Early in August, Brownlow learned from Richmond friends that his time was about up. In a letter to the editor of the *Washington* (D. C.) *Republican,* widely reprinted by other Northern newspapers, Brownlow said:

An order has been made at Richmond to suppress the publication of the *Knoxville Whig,* but the notice has not yet been served on me. I have given them the devil in this day's paper, and I shall continue to say just what I please until my office is closed or destroyed by brute force.

He said further that his finances were exhausted and that letters containing subscription money were withheld by the Confederates. "And thus," wrote Brownlow, "I am driven to the wall with more subscribers on my list than the eight secession papers of East Tenn. But I will starve, or beg my bread of Union men, before I will surrender to this vile heresy of Secession."[12]

Still nothing happened, and the *Whig* continued to appear. Brownlow taunted the secessionists of East Tennessee about enlisting in the Confederate army, saying: "Ye who are the advocates of southern rights, for separation and disunion—ye who have lost your rights, and feel willing to uphold the glorious flag of the South in opposition to the Hessians arrayed under the despot Lincoln—come to your country's rescue! Come, gentlemen." He charged that the rich were holding back while "poor laborers and mechanics" were enlisting in the rebel army.[13]

Brownlow spoke his valedictory in a signed editorial on October 12, 1861, in which he said, "I am to be indicted before the grand jury of the Confederate court. . . . The indictment will be made because of some 'treasonable articles in late numbers of the *Whig*.'"

He explained he could retain his freedom by taking an oath or by giving bond, but he would not bow "to any power on earth." He said the only "offense" he had committed was his refusal to make war upon the United States and the real object of his impending arrest was destruction of the last Union paper in the eleven seceded states.

He chided the leaders of the Confederate government, pointing out that the entire press of the South "had come down in thunder tones" at the Lincoln administration when the *New York Day Book* and other papers friendly to the rebel cause were barred from the mails.[14]

The *Whig* editor's dream of being arrested and escorted to an orderly court was shattered when he was warned by friends he would never live to be tried. They said that persons offended by his newspaper were plotting to kill him. With a group of Union men—preachers and members of the state legislature who had voted against secession—Brownlow fled on a horse into the Smoky Mountains, hiding in a gorge and living on wild game. The hide-out was discovered, and Brownlow sought refuge in the home of a friend six miles from Knoxville.[15]

The Secretary of War of the Confederacy at that time was Judah P. Benjamin, born in St. Thomas, West Indies, who had the reputation of being "the brains" of the rebel government. While Brownlow was hiding in the mountains, Secretary Benjamin, on November 26, 1861, gave directions to Colonel W. B. Wood at Knoxville as to how "the traitors of East Tennessee" should be handled. His written order said:

First. All such as can be identified in having been engaged in bridge-burning are to be tried summarily by drum-head court-martial, and, if found guilty, executed on the spot by hanging. It would be well to leave their bodies hang in the vicinity of the bridges.[16]

Brownlow knew that a man's chances of surviving the "drum-head court-martial" were exceedingly slim. He sent a note to Brigadier General W. H. Carroll, saying he knew he had been suspected of burning bridges but that he was not guilty. He was willing to stand trial, Brownlow said, but he did not want to be "turned over to any infuriated mob of armed men."[17] In the meantime, Brownlow's friends in Richmond made application to Benjamin for a passport out of Tennessee for him.

General Carroll replied to Brownlow's note that he would grant him a passport into Kentucky if he would call at headquarters within twenty-four hours, that a military escort would be provided for a route to be designated by Major General George B. Crittenden. At the same time, Brownlow was given a copy of a letter written by Secretary Benjamin to Crittenden, which said:

I have been asked to grant a passport for Brownlow to leave the state of Tennessee. . . . I cannot grant him a formal passport, though I would greatly prefer seeing him on the other side of our lines, as an avowed enemy. I wish, however, to say, that I would be glad to learn that he has left Tennessee; I have no objection to interpose to his leaving, if you are willing to let him pass.[18]

With a new feeling of security, Brownlow came out of hiding and went to the headquarters of General Crittenden. That was on December 5. It was agreed that he should be started north on the morning of December 7.

On December 6, Brownlow was arrested and charged with treason on a warrant issued by a Confederate commissioner. The warrant said the charge of treason was based on editorials published in the *Knoxville Whig*. Brownlow was denied release under bond, although his friends offered to post one hundred thousand dollars. He immediately appealed to Crittenden, but the General sent word that the case was now out of his hands, inasmuch as the charge was filed by civil authorities. The editor was thrown into prison, charging that Secretary Benjamin had trapped him into surrendering.[19]

Brownlow wrote on December 16 a letter to Secretary Benjamin that posed a question. He said, "I am anxious to learn which is your highest authority, the Secretary of War, a major-general, or a dirty little drunken attorney. . . . Just give me my passports, and I will do for your Confederacy more than the devil has ever done, I will quit the country!"[20]

No answer came from Benjamin, and Brownlow, now convinced he was to be hanged, wrote a speech which he intended to read on the gallows. He berated the leaders of the Confederacy, calling them crooks and swindlers. Of Benjamin, he wrote, ". . . your Secretary of War, and one of the men engaged in deceiving me, was expelled from a New England college for stealing money and jewelry out of the trunks of his fellow-students." He ended this planned speech with these words: "Let me be shrouded in the sacred folds of the Star Spangled Banner."[21]

A new prison commander permitted Brownlow's family doctor to attend him. The physician said further exposure in the prison would result in the editor's death. Consequently, Brownlow was removed to his home with a guard posted at the door.

Brownlow was still too ill to appear when his case was called in court a few days later, but that did not matter in the final disposition of charges. The district attorney read to the court a letter from Secretary Benjamin, dated "December 22, 1861." The secretary said:

> I confess it did not occur to me that any attempt would be made to take him (Brownlow) out of the hands of the military authorities. This has been done, however, and it is only regretted in one point of view—that is, color is given to the suspicion that Brownlow has been entrapped and has given himself up under promise of protection which has not been firmly kept. . . . Under all circumstances, therefore, if Brownlow is exposed to harm from his arrest, I shall deem the honor of the Government so far compromitted as to consider it my duty to urge on the President a pardon for any offense of which he may be found guilty; and I repeat the expression of my regret that he was prosecuted, however evident may be his guilt.[22]

After hearing the letter read, the presiding judge remarked that, under the circumstances, he could do nothing but release Brownlow.

The Southern press howled at the disposition of the Brownlow case. The *Knoxville Register* said: "Brownlow was triumphant and Benjamin outwitted. In fact, we do not know whether to laugh or get mad with the manner in which Brownlow has wound the Confederate Government around his thumb."[23]

The *Columbus* (Ga.) *Times* said: "Now this hoary-headed and persistent traitor . . . deserves death and we vote to kill him."[24]

The *Nashville Patriot* said it would place the names of Brownlow and other "vile Tories . . . as high on the roll of infamy as their despicable bodies ought to be on the gallows."[25]

The *Richmond Examiner* advocated mob action, declaring that "if the inhabitants of the South have any real manhood . . . they will silence traitors with the halter or the pistol."[26]

Brownlow spent two months on a sickbed and in the latter part of February was on the road to recovery. He wrote to Secretary Benjamin for permission to pass through the Confederate lines. The order was issued on March 2, and the next day Brownlow left Knoxville for Nashville, escorted by ten soldiers and four civilians.[27]

It was twelve o'clock noon on March 15, 1862, when Brownlow walked toward the Union pickets under protection of a white flag. They knew the Parson. One of their favorite stories was that he had said he would fight the rebels "until Hell freezes over and then fight them on the ice."[28]

Upon catching sight of the American flag flying over Nashville, the Parson said he wished good will to every one except the "Hell-bound" rebels in Knoxville.[29]

Brownlow was hailed as a hero in the North. Crowds gathered to see him everywhere he went. Ohio received him in Columbus as "guest of the state," welcomed by Governor Tod. He spoke in Cincinnati and Dayton, then in Chicago and Indianapolis before going east to Pittsburgh, where the Mayor and city council greeted him.

A crowd headed by Governor Curtin heard the banished editor speak from his train at Harrisburg, Pa. Philadelphia gave him a rousing reception.[30] Upon arrival there, he was taken over by George W. Childs, book publisher, to write "the story of his martydom." He went into seclusion to work on his book at Crosswicks, N. J., and there he was joined by his wife and family, who had been permitted to leave Knoxville under a flag of truce.[31]

Later that year, Brownlow published his book under the jawbreaking title, *Sketches of the Rise, Progress, and Decline of Secession; With a Narrative of Personal Adventures Among the Rebels.* The publisher put the name on the cover as "Parson Brownlow's Book," and under that title it was discussed and publicized by the press. It made a small fortune for both the author and the publisher.

At Harrisburg, Brownlow had said:

My only ambition is to get up a new printing-establishment, and return to East Tennessee and resurrect my *Knoxville Whig*, the only Union Journal in the Confederacy at the time the Rebels crushed it out. I want to go back and aid in restoring that glorious state to the old Union again. I want to go back and point out to the triumphant Federal army such men as deserve to hang, and suitable limbs upon which to hang them! Nay, I desire to tie the rope around some of their infernal necks.[32]

The dreams of few men have been so fully realized. After the Union army took Knoxville, Brownlow went home and resumed publication of his newspaper, but with the name changed to *Knoxville Whig and Rebel Ventilator.* He was elected Governor of Tennessee in 1865 and served two terms. He resigned that office and sold his newspaper in 1869 to accept a seat in the United States Senate, where he served until 1875. Upon his return to private life, he bought back the *Whig* and edited it until his death in 1877.[33]

# 20 The Answer
## to a Greeley Prayer

Union successes in the West in the early months of 1862 were followed by a series of setbacks in the Eastern theater of war during the summer. General McClellan opened an offensive against Richmond in what was called the Peninsular campaign. The campaign was a disastrous failure, ending in a Confederate threat to capture Washington. The Army of the Potomac was thrown back into the defenses of Washington, and, although the rebel army did not win a decisive single engagement, the effect of the campaign as a whole was a triumph for the South. McClellan, with his splendidly trained and well-equipped army, was no match for Lee and Thomas J. (Stonewall) Jackson. Thousands of dead were left by both sides at Fair Oaks, Gaines's Mill, Frazier's Farm, Malvern Hill, and in the swamps of the James and the Chickahominy. Lincoln removed McClellan from command in favor of Major General John Pope, saw him defeated but not disgraced in the second battle on the old field at Bull Run, reversed himself and recalled McClellan to turn back Lee's invasion of Maryland and relieve Washington. The Confederates, flushed with their success, threatened Baltimore and, indirectly, Philadelphia.

The slavery issue was before the Thirty-seventh Congress all summer, and on June 17, 1862, it passed the Confiscation Act, an attempt to harmonize all shades of opinion, which declared the slaves of any person convicted of treason should go free. The Abolitionists demanded that Lincoln issue a proclamation of emancipation. Pressure groups took up the President's time and taxed his patience.

On the morning of August 20, 1862, the *New York Tribune* published an open letter to the President under the heading, "The Prayer of Twenty Millions." It began with, "To Abraham Lincoln, Pres. of the U. States," and was signed, "Horace Greeley."

The editor of the *Tribune* accused Lincoln of failure to enforce the new Confiscation Act, made an appeal that all slaves the army could reach be set free, and charged the President was subservient to the slave interests. He then addressed the President in these words:

What an immense majority of the loyal millions of your countrymen require of you is a frank, declared, unqualified, ungrudging execution of the laws of the land, more especially of the Confiscation Act. That act gives freedom to the slaves of rebels coming within our lines, or whom those lines may at any time enclose—we ask you to render it due obedience by publicly requiring all your subordinates to recognize and obey it.[1]

Perhaps unwittingly, Greeley provided Lincoln with the very opportunity he needed to explain to the country his exact stand on the issue of slavery. The President saw a way to take the North into his confidence and at the same time tell the South exactly why he sought to conquer the seceded states.

He wrote a reply to Greeley in the form of a personal letter and notified the editors of the Washington *National Intelligencer* that he had prepared an article for publication. James C. Welling, political editor of the *Intelligencer*, went over the letter with the President, word for word. At Welling's suggestion, one sentence was eliminated.[2]

Lincoln's motive in choosing the *National Intelligencer* to carry his answer to Greeley raises an interesting question. Edited by the distinguished William W. Seaton, it was one of Lincoln's favorite newspapers from early manhood, but with all its former nationalism it was only lukewarm to the Lincoln administration and made no secret of its sympathy for the slavery system. Lincoln might have chosen it to tease Greeley.

On Saturday, August 23, the *Intelligencer* published Lincoln's reply at the top of its editorial column, under the heading, "A Letter from the President." The President had ordered italicized the words he deemed most important. It follows in full:

> Executive Mansion,
> Washington, August 22, 1862.

Hon. Horace Greeley:

Dear Sir: I have just read yours of the 19th, addressed to myself through the New York Tribune. If there be in it any statements, or assumptions of fact, which I may know to be erroneous, I do not now and here controvert them. If there be in it any inferences which I may believe to be falsely drawn, I do not now and here argue against them. If there be perceptible in it an impatient and dictatorial tone, I waive it in deference to an old friend whose heart I have always supposed to be right.

As to the policy I "seem to be pursuing," as you say, I have not meant to leave any one in doubt.

I would save the Union. I would save it the shortest way under the Constitution. The sooner the national authority can be restored the nearer the Union will be "the Union as it was." If there be those who would not save the Union unless they could at the same time *save* slavery, I do not agree with them. If there be those who would not save the Union unless they could at the same *destroy* slavery, I do not agree with them. My paramount object in this struggle *is* to save the Union, and is *not* either to save or to destroy slavery. If I could save the Union without freeing *any* slave I would do it, and if I could save it by freeing *all* the slaves I would do it; and if I could save it by freeing some and leaving others alone, I would also do that. What I do about slavery and the colored race, I do because I believe it helps to save this Union; and what I forbear, I forbear because I do *not* believe it would help to save the Union. I shall do *less* whenever I shall believe what I am doing hurts the cause, and I shall do *more* whenever I shall believe doing more will help the cause. I shall try to correct errors when shown to be errors; and I shall adopt new views so fast as they shall appear to be true views.

I have here stated my purpose according to my view of *official* duty; and I intend no modification of my oft-expressed *personal* wish that all men everywhere could be free.

Yours,<br>A. LINCOLN.[3]

The *Intelligencer* carried a small editorial under the President's letter in which it directed some sharp sentences at the editor of the *New York Tribune*, commenting as follows:

When the very original idea of addressing in the *New York Tribune* a letter to President Lincoln, in the name and authority of "twenty millions" of American people, entered the head of Mr. Horace Greeley, we suppose he had little idea that his communication, if ever reaching the eye of his distinguished correspondent, would receive from that correspondent the honor of a response. Still less could he have expected or wished that the response should be of a nature to give so much satisfaction to the "twenty millions" of loyal men in whose behalf he assumed to speak, than he, their self-elected organ, is likely to find in it. We hope, however, that when Mr. Greeley has duly pondered the pithy sentences of the President's letter, he will be able to rejoin, if he proposes to continue the "correspondence" in a spirit which shall be slightly less arrogant, dictatorial, and acrimonious. "Twenty millions" of his countrymen have a right to claim this at his hands, in deference to the high office whose incumbent he ventures to arraign before the bar of public opinion in their name.[4]

Greeley ventured an answer on Monday morning, August 25, but Lincoln's clever fencing had him clearly on the defensive and he was compelled not only to declare his own good intentions but to offer an apology to the President. He wrote, "Nothing was farther from my thought than to impeach in any manner the sincerity or the intensity of your devotion to the saving of the Union."[5]

The administration newspapers attacked Greeley on the grounds that he presumed to be a dictator of policy. The *National Intelligencer* thought Greeley needed "a lesson in etiquette" and charged he was arrogant. *The New York Times* was more subtle, saying it was "a bold assumption" on Greeley's part to claim to represent twenty million people. The *Times* already had taken the wind out of Greeley's sails, saying on August 23:

Several days ago the President read to a friend a rough draft of what appears this morning as a letter to Horace Greeley. He said that he had thought of getting before the public some such statement of his position on the slavery question in some manner and asked the opinion of his friend as to the propriety of such a course and the best way to do it. The appearance of Greeley's "Prayer" gave him the opportunity.[6]

A sifting of the facts shows that Lincoln, moving so swiftly in his slow way, was far ahead of Greeley. The President had submitted to his Cabinet on July 22 a tentative draft for an emancipation proclamation. Secretary Seward suggested it be put aside until a more propitious time in view of the recent Union defeats in the field. Less than a month later, Lincoln learned that Greeley was writing a letter to him on the slavery question and that it would be published in the *Tribune*. He and his advisers decided the editor could be held off if he were given inside information.[7] They were too late, "The Prayer" appearing the next morning.

It was no secret to well-informed observers that the Lincoln administration was preparing to change its policy on slavery. On July 30, *The Press* of Philadelphia, edited by the President's confidant, John W. Forney, came out with a declaration for adoption of a national policy of emancipation. The editorial obviously was Lincoln's trial balloon. Forney, who had maintained a course parallel to Lincoln's conservatism, nationally recognized as a White House voice, would not have dared to make such a declaration without the Presidential blessing.[8]

It might be unfair to Greeley, although the conclusion is obvious, to assume that in publishing his "prayer" he was trying to beat Lincoln to the draw on emancipation and thus win for himself a portion of the reflected glory.

Lincoln's letter, clear as it was, found many persons trying to read between the lines in search of a hidden meaning. Slaveholders of the border states read in it a hint that the President intended to break with the Greeley faction of Abolitionists. To them, it appeared that Lincoln was in sympathy with their theory of the war.[9] The tone of the *National Intelligencer's* editorial shows this proslavery newspaper saw but little indication of emancipation in Lincoln's reply.

As late as September 13, Lincoln would not promise a proclamation of emancipation. A committee representing various religious denominations in Chicago called at the White House and urged him to act. He pointed out to the committee that there were 50,000 men from the border slave states serving in the Union army and that a proclamation might drive them over to the enemy. He asked them:

What good would a proclamation of emancipation from me do, especially as we are now situated? I do not want to issue a document that the whole world will see must necessarily be inoperative, like the Pope's Bull against the comet. Would my word free the slaves, when I cannot even enforce the Constitution in the rebel states?[10]

Within a week, the whole picture had changed. McClellan met Lee's invading army at Antietam Creek in Maryland near Sharpsburg on September 17. Losses were about thirteen thousand men on each side. Washington had hopes the Confederate army might be captured, but McClellan followed slowly and criticism of his delay robbed him of the plaudits he deserved for turning back the invasion. The South looked upon the battle as a draw, but the fact remains it was Lee who quit the field.

Lincoln knew that the time had come to use what would be called today his "secret weapon" against the slave states in insurrection. On September 22, he made his preliminary announcement of the Emancipation Proclamation, the instrument which he was to formally issue on the next January 1, 1863.

The first proclamation declared restoration of the Union still the objective of the war; that when Congress reconvened, he would ask legislation to reimburse any slave state, not in rebellion, which in the meantime would abolish slavery; that all persons held as slaves in any state then in rebellion should go free; that the Federal government, through its military and naval forces, would recognize the freedom of these slaves and that on the forthcoming January 1 he would designate the parts of the country to which the proclamation should apply.[11]

Reaction of the press to the preliminary announcement followed party lines with some slight exception. *The New York Times* took its usual conservative stand, defending the new policy on the grounds of political necessity. The *New York Herald* said Lincoln had given "a sop to the Abolitionists."[12] *The World* of New York declared Lincoln was "adrift on a current of radical fanaticism."[13] Horace Greeley's *Tribune* cried: "God bless Abraham Lincoln."[14] Medill's *Chicago Tribune* saw the impending Emancipation Proclamation in the light in which it is viewed today, saying in an editorial:

The President has set his hand and affixed the great seal to the grandest proclamation ever issued by man. He has declared after the first day of January next all the slaves in the then rebellious states shall be free. . . . So splendid a vision has hardly shone upon the world since the day of the Messiah. From the date of this proclamation begins the history of this Republic, as our Fathers designed to have it—the home of freedom, the asylum of the oppressed, the seat of justice, the land of equal rights under the law, where each man, however humble, shall be entitled to life, liberty and the pursuit of happiness. Let no one think to stay the glorious reformation. Each day's events are hastening its triumphs, and whosoever shall place himself in its way it will grind to powder.[15]

The *National Intelligencer*, which had crowed so loudly over Lincoln's reply to Greeley, found the preliminary announcement a bitter pill. It made an attempt to swallow it in these words:

. . . where we expect no good, we shall be only too happy to find that no harm has been done by the present declaration of the Executive. . . . The proclamation may be said to open issues too tremendous and to be fraught with consequences too undeveloped, to admit of calculation or forecast by any intelligence we can command.[16]

The editors of the *Intelligencer*, always in the past too dignified to engage in any controversy with another newspaper over a difference of opinion, attacked the *Boston Advertiser* because it changed its policy to laud Lincoln's action. The *Intelligencer* pointed out with sorrow that the *Advertiser* had deserted the old ranks for the new.[17] From that day, the *Intelligencer* was an avowed enemy of President Lincoln.

Fear of recognition of the Confederate States of America by European powers was ever present in Washington. The administration hoped a declaration of emancipation would weigh favorably on the side of the Union in the capitals of the Continent. All of Lincoln's foreign ministers had urged such a measure upon him. William L. Dayton, Minister to France, warned the President that a section of the foreign press might attempt to misstate his purposes in proclaiming emancipation and its results. Russell, British Foreign Minister, in a dispatch to Lord Lyons in Washington, called the Proclamation a war measure of a very questionable kind.[18]

The proslavery press in the North took especial note of the reaction of the British newspapers. *The Crisis* told its readers in the rural West that the powerful *London Times* was "savage" on Lincoln's announcement.[19] *The Crisis* told the truth. This is what the *Times* said:

Is Lincoln yet a name not known to us as it will be known to posterity and is it ultimately to be classed among the catalogue of monsters, the wholesale assassins and butchers of their kind? It (the Emancipation Proclamation) will not deprive Mr. Lincoln of the distinctive affix which he will share with many, for the most part foolish and incompetent, kings and emperors, caliphs and doges, that of being Lincoln—"The Last."[20]

The world-wide interest stirred by the President's announcement on September 22 found the *Cincinnati Commercial* smug in the satisfaction that it had performed one of the greatest news beats of the Civil War. Murat Halstead's newspaper accurately forecast the President's action almost six months before he took the step. On April 4, 1862, the *Commercial* published this one paragraph: "Before the first day of January, 1863, the President will declare general emancipation of the slaves of rebels a military necessity. When conversation and discussion at the capital of the nation assume that phase prominently as now, the fact may be considered significant."[21]

Apparently no one paid much attention at the time. Halstead was not a name in the East, but his politics, that of a Republican liberal, should have been the tip-off that he was not merely mouthing the views of a hopeful Abolitionist. Halstead himself may not have believed the story. He made no display of it, wrote no editorials about it.

In the interval between the preliminary announcement and the actual Proclamation, President Lincoln was subjected to a barrage of criticism that was unusual even for his administration. The Democratic press grew still more hostile, and even those newspapers of that party which supported the war regretted the change in policy. Under the heading, "The President and His Critics," the *Springfield* (Mass.) *Republican* published this story from its Washington correspondent:

Some one sent Mr. Lincoln a batch of newspaper criticisms upon him and his conduct of the war last week. In speaking about it to a friend, Mr. Lincoln said, "Having an hour to spare on Sunday I read this batch of editorials and when I was through reading I asked myself, 'Abraham Lincoln, are you a man *or* a dog?'" The best part of the story was Mr. Lincoln's inimitable manner of telling it. His good nature is equal to every emergency. The editorials in question were very able, and as bitter in their criticisms upon him as they were able; yet Mr. Lincoln smiled very pleasantly as he spoke of them, though it was evident that they made a decided impression upon his mind.[22]

The Proclamation, as issued on New Year's Day, 1863, excluded Delaware, Maryland, Kentucky, and Missouri, the border slave states that had remained loyal. The western part of Virginia—soon to be the state of West Virginia—Tennessee—always represented in the Federal Congress—and thirteen parishes in Louisiana held by Union forces, also were recognized as not in insurrection.[23]

# 21  A Vast Newspaper Sepulcher

LINCOLN'S FRIEND FORNEY, publisher of the Philadelphia *Press*, established the *Daily Morning Chronicle* in Washington on November 3, 1862, under circumstances that brought it close to the White House door. For about a year, Forney had published a weekly in the Capital, the *Sunday Morning Chronicle*, and he had merely to convert it into a daily.

The Union suffered reverses to the Army of the Potomac in the Peninsular campaign that were only partially canceled with the firm stand at Antietam Creek. Although McClellan stopped the invasion of Maryland, Lincoln was not satisfied with him and on November 5, 1862, transferred command of the army to Burnside. McClellan went to Trenton, N. J., to await orders, but the orders never came.[1]

McClellan was removed after Washington heard mysterious rumors that the General, idolized by the rank and file of his army, was sought after as a tool by persons who would have replaced Lincoln with a military dictatorship. The contemporary press was aware something of this nature was afoot immediately after the Battle of Antietam, Medill's *Chicago Tribune* saying on September 20:

The danger of wrecking the Republican institutions of this country in a military despotism is as imminent on the heels of a great success as after great disasters. The danger may be far off, but we are mistaken if there is not a well matured design on the part of a powerful and dangerous faction to accomplish a result over which all friends of liberty will mourn.[2]

The order for removal of McClellan came from the Secretary of War, "by direction of the President of the United States."[3]

The *Daily Morning Chronicle*, whose appearance was simultaneous with the shake-up of the army command, was founded at the suggestion of President Lincoln, who was disturbed over the attitude of Horace Greeley's *New York Tribune* and feared the effect its wavering editorial policy might have among the soldiers of the Army of the Potomac.[4] Ten thousand copies of the *Chronicle* went to the Army of the Potomac every day. The newspaper carried the name of D. C. Forney as publisher, but that is not to be taken seriously. D. C. was Daniel Forney, a cousin of John.

Washington was "a vast newspaper sepulcher" to John Forney, who had seen the rise and fall of more newspapers there than in any other city of like population and importance in the world.[5] His *Daily Morning Chronicle* prospered because, he admitted, it served "a reading army," and the press count was often 30,000 a day. He could have sold 100,000, but his facilities were limited. Public printing by contract ceased with the Lincoln administration, and the Washington newspapers were compelled to exist on their own efforts rather than on government subsidy.[6] However, the *Daily Morning Chronicle* got its share of government patronage, the pages filled with Federal notices and advertising testify.

A few months before the *Chronicle* became a daily, the Sunday newspaper ran afoul of the army censorship regulations and gained the unenviable name of being the only Washington newspaper suppressed, one edition feeling Secretary of War Stanton's iron fist. The editor of the *Sunday Morning Chronicle* was John Russell Young, still in his early twenties, sometimes secretary to the publisher, sometimes war correspondent, and sometimes managing editor of *The Press* at Philadelphia. The offending story appeared in the *Chronicle* on Sunday morning, March 16, 1862. It revealed troop movements.

The Washington correspondent of the *Philadelphia Inquirer* wrote this page-one story for his newspaper:

Washington, March 17—Secretary Stanton has today issued a written order to General James I. Wadsworth, who is now acting as military governor of the District of Columbia, directing him to suppress the number of the Washington *Sunday Chronicle* published yesterday and to take measures for the prevention of publication in its columns of any more information of army movements for the enemy.

It also directed the arrest of all connected with the paper, even to its compositors. The *Chronicle* is a spicy, enterprising sheet, owned by Colonel John W. Forney and edited by John R. Young, neither of whom was the author of the offensive matter in yesterday's issue. It is believed that this, being the first arrest of the kind, that the warning will be sufficient without harsher measures being resorted to and that the parties implicated will be released without a reprimand.[7]

Forney, who ran in and out of the White House and was as near to Lincoln as any man in journalism or politics,[8] probably had the President smooth things over with "Mars," as the Chief Executive liked to call the Secretary of War. Nothing further was heard of the case.

Young went to the White House at two o'clock one morning to show the President a Southern newspaper obtained from a rebel picket. The paper carried a report Charleston had fallen, big news if true. With another member of the *Chronicle* staff, he was admitted to the Executive Mansion by the sleepy doorkeeper, and their presence was announced to the President.

Lincoln came to the reception room clad only in a nightshirt and bedroom slippers, with his hair tousled. He sat on a lounge, nursed his knees, and listened with eyes half opened. Young read some excerpts from the paper, and when he had finished, Lincoln asked the date of the publication. When told, he replied he himself knew the city was still holding out two days after the paper said it had capitulated.

Young was embarrassed and offered apologies, but Lincoln eased his feelings by thanking him profusely for making the trip at that hour.[9]

Lincoln himself wrote, headline and all, a short story for the *Chronicle*, published on December 7, 1864, at the bottom of column two on the editorial page. After he prepared the copy, he handed it to Noah Brooks, Washington correspondent for the *Sacramento* (Calif.) *Union*, one of his closest friends, and asked him to see that it was printed "right away" in the *Chronicle*. He signed his name, "A. Lincoln," on the copy at Brooks's suggestion. The correspondent, who saw the souvenir value of the copy, retained the original as a memento.[10]

The headline said: "The President's Last, Shortest and Best Speech."
The text follows:

On Thursday of last week two ladies from Tennessee came before the
President, asking the release of their husbands, held as prisoners of war
at Johnston's Island. They were put off until Friday, when they came again,
and were again put off until Saturday. At each of the interviews one of the
ladies urged that her husband was a religious man, and on Saturday, when
the President ordered the release of the two prisoners, he said to this lady:
"You say your husband is a very religious man; tell him when you meet him
that I say I am not much of a judge of religion, but that, in my opinion, the
religion that sets men to rebel and fight against their Government because,
as they think, that Government does not sufficiently help *some* men to
eat their bread in the sweat of *other* men's faces, is not the sort of religion
upon which people can get to heaven." We have given as a caption for this
paragraph the President's own opinion of his little speech, which he considered his shortest and best, as well as his latest.[11]

Comparison of the text as written by Lincoln with the version that
appeared in the *Chronicle* reveals that the editor who handled it made
several changes in the copy, altering punctuation and changing the
name "Johnson's Island" to the incorrect "Johnston's Island." The word
"till" was changed to "until," and the word "to" was made to read
"until."

The *Chronicle*, with a fine disregard for history, did not tell its readers
the story was written by the President, not even admitting he wrote
the headline for it, but gave the impression it was the work of a member
of the newspaper staff.

The story was widely reprinted from the *Chronicle*, as Lincoln
probably hoped it would be, in both the Republican and Democratic
press. Classified as another Lincoln anecdote, it made a good filler for
editorial pages.

From the day it was established, the *Chronicle* engaged in a no-holds-
barred battle with the *National Intelligencer*, the former Whig newspaper which broke with Lincoln over the Emancipation Proclamation.
The fight ended in a knockout for the *Chronicle* in a little over two
years.

The *Intelligencer*, once one of the most highly respected newspaper
names, was edited by the aging W. W. Seaton, a Virginian whose
mother was a cousin of the patriot, Patrick Henry. From 1812 to
1860, Seaton and Joseph Gales, Jr., his brother-in-law, published the
*Intelligencer*. Gales died just before the outbreak of the Civil War,

and Seaton, then seventy-five years old, carried on the paper alone. The *Intelligencer* had a wide circulation in Virginia. As a daily record of Congress for half a century, the paper had no equal.

Seaton tried to ignore secession at first, and the word rebel never invaded his columns. The term insurgent was used. Election of Jefferson Davis as President of the Confederacy was published as routine news on page three.

The newspaper showed symptoms of alarm when Lincoln, speaking at Indianapolis, made a reference to retaking forts in South Carolina. Lincoln's use of the word "coercion" brought many letters to the editor from Southern readers, all dutifully published in the *Intelligencer*.

The paper shoved the advertising from page one and devoted almost all the page to the Lincoln inauguration. It said in an editorial that the inaugural address "leaves to conservative citizens good reason to expect a conciliatory course at the hands of the new President."[12]

When South Carolina batteries fired on Fort Sumter, the *Intelligencer* said:

We can only give expression to the profound sorrow with which we contemplate the melancholy spectacle of a fratricidal conflict, which, however begun or however ended, can bring only shame to every lover of his land, and only grief to every friend of humanity.[13]

The editorial was a masquerade for the views Seaton actually held. In 1864, when the *Intelligencer* was fighting Lincoln's bid for reelection, it charged him with responsibility for the war, saying:

Safely installed in the Executive Mansion, what did Mr. Lincoln do to assuage the "artificial excitement in the South" . . . ? Mr. Lincoln dispatched an expedition to Charleston Harbor for the purpose of reinforcing Major Anderson. . . . We all know what was the upshot of this expedition . . . which gave to the insurgents just the pretext they wanted for lighting up the flames of civil war.[14]

The *Chronicle,* always ready to defend the President, charged the *Intelligencer* was "consorting" with the Vallandighams.[15] The attack on Seaton continued when the *Chronicle* said: "The *National Intelligencer,* in becoming a 'Democratic' organ, made an immense leap from its lofty pedestal of immobile conservatism, upon which it had dwelt, like a Simon Stylites, for some thirty or forty years."[16]

Forney's paper further insulted the *Intelligencer* by classifying it with the *Louisville Journal* and the *St. Louis Republican,* saying that "it is the chronic habit of these papers to advocate an unsuccessful cause."[17]

On December 31, 1864, the *Chronicle* reported the *National Intelligencer* had "changed hands" and that the new owners were Allen, Coyle, and Snow. Sale of the *Intelligencer* was confirmed the next day when Seaton, in a signed statement, said the editorial management of the paper "passes into other hands." Welling, who helped Lincoln prepare his answer to Greeley in 1862, published "a card" in which he announced his "release from his labors in connection with this journal."

The new owners pledged "unwavering support" to the war policy of the Lincoln administration and added, "We have no taste, at this time, for the discussion of such issues as are represented by the Emancipation Proclamation."[18]

In one edition, the *Intelligencer* changed to a Lincoln newspaper that outstripped even the *Chronicle* in applauding everything the President did. When Lincoln began his second term, the *Intelligencer* said: "Our heart's deepest wish is that his present term may be a success commensurate with his responsibilities, and that he may WIN AND WEAR SUCH A CROWN OF GLORY AS SHALL RESULT FROM THE RE-ESTABLISHMENT OF THE AMERICAN UNION."[19]

It was of the opinion that the last paragraph of the inaugural address—with malice toward none; with charity for all—should be "printed in gold."[20]

No mention was made in the *Intelligencer* that Vice-President Andrew Johnson of Tennessee was in an obvious state of intoxication when he appeared to take his oath, but it cleverly revealed he had been drinking on his way to Washington. It reprinted from the *Cincinnati Gazette* the report of a speech made by Johnson in the Ohio city a couple of days before the Inauguration. The story said Johnson "looked somewhat worse for wear," and added:

The Vice-President did not respond in a clear voice, or, it seemed to us, with as clear a head as we have heard him on former occasions. It was with difficulty we could hear or understand him at all from where we stood.[21]

Politics and journalism were so closely interlocked that it was difficult to tell where one left off and the other began. Loyal editors all over the North felt no hesitancy in dashing off a personal letter to the President when they thought he needed the stimulation of their sage observations or when they had a bone to pick with him over the course of his administration. Letters from editors and publishers piled up in Lincoln's files until they numbered several hundred.

These letters contained requests for political or military favors in many instances; some reported the state of affairs as the writers pointed with pride or viewed with alarm, while others brazenly informed Lincoln how he should run the country to win the war.[22]

The President had a little cabinet in his office for use as a special letter file. The interior of the cabinet was divided into pigeonholes which were lettered in alphabetical order, but some were marked for one individual only. Horace Greeley had a pigeonhole all to himself, an honor held by no others but generals. One box was marked, "W. & W." and was reserved, Lincoln explained to a friend, for Thurlow Weed and Fernando Wood.[23]

Medill of the *Chicago Tribune* never spared the ink when he had a thought to transmit to Lincoln. One of the publisher's last letters to the President, dated Washington, January 15, 1865, was marked "private" and addressed to him as "Father Abraham." The editor began, "I am going home to Illinois in a few days and do not propose or desire to consume any of your time in personal interviews, but before leaving will jot down a few things, perhaps of no great account."

Then followed, under four long numbered sections, the publisher's suggestions on everything from Cabinet appointments to tax measures. He also told the President how to bring the Confederates to terms. First, he wanted Lincoln to turn Secretary of the Navy Gideon Welles out of the Cabinet in favor of General Butler. Second, he wanted General Frémont sent to France as ambassador. Third, he proposed a special session of Congress to act on Constitutional amendments. Fourth, he proposed taxes should be raised.

He added a recipe for victory, saying: "Lastly. Don't be in too much hurry for peace. Don't *coax* the rebel chiefs, but pound them a little more. When they are sufficiently whipped they will gladly accept *your terms*, and the peace then made will be enduring. . . . The starch is not sufficiently taken out of the devils yet."[24]

Another letter from Medill enclosed an editorial clipped from the *Chicago Tribune* of October 15, 1864, that boosted Chase for Chief Justice of the Supreme Court. Penciled on the margin of the editorial was this note: "Please run your eye over this."[25]

While Medill was full of advice that overflowed into the White House, other editors were complaining to Lincoln about a thousand and one things. For example, George Bergner, editor of the *Daily Telegraph* at Harrisburg, Pa., wrote to him on February 5, 1864, that "blunders" of the state provost marshal were blamed on Lincoln and that the editor had denounced the official in his paper "to save the administration from being disgraced." A batch of clippings was enclosed.[26]

Newspaper editors sometimes forwarded to President Lincoln letters sent to them which they believed to contain information of value to him. The editor of the *Washington* (D. C.) *Republican* sent this one to the White House:

Washington, Feb. 1, —64.

Editor Republican, dear sir

I hasten to say to you that I have of my own knowledge before leaving Richmond that the rebel authorities are taking steps to propose to the federal government to lay down their arms provided the President's amnesty is extended to their leaders. Let this be known in the South and the rebellion is at an end. You may make any use of this you think proper but please do not publish my name at present for obvious reasons. I am writing out a statement to-day for the government.

Yours truly
James Yates of Richmond[27]

The helpful attitude of the *Republican* showed it harbored no ill will toward the Lincoln administration for rough treatment of its editor in October of 1862. He was summoned to the War Department by Chief Detective Baker, who demanded the editor explain "how he got the news that a man in the War Department was giving the rebels information."

*The World*, in New York, reported that the editor of the *Republican* came close to being sent to prison, and the Democratic press made a mountain out of a molehill. The idea of "a traitor in the War Department" was planted in the public mind. The *New York Tribune* came up with a truthful story, explaining: "He (Baker) did not arrest the editor, as stated, but not improperly treated him with some roughness of manner, and made some foolish remarks about newspapers, such as are not uncommon in military circles."[28]

The *Washington Star* did not cut a spectacular figure in the Capital, but its excellent coverage of the scene there was often clipped and reprinted as "specials." The Washington *Constitutional Union* was always critical of President Lincoln and was assailed for its stand by Forney's *Chronicle*.[29]

Instead of writing to Lincoln, many editors and publishers went to see him in the White House, and almost every Northern journalist of prominence was a visitor there during the war. Frederick Douglass, Negro editor of *The North Star*, Rochester, N. Y., was among them.[30]

Sometimes an editor received a special invitation to visit President Lincoln. One was David R. Locke, editor of a small-town newspaper, the *Jeffersonian*, at Findlay, Ohio. Locke had admired Lincoln for years. He went to Quincy, Ill., in 1858 to hear him debate with Douglas and heard Lincoln speak in Columbus a year later.

He took over the editorship of the little *Jeffersonian* about the time the war began, and his genius flowered into a column, written in the form of letters signed "Petroleum V. Nasby." The column attracted immediate attention and was widely reprinted. From the obscurity of his dingy office, Locke was lifted to sudden fame and, in a few years, fortune.[31]

Lincoln liked the Nasby letters and in 1863 asked him whether there was any place he was capable of filling that he might want. The editor went to Washington as he was bidden and amazed the President by telling him he sought no favors. They spent an hour together in Lincoln's study.

Locke saw the President once more, in 1864, when he went to Washington to plead for the life of an Ohio soldier sentenced to be shot for desertion. His plea was granted.[32]

The President also read the humorous writings of R. H. Newell, who signed himself "Orpheus C. Kerr" (Office Seeker), and Charles F. Browne, whose pen name was "Artemus Ward," but Nasby was his favorite. When Lincoln read something by Nasby, written in the idiom of an illiterate backwoodsman, that struck him as especially funny, he would repeat it for days afterwards. When the politicians were rallying Negroes to fill the draft quotas in some places, Nasby was quoted as telling the country, "Arowse to wunst!" Lincoln went around the White House using that expression, much to his own enjoyment.[33]

# 22 "What Have We Gained?"

IN THE CLOSING WEEKS of 1862, when the first wave of defeatism overspread the North, it was the opinion of many persons that the South could not be conquered by force of arms. A fantastic idea took form, newspaper files of the Democratic press of that year prove, that if the

Union were not restored, the Middle and Western states would go with the South, leaving the states of New England and the state of New York to form a republic.

President Lincoln's preliminary proclamation of emancipation, his suspension of the writ of habeas corpus for all persons arrested under military authority, his removal of the Democrat Burnside from command, Confederate military gains, and the loss of thousands of Union lives: these gave opponents of the war fresh opportunity to complain.

The *Providence Post*, Democratic voice in the Rhode Island capital, seriously discussed the formation of a new nation on December 1, 1862, declaring it "the finale to which this administration is driving us." With the assertion the administration "is every day rendering a restoration of the Union more and more difficult," it belabored Lincoln, saying:

He empties Fort Warren and Lafayette of political prisoners, without a word of apology or explanation to their victims, and without the moral courage to rescind the unconstitutional order under which they were . . . arrested.

We have allowed personal rights and state rights to be trampled upon— we have allowed the country to be flooded with a currency which five years hence will not be worth the paper upon which it is printed—we have submitted to taxation such as Americans before never dreamed of—we have offered up hundreds of thousands of valuable lives. And what have we gained?[1]

Reprinted in the radical Democratic press, the editorial was given wide circulation in the North. War dissidents read it with relish. A few months later, the *Portland* (Me.) *Advertiser* expressed itself equally bluntly. It said, in part:

The fact is not to be disguised, however unpalatable to partisan politicians, that in Maine, New Hampshire, in the great state of New York, and in other states, the conduct of the war has rendered the war itself unpopular. . . . We verily believe that if the honest heart of the people of Maine could be fairly and freely expressed today, three-fourths of our entire population would vote the war, as conducted, a nuisance or a curse, and that they are only anxious to know how to change it and conquer an honorable peace.[2]

Medary's peace propagandist, *The Crisis*, spread the editorial over the land with this explanation: "We have before us the *Portland* (Me.) *Advertiser*, one of the most influential and able papers in New England. In its antecedents it is Old Line Whig. It is edited by F. O. Smith, formerly a member of Congress, and we believe he was once clerk to the Federal House of Representatives."

It cannot be denied that such newspaper expressions represented a segment of the population, but they certainly did not represent the majority. In New England, as in many other parts of the North, the man in the street was several steps ahead of the press in his national-policy views. The New England states were among the first to witness destruction by mobs of newspapers hostile to the Union. Riot rule, however, was confined chiefly to smaller centers of population, and in metropolitan Boston the Democratic press made utterances that would have brought ruin to newspapers elsewhere.

The weekly *Democratic Standard*, published at Concord, N. H., was wrecked by soldiers on August 8, 1861. The soldiers, members of the 1st New Hampshire Regiment, were incensed by an article that reflected on them. They demanded a retraction, and when it was refused stormed the office.[3] Found in the debris was a letter from the editor of the *New York Day Book*, asking the *Standard's* editor, John B. Palmer, for a list of Democratic newspapers.

The editor of *The Patriot*, also published in Concord, issued an extra on the mobbing in which he declared "it ought to have been done long ago."[4] Palmer was financially ruined. He published an open letter in Democratic newspapers, appealing for money to buy food for his family.[5]

On August 12, 1861, angry citizens raided the *Democrat*, at Bangor, Me., carried out type cases and other equipment, stacked them in the public square, and burned them. The *Whig and Courier* of Bangor, in reporting this removal of opposition, said: "The people have determined that a secession organ should not exist in our city."

There was an anticlimax to the destruction of the *Democrat*. J. Jones, a barber, met John Wyman on the street and asked him why he had made remarks about the *Democrat*. When Wyman said it was none of his business, Jones struck him in the face. The mob that sacked the *Democrat* then wrecked Jones's barber shop.[6]

The destruction of the *Democrat* was due to such editorial utterances as this, written by Editor Marcellus Emory: "As war has been determined upon by President Lincoln and his Cabinet to subdue the South, these states will ward off the blow as best they can. . . . He (Jefferson Davis) is one of the very, very few gigantic minds which adorn the pages of history of whom it may be said: 'Desperate courage makes one a majority.' "[7]

Emory purchased new equipment, and the *Democrat* was soon publishing again. In the spring of 1863, it passed along to its readers a poem of sixteen verses featured in Copperhead newspapers. This is a typical verse:

> You saw those mighty legions, Abe,
> And heard their manly tread;
> You counted hosts of living men—
> Pray—can you count the dead?
> Look o'er the proud Potomac, Abe,
> Virginia's hills along;
> Their wakeful ghosts are beckoning you,
> Two hundred thousand strong.[8]

On the night of August 20, 1861, Ambrose L. Kimball, editor of the *Essex County Democrat*, "a weekly secession sheet" at Haverhill, Mass., was taken from his home by a mob, covered with a coat of tar and feathers, and ridden through town on a rail. The town police and "good citizens" tried to save him but were repelled.

The mob forced Kimball to get down on his knees and make this declaration: "I am sorry that I have published what I have and I promise that I never will again write or publish articles against the North and in favor of secession. So help me God."[9]

The *Advertiser and Farmer* of Bridgeport, Conn., an outspoken opponent of the war and bitter enemy of President Lincoln, published editorials in the first months of war like this one:

What now is to be done? Stop the war! Withdraw your troops from the invaded states!! This is the first duty. Then guarantee the South the full enjoyment of their Constitutional rights!! The Constitution is the government— The President is but an agent to execute its provisions . . . and when he departs from these, he violates his oath and is himself the greatest of rebels.[10]

On August 24, 1861, Union soldiers broke into the *Advertiser and Farmer* office and tore it to pieces while a crowd of 5,000 looked on. Letters were found in the files to link prominent politicians in Hartford with the secession movement.[11] The paper resumed publication after refurnishing its plant, but it was more temperate in its antiwar policy.

Speaking for the administration in Boston was the *Daily Evening Transcript*, aided by the *Boston Traveller*. Opposed to them in politics was a strong group of Democratic newspapers, among them the *Courier*, which became downright Copperhead before the war ended. The cultured *Transcript* set its policy solidly behind Lincoln when it praised his inaugural address, saying: "The language is level to the popular mind—the plain homespun language of a man accustomed to talk with 'the folks' and 'the neighbors,' the language of a man of vital common sense."[12] The *Transcript* quoted other Massachusetts papers as lauding the President, among them the *Worcester Spy*, *Salem Gazette*, and the *Herald*, at Newburyport.[13] It also pointed out that the *Providence* (R. I.) *Journal*, a Republican journal that offset the political effect of the Democratic *Post*, said that Lincoln's "honest, simple, straightforward declarations of fidelity to the spirit of our government and Constitution must . . . awaken a response in every patriotic heart."[14]

The *Boston Post*, foe of Abolitionists, charged early in 1862 that Congress cut pay and increased working hours in the navy yards. It made a play for the white working class, saying: "The sympathizing roll up the white of their eye for the negro, but when it comes to northern mechanics, it is a horse of another color. . . . The people will get their eyes open after awhile and place a proper estimate upon the negro politician."[15]

A few months later, the *Boston Post* charged Horace Greeley was a war profiteer, "engaged in a large and very profitable gun contract." It added: "Greeley is the philanthropist who wanted dishonest contractors summarily hanged."[16] The charge obviously was baseless.

The *Boston Herald* joined the 1862 defeatism chorus with a tirade against Governor John A. Andrew, whose order sent the 6th Massachusetts Regiment to Washington at President Lincoln's call. The *Herald* said:

Had it not been for such men as Governor Andrew there would have been no war . . . and thousands who have perished . . . would be at home pursuing their peaceful avocations. It is about time this bombastic and fanatical stuff was played out.[17]

Growing more bitter against Lincoln and his administration each year, the *Boston Courier*, upset by the election of 1864, gave vent to this:

Gigantic efforts at corruption, unheard of attempts to intimidate voters, the forcible application of illegal tests of qualification—these have been the means by which the unscrupulous and profligate agents of the Administration and their besotted followers have endeavored to compel a people, born free, but grown too careless of their liberties, to submit to a yoke, which men worthy of freedom would regard as disgraceful as it is contemptible.[18]

The *Boston Pioneer*, described by the Copperhead press in the West as a "German Republican paper," came out strongly against Lincoln in the middle of the war with this declaration:

We think the support of Lincoln, under any circumstances, to be the most pernicious policy, and indirect treason to the Republic; and we hope that nobody who tries to deserve the name of radical will soil himself with participation in such treachery.[19]

After a wavering start, Samuel Bowles, editor of the *Springfield* (Mass.) *Republican*, took a stand for Lincoln and all his policies that made his newspaper, small in comparison with the big-city dailies, a national voice. At first a doubting Thomas of Lincoln's capabilities, Bowles became his idolator.

In the Wigwam at Chicago when Lincoln was nominated, Bowles looked upon the result there as "the triumph of politically available mediocrity over the superior talents of other candidates."[20]

Taking a leaf from Horace Greeley's notebook, the *Republican* said a week after Lincoln's election that South Carolina should be allowed to secede if it sought to do so peacefully, adding: "A Union that must be maintained by force is not desirable."[21] A few days before Lincoln was inaugurated, Bowles wrote to a friend that the President-elect was "a simple Susan" and that the men who nominated him had only their labor for their trouble.[22]

During the first months of war, the *Republican* strove to live down past declarations and advocated full military measures. It was highly critical of those who thought otherwise, saying in an editorial:

There are three ways in which a Northern man can give aid and comfort to the traitors who are making war on the Union. One is by joining them personally and helping them to fight their battles. Another is by remaining at home and stealthily sending them arms and ammunitions of war. And still another is affording them moral support by assuring them that the rebellion cannot be put down by force and by advocation of concessions to the traitors, or consent to the dissolution of the Union, if they cannot be coaxed back by concession and compromise.[23]

At the start of the war, the *Republican* had about 6,000 circulation, but a weekly edition, to which Bowles gave his personal attention, had a circulation of 12,000 scattered over several states.[24] Springfield was a war-boom town, the place where the famous rifle was manufactured. The city doubled in population, and the *Republican* doubled in circulation.[25]

Editor Bowles came to look upon Lincoln in a manner akin to worship, fully aware of the stature of the man. He said in an editorial:

Abraham Lincoln is the representative of the simple truthfulness and the honest and all-enduring patriotism of the American people. He is a man who believes in the people, believes himself to be the agent of the people, believes in the rule of the majority, believes in the power and prevalence of the right, believes in human equality, and believes that the Union can and will be saved from disruption. . . .

He stands out from all the men of his section, and his time—and not alone by reason of his office—as representative of the republicanism of the republic; the champion of democratic principle, the friend of the Union and the Constitution, and the foe of all class combination. . . . His way of serving the country is recognized as the only way.[26]

William Lloyd Garrison, editor and publisher of *The Liberator*, an Abolition weekly published at Boston, was one of the outstanding personalities of New England journalism. *The Liberator*, founded in 1831, flourished until slavery was abolished.[27]

George G. Benedict, editor of the *Burlington* (Vt.) *Free Press*, enlisted in the army, was commissioned a lieutenant, and helped repulse Pickett's charge at Gettysburg.[28] George G. Fogg, editor of the *Independent Democrat* at Concord, N. H., exerted wide influence in keeping his state in the Republican column. From 1856 to 1864, he was a member of the Republican National Committee. As a delegate to the national convention, he was a strong Lincoln man. After the election, he was appointed Minister to Switzerland by the President.[29]

North Carolina born Joseph R. Hawley, editor of the *Hartford Press*, is said to have been the first man to volunteer for military duty in the Civil War from Connecticut. When Lincoln called for troops, Hawley recruited a company, armed it at his own expense, and saw it accepted in twenty-four hours. In the Union shambles at Bull Run, Hawley kept his head and won commendation for his conduct. He rose to the rank of major general.[30]

W. H. Simpson, editor of the *Republican Journal* at Belfast, Me., was arrested on August 13, 1864, and taken before the United States District Court at Bangor to face an indictment that charged he gave aid and comfort to the enemy by publishing an editorial critical of the army draft. He pleaded not guilty, and the case was continued until the next term of court. He was released on personal recognizance for his appearance.[31]

One of the last newspaper mobbings while Lincoln still lived was staged in New England. It occurred on April 10, 1865, when the office of the *States and Union* at Portsmouth, N. H., was destroyed. The city was celebrating the great Union victory in Virginia. A mob, estimated at two thousand men, formed in front of the newspaper office and demanded that Editor J. C. Foster display the American flag. He was believed pro-Southern in his sympathies.

Foster, "pale with fear and rage," poked a flagstaff from a window and gave the colors a "slight toss with his hand." The mob was incensed at what it thought was Foster's disdainful attitude and rushed into the building.

Foster grabbed his office records and fled through a rear door. The mob carried out every piece of equipment in the plant and piled the wreckage in the street. The Mayor finally appeared on the scene, read the riot act to the mob, and it dispersed.[32]

Across the New England border in Canada, a newspaper that upheld the North was twice wrecked by a mob. On the night of December 19, 1861, the office of *The St. Croix Herald* at St. Stephen, New Brunswick, was torn up and a large quantity of the type destroyed.[33] The paper refused to change its policy, and on July 28, 1862, a mob tore the plant to bits. Office furniture was smashed, the press wrecked, the type scattered, and equipment thrown into the St. Croix River. Months elapsed before it could be refitted and resume publication. The *New York Tribune* commented in an editorial:

The lovely neutrality of Great Britain had another illustration a few days ago. . . . The printing office of *The St. Croix Herald* was destroyed by a mob. Reason: It has been in favor of the North while the vast majority of the subjects of Queen Victoria are anything that is opposed to the United States.[34]

# 23  A Governor's Backbone

CONGRESSMAN CLEMENT LAIRD VALLANDIGHAM of Dayton, darling of the radical Democratic press in Ohio, led the fight on the floor of the House against President Lincoln's impending Emancipation Proclamation. On December 5, 1862, he stirred the North by offering a series of resolutions in which he declared "that, as the war was originally waged for the purpose of defending and maintaining the supremacy of the Constitution and the preservation of the Union . . . whosoever shall attempt to pervert the same to a war of subjugation, and for overthrowing or interfering with the rights of the states, and to abolish slavery, would be guilty of a crime against the Constitution and the Union."[1] The House, by a vote of seventy-nine to fifty, tabled the resolutions.[2]

Vallandigham was a member of the extreme state-rights wing of the Democratic party, recognized by the loyal press as the outstanding Copperhead in the North. The New York *Sun* was one of the first newspapers to call the turn on him, saying in July of 1861:

The course of Mr. Vallandigham, M. C., from Ohio provokes severe comment. He is heels over head in love with the worst men of the South and intends to spare no pains to embarrass the administration, trouble its action and misrepresent its policy. He will be quite as likely to get himself into trouble.[3]

Vallandigham was born at New Lisbon, Ohio, in 1820, and received an academic education. He taught school at Snow Hill, Md., for two years and returned to Ohio in 1840. He was admitted to the bar in 1842, served in the state legislature, and edited the *Dayton Daily Empire* for two years. He ran for Congress in 1857 and was declared defeated. He contested the election and won, taking his seat May 25, 1858. He ran for reelection and won, serving until March 3, 1863.[4]

When Vallandigham went to Washington, the *Dayton Daily Empire* became his mouthpiece. The editor actually in charge of the *Empire* was J. F. Bollmeyer, but Vallandigham still controlled it and probably owned it. Vallandigham was an intimate of Samuel Medary, editor of *The Crisis,* and they were often seen together in Columbus, an association noted in observing Republican newspapers.

When Governor Dennison of Ohio prepared to answer Lincoln's call for troops after the fall of Fort Sumter, the *Empire* said:

Governor Dennison has pledged the blood and treasure of Ohio to back up a Republican administration in its contemplated attack upon the people of the South. . . . What right has he to make any such pledge? Does he promise to head the troops which he intends to send down South to butcher men, women and children of that section?[5]

That was the song the *Empire* sang in its daily and weekly editions, while in Washington, Congressman Vallandigham was making passionate speeches of the same stripe. By the fall of 1862, feeling was running high against the *Empire*, and businessmen of Dayton had withdrawn all advertising from it.[6]

On the morning of November 1, Editor Bollmeyer was shot to death in the street by Henry M. Brown, after an argument. The thirty-two-year-old editor was on his way to market with a basket on his arm. The two men had known each other for years.[7]

Brown was arrested and taken to jail. The city was thrown into turmoil. One report said the men quarreled over a dog, that one of Brown's sons had shot the editor's pet. Another said Brown disliked the editorial policy of the *Empire* and had threatened to shoot both Bollmeyer and Vallandigham.[8]

In the afternoon, a mob stormed the jail but was beaten back by the police, and the leaders were arrested. The town was quiet until nightfall when the mob re-formed. This time it brought two cannons, loaded with powder and scraps of iron. Again the mob stormed the jail and fought the police. Four rioters were shot. Mayor W. H. Gillespie, described as a "bosom friend of the deceased," sent a plea to Cincinnati for help. Five companies of regular troops came by special train and restored order at midnight.[9]

The Democrats of Dayton proposed that a monument be set up in honor of Bollmeyer, and a public fund was raised. When it was learned the editor had died penniless, the money was turned over to his widow and child.

In the neighboring town of Springfield, the Democratic Club passed a resolution saying Bollmeyer had been "murdered on the streets of Dayton by an Abolitionist because he dared advocate freedom of speech, liberty of the press, and the doctrines of the American Constitution." The resolution also said the slaying was a "natural result of the partisan animosities and vindictive teachings of the Abolition party." It referred to Bollmeyer as the "first victim of Abolition violence."[10]

Brown was tried for the slaying almost a year later. He insisted he shot Bollmeyer in self-defense and was acquitted. The Democratic press screamed in derision. The *Cincinnati Enquirer* called the trial a farce. The *Empire*, under a new editor, sadly reported there were "cheers and hurrahs" in the courtroom when the verdict was announced.[11]

Vallandigham's attempt to block the Emancipation Proclamation was made just a month after his editor was buried. He rose to new heights in his denunciation of the Lincoln administration after emancipation had been declared. On January 14, with time running out on him because of his defeat at the previous election by Major General Robert C. Schenck, he took the floor to denounce the war, saying in part:

A war for the Union! Was the Union thus made? Was it ever thus preserved? History will record that after nearly six thousand years of folly and wickedness in every form and administration of government, theocratic, democratic, monarchic, oligarchic, despotic, and mixed, it was reserved to American statesmanship in the 19th century of the Christian era to try the grand experiment, on a scale the most costly and gigantic in its proportions, of creating love by force, and developing fraternal affection by war; and history will record, too, on the same page, the utter, disastrous, and most bloody failure of the experiment.[12]

With the end of the Thirty-seventh Congress on March 3, 1863, Vallandigham returned to his home at Dayton and started a speaking tour that took him all over Ohio. He was heard by thousands, including some who listened out of curiosity, according to newspaper accounts. His speeches were published in their voluminous entirety in *The Crisis* and the *Empire*.

The editors of Ohio's Democratic press who followed in Vallandigham's footsteps took their papers down the road to ruin. More than a score of antiwar newspapers felt either the fury of mob violence or the hand of the Federal government. Although arrests were made frequently, they did not keep pace with public opinion, and in instances where the government failed to act, the people took matters into their own hands. Nowhere in the North was the purpose of the people to kill off that segment of the press injurious to the Union cause more prominently displayed than in Ohio.

The *Clermont County Sun*, published at Batavia, was one of the first newspapers in the state to feel the power of public opinion. In August of 1861, the *Sun* heard it was to be destroyed because of its secession sympathies. In a page-one editorial, the editor charged that the "Abolition clique has been urging the military necessity" of wrecking his plant.[13]

At midnight on August 22, 1861, a mob entered the office of the *Stark County Democrat* at Canton and left it a shambles because the editor, Archibald McGregor, was preaching opposition to the war. A public meeting of Democrats demanded that the Canton city council reimburse McGregor for his loss, and it appropriated three thousand dollars for a settlement.[14] The editor charged there were fourteen men in the mob and that all had been recognized. That fact may have had something to do with the council's willingness to pay. In an open letter, published in *The Crisis*, McGregor said the leader of the mob was

Lieutenant Edward Meyer, son of the Mayor. Nine men were arrested, including the lieutenant, and bond was posted for them by "prominent Republicans." The case ended there.[15]

McGregor was sitting in his office on Sunday morning, October 12, 1862, when Provost Marshal Anson Pease of Massillon and a file of soldiers entered. They were accompanied by W. K. Miller, Republican postmaster of Canton. Pease told McGregor he was under arrest, and the editor demanded to know by whose authority.

"No matter, come right along!" the postmaster told him.

As the editor was led away, he called out to a crowd on the sidewalk to witness his arrest as "another instance of Abolition tyranny." He was taken by train to Camp Mansfield, an army training base.

The editor's wife, Martha McGregor, took over the job of editing the paper. In a signed editorial, she appealed to the Democrats, "Falter not, for our cause it is just and conquer we must."[16]

Medary's *Crisis* squawked like an old hen whose chick has been snatched by a hawk. It said:

> The whole Republican press is jubilant. What a crew of modern devils these Abolition editors are. . . . A noble wife, a true woman, let tyrants blush. Mrs. McGregor, whose husband is in a military prison for no cause whatever but that he is a Democrat, is filling her husband's post admirably.[17]

McGregor was held at camp, where he was treated as a guest, until the first of November when he was released with "nothing being proved" against him. Canton Democrats received him with "demonstrations of great joy."[18]

*The Mirror*, a Democratic paper published at Marion, was hanged in effigy in front of its own office on a September evening in 1861. Democrats came running and dispersed the crowd.[19] During that same month, the *Jackson Express* escaped destruction when a friend tipped off the editor that a mob was coming. Democrats formed a cordon around the office, and the attack did not materialize.[20]

Reverend Sabin Hough, "a clergyman of Swedenborgian persuasion," was arrested at Cincinnati on a charge of treason in September of 1861. His newly established weekly, *The Banner of Reunion*, was suppressed. Hough was taken off to prison.[21] A Cincinnati newspaper laid his arrest to an editorial in which he said: "There is no need of this war, nor any reason why it should continue. It cannot and will not bring back the states that have withdrawn."[22] The *Bucyrus Forum* was damaged by an excited crowd of partisans on September 8, 1861.[23]

When the editors of radical Democratic newspapers found a story that would fit any community, such as propaganda that made fun of Abolitionists, they passed it around. The *Ohio Patriot* of New Lisbon published a story of this character that was widely reprinted. It said in part:

One of the kind of Abolitionists we have spoken of . . . had a house dog . . . which was a great favorite in the family. He takes the *New York Tribune* and . . . generally gets everything wrong. Reading over the tax bill, he conceived the idea that the law had passed taxing dogs a dollar a head. . . . This lousy, ranting Abolitionist . . . murdered his poor, dumb dog to cheat the government out of a dollar. He is a patriot. . . . The Democrat who pays his taxes and wants an adjustment of the difficulties to save human life and money is a traitor.[24]

On a Sunday morning in the latter part of June, 1862, two men drove into Circleville in a carriage and registered at the hotel. They sat around until eleven o'clock that night when they went to the home of John W. Kees, editor of the *Circleville Watchman*, a violently antiwar weekly newspaper, and told him he was under arrest by order of the War Department. Kees asked to see the warrant; it was signed by C. P. Wolcott, an assistant Secretary of War, and was directed to William Scott, a Cincinnati provost marshal.

Kees had retired, and the officers ordered him to dress quickly. His wife asked for time to pack clothing for him, but he was placed in a carriage and driven off. Before they left town, the officers ordered the *Watchman* office locked for four months, with the keys held by some "trusty person." Taken to Columbus, Kees was put aboard an eastbound train at three o'clock in the morning.[25]

When Circleville awakened and found the editor gone, there was much excitement among the Democrats. They called a "large and enthusiastical" meeting, in which it was resolved to establish a new Democratic newspaper and a series of resolutions was passed. One said: "We denounce the illegal and despotic suppression of the *Circleville Watchman* as a tyrannical attack upon the liberties of speech and the press, for the purpose of influencing the coming October elections. . . . We have no language severe enough to portray our detestation of these corrupt tools, who plot in secret conclave the injury of their fellow citizens."

The Democrats also pointed out that "kidnapping is in Ohio a high crime and aiding and abetting the same a penitentiary offense." They insisted the Constitution guaranteed that the trial of all crimes, except in cases of impeachment, shall be by jury.[26]

The next act in the Ohio drama was forecast by Joseph Olds of Circleville when he wrote a letter to his father, Dr. Edson B. Olds, of Lancaster, a former Democratic Congressman. Joseph said the Republicans were jubilant and "it is in their mouths that you are to go next."[27] The letter was published in *The Crisis* on July 9.

On August 12, Provost Marshal Scott went to Lancaster with a warrant for the arrest of Edson Olds, signed by Wolcott, which charged "disloyalty, using treasonable language and interfering with enlistment."

Scott and his assistant reached the home of Dr. Olds at ten o'clock that night. Olds was in bed, and his daughter and son-in-law, who lived with him, tried to keep the officers from entering his room. Scott crashed the door, and a fight started. The uproar awakened the neighbors, and someone raised a cry of "fire." The yard was crowded with people when the officers emerged from the house with their prisoner. A man asked Olds whether they should attempt to take him away from the officers, and Scott threatened, with drawn pistol, to kill the first person who made a move. The prisoner was taken to Columbus.

The next afternoon, Olds was placed on a train en route to New York and Fort Lafayette.[28]

"Dr. Edson B. Olds, the traitor, has been arrested and sent to Fort Lafayette," said the *Cincinnati Commercial* in language the Republicans liked to read. "Dr. Olds was the meanest and noisiest of the nest of traitors in Fairfield county."[29]

*The Crisis* gave the Democratic version under these headlines: "Another Constitutional Outrage—Dr. E. B. Olds Kidnapped—The Liberties of the People in Danger." The story said Olds was "dragged from his bed and the bosom of his family . . . by Wm. Scott and other hired tools of the Lincoln, unscrupulous and despotic administration."[30]

The Democrats at Circleville in the meantime launched their new paper, the *Circleville Democrat*. Kees wrote to the editor from Washington, and the *Democrat* quoted him as saying: "I am once more at liberty, without trial or accusers, and if I shall regain my health, hope to return to Circleville in a few weeks."[31] He had been held in Old Capitol.

The condition of Kees's health was much worse than he indicated. A few weeks later, *The Crisis* said:

We regret to learn that Mr. Kees, late editor of the *Circleville Watchman*, has from his late persecution and confinement in an eastern bastile, become a raving maniac and is at present in the Lunatic Asylum of this city. This is a sad affair for his wife and children.[32]

After the arrest of Dr. Olds, the two Lancaster newspapers, the Democratic *Eagle* and the Republican *Gazette*, exchanged hot words. The *Eagle* said the *Gazette* had misquoted one of Olds's speeches, and the *Gazette* retorted with a prophecy that the editor of the *Eagle* would soon be arrested.

The Governor of Ohio was David Tod, elected by the Republicans although he was a Democrat and vice-president of the Charleston convention in 1860. Tod was a strong supporter of the Union and lent all his strength and the power of the state to the Lincoln administration. On August 29, 1862, he sent to Charles Roland, editor of the Lancaster *Eagle*, a note which said: "I desire an interview with you. Please call upon me Monday morning."[33]

Roland appeared as requested. Tod went directly to the point. He told the editor the "general course" of the *Eagle* had been objectionable; that its policy on enlistment and its attitude toward the arrest of Olds were wrong. The Governor said he himself ordered Olds taken into custody.

Tod said he especially disliked the wording of handbills published by the *Eagle* to advertise a meeting of Democrats to protest Olds's arrest. He had intended to order the arrest of Roland and have him sent to Fort Warren at Boston but on second thought decided to have a talk with him. He demanded Roland tell him whether he planned to continue publication "in the spirit of the handbills," adding: "If you do, you shall be arrested. I have the backbone to do it!"

"I supposed," the editor replied, "I was living under a government of written constitutions and laws, and in the publication of the *Ohio Eagle* I have adopted them as my guide."

"I am to be the judge," said Tod, "of what you may and what you may not publish, constitutions and laws notwithstanding. Unless you agree not to publish the *Eagle* in the spirit of the handbills, it will be suppressed, regardless of consequences."[34]

The Governor turned on his heel and left the room. Roland went back to Lancaster and wrote a story that featured Tod's "backbone." The heading was, "Our Interview With Governor Tod." It ruined Tod's political career.

The radical wing of the Democratic press detested the Governor because he quit the party to support Lincoln. He was immediately dubbed "Backbone" Tod. When the time came for renomination, he was passed by, a matter of "deep regret" to President Lincoln.[35] Upon the resignation of Secretary of the Treasury Chase, President Lincoln nominated Tod for the office, but he declined, pleading ill health.[36]

The Cabinet seat went to William P. Fessenden. Tod died four years later at sixty-three.

For months after Tod's interview with Roland, the Democratic editors ridiculed the Governor, one of their choice bits being some verses that went like this:

> Once on a time there was a Tod,
> Governor Tod with a backbone;
> He ruled and reigned with iron rod,
> And laughed to hear his victims groan.
> > Tody, Tod, Tod, O! Gov'nor Tod,
> > What a backbone has Gov'nor Tod.
>
> Saucy Charles Roland, how dare you,
> Print the *Eagle* against my will?
> Quoth Davy, the king, in a rage, too,
> An omen to Charley of ill.
> > Tody, Tod, Tod, O! Gov'nor Tod,
> > A stiff backbone has Gov'nor Tod.[37]

"Saucy Charles Roland" escaped arrest, but he could not escape the wrath of Lancaster boys serving in the Union army. On a cold Saturday night in January of 1864, a group of veterans home on furlough broke into the *Eagle* office and wrecked it from top to bottom.[38]

While Dr. Olds was in Fort Lafayette, he was elected to the Ohio legislature at a special election to fill a vacancy. He came home from prison to be greeted by a crowd of 12,000, according to the *Eagle's* estimate.[39] He brought suit against Tod on charges of kidnaping and later asked personal damages of one hundred thousand dollars, but nothing came of either action. Editor Kees, having miraculously recovered his mental faculties, vainly brought suit against the Governor for thirty thousand dollars.[40]

The Columbus *Ohio Statesman* on April 24, 1864, carried this item: "John W. Kees, late of the *Circleville Watchman*, left last night for Nevada to seek his fortune in that remote land of promise."

A. R. Van Cleaf, editor of the *Lebanon Citizen*, "the organ of the Democratic party in Warren county," was asleep in his boardinghouse on the night of August 12, 1862, when told a mob was wrecking his newspaper office. By the time he got there, a crowd of more than two hundred persons had stoned the building, breaking the windows and doors. The type was in the street.

Unable to publish for a few days, Van Cleaf wrote an "Address to the People," printed by the *Dayton Daily Empire*. He charged the mob was incited by the editor of the *Western Star*, Lebanon's Republican newspaper. The editor of the *Western Star* was Dr. James Scott, a member of the state legislature and candidate for Congress.[41]

The *Republican*, published at Marietta, was not all its name implied and in March of 1863 was visited by a mob. *The Crisis* reported that the *Republican* was wrecked by "Abolition mobites."[42]

The *Cincinnati Enquirer* reported in August of 1863 that J. G. Doren, "the amiable and gentlemanly editor of the *Brown County Argus*, was lately set upon by a gang of Abolition ruffians in Ripley township—the only Abolition one in the county—and was shockingly beaten by them."[43] A mob, said to have consisted of Republicans, scattered the type of the *Cadiz Sentinel* a month later.[44]

The *Mahoning Sentinel*, published at Youngstown by John M. Webb, was sacked by a mob of civilians and Union soldiers the night of January 28, 1864. Webb told the story of the mobbing in what he called a "diminutive extra" published on the press of his Republican rival, the *Youngstown Register*. He complained the mob threw type cases out the windows, "which they had failed to open." He printed a long list of damage and added, "In short, our office is a wreck."[45] The full flavor of the times was caught by *The Crisis* in its biased account of the mobbing, saying:

A squad of drunken soldiers, intoxicated and instigated by the Abolitionists of Youngstown, entered and totally destroyed the office of the *Mahoning Sentinel* at Youngstown, Ex-Governor Tod's place of residence. The *Sentinel* refused to join the Abolition party when Tod did, and thereby incurred the undying hatred of that renegade.[46]

The *Toledo Commercial* reported the Youngstown mob actually consisted of only five soldiers and that three of them were Democrats when they enlisted in the army.[47]

Another newspaper mobbing was staged at Wauseon three weeks later, on February 18. The *Ohio Democratic Press* had suspended publication, owing to lack of financial support, but left a record of strong opposition to the war. Company K, 38th Regiment, Ohio Volunteer Infantry, an outfit enrolled in that part of Ohio, came home on furlough and did the job. The Wauseon correspondent of *The Crisis* wrote, "The *Press* office is a perfect wreck. Thus we drift along."[48]

By this time, the Northern press was amazed at the chain of events against the peace newspapers in Ohio. The *Boston Courier* said: "The mobbing of the Democratic newspapers has been revived as a pleasant Republican pastime."[49]

But the mobs still had work to do. On a Saturday night in March of 1864, soldiers destroyed the office of the *Democrat* at Greenville. The mob extended its operations next door to the law office of William Allen, a former Democratic United States senator. *The Crisis* made its usual comment: "Republicans incited soldiers to do the job."[50]

M. P. Bean, editor of the *Ohio Messenger* at Fremont, stopped publication of his newspaper in the early days of the war, took a commission in the Union army, raised a regiment of volunteers, and went to the front. He later returned to Fremont, resuming his work as editor. On the night of April 14, 1864, his press was beaten into old iron, kegs of ink were spilled, and the type scattered the length of the main street of the town. No witnesses could be found, and Fremont heard rumors that Bean himself wrecked his plant for political effect. Bean denied the charge in a public statement.[51]

At Hamilton, John McElwee, editor of the *True Telegraph*, ran a paper that was for peace at any price. On July 21, 1864, he said in an editorial:

It is our subtle conviction that the war, if protracted, will bring anarchy upon the North, and ultimately some form of despotic government. . . . With this understanding of the issue before us, who . . . shall gainsay our right to discuss it fully and freely?[52]

The arrest of McElwee on November 14, 1864, revealed that he had been indicted by the grand jury for the Southern District court of Ohio on four counts of treason. He was taken to Cincinnati, arraigned before Judge Humphrey H. Leavitt, and he gave bond for three thousand dollars, signed by Alexander Long, an Ohio Democratic Congressman.[53]

McElwee defied the government in an editorial that said: "Come what punishment may, nor jot nor tittle will we abate of the opinion set forth in the article which seems to form the principal count of the indictment."[54]

People in Hamilton talked of the difference between the editor of the *True Telegraph* and the editor of the *Hamilton Intelligencer*, the Republican paper. Minor Millikin, who purchased the *Intelligencer* soon after he was graduated by Miami University at Oxford, Ohio, in 1858, sold it when war came and enlisted in the 1st Ohio Cavalry. He rose to colonel and was killed at the Battle of Stone River. He was a college classmate of Whitelaw Reid, who covered Stone River for the *Cincinnati Gazette*.[55]

On March 22, 1865, *The Crisis* said: "The *Cleveland Plain Dealer* has succumbed to the pressure of the times and has ceased to exist." That story marked the end of the road for an interval of a newspaper that changed during the war from Union Democracy to the brand taught by Vallandigham. The paper had attempted the impossible—defense of slavery in the Western Reserve, a section predominantly Abolitionist. Under its founder, Joseph W. Gray, the *Plain Dealer* supported Douglas for President. Because of that stand, Gray was removed as postmaster of Cleveland by President Buchanan.[56]

The other Cleveland dailies, the *Herald* and the *Leader*, were Republican. With the outbreak of war, Gray took his cue from his hero Douglas, backed the Lincoln administration and all steps taken to put down the rebellion. He supported Tod for governor and accused Vallandigham of playing with treason.[57]

Gray died on May 26, 1862, from the effect of having been accidentally shot in the eye by his son with a toy pistol. The *Plain Dealer* passed into the hands of Gray's nephew, John S. Stephensen, chairman of the Cuyahoga County Democratic central committee, who abruptly changed the policy of the newspaper.[58]

This about-face caused the *Leader* to make some nasty remarks under the heading, "The Dog Returns to His Vomit."[59] The *Plain Dealer* became the northern Ohio voice for Vallandigham and published all his speeches, while assailing the Lincoln administration, becoming most bitter in 1864. It called Lincoln a "dangerous character" and listed fourteen reasons why he should not be given a second term.[60]

The *Plain Dealer* quit on either March 7 or 8, 1865—the date is not clear—and on March 10 Gray's widow asked the court to remove Stephensen as the administrator of the estate. The suit forced the resignation of Stephensen.[61] On the following April 9, a joker went to the deserted *Plain Dealer* office and raised a white flag.[62] On May 3, 1865, *The Crisis* said: "Hon. Wm. W. Armstrong, late secretary of state of Ohio, has revived the *Cleveland Plain Dealer* and will publish it as a Democratic newspaper."

On the editorial page of the *Cincinnati Gazette* of April 4, 1863, an article headed "The Two Enquirers," said in part:

We have before us a copy of the *Knoxville Register* (rebel) which contains a letter from Richmond on the 8th of March, devoted to the *Richmond Enquirer* and the *Cincinnati Enquirer*. The writer says the latter is the better of the two.

The *Cincinnati Enquirer* was the leading Democratic organ in the Ohio Valley, with a circulation in three states—Ohio, Indiana, and Kentucky—and it had no party rival in Cincinnati. The editor was James

J. Faran, and associated with him was the wealthy Washington McLean. Faran, as postmaster of Cincinnati, met with the same treatment from President Buchanan that was accorded Gray at Cleveland; he was removed because the *Enquirer* supported Douglas.[63]

It appeared at the start of the war that the *Enquirer* might support Lincoln. Then it was in the War Democrat category, but it slipped gradually and ended up in the Vallandigham camp.[64]

The *Enquirer* was looked upon as undesirable by generals in some military districts. Burnside banned it from Kentucky in 1863. The *Enquirer* carriers took their papers across the Ohio River as usual but were promptly relieved of them by the provost marshal. Postmasters were told they must not deliver the *Enquirer* to Kentucky subscribers.[65]

The *Enquirer* was stamped as contraband in Kentucky after a widely publicized outburst against it in Indiana. Feeling against the newspaper came into the open at Milford when the women of that town addressed a petition to "President Lincoln and General Horatio G. Wright" or "those in authority whom it may concern," asking the *Enquirer* be suppressed. The petition said: "We firmly believe that the *Enquirer,* and other papers of the same character, are the chief instigators of all secret rebellion in the North."[66]

A few days later, March 8, 1863, the *Enquirer* published a story that was declared an insult to wives of soldiers. It was described by the *Cincinnati Gazette* as:

A long and laborious effort to convince the soldiers that the war is carried on solely to create offices and rich contractors and benefit the negro. . . . It held out to the soldiers in the field the picture of their families neglected in the midst of the fortunes accumulated by the designing supporters of the war at home, their wives and children, their widows and orphans coming to want, while the Aid Societies were only means to prostitute their wives.[67]

According to the *Gazette*, this is what the *Enquirer* actually said:

. . . they (the soldiers) come back to find their places filled, their families possibly scattered, their wives perhaps under the care of some charitable agent of an Aid Society, who has found that there are more ways than one to administer consolation.[68]

The slur on soldiers' wives aroused indignation in Indianapolis. In response to a notice in the *Indianapolis Daily Journal,* a crowd gathered at a main intersection on the night of March 16 and heard Colonel A. D. Streight of the 51st Indiana Regiment denounce the *Enquirer* and urge boys to stop selling it.[69]

Two days later, soldiers met the Cincinnati train bringing newspapers into Indianapolis and seized all copies of the *Enquirer*, throwing them into Pogue's Run. One newspaper boy got away with his bundle by outfooting the soldiers down an alley.[70]

Major General Henry B. Carrington, in command of the District of Indiana, paid the news agent for loss of his *Enquirers* and arrested several soldiers. He issued a statement that only the government could take action against a newspaper.[71]

The *Enquirer* was compelled to publish a retraction of the offending article on March 19. The editor blandly explained he had not read the story in question until he saw it reprinted from the *Enquirer* by the *Nashville* (Tenn.) *Union*. The *Cincinnati Gazette* remarked that "this excuse is exceedingly lame."[72]

The Columbus *Ohio State Journal* said it was "our candid opinion" that the *Enquirer* "ought not to be allowed to circulate anywhere." The editorial continued: "It is a paper directly in aid of the rebellion to the extent that it opposes the government and discourages the war. Of this fact there can be no mistake or doubt."[73]

While trying to capture the Confederate raider, Major General John H. Morgan, in his dash across southern Ohio in 1863, state militia, stationed at Jackson, wrecked the office of the *Jackson Express*, a Democratic weekly.

After repairs were made, Editor Bowen said in an editorial that a crowd cheered as type was thrown into the street. "They thought," he wrote, "it a suitable time to hold a jubilee over the destruction of a printing office."[74]

# 24 The Prentice Story

IN A THREE-DAY battle that opened December 31, 1862, along Stone River near Murfreesboro, Tenn., the Confederates were defeated, with a total loss on both sides of more than twenty thousand men.[1]

The victory was a balm to the North, still reeling under the shock of General Burnside's bloody blunder at Fredericksburg, Va., on December 11.[2] But far more important, it marked the last major Confederate attempt to recover Kentucky, a state which had vainly hoped to keep out of "this unnatural strife."[3]

The Kentucky press was preponderantly pro-Southern and wholly out of step with the masses, whose choice of Union men for elective offices kept the state out of the Confederacy, although many young men "went South."

Shortly after Stone River, President Lincoln expressed his admiration of the loyalty and bravery of "Kentucky sons" bearing Union arms.[4] He could hardly have said the same thing of the newspaper editors.

Three days before the fighting opened along Stone River, *The New York Times* said:

> Maj. Prentice, a son of the editor of the *Louisville Journal*, recently came into Gen. Rosecrans' lines below Nashville. He appeared very anxious to see the *Journal* and sent word to his father that he was still "fat, saucy and rebellious."[5]

Major Clarence Joseph Prentice, serving in the Confederate army, was the younger son of George D. Prentice. He enlisted in the rebel army as soon as war broke out. The other son, William Courtland, who lived on a farm near Louisville, joined the Confederate General Morgan's cavalry in the summer of 1862. Less than a month after he enlisted, he was killed in battle at Augusta, Ky., and his body was sent home for burial.[6]

His father wrote an editorial that was reprinted many times in the North. It said in part:

> Oh, if he had fallen in his country's service, fallen with his burning eyes fixed in love and devotion upon the flag that for more than three-fourths of a century has been a star of worship to his ancestors, his early death, though still terrible, might have been borne by a father's heart; but alas, the reflection that he fell in armed rebellion, against that glorious old banner, now the emblem of the greatest and holiest cause the world ever knew, is full of desolation and almost of despair.[7]

The father of those two rebel soldiers was born in Connecticut in 1802. He was graduated from Brown University and admitted to the bar but never practiced. He edited the *New England Weekly Review* for two years. In 1830, he wrote a campaign biography for Henry Clay, and the Kentucky Whigs invited him to publish a newspaper in Louisville. He founded the *Journal* and became an outstanding journalist ten years before Greeley launched the *New York Tribune*.[8]

Prentice married Harriette Benham, member of a prominent Cincinnati family.

By 1860, Prentice was recognized in both America and Europe as a poet and wit. His editorial paragraphs were collected in a book, *Prenticeana*.[9] The story of the press of Kentucky during the Civil War revolves around him.

Prentice and his newspaper did not support Lincoln in 1860, but even before he was elected, the Louisville editor began to pester him with unsolicited advice and later requests that ranged from advance copies of his speeches to political jobs. On October 26, 1860, Prentice wrote to Lincoln, saying:

There is evidently a very strong probability of your being elected to the Presidency by the popular vote. Whilst I have the strongest confidence in both your personal and political integrity, and have at no time hesitated to express it in my paper, I have warmly opposed and am still opposing your election because I greatly fear its influence upon the Peace of the country. You undoubtedly know the condition of public sentiment in the far South as well as I do. I dread lest, almost as soon as the fact of your election shall be proclaimed, a desperate blow will be struck for the dismemberment of the Union. Under these circumstances I take the liberty of suggesting to you whether it will not be advisable for you to prepare a letter to some friend, which, in the event of your election, shall be published at once. A letter setting forth your conservative views and intentions and therefore calculated to assure all good citizens of the South to take from the disunion its early excuse or pretext for treason.

I hope I am not presuming too far in thus addressing you. If I am, pardon me.[10]

Lincoln's reply is dated "October 29." He called Prentice's attention to the fact that his newspaper was supporting Douglas and said that if he tried for a month he could make himself no clearer than his speeches already published.[11]

Prentice wrote to Lincoln again on January 24, 1861, and tried to explain why he had opposed his election, insisting he brought "some odium" on himself because he spoke kindly of him. He promised to do Lincoln justice in the event of disunion.

The last half of the letter was a request that Lincoln appoint John J. Piatt, a friend whom he described as a poet and a genius, to some office. Piatt was engaged to a "poetess," but they were too poor to marry. If Piatt got the job, they could wed and their first son would be named for either Prentice or Lincoln![12]

And again, on January 31, Prentice sent a letter to Lincoln. This asked for an advance copy of the inaugural speech. Lincoln replied he was still working on it but would send him a copy if he remembered.[13]

Just as Lincoln was preparing to leave Springfield for Washington, Prentice wrote to him again, his letter this time covering many sheets of paper, in the editor's scrawling and almost illegible hand. He again begged jobs. This is the letter, in part:

Louisville, Feb. 8th, 1861.

My Dear Sir,

I have been intending to meet you at Indianapolis and to seek a personal interview with you, but I well know that heavy demands will be made upon your time and attention by those who think that they have claims upon you. . . .

I have received no answer to the letter I wrote you a few days ago, suggesting that you let me have a copy of your inaugural address before its delivery to be published immediately afterwards. By doing this you can secure the document in this section against the murderous mutilations of the telegraph, and I think it is desirable.

I beg you to bear in mind what I wrote to you in regard to my excellent Republican friend, John J. Piatt of Illinois. Knowing the warmth of your heart, I cannot doubt that the circumstances which I mentioned to you will enlist your feelings strongly in Mr. Piatt's behalf and induce you to do the very best that you can for him. He is, as I told you, a man whose genius is scarcely equalled except by that of the lovely young woman whom he wishes to be able to marry. If I could make them happy I would do it at any sacrifice; and you can do it without a sacrifice. . . .

And now, my Dear Sir, I have one more request to make of you, and probably but one. I have a brother in Washington, Rufus Prentice, whom I love very dearly. . . .

My brother is one of the best men in the world. . . . He is old and poor and has had for many years a sick wife as well as a family of children dependent upon his earnings. He sorely needs office, and I do not know what he could possibly do without it. He has always been a Republican in principle. . . .

The portents, Mr. Lincoln, are dark, and I know not what the future is to be. I trust to God Kentucky may stay in the Union. I have every confidence in your official and personal integrity and I hope I need not say that I shall take great pleasure in performing the important duty of doing liberal justice to your administration. I recognize no party now but the Union Party.

Earnestly hoping that you will excuse my intrusion and give a kind regard to my suggestions, I remain,

Very truly yours,

G. D. Prentice.[14]

Piatt, who was a native of Indiana, not Illinois, got a job, a clerkship
in the Treasury Department at Washington, and held it for six years.
He married the "poetess," Sarah Morgan Bryan, and their combined
output of poetry filled many volumes.[15]

Lincoln saw Kentucky—one of the four border slave states—as the
keystone in the Union wall against the South. He thought the result
of the whole war just about hinged on which way Kentucky would
swing.[16] On April 15, 1861, in answer to Lincoln's call for troops, Governor Beriah Magoffin, who was posing as a neutral, answered that
Kentucky would "furnish no troops for the wicked purpose of subdu-
ing her sister southern states."[17] Learning that Magoffin turned Lincoln
down, Jefferson Davis asked the Kentucky Governor to send a regiment to Harpers Ferry. Although he denied the request, he saw to it
that Blanton Duncan, at the head of a regiment of volunteers, read the
message. Duncan and his men joined the Confederate forces.[18]

If President Lincoln entertained hopes of support from Prentice, he
was due for a shock. Even the *Cincinnati Enquirer* was surprised, noting the *Louisville Journal* "has gagged at the late war proclamation of
the President and most indignantly refuses to swallow it."[19] The
*Journal* editorial said:

If Mr. Lincoln contemplated this policy in the inaugural address, he is a
guilty dissembler; if he has conceived it under the excitement raised in the
seizure of Fort Sumter, he is a guilty hotspur. In either case, he is miserably
unfit for the exalted position in which the enemies of the country have
placed him.[20]

Prentice offered his solution for the state's troubles in an editorial
that said: "Arm Kentucky, efficiently but rightfully and fairly, with
the clear declaration that the army is not for offense against either
the Government or the seceding States, but purely for defense against
whatever power sets hostile foot upon the actual soil of the Commonwealth."[21]

The Congressional elections proved the people of Kentucky loyal
to the Union. Every district but one chose a Union man. In August,
the election of members of the state legislature brought a similar result.
On September 5, 1861, the legislature was notified a Confederate army

had invaded Kentucky. That ended the neutrality policy.[22] Magoffin opposed all measures to expel the Confederates and resigned the next year.

The *Frankfort Yeoman* thought the people were being misled by Northern propaganda and said: "The only safe rule for the people to follow is to believe nothing published in the Lincoln newspapers."[23]

The *Nicholasville Democrat* spoke too loudly for the Confederacy, and on a Saturday night in May of 1861 a small mob entered the office, pied the forms, gathered the type in buckets, and dumped it in the street.[24] The *Louisville Express* was suppressed and the editor and publisher arrested by Brigadier General Jeremiah Tilford Boyle, a former Kentucky attorney, "on account of the general tone of the paper being calculated to aid the rebellion."[25]

Two newspapers published at Georgetown, Ky., both of Southern sympathy, went out of business in August in 1861.[26] M. H. Cofer, editor of the *Elizabethtown Democrat*, was one of the first Kentucky newspaper men to join the Confederate army.[27]

The *Kentucky Statesman* at Lexington, "one of the bitterest and most unscrupulous advocates of treason in Kentucky," according to the *Cincinnati Gazette*, quit for the duration of the war in the fall of 1861.[28] Its last editorial said:

When the time comes that a free man can utter his sentiments without the Bastile in his face, this paper will assume its old position. . . . A free press has ever been the foe most dreaded by all usurpers. We hope it may be free again in this country.[29]

Prentice's chief competitor in Louisville was the *Daily Courier*, edited by Walter N. Haldeman. The *Courier* was the mouthpiece of Governor Magoffin and outright advocate of secession. The tone of the *Courier* was unchanged as the state swung into the Union column, and on September 18, 1861, it bluntly stated in an editorial:

We therefore deliberately pronounce the assumption of any authority over Kentucky by the Lincoln government or by the present legislature under it, as a usurpation, and revolutionary, and which no citizen of Kentucky is bound to obey.[30]

That was the last straw. In an order issued that same day, the Postmaster General barred the *Courier* from the mails, calling it an "advocate of treason."[31]

The *Courier* was reestablished at Nashville, Tenn., behind the Confederate lines, where it enjoyed the liberty of publishing degrading insults to people of the Northern states. This editorial, published the following March, is typical:

This has been called a fratricidal war by some, by others an irrepressible conflict between freedom and slavery. We respectfully take issue with the authors of both these ideas. We are not brothers of the Yankees, and the slavery question is merely the pretext, not the cause of the war.

The Norman cavalier can not brook the vulgar familiarity of the Saxon Yankee, while the latter is continually devising some plan to bring down his aristocratic neighbor to his own detested level . . . when, owing to divisions in our ranks, the Yankee hirelings placed one of their own spawn over us, political connection became unendurable, and separation necessary to preserve our self-respect. . . . Incapable of self-government, they will inevitably again fall under the control of the superior race.[32]

The abandoned plant of the *Courier* at Louisville was sold at auction to the *Louisville Democrat* for $6,150.[33] The migratory *Courier* was also published for a time at Bowling Green.[34]

The third largest Louisville newspaper was the *Democrat*, edited by John H. Harney, who at first supported the Union and then veered off to the Peace Democrats over the Negro question.[35] The policy of the *Democrat* had become clear by 1862. An editorial said: "The Abolitionists propose to elevate the black race. Nothing but hemp could do the same thing properly for them."[36]

After the Union government was solidly established in Kentucky, Prentice and his *Louisville Journal* still tried to walk down the middle of the road. In 1862, he was saying, "We are for the Constitution as it is and the Union as it was. We speak purely as American patriots. Let Abolitionists and secessionists alike take heed."[37] The *Allen County* (Lima, Ohio) *Democrat* lauded Prentice and said: "That's the doctrine of all conservative men and especially of the Democracy throughout the country."[38]

About the time his son was killed at Augusta, Prentice took a hand—just what he did is not clear—in the state election in Ohio and incurred the hatred of Samuel Medary, editor of *The Crisis* at Columbus. Heretofore, Prentice and Medary had seen eye to eye with their policy of "the Constitution as it is and the Union as it was." Medary was no ordinary antagonist; crafty and cunning, he could express himself as clearly as any editor of his day. After the election, in which the Democrats gained a margin at the polls, Medary published an open letter to Prentice in which he charged the editor of the *Louisville Journal* sent "venomous missiles" into Ohio, aimed at the publisher of *The Crisis*. The letter said:

You use the words "traitor" and "treason." . . . A tree is generally known by the fruit it bears. You had two sons in the southern army, one of whom was recently killed at Augusta, Kentucky. The editor of *The Crisis* has a son in the Northern army, who was in Kentucky at the same time your son was killed fighting on the other side. Now, in the chances and accidents of war, your son might have killed our son or vice versa, and yet you called us a "traitor." Now, were you in such straits, that to clear your skirts of the charge of teaching your sons treason, you were driven to this vulgar exhibition of yourself to save your reputation among your abolition friends, who have you in their pay . . . ? You went begging amongst the abolitionists not long since and in Philadelphia alone they raised you forty thousand dollars! How much do you expect to get out of them for your vile abuse of the editor of *The Crisis*, who sent a son into Kentucky to save your rotten carcass from the daggers of your own flesh?[39]

The following spring, Prentice was the target of a whispering campaign that got into print. While he was visiting Eastern cities, the *Chicago Times* reported he was on his way to Europe, having converted all his property into gold. The *Times* charged he was told by his son in the rebel army that Kentucky would be overrun by the Confederates.[40]

The *Cincinnati Gazette* took note of these rumors in an editorial, saying it had attempted to ascertain the truth. It found the Cincinnati correspondent of the *Chicago Times* wrote the story and that he said he obtained the information from the managing editor of the *Cincinnati Enquirer*.[41]

Prentice was in New York and took his troubles to Horace Greeley. He replied to the charges in this letter published by the *New York Tribune*:

Sir: The author of a letter in your paper today says that I am on my way to Europe, that last Saturday I paid 178 for gold in Louisville, and that I believe the rebels will have complete possession of Kentucky during the present month. Please afford me space in your columns to say that I have no thoughts of going to Europe, that I was not in Louisville last Saturday, and never bought gold at 178 in my life; and, that I have at no time believed that the rebels would have complete possession of Kentucky during this month or any other month. I have said that, if, as some claim, Kentucky was invaded by a rebel force of 40,000 men, they might overrun the State,

unless the Federal troops should be re-enforced; but, in the first place, I
have not believed that the invading force was even a tenth part of 40,000,
and in the second place, I have not seriously doubted that any needed reenforcements would be forthcoming.

Respectfully, Geo. D. Prentice

Astor House, New York, March 6.[42]

The story refused to die. On March 12, the *Cincinnati Gazette*
quoted the *Enquirer* as saying its managing editor could prove the story
was true on the word of two witnesses. Prentice went from New York
to Washington, where he wrote a letter on March 14 to *The New York
Times,* offering further explanation and denial. He wrote, "I have a boy,
who—God forgive him—is a Colonel or Major in the rebel army." He
explained his son was wounded at Murfreesboro and that Mrs. Prentice,
the boy's mother, went to see him in the hospital, passing through both
the Union and Conferedate lines at Nashville. Mrs. Prentice, he said,
brought back with her an unsealed letter from the wounded son, and
this probably was the origin of the story that the boy advised him to sell
out and go to Europe.[43]

Meanwhile, the *Cincinnati Gazette,* with a hawklike eye on Prentice,
said: "One of the editors of the *Louisville Journal* has been enjoying
a rich clerkship at Washington. . . . The unconditional Union men
of Kentucky demand his replacement."[44] That obviously was a blow at
John Piatt, the Lincoln appointee. Piatt was a printer by trade, having
served his apprenticeship on the *Ohio State Journal* at Columbus.

What was purported to be a letter from a "Kentucky Soldier" to
Prentice was published by the *Cincinnati Gazette.* It charged Prentice
conducted the *Louisville Journal* for more than thirty years "patrioti-
cally and bravely" but that since 1861 he had maintained a neutrality
that helped no one. While purporting to support the government, the
letter said, Prentice inadvertently helped the South.[45]

Prentice came out firmly against Lincoln for reelection in 1864. Not
only did he refuse to support him, but he opened a violent and personal
attack. This is a typical *Journal* editorial during the campaign:

If the loyal people of the Union do not set the seal of their condemnation
upon Abraham Lincoln at the ballot-box, they will become speedily not
only the most wretched, but the most despised people in history. With
thickening and revolting evidences of his incompetency and faithlessness,
however, the people can not fail to set the seal of their condemnation upon
him at the ballot-box. Let them set it so broad and deep that time will never
efface the impression.[46]

Most surprised of all at Prentice's attitude was the anti-Lincoln *Cincinnati Enquirer*, which pointed out that for the first time in history the *Louisville Journal* had hoisted the Democratic flag after having served for decades as the Whig organ of Kentucky.[47]

Just before the election, the *Louisville Journal* said: "The *New York Tribune* says Lincoln and Johnson were both born in slave states and are representatives of the class known as 'poor whites.' " The *Journal* editorial took it on from there, stating:

They never have improved their condition, unfortunately. On the contrary, they have steadily deteriorated, until at last they have reached the lowest depths of mortal shabbiness in the leadership of the Abolition party. What a warning to ragamuffins!

We hardly need say that *"poor whites"* is a phrase current amongst the negroes of the South, signifying not white people who are poor, but white people who are poor without being respectable. It means white people who are beggars and thieves.[48]

Were it not for Prentice's own admission, later written in bitter anguish, that the decision to oppose Lincoln in 1864 was his and his alone, the supposition might arise that Paul R. Shipman, described as associate editor, was mainly responsible. After Lincoln's election, Shipman resigned with the statement, "I deem it my duty to retire."[49]

The *Cincinnati Gazette* commented:

The proprietors of the *Louisville Journal* have kicked out Paul R. Shipman and George D. Prentice takes the helm. But the loyal people have no more confidence in the latter than in the former. Both have proved recreant to the Union cause. They made their bed with rebel sympathizers and they will not soon be able to cheat Union men again.[50]

Announcement that Shipman was no longer connected with the *Journal* was followed by his arrest on order of Major General Stephen G. Burbridge, and he was sent through the lines into the Confederacy. Shipman's exile was of short duration, Burbridge permitting him to return in a few days with an unconditional release.[51]

The Republican press noted with satisfaction when the *Journal* then came out in favor of emancipation for Kentucky, but why it never knew.

During the fateful year of 1864, when Prentice was doing everything in his power to bring about the defeat of Lincoln, the President had in his possession a letter from Mrs. Prentice in which she begged permission to visit her son Clarence in Richmond. This is the letter:

Louisville, Jan. 18th, 1864

Hon. President Lincoln,

Sir, I have as you know a son, an only and most dearly beloved son in the Southern army; and I know, am well assured, that if I can reach Richmond I shall be enabled to procure for him an honorable discharge from the army and an opportunity of being once more united (in a foreign land) to his mother and child. I ask you now for the permit to go south, and Oh!, Mr. Lincoln by the love you bear to your dear ones who are yet spared to you as well as that you bear for those whom God has called to await you in another and a happier world, grant my petition. Let me go, and if I should fail in the main object of my journey, still I shall once more see my child face to face, and his little boy may take away a memory of his father, which otherwise he may never have.

You may trust my honor for taking nothing contraband nor compromising my government by letter or word of mouth. Yield to my entreaties and receive the ever grateful remembrance of yours respectfully,

Harriette B. Prentice.[52]

The story has persisted, nourished by romantic writers, that Clarence Prentice was arrested as a spy by the Union army and ordered to stand trial by court-martial by General Burnside. The penalty in such a case would be death. The distraught father, so the story goes, sent a telegram to President Lincoln, then went to Washington to make a personal appeal for his son's life. The editor was "smilingly received" by the President, who assured him the order for the court-martial had already been dissolved. Lincoln was quoted as saying, "Did you think I'd let them hang your boy?"[53]

It is a beautiful story, but it is not true.

Early in October of 1864, one of General Burbridge's scouting parties captured a Confederate soldier near Louisa, Ky., who identified himself as J. K. Johnson, a member of Company E, 8th Kentucky (Confederate) Cavalry. Johnson stumbled into their camp at night, mistaking them for rebel bushwhackers. When he was searched, two official documents were found in his pockets. One was an order that authorized Johnson to swear Kentucky recruits into the Confederate service, the other a permit issued at Richmond by the Confederate War Department for George D. Prentice of the *Louisville Journal* to visit his son, Lieutenant Colonel Clarence J. Prentice.

A Kentucky correspondent of the *Cincinnati Gazette* sent his newspaper what he said was a "*verbatim, et literatim*" copy of the pass to Prentice. It follows:

Confederate States of America,
War Department,

Richmond, Va., Sept. 10, 1864.

Mr. George D. Prentice of Louisville, Ky., is authorized to pass the Confederate lines to Pound Gap, in Southwestern Virginia, on a visit to his son, Lieutenant-Colonel Clarence J. Prentice. By order,

J. A. Campbell,
Assistant Secretary of War.

Regarding the above as most satisfactory to you, you will be received at any other point, and by flag-of-truce boat if preferred. By authority,

E. M. Bruce,
Headquarters Morgan's Brigade,
September 16, 1864.[54]

While Prentice was negotiating with the Confederates for papers to carry him to Richmond, he was pulling strings in Washington to obtain a pass. On October 23, 1864, he wrote this letter to Secretary of State Seward:

I received your kind letter, informing me that you had referred to President Lincoln my application for a pass to visit my son, with a recommendation that the pass should be granted. And I have since been awaiting very anxiously, but have heard nothing further upon the subject. May I not presume to ask of you to see the President in person and ascertain for me whether my earnest request cannot be granted.

My only son, an erring one to be sure, is about to be tried for his life. He and his counsel are deeply anxious to see me before the trial, and I am painfully anxious to see them. I am in exceedingly feeble health, the springs of my life are fast failing, and, if I do not see my child soon, I certainly never shall. My paper opposes Mr. Lincoln's reelection, but I do not think that he is capable of indulging revenge or resentment by refusing to permit an almost dying father to have an interview with a son in mortal peril.

If the President is under the strange delusion that I would or could use for disloyal purposes any privilege he might accord to me, I have of course nothing to say. The necessity I felt myself under of opposing him or consenting to his being opposed in the *Louisville Journal* was certainly one of the most painful of my life.

Most respectfully yours,
Geo. D. Prentice.

P. S. An early answer from you will command my warmest thanks. G. D. P.[55]

Only the signature of that letter is in Prentice's hand. He suffered a disease of the fingers that kept him from doing much writing. Two days later, October 25, Prentice dictated another letter to Seward, saying:

Capt. Babtist, who formerly served under my son in the Confederate Army and is now a prisoner of war at Johnson's Island, writes to me some facts which would be of vast importance to my erring child in his approaching trial for his life, and which Capt. B. says he would state on oath before the court if he could be paroled to the Southern Confederacy or exchanged. Exchanges, I believe, are now going on, and I think that the exchange of Capt. Babtist would sub-serve the cause of truth, humanity and justice.

He wrote a postscript almost as long as the letter itself, saying:

I enclose you one of several letters that I have received from Capt. Babtist in relation to my son's case. It seems to me that the interest every man ought to feel in our common humanity should induce our authorities to parole or exchange Capt. B. in order to prevent an innocent young man from being doomed to an unjust and terrible punishment.[56]

On October 30, 1864, while Prentice was pleading for Lincoln's help, the *Louisville Journal* published an insult, one of a long series, to Parson Brownlow, the President's stout friend who was doing great work for the Union with his *Knoxville Whig and Rebel Ventilator*. The *Journal* said that Brownlow, "having received office from Lincoln, now declares his approbation, as we understand it, of all that Lincoln has done and all he may do hereafter. Every such man has his price."

Brownlow replied to Prentice in an open letter, pointing out to him that it was addressed "*to you.*" It revealed that Prentice's son was charged with murder! Brownlow opened by saying he had been "repeatedly assailed" by the *Louisville Journal* but had not replied until Prentice made a "direct charge of bribery and corruption which needs to be ventilated by a statement of facts." He explained he held a minor office "to serve my friends in East Tennessee" but that the pay was not equal to the labor performed.

Prentice, Brownlow charged, "had moved Heaven and earth" in a futile effort to obtain contracts for supplying the Army of the Cumberland, writing "sickening and flattering" stories for his newspaper about Major General W. S. Rosecrans.

When Prentice's efforts to obtain the contracts failed, Brownlow said, the *Louisville Journal* bolted the Lincoln administration. "While you were interested in contracts," wrote Brownlow, "you were as good a Lincoln man as I was." The editorial continued:

My two sons entered the Federal army and one of them is now at home on crutches, because of wounds received in leading his regiment of cavalry in a charge upon Wheeler's forces in Middle Tennessee. My other son was in General Gillem's command, and was in the fight when the great Kentucky horse-thief, Morgan, was killed, under whom and with whom your sons have been fighting against the Government upon whose bounty their rebel mother and contract hunting father are living. One of your sons was killed in Kentucky while on a horse-stealing expedition under rebel officers. Your other son is now on trial in Virginia for the murder of a brother rebel by the name of White. Your wife is an avowed rebel, and ought to be sent South by the Federal authorities; and you are but one degree removed from a rebel and a traitor, having completely played out.[57]

When Prentice wrote to Secretary Seward that he did not think Lincoln was "capable of indulging revenge or resentment," he put his finger on one of the President's finest traits. His request for a pass was granted. A wire story out of New York on December 3, 1864, said:

The *Richmond Whig* of Nov. 30th notices the arrival of George D. Prentice, of the *Louisville Journal*, at the Spottswood Hotel, on a visit to his son in the rebel service. Mr. Prentice makes his visit by permission of the authorities on both sides.[58]

On December 9, 1864, the *Louisville Journal* published a momentous announcement. It said: "We have dissolved our alliance with the Democratic party, for it was never intended that we should merge ourselves into the ranks of our lifelong opponents."

Lieutenant Colonel Prentice was neither hanged nor shot and continued in the Confederate service until the end of the war.[59]

That is the Prentice story, but still to be solved is the question why the editor fought Lincoln in 1864. There may have been pressure from Richmond, which held his son's life in its hands. His letter of October 23, 1864, would so indicate.

The military, charged with keeping order in Kentucky, enjoyed a free hand in excluding from the state those radical Democratic newspapers whose influence was believed injurious to Union interests. The order barring the *Cincinnati Enquirer* was issued on March 5, 1863, by General Burnside.[60] At the same time, General Rosecrans barred the *Enquirer* and the *Chicago Times* from circulating in the Army of the Cumberland.[61] The ban on the *Enquirer* in Kentucky was not lifted until April 4, 1865.[62]

In a sweeping order issued in November of 1864, the military placed these newspapers on the contraband list in Kentucky: *New York Day Book*, New York *Freeman's Journal*, *New York Daily News*, New York *Metropolitan Record*, and the *Chicago Times*.[63]

Thomas E. Bramlette, elected Governor of Kentucky on a Union ticket in 1863, took his troubles on the slavery issue to the White House in the spring of 1864. He was accompanied to Washington by Archibald Dixon, former Kentucky senator who served the unexpired term of Henry Clay, and A. G. Hodges, editor of the *Frankfort Commonwealth*, a Lincoln newspaper.

The President granted a long interview to them and remarked at the close he was apprehensive that "Kentuckians felt unkindly toward him, in consequence of not properly understanding the difficulties by which he was surrounded in his efforts to put down this rebellion."

Editor Hodges agreed with him that he was "greatly misunderstood" by many persons in Kentucky. He suggested to Lincoln that he "write out the remarks" he had just made to Bramlette and Dixon for publication in the *Frankfort Commonwealth*.

The Kentuckians returned home, and in due time Lincoln's article for the Frankfort newspaper reached Hodges. It was dated "April 4, 1864." The President said: "I am naturally anti-slavery. If slavery is not wrong, nothing is wrong. I cannot remember when I did not so think and feel. . . . I claim *not* to have controlled events, but confess plainly that events have controlled me."[64]

The *Commonwealth's* story of the interview and the text of Lincoln's article were newspaper sensations, reprinted by the leading papers of the country. *The New York Times* said: "The letter of President Lincoln to the editor of the *Frankfort Commonwealth* is a new and admirable specimen of his ingenuous character, and of his remarkable aptness in stating the truth."[65]

During the presidential campaign of 1864, Thomas B. Pettit, editor of the *Owensboro Observer*, was arrested by the military. He was taken to Cairo, Ill., where, in an interview with the editor of the *Cairo Democrat* he charged he was seized because he told Kentuckians to vote against Lincoln and that he probably would be sent into the Confederate lines.[66]

Pettit spoke the truth, so far as his destination was concerned. He was not heard from again until the *Richmond Enquirer* said: "Thomas B. Pettit, editor of the *Owensboro* (Ky.) *Observer*, has reached this city, not, however, as a peace commissioner, nor with the remotest idea of entertaining peace sentiments toward Abraham Lincoln, but as an exile, for daring to be an independent man."[67]

General Burbridge suppressed the *True Presbyterian*, published at

Louisville, on November 19, 1864, and the editor, Reverend Stuart Robinson, fearful of imprisonment, fled to Canada. The *True Presbyterian*, said a leading Northern paper, "formerly was the denominational organ of the Presbyterians, but it has been sustained by rebel sympathizers of all classes and creeds since the rebellion commenced."[68]

The fugitive preacher sent an appeal to President Lincoln through Dr. Phineas D. Gurley, pastor of the First Presbyterian Church in Washington. He wrote a letter to the President from his hiding place in Canada and sent it to Dr. Gurley to deliver.[69] When Dr. Gurley handed the letter to Lincoln, he included a note in which he described the Reverend Mr. Robinson as a "great rebel." He added that he knew nothing about the policy of Robinson's paper.[70]

In his letter, the Reverend Mr. Robinson denied his newspaper contained political or military discussion and blamed the "personal malignity" of Dr. Robert J. Breckenridge for the suppression. He admitted he had not supported Lincoln, but asked him to countermand "the foolish order."

Dr. Breckenridge was stumping Kentucky and Ohio for the Lincoln ticket, although he had two sons in the Confederate army. Robinson received no reply from the White House. He had to wait until the war was over to regain control of his paper.[71]

# 25  "The Fire in the Rear"

THE ILLINOIS DAILY STATE JOURNAL of Springfield started 1863 by advocating a second term for President Lincoln. Speaking in ecstasy after the Emancipation Proclamation went into effect, the *Journal* said:

> This great man, whom it is not extravagant to say is God-like in his moral attributes, child-like in the simplicity and purity of his character, yet manly and self-relying in his high and patriotic purpose—this man who takes no step backward—let him consummate the grandest achievement ever allotted to man, the destruction of American slavery.[1]

The *Journal* was the only newspaper in the country that blindly followed with admiration and constant devotion the sure progress of

Abraham Lincoln to his triumph. Edited by his friend, Edward L. Baker, Harvard Law School graduate,[2] the *Journal* fought just as savagely for Lincoln after he had gone to Washington as it did in the days when he spent his evenings in the city room and gave the editor a hand by writing editorials. It fought "the fire in the rear," the opposition to the war in the Northwest, that Lincoln feared more than the military might of the South.[3]

Lincoln's use of the expression, "the fire in the rear," may have stemmed from an editorial published in the *Detroit* (Mich.) *Free Press* in the January before he took office. The *Free Press* said:

If troops shall be raised in the North to march against the people of the South, a fire in the rear will be opened upon such troops which will either stop their march altogether, or wonderfully accelerate it. If war shall be waged, that war will be fought in the North . . . here in Michigan, and here in Detroit, and in every Northern State.[4]

That sentiment against a war was not uncommon. On the very day the *Free Press* made its stand plain, the *Joliet* (Ill.) *Signal* published an editorial of striking similarity, saying:

We learn that the Black Republican artillery company at Plainfield are drilling for service. They are making ready to go down South to subdue the Southern people. Well, let them go—but in their journey they should avoid passing through this city for fear that they and their cannon might be tumbled into the river.[5]

"The fire in the rear" burned as brightly in Lincoln's home city of Springfield as it did in any Northern community, the flames fed by the *Illinois State Register*, edited by his lifelong enemy, Charles H. Lanphier, the Virginian. The Democratic *Register* did not like a single act performed by Lincoln and approved not one word he uttered. Lanphier left the *Register* on November 24, 1863, when he won a minor political office at the polls.

Lanphier, in Lincoln's own words, was a man unworthy of credit in political matters.[6] He was hotheaded, drank rather heavily, and carried a pistol. At a political rally in Springfield on September 3, 1863, he pulled his gun on "an unarmed gentleman from the country," but spectators interfered and prevented a shooting.[7]

Lanphier and Baker staged a duel for several years with printer's ink at a distance of about one square. The *Register* called the *Journal* "the Abolition sheet in this city." The *Journal* identified Lanphier as "the agent of Jeff Davis who presides over the Copperhead sheet in this city."

In the *Register*, President Lincoln was "the ineffable despot, who, by some inscrutable dispensation of providence presides over the destinies of this vast republic." When he bid for reelection, it said: "The doom of Lincoln and Black Republicanism is sealed. Corruption and the bayonet are incompetent to save them."[8]

Lincoln's victory was a blow to the *Register*. Its editorial said: "Believing, as we do, that this result is the heaviest calamity that ever befell this nation; regarding it as the farewell to civil liberty, to a Republican form of government, and to the unity of these states, it is useless to say that his election has filled our hearts with gloom."[9]

Lincoln remembered his friends on the *Journal*. Simeon Francis, whose place Baker took in 1855, went to Oregon where he was editor of the *Oregon Farmer* when war came. The President made him a paymaster in the United States Army, a position he held until 1870.[10]

Baker was appointed a United States marshal for southern Illinois, was reappointed in 1865, but was removed by President Johnson.[11] William H. Bailhache, associated with Baker in the *Journal*, received a commission as captain in the army quartermaster department of the Army of the Tennessee.[12] His place on the *Journal* was taken by David L. Phillips, a former Baptist minister, radical Republican and personally devoted to Lincoln.

It was Phillips who proudly wrote: "It will be my recollection that in those long, dreary years of blood and carnage, not one disloyal sentence ever found utterance in the columns of the *Journal*, nor one discouraging word to the heroic men who fought the great battles of the Union."[13]

Anti-Union sentiment was so strong in southern Illinois in the early days of secession that the well-informed Charles H. Ray of the *Chicago Tribune* was fearful the state might be torn asunder if the Ohio River became the dividing line between the North and the South.[14]

An early proposal to form a Northwest Confederacy was seriously considered and boosted by the minority Democracy through newspapers that included the *Joliet Signal*, the Democratic *Carthage Republican*, the Lewiston *Fulton Ledger*, the *Cairo Gazette*, the *Macomb Eagle*, and the *Quincy Herald*.[15] The *Carlinville Spectator* saw Lincoln as "the vulgar, swaggering usurper at Washington."[16]

The *Peoria Demokrat*, a German language newspaper, was barred from the mails by the Postmaster General in the fall of 1861. The *Peoria Transcript* charged the *Demokrat* was in open sympathy with secessionists and that legal advertising placed in it by the antiadministration city council of Peoria encouraged this policy.[17]

The *Quincy Herald* spoke for William A. Richardson, elected Democratic United States Senator in 1863. Philip Snyder, editor of the Quincy *Daily Whig and Republican*, waged unceasing editorial war with a procession of editors of the unstable *Herald*. Noting on August 13, 1863, that the latest *Herald* editor "quit in disgust," he said a former proprietor, Brooks, was again in charge. "The dog has literally returned to his vomit," wrote Snyder.[18]

Snyder finally met his master in the person of Colonel I. N. Morris, who beat him with a cane and chased him into a store in return for an uncomplimentary article in the *Whig*. The Springfield *Register* reported the affair, saying: "They do say he made even better time than the *Chicago Tribune* editor made at Bull Run."[19]

M. Mehaffey and F. Odell, editors of the *Democratic Standard* at Paris, were arrested by government agents on August 8, 1862, their seizure following a blanket order issued that day by Secretary of War Stanton, aimed at persons who discouraged volunteering or gave aid and comfort to the enemy. A United States marshal and two deputies made the arrests after they warned a crowd at the newspaper office not to interfere.

They also had a warrant for the arrest of Amos Green, an attorney. He fled to Indiana but was captured and returned. When searched, his pockets gave up copy for *Standard* editorials and letters from Vallandigham.[20]

The marshal locked the office of the *Democratic Standard* and gave the keys to local officers for safekeeping. He shipped his prisoners by train to Old Capitol at Washington. In its story of the arrests, the Springfield *Journal* said the *Democratic Standard* was established after war began to "break down" the *Democratic Blade*, a Union newspaper.[21]

Mehaffey and Odell were charged with "treasonable practice," and Green was accused of having purchased arms to resist army conscription.[22]

The *Bloomington Times* was reported mobbed on August 22, 1862. Office equipment was destroyed. The New York *Journal of Commerce* later charged the act was performed by Republicans and the editors were "ill treated."[23]

Union cavalrymen, hunting deserters, rode into Olney on the night of August 30, 1863. Finding no deserters, they tormented the Democratic editor of the *Olney Herald* by mixing his type and throwing equipment into the street. Brigadier General Jacob Ammen caught them in the act, put them all under arrest and made them pay damages. The money was deducted from their pay.[24]

The Jerseyville *Democratic Union* was in the habit of denouncing President Lincoln as "a worse traitor than Jefferson Davis." A Colonel Hildebrand, described as a Douglas Democrat, sent a squad of soldiers into Jerseyville to "frighten" the editor. Taking flight, the editor remained hidden until the soldiers departed, when he returned to write a glowing account of his encounter with the military.[25]

The *Alton Telegraph* read the editor's story and observed that he "should be either in prison or the insane asylum at Jacksonville, it is not quite clear which."[26]

The Springfield *Journal* said that the *Logan Sun* ("a secession paper," published at Lincoln), "has gone down amid clouds and thick darkness," and the editor, W. H. G. Burney, "has gone to parts unknown."[27]

J. B. Durham, editor of the *Kankakee County Democrat*, entered the service in 1862, and his newspaper went out of business.[28] The editor of the *Illinois Free Press* of Hillsboro enlisted, and the *Canton Register* was forced to suspend publication when every man in the office capable of bearing arms volunteered for service in the Union army.[29]

After writing a farewell editorial in which he told his subscribers he was going to see what he could do for his "affectionate relative"—meaning Uncle Sam—the editor of the *Carbondale Times* donned a blue uniform.[30] The *Alton Telegraph* suspended publication for a short time in August of 1862 because of loss of men to the army.[31] D. W. Lusk, editor of the *Shawneetown Mercury*, a Democratic newspaper, entered politics as a candidate for the Illinois state legislature, taking for his slogan: "Down with treason wherever found."[32]

The *Volksblatt* of Belleville was mobbed twice. Civilians wrecked it on a March night in 1863, breaking up the forms, throwing type in all directions, and smashing windows.[33] The German language daily still attacked President Lincoln, and soldiers of the 9th Illinois Regiment raided it on the afternoon of May 19, 1864. They destroyed all equipment, including the press.[34]

J. B. Danforth, editor of the *Rock Island Argus* and "an exponent of Democratic principles," was beaten by three men, one of whom was a major in the Union army, on his way home to dinner on a cold February day in 1864.[35] The Democrats of Rock Island called an indignation meeting that packed the courthouse. The bruised and sore Danforth, escorted to the meeting by a committee, responded with a speech on rights of the press and freedom of speech.[36]

During the presidential campaign of 1864, the *Chicago Times* and the *Missouri Republican* of St. Louis, both strongly anti-Lincoln, pointed to the 22d Illinois Regiment as typical of soldiers in the field opposed to a second term. The outfit obtained a furlough that sent home 290 men. The *Times* and *Republican* said 210 favored the Democratic ticket while only 80 would vote for Lincoln.

En route home, the furloughed men passed through Chester, where the *Picket Guard*, a newspaper that denounced Lincoln, was published. They destroyed the newspaper office in one of the most spectacular cases of its kind in the Midwest.[37]

The Springfield *Journal* published the story of the mobbing and right beside it the story clipped from the *Times* and *Republican* that claimed the regiment was Democratic. The *Times* came back with the retort that the paper was destroyed by the eighty Lincoln men.[38]

The *Alton Democrat* offered the startling suggestion of retaliation, saying:

Let a committee be appointed . . . to wait immediately upon prominent members of the Abolition party in Chester and demand that they make good one-half of the loss of the *Picket Guard*, and in case they decline so doing, let another committee proceed to the office of the *Randolph County Democrat* and reduce it to precisely the same condition.[39]

Fifteen hundred persons turned out for the meeting, most of whom were Democrats. The Republicans were represented by a committee. Funds to finance repairs to the *Picket Guard* office were pledged by the Republicans, and the *Chester Democrat*, a Republican paper, granted the use of its facilities to the *Guard* until the plant was restored. The Democrats pledged protection of the Republican newspaper.[40]

The *Waterloo Advocate* covered the meeting at Chester, its reporter ending his story thusly: "The Chester Cornet Band enlivened the day with music. In the evening all parties adjourned, feeling that it is much better to meet and settle difficulties in an amicable manner than to resort to force."[41]

The editor of the *Gallatin County Democrat* peered from his office on August 19, 1864, and saw a squad of soldiers of the 139th Illinois Regiment. Lieutenant J. E. Chapman entered and informed the editor he was under arrest and would be taken to Caseyville, Ky., to face Brigadier General Eleazar A. Paine. The General was a West Pointer, a friend of President Lincoln, whom he had known while practicing law in Illinois.

The editor argued that the soldiers had no right to take him out of the state, but he and his assistant soon found themselves aboard an Ohio River transport. They were held in a prison from Sunday until Tuesday morning when they were taken before the General. The only thing Paine said to them was, "I am going to send you damn sons of bitches home."

After his release, the editor was told he was suspected of membership in the underground Sons of Liberty but that evidence against him was lacking. He went home and wrote an editorial that charged "dirty Abolition thieves" had him arrested in an effort to obtain control of his newspaper.[42]

In midsummer of 1864, the disappearance of A. D. Davies, editor of the Rushville Times, a Democratic newspaper, created a minor sensation. A tear-jerking letter from Davies, in which he said farewell to his family and the world in general, gained still more publicity for the case. He explained he was held by Union forces in Missouri, unjustly condemned to death as a rebel spy. The Democratic newspapers published his letter, but the Republicans were skeptical.

A few weeks later, the Schuyler Citizen solved the mystery. It said:

A. D. Davies, ex-editor of the Rushville Times, and the whilom adviser of the Democracy of Schuyler, wrote an affecting farewell to his family in this place, a few weeks since, just on the eve (so he stated) of his execution as a rebel spy, near Warrensburg, Mo. From letters just received from that place, the information comes that it was not a leaden bullet with which he was shot. How he was shot may be inferred from the fact that he has lately been married to another woman in or near that place. We presume there is room in the penitentiary for one or more subjects.[43]

"The fire in the rear" never lacked for fresh fuel from the anti-Lincoln press in Wisconsin, where the leading opponent of the war for the Union was the notorious Marcus Mills (Brick) Pomeroy. As editor of the La Crosse Democrat, his name ranked with Manton Marble of the New York World, Wilbur F. Storey of the Chicago Times, Samuel Medary of The Crisis, Benjamin Wood of the New York Daily News, and Lanphier of the Illinois State Register. A native of Elmira, N. Y., Pomeroy established the La Crosse Democrat in 1857 and published it until 1864 when he returned east.[44]

Pomeroy's editorials, as bitter as any written in the deep South, enjoyed wide reprinting in the extreme radical section of the Democratic press. This is typical:

Lincoln has called for five hundred thousand more victims! On the 5th of September half a million men are to be drafted. . . . Let the women buy mourning goods now, for in a month or so there will not be enough money in this country to use for that purpose. . . . Patriotism is sick! The nation is discouraged. Half the men sent before have been lost to us in the country. . . . It is now revolt, Canada or fight. Let us see what the people will do. . . . Only one half a million more! Oh, that is nothing. We are bound to free the niggers or die . . . ! Continue this administration in power and we can all go to war, Canada, or to hell before 1868.[45]

Pomeroy, twenty-seven years old when the war broke out, fought Lincoln's bid for reelection by declaring he "has swapped the Goddess of Liberty for the pate and wool of a nigger. He has swapped a land of peace for a desert of graves. . . . He has swapped all these as he once swapped jokes in an old saloon in Illinois."[46]

Pomeroy's play on the word "swap" was a reference to Lincoln's reply to a delegation from the National Union League on June 9, 1864, when he said "they have concluded that it is not best to swap horses while crossing the river."[47]

The *Detroit Free Press* insisted only the rich would benefit from a struggle between the North and the South. It belittled the claims of the Republican press that the country was prosperous in the midst of a great conflict.[48]

It finally drifted into the Vallandigham camp, declaring the Copperhead politician "has ever been the able, eloquent and gallant advocate of the policy and the party, and the administrations that have governed and made the country what it was as an unrivalled example of peace, liberty, prosperity, national greatness and glory, from 1800 until the Republicans came into power."[49]

The *Michigan Journal* of Detroit bolted from the Lincoln ranks in the campaign of 1864, as did the *Ann Arbor Journal*, whose editor, E. C. Seaman, explained he had "frequently expressed our dissent from the Abolition policy of Mr. Lincoln."[50]

An imposing list of Democratic newspapers was wrecked by Union soldiers in Indiana, where the Sons of Liberty, a Confederate fifth column, flourished. On October 21, 1861, two companies of the 43d Indiana Regiment, stationed at Camp Vigo, marched into nearby Terre Haute and destroyed the office of the *Journal and Democrat*.

First reports from Terre Haute charged the soldiers made attacks on eight private homes after wrecking the newspaper office. Public indignation subsided the next day when it was correctly stated that the "homes" were houses of ill fame. Colonel George K. Steele, commander of the 43d, promised a court of inquiry, and the incident was forgotten.[51]

The *Journal and Democrat*, described as "an organ of Vallandigham and Voorhees," ceased publication less than a year later when a Republican newspaper noted that it had "died."[52] Daniel W. Voorhees was a Democratic Congressman.

The editor of the *Lafayette Argus*, "a secession sheet," was beaten in a fight with a recruiting officer who took offense at the attitude of the newspaper toward enlistments in the Union army in the fall of 1861.[53]

Soldiers of the 5th Indiana Cavalry broke into the office of the *Rockport Democrat* at nine o'clock in the evening late in January of 1863 and destroyed the type cases and furniture but left the press intact. Editor Jones told the *Indianapolis Daily State Sentinel* that "no cause as yet has been assigned for the hellish act."[54] The *News*, published at Columbia, reported in March of 1863 it had been "mobbed by Republicans."[55]

On Sunday morning, March 15, 1863, troop trains carrying 800 paroled soldiers to St. Louis stopped in Richmond, Ind., to remain in the yards until Monday noon. The soldiers, formerly members of Illinois and Wisconsin regiments, had been exchanged after their capture in the fighting around Murfreesboro. They were fed and entertained by the people of Richmond. That night, some of them wrecked the plant of the *Jeffersonian*, a Democratic newspaper hostile to Lincoln.[56]

J. R. Elder, the editor, charged Abolitionists plied the soldiers with liquor, told them the *Jeffersonian* was a "secession sheet," and led them to the building.[57] When the soldiers reached Indianapolis, they read what the *Sentinel* said about their actions in Richmond. Only the fact that a heavy guard was posted around the building saved it from a mobbing.[58]

The *La Porte Democrat*, said by party newspapers to have been "mild in its strictures upon the administration," was sacked by members of the 29th Indiana Regiment on the night of February 16, 1864. After tearing the office to pieces, the soldiers left town on a train. Editor McDonald charged the attack was instigated by Republicans and that one of them, a member of the town council, led the soldiers to the office. Editor Millikin of the *Union*, La Porte's Republican newspaper, offered use of his plant to the *Democrat* until it could be refitted.[59]

Members of the 24th Indiana Regiment mobbed a Democratic newspaper on March 1, 1864, tried to destroy another, and threatened a third. En route through southwestern Indiana by train, their first stop was at Vincennes, where they visited the *Western Sun*. They smashed the press, dumped the type cases, and broke every window in the building, all this in midafternoon. The *Gazette*, Vincennes' Republican paper, said: "We regret our city was the scene of an act of lawless violence."[60]

Their mission accomplished, the soldiers, about thirty in number, marched back to the train. The next stop was Princeton, home of the *Union Democrat*, another anti-Lincoln newspaper. Already in town was Company H of the 17th Indiana and Company D of the 42d Indiana. The men of the 24th were preparing to attack the newspaper when those of the 17th and 42d decided—probably just for the fun of it—to defend the building. A lively fist fight followed, but the *Union Democrat* stood unscathed through it all.[61]

The train carried the 24th on to Evansville, where some of its members threatened to destroy the *Daily Times*, a newly established Democratic evening newspaper, but nothing happened.[62]

Traveling south on a train out of Indianapolis, the 29th Pennsylvania Regiment stopped in Franklin on a March day in 1864. The newspaper there was called the *Franklin Herald*, Democratic and anti-Lincoln, and had been mobbed a few weeks previously by soldiers passing through town. It was just getting started again, having been refitted, when the Pennsylvanians arrived. They marched to the *Herald* office, riddled it, and ran back to the station to catch their train, bound for the front.[63]

General Grant, who had just received his commission as commander of all the Union armies from President Lincoln, chanced to be at one of the stations when the train bearing the 29th pulled in. He was making a quick trip to Nashville to confer with Sherman, who was to take his place in the West.[64]

Told of the newspaper mobbing staged by the Pennsylvanians on the way down, Grant asked, "Are any of the men sober?"

"A few," was the reply.

The commander of the armies ordered the soldiers who had participated in the mobbing placed in one car with the doors locked and a guard on either platform. They were still under arrest when they arrived at Louisville, Ky.[65]

Editors of other Democratic newspapers in Indiana had their troubles. John E. Bowen, editor of the *Petersburg Record*, shot and wounded a man named Donahue in a street fight. Bowen claimed that Donahue and "another Abolitionist" called him "grossly insulting names."[66]

The editor of the *Albany Ledger* published the identity of the brigades and divisions to which various Indiana regiments were attached in 1862. An order for his arrest, under the 57th Article of War, was issued by General Rosecrans, and he was ordered to report to Major General Horatio G. Wright at Cincinnati. He was released when he told the General he copied the story from another newspaper but was warned against further offense.[67] The fact that the *Albany Ledger* was a Democratic paper supporting the war probably served as a mitigating circumstance in the case.

A "fire in the rear" burned so brightly on the far-off west coast that it quickly drew the attention of Washington. Spurred by a dream of a Pacific republic if the Union fell apart, California and Oregon Democratic editors of the radical wing threw their weight to the South. They were led by disgruntled politicians. United States Senator William M. Gwin was the moving spirit of the California fantasy.[68]

In February of 1862, the long arm of the Lincoln administration barred from the mails the *Los Angeles Star*, the *San Jose Tribune*, the *Tulare Post;* the *Equal Rights Expositor*, and the *Post*, both of Visalia; the *Argus* and the *Democrat*, both of Stockton; and the *Mountain Democrat* of Placerville.[69]

The *Expositor* published a still-quoted editorial in 1862, saying: "O Lord we thank Thee for letting the rebels wallop us at the Battle of Pittsburg Landing."[70] It later was mobbed by Union soldiers, the press shattered, and the pieces scattered in the street.[71]

Henry Hamilton, *Los Angeles Star* editor, was arrested in October of 1862 and taken to San Francisco where he was in the custody of a provost marshal for a few days. Welcomed home by a barbecue, he ran for state senator and was elected in 1863. His newspaper failed for lack of public support the following year.[72]

The leading dreamer in Oregon was Joseph Lane, nominated for Vice-President on the ticket with Breckinridge. His followers were those who refused to vote for Douglas, having held a separate state convention.

Lane envisioned a new nation founded on a plan of aristocracy that resembled ancient Venice, with all power held by nobles. In this scheme, the white inhabitants would perform no labor, all work to be done by Negroes or other persons with dark skin.[73]

Editors of the Democratic newspapers that followed Lane were hit by a sweeping order that barred their publications from the mails on April 30, 1862. The order was issued by Brigadier General George Wright, commanding the Department of Oregon.[74]

Those barred were the *Albany Democrat*, the *Southern Oregon Gazette*, the *Eugene Democratic Register*, the *Albany Inquirer*, the *Portland Advertiser*, and the *Corvallis Union*. By permission of the military, the *Albany Democrat* resumed publication in February of 1863. Later that same year, the *Eugene Democratic Register* reappeared under the name of the *Democratic Review;* the *Democratic State Journal* at The Dalles, an anti-Lincoln newspaper, was sold and became a supporter of the Union.

With the tide of secession sentiment stemmed, new Union newspapers sprang up to replace those barred from the mails for disloyalty. They included *The State Republican,* Eugene City, and the *Union Crusader,* later called *The Herald Of Reform,* also published at Eugene City.[75]

# 26 Editor Boileau Regrets

THE PHILADELPHIA EVENING JOURNAL, five years old when the war began, came to an inglorious end in 1863 in a case that stirred the seaboard. On January 20, the Democratic *Journal* carried an editorial headed "Davis' Message." It opened with this sentence: "The third annual message of Jefferson Davis to the Confederate congress and Abraham Lincoln's last message to the United States Congress provoke a comparison quite damaging to the intellectual capacity of the Federal President."

Continuing, the editorial recalled several speeches made by Davis on a tour of Southern cities and declared that *The New York Times,* "generally pretty candid, except when engaged in a political campaign," had referred to the Confederacy chief's addresses as "crushingly truthful." It added: "Subsequent events (Union defeats) have proved that they were 'crushingly truthful.' "[1]

Just after midnight on January 28, Albert D. Boileau, editor and publisher of the *Journal,* was arrested at his home by soldiers and whisked out of the city.

The arrest caused great excitement, particularly among newspaper men, owing mainly to the secrecy under which the government operated. The Philadelphia newspapers knew neither why Boileau had been arrested nor where he had been taken. It was at first believed he was imprisoned in Washington, one of the papers saying: "The columns of the *Journal* have recently been filled with articles abusing the government and bitterly denouncing the administration, and it is probable that to this fact Mr. Boileau owes his sudden and involuntary visit to Washington."

In the afternoon following Boileau's arrest, the provost marshal and a file of soldiers marched into the *Evening Journal* office and took possession, preventing further publication. The soldiers stacked their arms in the city room and made themselves at home.[2]

Two days after Boileau was taken away, a dispatch out of Baltimore said he was in Fort McHenry and that Philadelphia and Baltimore friends had visited him. The story said Boileau had written "a conservative and loyal letter" to Major General Robert C. Schenck.

Then the full story was published by the Philadelphia newspapers. Boileau had been seized and his newspaper suppressed by special order of General Schenck, commander of the Middle Department, which included the city of Philadelphia. The officer in charge at Philadelphia was Brigadier General William R. Montgomery, an old West Point man on the verge of retirement, and to him was delegated the arrest of Boileau. This is the order as written by General Schenck:

> Headquarters of Eighth Army Corps, Baltimore,
> Monday, January 24, 1863.
> Special order No. 9

Brigadier-General Montgomery will immediately arrest and send under a sufficient guard to Fort McHenry, Baltimore, Albert D. Boileau, the publisher and editor of the Philadelphia *Evening Journal*, for the publication of an editorial article under the title of "Davis' Message," in his paper of January 20, 1863, and for the publication of other articles of like dangerous character tending to the support and encouragement of Rebellion against the Government of the United States. He will also take measures to suppress the publication of the Philadelphia *Evening Journal*, the paper in question, until further orders.[3]

General Schenck's headquarters in Baltimore permitted Boileau's letter to fall into the hands of the press. Dated "February 1, 1863, Headquarters of the Middle Department," it said in part:

I, Albert D. Boileau, citizen of Philadelphia, and editor and publisher of the *Evening Journal*, now confined in Fort McHenry . . . do hereby freely and voluntarily express my regret for the publication of that article, or of any other article of like tendency or character, and do distinctly disavow such articles being published with my proper authority or knowledge . . . and I hereby give to Major-General Robert C. Schenck . . . my sacred parole of honor, that upon being discharged . . . I will not write, print, or publish any articles having such dangerous character. . . . And . . . these declarations and pledges are made to relate as well to the *Democratic Leader*, made up from the *Daily Philadelphia Evening Journal*.[4]

Within twenty-four hours after Boileau was arrested, Judge James R. Ludlow, "a Democrat of well known partisan conviction," called attention of the Philadelphia grand jury to the case and ordered that it be "examined." The jurist admitted he was acting "alone" and said he would take the responsibility. General Montgomery and the provost marshal were summoned to testify.

The grand jury acted quickly and on January 30 handed down a "presentment" cautiously worded. The jury stated that while it "could not conscientiously do anything" that would weaken the government to suppress "this most wicked and causeless Rebellion," yet it felt it was duty-bound to enforce all laws for the protection of life, the security of property, and the liberty of the citizens.

Judge Ludlow read the "presentment" and told the grand jury, "I shall direct the district attorney . . . to frame such bills of indictment as he may find to be necessary. . . ." There the matter rested for a few days until the next term of court when Judge Alison was on the bench. He disposed of the "presentment" in a few words, saying, "It was unwise, it was unnecessary, it was injudicious."

Democratic members of the state legislature, in session at Harrisburg, made an unsuccessful attempt to force the Governor to go to Washington and demand the release of Boileau.[5] Meanwhile, Boileau came back to Philadelphia, a free man, ending the whole affair. The editor's written apology to General Schenck won his release, but it also was his undoing; he was laughed at by his opponents, despised by those with whom he had previously stood.

The New York *World*, spokesman for all Lincoln hating newspapers, read Boileau out of their lists, saying in a sarcastically written editorial:

Mr. Albert D. Boileau has made a solemn promise, "all of his own accord," to Major General Schenck. . . . In obtaining his release by an act which consigns him . . . to the contempt of honest men and the scorn of the loyal, he has (and this is the only view in which his action has more than a petty personal significance) prevented the Government from righting its wrong, and enabled it to establish another precedent for lawless despotism.[6]

The loyal Union newspapers of Philadelphia said very little thereafter about the accused editor; all they had to do was reprint the *World* editorial to perform an act of execution on both Boileau and his *Evening Journal*. Publication of the *Evening Journal* ceased.

The radical wing of the Democratic party in Philadelphia was left without a voice. That situation brought about the appearance of *The Age*, a morning daily newspaper, on March 25, 1863, not long after the Boileau episode.

The theme of *The Age* from the day of its launching was that slavery was established on the American continent by God "for wise purposes in the Divine mind—to make it the nursery of civilization, from which, in His own good time, should be taken the instruments through which benighted Africa was to be colonized, civilized and Christianized."[7]

The newspaper was backed by wealthy Democrats, three of whom, Adam J. Glossbrenner, William H. Walsh, and Francis J. Grund, were identified as members of the firm. Grund was editor. The office of *The Age* was several times menaced by mobs, and it was saved each time by the police.[8] Grund resigned in July of 1863, when he could no longer stomach his own editorials, and joined the Republican party.[9]

In Harrisburg, the Pennsylvania capital, the Democratic newspaper was the *Patriot and Union*, known for its antiadministration utterances. The daily's reputation finally led it into trouble, perhaps in this case unjustly. On August 4, 1862, a handbill was posted around the city, announcing "the great General James Lane" was in town to address the Negro citizens and recruit for the army. It was signed "J. H. Tomkins, Recruiting Officer for Lane's Colored Regiments."[10]

The people of Harrisburg became highly excited over the handbills, and a rumor spread that they were the work of the *Patriot and Union*. There was no meeting, and Lane was not in town.[11]

At four o'clock in the morning of August 6, Lafayette C. Baker, chief of the United States Secret Service, with Captain I. Dodge, provost marshal of Harrisburg, the chief of police of that city, and a file of Union soldiers routed the editors and staff members of the *Patriot and Union* out of bed and placed them under arrest. Those arrested were Ormond Barrett and Thomas C. MacDowell, editors and owners of the newspaper, J. Montgomery Foster, assistant editor, and M. J. Jones, city editor.

MacDowell was seized first. They showed him a paper signed by Major General H. W. Halleck, General in Chief, ordering that the editors be taken to Washington and tried before a military commission for publishing a handbill that discouraged enlistments. The order also stated that the "presses, type, fixtures, and all the property" of the *Patriot and Union* were to be seized.

The four men were given an hour to get ready and appear at the Mayor's office. At six o'clock, they were marched off to the depot by soldiers and placed on a train for Washington. Upon entering the coach, they were turned over to Brigadier General James S. Wadsworth, military governor of the District of Columbia, who had come to Harrisburg to supervise the arrests.

When they reached Washington, their baggage was searched and they were taken off to Old Capitol prison. On August 23, they were taken before Judge Advocate L. C. Turner for examination. The hearing was a farce. The editors demanded to see the affidavit upon which they had been arrested; they also asked for a copy of the specific charges against them and the names of their accusers. Turner told them he was unable to produce any evidence and released them.

The four left Washington the following morning and arrived in Harrisburg that afternoon, having been imprisoned eighteen days.[12]

While they were in prison, the radical element of the Democratic press took up their case with a denunciation of the administration. The *New York Evening Express* wanted to know why Wendell Phillips, the Boston Abolitionist, had not been arrested. It pointed out that Phillips was an advocate of disunion because he wanted the North detached from slaveholding territory. The *Express* spoke of Lincoln as "the present turtle at the head of the government."[13]

*The Crisis* at Columbus, Ohio, explained—and may have told the truth —that the *Patriot and Union* had nothing to do with the handbills and that "the whole thing was evidently a hoax, probably gotten up by some boys for the sake of a little sport." And as for discouraging enlistments, said *The Crisis*, why was not some action taken against William Lloyd Garrison's Boston *Liberator?* It quoted from an Abolition speech made at Milford, Mass., and published in *The Liberator*, in which the speaker was alleged to have said:

Believe yourself too sacred to be shot down like dogs by Jeff. Davis . . . in the cause of slavery! Die, rather at home, in the arms of loving mothers and affectionate sisters. Nay, be shot down if you must, at home, and die like a Christian and have a decent burial, rather than go and die in the cause of a Union and government based on slavery, which should never have been formed. . . .[14]

When the train bearing the *Patriot and Union* editors reached Harrisburg, more than a thousand persons were at the station to meet them.

"Marched from the city under an escort of gleaming bayonets to the railroad depot," *The Crisis* reported, "they returned amid the plaudits of the men and waving of handkerchiefs of the ladies."[15]

Elsewhere in Pennsylvania, Democratic newspapers found it unprofitable to oppose the war. The *Sentinel*, at Easton, that stood for peace and compromise, was wrecked by a mob on August 19, 1861. The editor of the Easton *Argus* was visited by the mob and told to change his policy.[16] Editor Neiman of the *Sentinel* was later elected to the state legislature as a Democrat from Northampton County.[17]

In Allentown, on August 22, 1861, a mob threatened to destroy the offices of both the *Democrat* and the *Republikaner*, a German language newspaper. They were saved by the sheriff.[18]

The *Republikaner* at Pittsburgh, edited by L. W. Koelkenbeck, was warned by the United States district attorney in August of 1861 that the paper was "decidedly inimical to the interests of the government" and "the cause of much annoyance to the Union citizens of Allegheny county."[19]

The *Carbon Democrat* of Mauch Chunk was mobbed on August 31, 1861. The Carlisle *American Volunteer* suffered mob action on October 24, 1862. The editor of the Bellefonte *Watchman* was arrested by order of the government on August 15, 1863. The Huntingdon *Monitor* was mobbed May 20, 1863, just a week after the *Mentor* at Kittanning suffered the same fate.[20] The *Mentor* resumed publication, still defiant. In a few weeks it was saying: ". . . when we look at the vacant chair, or new made graves of those who have died, let us remember that all these we owe to Mr. Abraham Lincoln and the party that supports him."[21]

The *Crawford Democrat* at Meadville was successfully defended from mob attack on February 5, 1864.[22] The *Northumberland County Democrat* at Sunbury was wrecked by a mob on January 18, 1864. In reporting the Sunbury mobbing, the *Patriot and Union* hailed Editor Purdy as "a man of distinction." Purdy had his paper going again soon.[23]

Two months later, soldiers of the 4th Pennsylvania Volunteers, a Shamokin company, threatened to wreck the Sunbury newspaper but were halted by their captain after they smashed the front door.[24]

The *Lebanon Advertiser* was damaged by a mob in early 1864.[25] The *Valley Spirit*, a Democratic newspaper, was destroyed in the burning of Chambersburg by Confederate raiders in July of 1864.[26]

# 27 "A Wily Agitator"

THE YEAR 1863 saw the Confederacy take the offensive and make its supreme effort. It saw Fort Sumter shelled by a Union fleet, the great battles of Chancellorsville and Chickamauga, the siege and capture of Vicksburg by Grant, and a new state, West Virginia, born of Virginia's secession labor pains. It saw Lee turned back at Gettysburg.

Linked with the Confederate military strategy was the effort of those in the North who opposed the war and hated Lincoln to stir unrest on the home front. The opposition press in the Union states screamed more loudly than ever that Lincoln was destroying all personal liberty, that free speech and freedom of the press no longer existed. The charge of lost liberties found thousands of gullible and willing listeners in the North.

Editors of Copperhead newspapers had exhausted their supply of adjectives in acrimonious editorials by 1863, only to find popular opinion among the masses still was on the President's side. They adopted new tactics, stirring dissension and attempting to make the people lose faith in their leaders. Criticism and ridicule of Lincoln were maintained, while individuals, generals, and department heads were singled out as targets.

Clement L. Vallandigham, his term in Congress having expired, took his fight to the people. Puffed by editorial praise of the peace papers and flattered by the flood of publicity that followed his every movement, he ranted and raved against Lincoln, apparently daring the government to arrest him.

General Burnside, transferred to command of the Department of the Ohio after his defeat at Fredericksburg, kept his eye on Vallandigham. On April 13, 1863, he issued General Order No. 38, which said in part:

. . . hereafter all persons found within our lines who commit acts for the benefit of the enemies of our country will be tried as spies or traitors, and if convicted will suffer death. . . . The habit of declaring sympathies for the enemy will no longer be tolerated in this department. Persons committing such offenses will be at once arrested, with a view to being tried as above stated or sent beyond our lines into the lines of their friends.[1]

Burnside's order was the subject of widespread comment in the Democratic press. That it was aimed at Vallandigham, there could be no doubt, and he prepared for a showdown. The peace wing of the Democratic party was especially strong at Mount Vernon, in Knox County, Ohio, and he announced he would speak there on May 1.

Every effort was made to publicize the meeting. A stand was set up in a field, decorated with pictures of butternuts, one of the insignia worn by Peace Democrats. Newspaper reports say thousands heard Vallandigham. Hundreds wore Copperhead badges, made from pennies. A large banner carried by a township delegation bore the words: "The Copperheads Are Coming."

On the platform with Vallandigham was Congressman S. S. Cox, formerly editor of the Ohio Statesman at Columbus and critic of Lincoln, although a supporter of war measures. Cox won fame as an editor by writing a sophomoric editorial on the beauties of a Columbus sunset that made the whole country laugh when it was reprinted by many newspapers. He was known thereafter as "Sunset" Cox.[2]

General Burnside sent members of his staff in civilian dress to hear Vallandigham. They carried their reports back to the General, and Vallandigham returned to his home at Dayton. Word got around that Burnside's men had been at Mount Vernon, and arrest of Vallandigham was expected momentarily.

General Burnside sent a full company of the 115th Ohio Regiment to Dayton by special train, leaving Cincinnati shortly before midnight on May 4. Upon arrival at Dayton at three o'clock in the morning, the soldiers marched to the Vallandigham home, and an officer pounded on the door.

Vallandigham poked his head from a second-floor bedroom window. The officer said they had come to arrest him and demanded admittance. Vallandigham replied he would not open the door and began to call in a loud voice, "Asa! Asa! Asa!" His cry was answered by a pistol shot fired from a rear window, a prearranged signal to his friends. The soldiers broke into the house and found Vallandigham in his nightshirt. The officer told him to get into his clothing. Fire bells were ringing all over the city, and a crowd began to gather in front of the house.

Vallandigham was marched off to a waiting train, taken directly to Cincinnati, placed in a military prison, and there all visitors were denied access to him.[3]

The arrest left Dayton in an uproar. By noon, wagons and carriages filled with Vallandigham followers were arriving in town. At dusk, a mob of five or six hundred men, hooting and yelling, attacked the office of the *Dayton Daily Journal*, a Republican newspaper that despised Vallandigham. Bullets broke the windows of the building, and blazing torches were tossed inside.

Fire started in the *Journal* building and spread rapidly. It destroyed a hat store, a shoe store, the office of a church publication, a livery stable, a meat market, and a leather store. The firemen were helpless. Their engines had been put out of commission and the hose slashed to ribbons.

City officials telegraphed to Cincinnati for troops, and Burnside had a company in Dayton by ten o'clock. With engines repaired under protection of soldiers, firemen finally halted the conflagration.[4]

Lewis Marot, editor and publisher of the *Journal*, missed only one day's publication. The paper came out on May 7, with four pages, eight by twelve inches, printed on a hand press. An editorial declared Dayton city officials were guilty of treason and cowardice. The *Journal* also charged that the mob assembled at the office of the *Dayton Daily Empire*, where a cannon was fired in the street, as a signal to attack the Republican newspaper.[5]

The *Empire* protested Vallandigham's arrest in an editorial that lashed the military officials and was suppressed at once by General Burnside. Its editor, William T. Logan, followed his hero to prison at Cincinnati. Copies of the *Empire* that contained the editorial sold on the streets of Dayton for fifty cents each.[6]

Dayton and Montgomery County were placed under martial law, and the jails were filled with mob suspects.

Vallandigham spent his first day in prison writing an address to the Democrats of Ohio and managed to get it into the hands of his party press. Dated "military prison, Cincinnati, May 5th, 1863," it said in part:

I am here in a military bastile for no other offense than my political opinions, and the defense of them, and of the rights of the people, and of your constitutional liberties. Speeches made in the hearing of thousands of you in denunciation of the usurpations of power, infractions of the Constitution and laws, and of military despotism, were the sole cause of my arrest and imprisonment. I am a Democrat—for the Constitution, for the law, for the Union, for liberty—this is my only "crime." For no disobedience to the Constitution; for no violation of law; for no word, sign, or gesture of sympathy with the men of the South, who are for disunion and southern independence, but in obedience to their demand as well as the demand of northern abolition disunionists and traitors, I am here in bonds today; but "Time, at last, sets all things even!"[7]

General Burnside moved swiftly and ordered Vallandigham tried the next day, May 6, by a military commission. This form of trial differed from a court-martial in that a military commission sat only under special orders, was limited to a particular case, and had no rules of evidence or any rule of decision. The charge was that Vallandigham had publicly expressed "in violation of General Order No. 38 . . . his sympathies for those in arms against the Government of the United States, declaring disloyal sentiments and opinions, with the object and purpose of weakening the power of the Government in its efforts to suppress an unlawful rebellion."

It was specified Vallandigham said the war was wicked, cruel, and unnecessary, that it was a war to crush liberty and set up a despotism, that it was a war to free the blacks and enslave the whites.

He also was charged with saying President Lincoln rejected a plan to end the war the day before the Battle of Fredericksburg. Still another charge said that Vallandigham declared the government was about to appoint military marshals in every district "to restrain the people of their liberties, to deprive them of their rights and privileges." He faced the accusation of having said he spit on General Order No. 38 and trampled it underfoot.[8]

When asked to enter his plea, Vallandigham refused and requested the commission to compel the attendance of Fernando Wood of New York. He asked that Wood be directed to produce a letter he received from Richmond, purportedly containing a proposition for return of Southern Senators to their seats in Congress and to show a letter from President Lincoln declining to entertain the plan. Instead, the commission granted Vallandigham three hours to consult with his attorney, George E. Pugh, former United States Senator from Ohio.[9]

After the recess, introduction of testimony began, and General Burnside offered as witnesses the officers who heard Vallandigham at Mount Vernon. Captain H. R. Hill said he stood within six feet of Vallandigham and heard him say General Order No. 38 was "a base usurpation of arbitrary authority," that he despised it and spit on it. Hill described the decorations on the platform, and the judge advocate interposed to ask Vallandigham whether it was not true the butternut was an emblem of the Confederacy. Vallandigham said he was not aware of it.

Courtesy The Historical Society of Pennsylvania

John W. Forney, editor of *The Press*, Philadelphia, and *Daily Morning Chronicle*, Washington.

Engraving from *Parson Brownlow's Book*

W. G. "Parson" Brownlow, editor of the *Knoxville* (Tenn.) *Whig.*

Courtesy Ohio State Archaeol. and Hist. Society

Clement L. Vallandigham, Ohio newspaperman and Copperhead politician banished by Lincoln.

Courtesy Frederick H. Meserve

Thurlow Weed, editor of the *Albany Evening Journal.*

Courtesy Frederick H. Mese

The Lincoln of Gettysburg. Photo by Gardner on November 15, 1863, four da
before he spoke in Pennsylvania.

Captain John A. Means testified he heard Vallandigham say he spit on General Order No. 38 and heard him refer to the President as "King Lincoln."

Congressman Cox was the only witness for Vallandigham. He admitted he was on the speaker's platform but heard no "epithets" applied to General Burnside, whom he described as "an old friend of mine." Cox said he could not recall that Vallandigham said anything about spitting on General Order No. 38 or trampling it underfoot. The commission studied the evidence for three hours and reached a verdict of guilty.[10]

Before the verdict was made public, Vallandigham sought to obtain his release by asking for a writ of habeas corpus in the United States circuit court on May 11. His action brought to a head the controversy that centered on this form of legal writ. Only two months before, Congress enacted legislation authorizing the President to suspend the privilege of the writ of habeas corpus in any case throughout the United States or any part thereof, whenever in his judgment the public safety required it. The motion for the writ was denied by Judge Humphrey H. Leavitt, a Democrat appointed to the Federal bench during the Jackson administration. In a lengthy decision, Judge Leavitt held that Burnside, acting as an agent for President Lincoln, had a perfect legal right to arrest and hold Vallandigham.[11]

The President was watching the case closely and decided not to use his power of suspension of habeas corpus. He told Secretary of War Stanton he had conferred with Secretary of State Seward and Salmon P. Chase, Secretary of the Treasury and Republican leader in Ohio, and they were of the opinion a suspension should not be ordered. Secretary Chase, said Lincoln, did not think Judge Leavitt would honor Vallandigham's application for release.[12]

The President was overjoyed when Judge Leavitt denied the writ of habeas corpus and declared the decision was worth three victories in the field.[13]

When Attorney Pugh argued for Vallandigham's release, General Burnside submitted to the court an "explanation and defense" of his action. It was a novel paper, saying in part:

If I were to find a man from the enemy's country distributing in my camps speeches of their public men that tended to demoralize the troops, or to destroy their confidence in the constituted authorities of the government, I would have them tried and hung if found guilty and all the rules of modern warfare would sustain me. Why should such speeches from our own public men be allowed . . . ?

It is said that the speeches which were condemned have been in the presence of large bodies of citizens, who, if they thought them wrong, would have then and there condemned them. That is no argument. These citizens do not realize the effect upon the army of our country, who are its defenders. They have never been in the field, never faced the enemies of their country. . . .

There is no fear of the people losing their liberties; we all know that to be the cry of the demagogues and none but the ignorant will listen to it. . . . I call upon the fathers, mothers, brothers, sisters, sons, daughters, relatives, friends and neighbors of the soldiers in the field, to aid me in stopping this license and intemperate discussion, which are discouraging our armies. . . .

These are substantially my reasons for issuing General Order No. 38. . . .[14]

The military commission sentenced Vallandigham to imprisonment in a fortress for duration of the war. General Burnside approved the finding and the sentence and designated Fort Warren, Boston, as the place of incarceration.[15]

Hundreds of political arrests were made by the Federal government, but none caused the excitement of the Vallandigham case. It was the topic of the day, sharing newspaper space with the Battle of Chancellorsville and the death of "Stonewall" Jackson, the great Confederate General.

The Democratic press, screaming for months that Lincoln was endangering the liberties of the people, the right of free speech and print, pointed to the Vallandigham arrest as a prophecy come true. That attitude was supported by some of the most important Republican editors, and a great chorus of "lost rights" rose to the high heavens.[16]

Even the administration press was divided. *The Crisis* gleefully reported that "every Republican paper in the city of New York opposes the arrest of Mr. Vallandigham except the *Times*. This speaks volumes."[17]

The *Cincinnati Gazette*, which covered the arrest and trial carefully, said: "Our eastern contemporaries, who have commented on this arrest as unnecessary, do not appreciate the entire situation."[18] From Washington, in a special dispatch, came a hint of Vallandigham's ultimate fate:

General anxiety has been expressed here lest the decision of the court-martial in Vallandigham's case should have the effect to make a martyr of him. On this account it was earnestly hoped that the result would be an order to send him down beyond Rosecrans' line and dump him into the territory of his friends, the rebels, with due notice that if caught back on our side he would be treated as a spy.[19]

George D. Prentice's *Louisville Journal* said it was a mistake to suppose the excitement aroused by the Vallandigham arrest came from sympathy with his "peculiar views," but on the contrary, "it arises in spite of a decided antipathy to those views, as is shown conclusively by the fact that the feeling is shared by such Republican champions as the *New York Tribune*, the New York *Evening Post*, the New York *Commercial Advertiser*, the *Albany Statesman*, the *Boston Advertiser*, the *Boston Traveller*, the *Springfield Republican*, and, in short, by the ablest and most influential champions of the Republican party, backed, as the New York *Evening Post* avows, by at least three-fourths of the Republican party itself."[20]

The *National Intelligencer* at Washington charged Judge Leavitt with ignorance of the law, saying:

. . . as if to shut the door against any such proceedings as those instituted by Gen. Burnside, it (Congress) passed an act, approved March 3, 1863, expressly "relating to habeas corpus and regulating judicial proceedings in certain cases. . . ." Judge Leavitt, in refusing to grant the writ . . . , stated that he had not seen this law, which was cited in court by Mr. Pugh. . . . And when a judge of the United States is ignorant of the legislation of Congress on this head, surely Gen. Burnside may be excused for not knowing that Congress, by the act of July 17, 1862, had expressly provided for the trial by the courts of the offense he alleges against Mr. Vallandigham.[21]

Public meetings of indignation at the arrest of Vallandigham were held, one of the largest being staged in New York's Union Square. The meeting, called a "ridiculous demonstration" by *The New York Times*, heard several speakers, one of whom was James McMaster, editor of *Freeman's Journal*. None of the "big names" of the Democratic party in New York appeared, the *Times* observed.[22]

The source of the order for the arrest was one of the main points of speculation. President Lincoln was, of course, blamed by the critical press. A story out of Washington by the *Cincinnati Gazette's* "Agate," on May 25, stated the facts correctly but drew little attention. It said:

General Burnside certainly acted under no orders from Washington, either in making the arrest or in confirming the sentence of the court-martial. . . . Some of the more prominent members of the Government regretted the arrest. . . . Neither arrest nor punishment was an Administration measure. . . . His (Vallandigham's) friends may erect his tombstone, for he is dead.[23]

"Agate" was Whitelaw Reid, former Xenia newspaper editor, now war correspondent and Washington writer for the Cincinnati paper. Reid, like his contemporary writers, referred to Vallandigham's trial as a court-martial when he should have used the term "military commission."

On May 19, Brigadier General E. R. S. Canby, attached to the War Department, wired General Burnside that the President "directs that without delay" Vallandigham be sent to the headquarters of General Rosecrans, there to be sent beyond the Union lines.

The order stated that in the event Vallandigham returned he should be arrested and kept in prison as his sentence specified.[24] The morning papers of May 26, carrying a story out of Murfreesboro, said the order had been executed. They quoted Vallandigham as saying to the Confederate army pickets who received him, "I am a citizen of Ohio and of the United States. I am here within your lines by force and against my will. I therefore surrender myself to you as a prisoner of war."[25]

One more step was taken in the courts for Vallandigham. At the next session of the United States Supreme Court, an application was made by Attorney Pugh for a writ of *certiorari* to bring up the proceedings of the military commission for review. The motion was denied on grounds no such writ could be issued by the Supreme Court to a military commission, the court not having jurisdiction over the proceedings of such a body.[26]

New York Democrats, headed by Erastus Corning, met at Albany on May 16 and passed resolutions critical of the administration in the handling of Vallandigham. One resolution said that "we denounce the recent assumption of a military commander to seize and try a citizen of Ohio . . . for no other reason than words addressed to a public meeting, in criticism of the course of the Administration, and in condemnation of the military orders of that general."

It was also declared that "this assumption of trial by a military tribunal, if successfully asserted, not only abrogates the right of the people to assemble and discuss the affairs of Government, the liberty of speech and of the press, the right of trial by jury, the law of evidence, and the privilege of habeas corpus, but it strikes a fatal blow at the supremacy of law and the authority of the state and Federal constitutions."

The Albany Democrats told the President that "in the election of Governor Seymour, the people of this state, by an emphatic majority, declared their condemnation of the system of arbitrary arrests, and their determination to stand by the Constitution."[27]

Corning mailed a copy of the resolutions to the White House on May 19, and Lincoln, promising a "respectful response," acknowledged receipt of it in a telegram on May 28.[28] The President did not reply for two weeks. When he finally answered, he pointed out first that Vallandigham was trying to prevent the raising of troops and was encouraging desertions from the army. Then with a few plain words he cut through to the heart of the matter. He put this question to Corning:

"Must I shoot a simple-minded soldier boy who deserts, while I must not touch a hair of a wily agitator who induces him to desert . . . ? I think that, in such a case, to silence the agitator and save the boy is not only constitutional, but withal a great mercy."[29]

Corning tried to belittle the President's reply by saying it was couched in "misty and cloudy forms of expression." He charged freedom of the press had been denied and that "in repeated instances newspapers have been suppressed in the loyal states because they criticized, as constitutionally they might, those fatal errors of policy which have characterized the conduct of public affairs since your advent to power."[30]

Ohio Democrats joined the New Yorkers in assailing the President. In a state convention on June 26, they passed resolutions of protest and sent them, with a long letter, to President Lincoln. They contended Vallandigham was a "prominent candidate" for the gubernatorial nomination in Ohio at the time of his arrest and Burnside's action was an insult to the state. They said:

If freedom of speech and of the press are to be suspended in time of war, then the essential element of popular government to effect a change of policy in the constitutional mode is at an end. The freedom of speech and of the press is indispensable, and necessarily incident to the nature of popular government itself. If any inconvenience or evils arise from its exercise, they are unavoidable.

The letter was signed by a group of Democrats who called themselves "the Ohio Committee."[31] Among the signers was George H. Pendleton, Ohio Congressman who later ran for Vice-President against Lincoln. Pendleton's wife Alice was the daughter of Francis Scott Key.

Although Lincoln's days and nights during the last week of June were filled with anxiety as Lee's army moved north to Gettysburg, he took time to make another explanation of policy on Vallandigham. He offered to revoke Vallandigham's sentence under certain conditions—that members of the "Ohio Committee" pledge themselves to do nothing to hinder the army or navy and that each was to do all he could to see that the armed services were well equipped and well fed.[32] This the committee, to a man, refused to do.[33]

It was generally agreed by now that President Lincoln had not actually ordered the arrest of Vallandigham but that he had not said he should be left to run at large, and, once the arrest had been made, he stood behind it. In his letter to the New York Democrats, Lincoln said that, left to his own discretion, "I do not know whether I would have ordered the arrest." He added, however, that he could not shift the responsibility from himself and that he must practice "a general directory and revisory power in the matter."

Meanwhile, General Burnside, disgusted by the upheaval that followed the arrest and trial, informed the President he was ready to give up his command of the Department of the Ohio. On May 29, Lincoln told the General by telegram that he would let him know when he wished to remove him. He said the whole Cabinet regretted "the necessity" of the arrest and that some doubted whether it was necessary, but all were for seeing him (Burnside) through with it.[34]

Martial law continued in Dayton until June 21 when it was lifted by General Burnside. Meanwhile, Editor Logan of the Dayton Daily Empire lay in prison at Cincinnati.[35] Logan's trouble was that he had spoken too bluntly in his editorials. If his pen had been as talented as that of Bryant of the New York Evening Post, he could have upbraided Lincoln and Burnside so politely he might have escaped arrest. Bryant's Post said:

Under the provisions of these statutes (acts of Congress), Vallandigham is a prisoner of State and the Secretary of War is bound to report him as such to the Circuit Judge of the district in which his supposed offenses were committed, to be regularly tried by the civil tribunal. There is no escape from the plain demands of the law, even if there were a desire to do so, which we cannot suppose, and we expect to hear in a few days that the culprit has been handed over to the only legitimate authorities.[36]

The burned-out Dayton Daily Journal, with borrowed equipment, appeared every day and was "the same fearless denouncer of treason, the same hater of Copperheads, Butternuts, and incendiaries who would lay the North in ashes that the supremacy of slavery propagation may be maintained," the Cleveland Herald reported.[37]

Editor Marot was offered financial assistance of Dayton businessmen to establish a new plant, but he declined and took a job on the *Inter-Ocean* at Chicago. A committee of Republicans organized a stock company and offered editorship of the newspaper to W. D. Bickham, war correspondent of the *Cincinnati Commercial*. Bickham, a soldier of fortune, viewed the ashes of the *Journal* and announced he was ready to go to work.[38]

Two brothers, Thomas and William Hubbard, bought the *Dayton Daily Empire*, taking it over from Jonathan Kenny, who operated it briefly after Logan went to prison. The Hubbards formerly published the *Logan* (Ohio) *Gazette*, a Democratic newspaper of the Copperhead species that folded with the 1863 fall elections. Under them, the *Empire* continued to sing the praises of Vallandigham.[39]

On March 3, 1864, less than three months after the Hubbards assumed proprietorship, the *Empire* office was mobbed and wrecked by Union soldiers and civilians. For three days, the *Empire* had been attacking Lincoln in long editorials. At noon, fifteen soldiers and several men in civilian clothing broke into the composing room of the *Empire*, threw type in all directions, and manhandled the Hubbards. They threw a heating stove out the window, but hot coals set the building on fire.[40]

A crowd poured into the building, extinguished the fire, and pleaded with the soldiers to stop their work of destruction. The soldiers and their leader, Captain Badger of the 44th Ohio Regiment, left the newspaper office and went to the county courthouse where he made a speech in the public square. A reporter for the *Cincinnati Enquirer* gave this version of Badger's speech:

Fellow citizens, by the great God (hiccup) and Resurrector of everybody, I swear (hiccup) I am responsible for all this! and God damn you, I led this whole thing. These men (hiccup) are under my control and I am responsible. God damn you, two hundred veterans, such as we are, are worth one thousand citizens. There is no line of distinction (hiccup) between the Administration and the Government and I tell you, by God, if any action is taken against me and my men here, the city of Dayton shall suffer.[41]

Two Dayton men spoke when Badger finished, telling the crowd to be calm. They apparently had the situation in hand till some person jeered that the government was protecting "niggers." In a wild fight that followed, a dozen shots were fired. A spectator was killed and two soldiers wounded.

The provost marshal telegraphed to Cincinnati for troops, and Major

General Samuel P. Heintzelman sent 300 soldiers. Captain Badger, arrested by city officials, was turned over to the army to face charges. A coroner's jury ruled that the spectator killed came to his death by "persons unknown."[42]

The *Empire* printers gathered up their scattered type and put a paper on the streets the next day. It carried a news story and an editorial on the mobbing. The editor displayed remarkable self-control when he wrote this simple headline, "Another Riot." The editorial charged Badger was drunk and that the soldiers "screwed up" their courage with drink.

When the *Empire* was mobbed, Vallandigham was living in a hotel at Windsor, Canada, awaiting a chance to sneak back into the United States. After he was received within the Confederate lines, he was transferred to Richmond by Major General Braxton Bragg. The Confederate capital was cool to Vallandigham, and he fled, with approval of the South, to Bermuda and later to Canada.

On March 11, 1864, eight days after the attack on the *Empire*, "The Great Unhanged," as Vallandigham was called by Ohio Republican newspapers, sent a message from Windsor to the Hubbards in which he offered his sympathy at the loss suffered and gave this dubious advice: "There is, therefore, but one remedy for past and preventative of future injuries; and that is, instant, summary and ample reprisals upon the persons and property of the men at home, who, by language and conduct, are always exciting these outrages."[43]

Just two days before, on March 9, the *Empire* carried an editorial that charged President Lincoln had tried to muzzle the opposition press but, having failed, permitted soldiers to raid newspaper offices. This editorial bears every sign of having been written by Vallandigham, and it is probable it came in the same mail with the message of condolence. It said:

Abraham Lincoln has assaulted the dearest rights of the people in a variety of ways. He has imprisoned, threatened, or banished those public men whose voices were dangerous to the consummation of his purpose. He muzzled the press by the edicts of his Secretary of War. That bond being broken, he allowed his military generals to issue such orders as they please to effectuate the same purpose. Both these methods having failed, he smiles complacently while a few disorderly soldiers, in various parts of the country, instigated and deceived by lying Republican politicians, attempt to destroy the material with which the voice of the people is expressed. Vain hope of tyrants! A thousand presses might be destroyed, yet the voice of the people would still live and seek a thousand new engines to make itself heard. The type may go to destruction, but the thoughts of the people will survive, and until the art of printing becomes one of the lost arts, the people will have their thoughts heard and will make their wishes known and respected. If every Democratic press were destroyed tomorrow, every Democrat would be only confirmed in his antagonism to the present administration, and thousands of true men would join their ranks for the first time.

The rage of Lincoln against the press that is not subservient to his green money is impotent and comparatively harmless.[44]

The administration was upheld in the state elections of 1863. Republicans won in Vermont, California, and Maine. Governor Curtin of Pennsylvania was reelected, a Republican governor and legislature chosen in Iowa, and the result was similar in Wisconsin, Minnesota, and Michigan. The Republican majority in New York was 30,000, and in Massachusetts it was 40,000. Maryland backed the administration with 20,000 votes to spare.[45]

Nominated for governor by the peace wing of the Ohio Democratic party, Vallandigham ran as an "exiled martyr" against a fusion ticket headed by John Brough, a former newspaperman and War Democrat. He was defeated by more than one hundred thousand votes, giving Brough the greatest majority for governor in any state up to that time.[46]

In June of 1864, just a year after he was banished, Vallandigham stole back to Dayton, making his way across the Canadian border with a pillow under his coat to make him look like a fat man, a disguise that fooled no one. Government agents ignored him.

# 28 "Insults and Grimaces"

SOON AFTER GENERAL BURNSIDE issued General Order No. 38, one of his subordinates, Brigadier General Milo S. Hascall, military head of the District of Indiana, Department of the Ohio, broke into the newspaper headlines with General Order No. 9, aimed at the press and speakers in his area.

General Hascall proclaimed his intention to enforce Burnside's order, whose provisions, he said, were being violated "by well-meaning men, who are led astray by newspapers and public speakers." Order No. 9 continued: "There is no use in trying to dry up the stream while its fountains are allowed to flow."[1]

The Indiana General's flat ultimatum stirred protest in the anti-administration press all over the North. No military man had ever before, except in instances where martial law was in effect, used such plain language in addressing the civilian population. The word was passed that a "press dictator" had been appointed in Indiana.

General Hascall was a West Pointer, class of 1852, practicing law in Indiana when the Civil War broke out. He reentered the army, fought in the western Virginia campaign of 1861, and led his own division at Stone River, where he was wounded. His transfer to Indianapolis followed.[2]

A brave soldier but a poor politician, Hascall also was a man of few words. On May 6, 1863, he wrote to the editor of the Columbia City (Ind.) News, saying:

A copy of your paper of May 5 has been handed to me and my attention called to your comments on General Order No. 9 from these headquarters. You can now take your choice: publish an article taking back your threats of resistance to that order and your comments designed to destroy its usefulness, and hereafter publish a loyal paper, or you can discontinue the publication of your paper until further orders. Any violation of this order will receive prompt attention.[3]

Two days later, the editor of the South Bend (Ind.) Forum received this note from General Hascall:

A half dozen copies of your paper of the 3rd inst. have been sent to me marked, in which you boast of your intention to violate General Order No. 9 from these headquarters. You can now publish an article retracting this and publish a loyal paper hereafter, or you can discontinue publication till further orders. . . .[4]

Copies of Hascall's letters fell into the hands of the Democratic press and were soon in the national spotlight. James Brooks, editor of the New York Evening Express, leaped to the attack. His specialty was employment of what he called "newspaper pellets" on the "Lincoln tools." Brooks and his brother, Erastus, co-owner of the Express, were natives of Portland, Me. James studied law, became a Washington correspondent for the Portland Advertiser, and married Mrs. Mary

Randolph, a wealthy widow, of Richmond, Va. He entered politics, served in the New York legislature, then went to Congress for two terms. Brother Erastus, also a Washington correspondent, became a New York state senator. While in Albany, he tried to put through legislation that would have stripped Roman Catholic bishops of the title to church property and real estate. James and Erastus founded the *Express* in 1836 when both were in their early twenties.[5]

Their opposition to the war was based on a policy that it was better to lose the Southern states than fight. They looked upon Lincoln as a "trouble maker," who entered Washington "as a thief in the night."[6] Their newspaper was one of those visited in New York on April 18, 1861, by a shouting crowd that demanded it display the American flag. The brothers quickly complied,[7] but their editorial policy remained unchanged. The *Express* never deviated from its contention that the inauguration of Lincoln sounded the "death-knell of the Union."[8]

James Brooks opened his attack on General Hascall in an editorial which said:

In Indiana, a little primitive village attorney, who could not earn a living by law, was made a brigadier general. Hascall is his name and to him is given dictatorial power in the great state of Indiana. This Hascall, the story goes, suppressed one journal because the editor called him a "donkey," and stopped another because the printer had commenced his name with an R, instead of an H, which the editor said was a typographical error.[9]

All over the North, the antiadministration press howled at Hascall. The New York *World*, in telling of his action against newspapers, said they had fallen before the General's "royal frown."[10]

General Hascall saw the editorial in the *Express* and wrote a blistering letter to the editor. The letter was so unusual that Brooks thought some person might be playing a joke on him. He wrote to the General for verification before making formal reply. Hascall assured him the letter was not a forgery.

To the delight of the Democratic press, Brooks published the correspondence between him and the General, with this note of explanation:

Some days since, the editors of the *Express* received a letter from Brigadier General Hascall, dated Indianapolis. Never having heard of this military gentleman until his now famous "Order No. 9" came out, we thought that, when he sent us the following letter, some one was making a fool of him and his profession, and, therefore, we wrote to inquire if the letter was genuine or a forgery. In a scurrilous reply, he admits the letter to be genuine. We, therefore, publish the letter, and our reply, which we have mailed for him today.

This is the letter that aroused Brooks's curiosity, as reprinted in the *Express:*

Gents: Some one has been kind enough to inclose a slip containing a copy of my order no. 9, and your remarks thereon. They are exceedingly witty and smart, and in your judgment, probably, dispose of the whole case. It may surprise you some to know that the order was issued after mature deliberation and consultation, and is being, and will be, carried out to the letter. It is fortunate for you that your paper is not published in my district.

In Brooks's reply to Hascall, a letter of some length, the editor boasted the *Express* would be safe even if the General was in command of the New York district because Governor Seymour would find "a place in the Tombs" for him in the event of interference with the newspaper. It said in part:

If you have any surplus military talent yet undeveloped, would it not be wiser first to flesh your maiden sword in the field upon the enemies of your country before you distinguish yourself as Gaoler or Executioner?[11]

The press reported on June 7, 1863, that General Hascall had been relieved of the Indiana command and would probably go into the field. His last act at Indianapolis was to revoke General Order No. 9.[12] The report was current that he was removed because his letter to the *New York Evening Express* was considered "unofficer-like."[13]

Brooks's next step was to cause trouble for General Schenck, commander of the Middle Department, in Baltimore. Schenck was wrestling with a serious situation, Confederate raids into Maryland keeping the city in a state of constant alarm. Lee was preparing for the invasion that led to Gettysburg.

Schenck issued an order that barred several antiadministration newspapers from his Department, among them the *New York Evening Express.* About the time the order was issued, several regiments of New York troops arrived in Baltimore to bolster the city's defenses.

According to *The Crisis* and other Copperhead newspapers, Brooks appealed to Governor Seymour, his political friend, who notified Schenck that unless the order against the *Express* and the other barred

New York newspapers was rescinded, he would recall the New York regiments. Schenck had no alternative but to remove the barrier against the newspapers, explaining that one of his aides had issued the order "by mistake."[14]

By stirring a tempest when the North was threatened with invasion, Brooks won another victory for the anti-Lincoln press. He exulted in a long letter to Schenck, publishing it in the *Express*, to be reprinted by Democratic newspapers.

The letter, dated "June 22, 1863," spoke of Schenck as "an actor in the midst of a great tragedy." Brooks pointed out to him that they had served together as Whigs in Congress in 1849 to 1851 and would meet again as members in the next session. He charged Schenck devoted his time to preparing an "Index Expurgatorious of Newspapers" when he should have been fighting. He added this insult: "Sir, the true ambition of a great general should be to stop bullets, not newspaper pellets! A general that cannot stand a little paper wadding can never stand an enemy's battery."[15]

Brooks bragged in his letter that the *New York Evening Express* was essential to army reading because it inspired the troops with "patriotism and principles," but the files of the newspaper told another story. A description of the draft published in the *Express* on August 12, 1863, could hardly be classified as inspirational. It said:

The conscription is a horror—as horrible to Republicans, drafted, as to Democrats or others—the horror of horror to all, torn off from home, household, father, mother, wife, children—and such a horror as no human language can well paint. It is slavery, accursed slavery, in its most frightful form. Hence, whoever is conscripted, is, necessarily, penned up, as cattle are penned up, barricaded, guarded—surrounded by armed men, swords ready to be drawn, bayonets pointed, muskets loaded.[16]

The candidacy of Vallandigham for governor of Ohio gave Brooks further excuse to spread the Copperhead doctrine, with publication of his speeches and reference to him as a martyr. The *Express* quoted the *Cincinnati Enquirer* as forecasting a Vallandigham triumph in the election booths.[17]

The *Express* uncovered an effort by Republican postal officials to help beat down the virulent Copperhead press in New York State in late summer of 1863. The exposure added some weight to the charge often made by Democratic editors that the Post Office Department was hostile to the antiadministration press. Brooks published in his *Express* what was purported to be a circular signed by Abram Wakeman, postmaster of New York City, Benjamin Field, and Henry R. Low.

The *Express* charged this circular was intended "to convert the whole Post Office Department into one grand electioneering machine." It charged further that subordinate postmasters understood they must follow the orders in the circular or face dismissal on the grounds of being "enemies of the Union." This is the circular as reproduced:

> No. 73 Trinity Building,
> New York, August 4, 1863.

To ........................., Postmaster at ........................

Dear Sir: The subject of an increased circulation of loyal journals has been strongly urged by prominent Union men throughout the state. . . .

To do this work well, the whole state should be thoroughly canvassed, and every family not thus provided should be induced to subscribe to some loyal journal.

When a family may not feel able to pay the full price of subscription, it is believed that the liberal local men of your vicinity would make up a deficiency if called upon to do so, a little labor in each locality providing the proper sum for this purpose.

The purported circular listed the "leading loyal journals of this city and Albany" and quoted the subscription prices. The papers named were the *New York Tribune, The New York Times,* New York *Evening Post, Abena Zeitung* (German), *New Yorker Democrat* (German), *Albany Evening Journal,* and the *Evening Standard and Statesman* (Albany). No effort was made to discriminate among loyal newspapers, the circular said, the committee's aim being to "bring within the reach of all who will read a journal heartily devoted to our country's salvation."

Postmasters were instructed to send their subscription orders to Sinclair Tousey, 121 Nassau Street, in charge of all distribution.[18]

The *Express* launched a countermeasure against the circular, saying it was the duty of every Democrat to see that his neighbors were supplied with reading matter "to counteract this extensive movement of official power." In a plea addressed to "Democrats and all friends of free government and constitutional liberty," Brooks said, "Now is the time and now is the hour or it may be too late forever to save yourselves from the reign of Tyranny preparing for your necks and those of your children after you." He added: "Give your postmaster to understand that it is his sworn duty to deliver promptly, and without insults and grimaces, all papers that come to his office, whether Democratic or Abolition, or abide the consequences."[19]

Brooks received the accolade of the Democratic press for his journal-istic enterprise. His story of the circular was eagerly reprinted, and other editors added charges, Medary of *The Crisis* insisting money sent to Democratic newspapers was no longer safe in mail bags and that "Democrats have been compelled to threaten personal violence . . . before they could get their papers delivered."[20]

In at least one community, the Union people resorted to violence to prevent circulation of the opposition press by a postmaster. On August 12, 1864, a "mob of Republicans" raided the post office at Milford Center, in Union County, Ohio, sorted out the Democratic newspapers, and burned them in the public square.[21]

# 29 "A Triumph of Treason"

AT FOUR O'CLOCK ON the morning of June 3, 1863, Federal troops, acting on orders of General Burnside, marched into the office of the *Chicago Times*, stopped the press, told all employees to leave, and took posses-sion of the establishment.[1]

Seizure of the *Chicago Times* was the climax of public agitation that had been growing for some months. On June 25, 1862, Governor Oliver P. Morton of Indiana singled out the *Times* as one of the news-papers against which the Lincoln administration should act. He told Secretary of War Stanton that the *Times* and other newspapers of its kind were doing "incalculable injury" in the North.[2] Governor Richard Yates of Illinois complained to Stanton against the *Times,* telling him that loyal citizens demanded its suppression.[3]

The editor of the *Chicago Times* was Vermont-born Wilbur Fiske Storey, forty years old, tall and muscular, with thick white hair and a white beard, and was looked upon as the "very ogre of Copper-headism."[4]

Storey was a printer by trade, having become an apprentice at the age of twelve. He edited two country weeklies in Indiana and later established *The Patriot* at Jackson, Mich., a venture that won him the postmastership there for supporting James K. Polk. Twice he operated drugstores, and for a time he studied law. He was a Michigan state-prison inspector when he took over the *Detroit Free Press* in 1853. Under his direction, the *Free Press* prospered and became one of the leading Democratic newspapers of the West.

On June 8, 1861, he bought the *Daily Chicago Times* from Cyrus H. McCormick, changing the name to the *Chicago Times*. He took with him to Chicago a large part of the *Free Press* staff.[5] Soon the *Times* was prospering with a growing circulation and increased advertising.[6] From 1854 to 1860, the *Times* was the mouthpiece for Stephen A. Douglas, with James W. Sheahan as editor.[7]

From the day Storey took charge of the *Times*, his editorials revealed opposition to all forms of Negro emancipation. He made a feeble effort to support the Union war effort, but he broke completely with President Lincoln when he announced his emancipation plan in September of 1862. Storey termed the plan "a monstrous usurpation, a criminal wrong, and an act of national suicide."[8] When the Proclamation was formally issued, the *Times* said: "It will be known in all history as the most wicked, atrocious and revolting deed recorded in the annals of civilization."[9]

Storey advocated peace and flatly demanded the war be brought to an end. He declared soldiers's lives were sacrificed without cause and responsibility of all further conflict should rest upon Lincoln.[10] He became a leader in the ranks of the Vallandigham forces.

General Burnside's directions for suppression of the *Chicago Times* were contained in General Order No. 84, issued at his headquarters of the Department of Ohio at Cincinnati, on June 1, 1863. That order also excluded the New York *World* from the Ohio Department. It said:

1. The tendency of the articles and opinions habitually published in the newspaper known as the New York *World*, being to cast reproach upon the Government, and to weaken its efforts to suppress the rebellion, by creating distrusts in its war policy, its circulation in time of war is calculated to exert a pernicious and treasonable influence, and is, therefore, prohibited in this department.

2. Postmasters, news agents, and all others, will govern themselves by this order, as any person detected in forwarding, selling, or in any way circulating the paper referred to, will be promptly arrested and held for trial.

3. On account of the repeated expression of disloyal and incendiary sentiments, the publishing of the newspaper known as the *Chicago Times* is hereby suppressed.

4. Brigadier General Jacob Ammen, commanding the district of Illinois, is charged with the execution of the third paragraph of this order.[11]

General Burnside followed his order with a telegram to Storey, notifying him of the action, on June 2. The wire said: "You are hereby notified that I have issued an order stopping the publication of your paper, which order will be published in the morning papers of this city today. You will please govern yourself accordingly."[12]

When General Ammen received the suppression order, he directed Captain James S. Putnam, commanding Camp Douglas, Chicago, to carry it into effect. Putnam warned Storey on the night of June 2 not to publish his paper the next morning.

Storey kept his staff at work while he applied to Judge Thomas Drummond of the United States circuit court for an injunction to prevent Putnam from interfering with publication. Drummond issued the writ after midnight; it directed the Captain to take no further steps to execute Burnside's order until the application for a permanent injunction could be heard in open court that day.[13]

Storey returned to his office and continued preparations to publish as usual. He posted mounted lookouts on the road to Camp Douglas to warn of the approach of the military in the event that seizure was attempted.

Army headquarters at Camp Douglas received this supplementary order from General Burnside: "I have issued an order suppressing the *Chicago Times*. You will see that no more publications of it are made; and, if necessary, you will take military possession of the office."[14]

The *Times* was about ready to go to press when the lookouts galloped up with the news that two companies of the 65th Illinois Infantry, under command of Captain McDonald, were on their way. Storey ordered the forms locked. They were slammed on the press, and 8,000 papers had been run off, some of them already on the street, when the soldiers rushed in.[15]

When court opened that morning, Storey made a new plea for action to restrain the military authorities, but Judge Drummond refused to open the injunction hearing on the grounds that the defendant, Captain Putnam, had not been notified.[16] Judge Drummond issued this statement from the bench:

I may be pardoned for saying that, personally and officially, I desire to give every aid and assistance in my power to the government and to the administration in restoring the Union, but I have always wished to treat the government as a government of law and a government of the Constitution, and not a government of mere physical force. I personally have contended and shall always contend, for the right of free discussion, and the right of commenting, under the law and the Constitution, upon the acts of the officers of the government.[17]

That afternoon, there was excitement in the state legislature at Springfield when it learned troops occupied a Chicago newspaper office. After long debate, resolutions censuring the seizure were passed by a vote of forty-seven to thirteen.

The resolutions charged Burnside's order was a direct violation of the Constitution, saying it "threatens an act so revolutionary and despotic as contrary to liberty, destructive of good government, and subversive of constitutional and natural rights, and that, if carried into effect, we consider it equivalent to the overthrow of our form of government, and the establishment of a military despotism in its stead."

With its approval of the resolutions, the legislature requested withdrawal of the order and "the disavowal thereof by those in power, as the only course which can be pursued to reassure our people that constitutional freedom, so dear to their hearts, has not ceased to be."[18]

Prominent Republicans and businessmen attended a meeting in the circuit court room at Chicago that same afternoon at which a petition addressed to President Lincoln to revoke the order of suppression was signed by everyone present. Carrying more weight, perhaps, was the request for revocation telegraphed to President Lincoln by Senator Lyman Trumbull, a former Democrat who joined the Republicans and worked for the election of Lincoln, and Isaac N. Arnold, a Republican Congressman and close friend of the President.[19]

That evening, a mass meeting was staged in the courthouse square, where speeches were made by representatives of both political parties. Resolutions were passed, one charging Burnside's suppression of the Times was "without warrant of law" and predicting that "it will forthwith be rescinded by the President." It was claimed 20,000 persons were in the square.[20]

The philosophy of retaliation was expressed by some of the hotheaded Democrats, and threats were made to mob and burn the office of the Chicago Tribune, outspoken enemy of Storey and his Times. Members of the Knights of the Golden Circle circulated in the crowd, and an inflammatory handbill was passed in an effort to excite the Copperheads to violence against the Tribune.[21] The Chicago militia, called out in full force, had a quieting effect.

The next day, June 4, Storey received a telegram from Burnside which said: "By direction of the President of the United States, my order suppressing the circulation of your paper is revoked. You are at liberty to resume its publication."[22]

The General also sent a telegram to Manton Marble, editor of The World, saying: "Having been directed by the President of the United States to revoke that part of my order suppressing the Chicago Times, I have revoked the entire order and your paper will be allowed its circulation in this department."[23]

Lincoln was "embarrassed" by Burnside's suppression of the newspaper; while he desired to do right by the military and give it every support, he was faced by the question of liberty of the press. He was reflecting over the course he should follow when he received the telegram from Trumbull and Arnold. His order to revoke the suspension resulted.[24]

All members of the President's Cabinet regretted Burnside's action.[25] On the very day Burnside issued the suppression order, Secretary of War Stanton was writing to him that Lincoln was displeased with General Hascall's actions in Indiana.[26] Just then Stanton got word that the Times had been suppressed. After talking it over with the President, Stanton added a postscript to say Lincoln thought the General should revoke the order, that suppression would do more harm than good, and that he asked to be consulted on all newspaper questions.[27]

It is apparent Burnside did not accept the suggestion to act immediately. When, on June 4, Lincoln got the wires from his friends in Chicago, he directed Stanton to "revoke or suspend" the order.[28]

Joseph Medill and his Chicago Tribune, unwavering supporters of the Union, were indignant. The Tribune declared the President's action in revoking the suspension was as "unexpected" as Burnside's had been. It said:

Yesterday, before the revocation was announced, a clear majority of citizens were in favor of the order and resolved it should be enforced against mob opposition. The revocation is felt to be a most unfortunate blunder. As the matter stands it is a triumph of treason.[29]

The World said the Tribune owners wanted the order lifted because they feared the Tribune office might be mobbed by "popular" violence, meaning by friends of the Times. The heated reply in the Tribune said:

This is a point blank fabrication. No living human being that owns a dime's interest in the Tribune . . . knew that such a dispatch was prepared until after it was sent. Nor do we believe that any person that signed the dispatch feared the destruction of the Tribune by popular violence. Our proprietors and friends feel perfectly confident of their entire ability to expel any number of Copperheads that might attempt its destruction.[30]

An accompanying editorial carried a barb for Lincoln, saying:

But the time for mere compromise candidates has passed. . . . Better a thousandfold, in such times as these an occasional exercise of arbitrary power, if directed to the preservation of the Constitution and the enforcement of laws, than a timid, vacillating policy—one that permanently or for the moment destroys the confidence of all loyal, honest men in the wisdom and energy of the government.[31]

Although burning with indignation, Editor Medill the next day published an editorial that said blame for the "triumph of treason" did not rest on the President. The *Tribune* said:

He probably had not seen the *Times* and rarely reads any newspaper. On Thursday night, when all prudent men knew that serious trouble was expected, our business offices were protected against rebel bullets by a proper barricade. . . . Now that it again has free license to belch its treason, we give the same counsel but let its dupes remember . . . they will find the *Tribune* fully prepared to welcome them with sharp sounds and sudden illuminations.[32]

The *Times* also armed itself against mob violence. Storey purchased a supply of rifles and grenades, and he had a long hose attached to the boiler to scald a mob with steam.[33]

Storey, contrary to popular belief, was not overjoyed when the President revoked Burnside's order. He regretted that Lincoln stepped in to take the case out of the hands of the courts. He held the opinion that, had the application for an injunction against the military been heard, it would have been granted.[34]

As the *Tribune* predicted, the *Times* continued to "belch its treason." It sent a reporter to Windsor, Canada, to obtain an interview with Vallandigham and gave the then candidate for governor an opportunity to make what he called "an address to the people of Ohio." The *Times* reporter tried to file his story on the wire at Buffalo and was turned down. This incident was portrayed by the *Times* as a "government interdict laid on the telegraph on all messages from Mr. Vallandigham." The *Times* also charged its reporter was trailed by Federal detectives throughout his trip. Failing to get his story off to Chicago by express, the *Times* man finally carried it home in his pocket, the newspaper insisting he was afraid to put it in the mails, thinking it might be "stolen."[35]

The *Tribune* lampooned the journalistic enterprise of its Copperhead rival by saying Vallandigham was offered a job on the *Times* by Storey. An imaginary interview was printed, saying Storey went to see Vallandigham. The *Tribune's* colorful language said: "The arch traitor and Copperhead secession promulgator for Illinois, on his return from the east on last Hangman's Day, called upon Jeff Davis's pimp at Windsor to offer his condolence at his defeat."[36]

When Grant was chosen by the President to command all Federal armies, the *Times* charged he did it to keep him from running against him at the next election. Storey now saw Lincoln as "a blunderer, a charlatan, a temporizer, a man who jokes when a nation mourns, a crude, illiterate, bar-room witling."[37]

A visit to Chicago by Burnside in 1864 gave the *Times* opportunity to greet him with these words:

The butcher of Fredericksburg and attempted assassin of the liberty of speech and of the Northwest is coming to Chicago. . . . He was not the head butcher and assassin; he was only the creature, the mean instrument, the puppet, the jumping-jack of the principal butchers and assassins.[38]

When Lincoln was inaugurated for his second term, the *Times* said that "the partially honest coward . . . has been transformed into the unblushingly corrupt bully."[39] It scoffed at the beautiful words of his address, saying: "We did not conceive it possible that even Mr. Lincoln could produce a paper so slip-shod, so loose-jointed, so puerile, not alone in literary construction, but in ideas, its sentiments, its grasp."[40]

While controversy over suspension of the *Chicago Times* was raging, President Lincoln read in the *Daily Morning Chronicle* at Washington an article on Storey's newspaper in which the facts were garbled. He felt it did not do justice to James Sheahan, editor of the *Times* in the days when it represented Douglas. He wrote a letter to the editor of the *Chronicle*, giving a thumbnail history of the *Times*, but did not permit use of his name. In the letter he referred to himself as "an Illinoisian," who happened to know "much of the article is incorrect."[41]

The letter revealed Lincoln's intimate knowledge of the Chicago newspaper scene. He had good cause to clear Sheahan of any connection with Storey's *Times*. Sheahan was now editor of the *Chicago Post*, a Democratic newspaper that supported the war.[42]

In 1864, when the pacifist wing of the Democratic party was doing its utmost to save slavery with a negotiated peace, an editorial in the *Chicago Post* attacked the movement in no uncertain terms. It charged Northern Democrats were trapped in 1860 by a platform manufactured for them by "Messrs. Davis, Benjamin, Hunter & Co.," then asked:

Will an appeal for a peace party and a peace platform coming from the same men deceive anyone now . . . ? Will the Democrats take up the burden repudiated in 1860?

Will they, by raising the white flag now, give strength to the rebellion, and weaken the arms of Grant and Sherman, who are now striking that rebellion to earth?

The editorial demanded the Confederates lay down their arms before asking for peace and told the Northern Democrats to insist "that the Union shall be one and indivisible." It continued: "This is the only kind of peace that the Democracy can favor without self-destruction."[43]

Editors of Republican newspapers read the declaration of the *Post* with much interest and gave it wide distribution by reprinting it. That editorial, coming from a Democratic newspaper, was of more value to Lincoln's war effort than a thousand similarly worded in an outright Republican journal in which such utterances were expected because of party affiliation.

# 30  "A Marvel
# to the Future Historian"

BEHIND THE STRUGGLE for western Virginia that resulted in the formation of a new state which was admitted to the Union in early summer of 1863, there lies the story of a loyal Union press persecuted by a fanatical Federal general it dared to criticize.

When Virginia, on April 17, 1861, passed the Ordinance of Secession, Governor John Letcher notified Mayor Andrew Sweeny of Wheeling to seize all Federal and public buildings and documents in the name of the state of Virginia, he received this reply, seeming to speak for the whole northwestern portion of the state: "I have seized the custom house, the post office, and all public buildings and documents, in the name of Abraham Lincoln, President of the United States, whose property they are."[1]

After Confederate forces were driven south by Union armies led by

McClellan and later by Rosecrans, the Richmond government made only feeble efforts to retaliate, apparently deciding the extreme western part of the state could not be successfully defended.

Delegations representing forty western counties held a Union convention at Wheeling on June 11, each delegation taking an oath to defend the Constitution of the United States. The next day, all allegiance to the Confederacy was repudiated and Frank H. Pierpont appointed Governor.[2]

The pro-Union sympathy of the people flared against the opposition press on May 20, 1861, when a mob, said to consist of "Republicans," wrecked the office of the *Parkersburg News*.[3] The *Wheeling Union*, described as a "secession paper of long standing," went out of business on May 29. The *Cincinnati Enquirer*, reporting the voluntary suspension of the *Union*, said: "The public feeling in Wheeling is overwhelmingly for the Federal Union and would not sustain a print which advocated contrary doctrines. The vote of Ohio county, in which the city of Wheeling is situated, was as follows: For the Ordinance of Secession—157; Against the Ordinance of Secession—3368." Added the *Enquirer:* "We do not wonder."[4]

A charge that A. W. Campbell, postmaster at Wheeling and editor of the *Wheeling Intelligencer*, held up distribution of *The Crisis*, published at Columbus, Ohio, was made by Editor Medary on June 11, 1862. *The Crisis* said that Campbell was "a rabid follower of old John Brown and should be removed from the office position he now disgraces."[5] *The Crisis* attacked the formation of the new state as unconstitutional, and it was barred from the mails in West Virginia "for disloyalty to the government of the United States."[6] The charge probably was based on the fact that *The Crisis*, always pro-Southern, refused to recognize the new state and spoke of it as "western Virginia."

The *Cincinnati Enquirer* was barred from the District of the Kanawha by Captain J. L. Hill, provost marshal of Charleston, and the paper retorted that this was a big thing for a little captain to do but that the government "will probably make him a major general for his war on the *Enquirer*."[7]

The *Wheeling Press* was temporarily suppressed by military authorities on December 2, 1862, when its issue of that date carried an article on taxation and national debt that was held damaging to the Union cause.[8]

In May of 1864, Major General David Hunter, a radical Abolitionist, was placed in command of the Department of West Virginia. A graduate of West Point and a major at the outbreak of war, he rode with Lincoln from Springfield to Washington as an official member of the party. He broke into the news at Buffalo when caught in a surging crowd that tried to see the next President and suffered a dislocation of the collarbone. He fought at Bull Run as a brigadier general and was wounded.

As commander of a department that included Georgia, Florida, and South Carolina, he declared those states under martial law—although they were held by the Confederates—and announced that all slaves were "forever free." That order, issued May 9, 1862, was annulled by Lincoln ten days later.[9]

Hunter received the West Virginia command after Major General Franz Sigel was defeated in the Battle of Newmarket by the rebel General Breckinridge. He gathered a force of 20,000 men and moved up the valley on Lynchburg. He met the rebels at Piedmont and routed them, leaving the road clear to his objective. Lee saw the danger and detached a part of his army to stop Hunter, although he was facing Grant at Cold Harbor.

Hunter extended himself too far and, without sufficient rations and short of ammunition, dared not risk a battle. For some unexplained reason, he started northwest down the Kanawha instead of going north. The retreat became one of the most tragic in American history. It paved the way for Lieutenant General Jubal Early's near capture of Washington.[10]

Out of the retreat there developed a war between Hunter and the press that set the nation to talking. Party politics was forgotten by the newspapers as they joined to blast Hunter. The *New York Herald* charged he was to blame for all the disasters in the Shenandoah Valley and was responsible for the invasion of Maryland by Early because he left "the back door open." The *Herald* called Hunter one of Lincoln's "pet generals."[11]

The staunchly Republican *Cincinnati Commercial* made even more severe charges against Hunter, saying:

> Gen. Hunter's retreat to the Kanawha has opened the Shenandoah gate to the rebel. . . . His "vigor" has been manifested chiefly in his proclamations, and in house-burning and other performances of a nature no true soldier would be guilty of.[12]

The *New York Tribune* charged dispatches mailed by its correspondent with Hunter's army failed to reach New York, although he wrote a daily news letter. The inference was that Hunter rifled mail bags, trying to keep the horrors of the retreat out of the public print.[13]

The *New York Daily News* gloatingly reported Hunter stole a bronze statue of George Washington at Lexington, Va., set up by the state in 1788. The *Wheeling Register* supplemented this report, stating Hunter brought a statue of Washington back to Wheeling and that the pedestal was broken in three pieces.[14] A story that Hunter sacked the Virginia Military Institute, destroyed its valuable library, and did the same to Washington College, where letters autographed by George Washington were carried off, was published by the Columbus *Ohio Statesman*, a War Democrat newspaper.[15]

The *Statesman*, speaking for conservative Democrats of the Northwest, published a list of charges against Hunter and called him a "square-headed, imbecile, addle-brained negro maniac," whose stupidity might result in the loss of the city of Washington.

The newspaper charged that many of Hunter's soldiers died of starvation on the retreat and exhausted men were left to perish. Suffering of the troops, said the newspaper, was "beyond description." It said that rations intended for the men were fed to Negroes who followed the army and ambulances and provision wagons were emptied to make room for "contrabands." The *Statesman* reiterated the charge, already widely circulated, that Hunter publicly horsewhipped two sick soldiers whom he accused of offending Negroes.[16]

According to the *Cincinnati Enquirer* and other newspapers, the soldiers, too ill to keep up with their column, took a horse from a Negro and forced him to walk in the lines of stragglers. The Negro complained to Hunter, who ordered the soldiers punished by whipping. They were tied to a tree and flogged.[17]

One of the newspaper men close to the scene was Editor Wharton of the *Parkersburg Gazette*. He was an early antislavery man in western Virginia and outspoken supporter of the Union. His loyalty to the North was without question. He saw Hunter's starved and exhausted troops pass through Parkersburg. Sadly he wrote:

General Hunter, with his command, has principally passed through our city. . . . We have found among them old acquaintances and friends and we are sorry to see so much suffering among them. They are completely worn out and many in the division have died of starvation. Among officers and men we are sorry to say a large portion of the suffering is attributed to the neglect and indifference of General Hunter. In the whole command we have not found an officer or man who spoke well of his skill as a general or his humanity to his soldiers.[18]

Hunter flew into a rage when he read the *Gazette* editorial. He arrested Wharton, suppressed his newspaper, and seized and burned all copies of the edition that had offended him. Wharton was taken to a military prison in Cumberland while his office was ransacked and all records destroyed at Hunter's direction. Public indignation against the General rose to a new high. Governor Arthur I. Boreman of West Virginia telegraphed a demand to Secretary of War Stanton that Wharton be released instantly. Wharton returned to Parkersburg within the week.[19]

But the damage could not be repaired so easily. The Democratic press could not refrain from laughing at Wharton's predicament. As an editor who fought secession and whose name was known throughout the border states, the sight of him being carted off to prison by one of the Union's own generals was most amusing to those who had been the targets of his sharp, pointed pen. The *Cincinnati Enquirer* published a diatribe against him under the head, "How a Tool of Power Has Been Hoisted on His Own Petard." It said in part:

The notorious editor of the Parkersburg, Va., *Gazette*, after three years of relentless persecution of citizens of that place who differed with him in political sentiment, has at last come to grief in a way he least anticipated. He has fallen a victim to that military proscription which he and his party have been and are applying to the Democracy. Last week he was arrested by order of General Hunter . . . in consequence of an editorial notice of Hunter's disastrous campaign, which did not set well on the General's stomach.

Of all the petty tyrants with whom this war has cursed people, none has so delighted in hounding down everyone within reach of his influence, who did not think politically as he did. . . . It was chiefly through this man's instrumentality that the circulation of the *Cincinnati Enquirer*, Medary's *Crisis* and other Democratic papers were suppressed in that city and bogus state. The Democracy of that section have been denied any reliable Democratic paper for the past two years. . . . So long as this tool of the Administration served the "boor" at Washington by aiding to tyrannize over a whole community, his acts were applauded and rewarded.[20]

Postmaster Campbell's *Intelligencer* at Wheeling was disgusted by Hunter's conduct, although it was cautious in its comment, fearing, no doubt, that it might be the next to fall before his fanatical wrath. It said: "Wharton, we all know, is a loyal man and, of course, it was for no act of intentional aid and comfort to the enemy that he was arrested. . . . The arrest of Wharton has stirred up a great deal of feeling among the Union men."[21]

The editor of the *Intelligencer* had just witnessed the arrest and imprisonment of three members of the staff of his Democratic opposition, the *Wheeling Daily Register*, by Hunter. About the time Wharton was taken into custody, William H. Oxtoby, city editor of the *Register*, was taken off to the "Atheneum," used as a military prison in Wheeling, and placed in solitary confinement. Then on the afternoon of July 9, 1864, Lewis Baker and O. S. Long, editors and publishers of the *Register*, were at work in their office when a squad of soldiers, with fixed bayonets, led by Captain Ewald Over, commandant of the Wheeling post, and Lieutenant Henry Knapp, a provost marshal, entered and displayed an order signed by Major General David Hunter.

Baker was copublisher of the *Ohio Statesman* at Columbus, one of the papers most critical of the General. He and Long were marched off to "the filthiest dungeon in Virginia," and their newspaper was suppressed.[22]

Up in Columbus, Baker's *Ohio Statesman*, at a safe distance from Hunter, denounced him, saying: "That such a blundering, vicious, odious, rapacious and imbecile tyrant as Hunter is allowed to hold supreme power over a people who were once free is a wonder to the present and will be a marvel to the future historian."[23]

The *Wheeling Intelligencer* was far from happy at this summary elimination of its opposition. It wondered why Hunter suppressed the *Register* while he permitted the *Chicago Times* and the *New York Daily News* to circulate in his department. It said in an editorial:

So far as we have observed there has been nothing unusual in the paper of late. . . . He has given it notoriety that it would never have otherwise enjoyed, and also, in addition, a new lease on life, if it ever starts again. As it was, it had not sufficient strength to run through the summer.[24]

On the ninth of July, when Hunter was suppressing the *Register*, Jubal Early and his hard-fighting Confederates defeated Union forces under General Wallace at the Monocacy. Washington lay before him, unprotected, except for a few forts manned by militia and convalescents from the hospitals. On the evening of July 11, with Early in sight of the Capital, heavy Union reinforcements from Grant's command steamed up the Potomac.

President Lincoln was at the wharf to greet the troops as they disembarked. He was munching on a piece of army bread, having skipped his evening meal at the White House in his anxiety.

His face lighted up at the sight of the troops. "It is the old Sixth Corps," he said. "The danger is over."

On the twelfth, Early was repulsed at Fort Stevens, and, under cover of darkness, he recrossed the Potomac. He left many dead behind, but he took with him 5,000 horses and almost 3,000 fat cattle.[25]

General Hunter had run his course. He was relieved of command and given leave of absence. Grant chose the man to fill his place, Major General Philip H. Sheridan, who took over on August 7.[26]

The *Ohio Statesman* hailed the news that Sheridan had replaced Hunter with the hope that Baker, Long, and Oxtoby would soon be released.[27]

On September 2, the *Statesman* said happily that Sheridan had freed the three men and that Baker had sent word he was out of prison again "until some petty tool of Abraham Africanus sees fit to again attempt to wreak the black malice of a rotten heart upon my personal liberty."[28]

# 31 "The Torch
# That Lit the Flame"

ENACTMENT OF THE conscription act in the last session of the Thirty-seventh Congress set off a new explosion of the Copperhead press against President Lincoln and his administration in 1863. The act ended the peace faction's hopes of seeing the Union army dwindle away under the old system of volunteering. Need for such legislation was obvious if the war was to be carried to a successful conclusion.[1]

A year before, President Davis of the Confederate States put through a draft bill at Richmond which placed at his disposal for military use every man between the ages of eighteen and thirty-five.[2]

While the peace wing of the North's Democratic press accused Lincoln of operating a slaughterhouse, it remained suspiciously silent on conscription in the South.

As enacted by the Federal Congress, the conscription law provided for enrollment of all men between the ages of twenty-one and forty-five but contained a provision that a drafted man might furnish a substitute or, on payment of three hundred dollars, be discharged from further call. The commutation clause caused unrest among the poorer classes.[3] Registration began July 1, 1863.

Meanwhile, General Grant opened a drive on Vicksburg the first of May, and Major General Joseph Hooker, who succeeded Burnside as commander of the Army of the Potomac, crossed the Rappahannock to strike Lee. At Chancellorsville, May 2 and 3, the Union army was defeated. Hooker recrossed the river, and the way was open for the Confederacy's carefully planned invasion of Pennsylvania. Lincoln removed Hooker from command on May 27, and Major General George G. Meade was given the responsibility of stopping Lee.

The Army of the Potomac paced Lee as he moved north, parallel with his route. The two great armies collided at Gettysburg, July 1 to 3. Lee turned back to his native Virginia, and the invasion, on which the South had staked so heavily, was ended.

The invasion was timed with an impossible peace offer from the Confederacy.[4] A concerted effort by the Copperhead press and Peace Democrats to excite the Northern population, already in ferment over the draft and the arrest of Vallandigham, added to the tumult of the hour.

On the Fourth of July, when Lee's army was dragging itself from the battlefield, the North was electrified by news that Vicksburg had fallen. But the national holiday also heard voices in the North declaring the people had lost their liberties. Franklin Pierce, former President of the United States, spoke to 25,000 at Concord, N. H., denouncing the war as "sectional and parricidal."

"Even here in the loyal states," he said, "the mailed hand of military usurpation strikes down the liberties of the people, and its foot tramples on a desecrated Constitution."

His chief lament was for Vallandigham. He charged the policies of the Lincoln administration were such that "it was made criminal for that noble martyr of free speech to discuss public affairs."[5] The Democratic press made a big fuss over the former President's address.

New York's Governor Seymour—who deplored the election of Lincoln as a "great calamity," made formal protests against "arbitrary arrests," and vetoed a bill to permit soldiers in the field to vote on grounds it was unconstitutional[6]—spoke before a large audience at the Academy of Music in New York City.

He asserted that not only was there a "bloody civil war" in progress but that a "second revolution" was threatening in the North because of the hostility between the two political parties. Then he said, "Re-

member that the bloody, and treasonable, and revolutionary doctrine
of public necessity can be proclaimed by a mob as well as by a government."⁷

Benjamin Wood, Democratic Congressman and editor of the *New
York Daily News*, published an editorial attack on President Lincoln,
charging he was trying to preach "passive submission," through the
columns of Forney's *Chronicle* at Washington. The editorial spoke
of the *Chronicle* as "the salaried organ of the bloodstained criminals at
Washington." It continued:

That a people, who, in the incredibly short space of seventy years, have
risen from the condition of a dependent colony, to be one of the most important and commanding powers of the earth, should have surrendered
that dearest prerogative of American citizens—the right to criticize the action of those whom they place in power—into the hands of the vilest
political faction that ever conspired for the overthrow of human freedom,
is certainly one of those anomalies in the history of a nation, which strongly
reminds one of the crowning incidence of some grotesque dream. And yet
this is precisely the sort of entertainment which the American people have
been invited to partake of by His Excellency Abraham Lincoln.⁸

On Friday, July 10, the city of New York was tranquil. The newspapers were still carrying reports from Gettysburg and Vicksburg.
There were stories about prominent New Yorkers killed in battle.
Drawing for the conscription was to start on the morrow, July 11. A
New York *World* editorial said the draft "promises to be a very mysterious business. . . . We have no assurance that it is to be an equal
conscription . . . how do we know but the secret instructions of the
provost marshals are to conscript heavily in the Democratic districts
and lightly in the Republican districts?"⁹

At ten o'clock on Saturday morning, about one hundred and fifty
men gathered at the office of the provost marshal of the Ninth Congressional District, Forty-sixth Street and Third Avenue, to see the first
names pulled from the wheel in New York. A squad of police was on
duty. The provost marshal read the order for the draft issued by President Lincoln, and the drawing began. Names were pulled from the
wheel until four o'clock in the afternoon when the drawing was
adjourned to Monday morning. A total of 1,236 names had been drawn,
with 264 still to be picked for the quota.¹⁰

Wounded soldiers from Gettysburg were pouring into the seaboard
cities, and New York took its share. Over Sunday, a train arrived in
Jersey City with 700 on their way to Fort Schuyler Hospital. A group

of New Yorkers met the train with food and brandy. They helped carry stretchers from the train to the waiting ship. A reporter for the *New York Tribune* wrote, "The wounded did not complain. They seem proud of the fact that they had participated in the fight at Gettysburg."[11]

Monday morning came and the resumption of the draft drawing. Three leading morning newspapers, all Democratic and all outspoken against President Lincoln, made it their business, as if by prearranged plan, to publish long editorials against the draft. *The World* said:

An administration ordinarily sensible and capable of subordinating party to patriotism would never for a moment have permitted such an act as the act of conscription to be so enforced as to create the impression that the greatest city in the nation—a city which has poured out its blood and treasure without stint or measure—is to be mulcted in largely more than its due proportion of men. . . .

(The draft is) . . . a measure which could not have been ventured upon in England, even in those dark days when the pressgang filled the English ships-of-war with slaves, and dimmed the glory of England's noblest naval heroes—a measure wholly repugnant to the habits and prejudices of our people.[12]

*The World* editorial obviously was written by Manton Marble. His writing was marked by a habit of dragging in English law and custom when he wished to appear profound.

The *Journal of Commerce* published an editorial of equal length, saying: "It is a melancholy fact that war, sad and terrible as it is, becomes oftentimes the tool of evil-minded men to accomplish their ends. . . . The bloodshed counts as of no value in their measurement. The mourning it produces causes no impression on their sensibilities."[13]

Wood's *New York Daily News* contended the city was being asked to furnish more men than the quota required. A vicious editorial said:

The manner in which the draft is being conducted in New York is such an outrage upon all decency and fairness as has no parallel and can find no apologists. . . . The proper quota to be drawn from this city would be about twelve thousand. Instead of this number, however, over twenty-two thousand are being drafted. . . .

The miscreants at the head of the Government are bending all their powers . . . to secure a perpetuation of their ascendency for another four years, and that triple method of accomplishing this purpose, is to kill off Democrats, stuff the ballot boxes with bogus soldier votes, and deluge recusant districts with negro suffrage. . . .

The people are notified that one of about two and a-half of our citizens are destined to be brought off into Messrs. Lincoln & Company's carnel (sic) house. God forbid. We hope that instant measures will be taken to prevent the outrage. . . .

If the workingmen of this city are disinclined to be forced into a fight for emancipation, let them clamor so loud for peace that their voices shall be potential with our rulers.[14]

When the drawing was resumed at ten o'clock that morning, the "instant measures" suggested by Wood were taken by the mob which Seymour had idly discussed. About one hundred names were drawn when a shower of bricks crashed through the windows of the draft quarters. A screaming mob poured into the room, carrying everything in front of it.

While a mob of four or five thousand milled outside, the leaders poured turpentine on the floor and threw a match on it. In a matter of seconds the building was a mass of flames. Women and children living on the upper floors fled for their lives. Firemen were not permitted by the mob to attach hose to the hydrants until the building was consumed. Four days and nights of murder and pillage followed, rioting that has no equal in American history.

Mobs roved the city, directed by men on horseback. Negroes were beaten to death, some of them burned alive. The police were almost powerless, outnumbered but not outfought. Mayor George Opdyke, Republican mayor who succeeded Fernando Wood, called "loyal citizens" to serve as special policemen. Convalescent soldiers and others on furlough were called for service by Major General John E. Wool, eighty-year-old commander of the Department of the East, but the men in the Union blue uniforms were marked by the mobs. Many were beaten to death. General Wool's appeal was made because there was no militia in the city, all companies having been sent into Pennsylvania to face Lee in the event of a break-through at Gettysburg; Seymour received the call for help from the Secretary of War on June 15, and his response was immediate.

Newspaper reporters who mingled with the mobs said they were made up, for the most part, of foreign-born Irish workingmen but that they appeared to be directed by a mastermind. The press also noted that the most heroic police officers, some of whom died in the rioting, bore Irish names.[15]

Not until Thursday evening, with the city patrolled by troops rushed to the scene, did the rioting cease. Estimates of the dead ran as high

esy Ohio State Archaeological and Historical Society

el Medary, editor of *The Crisis*, at nbus, Ohio.

Courtesy Chicago Historical Society

Wilbur F. Storey, editor of the *Chicago Times*.

From Harper's *Pictorial History of the Civil War*

e charge mob trying to destroy *New York Tribune* office. An incident during the draft riots of July, 1863.

The New-York Times.

VOL. XIV.....NO. 4290.  NEW-YORK, SATURDAY, APRIL 15, 1865.  PRICE FOUR CENTS

## AWFUL EVENT.

### President Lincoln Shot by an Assassin.

**The Deed Done at Ford's Theatre Last Night.**

**THE ACT OF A DESPERATE REBEL**

**The President Still Alive at Last Accounts.**

**No Hopes Entertained of His Recovery.**

**Attempted Assassination of Secretary Seward.**

**DETAILS OF THE DREADFUL TRAGEDY.**

EUROPEAN NEWS.

**TWO DAYS LATER BY THE EUROPA.**

**The Insult to Our Cruisers by Portugal.**

**The American Minister at Lisbon Demands Satisfaction.**

**Dismissal of the Commander of Fort Belem Requested.**

**Further Advance in Five-Twenties.**

FINANCIAL AND COMMERCIAL.

---

The Daily Ohio Statesman

VOL. XXXII.  COLUMBUS, OHIO, MONDAY MORNING, APRIL 17, 1865.  NUMBER 24

**Assassination of President Lincoln and Secretary Seward.**

**FULL PARTICULARS**

Courtesy Ohio State Archaeological and Historical Society

Newspapers in mourning dress for President Lincoln. Column rules turned in *New York Times* and Columbus *Daily Ohio Statesman*.

as a thousand, with other thousands injured. The loss in property was estimated as high as three million dollars.[16] Boston and other cities reported rioting of a less serious character.

The office of the *New York Tribune* narrowly escaped destruction by fire. On Monday afternoon, while a mob was burning a Negro orphanage at Fifth Avenue and Forty-sixth Street, another formed downtown in Printing House Square, singing "Hang Horace Greeley to a sour apple tree," to the tune of *John Brown's Body*. Just before darkness, the mob groaned and shouted and began to hurl bricks through the *Tribune* office windows. It forced its way into the building, piled paper in the business office, and set it on fire. A company of police came on a run across the park and clubbed the rioters until they ran. Others extinguished the fire. The *Tribune* blamed "foreign rowdies."[17]

Hearing another attack was planned on "the Abolition newspaper," Greeley ordered steps taken for defense; a howitzer was secured and set up at the Spruce Street corner. The weapon was in charge of a United States Navy midshipman.

Similar measures were taken by *The New York Times*. The building was brilliantly illuminated and a Gatling gun placed in the main entrance. One of the men who manned it through the night was Leonard W. Jerome, father of the girl who later became the mother of Winston Churchill. Jerome was a *Times* stockholder.[18]

Across the Hudson in Newark, N. J., a mob, incited by a speaker who declared the arrest of Vallandigham was unconstitutional, stoned the office of the *Mercury*, a Republican newspaper. Leaders of the mob insisted an American flag be raised over the building, contending the Democratic *Newark Journal* had once been compelled to do so.[19]

While the mob fury was raging, *The World* on Tuesday spoke lightly of the attack on the *Tribune* and charged that Greeley, afraid to enter his office, cowered in a restaurant all day and left it in disguise. Greeley replied that *The World*, the *Journal of Commerce*, and the *Daily News* had incited the rioting. He picked up their inflammatory editorials of Monday morning and reprinted them under the heading, "The Torch That Lit The Flame."

The *Tribune* also assailed the *New York Herald* in a short editorial that said: "The *New York Herald* of yesterday had not one editorial word concerning the mob which its counsels had originated and inflamed. Nothing which it could have said was so significant as this silence. The rioters knew that they had the sympathies of the *Herald*."[20]

*The World* returned to the attack against Greeley with a reference to the "torch" headline. It said:

It might have been supposed that the lowering approach of the rude vengeance they have courted would have made these people feel at last how mad their course has been. It might have been supposed that the Editor of the *Tribune*, trembling all day long in the safe umbrage of a friendly restaurant, and breaking at last under cover of darkness to his home, might have been led by these long hours of seclusion to fling away the torch he had so long and thoughtlessly brandished.[21]

Speaking in the third person, Greeley replied: "He may be murdered, as *The World* threatens, but he does not expect to be frightened." He flatly denied that he hid in his favorite restaurant, Windust's.[22]

Greeley lived in Chappaqua. When he finally got home on Saturday evening, he learned his family had been in jeopardy. Mrs. Greeley, when told that toughs in the drinking taverns along the Hudson were plotting to kill her and the children and burn the house, set a deathtrap for a mob. She obtained a keg of gunpowder from Ossining (then called Sing Sing). The head of the keg was knocked in and a train of powder poured to a point near the house. She planned to let the mob enter, then run for safety, setting fire to the powder train. The mob came that evening, glared at her from the farm gate, then went away.[23]

Drafting was resumed on August 19, in the presence of thousands of troops and three batteries of artillery. There were no riots.

# 32  "Oh, Thou Noble Patriot!"

ON THE MORNING OF July 27, 1863, Captain F. W. Hurtt, an assistant quartermaster of the United States Army, stationed at Cincinnati, was placed under arrest by order of General Burnside, charged with irregularity in his accounts and with having appropriated government funds to his own use.[1]

The story of the arrest filed out of Cincinnati that day consisted of only a few lines, owing to military secrecy that cloaked the specific charges, but it was big news for every newspaper in the North and especially interesting to the Democratic press. Captain Hurtt was principal owner and senior editor of the *Ohio State Journal* at Columbus, a Republican daily known as "the Lincoln organ" in the state.

As the *Logan* (Ohio) *Gazette* (Democratic) had said some time before: "The editor of the *Journal* is a consummate ass. Nevertheless, as conductor of the central Republican organ of the state, his position gives him some consequence."[2]

Hurtt was a Cincinnatian who became a partner in the *Ohio State Journal* with Henry D. Cooke in November of 1858 when the latter gave up the *Daily Commercial Register* at Sandusky, Ohio, to take over the capital city newspaper. The name of the firm was Cooke, Hurtt & Co. Cooke went to Washington in July of 1861 to become associated with his brother, the wealthy Jay Cooke, in handling government financing. Hurtt became editor and took as a junior partner in the firm a writer and editor, Isaac J. Allen.[3]

Under Hurtt's editorship, the *Journal* continued its solidly Republican policy, lending all support possible in print to the administration and enjoying revenue that came from Federal advertising. It fought with the *Cincinnati Enquirer*, the *Cleveland Plain Dealer*, and the Columbus *Ohio Statesman*, the state's leading representatives of the Democratic party, but its chief enemy was Medary's nationally circulated *Crisis*.

Hurtt left the editorial chair in March of 1862 to take a commission as captain in the army. Employees of the *Journal* purchased a handsome military saddle and other trappings of the mounted warrior, which they presented to Hurtt as a farewell gesture. He reported to General Rosecrans, then commanding the Department of the Ohio, and was assigned to duty at Clarksburg, in western Virginia, as a brigade quartermaster.[4]

The arrest of Captain Hurtt gave Democratic editors opportunity to reiterate their old charges that the war was being waged for the benefit of Republican contractors. It made the heretofore highly respectable *Journal* a laughing stock. The case was dubbed "the great Hurtt theft at Cincinnati" by opposition editors, who speculated over the exact charges, which the army refused to reveal. *The Crisis* published all the information it could obtain under the headline, "One of the Proprietors of the Ohio State Journal Arrested for Stealing Government Funds."

"The *Ohio State Journal*, our readers need not be told," said *The Crisis*, "is the central organ of Republicanism in this state, and has just ordered a purchase of new type. Captain Hurtt is one of the principal proprietors. The mystery of how he raised the wind is thus explained."[5]

In the weeks that followed, with the army still maintaining secrecy, the Democratic press kept the case before the public by calling it "the most magnificent fraud and swindle of the war." It circulated the rumor that "one of the editors" of the *Journal* paid almost fifty thousand dollars for property just before "the arrest." It also recalled that the *Journal* had denounced Hurtt's predecessor in the quartermaster office, calling him a Copperhead and disloyal, until he was removed and the assignment given to the editor.

The *Cincinnati Enquirer* broke the complete story, with detailed charges and specifications, on Sunday morning, December 6, 1863. How the *Enquirer* came into possession of the secret documents was a matter of conjecture. The story revealed Captain Hurtt faced four charges, containing seventeen separate specifications. They were:

Selling, without proper orders for that purpose, embezzling and misapplying commissary and quartermaster stores, belonging to the United States (three specifications).

Conduct unbecoming an officer and a gentleman (seven specifications).

Stealing, embezzling and misappropriating and applying to his own use, money or other property of the United States (six specifications).

Conduct to the prejudice of good order and military discipline (one specification).

The first specification under the second charge said that Hurtt purchased horses and forage for the government "from and through one S. H. Dunan, connected with him in business in the *Ohio State Journal* for the stated purpose of benefitting their own private pecuniary interests, and held to relieve the *Ohio State Journal* from debts which greatly threatened its solvency, he, Captain Hurtt, being at that time in correspondence with said Dunan, would make out the bills, receipt them, and pay the parties from whom the supplies were bought; that said parties would not know how much he, Dunan, got; and that he, Dunan, would keep back the profits which accrued, and advise Captain Hurtt as to certain profits to be realized. . . ."

One of the specifications in the second charge involved the feeding of troops at Camp Chase, on the west side of Columbus. It charged that Hurtt and Dunan speculated in the sale of rations and "on discovering that the cost of the rations furnished reduced too much their net profits, they concluded to increase their profits by furnishing rations of an inferior quality. . . ."

That charge also said that Hurtt corresponded "with one H. D. Cooke, of the firm of Jay Cooke & Co., bankers, Washington, D. C., requesting favors of said Cooke . . . to have him, Hurtt . . . charged with heavy disbursements of the government funds, and assured said Cooke that if he, Hurtt, succeeded in his plan, it would be all right for him, Hurtt, and for said Cooke. . . ."

A specification under charge two, said Hurt in a letter to Cooke, expressed distrust in the stability of the government. He was quoted as having asked Cooke, "What is there yet in store for us? I am anxious to know how you people near the throne feel."

In the third charge, specification four said a reporter sent as a war correspondent to Memphis was carried on the army's payroll by Hurtt as a cashier in the quartermaster department. It further said that the reporter, D. I. Manley, devoted his time to looking over the market for goods to be sold to army sutlers at Hurtt's direction.

Charge four took note of the attacks made by the *Journal* on a Captain Dickerson to bring about his removal from the position to which Hurtt succeeded.[6]

The *Journal* tried to defend its editor by saying the story published by "that Copperhead institution known as the *Enquirer*" did not state the case correctly and was a "simple libel."[7] Captain Hurtt issued a statement, addressed "to the public," published for him by the *Cincinnati Gazette*, to say he could vindicate himself "before any just tribunal." The *Gazette*, always Republican, ran the statement by Hurtt, but it also reprinted the lengthy charges against him as revealed by the *Enquirer*.[8]

Hurtt went on trial before a court-martial on February 2, 1864. *The Crisis* was happy to say: "We have never lost confidence that Secretary Stanton would bring these army thieves to the work, if not overruled by those around him."[9]

Hurtt was found guilty of virtually every charge and specification, but no public announcement was made. It was finally reported the verdict had been placed before President Lincoln for approval, and *The Crisis* said: "This may account for the frequent eulogies in the *Journal* on Old Abraham."[10]

The New York *World* accused Secretary Stanton of having interceded with the President on behalf of Hurtt. The Secretary replied in this dispatch:

Washington, June 9—The libelous article in the New York *World* this morning, stating that the Secretary of War had been endeavoring to shield Captain Hurtt from the operation of the finding of the court-martial is false, and refuted by the fact that Secretary Stanton approved the finding immediately upon its being received from the Judge Advocate General. Captain Hurtt was convicted and the record is before the President for approval.[11]

Lincoln affirmed the proceedings, and Hurtt was sentenced "to be dishonorably dismissed from the service of the United States, with the loss of all pay and allowances now due or to become due."[12]

While the controversy over Hurtt was at its height, his partner Allen was appointed United States Consul at Bangkok, Siam, and this was too much for even the *Cincinnati Commercial*, Murat Halstead's Republican newspaper, which said:

Judging from the article in the *Cincinnati Gazette* of yesterday, on Bangkok, the capital of Siam, to which place Isaac Jackson Allen, editor of the *Ohio State Journal*, has been appointed consul, it would be a locality admirably adapted for a summer residence for Captain F. W. Hurtt, Mr. Allen's partner, a gentleman whose distinguished public services have been dispensed with, with advantages to the country. If Allen insists upon the appointment as representing at once a decree of Providence and his country's call, Hurtt might as well go along, and have the *State Journal* issued at Bangkok. It would be about as valuable in American affairs published in Bangkok as in Columbus, and there is no telling what it might do for the Siamese.[13]

The *Toledo Blade*, whose support of Lincoln throughout the war was unwavering, asked with righteous indignation:

. . . how long is the name of F. W. Hurtt to remain at the head of the Union paper at the capital of Ohio, a scandal upon that city and the loyal men of the state? It would seem that somebody beside a convicted swindler of the government should control the *Journal*.[14]

A Union soldier lying wounded in Washington Park Hospital in Washington, D. C., heard about the Hurtt case and wrote a letter to the editor of the *Cincinnati Commercial*. He signed himself, "Ezra Howe, Company B, 52d Ohio V. I. One who lost his right arm at Chickamauga."

"During the time Captain Hurtt was being tried for stealing his tens of thousands from the government," he wrote, "a private soldier by the name of Shay was tried for stealing a pair of boots, and although he proved a first-rate character as a soldier and a man, he, the poor private, was sentenced to the Dry Tortugas with a ball and chain to his leg, at hard work, for three years with a loss of all pay, bounty, etc."[15]

A soldier fighting with Sherman in Georgia wrote a letter to the

editor of *The Crisis*, beginning, "Atlanta (in the distance) Aug., '64."
He wanted to know:

> What has become of poor Captain Hurtt of the *Ohio State Journal?* What
> a magnificent advertisement for that paper! Oh, thou noble patriot![16]

There was a similarity between the Hurtt case and one that involved
the New York *Evening Post*, William Cullen Bryant's newspaper. The
*Post* was owned by Bryant, Parke Godwin, his son-in-law, and Isaac
Henderson. Bryant and Godwin were the literary talent while Henderson, the business manager, chased the dollars. Godwin disliked Henderson for sufficient reasons; the Bryant and the Henderson families
fought for possession of the newspaper, with the business office trying
to wrest editorial direction from the news room.[17]

Early in 1864, the *Evening Post* figured in an odoriferous war-contract
scandal because of Henderson's extracurricular money-making activities. Through political connections, he succeeded in having himself
appointed navy agent in New York, a responsible position that included
Federal contracting. In January, he was dismissed from the office by
Secretary of the Navy Welles, charged with having accepted commis-
sions illegally.[18]

Henderson was ousted with the full approval of President Lincoln
and despite Bryant's personal intervention at the White House in defense of his business manager.[19] Instead of going to Washington, as he
had in times past to see the President, Bryant wrote a letter and received
in reply a stinging rebuke. To Bryant's plea that the Henderson case
be handled with leniency, Lincoln skinned him by saying, ". . . may
I ask whether the *Evening Post* has not assailed me for supposed too
lenient dealings with persons charged with fraud and crime?"[20]

The man responsible for the charges against Henderson was Thurlow Weed, the Albany editor. He made a private investigation and
took his information to Secretary Welles. Henderson was tried in
Federal court in May of 1865. The case collapsed, and the jury voted
for acquittal without retiring.

The jury verdict did not change the opinion of Godwin, who
thought Henderson guilty, not only in the navy case, but in handling
the financial affairs of the *Evening Post*, and he told Bryant so in a
letter after the trial.

Godwin estimated Henderson's profits in the questioned transactions
at one hundred thousand dollars. Even if Henderson were innocent,
Godwin said, he was a source of embarrassment to the *Evening Post*
and nine-tenths of the public thought the charges were true.

The incongruity of Godwin writing a letter to Bryant was explained by the son-in-law's statement that he heard Mrs. Bryant express confidence in Henderson and took this method of protesting to avoid any chance of being misunderstood.[21]

# 33  Some "Dish-watery Utterances"

AT DUSK OF WEDNESDAY, November 18, 1863, a special train of four coaches puffed into the little town of Gettysburg, bringing from Washington an official delegation to dedicate on the morrow a soldiers's national cemetery on the battlefield where in July the Union army turned back Lee's invasion.

It had been raining all afternoon, but the clouds disappeared with the early darkness and the moon shone on the scarred ground for which the armies had struggled.[1]

Passengers alighting from the train included Cabinet members Seward, Usher, and Blair; Senators, Congressmen, high-ranking officers representing the army and navy, foreign ministers, a military guard, newspaper correspondents, and President Lincoln and his two private secretaries, Nicolay and Hay.[2]

Gettysburg was in a state of chaos and excitement, filled to overflowing with thousands come to witness the dedication. Special trains arrived every hour, bringing passengers from New York, Philadelphia, and Western cities. Horse-drawn vehicles brought visitors from the countryside for miles around. Governors and their suites from states whose troops had participated in the battle were in the crowd. Hotels and rooming houses were jammed, and the people of Gettysburg, doing everything they could to accommodate the crowd, took visitors into their homes.[3] Some said this "invasion" was almost as bad as the first. Visitors were thankful if they could find a corner in a tavern.[4]

In the crowd at the station to meet the special from Washington was John Russell Young of the Forney newspapers in Philadelphia and the Capital. He greeted his employer, noting he had taken "the lead" in the presidential party.[5] Forney had been drinking during the long ride. Politician Wayne MacVeagh talked plainly to the President on the way up, and Forney said Lincoln needed telling sometimes.[6]

David Wills of Gettysburg, whose suggestion that a national cemetery be established was taken up by Governor Curtin of Pennsylvania, had the honor of playing host to the President and was at the station to receive his distinguished guest. The rest of the party went in all directions, looking for supper and lodgings. Hay was stopped by newspaper correspondents who asked for copies of the speech the President was to make. He explained over and over that he had no copy to give them and had no idea what the President was going to say.[7]

Hay ate an oyster supper at a place near the college campus and went from there to the courthouse where a group of marshals was making its arrangements to handle the crowd at the battlefield. Forney was there, and he invited Hay and some of his other friends to go to his room for a drink. Later they stood outside and watched parading bands serenade President Lincoln, Secretary Seward, and other prominent men.[8] Lincoln appeared in the door of the Wills home and said he would make no speech because he had "nothing to say."[9]

Nicolay came along and went upstairs with Forney and the others where they had some more drinks. Feeling jubilant by that time, they broke into song with *John Brown*, and Nicolay did a solo of *Three Thieves*.

Someone said Forney should be serenaded with the other celebrities, and Nicolay went to find a band. Forney told Hay that if he spoke he was going to speak his "mind." Just then the music blared outside.

The publisher assumed a pose of great dignity. He wanted to know whether there were reporters in the crowd and ordered Hay to find out. When told there were newspaper men present, he asked whether they were friendly. That was a hard question to answer, and the suggestion was made that he be careful. The crowd outside, meanwhile, was calling for him.

Forney fortified himself with another drink, in which his guests joined, and said he was ready to go. They went downstairs, and Forney stood on the doorstep, with Hay on one side, Young on the other. Several reporters separated from the crowd and came into the hall.

The publisher really gave the crowd a piece of his mind as he had threatened. He chided it for apathy toward the President, saying the cheers he had just heard were louder than those given for Lincoln.

He told his listeners they owed their country to that "mysterious man."[10]

After Forney finished, Young implored the reporters in the hall to forget what they had just heard, explaining the publisher might reconsider his words after he sobered up.[11] Forney and his party went back to his room where they sang *John Brown* until it was time to go to bed.[12]

During the evening, in a room shielded from the wild celebration in the streets, Edward Everett of Massachusetts, brought to Gettysburg to deliver the address of the occasion, received the press for an interview. Everett was the candidate for Vice-President on the Constitutional Union ticket headed by John Bell in 1860 and the most noted orator of his time. His carefully prepared address had been sent out in advance to the newspapers and already was in type, to be held for release.

He entertained his visitors with stories of his days in Europe, how kind Lord Byron was to him in Venice and how he missed seeing Napoleon because he was at Waterloo. He was in his seventieth year, with long white hair, and as he talked he gesticulated with a cambric handkerchief.[13]

Gettysburg awakened the next morning to a raw November day. At midmorning, a regiment of cavalry, two batteries, and a regiment of infantry formed in the street for the parade to the battlefield. Except for the military, the procession was a ragged affair, with every one to get there as best they could. Everett rode in a carriage, wrapped and bundled against the chill.

The newspaper correspondents hired horses and rode to the Wills home to meet the President. When Lincoln emerged, they cheered, and he smiled happily. He mounted his horse and rode off with the escort, Secretary Seward bouncing along behind, trying to find a place in the procession.

After greeting the President, the reporters, who had work to do, spurred ahead of the parade and were in the seats assigned to them on the speaking platform before the slowly moving column came in sight.[14]

Before the President arrived, a reporter for a Democratic newspaper caused a scene by standing at the front of the platform with his hat on and smoking a cigar. He made some remarks that were out of place and laughed at reporters who tried to quiet him. He loudly declaimed that this was a free country and that he would wear his hat and smoke wherever he pleased. The correspondents threw him over the railing.[15]

Order was restored by the time the President took his seat between Everett and Secretary Seward. Shouts of welcome greeted him, and the press gallery stood until he sat down. The correspondents enjoyed the show because their task for the day was not difficult; Everett's oration was out of the way, and even the prayer to be delivered by the Reverend Thomas H. Stockton, chaplain of the House of Representatives, was issued in advance. They still did not know what Lincoln would say, but not much was expected from him.[16]

A press-association story thus described the events of the next two hours:

Hon. Edward Everett was then introduced and proceeded with a discourse occupying two hours and four minutes in the delivery. . . . Perhaps the most attentive and appreciative listener was Mr. Lincoln himself. He seemed to be absorbed in profound thought till the speech was broken by a mistake of the orator in saying General Lee when he should have said General Meade, which mistake caused the President to turn to Seward and with a loud voice say, "General Meade." The orator seemed not to hear him at the time, but the President corrected loud enough to secure a correction. . . .

The crowd was packed so densely that the marshals who sat on their horses amid the multitude could not move. . . .[17]

When Everett finished, flushed and exhausted, Lincoln and Seward shook his hand. Others threw a blanket around him and led him to his chair while the band played.[18] Lincoln was to speak next.

Young, sitting only a few feet from the President, had his little worries. He wondered how long the address might be. Still unable to obtain an advance from Hay, he knew he must take it down in shorthand. Forney had promised him a tour of the battlefield as soon as the ceremony was over. If the President made a long address, it meant hours of transcribing notes. Lincoln rose to speak. Young poised his pencil over his pad.[19]

Cheers greeted the President as he stepped to the front of the platform. He stood for a moment, waiting for the applause to cease. Slowly and deliberately he adjusted his glasses, took from his pocket a sheet of paper, and unfolded it. He began to read in a high-keyed voice, each word spoken distinctly.[20]

Young, a trained shorthand reporter, listened automatically, his interest centering on a photographer who had set up his camera directly in front of the President.

"Four score and seven years ago," Lincoln began, "our fathers brought forth on this continent a new nation, conceived in liberty, and dedicated to the proposition that all men are created equal."

The photographer peered through his lenses, made some adjustment, fiddled with the black cloth over his camera, and stared at the President, hoping he would strike a moment's pose for a picture. The President read on:

Now we are engaged in a great civil war, testing whether that nation, or any nation so conceived and so dedicated, can long endure. We are met on a great battlefield of that war. We have come to dedicate a portion of that field as a final resting-place for those who here gave their lives that the nation might live. It is altogether fitting and proper that we should do this.

Lincoln did not appear conscious of the man with the camera. The photographer's most entreating looks at him brought no reaction. The President continued to read, holding the paper in front of his face.

But in a larger sense, we cannot dedicate—we cannot consecrate—we cannot hallow—this ground. The brave men, living and dead, who struggled here, have consecrated it far above our poor power to add or detract. The world will little note nor long remember what we say here, but it can never forget what they did here. It is for us, the living, rather, to be dedicated here to the unfinished work which they who fought here have thus far so nobly advanced. It is rather for us to be here dedicated to the great task remaining before us—that from these honored dead we take increased devotion to that cause for which they gave the last full measure of devotion; that we here highly resolve that these dead shall not have died in vain; that this nation, under God, shall have a new birth of freedom; and that government of the people, by the people, for the people, shall not perish from the earth.[21]

The President finished, abruptly so it seemed, and turned away. Desperately the photographer snatched at the black cloth over the camera, but he was too late. The President walked back to his chair. The crowd around the platform, watching the photographer instead of the speaker, broke into laughter at his obvious dismay in failing to obtain a picture.[22]

Young could not believe the President was through, and he leaned across the aisle to ask him whether he was going to continue. The President replied he had nothing more to say.[23] Word was passed to the press gallery that the *Associated Press* had the manuscript. This meant the text would be wired to all papers served by the news organization. Young did not bother to transcribe his notes and left to join Forney on a sightseeing trip.[24]

When Young later read the text of the address as recorded by the *Associated Press*, he was surprised to see the word "applause" in five separate places. The words "long applause" appeared at the end. He could not recall any applause during the time the President spoke, but he did remember distinctly the laughter at the photographer.[25]

The newspapers's treatment of President Lincoln's ten sentences of 272 words was exactly what might have been expected under the circumstances. They had been led to believe the Everett oration would be important; their page forms were ready with type set previously from his advance text. All they needed was a descriptive lead and some mention of Lincoln to complete the picture for their readers.

The big dailies published Lincoln's address but made no special effort to set it apart typographically. In many newspapers, the address was used as a "shirttail" on Everett.

The impression that Lincoln's few words were overlooked by the press is erroneous. As a matter of fact, his address was more widely circulated than the thousands of words spoken by Everett. Hundreds of country weeklies, that had neither space nor facilities of composition to handle the Everett effusion, found the President's "little speech" exactly suited to their purpose.

The *Philadelphia Inquirer* published Lincoln's address as taken down by its own shorthand reporter. It would appear that he heard poorly or was unable to transcribe his notes correctly. His version said in part:

The world will little know and nothing remember of what we see here, but we cannot forget what these brave men did here. We owe this offering to our dead. We imbibe increased devotion to that cause for which they here gave the last full measure of devotion; we here might resolve that they shall not have died in vain.[26]

In the editorial comment that followed the news stories, the press pursued the same old pattern—politics dictated the discussion. The next day's remarks by the Republican press on Lincoln's address indicated a general feeling of satisfaction. But Samuel Bowles's *Springfield* (Mass.) *Republican* made journalistic history with immediate recognition of the immortal words. The day after the address was delivered, the *Republican* said it was "a perfect gem, deep in feeling, compact in thought and expression."[27]

The comment in the Democratic press ran true to form. It assailed the address, just as it had ridiculed everything else the President uttered on public occasions. The *Chicago Times* said: "The cheek of every American must tingle with shame as he reads the silly, flat and dish-watery utterances of the man who has to be pointed out to intelligent foreigners as the President of the United States."[28]

At Harrisburg, only 36 miles from Gettysburg, the *Patriot and Union* spoke bitterly:

We pass over the silly remarks of the President; for the credit of the nation, we are willing that the veil of oblivion shall be dropped over them and that they shall no more be repeated or thought of.[29]

In England, the *London Times* said:

The ceremony was rendered ludicrous by some of the sallies of that poor President Lincoln.[30]

And that was just what the public expected those newspapers to say. In 1862, the *Patriot and Union* editors were held for a few weeks in a Washington prison. In July of 1863, troops seized the *Chicago Times* temporarily. For the *London Times* to have said anything differently would have been in the category of news.

The *Ohio State Journal* of Columbus was the only newspaper in the country to make the President's address the feature of the Gettysburg dedication story. Isaac J. Allen, one of the editors and copublisher, went to Gettysburg with the press party aboard Governor David Tod's special train. His story was published in the *Journal* on the morning of November 23, four days after the dedication. It said:

The President's calm but earnest utterances of this brief and beautiful address stirred the deepest fountains of feeling and emotion in the hearts of the vast throng before him, and when he had concluded, scarcely could an untearful eye be seen, while sobs of smothered emotion were heard on every hand.

At our side stood a stout, stalwart officer, bearing the insignia of a captain's rank, the empty sleeve of his coat indicating that he had stood where death was reveling, and as the President, speaking of our Gettysburg soldiers, uttered that beautifully touching sentence, so sublime and so pregnant of meaning—"The world will little note nor long remember what we say here, but it can never forget what they did here"—the gallant soldier's feelings burst over all restraint, and burying his face in his handkerchief, he sobbed aloud while his manly frame shook with no unmanly emotion.

In a few moments, with a stern struggle to master his emotions, he lifted his still streaming eyes to Heaven and in low and solemn tones exclaimed, "God Almighty, bless Abraham Lincoln!" and to this spontaneous invocation a thousand hearts around him silently responded "Amen."[31]

Allen's story indicates that he was standing in the crowd and did not occupy a seat on the platform with the press corps. No other reporter at Gettysburg had anything like this story to tell. While it may have been true, the sincerity of the writer is to be doubted. At that time, Allen's partner in his newspaper was under arrest and awaiting a court-martial at Cincinnati on charges of embezzlement and theft of funds while serving as a captain in the quartermaster department. Allen himself was striving for a presidential appointment and was later named Consul at Bangkok, Siam.

# 34 "A Hideous Dream"

IN MAY OF 1864, when the North held its breath to await the outcome of Grant's onslaught against Lee's Army of Northern Virginia—a campaign timed with Sherman's first moves toward Atlanta—two money-mad newspaper men created a crisis for the press with a faked presidential proclamation. It resulted in Lincoln signing an order to suppress newspapers, the only recorded instance of such an act on his part.

By mere chance, the New York *World*, recognized leader of the radical opposition to Lincoln, and the New York *Journal of Commerce*, a Democratic paper known for Southern sympathies, were the victims of the trick, although it was aimed at all New York morning newspapers. Less than a year previously, *The World* helped stir the draft riots by ridiculing the President's registration proclamation, saying he had issued "a number of unnecessary and mischievous proclamations."[1]

It was a "mischievous proclamation" that tripped *The World*.

Editor of *The World* was Manton Marble, not yet thirty, a former member of the New York *Evening Post* staff. *The World* was established in 1860 as a Republican newspaper. It was not a financial success, owing to misdirection, and the stockholders got out from under it. When its tangled financial affairs were finally unwound, Mayor Fernando Wood of New York and August Belmont, the banker, both Democratic and hostile to Lincoln, held the reins. The politics of the newspaper changed abruptly from Republican to radical Democratic. Marble, a journalist who could meet Bennett, Raymond, and Greeley on even terms, was placed in charge. In a short time after he took over, *The World* stood fifth in circulation in New York.[2]

Marble was born in Worcester, Mass., was graduated at the University of Rochester in 1855, and entered newspaper work in Boston. He went to New York and worked for Bryant, then toured the Red River country for *Harper's Magazine*. From there he went to *The World* where he was appointed editor in chief in 1862.[3]

A defender of Vallandigham, he challenged the arrest in an insolent open letter to Lincoln, aping Greeley's "Prayer of Twenty Millions," but was ignored.[4] Forney's Washington *Chronicle* described *The World* and Marble thusly:

The most malignant, the most brutal, the most false and scurrilous of all the assailants of the President and of the Republican party during the past year or two, has been the New York *World*. Its editor-in-chief is one Manton Marble, a mercenary scribbler, who has no scruple in admitting that he writes for pay, and for the party which pays the most. . . . Marble is not the owner of the *World* newspaper. He is merely employed by unknown Copperhead capitalists at so much per week.[5]

In their morning editions of May 18, 1864, *The World* and the *Journal of Commerce* published a purported presidential proclamation that set May 26 as a day of fasting and prayer and called for a draft of 400,000 men. It said:

Executive Mansion,
May 17, 1864.

Fellow Citizens of the United States:—

In all seasons of exigency, it becomes a nation carefully to scrutinize its line of conduct, humbly to approach the throne of grace, and meekly implore forgiveness, wisdom and guidance.

For reasons known only to Him, it has been decreed that this country should be the scene of unparalleled outrage, and this nation, the monumental sufferer of the Nineteenth Century. With a heavy heart, but an undiminished confidence in our cause, I approach the performance of a duty rendered imperative by my sense of weakness before the Almighty, and of justice to the people. . . .

In view . . . of the situation in Virginia, the disaster at Red River, the delay at Charleston, and the general state of the country, I, Abraham Lincoln, do hereby recommend that Thursday, the 26th day of May, A.D., 1864, be solemnly set apart throughout these United States as a day of fasting, humiliation and prayer.

Deeming furthermore that the present condition of public affairs presents an extraordinary occasion, and in view of the pending expiration of the service of (100,000) one hundred thousand of our troops, I, Abraham Lincoln, President of the United States, by virtue of the power vested in me by the

Constitution and the laws, have thought fit to call forth, and hereby do call forth, the citizens of the United States, between the ages of (18) eighteen and (45) forty-five, to the aggregate number of (400,000) four hundred thousand, in order to suppress the existing rebellious combinations, and to cause the due execution of the laws.

And, furthermore, in case any state, or number of states, shall fail to furnish, by the fifteenth day of June next, their assigned quota, it is hereby ordered that the same shall be raised by an immediate and preemptory draft. . . .[6]

No other newspapers had a word about a proclamation, and it appeared at first that *The World* and *Journal of Commerce* had scored a sensational news beat. Wall Street read the proclamation, and gold began to climb as soon as trading started.[7]

Excitement in the Street mounted. A crowd of traders and brokers assembled at the office of the *Journal of Commerce*, Wall and Water Streets, and called on the newspaper to affirm or deny the proclamation. David M. Stone, financial editor and one of the owners, insisted it was genuine. He said the proclamation was transmitted over the wires of the *Associated Press* and therefore authentic.[8]

While Stone was trying to placate the brokers, General McClellan elbowed his way through the crowd and entered the newspaper office. Although in civilian clothing, he was recognized by many persons, and a new crop of rumors sprouted.[9]

Two telegraph systems, owned by separate companies, were in operation. One was the American Telegraph System, whose wires ran directly into the War Department building in Washington and was under Federal control. The other was the Independent Telegraph Company, a younger concern, rival of the American and, lacking government patronage, not so prosperous.[10]

M. S. Roberts, manager of the New York office of the American System, checked his files and found no proclamation from Washington had been carried during the night. He wired the War Department for explanation.

Major General John A. Dix, commander of the Department of the East, wired Secretary of State Seward about the proclamation and asked proof of its authenticity. The published proclamation bore the signature of both Lincoln and Seward. The General asked an immediate answer, saying it was steamer day, meaning the day of departure for Europe of ships carrying the latest newspapers. He feared the effect of such a proclamation in London and Paris.[11]

Meanwhile, General Dix was making his own investigation. He soon learned the two newspapers had been tricked with a cleverly executed forgery. He informed Stanton that the forgery was received by city newspapers at four o'clock in the morning, that it was written on paper used by the *Associated Press,* and that none of the "responsible editors" of *The World* or *Journal of Commerce* were at the offices when the copy came in. The *New York Herald* started its press run with the forgery in type, the General said, but it was detected and all copies containing it were destroyed, none reaching the public there. He promised an early arrest.[12]

Manton Marble was routed out of bed, rushed to his office, and stopped the sale of papers over the counter. He called back the bundles marked for the *Scotia,* the steamer preparing to sail, and made the purser surrender his free copy. *The World* and the *Journal of Commerce* posted notices on their bulletin boards that the proclamation was a forgery. The *Associated Press* transmitted a denial of the proclamation to almost every daily paper in the North, from Maine to California.[13]

Marble and William C. Prime, editor of the *Journal of Commerce,* went to General Dix's headquarters and told him all they knew about the proclamation. The General believed their story, and the editors went to their offices. The staffs reported for work as usual.[14]

The *Associated Press* and its member papers in New York offered a reward of one thousand dollars "for such evidence as may lead to the conviction of the author of the fraudulent document."[15]

The forged copy was carried by a boy to *The New York Times,* the *New York Tribune,* the *New York Herald, The World* and the *Journal of Commerce.* The boy failed to leave the copy at the *Tribune* because the editorial rooms were locked and he could not find the composing room. The *Herald* admitted it had to destroy 20,000 copies that carried the forgery.[16]

When the boy left the copy at *The New York Times* office, it was sent to the night editor. It was written in a hand he did not recognize, and he sent it to the *Associated Press* office, 145 Broadway, with a note asking its origin. He received this reply: "The proclamation is false as hell and was not promulgated through this office. The handwriting is not familiar."

The *Times* did not blame Marble and Prime, saying: "We do not believe that the editor of either of those journals in question is in the least amenable to so grave a charge."[17]

The curiosity of the *Times* was aroused, and the night editor sent a messenger to its nearest neighbor, the *Tribune*, just across Printing House Square, to see what it knew about the strange copy. There it was learned the *Tribune* had not received it.

"Our own remoteness from the offices of other papers," wailed the *Journal of Commerce*, "forbade any such comparison of notes by our employees."[18]

Official Washington reacted as though it heard a fire bell in the night. What was going on in New York? Was this a Copperhead plot to set off new draft riots? The reputation of *The World* did not preclude such a possibility. The *Journal of Commerce* also bore a bad name in Washington's eyes. Under the editorship of Gerard Hallock, it was for years a propagandist for slavery and defender of Southern rights. As one of the five New York newspapers named in a Federal grand jury "presentment" in August of 1861, it was branded disloyal to the government and barred from the mails.[19]

The newspaper regained its mailing privileges by announcing a re-organization of the firm and the retirement of Hallock. He was said to have sold out to his associates.[20] In the proclamation forgery investiga-tion, it was revealed Hallock still retained his interests.[21] In the early days of the war, he unfurled an American flag from a window of the *Journal of Commerce* building to a crowd that demanded a display of colors.[22]

A conference was called in the War Department office, and President Lincoln directed Secretary Seward to draw up an explanation to the public. The statement as written by Seward declared the proclamation "an absolute forgery" and that no paper of that kind had either been proposed or written by the head of any department of the government. Copies were sent to New York newspapers and mailed to the American ministers in London and Paris.[23]

Secretary of the Navy Gideon Welles, as a former editor, had a newspaper man's interest in the action that followed. He noted in his diary that Seward wanted extreme action taken against *The World* and the *Journal of Commerce* and that Stanton agreed. Lincoln, he said, yielded to please his Secretary of State.[24]

An order for arrest and imprisonment of the "editors, proprietors and publishers" and seizure of the newspaper offices "by military force" was drawn up and signed by Lincoln and Seward, dated "Executive Mansion, May 18, 1864."[25]. Governor Richard Yates of Illinois heard about the proclamation and wired the President for confirmation. Lincoln wired back that if any such proclamation appeared it was a "forgery."[26]

For some unaccountable reason, the proclamation was spread over the country by New York wire services, although quickly countermanded in the *Associated Press* denial. D. H. Craig, general agent of the New York *Associated Press*, was later accused by some newspapers of having permitted the story to be filed, an accusation probably unjust in view of his exertions to warn the country against it.

In far-off New Orleans, occupied by Union forces and under martial law, the *Picayune* and the *Courier* obtained the forgery via Cairo, Ill., and published it. They were immediately suppressed by Major General Nathaniel P. Banks, commander of the Department of the Gulf. General Banks directed the disastrous Red River expedition mentioned in the forgery, a failure that resulted in his removal and subsequent resignation from the army. His order suspending the papers was said never to have been revoked.[27]

Washington assumed the proclamation was forged in the Capital and transmitted by telegraph to the *Associated Press* office in New York. When a check of the night file of the American System in both Washington and New York cleared its employees of any complicity in a plot, Secretary Stanton jumped at the conclusion the forgery was transmitted over the wires of the Independent.

He sent Major Thomas T. Eckert, superintendent of military telegraphs, and a squad of soldiers to the Independent office in Washington, with a demand that James N. Worl, head of the office, hand over to him a copy of all messages and news reports of recent days. Worl was indignant that his firm should be suspected and refused to turn over the records. Major Eckert ransacked the office, arrested Worl and his staff, and locked them in Old Capitol prison.[28]

Stanton wired Dix in New York to seize the Independent offices there, including those at Cedar and Nassau Streets, in the "gold room" in William Street and in the Broker's Exchange. All employees were to be arrested and held in Fort Lafayette. Similar orders were sent to General Wallace at Baltimore and to Brigadier General George Cadwalader in Philadelphia, to Harrisburg and to Pittsburgh.[29]

The Secretary of War suspected the forgery might have originated in a news bureau operated by Henry Villard, political writer and war correspondent; Adam S. Hill, news writer and later a professor at Harvard University; and Horace White, Lincoln's faithful friend of Illinois days. He ordered Villard taken into custody and held him for two days at the provost marshal's headquarters. Hill was kept under surveillance. White was called into Stanton's private office and grilled.[30]

Dix, upon receipt of the order signed by Lincoln, had no alternative but to arrest the editors and suppress the newspapers. He sent soldiers to the newspaper offices just as work was starting on the next day's edition. Hallock was arrested at his desk in the *Journal of Commerce* building and taken to Dix's headquarters where he was received "with great courtesy." He wrote a farewell letter to his family, shook hands all around, and was taken to the Battery to await transportation to Fort Lafayette.

Prime had left the *Journal of Commerce* office for the evening but heard Hallock was in custody and went to army headquarters. He was in Dix's office when the General was informed the order for the arrests had been recalled by Washington but that the seizure of the newspapers was to remain in effect.

Stone, who worked only on the day side, was at his home in Brooklyn when he learned of the arrest of Hallock. He went back to Manhattan. Meanwhile, soldiers went to his home and told his wife they had come to take him to Fort Lafayette. Informed by the General that he was not to be arrested, Stone went to the *Associated Press* office where he found Hallock and Prime.

Manton Marble was not arrested, the order being recalled before he could be located. The General warned the four men not to try to enter the offices of their newspapers.[31]

President Lincoln's reconsideration of that portion of the order which called for arrest of the editors probably was taken upon the advice of Dix, who had the case in hand from the start. The early arrest he promised may have been accomplished a few hours after the forgery appeared, although it was not until two days later that the *New York Tribune* heard a suspect was in Fort Lafayette. On Saturday morning, May 21, the *Tribune* said it "understood" that Joseph Howard, "one of the editors" of the *Brooklyn Daily Eagle*, had been arrested.

The *Tribune* "understood" correctly. Howard, city editor of the *Brooklyn Daily Eagle*, was in a cell at Fort Lafayette, the confessed forger of the proclamation. Also in Fort Lafayette was a reporter for the *Eagle*, Francis A. Mallison, who admitted he participated in the hoax. Mallison was arrested by two detectives on Saturday morning, May 21, while on his way to a precinct house to report for the army draft.[32]

This was the same Howard who, as a reporter for *The New York Times*, wrote that Lincoln "wore a Scotch plaid cap and a very long military cloak, so that he was entirely unrecognizable" on his secret night ride through Baltimore en route to Washington in February of 1861.

Howard was a baldish, pale, slender man about thirty-five years old. He was of medium height, had dark eyes, and wore a mustache. With a recognized talent for writing, he held a series of good jobs, first with the *Boston Journal*. While working for the *Journal*, he covered a strike of shoemakers at Lynn, Mass., and attracted the attention of *The New York Times*. He held down the city desk at the *Times* and won the choice assignment of traveling with the Prince of Wales when he toured the country just before the Civil War. He also served as a correspondent for the *New York Tribune*. He next appeared on the *New York Daily News* as one of Benjamin Wood's bright boys and wrote a series of inflammatory interviews with workingmen just before the draft riots. From the *Daily News* he drifted to the *Brooklyn Daily Eagle*.[33]

Mallison told all after his arrest. He said he and Howard met in a private home in Brooklyn on the night of May 17 and that he prepared the forged proclamation in *Associated Press* style from Howard's dictation. He said they separated about eleven o'clock and that he took the copy to New York and directed its distribution to the newspapers. The stylus he used in manifolding the copy was stolen from the editorial room of the *New York Tribune*.[34]

*The World* and the *Journal of Commerce*, unable to publish, prepared statements of explanation to the public, published for them by the other New York newspapers. The *Journal of Commerce* said it usually closed its forms at half-past three every morning, although late *Associated Press* dispatches were often received after the last page had gone to the pressroom. If no editor was around, the foreman would act in his stead and decide whether it was worth pulling back the page for a make-over. The copy was always brought by a runner from the *Associated Press* office, and the foreman could readily recognize it because of the characteristic manner in which it was prepared.

It was about half-past three on Wednesday morning, May 18, when the foreman ordered the last form closed and dismissed his printers, "the entire night force of editors and proof readers having already left." As the printers were leaving the building, a boy appeared with a batch of copy, supposedly from the *Associated Press*. The foreman glanced at it and saw it was a proclamation signed by the President. He rounded up enough compositors to put the proclamation in type, called back a form, and made it over.

He ordered the change made "on the fly," that is, the press was to continue to run until the make-over was cast and ready.

All this happened, the paper explained, at that moment "well known to newspaper men as one of the most critical in the day's history of a newspaper." A situation almost identical obtained in *The World* office.[35]

"This, we know," said the *New York Tribune*, "is a truthful statement of the facts." It said the forgery caused no havoc except in Wall Street "where no lie is so big that it cannot be swallowed." The *Tribune* commented further in an editorial:

The real facts which led to the publication of this monstrous forgery were not, we presume, known yesterday in Washington, or the suspension of the two journals would not, we suppose, have been ordered. The order, no doubt, will be revoked today. We hope it will, for certainly no journal should be punished for a mistake which might have very innocently been committed by the most loyal paper in the land.[36]

The *New York Daily News* asked: "For what crime have these offices been thronged with soldiers . . . ? The idea that any one connected with these journals had anything to do with the forgery of the proclamation is too preposterous to be entertained by any sane mind."[37]

The *Tribune* replied to the *Daily News* by reminding it of its own attitude on the war. "We can't quite understand," said the *Tribune*, "how it is that victims of a forger are severely punished, while the daily utterances of such vallainous, traitorous, and utterly preposterous calumnies, calculated to shake the very pillars of the State, go utterly unrebuked. Can any one explain?"[38]

Two days after the forgery appeared, Dix had the case solved and a written confession from Howard. He telegraphed Secretary Stanton full details of the plot and pointed out the newspapers had been tricked.

The General's telegram was shown to President Lincoln. He told Stanton to inform the General that, while editors were responsible for what appeared in their newspapers, he did not intend to be vindictive and that *The World* and the *Journal of Commerce* should be handed back to them.[39] The suspension was lifted by Dix at eleven o'clock on Saturday morning, May 21. Not a wheel had turned in either plant since Wednesday. Neither paper had a Sunday edition; thus they could not reappear until Monday morning.[40]

Dix also informed Secretary Stanton that the New York offices of the Independent Telegraph Company were cleared, and he authorized the release of all employees. In other cities where Independent employees had been carted off to prison, they also were released. The wire offices were held forty-eight hours longer.[41]

Secretary Stanton or some other official high in the government put a finger on the press at Washington. The capital correspondent of the New York *Commercial Advertiser*, a Republican newspaper loyal to the Union, wired his office: "We of the press are semiofficially cautioned not to criticize the recent newspaper seizure in New York. It is very easy to write about the liberty of the press, but one's personal liberty is more desirable these broiling days. Discretion is the better part of valor—mum's the word."[42]

With full resumption of the New York press on Monday morning, May 23, there was big news to publish. Headlines said: "Grant Making Flank Movement—He is Trying to Force Lee Out of his Entrenchments—Lee Probably South of the North Anna—He is Having a Tough Time."

A correspondent with Grant's army heard soldiers singing in the dead of night, a swelling chorus that "shook the forest's gloom." He heard the words of their song:

> The Union forever, hurrah, boys, hurrah;
> Down with the traitors, and up with the stars.

The New York newspapers also told of the arrest of Samuel Medary, editor of *The Crisis*, at Columbus, Ohio. His arrest revealed he had been secretly indicted on a charge of conspiracy against the government by a Federal jury in Cincinnati.[43]

But the bogus proclamation was still the talk of the town. An enterprising merchant used it in his advertising, saying: "Not a bogus proclamation—Official from Geo. C. Haffet & Co. Whereas Golden Bitters are the best tonic in town, etc."[44]

The full story of Howard and Mallison began to unwind. Their confessions revealed they bought gold on Tuesday in Wall Street and planned to sell it on Wednesday in the wake of their proclamation when the price shot skyward. Howard, said the *New York Herald*, had lost money in stock gambling operations and was trying to recoup. Persons other than Howard may have profited, one rumor said, he himself admitting he drank champagne with a stock operator, "one of the most prominent Republican politicians," the night after the forgery appeared.[45]

In their first issues after the suspension, *The World* and the *Journal of Commerce* spoke at great length of their troubles. The *Journal of Commerce* ignored President Lincoln by name and thanked the New York press for moral support, still insisting it was guilty of no crime and stated:

The press of New York City, excepting only the *Times*, was frank and out-spoken in condemning the whole proceeding. Especially should it be noted that the *Tribune*, *The Post*, *The Sun* and the *Commercial Advertiser* were true to old and noble principles. We regret that *The Post* subsequently lent its columns to a correspondent whose pen overflowed with folly, falsehoods and malignity.

The newspaper claimed to have published more than fifty thousand dollars worth of "gratuitous advertising" for the Lincoln administration, "every order coming to us in almost facsimile of this forged dispatch, and with no verification whatsoever." It continued:

There is scarcely a night in the year that the War Department does not send us, on manifold paper, now in this and now in that handwriting, at 1, 2, 3 or 4 o'clock, some such proclamation or order. If we should refuse to publish one of these we should be denounced as Copperheads. If we demanded verification or pay, we should be hooted at as traitors.

It had a lot to say about the "ingenious scamp" who caused the trouble. It ignored Mallison, whom the newspapers looked upon as the tool of Howard, and said:

. . . the guilty individual was educated in the newspaper business on *The New York Times* and is familiarly known as Howard of the *Times*. He was a thorough newspaper man, familiar with all the facts necessary to accomplish his purpose. He was a favorite contributor to *The Independent*, president of the First Republican Association in Brooklyn, long a member of the Rev. Mr. Beecher's church, member of the Republican committee of King's county, and employed lately in a subordinate position on the *Eagle*. He is well known in radical circles, intimate associate of the most eminent of their politicians.[46]

Manton Marble spent his time during his enforced idleness in writing a letter to President Lincoln, several columns long, which he published in *The World*. While the *Journal of Commerce* merely sobbed on the public shoulder, Marble addressed Lincoln in terms of cold anger, studded with personal insult. He accepted full blame for publishing the fake proclamation but said, "No newspaper in the country but would have been deceived as we were."

"That proclamation was a forgery," wrote Marble, "written by a person who, ever since your departure from Springfield for Washington in 1861, has enjoyed private as well as public opportunities for learning to counterfeit the peculiarities of your speech and style, and whose service for years as a city editor of the *New York Times* and the *New York Tribune* acquainted him with the entire newspaper machinery of the city, and enabled him to insert his clever forgery into the regular channels by which we receive news."

He charged that the troops occupying *The World* office damaged the property and stole some of the equipment, then said:

> Not until today has *The World* been free to speak. But to those who have ears to hear, its absence has been more eloquent than its columns could ever be. . . . Had the *Tribune* and the *Times* published the forgery . . . would you, Sir, have suppressed the *Tribune* and the *Times* as you suppressed *The World* and the *Journal of Commerce?* You know you would not. If not, why not? Is there a different law for your opponents and for your supporters? Can you, whose eyes discern equality under every complexion, be blinded by the hue of partisanship?

He demanded that the President tell him whether he believed a newspaper like *The World* "could afford" to publish a forgery knowingly. "Such a trick," said Marble, "would hardly have succeeded in Sangamon county, Illinois." He declared the forgers were President Lincoln's own "zealous partisans," adding:

> Joseph Howard . . . was a Republican politician and a Loyal Leaguer, of Brooklyn. Consider, Sir, at whose feet he was taught his political education, and in whose cause he spent his political breath. Mr. Howard has been from his very childhood an intimate friend of the Republican clergyman, Henry Ward Beecher, and a member of his church. He has listened year in and year out to the droppings of the Plymouth sanctuary. The stump speeches which there follow prayer and precede the benediction he for years reported in the journal which is your devoted organ in this city. For years he was the city editor of that journal, *The New York Times;* for a long time he was the Washington correspondent of the chief abolition newspaper of the country, the *New York Tribune* . . . he represents himself a favorite visitor at the White House since your residence there.[47]

Howard, who was said to have been arrested at his desk in the *Brooklyn Daily Eagle* city room,[48] wrote a series of silly stories about his experiences and smuggled them out of prison to appear in the *Eagle* with the by-line, "Dead Beat." He jokingly informed the public that he was sent to Lafayette because the government was making improvements on Staten Island and wanted somebody to watch the architects "to see that they didn't pocket the bricks."

He described an imaginary meeting of the Cabinet, saying:

A meeting of the Cabinet was called at the White House. Secretary Stanton introduced the subject. The President said it reminded him of a story he once heard in Illinois. A man who lived in Sangamon county, in conversation with a medical student, said he didn't believe in vaccination. Says he, "It don't do a child a bit of good. I had a child vaccinated once, and in three days after it fell out of a window and broke its neck."[49]

All over the North, the press, both Democratic and Republican, kept the story alive for days with long and earnest comment. The Copperhead newspapers maintained there was some connection between the New York seizure and the arrest of Medary. The *Atlas and Argus*, Democratic organ at Albany, said: "We believe that the occasion was seized upon, and the outrage has been persisted in, for the purpose of intimidating the press. The simultaneous seizure of Governor Medary of the Ohio *Crisis*, upon some false accusation and in violation of law, confirms this suspicion."

The newspaper suggested that the New York delegation in Congress leave its seats and go home and thought the Ohio delegation should do likewise.[50]

The radical Republican press of the Midwest, represented by the *Cincinnati Gazette*, believed that suspension of *The World* and *Journal of Commerce* was a drastic measure. The *Gazette* said: "To the credit of the press of the country, it may be said that the suppression . . . was disapproved by all the papers . . . that we have read."[51]

There was some political fence mending in Washington. Secretary Stanton invited the Independent Telegraph Company to connect its wires with the War Department offices, a move that gave it a share of government business.[52] On May 24, Stanton wrote to the Independent Company that "the satisfactory arrangements made by your company with this department will, I hope, do much toward inspiring the public with a just confidence in your telegraphic line, and the loyalty, prudence, and discretion of its management."[53]

The *Advertiser and Farmer*, Democratic newspaper at Bridgeport, Conn., made its own interpretation of Stanton's action. After complaining over the arrest of "that gallant old standard-bearer and pillar of democracy, Ex-governor Sam Medary of Ohio," it said: "The *Rochester Democrat* states that the Secretary of War told its editor that he had now got the telegraph under his control and he wished that he had the newspapers also."[54]

The Washington news agency operated by Villard, White, and

Hill broke out in a rash of exclusive stories whose source obviously was the White House and the War Department.[55]

The Democrats in New York State tried to make political capital of the newspaper cases. Governor Seymour, always ready to strike the Lincoln administration, caused the case to be presented before a grand jury, hopeful of an indictment against General Dix and members of his staff. The grand jury found no indictment but passed a resolution saying the matter should be investigated.

Seymour then ordered the district attorney of New York County to prosecute the officers before a city magistrate. Warrants were issued, charging Dix and members of his staff with kidnaping and inciting to riot. There were no actual arrests, but they were claimed to have been made technically.

The case came up for trial early in August before Judge A. D. Russell. The kidnaping charge, it was revealed, was based on the arrest of Hallock. As for "inciting to riot," the district attorney pointed to crowds of curious in front of the seized newspaper offices.

The defense argued there was no case, the grand jury having failed to return an indictment; that a state of war existed all over the country, not alone where battles were fought; that the Federal government and not the state held the war powers; that the authority of the President in time of war had been upheld in the Supreme Court; that imprisonment not through the regular channels of law had been authorized by Congress in the Habeas Corpus Act of 1863.

The case went round and round, but in the end it was right back where it started with Judge Russell ruling that Dix and the others should be held "subject to the action of the grand jury."[56]

In rendering his decision, Judge Russell spoke especially of the Habeas Corpus Act, observing that the defendants had placed themselves under certain provisions of it. "If that provision is constitutional," said Judge Russell, "it assimilates the President of the United States, during the existence of the present rebellion, to an absolute monarch, and makes him incapable of doing any wrong. This is a very novel and startling doctrine to advance under a republican form of government."[57] There is no record of further action in the case.

On August 22, Lincoln told Secretary Stanton he wished to "oblige" Henry Ward Beecher by turning Howard out of Fort Lafayette. He wanted to know what Stanton thought of the idea. Stanton replied he had no objection but wondered whether it was the "proper time." Lincoln let the matter rest until the next day when he sent a note to Stanton, directing that Howard be discharged.[58]

Wearing a three-month prison pallor, Howard left Fort Lafayette and went about his business. Later in life, he became one of the best-known reporters on New York newspapers and was elected president of the International League of Press Clubs in 1897.[59]

Perhaps events shaped themselves just as Prime hoped when he wrote for his *Journal of Commerce*, "God grant that we may live and work, till this story is remembered as a hideous dream."[60]

# 35 "Lincoln Is Already Beaten"

WHILE LAUNCHING GRANT and Sherman on a full-scale offensive against the Confederacy in the spring of 1864, Lincoln also began his fight for a second term. Dissension within the ranks of the Republican party was the only serious threat. Radical Republicans opposed Lincoln because, they said, he was too slow to adopt their theories. Editors of administration newspapers did not think he could win.

The President also faced the possibility of a war with France, resulting from French occupation of Mexico, where Louis Napoleon had enthroned a puppet emperor.[1]

From November of 1862, when General McClellan was removed from command by Lincoln and told to await orders that never came, it was correctly assumed he would seek the Democratic nomination for the Presidency. Republicans feared him, thinking all factions of the opposition would flock to him. He was the darling of War Democrats, secret hope of the Copperheads.

Forney's *Press* in Philadelphia and his *Chronicle* in the Capital opened editorial guns on McClellan in February, at the same time advocating a second term for Lincoln. They sounded the keynote for the Lincoln newspapers by charging that the South wanted McClellan elected.

The choice of the radical Republicans was General Frémont, first presidential candidate of the new party, defeated by Buchanan in 1856. He was a bitter enemy of Lincoln, their estrangement dating back to the President's annulment of the General's proclamation of emancipation to the people of Missouri in the first year of the war. Frémont had been awaiting orders since the middle of 1862, when he refused to serve under Major General John Pope "for personal reasons." He was ripe for picking when the radicals approached him with a proposal to run against Lincoln.

Answering a call addressed "to the Radical Men of the Nation," 350 so-called delegates met at Cleveland on May 31 and nominated Frémont, with John Cochran, who served in the Union army as a brigadier general until physically incapacitated in 1862, as his running mate.

One of the planks in the radical platform demanded the confiscation of rebel property and its distribution among "the soldiers and actual settlers." Frémont repudiated the confiscation policy in his letter accepting the nomination.[2]

Frémont's candidacy appealed to the German language press, and many of their newspapers deserted Lincoln for him. Among them were the *Michigan Journal*, Detroit; *Deutsche Zeitung*, Peoria, Ill.; *Wisconsin Democrat*, Milwaukee; *Staats Zeitung*, Dubuque, Iowa; *German American*, New York, and *Der Tagliche Demokrat*, Davenport, Iowa.[3]

Among others deserting Lincoln was the *Illinois Staats-Anzeiger* of Springfield, a newspaper once secretly owned by him. In announcing its break with Lincoln, the newspaper said:

Reviewing the history of the past four years, nothing is left to us but to cut loose decidedly and forever from Lincoln and his policy and to *protest against his reelection under all circumstances and at any price*. No reasons of expediency can influence us to ever accept Lincoln as our President again. If a portion of the so-called Republican party is, nevertheless, blind enough to cling to Lincoln, we shall not be induced to do so by their cry that we break up the party. On the contrary, they will have broken it up. They must bear the responsibility if a Democratic candidate is elected.[4]

A week after Frémont was nominated, the regular Republicans convened at Baltimore on June 7, their assemblage bearing the attractive title of National Union Convention. Fear of some party leaders that Lincoln would have to fight for the nomination had been pretty well erased by the departure of the radicals, although some faint effort was made to have the convention postponed until later in the summer. The opposition had many of the cards, but Lincoln held an ace: Henry J. Raymond, editor of *The New York Times*, was chairman of the platform committee and leading spirit in the convention.

The *Times* flayed the Frémont convention. "Hostility to Abraham Lincoln was its mainspring and motive-power," an editorial said. "It was a congregation of malcontents—of men who had griefs, and who sought revenge." And the *Times* predicted: "Abraham Lincoln will be renominated by acclamation."[5]

On the first ballot, Lincoln received the vote of every delegation except Missouri, which honored General Grant, then switched to make the nomination unanimous. Andrew Johnson, military Governor of Tennessee, was chosen over Hannibal Hamlin for Vice-President.[6]

Only one newspaper in the North saw the political situation with the crystal clearness in which it can be viewed today. The *Philadelphia Inquirer* said in an editorial:

> Mr. Lincoln's renomination is clearly the work of the people of his party. The politicians *may* have been for him; if they were, they *followed*, instead of leading the people. Whatever may be the differences of opinion as to his policy or his administrative ability, it is clear that for some paramount reason he has a powerful hold on the popular heart; and that reason is the firm belief in his integrity and patriotism, and the absolute singleness of purpose with which he has striven for three long years to restore the Union.[7]

The New York *World* reviled Lincoln for days after the nomination, climaxing the new attack with this editorial venom:

> The American people are in no mood to re-elect a man to the highest office whose daily language is indecent, and who, riding over the field of Antietam, when thirty thousand of his fellow citizens were yet warm in their freshly made graves, could slap Marshal Lamon on the knee, and call for the negro song of "Picayune Butler." The war is a serious business to men whose sons have bitten the dust, whose brothers are under the Virginia hill-sides; it is a very serious business to women whose children have come home to them maimed for life, or whose husbands pine in the hospitals or have perished in the swamps of Virginia. They cannot be reminded of a smutty song; they cannot tread on fresh graves and grin and roar over a ribald nigger song. . . .[8]

The next day, *The World* published an article under the heading, "Lincoln Upon the Battlefield," purportedly clipped from a newspaper represented to be the *Essex Statesman*, but not further identified. This article was supposed to be an accounting of the alleged battlefield incident *The World* discussed the day before in an editorial. It follows:

> We see that the papers are referring to the fact that Mr. Lincoln ordered a comic song to be sung upon the battle-field. We have known the facts about the transaction for some time, but have refrained from speaking them. As the newspapers are now stating some of the facts we will give the whole.
>
> Soon after one of the most desperate and sanguinary battles, Mr. Lincoln

visited the Commanding General and the army. While on his visit the Commanding General, with his staff, took him over the field in a carriage and explained to him the plan of the battle, and the particular places where the fight was most fierce. At one point the Commanding General said, "Here on this side of the road five hundred of our brave fellows were killed, and just on the other side of the road four hundred more were slain, and right on the other side of that wall five hundred rebels were destroyed. We have buried them where they fell."

"I declare," said the President, "this is getting gloomy. Let us drive away." After driving a few rods the President said, "This makes a feller feel gloomy. Jack (speaking to a companion), can't you give us something to cheer us up? Give us a song, and give us a lively one." Thereupon Jack struck up, as loud as he could bawl, a comic negro song, which he continued to sing while they were riding off from the battle-ground, and till they approached a regiment drawn up, when the Commanding General said, "Mr. President, wouldn't it be well for your friend to cease his song till we have passed this regiment? The poor fellows have lost more than half of their numbers. They are feeling very badly, and I should be afraid of the effect that it may have on them." The President then asked his companion to stop his singing till they got by that regiment.

We know that this story is incredible, that it is impossible that a man who could be elected President of the United States could so conduct himself over the fresh-made graves of the heroic dead. When this story was told us we said that it was *incredible, impossible,* but the story is told on such authority that we *know* it to be true. We tell the story that the people may have some idea of this man, Abraham Lincoln, who is a candidate for four more years of such rule. If any Republican holds up his hands in horror, and says this story *can't* be true, we sympathize with him from the bottom of our soul; the story *can't* be true, of any man fit for any office of trust, or even for decent society; but the story is every whit true of Abraham Lincoln, *incredible* and *impossible* as it may seem.[9]

Carried by *The World's* national circulation, the story was spread all over the North. It was reprinted by the leading Copperhead newspapers, the *Chicago Times, The Crisis,* and others of their ilk. As though there was a general understanding among editors who published the story, no one raised the question what and where was the *Essex Statesman.*

It is now believed such a newspaper never existed, authorities in this field being unable to find a trace of it other than its mention in *The World.* The word *Essex* has been used in the names of many newspapers

at various times in the eastern United States. There have been news-
papers called the *Essex Reporter, Essex Advertiser, Essex Times,* and
the *Essex Republican,* published at different periods at Elizabethtown,
N. Y. There was an *Essex Standard* at Elizabeth, N. J., while Haverhill,
Mass., had an *Essex County Democrat.* Nowhere is there record of an
*Essex Statesman.*

The history of *The World* under Manton Marble's direction makes
it easy to believe that the story was prepared in his office and made to
appear as reprinted to give it added interest. Whatever the source of the
story, it was a grand success from Marble's point of view. It set the
country to talking, and it hurt Lincoln deeply, perhaps more than any
slur published about him.

Ward Hill Lamon, who was accused of singing, observed that Lincoln
could not bring himself to read the bitter comment. He suggested the
President issue a refutation, but he demurred. Many persons wrote to
Lincoln and Lamon about the alleged episode, and again the marshal
wanted to speak publicly, but the President told him to keep silent.[10]

Day after day, *The World* made reference to the Antietam tale,
working it into fresh stories about the administration. On September 9,
1864, *The World* said:

While the President was driving over the field in an ambulance, accompanied by Marshal Lamon, General McClellan, and another officer, heavy
details of men were engaged in the task of burying the dead. The ambulance
had just reached the neighborhood of the old stone bridge, where the dead
were piled highest, when Mr. Lincoln, suddenly slapping Marshal Lamon on
the knee, exclaimed: "Come, Lamon, give us that song about Picayune
Butler; McClellan has never heard it." "Not now, if you please," said General
McClellan, with a shudder; "I would prefer to hear it some other place and
time."[11]

A man who signed himself "A. J. Perkins" clipped that story from
*The World* and sent it to Lamon in a letter, saying he should like to
know just what happened on the battlefield. Lamon wrote a long reply
to Perkins but decided to submit it to the President before mailing it.
The President read Lamon's letter and shook his head. Taking up a pen,
Lincoln rewrote it. Lincoln had Lamon say the President asked him to
sing a "little sad song," but not while on the battlefield. Someone in
the party, not President Lincoln, later called for "Picayune Butler,"
and Lamon sang it. At no time did he sing on the battlefield. The letter
finished, Lincoln handed it to Lamon, telling him not to mail it.[12]

Examination of the President's visit to the Antietam field two weeks after the battle reveals him as doubly careful of his words and actions. He was followed by the press wherever he went, and a *New York Times* reporter heard him say: "In my present position it is hardly proper for me to make speeches. Every word is so closely noted. . . ."[13]

Grant lost thousands of men in Virginia, and the offensive bogged down. The administration based election hopes on collapse of the Confederacy, with the capture of both Richmond and Atlanta expected during the summer. But the stubborn defenders of the Southern strongholds, with an eye on political events in the North, thinking defeat of Lincoln at the polls might bring a compromise peace, refused to yield.

Conduct of the New York press, especially of those newspapers that professed to support the Lincoln administration, disgusted Gideon Welles, who sat in Washington writing in his diary as though he were Father Time. On August 13, 1864, he told himself none of the papers was sincere. He put Raymond down as a mercenary, Greeley as an enemy of Lincoln, Bryant as well-meaning but old.[14]

*The World,* amused by the antics of Greeley, Bryant, and others, said:

> It would be difficult to determine which are more damaging to the prospects of Mr. Lincoln in his candidacy for reelection—the heavy blows in front which his manly opponents are dealing, or the stabs in the back inflicted by his professed friends.[15]

Even *The New York Times* came in for a scorching for its attitude on Lincoln, *The World* saying that Raymond's newspaper "does not exactly pronounce him a fool, but it does the nearest thing to it in referring to him as a man of open nature."[16]

Thurlow Weed, an editor whom Lincoln trusted, carried to him a warning that reelection was impossible. He took with him to the White House Henry Raymond's opinion that all was lost unless the administration could stage some bold stroke. Raymond said the people wanted peace, the Albany editor informed the President, and suggested commissioners be sent to Richmond to offer peace on the basis of a restored Union.[17]

Raymond himself went to Washington to press the peace-commission step, telling the President he was willing to serve as a commissioner.[18] But Raymond did not permit his own doubts to get into the columns of the *Times,* which long since had earned the title of "administration journal."[19]

Meeting in secret, when fortunes of the Union were at ebb tide, a group of New York Republicans, styling themselves "unconditional supporters of the National Government," started a movement for the withdrawal of Lincoln and substitution of another candidate. They issued a call for a convention to be held at Cincinnati on September 28. Foremost in the movement was George Opdyke, former mayor of New York.[20]

Horace Greeley was unable to attend the first meeting of the committee, held at the Opdyke home, but he sent his regrets in a letter dated August 18, 1864, saying:

I must go out of town tomorrow evening and cannot attend the meeting at your house. Allow me to say a word.

Mr. Lincoln is already beaten. He cannot be elected. And we must have another ticket to save us from utter overthrow. If we had such a ticket as could be made by naming Grant, Butler, or Sherman for President, and Farragut as Vice, we could make a fight yet. And such a ticket we ought to have anyhow, with or without a convention.[21]

H. Winter Davis, Abolitionist Congressman from Maryland, was one of the politicians in the plot against Lincoln, helping to contact men throughout the North whom he thought might be receptive to the movement. But one of the real busybodies was Whitelaw Reid, Washington correspondent for the *Cincinnati Gazette* and House Librarian by virtue of a sop from Lincoln. On September 2, 1864, writing on stationery of the *Gazette*, he replied to Opdyke's letter as follows:

Yours of the 25th inst. arrived here during my absence in Chicago, which must excuse my tardy reply. That which I could do in the direction you indicate has been done in inducing the *Gazette* to come out for Mr. Lincoln's withdrawal. The article has been telegraphed east, and I hope has done some good. . . .[22]

Richard Smith, editor of the *Gazette*, Reid's employer, wrote to Opdyke on August 27, saying in part:

The people regard Mr. Lincoln's candidacy as a misfortune. His apparent strength when nominated was fictitious, and now the fiction has disappeared, and instead of confidence there is distrust. I do not know a Lincoln man. . . .

The withdrawal of Lincoln and Fremont and the nomination of a man that would inspire confidence and infuse life into our ranks would be hailed with general delight.

While the people crave for a new candidate, they would regret any movement that would fall short of this result. If the move should be made, and then Mr. Lincoln refused to withdraw, our condition would be a great deal worse than it is now. Consequently a convention to *force* Lincoln from the track would not be popular, but would be disastrous. . . .

The course, then, should be to bring about Mr. Lincoln's withdrawal in advance of a call for a convention. This may be done if men near the throne will cooperate with you. . . . Military success of a decisive character would help us largely.[23]

Thus was provided a perfect setting for the nomination of General McClellan by the Democrats at Chicago on August 29.

About two hundred and fifty delegates formally named McClellan and adopted a platform that declared the war for the Union a failure and called for "immediate efforts" to end hostilities. The platform avoided any promise that the war would be carried on in event of failure to restore the Union. The platform was the brain child of Vallandigham, master spirit behind the convention, ably supported by Governor Seymour of New York. Vallandigham did his work too well. McClellan, to his credit, repudiated the platform by saying:

I could not look in the face of my gallant comrades of the army and navy, who have survived so many bloody battles, and tell them that their labors and the sacrifice of so many of our slain and wounded brethren had been in vain; that we had abandoned that Union for which we have so often periled our lives . . . no peace can be permanent without the Union.[24]

While the secret movement against Lincoln was under way and the Democrats were nominating, Sherman took Atlanta. Opposition to Lincoln within his party melted in the bonfires of celebration, the Cincinnati convention call forgotten. Frémont withdrew at request of a committee of Republicans.

During the time he was a candidate, Frémont supporters established a campaign newspaper in Washington called the *New Era*. The paper was designed to compete with the *Washington Republican*, which was supporting Lincoln. The *Republican* made it the butt of a nationally circulated joke by referring to it as the *New Error*.

An unsung defender of the Union and the war policies of the Lincoln administration in New York was *The Sun*, a newspaper of more than fifty thousand circulation, larger than that of some of the more widely known dailies. It was a strictly local newspaper, its voice seldom heard by the nation.

True to its role of friend of the workingman, *The Sun* resented criticism of the Republican ticket in 1864 as "a rail-splitter and a tailor." It took the stand both men should be honored for rising from humble spheres.[25]

# 36 The Belling of the Cats

HORACE GREELEY WAS a prophet of doom in that summer of 1864. He thought the South could never be defeated and that the only hope for the North rested in a compromise that could restore the Union. While engaged in the secret movement to throw Lincoln overboard in the midst of the heated campaign, he participated in an abortive peace maneuver that backfired to mark the complete political disintegration of the chameleonic editor.

On July 5, Greeley received a letter from George N. Sanders, written at Niagara Falls, on the Canadian side, saying that he, Clement C. Clay of Alabama, and James P. Holcombe of Virginia desired to visit Washington and sought full protection. The purpose of the proposed visit was not discussed, but Greeley was told by sources not disclosed that the three men constituted a Richmond commission authorized to discuss peace. Greeley rose quickly to the bait by forwarding the application to President Lincoln. Not content to merely drop the matter in the presidential lap, Greeley urged Lincoln to respond and even proposed terms to be offered. He told the President:

I do not say that a just peace is now attainable, though I believe it to be so. But I *do* say that a frank offer by you to the insurgents of terms which the impartial must say ought to be accepted, will, at the worst, prove an immense and sorely needed advantage to the national cause. It may save us from a Northern insurrection.

There was nothing naïve about Lincoln. He shrewdly deputed Greeley to go to Niagara to confer with the alleged commissioners and sent his secretary, John Hay, along to watch the proceedings. Greeley was to ascertain whether the three men were duly accredited agents; if they were, Lincoln would grant them safe conduct to Washington. Sanders admitted he was not dealing for Davis but insisted he had a clear understanding of the South's views for peace.

Thereupon, Lincoln sent a message addressed "to whom it may concern" to the Canadian visitors. It said:

Any proposition which embraces the restoration of peace, the integrity of the whole Union, and the abandonment of slavery, and which comes by and with an authority that can control the armies now at war with the United States, will be received and considered by the executive government of the United States, and will be met by liberal terms on other substantial and collateral points, and the bearer or bearers thereof shall have safe-conduct both ways.

The next move by the trio at Niagara revealed their purpose. They issued a manifesto in which they charged an offer of peace had been spurned by the Lincoln administration. Lincoln had, however, saved the day by addressing his note "to whom it may concern," thus taking no official notice of the delegation.[1]

Greeley was used as a dupe by the Confederacy in its efforts to further the chances of a Democratic victory at the polls in November. By Clay's own admission, he and his partners were in the "confidential employment" of the Richmond government and in contact with Democratic leaders in the North. They drew up a platform and an address in hope of having it presented to the National Democratic Convention at Chicago.[2]

After the Niagara Falls fiasco, the country was filled with ugly rumors that grew out of the charges made by the Confederates. Raymond of *The New York Times* called for publication of all correspondence in the case in his newspaper on August 4. He followed that with a letter to the President on August 5 in which he said:

I enclose an article from the *Tribune* of this morning. It seems to me that the public interest would be served—& certainly your action would be vindicated, which amounts to the same thing—by the publication of the correspondence in question.

If you concur in this opinion & see no objection to such a course I shall be very glad to receive from you a copy with authority to publish it.[3]

Greeley also wanted a copy of the correspondence, and he wrote to Hay for it. The reply came by telegram from President Lincoln. He told the editor he would be glad to see the letters published "with the suppression of a few passages." He asked Greeley to come to see him.[4]

Greeley answered two days later, saying he agreed to the editing of the letters before publication. He said he would be glad to come to Washington, but he feared such a visit would result "in further mischief," since his "bitterest personal enemies" were close to the President.[5]

The next day, August 9, the President forwarded to Greeley a privately printed copy of the correspondence. He had drawn a red pencil through the parts he wished suppressed, explaining they might "give too gloomy an aspect to our cause, and those which present the carrying of elections as a motive of action."[6]

Greeley answered immediately, first explaining he was writing a letter because he knew the War Department read his telegrams before they reached Lincoln. His letter said in part:

I will gladly come to Washington whenever you apprise me that my doing so may perhaps be of use. But I fear that my chance for usefulness has passed. I *know* that nine-tenths of the whole American people, North and South, are anxious for Peace—Peace on almost any terms. . . .

I know that, to the general eye, it now seems that the Rebels are anxious to negotiate, and that we repulse their advances. . . .

I firmly believe that, were the election to take place tomorrow, the democratic majority in this state and Pennsylvania would amount to 100,000, and that we should lose Connecticut also. . . .

What, then, can I do in Washington? Your trusted advisers nearly all think I ought to go to Fort Lafayette for what I have done already. . . . The cry has steadily been—No truce! No Armistice! No negotiation! No mediation . . . ! I never heard of such fatuity before. There is nothing like it in history.

I beg you, implore you, to inaugurate or invite proposals for Peace forthwith. And, in case Peace cannot now be made, consent to *an Armistice for one year.* . . . Meantime, let a National Convention be held, and there will surely be no more war.[7]

The correspondence between Greeley and Lincoln did not get into print until 1890 when Nicolay and Hay published it.

The North also had its "unofficial commissioners." With the blessings of the administration, but carrying no credentials, James Roberts Gilmore, author and magazine editor, and James F. Jaquess, an army colonel and preacher, went to Richmond in hope of obtaining a peace feeler.

They drew from President Davis the statement that "the war must go on till the last of this generation falls in his tracks, and his children seize his musket and fight our battle, unless you acknowledge our right to self-government. We are not fighting for slavery; we are fighting for independence, and that or extermination we will have."

Such an explicit exposition of the aims of the Confederacy emasculated the peace group in the North and did much to ensure a second term for Lincoln.[8]

Greeley still was unconvinced and continued to press the movement for a substitute Republican candidate for President. He headed a committee of three that wrote letters to the "loyal governors" to learn whether they believed Lincoln could be reelected. These letters were dated September 2, 1864, and were marked "private and confidential."

Three questions were propounded to the governors; whether they thought the reelection of Lincoln was a probability; whether Lincoln could carry "your state"; whether the interests of the Union party required a substitute candidate.

The letters were signed by Horace Greeley, editor of the *New York Tribune;* Parke Godwin, editor of the New York *Evening Post,* and Theodore Tilton, editor of the New York *Independent.* It was requested that all replies be addressed to Tilton. Secrecy was promised.

One of the first replies came from Governor A. W. Bradford of Maryland, an earnest Union man who served as a delegate to the futile Peace Congress in 1861. Writing from Annapolis on September 6, 1864, Bradford said he could reply in the affirmative to the first and second questions, and, as for the third, he believed Lincoln was the only man who could win.

He slapped down the committee by adding that no candidate "brought out under the auspices of the leaders most conspicuous in their objections to Mr. Lincoln" had a chance.[9]

On the very day Bradford was writing to the committee, Greeley's *Tribune* carried an editorial two columns long in which it proclaimed to the world:

Henceforth, we fly the banner of ABRAHAM LINCOLN for the next President. . . . We MUST reelect him, and, God helping us, we will.[10]

There must have been a reason for such an abrupt change in attitude. The fall of Atlanta may have had a bearing on it. Replies from the governors could not have yet been received. The explanation lies in the story that President Lincoln, who knew Greeley's greatest weakness was ambition to hold public office, suddenly dangled one in front of him.

George G. Hoskins, a young Republican politician, member of the New York state legislature and postmaster of Bennington by appointment of President Lincoln, dropped into the *New York Tribune* office to see Greeley. The editor told Hoskins about the President's telegram that urged him to come to Washington. Hoskins was amazed to hear Greeley say he did not intend to go. He argued Greeley must accept the invitation, if only out of respect for the Chief Executive.

Greeley still refused to listen. Always the opportunist, Hoskins suggested he go to Washington as spokesman for the editor and find out why the President wished to see him. Greeley raised no serious objections, and Hoskins, eagerly grabbing the excuse to call on Lincoln, went to the White House.

The President and the small-town politician had a long talk about Greeley. During the conversation, Hoskins got the idea that Lincoln intended to appoint Greeley to his Cabinet if he won the election, the President having mentioned something about Benjamin Franklin, an editor, and the office of Postmaster General.

Hoskins hastened back to New York, bursting to break the good news to Greeley. The editor believed Hoskins's story but insisted Lincoln would not keep his word. Hoskins, admirer of the President, told Greeley he would stake his life on it.[11]

While the *Tribune* did all it could to "fly the banner of Abraham Lincoln," Greeley made stump speeches to advocate his reelection. On September 24, the *Tribune* said "the only effective Peace Commissioners" were Grant, Sherman, Sheridan, and Farragut.

Three days later, the *Tribune* was repelled at the very thought of a cessation of hostilities in an effort to find peace. It said: "An Armistice! The idea of one springs from folly or treason."[12]

After a sputtering start, William Cullen Bryant and his New York *Evening Post* finally got behind Lincoln's candidacy for reelection. Bryant was one of the Republican radicals whose faultfinding with Lincoln's administrative policies did him more damage than even the Democrats were able to muster. He was one of those who called for a postponement of the Republican nomination until September, making his stand clear in a letter to the Republican Executive Committee on March 25, 1864.[13] His letter was publicized in a story printed on page one of *The New York Times* on May 6.

Just why Bryant did this is not clear, he himself insisting in a letter to a friend on June 15 that he did not doubt Lincoln would be re-elected.[14] It is probable he had secret hopes for the nomination of Chase, his close friend and fellow radical who had broken with the President.

Although it may be unfair to the lofty minded Bryant, it might not be going too far afield to conclude that the nasty scandal in which the *Evening Post* was involved by its business manager in January of 1864 shaped the poet's policy on a second term for Lincoln.

In April of 1864, the *Evening Post* lent itself, according to the proud boast of the Copperhead *Crisis*, to help spread one of the dirtiest specimens of anti-Lincoln propaganda to appear during the Civil War, not excepting the Southern press. It reprinted this article from *Brown-son's Quarterly Review:*

Mr. Lincoln evidently knows nothing of the philosophy of history, or of the higher elements of human nature. He imagines that men act only from low and interested motives. . . . His soul seems made of leather, and incapable of any grand or noble emotion. Compared with the mass of men, he is a line of flat prose in a beautiful and spirited lyric. He lowers, never elevates you. . . . You ask not, can this man carry the nation through its terrible struggles? But can the nation carry this man through them and not perish in the attempt . . . ?

Even wisdom from him seems but folly. . . . He is a good sort of man, with much natural shrewdness and respectable native abilities; but he is misplaced in the Presidential chair. He lives and moves in an order of thought, in a world many degrees below that in which a great man lives and moves. We blame him not because he is mole-eyed and not eagle-eyed, and that he has no suspicion of that higher region of thought and action in which lie the great interests and questions he is called upon to deal with as President of the United States.[15]

The article was reprinted by *The Crisis* with emphasis placed on its having appeared in the *Evening Post.* Orestes A. Brownson, editor of the quarterly that bore his name, was a former Democrat who joined the Republican party in 1860 and made campaign speeches in behalf of "the honest backwoodsman of Illinois."[16]

Brownson was a native of Vermont, reared as a disciple of Puritanism. He joined the Presbyterian church and later became a Universalist minister. Still later, he entered the Roman Catholic communion. His writings during the Civil War raised the question of his orthodoxy, and the matter was referred to Rome, the Pope delegating Cardinal Franzelin to make an investigation. The Cardinal reprimanded Brownson by suggesting that he be more moderate in his language. Brownson's two sons were killed fighting for the Union, and his biographer says this loss, combined with his anxiety for the safety of the country, so impaired his health that he was compelled to suspend the *Review* late in 1864 for a period.[17]

Bryant never came out editorially against Lincoln. Finally, the *Evening Post* fell into line with the administration dailies. On September 20, it said in an editorial:

He has gained wisdom by experience. Every year has seen our cause more successful; every year has seen abler generals, more skillful leaders, called to the head; every year has seen fewer errors, greater ability, greater energy, in the administration of affairs. The timid McClellan has been superseded by Grant, the do-nothing Buell by Sherman; wherever a man has shown conspicuous merit he has been called forward; political and military rivalries have been so far as possible banished from the field and from the national councils. . . . While Mr. Lincoln stays in power, this healthy and beneficial state of things will continue. . . .[18]

Strong support of the war by the *Evening Post* was its outstanding characteristic, and the opposition to Lincoln was something apart from Bryant's faith in the Union. All administration war measures, such as the draft, war financing, increased taxation, and all steps toward emancipation, received full commendation.

Bryant spoke violently to protest the efforts of Greeley and others for a negotiated peace. When the *Tribune* editor went to Niagara Falls, the *Evening Post* scoffed: "The most effective peace meetings yet held are those which Grant assembled in front of Vicksburg, which Meade conducted on the Pennsylvania plains, which Rosecrans now presides over near Tullahoma; their thundering cannons are the most eloquent orators, and the bullet which wings its way to the enemy ranks the true olive branch."[19]

The *Evening Post* was an ardent admirer of Grant and defended him from recurring charges made by temperance groups that he drank heavily. After the surrender of Vicksburg, it eulogized him as the General who had won more victories than any other. It added: "If any one after this still believes that Grant is a drunkard, we advise him to persuade the Government to place none but drunkards in important command."[20] That story was probably the source of the legend that Lincoln said if he knew what brand of whisky Grant drank he would see that the other generals got a barrel each.

Bryant began to move away from Lincoln early in the war when he refused to accept the President's patience on the question of emancipation. When Lincoln quickly revoked Frémont's proclamation in 1861, Bryant was deeply offended. Almost all criticism of Lincoln by the *Evening Post* until September of 1862 was based on his failure to free the slaves by governmental decree.[21] From that time on, he was criticized on almost any excuse.

Of Lincoln's second inaugural address, the *Evening Post* sarcastically observed that it had the "merit of brevity." It continued: "It will be a disappointment to perhaps a majority of readers that nothing is said in this prelude to a new administration to indicate the policy by which it will be guided."[22]

Lincoln's policy was clear enough—malice toward none; with charity for all—but the *Evening Post* gave no sign of recognizing it. The last time the *Evening Post* had a chance to criticize Lincoln was on April 12 when it commented editorially on his far-reaching address, carefully prepared, to celebrants on the White House lawn. Bryant's newspaper said: "The President being called upon by a popular assembly last evening, was of course bound to make a speech, which he did, and as he had nothing to say that could be said properly on such occasion, he succeeded in saying it to admiration."[23]

On May 20, 1864, two days after the New York *World* and the *Journal of Commerce* published the bogus presidential proclamation, the *New York Herald*, James Gordon Bennett's newspaper, published what has been called the "ghoul editorial."

It appeared after a National Union mass meeting in New York, which the *Herald* described as "a gathering of ghouls, vultures, hyenas and other feeders upon carrion" and authorized by "the great ghoul at Washington." The *Herald* charged that "these ghouls thought only of Lincoln's renomination, the control of the Baltimore convention and their own chances for petty offices." It continued:

If Lincoln's re-election were not impossible; if the blunders he has committed and the criminalities for which he is responsible had not placed him out of the Presidential ring; if the people had not long ago decided that General Grant is to be our next President, this ghoul-like meeting would alone destroy his chances and render his defeat a foregone conclusion. The trick of claiming credit for carnage, and trying to make capital out of wholesale slaughter was too transparent and too boldly played. In ancient times the ghouls stole slyly to their abominable festivals at midnight, by the pale glimmer of the sickly moon; but these modern ghouls parade themselves in open day, advertise their purposes in the daily paper, and gather publicly in a hall lit with the blaze of gaslight as if anxious to be universally abhorred and despised. The head ghoul at Washington had not sense enough to forbid the meeting. The ghouls and vultures here had not sense enough to postpone it. . . . Could the force of unblushing depravity much further go?[24]

Before the voters went to the polls in November, the *Herald* was supporting Lincoln. The President performed a great political feat to win Bennett's backing, said Alexander K. McClure, publisher of the *Chambersburg* (Pa.) *Repository*, who knew more about the stunt than any man of his time.[25] Lincoln made three attempts to get Bennett in his corner; the third, in the crucial year of 1864, was successful.

The first was in June of 1860 when Joseph Medill of the *Chicago*

*Tribune,* acting on his own, promised to see Bennett while on a trip to New York and "dicker" with his "Satanic Majesty" for his support in the campaign. Medill told Lincoln he suspected that Bennett wanted "social position."[26]

If anything came of the planned interview in New York, it was not appreciable during Lincoln's first campaign. The *Herald* was Democratic and not kindly disposed to the new party. Its tone was distinctly pro-Southern.

At outbreak of war, a howling mob at Fulton and Nassau Streets compelled Bennett to display the American flag. After that, he kept a stack of loaded rifles in his office.[27] He also softened the policy of the *Herald* toward the North, saying the South "wantonly and wickedly inaugurated hostilities."[28]

Bennett had an excellent newspaper, probably the best by far in America at that time, read wherever English was spoken. With the *Herald's* European circulation in mind, Lincoln wanted the foreign chancelleries to have a proper impression of the cause and purpose of the conflict. He decided his emissary to Bennett should be Thurlow Weed of the *Albany Evening Journal.* He called Weed to Washington and explained he had been chosen for the delicate job because he had experience in "belling cats."

Bennett and Weed had not spoken for more than thirty years, but the Albany editor accepted the assignment because he looked upon Lincoln's request as an order. Weed contacted a mutual friend of Bennett and himself. The result was that Bennett invited Weed to his home for dinner where he submitted to a harangue against Seward, Greeley, and others, including himself, as having been instrumental in bringing on the war.

When they finally got around to discussing the purpose of Weed's visit, Bennett showed a favorable reception. Weed went back to Washington to report and found Lincoln "greatly gratified."[29]

Bennett wanted something, too, and he planned a counterproposition by envoy, just as Lincoln had done. He summoned his best reporter, Henry Villard, then covering Washington, to give him instructions.

Villard was to tell President Lincoln that the *Herald* thereafter would stand for suppression of revolt in the South by force of arms and would support any war measures advocated by the government and enacted by Congress. He was to offer to Secretary of the Treasury Chase the fine yacht owned by the Bennetts as a gift to the revenue service on condition that James Gordon Bennett, Jr., be appointed a lieutenant in the naval service.[30]

Villard did his work well. Young Bennett went to Washington and was introduced to the President by Secretary Seward. Lincoln wrote a letter of introduction which Bennett carried with him to Secretary Chase's office. A commission was granted, and Bennett served until May 11, 1862, when he resigned.[31]

Bennett, Sr., supported the war effort, as pledged, but still he looked upon Lincoln as a conservative misled by a gang of radicals. As for personal relationship between the two men, there appears to have been none, except through correspondence, in which Lincoln took the lead.

Under date of September 22, 1861, Lincoln wrote a letter to Bennett to explain what appears to have been a misunderstanding over credentials for a *Herald* war correspondent. On May 21, 1862, Lincoln again wrote to Bennett, this time defending Secretary of War Stanton against the *Herald's* charge that he mixed politics with his duties. The President thanked Bennett for "able support."[32]

When the early fall elections of 1862 showed a trend to the Democratic party in the key states of Pennsylvania and Ohio, the *Herald* spoke of the result as a "revolution" and said it was due to loss of personal liberties. Bennett charged the government was responsible for "summary arrests and arbitrary imprisonments without trial" and said one of the contributing causes of political losses was suspension of the Habeas Corpus Act in loyal states. A *Herald* editorial gave advice to Lincoln but did not attack him, saying:

> . . . the great movement of the people . . . will enable the President, who is honest, to carry out the Conservative policy which he had contemplated from the beginning, and to apply the proper remedy to the evils we have enumerated. Heretofore he has been intimidated by assaults upon his family (Cabinet). . . . But now that it is proved by the elections that the radicals are powerless, and that he has the people to stand by him in defense of the Constitution, he can get rid of his imbecile cabinet.[33]

During 1863, the *Herald* became increasingly bitter against Lincoln and in 1864 began to boom Grant for his successor. Its sorry efforts in behalf of the General, who was too busy fighting to pay attention to politics, were climaxed by the horrible "ghoul" editorial.

Some time after he was nominated for a second term, Lincoln put his finger on Bennett to prevent his possible support of McClellan by offering him political preferment. Those who have explored the mystery say the prize was the French ambassadorship. The story sounds reasonable; as Medill once said, the one thing Bennett wanted that he could not buy with money was social position. Not even the President's official family knew of any transactions between him and Bennett. International circles buzzed when the secret began to leak out early in 1865.

It may have been—and this is pure supposition—that Henry Wikoff, a strange and mysterious man, known in the capitals of Europe as well as in Washington, performed the contact work between Bennett and Lincoln.[34] Wikoff, an author, diplomat, and a man about many towns, was such a striking personality that *Vanity Fair* gave over all of page one to a cartoon of him and dubbed him, "The political Paul Pry."[35]

The *Herald* did not change overnight to an administration journal; Bennett was far too clever for any step so crude. His editorials for several days discussed the qualifications of the candidates and presented the picture of having reasoned its way behind Lincoln.

On February 20, 1865, Lincoln sent a note to Bennett, saying he proposed to send his nomination for the Paris post to the United States Senate.[36] Bennett did not accept the appointment. He turned it down in a letter written in his own hand two days after the second inaugural, saying:

Fort Washington 6th March 1865

To His Exelency (sic)

The President of the United States

My Dear Sir

I have received your kind note in which you propose to appoint me Minister Plenipotentiary to full (sic) up the present vacancy in the important Mission to France. I trust that I estimate, at its full value, the high consideration which the President of the United States entertains and expresses for me by proposing so distinguished an honor. Accept my sincere thanks for that honor. I am sorry however to say that at my age I am afraid of assuming the labors and responsibilities of such an important position. Besides, in the present relations of France and the United States, I am of the decided opinion that I can be of more service to the country in the present position I occupy.

While, therefore, entertaining the highest consideration for the offer you have made, permit me most respectfully to decline the same for the reasons assigned.

I am, My Dear Sir

With sentiments of the highest respect, your most

Obt. Sert.

James G. Bennett[37]

Bennett, with modesty never before displayed, published nothing in his newspaper of the tendered appointment or his refusal to accept it. The President placed the letter in his files where it remained a well-guarded secret for more than eighty years.

At the time Lincoln is supposed to have secretly offered the French ambassadorship to Bennett, the assignment was held by William L. Dayton, a Republican appointed by Lincoln in 1861; there is no evidence that the President planned to recall him or that he intended to resign. He died suddenly on December 1, 1864, after a hearty dinner at the home of a friend.[38] His death created a vacancy, but that was a month after the election and at least four months after Bennett began to beat the drums for Lincoln.

On March 4, 1865, Bennett published a flattering tribute to the President, carefully avoiding any mention of the *Herald's* early stand on the issue of renomination. The *Herald* said the first three years of Lincoln's stay in the White House were not productive of the probability that he would be selected to run a second time and that "the magnates of his party laughed at the proposition when first thrown out by the *Herald*." It continued:

It was as amusing as one of Old Abe's jokes. But with the approach of the Baltimore convention, the radical dignitaries of their party began to discover their mistake. They were outwitted and outgeneraled completely. They became mutinous; they threatened secession; they tried it in a feeble experiment or two, but they were subdued—from Chase and Fremont, Wade and Winter Davis, down to Bryant and Greeley.

He is a most remarkable man. . . . He has proved himself, in a quiet way, the keenest of politicians, and more than a match for his wily antagonists in the arts of diplomacy. . . . Plain common sense, a kindly disposition, a straight forward purpose, and a shrewd perception of the ins and outs of poor weak human nature, have enabled him to master difficulties which would have swamped almost any other man. Thus today, with the most cheering prospects before him, this extraordinary rail-splitter enters upon his second term the unquestioned master of the situation in reference to American affairs, at home and abroad.[39]

Although that editorial has stood the test of time in its description of Lincoln, Bennett still did not understand him. The next day, in commenting on Lincoln's second inaugural address, the *Herald* said:

. . . we are inclined to receive this inaugural simply as the necessary speech which the occasion demanded—a little speech of "glittering generalities," put in to fill up the programme, and as nothing more.[40]

Months later, *The Crisis*, once so eager to publish Bennett's attacks on the Lincoln administration in the dark days of the war, said in an editorial:

It has transpired that BENNETT, of the *New York Herald*, at the beginning of the war, in a letter to President Davis, of the Confederate States, offered to support the policy of his government for the sum of fifty-thousand pounds sterling, to be paid abroad. Mr. Davis indignantly spurned the offer, on the ground of the *Herald's* utter lack of political weight and influence, its probable treachery, its certain cowardice, and its general infamy. This accounts for the extraordinary malignity of the *Herald* against the South during the war, and its present anxiety for the execution of Mr. Davis and his associates.[41]

Thurlow Weed, President Lincoln's trouble shooter during the first two years of the war, drifted away from him in the fall of 1863. The file of correspondence between them reveals the President as always eager for the editor's advice on political matters. Lincoln's respect for Weed is plain, and it is interlaced with a hint of affection. The two battle-scarred veterans of the political ring had much in common.

Lincoln chose him for an important assignment in 1861 when he sent him to Europe with Archbishop John Hughes of New York and Bishop J. H. McIlvaine, the former a Catholic, the latter a Protestant, to use their influence with foreign governments not to intercede in behalf of the Confederacy.[42]

A letter pleading for a resumption of their friendly relations was written by Lincoln to Weed on October 14, 1863. Lincoln said he feared that he had in some manner injured him. The President declared he never felt unkindly toward him and he was sure they could reach a new understanding by talking it over.[43]

Another Lincoln to Weed letter, dated March 25, 1864, indicates the first rupture was patched up and a new one had arisen. This time, Lincoln said he was surprised to learn Weed was hurt because one of his suggestions had not been followed. The President asked him to explain.[44]

If a story published by the *New York Herald* was true, Weed's absence from White House circles the second time may have been due to his desire to avoid Mrs. Lincoln. The story appeared in the *Herald* shortly after Lincoln asked Weed how he had been "wounded." The editor may have been "wounded" by Mrs. Lincoln's broomstick.

According to the *Herald*, Weed and some other men were in the lobby of a New York hotel, talking with the proprietor. One of the men remarked he had heard that General Halleck and Secretary of War Stanton had decided to get Mrs. Lincoln out of Washington by sending her home to Springfield.

In the laughter that followed, Weed was reported to have commented that he did not know whether the story was true, "but she ought to have been sent away long ago." Mrs. Lincoln was registered at the hotel, and a friend who overheard the men talking carried the story upstairs to her.

The next time Weed was in Washington, so the *Herald* related, he went to the White House. He was met by the First Lady, who accused him of talking about her, struck him with a broomstick, and ordered him out of the White House.[45]

Whatever "wound" Weed suffered, it had healed by election time. He made one of the final appeals in behalf of Lincoln in an electioneering stunt that took the form of a letter written by him to Abram Wakeman, New York postmaster. The letter was published in *The New York Times*, which called attention to it in an editorial that said:

Among the many prominent and influential Union men who doubted the wisdom of renominating and reelecting President Lincoln, none was more conspicuous than Thurlow Weed, of this state. His long experience in the field of practical politics, his wide and intimate acquaintance among public men, and his marked ability as a writer, gave his expressions a high degree of importance.

He has just published a letter, which we copy in another column, giving the reasons at length which led him, in spite of his former doubts, to regard the election of Lincoln and Johnson as absolutely essential to the salvation of the country. . . .[46]

Weed's letter said in part:

Gen. McClellan is wholly inexperienced in civil duties. Let us not consign all there is left of this priceless government and precious Union to the hands of those who are impatient for an ignominious shameful peace upon the best attainable terms, whether they conspire at Chicago under Vallandigham and Wood, or in Canada under Sanders and Greeley.[47]

# 37 A Son of Liberty

STRIKING AT THE roots of a conspiracy whose leaders planned at least two uprisings against Federal authority that never materialized, government agents broke the subversive secret organization known as the Sons of Liberty immediately after the Democratic national convention at Chicago.

The gathering at Chicago included hundreds of disaffected men of the Northwestern states, and mingling with them were countless Confederate spies who had infiltrated by way of Canada. The spies planned to use the excitement of the convention to screen them while they plotted a prison break at Camp Douglas where 8,000 captured Southerners were held. The proposed break was abandoned when the spies and their friends in the Sons of Liberty discovered their plans were known to the camp commander.[1]

The Federal government, operating with a sensationally effective counterespionage force, followed every move made by the Sons of Liberty in Kentucky, Ohio, Indiana, Illinois, Missouri, and Wisconsin, states where the great Northwest conspiracy existed. On September 7, 1864, Harrison H. Dodd, grand commander of the Sons of Liberty in Indiana, was arrested and jailed at Indianapolis. Dr. William Bowles, Andrew Humphreys, L. P. Milligan, Stephen Horsey, Horace Heffren, and William H. Harrison were rounded up and jailed as Dodd's lieutenants.[2]

The Sons of Liberty invited into its membership all men who opposed the war and were willing to stand for peace at any price. While it courted the Democratic party and some of its leaders directed the Chicago convention behind the scenes, it was actually a fifth column for the Confederacy. War Democrats were despised. That attitude was expressed on the Chicago convention floor when a speaker from Ohio declared there was no difference between a War Democrat and an Abolitionist. "They are links of one sausage," said the speaker, "made out of the same dog." A storm of applause followed.[3]

The Sons of Liberty was organized as successor to the played-out

Knights of the Golden Circle and the American Knights. The national head of the organization was a newspaper man, Phineas C. Wright, who stepped aside on February 22, 1864, for Clement L. Vallandigham, then a political exile in Canada.[4] Vallandigham slipped back into the country the following June.

His work in the West done, Wright went to New York after turning over the reins to Vallandigham and became chief editor of the *New York Daily News*, the Copperhead sheet run by the Woods. To say the Wood brothers were not aware of Wright's connections would be nothing short of ridiculous. The war course of the *News* would indicate that Wright was hired because of his connections.

He took up his editorial duties on January 18, 1864, and there is evidence that he spent his first day on the job writing a circular letter which was mailed to leaders of the Sons of Liberty all over the North. The letter, dated "January 18," gave the *Daily News* office, 19 City Hall Square, as the place of origin. Wright wrote that the newspaper was fighting usurpation of power by the Lincoln administration and that it was to be "our" newspaper. He urged all Sons of Liberty to obtain new subscribers for the *Daily News*.[5]

Wright was one of a series of men who held the post of editor of the *Daily News* during the Civil War. One of the first was George F. Thompson. He was arrested by government agents on June 10, 1862, his house searched, and his private papers examined. He was then taken to Washington where publisher Benjamin Wood, serving in Congress, was under investigation by the House Judiciary Committee. The government released Thompson on parole. At the time of his arrest, he was serving as private secretary to brother Fernando, Democratic mayor of New York.[6]

Before Phineas Wright went east, he succeeded in linking the Sons of Liberty to the high counsels of the Democratic party in Indiana. J. J. Bingham, editor of the *Indianapolis Daily State Sentinel* and chairman of the Democratic state committee, whose pro-Southern editorials marked him as an opponent of the war, was gathered into the Sons of Liberty fold by Wright's clever manipulation.

Wright was introduced to Bingham by Harrison Dodd, who took him to the *Sentinel* office, in the spring of 1863. They asked Bingham to join the secret order, but he did not take the step. The following November, he took the oath when Dodd bribed him with an offer of "financial support" for the *Sentinel*. Bingham promised to make his newspaper the mouthpiece for the Sons of Liberty in Indiana. He was appointed chairman of the "committee on literature."[7]

Bingham fitted smugly into his new role. His newspaper had led the opposition press in Indiana, critical of President Lincoln and all his policies. Following a county Democratic convention at Indianapolis on August 31, 1861, a mob of Union supporters, incensed at "sentiments expressed" in the meeting, visited the homes of several prominent citizens that night and compelled them to take an oath of allegiance to the government.

Those called out of their houses and forced to perform included Dr. W. S. Pierce, John Carlisle, Samuel Parrott, and Bingham. The Mayor and the chief of police "countenanced these proceedings," although fully aware of what was going on.

Bingham was at supper when the mob reached his home. He was informed that articles in the *Sentinel* favored disunion and that he must prove his loyalty by swearing allegiance. Bingham promised to meet the "committee" at a justice of the peace's office.

About an hour later, Bingham showed up, but the magistrate was absent. He was escorted to the Mayor's office where he repeated an oath used by the state militia, a copy of no others being available.[8]

The farce was finally ended by the sheriff of Marion County, who called on the Governor for military aid. Fifty regulars of the 19th Regiment responded and were stationed in the Circle.[9]

A temporary blanket of censorship was thrown over the *Sentinel* in 1863 by Brigadier General Henry B. Carrington, commander of the District of Indiana. General Carrington charged that the *Sentinel* filed misleading stories on the wires in reporting a fight between troops and civilians over the arrest of an army deserter. Telegraph companies were directed not to transmit any dispatches from the *Sentinel*.[10]

Upon his return from Canada, Vallandigham went directly to Hamilton, Ohio, where he spoke before a Democratic meeting. Across the line in Indiana, the Sons of Liberty, made bold by the return of their commander, planned a grand uprising tentatively set for August 16.

Dodd ordered Bingham to announce in the *Sentinel* a call for a Democratic mass meeting in Indianapolis on the date specified for the revolt, explaining that outbreaks were planned elsewhere on the same date. Bingham flatly refused, contending that violence created by the Sons of Liberty would have repercussions at the forthcoming Democratic convention.[11]

The editor acted quickly to save the Democratic party in Indiana. He called the party leaders and laid the plans for the revolt before them. The result was that the plot was called off.[12] Bingham later claimed he quit the Sons of Liberty the previous February. Were the story to end right here, he might be credited with having acted in the best interests of his country, at least in the interests of his party. But subsequent events proved he still was a Son of Liberty at heart.

Dodd and the six others arrested, all charged with conspiracy against the government, went on trial in Indianapolis before a military commission on September 22. With separate trials ordered for each defendant, Dodd was the first called. He entered a plea of not guilty. The government began presentation of its case and put the first witness on the stand.

Dodd's eyes must have popped out. The witness was Felix Grundy Stidger, an enlisted man in the Union army, a Kentucky-born farmer in his late twenties. Dodd knew him well. To him, Stidger was the "Grand Secretary of the Kentucky Grand Council of the Sons of Liberty."[13]

If Dodd had entertained any hope of acquittal, it sank when he faced Stidger, who had discarded his civilian clothing for the army blue. Dodd had been tracked down by one of the army's most clever and trusted spies.

Although Bingham, as a high-ranking member of the Sons of Liberty, knew exactly why Dodd and the others were on trial and the extent of their guilt, he charged in an editorial that the proceedings were a mockery and purely political. The editorial said in part:

It (the trial) was gotten up for partisan purposes, hence there will be no effort made to prosecute it vigorously. The government claims to have been in possession of a knowledge of the conspiracy charged upon Mr. Dodd and his associates for months, if we can believe its witnesses. . . .

The trial of Mr. Dodd before a military commission is a mockery. Indiana adheres to the Federal government. Never has there yet been a time when the mandates of her courts could not be enforced by the civil authorities. The Constitution of the United States, and even the acts of a Republican Congress, provide for the trial and punishment of the crimes charged against Mr. Dodd by the civil courts. . . .

Mr. Dodd is going through the form of a trial before a totally irresponsible body or commission. In the light of the laws of the land it is usurpation. . . . A people who will permit their rights to be trampled on are unworthy of liberty.[14]

On October 5, two days after the editorial appeared, Bingham was taken into custody by military officials. The next editorial he wrote appeared in the *Sentinel* on October 6 and was signed, "J. J. Bingham, in prison, October 5, 1864." It was strangely reminiscent of the statement issued by Vallandigham from a prison cell about a year and a half previously. Bingham wrote:

Today I was arrested by order of Major General Hovey, the Military Governor of Indiana, and confined in a military prison. Upon what accusation I know not. . . . While occupying the position of editor of the *Sentinel,* I have counselled obedience to law. . . . I am cast down, but not destroyed, a victim of arbitrary power. I am a military prisoner. From a cell, I urge every true man of Indiana . . . to return, in the rapidly approaching elections, a conservative party to power as the only hope of restoring and maintaining our free institutions—the Constitution and the Union. If such is not the verdict of the people at the ballot-box next Tuesday, farewell to civil and religious liberty.[15]

The Indianapolis correspondent of the *Cincinnati Enquirer* hinted at a temporary black-out on telegraph dispatches concerning Bingham's arrest in his second-day story when he wrote, "Concerning this arrest, I attempted to telegraph you yesterday but failed."[16]

Bingham and Dodd were cell mates on the third floor of the Federal Building at Ohio and Pennsylvania Streets in the Indiana capital. During the night of October 6, Dodd escaped.

He lowered a string from his cell window to draw up a stout rope which some person in the street below very kindly tied to it. The rope was fitted with iron clamps to grasp the window bars. A reward of one thousand dollars for Dodd's recapture was offered by military officials.[17]

Dodd headed straight for the Canadian border and about two weeks later was reported "safe and sound" on the other side of the line.[18]

There was a great public hullabaloo over the escape, and the Republican press charged it was conclusive proof of Dodd's guilt. The military commission was unperturbed and went on to try its former prisoner *in absentia.* A sealed verdict was returned, approved by the commanding general, and forwarded to President Lincoln. Word soon got around that the verdict was death.[19] The rumor had a sobering effect on those who had laughed at the trial, reflected in the sudden grave tone of the opposition press.

The rumor was absolutely correct. Dodd was found guilty on all counts and sentenced to be hanged. The Judge Advocate General gave his approval to the verdict, and the case came to rest in President Lincoln's hands.[20]

The military commission took a short recess and reconvened on October 21 to try the other six. Heffren, who admitted he was deputy grand commander of the Sons of Liberty, and Harrison turned state's evidence and were placed on the stand as prosecution witnesses. Dr. James B. Wilson, heretofore not mentioned in the trials, appeared as a former member of the S.O.L. to testify for the government.

Harrison, self-confessed former grand secretary of the secret order, identified all papers and documents found in Dodd's office. Dr. Wilson revealed Vallandigham attended a council of S.O.L. officers and gave instructions on the political situation.[21]

The four remaining defendants, Milligan, Horsey, Humphreys, and Bowles, were due for still another shock. Editor Bingham began to squeal like a stuck hog, as Lincoln might have said, and went on the witness stand for the government.

The editor's recital was that of an innocent man who had strayed into bad company. But again he sold himself, trading the inside story of the plot for his liberty. He stepped from the witness stand a free man. The observing correspondent of the *Cincinnati Enquirer* noted that the "military gentlemen in authority" extended to the editor "all the courtesies possibly allowable." He also noted that the Republican press expressed no admiration for Bingham.[22]

Bowles, Horsey, and Milligan were convicted and sentenced to death; Humphreys was convicted and sentenced to life in prison.[23] Major General Alvin P. Hovey, commander of the District of Indiana, modified Humphreys's life sentence to restriction to townships in Green County, Ind., for the duration of the war. The townships were the one in which he lived and the one in which he did business.

Bingham, sitting again at his desk in the *Sentinel* office, lauded the General in an editorial, saying, "This act of General Hovey does credit alike to his judgment and heart and it will have a beneficial influence on the public mind."[24]

The death sentences of Bowles, Horsey, and Milligan were commuted reluctantly to life by President Andrew Johnson, who inherited the cases from Lincoln. Their attorneys carried an appeal to the Supreme Court, which ruled on April 3, 1866, that the men should not have been tried by a military commission. The decision annulled the whole proceedings, and the prisoners were released on April 10.

Milligan brought suit for damages against the members of the military commission and after three years of litigation was awarded five dollars.[25]

Phineas Wright did not escape the net spread for the Sons of Liberty. Federal officials took him from his desk in the *New York Daily News* office and lodged him in Fort Lafayette, where he was held for several months.[26]

Bingham's *Sentinel* continued strongly Democratic after the trials.

With the reelection of President Lincoln, it said in an editorial: "Yesterday gave the most convincing proof that the election franchise, which should be held sacred by every citizen, has become a farce."[27] It reprinted many articles clipped from the *New York Daily News* and the *New York World*.

The *Sentinel* soon was calling attention to the fact that Robert Lincoln, Harvard-student son of the President, was still not in uniform.[28] The accusation was not without basis of fact and was for months, before he entered the army as a captain on Grant's staff early in 1865, a common topic of newspaper writers.

Fortunately for the Union cause, the *Sentinel* opposition in the Indiana capital was the *Indianapolis Daily State Journal*, always loyal to the Lincoln administration. The *Journal* was edited by Colonel W. R. Holloway, a brother-in-law of Governor Oliver Morton. The Governor was an antislavery Democrat who joined the Republican party and served through the entire war as Indiana's chief executive. He helped direct the roundup of the Sons of Liberty plotters, one of whose aims was said to have been his assassination in the August conspiracy. The Governor was an editorial contributor to the *Journal*.

In November of 1864, when Sherman was leading his victorious army across Georgia in the famous march to the sea, the *Sentinel* published stories clipped from Southern newspapers that pictured his campaign as a dismal failure. The *Augusta* (Ga.) *Constitutionalist* of November 19, 1864, carried a long story under the headline, "Sherman—A Retreat!" and the *Sentinel* reprinted it, banner and all. While military officials paid no attention to such preposterous editing in the *Sentinel* office, the loyal *Journal* suffered because it reported Sherman too correctly.

On Tuesday morning, November 8, the *Journal* said in its lead editorial:

Officers who arrived in this city yesterday direct from Chattanooga report that General Sherman returned to Atlanta early last week, with five corps of his army, having left two corps in Tennessee under General Thomas to watch Hood.[29]

Sherman exploded with rage upon hearing that the Indianapolis newspaper had revealed to the enemy his exact movements and disposition of his troops. He wired the War Department at Washington to "catch that fool," meaning Editor Holloway. He advised the War Department to have the *Journal* publish misleading statements about his campaign to befuddle the enemy.[30]

Holloway was not taken into military custody, but it is entirely probable his arrest was ordered by Secretary Stanton. If the order was issued, it was blocked by Governor Morton. The *Lafayette* (Ind.) *Journal* said: "It is with profound regret that we learn that Colonel Holloway of the *State Journal* has been arrested on order of the War Department for publishing contraband intelligence of Sherman's recent movements."[31] The vigilant correspondent of the *Cincinnati Enquirer* telegraphed his newspaper: "Col. Holloway of the *Indianapolis Journal* has been placed under military arrest by order of Gen. Sherman for publishing contraband army correspondence."[32]

Holloway flatly denied he was in custody, saying, ". . . the report that we have been arrested by the military authorities for publishing contraband intelligence of Sherman's recent movements *is a canard.*"[33] In a nearby editorial, Holloway wrote that he had been talking again with the "gentleman from Atlanta" and had learned "many items of interest" concerning Sherman's plans which would "not be prudent to publish."

Two days previously, the *Journal* had tried to make amends for breaking military secrecy. It published an editorial in the same position of the one that caused the damage, saying:

> We had a conversation yesterday with a gentleman who had just arrived in this city direct from Atlanta, having left there on Friday, November 6th. Every arrangement has been made for a gigantic movement in some direction. . . . Sherman expresses the utmost indifference to Hood's movements, and says, "Thomas has sufficient troops to attend to him and prevent his returning South."[34]

Governor Morton left for Washington, and the *Enquirer* correspondent reported he went "to plead for the release" of the *Journal's* editor. He said further that the *Journal's* war correspondent, a man named Hooker, had been arrested by Sherman and put to sweeping the streets of Chattanooga with a ball and chain on his leg.[35]

The *Journal* itself put a foundation under the *Enquirer* story when it carried this brief item in a column of telegraph news out of Washington: "Governor Morton arrived at Washington yesterday and had an interview with the President."[36]

The New York office of the *Associated Press*, which should have known better, picked up from the *Journal* the damaging editorial of November 8, forcing Holloway to make another denial. Wearily he wrote, "The agent of the *Associated Press* at New York is decidedly behind the times in reference to Sherman's movements in the Southwest. On Sunday last, he telegraphed from New York to the West the substance of an editorial which appeared in the *Journal* several days previous."[37]

# 38 "A Blessed Martyr"

ON NOVEMBER 7, 1864, the day before the national election, Samuel Medary, editor of *The Crisis*, a weekly eight-page newspaper published at Columbus, Ohio, died at the age of sixty-three years. Although the newspapers were filled with election news during the next three or four days, the story of his death commanded space and editorial comment. As editor of one of the most widely quoted Copperhead newspapers of the Civil War period, Medary was a nationally known figure in both journalism and politics. He was the acknowledged voice of the Peace Democrats, whose cause he advocated until he drew his last breath. He engineeered the nomination of Vallandigham as Democratic candidate for governor of Ohio while he was in exile and helped arrange his secret entry into the country just before the Democratic national convention.

"A great and distinguished man has fallen in Ohio," said a leading Democratic newspaper. "Colonel Samuel Medary is dead. This news will fall with sudden, crushing weight upon his tens of thousands of friends in all parts of the Union, to whom his name had become almost a household word."[1]

For years before the war, Medary was known as the "Old Wheelhorse of Democracy," with recognized influence at the White House. He was born in Montgomery Square, Pa., in 1801 and went to Ohio as a schoolteacher when he was twenty-six. He boarded with the Simpson family at Batavia, in the southern part of the state. Mrs. Simpson had a daughter, Mrs. Jesse R. Grant, whose three-year-old son sat on Medary's knee during the evenings around the fire. The little boy was named Ulysses, known in history as U. S. Grant.[2]

Medary began his newspaper career with a small weekly and climbed steadily until he owned the *Ohio Statesman* at Columbus, a powerful party organ. As an original Jackson man, he had his confidence.

In 1844, as chairman of the Ohio Democratic delegation, Medary directed the nomination of James K. Polk at Baltimore. Jackson gave a letter to Medary, with instructions to present the name of Polk before the convention in the event of discord. When the proper time came, Medary produced the letter. Polk was nominated by acclamation.[3]

Medary served as temporary chairman of the Democratic national convention that nominated James Buchanan in 1856. President Buchanan appointed him Governor of the Territory of Minnesota. He served there in 1857 and 1858, then took over the same office in Kansas, the last to hold that place before the territory became a state.[4]

Returning to Columbus late in 1860, Medary launched *The Crisis* on January 31, 1861, telling the public in the first edition: "Be not surprised at my thus addressing you at this time."[5]

In a page-one editorial, Medary exposed his purpose in founding the paper and his attitude toward the South. After asking himself the question, "Has the South any reason to complain?" he answered, "Yes, we think it has, and it is our duty to state it. . . . I have a great many reasons for publishing this paper, as will more clearly appear to my readers as it progresses."

His first step in behalf of the South, carried in that same edition, was to attack moves for preparedness. He ridiculed passage of a bill by the legislature to raise 6,000 troops, pointing out the bounty would cost the taxpayers thirty thousand dollars. He wrote, "The sudden anxiety for military parade looks too much like hiding behind the glitter of war to escape detection in refusing amicable adjustment."[6]

*The Crisis* operated without a news service, either wire or mail, and all telegraph reports used were rewritten from the exchange desk.

Medary filled many columns with his own writings, devoting the rest of his space to stories and editorials clipped from other newspapers. His tools were a paste pot, scissors, and a pen filled with poison. The first issues were sprinkled with humor. Medary chuckled when a Western newspaper, in announcing the death of a local citizen, said: "He was a great admirer of Horace Greeley, but otherwise a very respectable man." Another story said a young lady had refused to enter an Eastern war plant because the guns had no breeches. Medary asked, "Why is a young lady examining an apple core like South Carolina?" The answer was: "Because she wishes to see seed (secede)."[7]

War brought no change in the editorial policy of *The Crisis*. Not one good word was said for the North; its leaders were berated, its people told the conflict was folly. While *The Crisis* did not praise the South or laud its leaders, it carefully avoided any criticism. It carried many columns clipped from English newspapers, and Medary editorialized favorably on the hostility exhibited by the foreign press to the Lincoln administration.

Clever bits of propaganda, usually containing one paragraph, were planted here and there in the newspaper. This one is typical: "A gentleman of intelligence who had been up to very recently strong for this war, remarked to us the other day that he was satisfied that the administration had designs behind the present war, hidden yet from the public eye."[8]

It was not long until Medary was compelled by public accusation to deny he was a member of the Knights of the Golden Circle, and from there he went on to contend that "slavery is constitutional and Abolition is not," a statement he picked up from the *Chicago Times*. From that date, October 10, 1861, he made clear the real purpose of his newspaper—perpetuation of human slavery, no matter what the cost or the ultimate fate of his country. He defended slavery and ridiculed with every word at his command those who would abolish it. His was one of the few newspapers in the North that referred to members of the colored race as "niggers."

Medary cultivated the Democratic press with flattering articles about editors who saw eye to eye with him. If they returned the compliment, he reprinted their editorials. He quoted the *Fremont* (Ohio) *Messenger* as saying: "Col. Medary has again become a power within the state. . . . No other man can make such a paper succeed. It is the best paper today for the people published in the country."[9]

But some editors of the little Democratic papers were deaf to Medary's harangue against the war. *The Crisis* noted, without comment, that Thomas L. Young, editor of the *Shelby County* (Ohio) *Democrat*, sold his paper and enlisted in the Union army.[10]

Medary, president of the Ohio Democratic convention in 1862, made a speech in which he denied he was a traitor to the Union. He said: "I sent one of my sons into the army and supported him for six months out of my own pocket, without the aid of a dollar from the government. And a son-in-law . . . was in the thick of the fight, having charge of a regiment, when Lyon fell at Springfield. And yet I am a traitor. Why am I called a traitor? Because I believe that the doctrines which were taught me, and which I have taught to thousands of others, are true and necessary to the welfare of the country."[11]

When President Lincoln made his preliminary announcement of the Emancipation Proclamation, Medary moaned, "We have at last hit upon the lower round of our national existence. . . . Sad is our fate and monstrous the depths to which we are precipitated."[12]

With the final Proclamation on January 1, 1863, Medary declared Lincoln was a "half-witted usurper, who, in an evil hour, was elected under the forms of the Constitution by a portion of the American people under the whip and spur of a set of fanatical and sectional politicians. . . ." He wrote that the Proclamation "is as much unlike anything else which ever emanated from the head of a government, civilized or savage, as its author is unlike any other man who ever rose from obscurity to an eminent position."[13]

*The Crisis,* with a national circulation, was a clearinghouse for all antiadministration propaganda. One of its chief activities was publication of every speech and every word uttered in public by Vallandigham. Medary's exchange desk was stacked high. His paper shows articles reprinted from every Peace Democrat and slavery-advocating newspaper in the North.

When the issue of emancipation came up in the summer of 1862, *The Crisis* published this tale under the heading, "The Last Lincoln Story":

The other day, a distinguished public officer was at Washington and in an interview with the President, introduced the question of slavery emancipation.

"Well, you see," said Mr. Lincoln, "we've got to be mighty cautious how we manage the nigger question. If we're not, we shall be like the barber out in Illinois who was shaving a fellow with a hatchet face and lantern jaws like mine. The barber stuck his finger into the customer's mouth to make his cheek stick out, but while shaving away, he cut through the fellow's cheek and cut off his own finger. If we don't play mighty smart about the nigger, we shall do as the barber did."[14]

*Political Alphabet* made its appearance in the spring of 1863 and was spread by *The Crisis.* Two of the twenty-six verses show its intent:

> A stands for Old Abe, who has made up his mind,
> To yield to the pressure that crowds him behind;
> And to aid the malignants in splitting the nation,
> Has issued his mandate of Emancipation.

> L stands for liberty, basely betrayed,
> By the party in power, and at once lowly laid;
> For the war power prevails, and the civil power dies,
> And the freedom of speech and press prostrate lies.[15]

This was supposed to be a humorous anecdote:

When Sheridan, found drunk in a coal hole and questioned as to his name, replied that his name was Wilberforce, he did a sufficiently impudent thing; but it wasn't a touch to the effrontery of Senator C. (or some other man) who, being picked out of a ditch by a watchman and told to give his name, replied in a gutter-al voice, "Don't you see I am Sewer'd!"[16]

With the explanation that it was found on the body of a "dead Yankee" at Antietam and published in the *Columbus* (Ga.) *Enquirer*, *The Crisis* printed a travesty on the Lord's Prayer:

> Our father who art in Washington,
> Abraham Lincoln be Thy name!
> Thy will be done in the North
> As it is in the South!
> Give us this day our daily
> Rations of crackers and bacon!
> And forgive our quartermasters
> And commissionaries; for thine is the
> Power, the niggers and the soldiers,
> For the term of three years—Amen.[17]

Another, *All For The Nigger*, appeared in *The Crisis*. Here is one verse and the chorus:

> We are taxed on our clothing, our meat and our bread,
> On our carpets and dishes, our tables and bed,
> On our tea and our coffee, our fuel and lights,
> And we're taxed so severely we can't sleep o'nights.
> *Chorus*
> And it's all for the nigger, great God can it be,
> The home of the brave and land of the free.[18]

One of the most widely reprinted bits of doggerel appeared in Democratic newspapers when Lincoln sought renomination. It was published in *The Crisis* as clipped from the *Cincinnati Enquirer*.

> We're coming, Father Abraham, we're coming by the score,
> To swell the grand convention in the town of Baltimore;
> All unconditional Union men, of no uncertain tone,
> Believe in necessity, the war-power and backbone.
> We're coming with instructions, from the loyal and the true,
> To do some heavy voting and pull the wires for you.

We're coming, Father Abraham, to make you doubly great,
    Another child of Destiny—conserver of the State—
Be. what you've been—do as you've done—tax, banish and proclaim;
    Joke, draft, arrest and shake your mane; you play no losing game.
From your supreme prerogative no right can be reserved,
    Of rights makes trifles, Father Abe, and the nation is preserved.[19]

During a heavy snowstorm about ten o'clock on the night of March 5, 1863, a mob of more than two hundred men, consisting mainly of soldiers from nearby Camp Chase, attacked and wrecked *The Crisis* office in the heart of downtown Columbus, only a square from the state capitol. The soldiers carried rifles with fixed bayonets. Two or three squads circled the door with a warning of sudden death if any person interfered, and the others broke into the building, tearing off the door and smashing the windows.

All furniture and office fittings were broken up, and the files and records were carried into the street and scattered by the high wind. By the time Brigadier General James Cooper arrived on the scene, the destruction was complete and the soldiers had melted into the crowd.[20]

While *The Crisis* office was being wrecked, another group made an attack on the *Daily Ohio Statesman*, a Democratic daily that supported the war but maintained an anti-Lincoln policy. That mob was battering the door of the press room when police appeared.[21]

*The Crisis* suffered no mechanical damage because it had no press and no composing room, all printing being done under contract with a job shop. It appeared as usual the next week to bluntly charge that the *Ohio State Journal* organized the attack and supplied liquor to members of the mob.[22]

The *Journal*, which Medary always called "the Lincoln organ," replied the charge was "false and untrue."[23]

Medary, in Cincinnati when his paper was mobbed, came home the next day. He was met at the station by a crowd and the blaring music of Hemmerbach's Brass Band. Men carried him on their shoulders to a waiting carriage, the horses were unhitched, and the crowd pulled the vehicle to a downtown hotel.[24]

Medary's own account of this incident was the theme of a gloating editorial. He wrote:

The three thousand bold, brave, daring men who met us at the railroad depot on our return after the disaster, and bore us with shouts which rang to the vaults of Heaven, upon their shoulders, were not, thank God, either rioters or burglars—they were freemen—and, knowing their rights, dared, in

this beautiful capital of ours, in face of executive scowls and military sur-
roundings, thus give public advertisement that they know how to defend
them, and that they intend to do it.[25]

Eight days after the mobbing, an attempt was made to burn *The
Crisis* office. A fire was set at the rear of the building but was discovered before it could spread.[26]

Medary then came forth with sensational new charges. He said Andrew Johnson, military Governor of Tennessee, and Joseph A. Wright,
former Governor of Indiana, visited Camp Chase two days before the
mobbing and spoke for three hours to the soldiers "in the wildest political harangue before enough men could be found to engage in the dirty
work."[27]

Colonel August V. Kautz, commanding the 2d Ohio Cavalry, the outfit accused of the mobbing, said his officers disavowed the affair, but he
admitted some of his enlisted men participated. He returned four bound
volumes of *Crisis* files to Medary.[28]

The radical Democratic press raged. The *Dayton Daily Empire*, controlled by Vallandigham, advocated that "for every Democratic printing press destroyed by a mob, let an Abolition one be destroyed in
turn." Wilbur F. Storey's *Chicago Times* said: "We have been silent
thus far, but . . . in every occurrence like that at Columbus, a reprisal
should be made."[29] The *Placer* (Calif.) *Herald* indignantly said: "No
gang of soldiers or mob of Abolitionists are strong enuf, thank God,
to effectively stop the expressions and thoughts of American freemen.
If the unhappy time should ever come, farewell then to civil liberty."[30]

About two weeks after *The Crisis* was mobbed, little Sarah Osgood,
a pupil in the intermediate public school, was asked by her teacher
during recitation period to read an essay before the English class. Sarah
read from her paper as follows:

On Thursday night a week ago yesterday about eleven o'clock P.M., a
crowd was seen gathering on a corner of one of our principal streets. It was
composed mostly of soldiers who were armed with stones and clubs. The
object of the gathering was to suppress a paper called *The Crisis*, very popular with the sesionists and a few Democrats. It is edited by one of the lowest
contemptible traitors that ever breathed and it is a burning shame that he
has not been living before this. For that is, he deserved the fate of all traitors.
Of course he was not here then no not he and well it was for his worthless
self that he was not. Some called it a mob, and said it was unlawful and an
outrage against a peaceful citizen, very likely it was all that and more, and
put it all together it was not half enough. They only battered winders and

broke open his office and tore up his papers but because they did not do it that is no sign they will not. I wonder how Union men are treated in the South? shot down and every species of torture and cruelty inflicted on their helpless family's. And here because our soldiers will tolerate it no longer and endeavor to put it down one of the curses of the land its editor is styled a blessed martyr and drawn in an old omnibus from the depot to his residence by twenty or thirty half-drunken admirers—I think if Lincoln would put an armed force into these northern states and drive every miserable traitors into their proper place he would do something better than he has yet.[31]

Medary obtained possession of the essay. He explained "some spirited Democratic girls," disciplined by their teacher for hissing when it was read, sent it to him. He published the paper in its "original form," offering it as "evidence of the excellent state of learning in our high school."

He railed against Sarah's teacher and the Columbus board of education, then bragged in an editorial that he had forced an apology. He offered this statement from the board as proof:

The Board of Education has inquired into facts connected with a composition read in the Intermediate Schools kept in the High School Building and published in *The Crisis*.

The Board is satisfied, from a written statement of the teacher, that she disapproves of the sentiments expressed in the composition alluded to—that it was an act of thoughtlessness, on her part, in permitting it to be read before the school, and deeply regrets having permitted it to be read.

The Board unanimously disapproves the sentiments expressed in the composition, and the failure of the teacher to suppress it. The repetition of such offense will not be tolerated in any teacher.[32]

Medary then publicly donned the badge of opponent to the Union cause. He explained in an editorial note, "We acknowledge from a young Democrat of Connecticut the receipt of a Copperhead emblem of liberty, nicely cut from an old cent."[33]

The arrest and trial of Vallandigham by General Burnside puzzled Medary. He said he could not understand how a Democratic general could do such a thing. He was further amazed when Federal Judge H. H. Leavitt, a Democrat appointed by Jackson, refused to release Vallandigham under a writ of habeas corpus, but he finally decided that the jurist was "a weak-kneed politician."

In midsummer of that year, *The Crisis* announced Medary was ill and had gone away for "some slight recess."[34] Three weeks later, in "A Word With Our Readers," he broke down and told all. He had been to

Canada to see Vallandigham, to whom he referred as "the gallant exile" and "Ohio's noble standard-bearer." He also revealed he had been in New York to see Governor Seymour. He discovered, he said, that "Horace Greeley is the real President of the United States" and that Lincoln had become his "subservient tool."[35]

When the Ohio Democrats were routed by the defeat of Vallandigham for governor, the more conservative elements of the party blamed Medary and his newspaper was on the verge of failing by the end of 1863. The Crisis had never carried advertising; now he solicited it with the statement: "We throw ourselves on the generous support of our friends."[36]

On May 20, 1864, two deputy United States marshals entered The Crisis office with a warrant for Medary's arrest. He had been secretly indicted by a Federal grand jury at Cincinnati on a charge of conspiracy against the government.[37] He was taken to Cincinnati where he appeared before Judge Leavitt and was released on a recognizance bond after his "friends of the Enquirer office" offered to post cash.[38]

From newspapers on the extreme state-rights wing of the Democratic party there poured a flood of defense and praise for Medary. The New York Daily News said Medary's friends would "laugh in very scorn" at the idea he was a conspirer. The New York Day Book promised that The Crisis, "the able and excellent journal," would continue. The Atlas and Argus of Albany, N. Y., saw his arrest as "one of those errors into which the administration . . . blunders from its mere want of intelligence and capacity." Freeman's Journal of New York said a charge of conspiracy against Medary was "outrageous and preposterous." The Age of Philadelphia thought Medary was indicted because he "dealt many and heavy blows upon the heads of Lincoln, Seward and Stanton." The Daily Courier and Union of Syracuse, N. Y., declared Lincoln was a despot, "cruel and unchecked."

The Metropolitan Record of New York called Medary a "brave and indomitable journalist." The Washington (Pa.) Examiner doubted Medary would ever come to trial. The Greensburg (Pa.) Argus said the indictment was "ridiculous." The Patriot at Wellesville, Ohio, said the arrest was "the richest joke of the season." The Iowa Courier said: "It has always been a mania with Lincoln to arrest American citizens without warrant and to suppress American papers without authority."[39]

And so it went in paper after paper. The enfeebled Crisis took a new lease on life. Medary increased the price of a year's subscription from two to three dollars. He announced his trial had been postponed until October.[40] The trial never took place.

Medary collapsed while making a speech in August but returned to his desk at intervals. The refusal of General McClellan as nominee of the Democratic party to accept the peace-at-any-price plank in the party platform brought down the editor's wrath. Medary noted with alarm that McClellan's letter of acceptance of the nomination said nothing about "an armistice or a cessation of hostilities." He charged McClellan "falls back on the war as commenced by Lincoln and which he then approved and approves still."[41]

In late October, Medary took to his bed, and it became apparent he had not long to live. Members of his family were summoned. All responded except his soldier-son, Lieutenant Charles Medary. The family appealed to Secretary of War Stanton, whom Medary had so often castigated, to find the young officer and send him home.

A prompt reply came from Stanton himself. He located the officer in an army hospital where he was recovering from injuries suffered when his horse fell on him. Stanton was happy to tell the family that he had granted a leave to Charles and that he was on his way to Columbus. He tendered his sympathy and expressed the hope that the editor might recover. When the lieutenant in the blue uniform reached the house, his father was dead.[42]

Medary would have refused to vote had he lived. A few days before his fatal illness, he took from the masthead of his newspaper the names of McClellan and George H. Pendleton, his running mate.[43]

Thousands of words of tribute and praise appeared in the Democratic press from coast to coast. It remained for the *Nevada Gazette* to offer rebuttal. An editorial headed "Traitor's Biography" said:

Sam Medary, of Columbus, Ohio is dead—"the Lord reward him according to his works!" He died on the seventh of November last. He was an accomplished political trickster, one of the vilest scoundrels that ever lived, and has ruined more young men through his wiles and false doctrines than any other man of his age and country. He was the political godfather of John G. Breslin, the great defaulter; of John B. Weller, the conspirator; of Vallandigham, Pendleton, Cox and other Ohio traitors, and at the time of his death was a high officer of the secret treasonable organization of the "Sons of Liberty," corresponding with the "Knights of the Columbian Star," of this State. When Sam Medary died one of the devil's own children went home to his father's house. The old scamp has left many heirs to his infamy, but none so thoroughly corrupt and depraved as himself.[44]

# 39 The Rules Are Turned

THE NEW YORK TIMES greeted November 8, 1864—Election Day—with these words: "The day has come—the day of fate."

Voters in twenty-five states loyal to the Union went to the polls to elect a President. There was not much doubt that Lincoln would be the winner over McClellan. State elections in some parts of the North, preceding by a few weeks that for the presidential electors, showed a strong Republican trend. In Indiana, Governor Morton was returned to office by a huge majority. Vermont again chose a Republican slate. Pennsylvania gained three Republican Congressmen. The result in Maine was a slight loss to the Republicans, but their victory in New York more than atoned; Seymour was defeated for reelection by Reuben E. Fenton.[1]

On the evening of Election Day, Washington was tense as it awaited the first returns. Charles A. Dana, former managing editor of the *New York Tribune* and an assistant Secretary of War, went to the War Department building about eight o'clock and found President Lincoln with Secretary Stanton in his office. A messenger was popping in and out of the room with telegrams on the first election results as they came off the wires in another part of the building.

Stanton took the telegrams from the messenger, then passed them to the President. The stern Secretary of War was in one of his gravest moods. Finally there was a lull in the flurry of telegrams, and Lincoln motioned to Dana to take a chair beside him. The President asked whether he had read any writings of Petroleum V. Nasby, and Dana replied diplomatically that he had not but had seen some of them.

The President said he was going to read a "specimen" and pulled from his coat pocket a thin, yellow pamphlet. As he began to read aloud, Stanton could not hide his impatience. The President paused now and then to glance at a telegram forced on him by Stanton but quickly resumed his reading. He kept on until Whitelaw Reid of the *Cincinnati Gazette* and some others entered the room. When Lincoln began a conversation with the new arrivals, Stanton left and beckoned Dana to follow him.

Out of the President's hearing, the Secretary of War spoke his mind plainly on what he thought of a Chief Executive reading "balderdash" while the fate of the nation was decided.[2]

Stanton might as well have relaxed. Lincoln was reelected by a landslide. McClellan carried only three states, Delaware, New Jersey, and Kentucky, a total of 21 electoral votes. Lincoln gathered in the others, 212 of them. His popular majority was almost half a million.[3]

Major victories for the Union on the battlefields followed the election. Major General George H. Thomas cut the Confederates to pieces in the Battle of Nashville, December 15 and 16. For the first time in the war, an entire army was destroyed. The war in the West was finished. Sherman headed for the Atlantic Coast, and cities began to fall before his advance, among them Charleston, on February 18, 1865.[4] It was now apparent the showdown would be between Grant and Lee at Petersburg, just south of Richmond. The Confederacy's master General, aided by the peculiar terrain, had so deployed his dwindling forces that Richmond was invulnerable to assault as long as he held Petersburg.[5]

The Confederacy made an attempt to arrange a negotiated peace early in February of 1865. It sent a commission whose members were Alexander H. Stephens, R. M. T. Hunter, and John A. Campbell to confer with President Lincoln and Secretary Seward in Hampton Roads. Stephens was Vice-President of the Confederate government. Lincoln refused to discuss peace on the basis of Confederate independence, and the commission returned to Richmond, still determined to fight to the bitter end.[6]

Lincoln's reelection patched all the holes in the Republican press front. Newspapers that held him so lightly during the campaign fell over themselves in their efforts to pay homage. The subject was discussed even in Congress.

The Washington correspondent of the *New York Daily News* filed a story under date of February 7, which said:

The Republican papers of this city strive with each other to see which of them shall bespatter Mr. Lincoln the most with the titles and attributes of royalty.

During the whole course of the recent peace negotiations, the President's powers in the matter were spoken of as supreme, and the *Chronicle* went so far as to speak of Mr. Lincoln as the sovereign head of a great nation, and of the President's having left his capital in his sovereign capacity to confer with the southern commission. Such language will be regarded with disapproval, and even with apprehension, by Democrats everywhere.

But it is regarded with far different feelings by the present Republican Congress. . . . A resolution condemning the use of such language to the President, and setting forth the fact that the President is not the sovereign authority, but that the sovereignty resides in the people, was laid over, the House refusing to consider it. Hence, by the decision of the House, it is now *en regle* to regard the President as having the capacity and powers of a sovereign. This is certainly an interesting fact in the history of our republican government, and it shows the progress we are making toward becoming a great nation.[7]

Horace Greeley went to Washington to attend the Inaugural. He returned to New York with the impression the President was showing physical fatigue under the strain of war. In Greeley's words, Lincoln was "weather-beaten."[8]

In a *New York Tribune* editorial a few days later, written probably by Greeley, the change in the President's physical appearance was discussed, and even the matter of his death was broached. It was a cold analysis, and no words were spared. Swarming office seekers who imposed on the Chief Executive, as well as the strain of the conflict, were blamed for the President's condition. The editorial said in part:

We are not, it is known, among the idolators, nor even the adulators, of Abraham Lincoln. He was not our first choice for President in 1860, nor yet in 1864. We are among those who hold that the rescue of our country from the grave perils which so lately shrouded her horizon will justly redound to the lasting honor of her Loyal Millions, not to that of any particular man, whether general or civilian. . . .

Mr. Lincoln touched the keynote of his career when, in a recent letter, he observed that he had not controlled events, but had been controlled by them. . . . His usefulness, his strength, his popularity, grew out of the fact that he accurately collects, apprehends, interprets, embodies the average sentiment of the American people. His bark, firmly anchored on the rock of American nationality, swings to the ebb and flow of the popular tide. . . . He is emphatically a man of the people, not in that highest sense which indicates one who unfolds and quickens their better aspirations, but in the readier acceptation of one who speaks as they think, and does as they desire today, though it may be inconsistent with what they thought yesterday and irreconcilable with what they will think tomorrow.

We believe it was quite possible to have selected a stronger man for Pres;

yet that does not conflict with the fact that his death or a permanent disability now would be a calamity—very generally and justly deplored. We cannot forecast the future which that bereavement would open; yet we think few Americans, even though disloyal, can wish to confront its realization.

If the President is to outlive the term in which he has just entered, a radical retrenchment must be promptly effected in the current exactions on his time and energies. He has been carried further toward the grave by his four years in the White House than he could have been by ten years of constant labor in the courts or on a farm. All who knew him in 1860 must have observed his air of fatigue, exhaustion and languor—so different from his old hearty, careless, jovial manner. . . .[9]

The war moved quickly to a climax. Sheridan took 5,000 prisoners at Five Forks, 12 miles southwest of Petersburg, on April 1. The Union victory cracked the heretofore impregnable defenses, and Lee, his army on the verge of starvation, decided to pull his troops out of Richmond and head west. The fall of Petersburg and evacuation of Richmond were recorded as of April 2 and 3. Jefferson Davis took to flight.[10]

Collapse of the Confederacy found Lincoln at City Point, and he went on into the fallen capital. He himself flashed the capture of Petersburg to the War Department.[11]

The President returned to Washington, and Grant and Sheridan went in pursuit of Lee. They overtook him at Appomattox Courthouse, and there he surrendered what was left of the once proud Army of Northern Virginia on April 9.[12] The war was over.

The North started to celebrate as soon as Richmond fell. In Washington, flags flew from all government buildings, guns thundered, bands paraded, and cheering throngs filled the streets. The news that Lee had surrendered his army reached the city late on the night of the ninth, which was Palm Sunday. The real celebration began early the next morning. One of the biggest crowds gathered on the White House lawn and yelled for Lincoln. He appeared, brushing away tears of joy. He said he would save his speech for later, meaning the formal celebration set for April 11, and asked the band to play the "captured tune of Dixie."[13]

Lincoln was ready with a prepared speech that covered many sheets of paper when the crowd came back on the night of April 11. To friends who wondered why he had prepared a formal address, he explained that the last time he made "an offhand speech," he used the term in speaking of the rebels, "turned tail and ran." This, he said, pained some "nice Boston folks," so he did not want to make the same mistake twice. The protest against the phrase was made by Senator Charles Sumner of Massachusetts, a Harvard graduate.[14]

With Lincoln at the White House that evening was one of his intimate friends, Noah Brooks, a Washington correspondent for the *Sacramento* (Calif.) *Union*, who wrote under the name of "Castine." Brooks had known Lincoln for a good many years, having made his acquaintance in Illinois. He was more than twenty years younger than the President, but a steadfast friendship sprang up between them. The reporter often visited the White House, and it was not unusual for him to have breakfast with the President. An understanding seemed to have been reached that Brooks was to join the President's secretarial staff during his second term.

The President knew by the cheering it was time for him to appear. He went to the second floor to speak from the center window overlooking the portico. Brooks hid behind a drapery and held a candle by which Lincoln read his speech, dropping the loose pages to the floor one by one.[15]

As if he knew the hours of his life were numbered as the pages of the manuscript from which he read, as if he knew this was his last opportunity to speak to his people, Lincoln spoke not to the crowd below, but to his country, both North and South. The speech was his plan for reconstruction. The throng on the lawn gave only polite applause; this was not the speech they had expected. It went over the heads of his listeners.[16]

When the noisy celebrants appeared two days before, Lincoln called for cheers for Grant and for the army and the navy. On the night of the eleventh, he was no longer thinking of military glory, that "attractive rainbow that rises in showers of blood."[17] He was a man of peace.

On April 14, Horace Greeley chanced to meet his friend, George G. Hoskins, in New York and took occasion to remind him that he (Greeley) still was not Postmaster General. Hoskins, feeling his word was in jeopardy, boarded a train that evening for Washington.[18]

After Hoskins left, Greeley wrote an editorial on Lincoln, a blistering attack. He sent the copy to the composing room, had it set up, proofed, and slugged to go in the next morning's paper. Then he went home, leaving Sidney Gay, managing editor of the *New York Tribune*, in full charge for the night as was his regular custom.[19]

Down at Washington, President and Mrs. Lincoln and two young people went to Ford's Theater to see a popular comedy, *Our American Cousin*. A few minutes after ten o'clock, John Wilkes Booth, an actor, sneaked into Lincoln's flag-draped box and shot him in the back of the head with a pistol. He was carried to a house across the street where he died the next morning shortly after seven o'clock.

Secretary Seward, lying injured in his home as result of a carriage accident a few days before, was stabbed by an assassin who forced his way into the house at the same hour the President was shot. Seward's son Frederick, who tried to defend him, also was severely wounded.[20]

The routine of the *New York Tribune* office was shattered when the telegraph wire flashed a bulletin that Lincoln had been shot. Managing Editor Gay was trying to make some sense from the garbled account of the shooting when the foreman of the composing room went to him with a proof, explaining he wanted him to see an editorial he might want to keep out of the paper. The proof was Greeley's "leader," something no one, not even the managing editor, was supposed to touch.

Gay told the foreman to hide both the proof and the type, and he placed them in his private locker. The next afternoon, when Gay reported for work, he was told "the old man" wanted to see him.

He stepped into Greeley's private office and met an outburst. The editor wanted to know why Gay had "killed" the editorial on Lincoln. The managing editor told him a mob would have wrecked the *Tribune* office if they had published it, and he added he thought the newspaper would have deserved destruction.

Greeley's chalk-white face turned livid, and he stalked out of the office. The editorial was never mentioned again.[21]

The death of Lincoln was the biggest news story that had ever broken in the United States. The end of the war was insignificant in comparison; that had been anticipated for months. Every man, woman, and child in America knew "Old Abe." The impact on the press was without precedent. As the only instrument to inform the public, it had the field to itself. The newspapers flooded the country with extras. There were remarkably few "sensation" stories; Secretary of War Stanton saw to that, with careful censorship of everything filed out of Washington.

Newspapers, Democratic and Republican alike, turned the column rules in time-honored custom. When Forney's *Daily Morning Chronicle* at Washington did not appear in heavy black rules, there were raised eyebrows and it was compelled to explain, saying:

Owing to the fact that the type of the *Daily Morning Chronicle* is arranged in cylinder form in order to print our enormous edition, we are prevented from using the ordinary straight rules for the purpose of placing our columns in mourning. This explanation is made in answer to several correspondents and will be perfectly understood by newspaper men.[22]

However, some bright person thought to use slugs at the top of each column, and the *Chronicle* appeared decently in black the next morning.

Republican newspapers flying flags in observance of the end of the war lowered them to half-staff. Copperhead journals over whose offices the American flag had not flown for years displayed the colors.

*The Age,* Lincoln hating and slavery-loving daily at Philadelphia, displayed a flag draped in black. Incensed at the sight, a crowd gathered in the street and threatened to mob the newspaper for what it considered an insult to the martyred President. The flag was taken down. In suburban West Chester, *The Jeffersonian,* anti-Lincoln and antiwar, was afraid to show a flag or display any sign of mourning, Editor John Hodgson explained.[23]

The *Boston Transcript* reprinted from the *Selma* (Ala.) *Despatch* an advertisement of the previous December that carried an offer to assassinate the President. The *Transcript* was indignant that any newspaper, even in the deep South, should have been guilty of publishing such an announcement.[24]

On the West Coast, the people's anger at the assassination took more violent form. Bells tolled all day Saturday, April 15, in San Francisco, and Union men thronged the town. Those who dared speak against Lincoln were roughly handled, and several attempted lynchings were stopped by police.[25]

The San Francisco correspondent of the *Chicago Times* saw the temper of the surly crowd and wired his newspaper: "The popular voice demands the enforcement of the strictest justice against all connected with the assassination and against obdurate rebel leaders."[26]

In the afternoon, a mob surged up Montgomery Street, bent on destruction of newspapers that had blasphemed Lincoln and were known to be anti-Union. The *Democratic Press* was the first victim. The *News Letter,* the *Monitor,* the *Occidental,* and *L'Union Franco Américaine* fell in order. *L'Écho de Pacifique* was threatened but was saved and put under guard.[27]

While the mob wrecked the offices and broke the presses, an immense crowd stood in the street, cheering and applauding. Calls were sent for police, but they arrived too late.[28]

An *Associated Press* story out of San Francisco the next day said:

The destruction of the Democratic newspapers last evening was not the result of any recent offensive utterance, but the sudden outburst of long pent up indignation at their opposition to the government all through the war. It was effected with such rapidity and was so unexpected that the authorities were able to do nothing to prevent it. . . .

Intense excitement prevailed all night. . . . It is reported that the Democratic papers at Marysville and Grass Valley have been mobbed.[29]

Major General Irvin McDowell, in command of the Department of the Pacific, restored order. He ordered arrest of any person expressing satisfaction over the assassination and suppression of any newspaper so offending.[30]

McDowell walked through the crowd just as the mob prepared to wreck *L'Écho de Pacifique*. He made a speech that was cheered wildly and brought an end to the rioting. It was reported as follows:

My Friends: When I came over the bay this morning and first heard the terrible news of this infamous and hellish act, I felt as I know you feel, and I do not wonder at your excitement. But I have a few words to say to you. . . .

I have tolerated many wrong things done by the public press in its attacks against the government and the administration of its affairs, feeling, under the circumstances, it was better to endure the evil than to apply so harsh a remedy as military power; but after this last devilish act, I feel that it is time to tolerate this course no longer.

While your course today was very wrong, it was very natural; and in interfering in the affairs of the press you have but anticipated me, and have, perhaps, saved me from some trouble, though I should have managed the matter in a different way.

Now, I want you to save me further trouble by dispersing and going quietly to your homes. . . .[31]

In the little town of Westminster, Md., 33 miles from Baltimore, a mass meeting of citizens was held in the courthouse on the evening of April 15. Two resolutions were passed. One said: "We will not tolerate the presence amongst us at any future date of certain young men who have committed treason by going South."[32]

The other resolution demanded that publication of the town's newspaper, the *Western Maryland Democrat*, be stopped immediately and the editor notified to leave the community.

Joseph Shaw was editor of the *Democrat*. All during the war, he had defended secession and assailed Lincoln. His personal reputation was soiled by gossip that he had "led to ruin a simple minded girl." His hands were deformed, having been born with no joints in his fingers. He lived at the village tavern and was a familiar figure around the bar.

An hour after the courthouse meeting disbanded, a group of men wrecked the *Democrat* office. After smashing the press, they piled the office equipment in the street and burned it. Shaw vanished during the excitement.

Westminster heard no more of the editor until he was seen in the railroad depot at Baltimore in a "highly nervous" condition. He was carrying two pistols and a dagger. As though talking to himself, he said repeatedly, "I'm going back! By God, I'm going back!"

He returned to Westminster on April 24 and went to his old room at the tavern. That night, five men went to his room on the second floor. Patrons at the bar heard the sound of a brief struggle and a pistol shot. The five men came downstairs, half carrying the editor. They let him slump to the floor where he died in a few minutes from a deep stab wound under his armpit.

A grand jury indicted the five men on a charge of manslaughter. When the case came to trial, they testified Shaw slipped from their grasp and fell on his own dagger. There was some testimony about Shaw's deformed hands and his inability to fire a pistol accurately. It was near suppertime when the case went to the jury. In a little more than an hour, the jury returned the expected verdict—all parties not guilty.[33]

On Easter Sunday, April 16, when Lincoln's body was lying at the White House, the *New York Herald* openly charged that the press must share the guilt of the assassination. It said in an editorial:

. . . it is as clear as day that the real origin of this miserable act is to be found in the fiendish and malignant spirit developed and fostered by the rebel press North and South. That press has, in the most devilish manner, urged men to the commission of this very deed.[34]

# 40 "All the Land Weeps"

THE FUNERAL SERVICE for Abraham Lincoln was held in the East Room of the White House on Wednesday, April 19, 1865. On the coffin was a shield that bore a silver plate with the simple inscription:

Abraham Lincoln
16th President of the United States
Born February 12, 1809
Died April 15, 1865.[1]

He had achieved the martyrdom the newspapers jokingly told him he missed four years and a few months before. To him now was "the glory that awaited him." The body of Abraham Lincoln left Washington on the morning of April 21, borne by a special train draped in black. The first stop was Baltimore. Then the train went to Harrisburg, then to Philadelphia, and then to New York. In every city, thousands stood in line for hours to look on the face of the man in the coffin. For twelve days and nights the journey continued—Albany, Utica, Syracuse, Buffalo, Cleveland, Columbus, Indianapolis, Chicago—before Abraham Lincoln was home in Springfield.[2]

The coffin was carried into a flower-strewn vault at Oak Ridge Cemetery, and a churchman said, "Chieftain, farewell! The nation mourns thee. Mothers shall teach thy name to their lisping children. The youth of our land shall emulate thy virtues. Statesmen shall study thy record and learn lessons of wisdom. Mute though thy lips be, yet they still speak."[3]

Thus on May 4, the form that had held the spirit of Abraham Lincoln passed from the sight of the world.

From the time of Lincoln's death until he was buried, the newspapers of the North poured forth a torrent of adulation and eulogy that has never been equaled before or since. The lines of political party vanished. It was no longer possible to determine the politics of a newspaper by what it said about Lincoln.

The newspapers that had been the President's greatest enemies published columns of beautiful tribute and insisted their grief was deep at his passing. *The World* said in New York:

Today every loyal heart must suffer the terrible shock, and swell with overburdening grief at the calamity which has been permitted to befall us in the assassination of the Chief Magistrate. The splendor of our triumph is robbed of half its lustre. It is a deeper loss than if our first soldier had fallen by a hostile bullet . . . more than if an army had perished in the shock of battle. For it is the Commander-in-chief of our armies and navies who has fallen; and he has fallen, not by the natural course of disease, nor in the accepted peril of war, but by the foul stroke of some unknown assassin. Our history has no parallel to this. Such grief as ours today is new to our nation's heart.[4]

"The whole people will mourn," said the New York *Journal of Commerce.* "The blow is struck at the heart of the nation, and it is felt in every fibre of the body, social and politic. In a moment like this it becomes us to bow before that God in whose hands are the destinies of nations, and the lives of rulers and people, and beseech His merciful care and guidance in our afflicted country."[5]

Here are a few sentences from a long editorial in a paper that had hated Lincoln, the *New York Daily News:*

We are stunned, shocked, horrified beyond measure at this fearful announcement. We find it almost impossible to credit the tragic story. Need we say with what deep abhorrence we view the criminal madness which actuated these deeds of blood? We have not time, at the late hour when we are writing, to go into an analysis of the profound emotions which we experience in common with a grieved and horror-stricken public . . . there can be but one feeling or expression on the subject.[6]

The *Boston Evening Courier,* recognized as the leader of Copperhead opinion in New England during the last year of the war, said:

No language of which we are capable could half express the horror and dismay with which the dreadful event of the day has affected us. . . . Of the death of Mr. Lincoln, we can say, with the most heartfelt sincerity, that no public event has so startled and overwhelmed us. . . . Let us bow humbly to the determinations of Providence and with all our understanding and best purpose of heart work out all which it yet remains for us yet to do for our afflicted and distracted country as citizens and men.[7]

The Union backing *Boston Journal* said:

Abraham Lincoln was the gift of God to this land if ever a man was so commissioned. He was taken out of obscurity and mysteriously advanced over statesmen to whom all the people had been almost solely looking for their Chief Magistrate. All his singular array of qualities vindicated the choice. No man since Washington ever so completely met the emergency amid which he arose. Great success crowned his efforts. He saw the leading hope of his life realized, for he testified his faith, a few hours before he fell, that war had really given way to peace. His mission, perhaps, had been fulfilled. . . .[8]

The *Boston Transcript*, always loyal to Lincoln, published many tributes and said: "The horror of the deed was all the more deepened by the fact that its victim was the kindliest of all great magistrates and seemed to fall a martyr to his own goodness of heart." The *Transcript* also published, without comment, Lincoln's Gettysburg Address.[9]

*The Sun* of Baltimore, which had long insisted Lincoln was a lunatic, admitted his death was a loss to the country, saying:

Not alone in the North, but doubtless to a very large extent in the South, had a trust grown up that Abraham Lincoln possessed the qualities of head and heart which would enable him as readily as any other citizen who could possibly have been chosen to the position, to successfully accomplish the important work of reconciliation.[10]

The *Baltimore American,* which changed its Democratic principles to support Lincoln throughout the war in a hotbed of secession, paid him one of the most beautiful tributes: "He has exchanged the laurel wreath of time for the crown of immortality."[11]

The *National Intelligencer* of Washington, D. C., which turned to Lincoln with a change of ownership a few months before the war ended, said in its first edition after he died: "Our heart stands almost still as we take our pen in hand to speak of the tragedy of last night. We have no words at command by which to express anything that we feel. . . . Our heart is too full to say more."[12]

Then on April 17 the *Intelligencer* said: "All of us feel as if we were passing through a horrid dream. . . . The public mind is so paralyzed by the fiendish murder that it is hardly in a mood to read anything but what relates to the details of that tragedy."[13]

The loyal *Chronicle* told Washington readers: "It is with feelings of profound horror, sorrow and indignation that we are called upon to announce to the country one of the most terrible tragedies of which history affords an example." The editor then boasted that "it was our privilege to see the great and good heart of Abraham Lincoln slowly giving up its life blood."[14]

The *Chronicle* was one of Forney's newspapers. In his Philadelphia journal, *The Press*, he published an editorial of mysterious content; it was all the more strange in view of Forney's personal association and intimate friendship with the President. He seemed to say—at least he implied—that the assassination might prove of benefit to the country in removing Lincoln at just the right time. The editorial said in part:

> The loss we have sustained—the loss of Abraham Lincoln, that good and great man—is one which has been determined on by God. It is—we say this with reverence, but unhesitatingly—to serve God's purpose that he has been taken from us. A sterner and less gentle hand may at this juncture have been required to take hold of the reins of Government.[15]

The *Philadelphia Inquirer* had stood by Lincoln so steadfastly that it did not need to rush into print with great editorial tributes to prove its love and admiration. It stated with authority that "John Wilkes Booth has not removed a tyrant, he has murdered a friend."[16]

The administration newspapers of New York, notably *The New York Times*, published editorials that would stand the test of time. The *Times* published several editorials, saying on April 17:

> To him it was but the ordinary course of life to do that which has made him illustrious. He had a habit of greatness. . . . If he had ambition, it was to serve his country. . . . He was independent, self-poised, steadfast. You always knew where to find him; you could calculate him like a planet. A public trust was to him a sacred thing. Sublimer moral courage, more resolute devotion to duty, cannot be found in the history of man than he has displayed for the salvation of the American Union. It was the sublime performance of sublime duties that made him so trusted, and which has given him a fame as solid as justice, and as genuine as truth.[17]

After declaring on April 16 that Abraham Lincoln had died "in the fullness of his glory" and that his name "will go down to future ages," the *New York Herald* published an editorial of more than two thousand words under the heading, "Abraham Lincoln's Place in History," on April 17, saying:

> He will take his place in a sphere far higher than that accorded to any mere conqueror; and, indeed, without speaking profanely, we may well say that, since the foundation of the Christian era, no more remarkable or pregnant passages of the world's history have been unfolded than those of which

Mr. Lincoln on this continent has been the central figure and controlling influence. . . .

While we all must mourn with sad and sickened hearts the success of the great crime which has removed our beloved and trusted President from the final scenes of the contest he had thus far conducted to a triumphant issue, let us not forget that by the circumstance of death the seal of immortality has been stamped upon his fame; nor is it any longer in the power of changing fortune to take away from him, as might have happened had he lived, one of the most solid, brilliant and stainless reputations of which in the world's annals any record can be found—its only peer existing in the memory of George Washington.[18]

Greeley's editorial on "Mr. Lincoln's Fame" in the *New York Tribune* read as though he was writing about his own conduct toward Lincoln. He said:

Without the least desire to join in the race of heaping extravagant and preposterous laudations on our dead President as the wisest and greatest man who ever lived, we feel sure that the discerning and considerate of all parties will concur in our judgment that Mr. Lincoln's reputation will stand higher with posterity than with the mass of his contemporaries—that distance, whether in time or space, while dwarfing and obscuring so many, must place him in a fairer light—that future generations will deem him undervalued by those for and with whom he labored, and be puzzled by the bitter fierceness of the personal assaults by which his temper was tested. . . .

. . . he sleeps the sleep of the honored and just, and there are few graves which will be more extensively, persistently visited, or bedewed with the tears of a people's prouder, fonder affection, than that of Abraham Lincoln.[19]

William Cullen Bryant wrote a poem, *Death of Lincoln,* published in his New York *Evening Post,* April 20, 1865. As he penned the lines, Bryant must have remembered the time he went down to Washington to tell Lincoln he thought the Union's military operations were too sluggish. The poet-editor, in a long talk at the White House, spoke his mind plainly. Lincoln listened to Bryant's criticism and "bore it well."[20]

*The Crisis* at Columbus, edited by S. A. Medary, son of the late publisher, said:

His private life was unobjectionable. He was a man of a mild and kindly nature, gentle and genial in his intercourse among men, solicitous to satisfy his own conscience and judgment and trustful of his fame in history. . . .

The time at which the deed was done was most fatal and deplorable. At no

season during his administration had President Lincoln been in so commanding a position of usefulness to his fellow men. His political opponents for
weeks had hesitated to criticise his public acts, and that class of dangerous
men who sought to gain his confidence and misguide his better judgments
and purposes, were kindly but firmly put aside. . . .

His course since the fall of Richmond, his recognition of the only elements
by which the commonwealth could be restored to her allegiance, the wisdom
and moderation which he brought to confront the mighty difficulties before
him, were all full of promise of the greatest good. . . .

That the bullet of a single brutal fanatic should be allowed to crush all
these glorious hopes and plunge the nation into the abyss of despair and
anarchy, confounds the reason and paralyzes the heart. . . . this is certain,
that unless all are at fault, generations yet unborn will curse the slavish
instrument of this awful catastrophe.[21]

Under a headline that consisted of a single word, "Aftermath," *The
Crisis* said a few days later:

Since the assassination of President Lincoln, we have examined nearly two
hundred Democratic journals, from every State and district in the Northern
States, and we have not been able to find in one of them an expression in the
remotest degree justifying that most horrible crime. On the contrary, every
Democratic newspaper that we have read assumes precisely the ground taken
by *The Crisis,* that the deed was an atrocious murder, a blunder as wicked as
it was unwise and as devilish as it was foolish.[22]

The *Dayton Daily Empire,* Vallandigham's old mouthpiece, would
have bolted its party to support Lincoln, if one can believe an editorial
that deplored his death. It said:

We regard this news as the worst that we have had to chronicle since four
years ago when Fort Sumter fell and the country was plunged into a civil
war. The death of Mr. Lincoln is regarded by us as a great national calamity. . . . We had opposed Mr. Lincoln in his lifetime. Yet just at this junc-
ture we had the expectation of lending him our support.[23]

The *Milwaukee Sentinel,* whose editor, Rufus King, was appointed
Minister to Rome at the start of President Lincoln's first administration
and resigned to enter the army as a brigadier general, declared the assassination was "the great crime of the age." It continued:

We look as yet in vain for a rift in the black cloud which He has stretched
above us. Just now it appears to us as if Mr. Lincoln were absolutely indispensable to the nation's future life and true greatness.[24]

The *Toledo Blade*, always loyal to Lincoln, was baffled and, making an attempt to explain the assassination, said in an editorial: "May it not be that a 'jealous God' has seen in us too great a disposition to attribute to human strength and wisdom the great blessings which He has granted to us within the past year? Have we not shown an indication to give our beloved and lamented Executive credit for results for which we ought to render thanks to God? Did we not make too much of an idol of the weak instrument which a kind Providence saw fit to use for our good?"[25]

On an editorial page black with turned rules, the *Cincinnati Enquirer*, which had increased in bitterness against the Lincoln administration from year to year, published two death editorials. The wording of them indicates one was directed to the North, the other to the South. The first said:

So sudden and overwhelming was this announcement that when our eyes first rested upon it, it seemed like some horrid and terrible dream from which we have just been awakened. . . . We doubt whether among all the warmest personal and political friends of Mr. Lincoln and Mr. Seward, there can be found one who is more deeply pained and shocked at this catastrophe, or one who has darker fears of its unfortunate results to the country, than ourselves.

The second editorial carried the headline, "A Great Calamity to the South." This is the editorial in full:

The death of Mr. Lincoln we regard as one of great calamity to the people of the South. The assassin could not have done an act of greater injury to them than the taking of the life of the President. Mr. Lincoln was inaugurating measures that would have restored them to the Union on terms that had due consideration for their feelings, their persons and their property. He was a power, and could have carried out his plans of restoration, in defiance of the opposition of the radicals of the party. The Southern people should, therefore, be as anxious for the punishment of the assassin as the people of the North, for he has done them a very great injury.[26]

Wilbur F. Storey's *Chicago Times*, a source of personal insult to Lincoln since 1861, insisted it regretted his death, saying:

It is hard to conceive of the occurrence of any event which would be so shocking to the sensibilities of the country, occasion sorrow so profound, and create apprehensions and forebodings so painful as the event which today absorbs all minds and agitates the public heart to its lowest depths. Since the 4th of March last a higher estimate has been put upon Mr. Lincoln's life, and more voices have ascended to Heaven that it might be spared than before . . . the future, the darkness of which was just beginning to yield to a glorious light, is again enveloped in utter night. . . . There are not on this day mourners more sincere than the Democracy of these northern states. . . . The Democracy may well mourn the death of Abraham Lincoln.[27]

Most interesting was the reaction of the *Illinois State Register* at Springfield, his political and personal foe since Lincoln was an obscure politician. It attempted to speak of him as a fellow townsman and succeeded only in making itself ridiculous. A tribute editorial said:

We forget the points of difference of the four years past, and think only of Abraham Lincoln, the kindly and indulgent man, beloved of his neighbors, and of the chief magistrate who has honestly followed the path that seemed to him best for the welfare of the people. . . .

No national calamity so serious as his death could have befallen us. The bitterest and most radical opponent of his administration cannot fail to recognize, in the mere political bearing of the event, the terrible solemnity of the blow we have received. While we mourn the loss of the genial and kindly neighbor we once knew so well, and mingle our tears and sympathies with those of his bereaved family, we all feel alike keenly the fresh perils to which the nation is subjected.[28]

It accompanied the death editorial with a biographical sketch in which it made this amazing misstatement of fact: "He spent two years at school in Stafford County, Va.; taught school and studied law for a time in Culpepper County, of that state, and removed to Illinois in 1830."[29]

While the President's body was lying in the White House, the *Register* published another editorial in which it declared: "We are dumb with sorrow."[30]

The sincerity of the moving editorial carried by the *Chicago Tribune* cannot be doubted because of the newspaper's support of Lincoln, both as a candidate and as President. Its eulogy said in part:

All the land weeps. For we loved none as we loved him. . . . Hitherto the name of Washington has stood first in war, first in peace, first in the hearts of his countrymen. His star shall not decrease, but that of another shall increase, until, richer and more heavenly than the fame of him who emancipated his country will be the glory of him who gave emancipation to an outcast race and people. The first was manly and patriotic; the last was Christ-like and divine. Those who are now young will live to see the dawning of the fame and power of the martyred Lincoln.[31]

In the fallen capital of the Confederacy, the *Richmond Whig* spoke for many people in the conquered states when it said that "the heaviest blow which has ever fallen upon the people of the South has descended." The editorial continued:

The decease of the Chief Magistrate of the nation at any period is an event which profoundly affects the public mind, but the time, manner, and circumstances of President Lincoln's death render it the most momentous, the most appalling, the most deplorable calamity which has ever befallen the people of the United States. . . . Just as everything was happily conspiring to a restoration of tranquility, under the benignant and magnanimous policy of Mr. Lincoln, comes this terrible blow.[32]

The tone was different in faraway Texas. The *Texas Republican*, published at Marshall, said editorially that "from now until God's judgment day the minds of men will not cease to thrill at the killing of Abraham Lincoln, by the hand of Booth, the actor."[33]

An editorial in the *Galveston News* said: "In the plentitude of his power and arrogance he was struck down, and is so ushered into eternity, with innumerable crimes and sins to answer for. . . . He sowed the wind and has reaped the whirlwind."[34] The editor of the *Dallas Herald* said: "God Almighty ordered this event or it could never have taken place. His purpose in it, as His purpose in the surrender of Lee's army remains to be seen."[35]

The European press, to which the assassination was an event of international importance, hung on every word from America, and the editors expressed their opinions of Lincoln in lengthy comment.

Tributes poured from the French press. "The death of Mr. Lincoln is a cause of mourning for all civilization," said the *Constitutionnel*. "The restorer of the American country . . . has paid for his victory with his blood," said the *Époque*.

"Without arming himself with dictatorial power, he passed victoriously through a crisis in which his country might have been destroyed," said an editorial in the *Journal des Débats*.

*Opinion Nationale:* "The American Republic never produced a better, a greater citizen."

*Presse:* "Lincoln was the personification of energy in the struggle and wisdom and power."

*Le Pays:* "We are not among those who approved of everything that has been done in Mr. Lincoln's administration. . . . We lament from the bottom of our hearts this cruel death."

*Siècle:* "The great republic will pursue the course of her glorious career. As for the man who has just paid with his life for the place which history reserves for him, by the side of Washington, he goes down to the grave followed by the regret of the whole world."[36]

The press in the British Isles published notable editorials. At Belfast, the *Ulster Observer* said: "The assassin's hand may take away life; it cannot wound that which is more precious and enduring than life—the reputation which is based on tried goodness and proven greatness." *Freeman's Journal* of Dublin said: "We doubt whether modern history contains a grander character than the humble lawyer of Illinois." The Dublin *Daily Express* said: "We cherish the memory of the second Washington."[37]

The Edinburgh *Caledonian Mercury* noted the effect the assassination of Lincoln had on the people of Scotland. "Not a few strong men wept as children, as if a common father had gone," it said. The *Glasgow Herald* exclaimed: "His fall is a loss to the world."[38]

The leading newspapers in England were racked with remorse that the true height of the man was not measured until he had fallen. The London *Morning Star* confessed:

We in England have something to feel ashamed of when we meditate upon the true greatness of the man so ruthlessly slain. . . . English writers degraded themselves to the level of the coarsest caricaturists when they had to tell of Abraham Lincoln. They stooped to criticize a foreign patriot as a menial might comment on the bearing of a hero. They sneered at his manners, as if Mirabeau was a beauty; they made coarse pleasantry of his figure, as if Peel was a posture-master; they were facetious about his dress, as if Cavour was a D'Orsay; they were indignant about his jokes as if Palmerston never jested. . . . History will proclaim, to the eternal humiliation of our country, how an influential section of the British press outbade the journalists of the South in their slander and invective against the great man who has been so cruelly slain; how his every action was twisted and tortured into a wrong, his every noble aspiration spoken of as a desire for blood, his personal appearance caricatured, his lowly origin made the theme for scorn by men as base-born as he, but without the nobleness of soul which made Lincoln a prince among princes; how even that proclamation which conferred liberty upon four millions of down-trodden slaves was reviled as a base effort to incite the negroes to servile war.[39]

The *London Daily News* said: "Mr. Lincoln's name is mentioned with regret by men who four years ago half believed he was the wretched imbecile he was described to be by the Richmond press. . . . In all time to come, not among Americans only, but among all who think of manhood as more than rank, and set worth above display, the name of Abraham Lincoln will be held in reverence."[40]

The *London Times* bowed reluctantly at Lincoln's grave and made this admission: "The education of a man whose early years have been spent in earning bread by manual labor had necessarily been defective, and faults of manners and errors of taste repelled the observer at the outset. In spite of all these drawbacks, Mr. Lincoln slowly won for himself the respect and confidence of all. His perfect honesty speedily became apparent."[41]

The London *Evening Standard* said painfully: "Now that he is dead, the good qualities of the unfortunate Lincoln seem to come into the foreground. We remember his honesty and his manliness; we do justice to his consistency; we give him all praise for the spirit of conciliation which he has shown. . . . We almost excuse his obstinacy in prosecution of the war."[42]

The *London Spectator* asserted that "the one man in America whose resolve on the crucial question was unchangeable, whose shrewdness statesmen definitely keener than himself could never baffle, whose gentleness years of incessant insult had failed to weary out, who, possessed of these qualities, was possessed also of the supreme power, and who had convinced even his enemies that the power would be exerted under the influence of these qualities, has been taken from his work."[43]

"He had nothing of the tyrant either in his office or his person," said the *Carlisle Examiner.*

The *Leeds Mercury* said: "History, which embalms few reputations so spotless and so sacred as his, will do justice to his memory."

The *Daily Post* at Liverpool declared: "There stands before the world a man whose like we shall not soon look upon again."[44]

For days, for weeks, for months and years, even for tens of years the press poured out a torrent of fine words about Abraham Lincoln.

# Footnotes

## CHAPTER ONE

1 *Sangamo Journal* (Springfield, Ill.), June 18, 1836.
2 Albert J. Beveridge, *Abraham Lincoln* (1928), Vol. I, p. 154.
3 *The History of Sangamon County, Illinois*, Inter-State Publishing Company, Chicago (1881), Chap. XI, pp. 213–240.
4 Beveridge, *op. cit.*, pp. 183–184.
5 *Ibid.*, footnote, p. 184.
6 *Sangamo Journal*, Jan. 28, 1837. Quoted by Beveridge, *op. cit.*, pp. 202–203.
7 Beveridge, *op. cit.*, p. 212.
8 William H. Herndon and Jesse W. Weik, *Abraham Lincoln* (1923), Vol. I, p. 212.
9 *Sangamo Journal*, June 24, 1837. Cited by Beveridge, *op. cit.*, p. 215.
10 *Ibid.*, Aug. 19, 1837. Also see *Complete Works of Abraham Lincoln* (1894), Vol. I, pp. 57–64. Sponsor's Edition, Lincoln Memorial University. Referred to hereafter as *Complete Works*.
11 *Sangamo Journal*, Sept. 30, Oct. 7 and 14, 1837. Cited by Beveridge, *op. cit.*, p. 217.
12 *The History of Sangamon County, Illinois, op. cit.*
13 Beveridge, *op. cit.*, p. 291.
14 *Illinois State Register* (Springfield), Jan. 29, 1841. Quoted by Beveridge, *op. cit.*, p. 291.
15 Herndon and Weik, *op. cit.*, p. 201.
16 *Ibid.*, p. 202. When Herndon was gathering material for his life of Lincoln, he searched the *Journal* files for the suicide poem, only to find a hole in the page where it had been clipped.
17 *Ibid.*, pp. 212–213.
18 *Ibid.*, p. 213. Also Beveridge, *op. cit.*, p. 333. He quotes the Weik Mss.
19 Beveridge, *op. cit.*, p. 287 and footnote, p. 335.
20 Paul M. Angle, *Here I Have Lived* (1935), pp. 115–116.
21 Herndon and Weik, *op. cit.*, p. 218.
22 Beveridge, *op. cit.*, footnote, p. 205.
23 *Sangamo Journal* of dates specified.
24 *Ibid.*, Aug. 26, 1842.
25 *Ibid.*, Sept. 9, 1842. Also Herndon and Weik, *op. cit.*, pp. 227–228.
26 *Complete Works*, Vol. I, footnote, p. 221. Also Herndon and Weik, *op. cit.*, p. 226. Also Beveridge, *op. cit.*, p. 343.
27 *Sangamo Journal*, Sept. 16, 1842. Also Herndon and Weik, *op. cit.*, pp. 228–229.
28 Herndon and Weik, *op. cit.*, p. 229.
29 Beveridge, *op. cit.*, p. 352. He cites Condon's *Life of Major Shields*, p. 49.
30 *Sangamo Journal*, Oct. 7 and 14, 1842.
31 Beveridge, *op. cit.*, p. 355. He cites statement made by James H. Matheny, May 3, 1866. Weik Mss.

## CHAPTER TWO

1 Albert J. Beveridge, *Abraham Lincoln* (1928), Vol. I, pp. 359–363.
2 William H. Herndon and Jesse W. Weik, *Abraham Lincoln* (1923), Vol. I, pp. 257–258. Herndon succeeded Stephen T. Logan as Lincoln's law partner and was secretary of the convention that nominated him.
3 Beveridge, *op. cit.*, pp. 382–383.
4 *Complete Works*, Vol. I, p. 278.
5 *Ibid.*, pp. 278–280.
6 Beveridge, *op. cit.*, p. 371. He quotes Lincoln's letter to Dummer, Nov. 18, 1845. Ms., Chicago Historical Society.
7 *Ibid.*, p. 372.

8 *Complete Works*, Vol. I, pp. 285–286.

9 *Ibid.*, pp. 286–288.

10 *Sangamo Journal* (Springfield, Ill.), April 23, 1846. Quoted by Beveridge, *op. cit.*, p. 376.

11 Beveridge, *op. cit.*, p. 381. He says newspapers of both parties failed to print any campaign speeches.

12 *New York Tribune.* Quoted by Beveridge, *op. cit.*, p. 388.

13 Beveridge, *op. cit.*, p. 398.

14 These newspapers are quoted by Beveridge, *op. cit.*, in footnote, p. 420.

15 *Complete Works*, Vol. I, pp. 316–317.

16 *Ibid.*, pp. 318–320.

17 *Baltimore* (Md.) *Patriot.* Reprinted by *Rockford* (Ill.) *Forum*, Jan. 19, 1848. Quoted by Beveridge, *op. cit.*, pp. 422–423.

18 Beveridge, *op. cit.*, pp. 423–424 and footnote, p. 424.

19 *Illinois State Register* (Springfield), Jan. 21, 1848.

20 *Complete Works*, Vol. I, pp. 327–347.

21 The *Sangamo Journal* changed its name on Sept. 23, 1847.

22 *Illinois State Register*, Jan. 7, 1848. Quoted by Beveridge, *op. cit.*, p. 430.

23 *Illinois Journal*, Feb. 10, 1848. Cited by Beveridge, *op. cit.*, p. 430.

24 *Illinois State Register*, Feb. 18, 1848. Quoted by Beveridge, *op. cit.*, p. 431.

25 *Missouri Republican* (St. Louis). Reprinted in *Illinois Journal*, Feb. 3, 1848.

26 *Illinois State Register*, Feb. 18, 1848. Cited by Beveridge, *op. cit.*, p. 431 (a typographical error gives the year as 1858).

27 *Ibid.*, March 10, 1848. Quoted by Beveridge, *op. cit.*, p. 432.

28 These newspapers are quoted by Beveridge, *op. cit.*, p. 432.

29 *Complete Works*, Vol. II, pp. 53–54.

30 Beveridge, *op. cit.*, p. 451.

31 *Appleton's Cyclopaedia of American Biography* (1888), Vol. II, p. 738. 6 vols., I–V (1888); VI (1889).

Hereafter referred to as *Appleton's.*

32 *New York Tribune*, Dec. 22, 1848. William Alexander Linn, *Horace Greeley, Founder and Editor of the New York Tribune* (1903), pp. 98–103; Carl Sandburg, *Abraham Lincoln, The Prairie Years* (1926), Vol. I, pp. 355–356.

33 *New York Tribune.* Quoted by Sandburg, *op. cit.*, p. 356.

34 *Complete Works*, Vol. II, p. 58.

35 Beveridge, *op. cit.*, p. 468.

36 *Ibid.*, p. 469.

37 *Boston Advertiser.* Quoted in *Complete Works*, Vol. II, p. 89.

38 *National Aegis* (Worcester, Mass.). Quoted by Beveridge, *op. cit.*, p. 473.

39 *Journal and Courier* (Lowell, Mass.), Sept. 18, 1848. Quoted by Herndon and Weik, *op. cit.*, pp. 288–289.

40 Herndon and Weik, *op. cit.*, pp. 291–292.

41 Gilbert A. Tracy, *Uncollected Letters of Abraham Lincoln* (1917), p. 34.

42 *Boston Atlas*, Sept. 23, 1848. Quoted by Herndon and Weik, *op. cit.*, p. 286.

43 *Ibid.*, Sept. 25, 1848. Quoted by Herndon and Weik, *op. cit.*, p. 286.

44 Beveridge, *op. cit.*, p. 476.

45 *Ibid.* He cites *Memoirs of Seward*, footnote, pp. 79–80.

46 Herndon and Weik, *op. cit.*, pp. 299–301.

47 *Ibid.*, p. 306.

48 *Complete Works*, Vol. II, pp. 129–130.

49 *Ibid.*, pp. 100–101.

CHAPTER THREE

1 William H. Herndon and Jesse W. Weik, *Abraham Lincoln* (1923), Vol. II, p. 32.

2 Albert J. Beveridge, *Abraham Lincoln* (1928), Vol. II, p. 72.

3 *Ibid.*, p. 231, and footnote.

4 *Free West* (Chicago, Ill.), Sept. 7, 1854. Cited by Beveridge, *op. cit.*, p. 233.

5 Beveridge, *op. cit.*, p. 234 and 238.

6  *Ibid.*, p. 238. Also see "Fragments" in *Complete Works*, Vol. II, pp. 182–187.

7  *Ibid.*, p. 242.

8  *Daily Illinois State Register* (Springfield), Oct. 4 and 5, 1854. Quoted by Beveridge, *op. cit.*, p. 243.

9  *Illinois Journal* (Springfield). Quoted by Herndon and Weik, *op. cit.*, pp. 37–38.

10  *Complete Works*, Vol. II, pp. 190–262, and footnote, p. 190.

11  Horace White, *Lincoln in 1854*. An address before the Illinois State Historical Society in 1908. Cited by Beveridge, *op. cit.*, p. 249.

12  *Ibid.* Cited by Beveridge, *op. cit.*, p. 244.

13  Beveridge asserts Lincoln wrote this editorial, and the writer agrees.

14  *Illinois Journal*, Oct. 19, 1854. Quoted by Beveridge, *op cit.*, in footnote, p. 273.

15  *Chicago Journal.* Reprinted by *Illinois Journal*, Nov. 3, 1854. Quoted by Beveridge, *op. cit.*, p. 272.

16  *Complete Works*, Vol. II, pp. 262–265.

17  Herndon and Weik, *op. cit.*, pp. 43–44.

18  Beveridge, *op. cit.*, p. 286.

19  *New York Tribune*, Feb. 9, 1855. Quoted by Beveridge, *op. cit.*, p. 290.

20  *Washington* (D.C.) *Sentinel*, Feb. 13, 1855. Quoted by Beveridge, *op. cit.*, p. 290.

21  This is the finding of Beveridge, *op. cit.*, p. 290.

22  Beveridge, *op. cit.*, p. 358.

23  *Illinois State Journal*, Feb. 25, 1856.

24  Herndon letter to Theodore Parker, April 28, 1856. Cited by Beveridge, *op. cit.*, footnote, p. 359.

25  Herndon and Weik, *op. cit.*, p. 52.

26  *Ibid.*, pp. 53–54.

27  Philip Kinsley, *The Chicago Tribune* (1943), Vol. I, pp. 54–57.

28  Beveridge, *op. cit.*, p. 363.

29  Ida M. Tarbell, *In the Footsteps of the Lincolns* (1924), pp. 335–336. Quotes Medill letter.

30  *Chicago Press.* Reprinted by *Illinois Daily State Journal*, June 3, 1856.

31  Beveridge, *op. cit.*, pp. 374–378. Quotes Whitney version.

32  *Ibid.*, pp. 398–399.

33  Cited by Beveridge, *op. cit.*, footnote, p. 416.

34  Herndon and Weik, *op. cit.*, pp. 38–39.

35  Gilbert A. Tracy, *Uncollected Letters of Abraham Lincoln* (1917), p. 57.

36  Herndon and Weik, *op. cit.*, p. 45.

37  Tracy, *op. cit.*, pp. 83–84.

38  Herndon and Weik, *op. cit.*, pp. 59–60.

39  *Ibid.*, pp. 61–64.

40  Beveridge, *op. cit.*, pp. 566–568.

41  *Ibid.*, footnote, p. 554.

42  *Ibid.*, pp. 556–557.

43  *Illinois Daily State Journal*, June 17, 1858.

44  John W. Forney, *Anecdotes of Public Men* (1874), Vol. II, p. 179.

45  *Complete Works*, Vol. III, pp. 1–15.

46  Herndon and Weik, *op. cit.*, p. 92. Horace White's own story.

47  Beveridge, *op. cit.*, p. 585.

48  *New York Tribune*, June 24, 1858. Cited by Beveridge, *op. cit.*, p. 585.

49  *Chicago Times.* Quoted by Beveridge, *op. cit.*, p. 585.

50  *Daily Illinois State Register*, June 28, 1858. Cited by Beveridge, *op. cit.*, p. 586.

51  Kinsley, *op. cit.*, p. 78.

52  *New Orleans* (La.) *Delta.* Reprinted by *Chicago Tribune*, July 5, 1858. Quoted by Kinsley, *op. cit.*, p. 79.

CHAPTER FOUR

1  Philip Kinsley, *The Chicago Tribune* (1943), Vol. I, pp. 79–80.

2  William H. Herndon and Jesse W. Weik, *Abraham Lincoln* (1923), Vol. II, p. 89. Horace White's story of the debates, pp. 88–132.

3  All facts concerning Hitt, Binmore, and Sheridan are taken from Edwin Erle Sparks, *The Lincoln-Douglas Debates of 1858* (1908), pp. 75–82.

Hereafter referred to in this annotation as Sparks.

4 *New York Tribune*, July 12, 1858. Reprinted by *Daily Illinois State Register* (Springfield). Quoted by Albert J. Beveridge, *Abraham Lincoln* (1928), Vol. II, p. 592.

5 Beveridge, *op. cit.*, p. 609. He cites Judd's letter to Trumbull, July 16, 1858. Trumbull Mss.

6 Kinsley, *op. cit.*, p. 80.

7 *Chicago Press and Tribune*, July 16, 1858. Cited by Kinsley, *op. cit.*, p. 80. Footnote says the *Associated Press* should not be confused with today's news service of same name. The *Chicago Tribune* was called the *Chicago Press and Tribune* from July 1, 1858, until after Lincoln's election in November of 1860, owing to a merger.

8 Kinsley, *op. cit.*, p. 81.

9 Beveridge, *op. cit.*, p. 556. He cites Nicolay's letter to Trumbull, Nov. 23, 1857. Trumbull Mss.

10 *Ibid.*, footnote.

11 *Ibid.* Cites Hatch's letter to Trumbull, Nov. 23, 1857. Trumbull Mss.

12 *Boston Traveller.* Quoted by Sparks, p. 58.

13 *New York Tribune*, July 12, 1858. Quoted by Beveridge, *op. cit.*, p. 628, footnote.

14 *Illinois Daily State Journal* (Springfield), July 23, 1858. Reprinted by Sparks, p. 55.

15 *Chicago Times*, July 30, 1858. Reprinted by Sparks, p. 56.

16 *The Press* (Philadelphia), Aug. 4, 1858. Reprinted by Sparks, p. 57.

17 *Chicago Times.* Reprinted by *New York Herald*, Aug. 3, 1858. Reprinted by Sparks, pp. 57–58.

18 *New York Herald*, Aug. 3, 1858. Reprinted by Sparks, p. 58.

19 Sparks, pp. 59–60.

20 Lincoln-Douglas correspondence of July 30–31, 1858. Sparks, p. 70.

21 Henry Villard, *Memoirs* (1904), Vol. I, p. 91.

22 Quoted by Kinsley, *op. cit.*, pp. 84–85.

23 *Chicago Times*, Aug. 22, 1858. Reprinted by Sparks, p. 82. He

wrongly identifies the paper as Aug. 25 issue.

24 *Chicago Tribune*, Aug. 24, 1858. Cited by Kinsley, *op. cit.*, p. 85.

25 *Chicago Times*, Aug. 25, 1858. Reprinted by Sparks, pp. 82–83.

26 *Galesburg* (Ill.) *Democrat*, Oct. 13, 1858. Reprinted by Sparks, pp. 83–84.

27 *Chicago Times*, Oct. 12, 1858. Reprinted by Sparks, p. 84.

28 *Quincy* (Ill.) *Whig*, Oct. 16, 1858. Reprinted by Sparks, p. 84.

29 Herndon and Weik, *op. cit.*, p. 89.

30 *Evening Post* (New York), Sept. 2, 1858. Reprinted by Sparks, p. 193.

31 *Chicago Times*, Aug. 29, 1858. Reprinted by Sparks, p. 189. Also Kinsley, *op. cit.*, p. 87.

32 *Chicago Sunday Tribune*, May 9, 1895. This is "A Reminiscence of Lincoln," written by Medill. Reprinted by Sparks, pp. 203–204.

33 *Complete Works*, Vol. III, p. 279.

34 *Ibid.*, p. 297. Also Sparks, p. 161.

35 Herndon and Weik, *op. cit.*, p. 110.

36 *Ibid.*, pp. 111–112.

37 *Burlington* (Iowa) *State Gazette*, Oct. 29, 1858. Reprinted by Sparks, p. 533.

38 *Illinois Daily State Journal* and *Galesburg Democrat*, Nov. 3, 1858.

39 Beveridge, *op. cit.*, p. 695, and Herndon and Weik, *op. cit.*, p. 125.

40 *Chicago Press and Tribune*, Nov. 10, 1858. Reprinted by Sparks, pp. 585–586.

41 Herndon and Weik, *op. cit.*, pp. 110–111.

42 Kinsley, *op. cit.*, p. 92.

43 *New York Herald.* Reprinted by *Illinois Daily State Journal*, Nov. 19, 1858. Reprinted by Sparks, p. 581.

44 *Peoria* (Ill.) *Daily Message.* Reprinted by *Daily Herald* (Quincy, Ill.), Nov. 15, 1858. Reprinted by Sparks, p. 582.

45 *Chicago Daily Democrat*, Nov. 11, 1858. Reprinted by Sparks, pp. 586–587.

46 Beveridge, *op. cit.*, p. 699.

47 *Chicago Press and Tribune*, Nov. 12, 1858. Quoted by Kinsley, *op. cit.*, p. 93.

48 *Ibid.*, Dec. 16, 1858. Beveridge, *op. cit.*, pp. 699–700.
49 *Complete Works*, Vol. XI, p. 111.
50 Gilbert A. Tracy, *Uncollected Letters of Abraham Lincoln* (1917), p. 104.
51 *Complete Works*, Vol. V, pp. 127–128.
52 These facts from Ernest E. Fast's introduction to "Reminiscences of Abraham Lincoln" by Thomas J. Pickett in *The Lincoln Herald*, Dec. 1943.
53 *Central Illinois Gazette* (Champaign), May 4, 1859. Quoted by Ida M. Tarbell, *In the Footsteps of the Lincolns* (1924), pp. 384–385.
54 Tarbell, *op. cit.*, p. 385. Stoddard letter, 1896.
55 *Appleton's*, Vol. V, p. 698.
56 Pickett, *op. cit.*
57 Herndon and Weik, *op. cit.*, p. 208. Letter in footnote. Also *Complete Works*, Vol. X, p. 80.
58 *Chicago Press and Tribune*, March 29, 1859. Quoted by Kinsley, *op. cit.*, p. 54.
59 Kinsley, *op. cit.*, p. 98. Cites Medill interview in *Saturday Evening Post*.
60 Gustave Koerner, *Memoirs* (1909), Vol. II, p. 80.
61 Kinsley, *op. cit.*, pp. 98–99. Quotes Medill correspondence.
62 David C. Mearns, *The Lincoln Papers* (1948), Vol I, p. 226.
63 Herndon and Weik, *op. cit.*, footnote, p. 161.
64 Edwin Erle Sparks, *The Lincoln-Douglas Debates of 1858* (1905), pp. 591–592.
65 Herndon and Weik, *op. cit.*, footnote, p. 161.

CHAPTER FIVE

1 Charles H. Workman, "Tablet to Abraham Lincoln at Mansfield," *The Ohio State Archaeological and Historical Quarterly*, Vol. XXXIV (Oct., 1925), pp. 505–521. An address, Sept. 22, 1925.
2 *Mansfield* (Ohio) *Herald*, Nov. 10, 1858. Quoted by Workman, *op. cit.*
3 Alfred E. Lee, *History of the City of Columbus* (1892), Vol. I, p. 424.

4 *Appleton's*, Vol. I, p. 718.
5 *Toledo* (Ohio) *Blade*, Nov. 6, 1858.
6 Ida M. Tarbell, *In the Footsteps of the Lincolns* (1924), pp. 382–384.
7 Workman, *op. cit.*
8 *Daily Commercial Register* (Sandusky, Ohio), Nov. 22, 1858.
9 Edwin Erle Sparks, *The Lincoln-Douglas Debates of 1858* (1908), p. 582.

CHAPTER SIX

1 Joseph P. Smith, *History of the Republican Party in Ohio* (1898), Vol. I, p. 87.
2 *Ohio State Journal* (Columbus), Sept. 9, 1859.
3 *National Democrat* (Cleveland, Ohio). Reprinted by *Ohio State Journal*, Sept. 5, 1859.
4 *Louisville* (Ky.) *Daily Journal*. Reprinted by *Ohio State Journal*, Sept. 14, 1859.
5 *Ohio State Journal*, Sept. 17, 1859. The Columbus speech is in *Complete Works*, Vol. V, pp. 140–189.
6 *Daily Ohio Statesman* (Columbus), Sept. 17, 1859.
7 *Ohio State Journal*, Sept. 17, 1859.
8 *Cincinnati* (Ohio) *Daily Commercial*, Sept. 17, 1859. Reprinted by *Xenia* (Ohio) *Torch-Light*, Sept. 21, 1859.
9 Royal Cortissoz, *The Life of Whitelaw Reid* (1921), Vol. I, p. 31.
10 *Xenia* (Ohio) *News*. Quoted by Cortissoz, *op. cit.*, p. 45.
11 *Ibid.*, p. 50.
12 Cortissoz, *op. cit.*, p. 50.
13 *Xenia News*. Quoted by Cortissoz, *op. cit.*, p. 50.
14 Daniel J. Ryan, "Lincoln and Ohio," *Ohio Archaeological and Historical Publications*, Vol. XXXII (1923), p. 64.
15 *Dayton* (Ohio) *Daily Empire*. Quoted by Ryan, *op. cit.*
16 *Xenia Torch-Light*, Sept. 21, 1859.
17 *Cincinnati* (Ohio) *Daily Gazette*, Sept. 19, 1859.
18 *New York Times*, Sept. 12, 1859. Reprinted by *Cincinnati* (Ohio) *Enquirer*, Sept. 16, 1859.
19 *Cincinnati Enquirer*, Sept. 16, 1859.

20  *Ibid.,* Sept. 18, 1859.
21  *Ibid.,* Sept. 20, 1859.
22  *Cincinnati Gazette,* Sept. 17, 1859.
23  *Ibid.,* Sept. 19, 1859.
24  *Cincinnati Commercial,* Sept. 19, 1859. For more about Halstead see Eugene H. Roseboom, *The History of the State of Ohio,* Vol. IV, "Civil War Era: 1850–1873" (1944), p. 201.
25  Philip Kinsley, *The Chicago Tribune* (1943), Vol. I, p. 97.
26  *Cleveland (Ohio) Plain Dealer,* Sept. 20, 1859. For more about the *Plain Dealer,* see Archer H. Shaw, *The Plain Dealer* (1942), p. 30.
27  *Mariposa (Calif.) Star.* Reprinted by *Cincinnati Gazette,* Sept. 15, 1859.
28  *New York Tribune,* Sept. 28, 1859.
29  *Ohio Statesman,* Sept. 22, 1859.
30  *Columbus (Ohio) Gazette,* Oct. 21, 1859.
31  *Appleton's,* Vol. I, pp. 404–407.
32  *Complete Works,* Vol. V, footnote, p. 260.
33  *Ibid.,* p. 272.
34  *Ibid.,* p. 286.
35  Albert J. Beveridge, *Abraham Lincoln* (1928), Vol. II, p. 294. Also footnote, pp. 294–295.
36  *Complete Works,* Vol. V, pp. 286–289.
37  *Chester County (Pa.) Times.* Reprinted by *Chicago Press and Tribune,* Feb. 23, 1860. Cited by Kinsley, *op. cit.,* p. 108.

### CHAPTER SEVEN

1  Lincoln spoke at Indianapolis, Ind., en route home from Cincinnati. For other speeches see *Complete Works,* Vol. V, pp. 236–256 and 260–281.
2  David C. Mearns, *The Lincoln Papers* (1948), Vol. I, p. 227.
3  *Complete Works,* Vol. V, pp. 258–259.
4  *Ibid.,* footnote, p. 293.
5  Mearns, *op. cit.,* p. 229.
6  *Daily Illinois State Register* (Springfield), Feb. 23, 1860.
7  Carl Sandburg, *Abraham Lincoln, The Prairie Years* (1926), Vol. II, p. 210; Philip Kinsley, *The Chicago Tribune* (1943), Vol. I, pp. 109–110, uses the same story and credits Sandburg.
8  *Chicago Press and Tribune,* Feb. 16, 1860.
9  Sandburg, *op. cit.,* p. 210.
10  *Complete Works,* Vol. V, footnote, p. 293. Also Mearns, *op. cit.,* p. 227.
11  *New York Tribune,* Feb. 25, 1860.
12  *Ibid.,* Feb. 27, 1860.
13  *Evening Post* (New York), Feb. 25, 1860.
14  Henry B. Rankin, *Intimate Character Sketches of Abraham Lincoln* (1924), p. 188. Also Sandburg, *op. cit.,* pp. 214–215.
15  *Ibid.,* pp. 189–192.
16  *Appleton's,* Vol. II, p. 30.
17  *New York Times,* Feb. 28, 1860.
18  *New York Tribune,* Feb. 28, 1860.
19  *Evening Post,* Feb. 28, 1860.
20  Allan Nevins, *The Evening Post* (1922), p. 261.
21  Ida M. Tarbell, *In the Footsteps of the Lincolns* (1924), pp. 374–375.
22  Richard S. West, Jr., *Gideon Welles: Lincoln's Navy Department* (1943), pp. 73–74.
23  *Ibid.,* pp. 75–87.
24  *Hartford (Conn.) Press,* March 6, 1860. Quoted by West, *op. cit.,* p. 81.
25  *Chicago Press and Tribune,* Feb. 27, 1860.
26  Sandburg, *op. cit.,* pp. 215–216.

### CHAPTER EIGHT

1  *New York Tribune,* May 22, 1860.
2  *Ibid.,* May 11, 1860.
3  *Ibid.,* May 22, 1860.
4  *Chicago Press and Tribune,* May 15 and 16, 1860.
5  *New York Times.* Reprinted by *Toledo (Ohio) Blade,* May 17, 1860.
6  *New York Tribune,* May 15, 1860.
7  *Ibid.,* May 17, 1860. Note that Greeley referred to Seward as Governor. It was general practice, although Seward was now United States Senator.
8  *Ibid.,* May 18, 1860.
9  *Cincinnati Commercial,* May 18, 1860.

10 *New York Tribune*, May 19, 1860.
11 *Cincinnati Commercial*, May 21, 1860.
12 *Ibid.* Also *New York Tribune*, May 19, 1860.
13 *New York Tribune*, May 19, 1860.
14 *Cincinnati Commercial*, May 21, 1860.
15 Daniel J. Ryan, "Lincoln and Ohio," *Ohio Archaeological and Historical Publications*, Vol. XXXII (1923), p. 126. He quotes Joseph Medill in *Saturday Evening Post* interview, Aug. 5, 1899.
16 *Cincinnati Commercial*, May 23, 1860.
17 *Appleton's*, Vol. I, p. 544. Also Ruth Gertrude Curran, "David Kellogg Cartter," *Ohio Archaeological and Historical Publications*, Vol. XLII (1933), pp. 105–115. Curran errs on p. 110 in saying Cartter was named Chief Justice of the United States Supreme Court.
18 *Cincinnati Commercial*, May 21, 1860.
19 *Chicago Journal*. Reprinted by *Cincinnati Commercial*, May 25, 1860.
20 *New York Times*. Reprinted by *Cincinnati Commercial*, May 26, 1860.
21 *New York Tribune*, May 19, 1860.
22 *Peoria (Ill.) Transcript*, May 21, 1860. Quoted by Philip Kinsley, *The Chicago Tribune* (1943), Vol. I, p. 121.
23 *Toledo Blade*, May 19, 1860.
24 *Albany (N. Y.) Evening Journal*, May 19, 1860.
25 All newspapers reprinted by *New York Tribune*, May 21, 1860.
26 *Ibid.*
27 *Ibid.*
28 *Ibid.*, May 25, 1860. Reprinted from *New York Times*. William Alexander Linn, *Horace Greeley, Founder and Editor of the New York Tribune* (1903), carries a condensation of the Raymond letter, pp. 180–182.
29 *Ibid.*
30 *Ibid.*
31 Linn, *op. cit.*, pp. 172–174.
32 *New York Tribune*, June 14, 1860.
33 *Ibid.*

34 *Albany Evening Journal*. Quoted by Linn, *op. cit.*, p. 172.
35 Linn, *op. cit.*, p. 182.

### CHAPTER NINE

1 *Harper's Pictorial History of the Civil War* (1866), p. 15. In two parts, pages consecutive. Used as *Harper's* and *Harper's*, II.
2 *Ibid.*
3 William Dean Howells, *Years of My Youth* (1916), pp. 199–201.
4 *Ibid.*, p. 202. Howells was seventy-nine when he wrote his *Years*. He did not name the law student.
5 Roy P. Basler, "James Quay Howard's Notes on Lincoln," *The Abraham Lincoln Quarterly*, Vol. IV (Dec., 1947), p. 386.
6 *Ibid.*, p. 395.
7 David C. Mearns, *The Lincoln Papers* (1948), Vol. I, pp. 257–258.
8 *Complete Works*, Vol. VI, p. 42.
9 The Robert Todd Lincoln Collection of the Papers of Abraham Lincoln (3143). Hereafter referred to as Robert Todd Lincoln Collection.
10 Mearns, *op. cit.*, pp. 272–273.
11 *Complete Works*, Vol. VI, pp. 21–22, 39, and 51. Also Mearns, *op. cit.*, pp. 274–275.
12 *New York Tribune*, Oct. 11, 1860.
13 *Ibid.*, Nov. 7, 1860.
14 *Ibid.*, Nov. 10, 1860.
15 *Harper's*, p. 18.
16 *New York Tribune*, Nov. 7, 1860. Dispatch dated "Springfield, Nov. 6, 3:30 P.M."
17 *Ibid.*, Nov. 8, 1860. Dispatch dated "Nov. 7."
18 *Ibid.* Bulletin dated "4:45 A.M."
19 *Ibid.*, Nov. 10, 1860. Dispatch dated "Nov. 6."
20 Mearns, *op. cit.*, p. 223.
21 *New York Tribune*, Nov. 11, 1860. Dispatch dated "Nov. 8."
22 *Ibid.*, Nov. 9, 1860.
23 *Ibid.* Term used by William H. Seward at Rochester, N. Y., Oct., 1858.
24 *New York Herald*, Nov. 8, 1860. Reprinted by *New York Tribune*, Nov. 10, 1860.

370

25 *New York Tribune*, Nov. 19, 1860.
26 *Ibid.*, Nov. 24, 1860.
27 All newspapers quoted were reprinted by the *New York Tribune*, Nov. 10, 15, 16, 17, 20, and 22, 1860.
28 *Richmond* (Va.) *Enquirer.* Reprinted by *New York Tribune*, Nov. 21, 1860.
29 *Harper's*, p. 16.
30 *Ibid.*, p. 22.
31 *American Annual Cyclopaedia* (1862), Vol. I, p. 687.

CHAPTER TEN

1 *Harper's*, pp. 39 and 41.
2 *The Crisis* (Columbus, Ohio), Feb. 7, 1861. The editor claimed the letters were reprinted from "a Lincoln paper." That is doubtful. He probably clipped them from the *Charleston* (S. C.) *Mercury.*
3 *Illinois Daily State Journal* (Springfield), Feb. 8, 1861.
4 *The Crisis*, Feb. 7, 1861.
5 *Ibid.*, Feb. 14, 1861.
6 *Ibid.*
7 Henry Villard, *Memoirs* (1904), Vol. I, p. 91 and footnote.
8 *Ibid.*, pp. 138 and 140.
9 *Ibid.*, p. 140. Villard says the New York *Associated Press* office proposed the Springfield assignment. A footnote explains that rules of the *Associated Press* compelled the *Herald* to share its news dispatches with member papers. Again there is disagreement. The *Herald* boasted that rival newspapers were stealing the Springfield dispatches.
10 *Ibid.*, p. 96.
11 *Ibid.*, p. 134.
12 *Ibid.*, p. 141.
13 *Ibid.*, pp. 142–144.
14 *New York Herald*, Feb. 5, 1861.
15 *Harper's*, p. 45. Also David C. Mearns, *The Lincoln Papers* (1948), Vol. II, pp. 333–457.
16 Villard, *op. cit.*, p. 147.
17 *Complete Works*, Vol. VI, pp. 74–75.
18 Mearns, *op. cit.*, pp. 338–339.
19 *Complete Works*, Vol. VI, pp. 83–84.

20 Mearns, *op. cit.*, pp. 374–375 and 415–417.
21 *Ibid.*, p. 399.
22 *Ibid.*, p. 346.
23 *Complete Works*, Vol. VI, p. 83.
24 *Illinois State Journal*, Dec. 12, 1860. Reprinted in *Complete Works*, Vol. VI, p. 78.
25 *Cincinnati Commercial*, April 2, 1861.
26 *Ibid.*
27 Paul M. Angle, *New Letters and Papers of Lincoln* (1930), pp. 204–205. Also W. E. Barton, *The Life of Abraham Lincoln* (1925), Vol. I, pp. 421–423. Also Albert J. Beveridge, *Abraham Lincoln* (1928), Vol. II, pp. 626–627, and footnote, p. 626.
28 Carl Sandburg, *Abraham Lincoln, The Prairie Years* (1926), Vol. II, p. 419.
29 Beveridge, *op. cit.*, footnote, p. 626.
30 Mearns, *op. cit.*, p. 363.
31 *The Crisis*, Feb. 7, 1861.
32 *Illinois State Journal*, Feb. 6, 1861. Reprinted by *New York Evening Express*, Feb. 11, 1861.
33 *New York Express*, Feb. 11, 1861.
34 *New York Tribune*, Feb. 13, 1861.
35 *Illinois State Journal*, Feb. 7, 1861.
36 *Daily Illinois State Register* (Springfield), Feb. 11, 1861.
37 *Charleston* (S. C.) *Courier*, Feb. 12, 1861. Quoted by *Harper's*, p. 32.
38 *Illinois State Journal*, Feb. 12, 1861.
39 *Illinois State Register*, Feb. 12, 1861.

CHAPTER ELEVEN

1 Henry Villard, *Memoirs* (1904), Vol. I, p. 149.
2 This is the text of the address filed by Villard for the *New York Herald* and shared with *Associated Press* newspapers. It was taken from the *New York Tribune*, Feb. 12, 1861. It checks word for word with Villard's own version as reprinted in his *Memoirs.*
3 *New York Tribune*, Feb. 12, 1861. Villard's *Associated Press* dispatch.
4 Villard, *op. cit.*, p. 149.
5 *Ibid.*, p. 150.

6 *New York Herald,* Feb. 12, 1861.
7 *New York Tribune,* Feb. 12, 1861.
8 *Harper's,* p. 45.
9 William Dean Howells, *Years of My Youth* (1916), pp. 193–194.
10 *Ibid.,* p. 236.
11 *Ibid.,* pp. 211–212.
12 *The World* (New York), Feb. 19, 1861. Story datelined, "Buffalo, Feb. 16, 1861."
13 William H. Herndon and Jesse W. Weik, *Abraham Lincoln* (1923), Vol. II, pp. 197–198.
14 *The World,* Feb. 19, 1861. Story datelined, "Buffalo, Feb. 16, 1861."
15 David C. Mearns, *The Lincoln Papers* (1948), Vol. I, p. 291.
16 The story of the dinner was in the *Illinois Daily State Journal* on Feb. 12, 1861. The apology was published the next day.
17 *The World,* Feb. 19, 1861.
18 New York newspapers of Feb. 21, 1861.
19 *New York Tribune,* Feb. 22, 1861.
20 Villard, *op. cit.,* p. 152.
21 Mearns, *op. cit.,* Vol. II, pp. 430–433.
22 *Ibid.,* pp. 434–435.
23 *Ibid.,* pp. 442–443.
24 *Complete Works,* Vol. VI, pp. 156–158.
25 *New York Tribune,* Feb. 23, 1861. Story datelined, "Baltimore, Feb. 22, 1861." Also *Harper's,* p. 46. Files of the Baltimore *Daily Republican* were reported missing when research on this subject was done.
26 Allen Thorndike Rice, editor, *Reminiscences of Abraham Lincoln* (1886), pp. 37–39.
27 *Ibid.*
28 *Cincinnati Commercial,* Feb. 25, 1861. Correspondence from Washington, Feb. 23, 1861.
29 *The Sun* (Baltimore, Md.). Reprinted by *The World,* Feb. 27, 1861.
30 *New York Tribune,* Feb. 26, 1861. Washington correspondence dated "Feb. 25, 1861."
31 *New York Herald.* Reprinted by *New York Tribune,* Feb. 25, 1861.
32 *New York Times,* Feb. 25, 1861.

p. 1. Also *New York Tribune* with credit "from the *New York Times,*" Feb. 25, 1861.
33 *The Sun,* Feb. 25, 1861.
34 *New York Herald,* Feb. 26, 1861.
35 *Cincinnati Commercial,* Feb. 25, 1861. Statement made in editorial.
36 *The Press* (Philadelphia), Feb. 26, 1861. Reprinted by *The World,* Feb. 27, 1861. Washington correspondence of Feb. 25.
37 *Lafayette* (Ind.) *Journal.* Quoted by *The World,* Feb. 27, 1861.
38 *Syracuse* (N. Y.) *Journal.* Reprinted by *The World,* Feb. 27, 1861.
39 *Louisville* (Ky.) *Courier.* Reprinted by *The Crisis* (Columbus, Ohio), March 7, 1861.
40 *Ibid.*
41 *Appleton's,* Vol. I, pp. 70–71.
42 *Harper's,* p. 61.
43 *Richmond Examiner,* April 23, 1861. Quoted by *Harper's,* p. 109.
44 *Richmond Whig,* April 23, 1861. Quoted by *Harper's,* p. 109.

CHAPTER TWELVE

1 Reprinted by *The Crisis* (Columbus, Ohio), July 2, 1862, from an English magazine.
2 *Commercial Advertiser* (New York). Reprinted by *The Crisis,* Sept. 12, 1861.
3 *Springfield* (Mass.) *Republican.* Reprinted by *The Crisis,* Feb. 26, 1861.
4 *New York Evening Express.* Reprinted by *The Crisis,* May 30, 1861.
5 *Sunday Dispatch* (Philadelphia). Reprinted by *The Crisis,* May 30, 1861.
6 Allen Thorndike Rice, editor, *Reminiscences of Abraham Lincoln* (1886), pp. 217–218.
7 *Ibid.,* p. 223.
8 *Ibid.,* pp. 223–225.
9 *Ibid.,* p. 226.
10 William Dean Howells, *Years of My Youth* (1916), p. 203.
11 Rice, *op. cit.,* pp. 228–229.
12 *Cincinnati Commercial,* April 1, 1861.
13 F. B. Carpenter, *Six Months in the*

*White House with Abraham Lincoln* (1867), pp. 153–154.

14 *Ibid.*
15 *Ibid.*
16 *Ibid.*, p. 49.
17 *Ibid.*, pp. 155–156.
18 *Complete Works*, Vol. IX, pp. 95–102. The letter was in the public press.
19 *London Times*, Sept. 17, 1863. Reprinted by *The Crisis*, Oct. 14, 1863.
20 *London Morning Post.* Reprinted by *The Crisis*, Oct. 5, 1864.
21 *Complete Works*, Vol. X, p. 211
22 *London Morning Post.* Reprinted by *The Crisis*, Oct. 12, 1864.
23 A. T. Andreas, *History of Chicago* (1885), Vol. II, p. 491.
24 *London Times* and *London Daily News.* Quoted by James Ford Rhodes, *History of the United States from the Compromise of 1850* (1904), Vol. III, pp. 504–509.
25 See William S. Walsh, *Abraham Lincoln and the London Punch* (1909).
26 See Rufus Rockwell Wilson, *Lincoln in Caricature* (1945).

CHAPTER THIRTEEN

1 *New York Times*, April 3, 1861.
2 Henry Luther Stoddard, *Horace Greeley, Printer, Editor, Crusader* (1946), pp. 211–212.
3 Don C. Seitz, *Horace Greeley, Founder of the New York Tribune* (1926), p. 200.
4 *New York Herald*, April 10, 1861.
5 *Evening Post* (New York), July 6 and 7, 1861.
6 *Ibid.* Quoted by Frank Luther Mott, *American Journalism* (1941), p. 344.
7 Ralph Ray Fahrney, *Horace Greeley and the Tribune in the Civil War* (1936), p. 2, introduction.
8 James F. Rhodes, *History of the United States from the Compromise of 1850* (1904), Vol. II, p. 72.
9 *New York Tribune*, Nov. 10, 1860.
10 *Ibid.*, Dec. 17, 1860.
11 Robert Todd Lincoln Collection (5258).

12 *New York Tribune*, Feb. 23, 1861.
13 *Ibid.*, April 15, 1861.
14 *Ibid.*, April 22, 1861.
15 Seitz, *op. cit.*, p. 229.
16 *Harper's*, p. 157.
17 *New York Tribune*, July 25, 1861.
18 *Ibid.*
19 Robert Todd Lincoln Collection (10921).
20 Stoddard, *op. cit.*, pp. 215–216. He describes the dramatic reading of the letter. Also see William Alexander Linn, *Horace Greeley, Founder and Editor of the New York Tribune* (1903), pp. 190–192.
21 Lloyd A. Dunlap, "President Lincoln and Editor Greeley," *The Abraham Lincoln Quarterly*, Vol. V (June, 1948), p. 108.
22 *New York Herald*, April 5, 1862. Quoted by Dunlap, *op. cit.*, p. 108.
23 Robert Todd Lincoln Collection (13856).

CHAPTER FOURTEEN

1 *Appleton's*, Vol. III, pp. 79–80.
2 J. Thomas Scharf and Thompson Wescott, *History of Philadelphia* (1884), Vol. III, p. 2007.
3 *Ibid.*, p. 2019.
4 *Ibid.*, p. 2025.
5 *Philadelphia Inquirer*, May 3, 1861.
6 *Ibid.*, July 23, 1861.
7 *Ibid.*, July 1, 1861.
8 *Ibid.*, Aug. 21, 1861.
9 *Daily Evening Bulletin* (Philadelphia), Jan. 8, 1861.
10 *Ibid.*, April 13, 1861.
11 *Ibid.*, April 26, 1861.
12 Scharf and Wescott, *op. cit.*, Vol. I, p. 753.
13 *Daily Evening Bulletin*, April 29, 1861.
14 Scharf and Wescott, *op. cit.*, Vol. III, p. 2031.
15 *Christian Observer* (Philadelphia). Reprinted by *Philadelphia Inquirer*, Aug. 23, 1861.
16 Scharf and Wescott, *op. cit.*, Vol. I, p. 777.
17 *Appleton's*, Vol. I, p. 711.
18 John W. Forney, *Anecdotes of Public Men* (1874), Vol. I, p. 374.

19 From history of *The Press* as published in that newspaper when Forney sold it in 1877. Quoted by Scharf and Wescott, *op. cit.*, Vol. III, p. 2026.

20 Scharf and Wescott, *op. cit.*, Vol. III, p. 2027.

21 Elwyn Burns Robinson, "The Press: President Lincoln's Philadelphia Organ," *The Pennsylvania Magazine of History and Biography*, Vol. LXV (1941), p. 158. This is a fully annotated history of *The Press*.

22 *The Press* (Philadelphia), March 5, 1861.

23 Forney, *op. cit.*, p. 167.

24 Robinson, *op. cit.*, pp. 163–164. He cites Cameron Mss.

25 *Ibid.*, footnote, p. 160.

26 *Ibid.*, pp. 161–167.

27 *The Press*, May 20, 1862.

28 *American Annual Cyclopaedia* (1862), Vol. I, p. 329.

29 Ray H. Abrams, "The Jeffersonian, Copperhead Newspaper," *The Pennsylvania Magazine of History and Biography*, Vol. LVII (1933), p. 260. *The History of Chester County* (1881), by J. Smith Futhey and Gilbert Cope, also gives a full account of *The Jeffersonian*.

30 *Philadelphia Inquirer*, Aug. 24, 1861.

31 Abrams, *op. cit.*, p. 272.

32 *Ibid.*, p. 277.

33 *The World* (New York). Quoted by Abrams, *op. cit.*, p. 275.

34 The writer acknowledges the assistance of Dr. Hans Sperber, professor in the language department of the Ohio State University.

CHAPTER FIFTEEN

1 *American Annual Cyclopaedia* (1862), Vol. I, p. 329.

2 *Ibid.*

3 Allan Nevins, *The Evening Post* (1922), pp. 301–302.

4 *American Annual Cyclopaedia* (1862), Vol. I, p. 480.

5 Frank Luther Mott, *American Journalism* (1941), p. 358.

6 *American Annual Cyclopaedia* (1862), Vol. I, p. 329.

7 *New York Herald*, Sept. 17, 1861. Also *The Crisis* (Columbus, Ohio), Sept. 16, 1863. *Appleton's*, Vol. IV, p. 148, says McMaster was in prison eleven months. There is a discrepancy here because the biographer says McMaster resumed publication of his paper April 19, 1862. *The Crisis* is the accepted authority.

8 *The Crisis*, Oct. 3, 1861.

9 *Appleton's*, Vol. VI, p. 148.

10 *New York Daily News*, June 11 and 28, 1861. Cited by Mott, *op. cit.*, p. 353.

11 *New York Day Book*, Aug. 28, 1861.

12 Mott, *op. cit.*, p. 353.

13 *New York Daily News*. Reprinted by *The Crisis*, July 8, 1863.

14 *New York Daily News*, May 23, 1864.

15 *Ibid*. Reprinted by *The Crisis*, May 18, 1864.

16 *Ibid.*, Feb. 17, 1864.

17 *The Union* (Somerset, Ohio). Reprinted by *The Crisis*, March 23, 1864.

18 Mott, *op. cit.*, p. 353.

19 *New York Daily News*. Reprinted by *The Crisis*, July 27, 1864.

20 The *New York Daily News* quit in 1906. The present paper of the same name is no blood relation to the one that made Benjamin Wood notorious and wealthy.

21 Mott, *op. cit.*, p. 354.

22 *New York Day Book*, April 4, 1861.

23 *The Sun* (Baltimore), Feb. 20, 1861.

24 *New York Day Book*, April 6, 1861.

25 *Evening Post* (New York), April 12, 1861. Reprinted by *New York Day Book*, April 13, 1861.

26 *New York Day Book*, April 13, 1861.

27 *New York Herald*. Reprinted by *New York Day Book*, Aug. 25, 1861.

28 *New York Day Book*, Aug. 27, 1861.

29 Mott, *op. cit.*, p. 354.

30 *Ohio State Journal* (Columbus), Sept. 5, 1861. The writer has no further information on Reeve.

31 *Brooklyn* (N. Y.) *Daily Eagle*, July 8, 1864.

32  *Spirit of the Times* (New York). Reprinted by *The Crisis*, Feb. 24, 1864.

33  *The Crisis*, Aug. 31, 1864.

34  *Spirit of the Times*. Reprinted by *The Crisis*, May 18, 1864.

35  *The True American* (Trenton, N. J.). Reprinted by *The Crisis*, Aug. 29, 1861. Story datelined "Aug. 24, 1861."

36  *New York Tribune*. Reprinted by *The Crisis*, Aug. 29, 1861.

37  *The Crisis*, Sept. 19, 1861.

38  *American Annual Cyclopaedia* (1862), Vol. I, p. 361.

39  *The Crisis*, Oct. 3, 1861.

40  *Ibid.*, Nov. 25, 1861.

41  *American Annual Cyclopaedia* (1862), Vol. I, pp. 329-330.

42  *Evening Journal* (Newark, N. J.). Reprinted by *The Crisis*, June 6, 1861.

43  *American Annual Cyclopaedia* (1865), Vol. IV, p. 422.

44  *Evening Journal*. Reprinted by *Illinois Daily State Journal* (Springfield), July 30, 1864.

45  *American Annual Cyclopaedia* (1865), Vol. IV, p. 422.

46  *Evening Journal*. Reprinted by *The Crisis*, Aug. 10, 1864.

47  *New York Tribune*, July 23, 1864.

48  *American Annual Cyclopaedia* (1865), Vol. IV, p. 422.

49  *The Crisis*, March 15, 1865.

50  *Ibid.*, March 8 and 15, 1865.

51  *Ibid.*, March 8, 1865.

52  *Evening Post*, May 20, 1863. Quoted by Allan Nevins, *American Press Opinion* (1928), pp. 277-280. Also by Nevins, *The Evening Post*, p. 302.

53  *The Crisis*, Sept. 12, 1861.

54  *Cincinnati Enquirer*, Oct. 6, 1864. A purported roundup of governmental, military, and civilian action against the press, all incidents blamed on "A. L." First published by New York *Journal of Commerce*. Erroneous and misleading. Used here as authority when checked elsewhere.

55  *New York Times*, March 25, 1862. Reprinted by *Cincinnati Enquirer*, Oct. 6, 1864.

CHAPTER SIXTEEN

1  *Harper's*, p. 165.

2  *Appleton's*, Vol. I, p. 144.

3  Allen Thorndike Rice, editor, *Reminiscences of Abraham Lincoln* (1886), pp. 171-173.

4  *Cincinnati Enquirer*, Sept. 17, 1861.

5  Rice, *op. cit.*, p. 590.

6  *Philadelphia Inquirer*, March 21, 1862. The paper carried a lengthy report with detailed testimony of the investigation, starting on page one.

7  *American Annual Cyclopaedia* (1863), Vol. II, pp. 480-481.

8  *Ibid.*, p. 509, and *New York Tribune*, June 9, 1862.

9  Rice, *op. cit.*, p. 227.

10  Don C. Seitz, *Lincoln the Politician* (1931), p. 374.

11  Noah Brooks, *Washington in Lincoln's Time* (1896), pp. 61-62.

12  *The Crisis* (Columbus, Ohio), Sept. 24, 1862.

13  *Complete Works*, Vol. IX, pp. 100-101.

14  *Ibid.*, in footnote, p. 95.

15  Brooks, *op. cit.*, pp. 62-63.

16  *Complete Works*, Vol. IX, p. 109.

17  James G. Randall, "The Newspaper Problem in its Bearing Upon Military Secrecy During the Civil War," *The American Historical Review*, Vol. XXIII (1918), pp. 303 and 308.

18  *American Annual Cyclopaedia* (1864), Vol. III, p. 425.

19  Randall, *op. cit.*, p. 310.

20  *Ibid.*, p. 487.

21  *Ibid.*, p. 312.

22  *Ibid.*, pp. 310-311.

23  *Ibid.*, p. 311.

24  *Ibid.*, pp. 312-313.

25  F. Lauriston Bullard, *Famous War Correspondents* (1914), pp. 402-406.

26  Randall, *op. cit.*, p. 313. He says no arrests appear to have been made. The writer states his case in the text.

27  Bullard, *op. cit.*, pp. 406-408.

28  *Springfield* (Mass.) *Republican*. Reprinted by *Cincinnati Gazette*, Nov. 28, 1864.

29  *Cincinnati Gazette*, Nov. 30, 1864.

30 *Appleton's*, Vol. V, pp. 90 and 131.
31 *Cincinnati Gazette*, Dec. 1, 1864.
32 *The Crisis*, Feb. 22, 1865.
33 James E. Pollard, *The Presidents and the Press* (1947), p. 367. He cites Ward H. Lamon, *Recollections of Abraham Lincoln*, pp. 224-225.
34 U. S. Grant, *Personal Memoirs* (1886), Vol. II, pp. 143-145.
35 *Appleton's*, Vol. VI, p. 13.
36 Grant, *op. cit.*, pp. 144-145.

CHAPTER SEVENTEEN

1 Lucy Lucile Tasher, "The Missouri Democrat and the Civil War," *Missouri Historical Review*, Vol. XXXI (1937), p. 402.
2 *Missouri Democrat* (St. Louis), Aug. 27, 1858. Cited by Tasher, *op. cit.*, p. 403.
3 *Ibid.*, May 19, 1860. Cited by Tasher, *op. cit.*, p. 403.
4 *Ibid.*, July 26, 1861, and Aug. 31, 1861. Cited by Tasher, *op. cit.*, p. 406.
5 *Appleton's*, Vol. II, p. 547.
6 Tasher, *op. cit.*, p. 406, cites Nathaniel Wright Stephenson, *Lincoln and the Union*, p. 196.
7 *Missouri Democrat*, Sept. and Oct. issues, 1861. Cited by Tasher, *op. cit.*, p. 407.
8 *Harper's*, p. 176.
9 *Ibid.*, footnote.
10 *American Annual Cyclopaedia* (1862), Vol. I, pp. 328-329.
11 *Ohio State Journal* (Columbus), Aug. 29, 1861.
12 *Cincinnati Gazette*, Aug. 22, 1861.
13 *Ibid.*, Sept. 19, 1861. Wire story of Sept. 17, 1861.
14 *Missouri Democrat*. Reprinted by *Cincinnati Gazette*, Sept. 3, 1861.
15 *St. Louis* (Mo.) *News*. Reprinted by *Cincinnati Gazette*, Sept. 3, 1861.
16 *Missouri Republican* (St. Louis). Reprinted by *Cincinnati Gazette*, Sept. 3, 1861.
17 *Cincinnati Gazette*, Sept. 3, 1861. Louisville, Ky., wire story.
18 *Ibid.*, Sept. 17, 1861. Wire story of Sept. 16, 1861. Also Philip Kinsley, *The Chicago Tribune* (1943), Vol. I, pp. 203-204.

19 *St. Louis News*. Reprinted by *Cincinnati Gazette*, Sept. 26, 1861.
20 *Cincinnati Gazette*, Sept. 25, 1861.
21 *Ibid.*, Oct. 18, 1861. *Cincinnati Enquirer*, Oct. 6, 1864, says the Reverend Mr. McAnally was arrested again on April 20, 1862, and sent to Old Capitol prison, Washington.
22 *The Crisis* (Columbus, Ohio), June 20, 1861, and July 18, 1861.
23 *Cincinnati Gazette*, September 19, 1861.
24 Tasher, *op. cit.*, p. 408.
25 *Dictionary of American Biography* (1929), Vol. III, p. 105.
26 *Appleton's*, Vol. III, pp. 49-50.
27 *Missouri Democrat*, June 27, 1863, and *Complete Works*, Vol. VIII, pp. 282-283.
28 *Missouri Republican*, July 14, 1863. Reprinted by *Cincinnati Enquirer*, July 15, 1863.
29 *Missouri Democrat*, July 11, 1863. Reprinted by *Cincinnati Enquirer*, July 13, 1863.
30 *Missouri Republican*, July 14, 1863. Reprinted by *Cincinnati Enquirer*, July 15, 1863.
31 *Missouri Democrat*. Reprinted by *Cincinnati Enquirer*, July 23, 1863.
32 *Complete Works*, Vol. IX, p. 27.
33 *Ibid.*, pp. 36-37.
34 *Missouri Democrat*, Feb. 3, 1864. Cited by Tasher, *op. cit.*, p. 409.
35 *Missouri Republican*, Feb. 5, 1864. Quoted by Tasher, *op. cit.*, p. 409.
36 *Missouri Democrat*. Cited by Tasher, *op. cit.*, p. 410.
37 *Cincinnati Enquirer*, Oct. 6, 1864.
38 *Appleton's*, Vol. V, p. 325.
39 *Chicago Times*. Reprinted by *The Crisis*, April 8, 1863.
40 *The Crisis*, May 13, 1863.
41 *Ibid.*, Nov. 12, 1862.
42 *Missouri Democrat*. Reprinted by *Cincinnati Enquirer*, July 18, 1863.
43 *Cincinnati Enquirer*, Oct. 6, 1864.
44 James G. Randall, *Constitutional Problems Under Lincoln* (1926), p. 491.
45 *Cincinnati Enquirer*, Oct. 6, 1864.
46 *St. Louis News*. Reprinted by *Illinois State Journal* (Springfield), Aug. 21, 1862.

47  *Dubuque* (Iowa) *Herald*, Aug. 15, 1862.
48  *Ibid.*
49  John A. Marshall, *American Bastile* (1874), p. 405.
50  *Ibid.*, p. 406.
51  *Ibid.*, p. 407.
52  *Ibid.*, pp. 407–408.
53  *Burlington* (Iowa) *Argus*. Reprinted by *The Crisis*, Sept. 10, 1862.
54  *Ibid.*, Sept. 16, 1862.
55  *Dubuque Herald*. Reprinted by *The Crisis*, Nov. 5, 1862.
56  Marshall, *op. cit.*, p. 409. Also Franc B. Wilkie, *Pen and Powder* (1888), pp. 9–10.
57  *Ibid.*, p. 415.
58  *The Crisis*, Nov. 26, 1862.
59  Wilkie, *op. cit.*, pp. 9–10.
60  *Dubuque Herald*. Reprinted by *Davenport* (Iowa) *Daily Gazette*, Jan. 10, 1863. Quoted by Wood Gray, *The Hidden Civil War* (1942), p. 122.
61  *Ibid.*, March 7, 1863. Quoted by Gray, *op. cit.*, references, Chap. VI, p. 252.
62  *Burlington* (Iowa) *Hawkeye*. Quoted by Gray, *op. cit.*, p. 68.
63  *The Crisis*, Feb. 17, 1864.
64  *Chicago Tribune*. Reprinted by *The Crisis*, March 11, 1863.
65  *Daily Press* (Kansas City). Reprinted by *The Crisis*, Oct. 17, 1862.
66  George E. Dummer in letter to Samuel Medary, editor of *The Crisis*. Published in *The Crisis*, April 9, 1862. Dummer wrote he planned to continue publication.
67  *Leavenworth* (Kan.) *Times*, Aug. 29, 1863. Reprinted by *Cincinnati Enquirer*, Sept. 3, 1863. Also *Illinois State Journal*, Aug. 31, 1863.
68  *The Age* (Philadelphia). Reprinted by *The Crisis*, June 3, 1863. The newspaper did not explain where the Mayor obtained his extraordinary authority.
69  This writer has no information as to whether Editor Anthony and Mayor Anthony were the same person. The Leavenworth postmaster at that time also was named Anthony.

70  *Cincinnati Enquirer*, Oct. 6, 1864.
71  *Leavenworth Times*. Reprinted by *The Crisis*, July 1, 1863.

CHAPTER EIGHTEEN

1   J. Thomas Scharf, *The Chronicles of Baltimore* (1874), pp. 587–594, gives a detailed account of the riot.
2   *Ibid.*, pp. 600–601.
3   Sidney T. Matthews, "Control of the Baltimore Press During the Civil War," *Maryland Historical Magazine*, Vol. XXXVI (June, 1941), pp. 150–170. A valuable study of the Baltimore press achieved by minute research.
4   *Baltimore American*, Jan. 3, 1860.
5   *Ibid.*, May 19, 1860.
6   *Ibid.*, June 25, 1860.
7   *Ibid.*, Oct. 30, 1860.
8   *Ibid.*, Nov. 19, 1860.
9   *Ibid.*, March 5, 1860.
10  *Ibid.*, July 22, 1861.
11  Richard Henry Spencer, editor, *Encyclopaedia of the State of Maryland* (1919), pp. 1–12.
12  Frank Luther Mott, *American Journalism* (1941), p. 360.
13  Scharf, *op. cit.*, pp. 622–624.
14  Spencer, *op. cit.*, pp. 1–12.
15  Text of telegram and other correspondence in case published in *Baltimore American* on Tuesday, July 1, 1862, and other newspapers of like date. Scharf also gives the correspondence, *op. cit.*, pp. 624–625, source not stated, probably the *American*.
16  *The World* (New York). Reprinted by *Baltimore American*, July 3, 1862.
17  *Appleton's*, Vol. IV, p. 82.
18  *Daily Exchange* (Baltimore), April 15, 1861.
19  *The South* (Baltimore). Quoted by Matthews, *op. cit.*
20  Matthews, *op. cit.*
21  *Daily Exchange*, Sept. 11, 1861.
22  Matthews explains that, although Secretary of War Simon Cameron ordered the arrests, the cases were placed under jurisdiction of the State Department and Hall and Howard had the distinction of be-

ing "prisoners of state." Their cases were handled by the State Department until Feb. 15, 1862, when they were transferred to jurisdiction of the War Department.

23 Scharf, *op. cit.*, p. 616.
24 Matthews, *op. cit.*
25 Scharf, *op. cit.*, p. 621.
26 Matthews, *op. cit.*
27 Scharf, *op. cit.*, p. 624.
28 *Baltimore American*, Aug. 22 and Sept. 18, 1862.
29 Scharf, *op. cit.*, p. 628.
30 *Ibid.*
31 *Ohio State Journal* (Columbus), Feb. 11, 1864.
32 *Baltimore American* and *The Sun* (Baltimore), Oct. 5, 1863.
33 Matthews, *op. cit.*
34 *Daily Gazette* (Baltimore), Nov. 11, 1863.
35 Scharf, *op. cit.*, pp. 628–629, and Matthews, *op. cit.*
36 *Baltimore American*, May 19, 1864, and Matthews, *op. cit.*
37 Matthews, *op. cit.*
38 Scharf, *op. cit.*, p. 631.
39 *Ibid.*, p. 632.
40 Matthews, *op. cit.*
41 *The Crisis* (Columbus, Ohio), April 20 and 27 and May 4, 1864. The Union List of Newspapers does not include the *Gazette*. The name probably disguised the old *Beacon*, silenced in May of 1863.
42 *Ohio State Journal*, Aug. 31, 1861.
43 *The Crisis*, Sept. 28, 1864.
44 T. J. C. Williams, *History of Frederick County, Maryland* (1910), Vol. I, pp. 251–252.
45 *Ibid.*, p. 250.
46 *Cincinnati Enquirer*, Oct 6, 1864.
47 *New York Tribune*, Aug. 25, 1861.

CHAPTER NINETEEN

1 *Complete Works*, Vol. VII, p. 119.
2 *Philadelphia Inquirer*, March 17, 1862.
3 *Ibid.*, Aug. 4, 1861.
4 W. G. Brownlow, *Sketches of the Rise, Progress, and Decline of Secession; With a Narrative of Personal Adventures Among the Rebels*

(1862), pp. 195–206. Hereafter referred to as Brownlow.
5 *Ibid.*, pp. 81–88.
6 *Appleton's*, Vol. V, pp. 229–230.
7 *Knoxville* (Tenn.) *Whig*. Quoted by Brownlow, p. 92.
8 *Ibid.*, May 14, 1861. Quoted by Brownlow, p. 108.
9 Brownlow, pp. 208–209.
10 *Knoxville Whig*, May 18, 1861. Quoted by Brownlow, pp. 110–111.
11 *Ibid.*, July 6, 1861. Quoted by Brownlow, p. 150.
12 *Washington* (D. C.) *Republican*. Reprinted by *Philadelphia Inquirer*, Aug. 22, 1861.
13 *Knoxville Whig*, Oct. 12 and 19, 1861. Quoted by Brownlow, p. 246.
14 Editorial quoted by Brownlow, pp. 249–255.
15 Brownlow, pp. 280–283.
16 *Ibid.*, p. 269. Brownlow says this letter was found in a mass of correspondence recovered in General F. K. Zollicoffer's camp after his army was routed.
17 *Ibid.*, p. 283.
18 *Ibid.*, pp. 293–294.
19 *Ibid.*, pp. 294–302.
20 *Ibid.*, p. 318.
21 *Ibid.*, pp. 330–337. *Appleton's*, Vol. I, p. 235, says Judah P. Benjamin entered Yale in 1825 but left three years later without a degree.
22 *Ibid.*, pp. 339–340.
23 *Knoxville* (Tenn.) *Register*. Quoted by Brownlow, pp. 342–345.
24 *Columbus* (Ga.) *Times*. Quoted by Brownlow, pp. 347–348.
25 *Nashville* (Tenn.) *Patriot*, Feb. 1, 1862. Quoted by Brownlow, p. 350.
26 *Richmond* (Va.) *Examiner*, Feb. 21, 1862. Quoted by Brownlow, p. 351.
27 Brownlow, pp. 370–371.
28 *Ibid.*, pp. 380–389. See Henry B. Rankin, *Intimate Character Sketches of Abraham Lincoln* (1924), for Brownlow statement.
29 Oliver P. Temple, *Notable Men of Tennessee* (1912), p. 315.
30 See newspapers of cities mentioned April 5 through 22, 1862.
31 Brownlow, pp. 436–447.

32 *Ibid.*, p. 438.
33 *Appleton's*, Vol. I, pp. 415–416.

CHAPTER TWENTY

1 *New York Tribune*, Aug. 20, 1862.
2 Allen Thorndike Rice, editor, *Reminiscences of Abraham Lincoln* (1886), footnote, pp. 525–526.
3 *National Intelligencer* (Washington, D. C.), Aug. 23, 1862.
4 *Ibid.*
5 *New York Tribune*, Aug. 25, 1862.
6 *New York Times*, Aug. 23, 1862. Quoted by Henry Luther Stoddard, *Horace Greeley, Printer, Editor, Crusader* (1946), p. 222.
7 James R. Gilmore, *Personal Recollections of Abraham Lincoln and the Civil War* (1898), pp. 75–76.
8 *The Press* (Philadelphia), July 30, 1862. Cited by Elwin Burns Robinson, "The Press: President Lincoln's Philadelphia Organ," *The Pennsylvania Magazine of History and Biography*, Vol. LXV (1941), pp. 157–170.
9 Rice, *op. cit.*, pp. 526–527.
10 *Harper's*, p. 207.
11 *Ibid.*, p. 208.
12 *New York Herald*, Sept. 27, 1862.
13 *The World* (New York), Sept. 24, 1862.
14 *New York Tribune*, Sept. 23, 1862.
15 *Chicago Tribune*, Sept. 24, 1862. Quoted by Philip Kinsley, *The Chicago Tribune* (1943), Vol. I, p. 252.
16 *National Intelligencer*, Sept. 23, 1862.
17 *Ibid.*, Oct. 31, 1862.
18 *Harper's*, p. 208.
19 *The Crisis* (Columbus, Ohio), Oct. 29, 1862.
20 *London Times*, Oct. 21, 1862. Reprinted by *The Crisis*, Nov. 26, 1862.
21 *Cincinnati Commercial*, April 4, 1862.
22 *Springfield* (Mass.) *Republican*. Reprinted by *Cincinnati Gazette*, Nov. 29, 1862. F. B. Carpenter, *Six Months in the White House with Abraham Lincoln* (1867), p. 230, tells a similar story, saying the

editorials were sent by Henry Ward Beecher, the Abolitionist, editor of the New York *Independent*.
23 *Harper's*, p. 208.

CHAPTER TWENTY-ONE

1 *Harper's*, II, footnote, p. 405.
2 *Chicago Tribune*, Sept. 20, 1862. Quoted by Philip Kinsley, *The Chicago Tribune* (1943), Vol. I, p. 252.
3 *Harper's*, II, footnote, p. 405.
4 *Dictionary of American Biography* (1931), Vol. VI, p. 527. The biographer is Roy F. Nichols.
5 John W. Forney, *Anecdotes of Public Men* (1874), Vol. I, p. 382.
6 *Ibid.*, p. 383.
7 *Philadelphia Inquirer*, March 18, 1862.
8 John Russell Young, *Men and Memories* (1901), Vol. I, p. 54.
9 *Ibid.*, pp. 57–58.
10 Noah Brooks, *Washington in Lincoln's Time* (1896), p. 299.
11 *Daily Morning Chronicle* (Washington, D. C.), Dec. 7, 1864.
12 *National Intelligencer* (Washington, D. C.), March 5, 1861.
13 *Ibid.*, April 13, 1861.
14 *Ibid.*, Sept. 29, 1864.
15 *Daily Morning Chronicle*, Sept. 20, 1864.
16 *Ibid.*, Oct. 1, 1864.
17 *Ibid.*, Oct. 6, 1864.
18 *National Intelligencer*, Jan. 1, 1865.
19 *Ibid.*, March 4, 1865.
20 *Ibid.*, March 6, 1865.
21 *Cincinnati* (Ohio) *Gazette*. Reprinted by *National Intelligencer*, March 6, 1865.
22 Scores of letters of this description are in the Robert Todd Lincoln Collection.
23 Brooks, *op. cit.*, p. 300.
24 Robert Todd Lincoln Collection (40032).
25 *Ibid.* (37267).
26 *Ibid.* (30176).
27 *Ibid.* (30079).
28 *New York Tribune*, Oct. 31, 1862. Washington correspondence, Oct. 30.

29 *Daily Morning Chronicle*, April 21, 1865.

30 Allen Thorndike Rice, editor, *Reminiscences of Abraham Lincoln* (1886), p. 185.

31 Osman C. Hooper, *History of Journalism in Ohio* (1933), pp. 159–161.

32 Rice, *op. cit.*, pp. 447–449.

33 Brooks, *op. cit.*, p. 109.

CHAPTER TWENTY-TWO

1 *Providence* (R. I.) *Post*, Dec. 1, 1862. Reprinted by *The Crisis* (Columbus, Ohio), Dec. 10, 1862.

2 *Portland* (Me.) *Advertiser.* Reprinted by *The Crisis*, Aug. 26, 1863.

3 *American Annual Cyclopaedia* (1862), Vol. I, p. 328.

4 *Boston Journal.* Reprinted by *Philadelphia Inquirer*, Aug. 12, 1861.

5 *The Crisis*, Oct. 3, 1861.

6 *Whig and Courier* (Bangor, Me.). Reprinted by *Philadelphia Inquirer*, Aug. 16, 1864.

7 *Democrat* (Bangor, Me.). Reprinted by *The Crisis*, May 2, 1861.

8 *Ibid.*, May 13, 1863.

9 *New York Day Book*, Aug. 21, 1861. Also *Philadelphia Inquirer*, Aug. 21, 1861.

10 *Advertiser and Farmer* (Bridgeport, Conn.). Reprinted by *The Crisis*, July 4, 1861.

11 *New York Day Book*, Aug. 26, 1861. Also *New York Tribune* as reprinted in *The Crisis*, Aug. 29, 1861.

12 *Boston Daily Evening Transcript*, March 5, 1861.

13 *Ibid.*

14 *Providence* (R. I.) *Journal.* Reprinted by *Boston Transcript*, March 5, 1861.

15 *Boston Post.* Reprinted by *The Crisis*, Jan. 29, 1862.

16 *Ibid.*, May 28, 1862.

17 *Boston Herald.* Reprinted by *The Crisis*, Jan. 29, 1862.

18 *Boston Courier.* Reprinted by *Boston Transcript*, Nov. 9, 1864.

19 *Boston Pioneer.* Reprinted by *Ohio*

20 *Statesman* (Columbus), March 10, 1864.

20 *Springfield* (Mass.) *Republican.* Quoted by Richard Hooker, *The Story of an Independent Newspaper* (1924), p. 86.

21 *Ibid.*, Nov. 15, 1860. Quoted by Hooker, *op. cit.*, p. 90.

22 George S. Merriam, *The Life and Times of Samuel Bowles* (1885), Vol. I, p. 318.

23 *Springfield Republican*, July 9, 1861. Quoted by Hooker, *op. cit.*, pp. 90–91.

24 Willard Grosvenor Bleyer, *Main Currents in the History of Journalism* (1927), p. 261.

25 Hooker, *op. cit.*, p. 88.

26 *Springfield Republican.* Quoted by Hooker, *op. cit.*, p. 98.

27 *Appleton's*, Vol. II, pp. 610–612.

28 *Ibid.*, Vol. I, p. 233.

29 *Dictionary of American Biography* (1931), Vol. VI, p. 485. Also James O. Lyford, editor, *History of Concord, New Hampshire* (1903), Vol. II, pp. 1016–1045.

30 *Appleton's*, Vol. III, p. 123.

31 *American Annual Cyclopaedia* (1865), Vol. IV, p. 422. The writer has no further information on this case.

32 *Portsmouth* (N. H.) *Chronicle.* Reprinted by *Daily Morning Chronicle* (Washington, D. C.), April 15, 1865.

33 *New York Tribune*, Dec. 21, 1861.

34 *Ibid.*, July 30, 1862.

CHAPTER TWENTY-THREE

1 *Appleton's*, Vol. VI, p. 227.

2 *Ibid.*

3 *The Sun* (New York). Reprinted by *State Capital Fact* (Columbus, Ohio), July 9, 1861.

4 *Appleton's*, Vol. VI, p. 227.

5 *Dayton* (Ohio) *Daily Empire.* Reprinted by *The Crisis* (Columbus, Ohio), April 18, 1861.

6 *The Crisis*, Nov. 26, 1862.

7 *Ibid.*, Nov. 5, 1862.

8 *Cincinnati Enquirer*, Nov. 3, 1862.

9 *Ibid.*, Nov. 2, 1862.

10  *The Crisis,* Nov. 26, 1862.
11  *Ibid.,* Oct. 7, 1863.
12  *Appleton's,* Vol. VI, p. 227.
13  *Clermont County Sun* (Batavia, Ohio). Quoted by *The Crisis,* Aug. 26, 1861.
14  *The Crisis,* Aug. 29, 1861.
15  *Ibid.,* Sept. 12, 1861.
16  *Stark County Democrat* (Canton, Ohio). Reprinted by *The Crisis,* Oct. 22, 1862.
17  *The Crisis,* Oct. 22 and 29, 1862.
18  *Ibid.,* Nov. 26, 1862.
19  *Ibid.,* Sept. 19, 1861.
20  *Ibid.,* Sept. 12, 1861.
21  *Ibid.,* Sept. 19, 1861.
22  *The Banner of Reunion* (Cincinnati, Ohio). Quoted by *Cincinnati Press.* Reprinted by *The Crisis,* Sept. 19, 1861.
23  *Cincinnati Enquirer,* Oct. 6, 1864.
24  *Ohio Patriot* (New Lisbon). Reprinted by *The Crisis,* July 9, 1862.
25  *The Crisis,* July 2 and 9, 1862.
26  *Ibid.,* July 9, 1862.
27  *Ibid.* A letter written by Joseph Olds to his father.
28  *Cincinnati Commercial,* Aug. 13, 1862.
29  *Ibid.*
30  *The Crisis,* Aug. 20, 1862.
31  *Ibid.,* Aug. 13, 1862.
32  *Ibid.,* Dec. 10, 1862.
33  The Governor's letter was published by the Lancaster *Ohio Eagle.* Reprinted by *The Crisis,* Sept. 10, 1862.
34  *Ohio Eagle.* Reprinted by *The Crisis,* Sept. 10, 1862. Governor Tod's statements in the interview were published in the *Ohio Eagle* and sworn to be true in an affidavit signed by two men present, Sheriff James Miller of Fairfield County (Ohio) and Tall Slough.
35  *Complete Works,* Vol. VIII, p. 326.
36  *Ibid.,* Vol. X, pp. 140–141.
37  *The Crisis,* Dec. 3, 1862.
38  *Ibid.,* Feb. 3, 1864.
39  *Ibid.,* Dec. 3 and 31, 1862.
40  *Ohio State Journal* (Columbus), Oct. 29, 1863.
41  *Dayton Empire.* Reprinted by *The Crisis,* Aug. 20, 1862.

42  *The Crisis,* April 1, 1863.
43  *Cincinnati Enquirer.* Reprinted by *The Crisis,* Aug. 28, 1863.
44  *Ibid.,* Oct. 6, 1864.
45  *The Crisis,* Feb. 10, 1864. It is probable Webb sent Medary a copy of the "extra."
46  *Ibid.*
47  *Toledo* (Ohio) *Commercial.* Quoted by *The Crisis,* March 9, 1864.
48  *The Crisis,* Feb. 24, 1864.
49  *Boston Courier.* Reprinted by *The Crisis,* Feb. 24, 1864.
50  *The Crisis,* March 9, 1864.
51  *Ibid.,* April 27, 1864. Letter to Medary from M. P. Bean.
52  *True Telegraph* (Hamilton, Ohio), July 21, 1864.
53  *Cincinnati Enquirer,* Nov. 15, 1864.
54  *True Telegraph,* Nov. 17, 1864. The writer has no further information on this case.
55  Edwin C. Taylor, "Whitelaw Reid in Columbus," *Ohio Archaeological and Historical Publication,* Vol. XVIII (1909), pp. 513–514.
56  Archer H. Shaw, *The Plain Dealer* (1942), p. 79.
57  *Ibid.,* pp. 135–140.
58  *Ibid.,* pp. 140–141.
59  *Cleveland* (Ohio) *Leader,* Oct. 21, 1862.
60  *Cleveland* (Ohio) *Plain Dealer,* July 23, 1864.
61  Shaw, *op. cit.,* p. 153.
62  *Ibid.,* p. 155.
63  Eugene H. Roseboom, *The History of the State of Ohio,* Vol. IV, "Civil War Era: 1850–1873" (1944), p. 337.
64  *Ibid.,* p. 409.
65  *The Crisis,* April 22, 1863.
66  *Cincinnati Gazette,* March 4, 1863.
67  *Ibid.,* March 18, 1863.
68  *Ibid.*
69  *Indianapolis* (Ind.) *Daily State Sentinel,* March 17, 1863.
70  *Ibid.,* March 19, 1863.
71  *Cincinnati Gazette,* March 19, 1863.
72  *Ibid.,* March 20, 1863.
73  *Ohio State Journal,* March 23, 1863.
74  *Jackson* (Ohio) *Express.* Reprinted by *The Crisis,* Aug. 5, 1863.

CHAPTER TWENTY-FOUR

1 *Harper's*, pp. 322–324.
2 *Ibid.*, pp. 415–416.
3 *Ibid.*, footnote, p. 105.
4 *Complete Works*, Vol. VIII, pp. 175–176.
5 *New York Times*, Dec. 26, 1862.
6 John J. Piatt, editor, *The Poems of George D. Prentice* (1875), xxxviii–xxxix. Also W. H. Venable, *Beginnings of Literary Culture in the Ohio Valley* (1891), pp. 400–401.
7 *Louisville* (Ky.) *Daily Journal*, Reprinted by *Illinois State Journal* (Springfield), Oct. 5, 1862.
8 Venable, *op. cit.*, pp. 386–391.
9 George D. Prentice, *Prenticeana* (1871). Foreword by G. W. Griffin the year after Prentice died.
10 Robert Todd Lincoln Collection (21050).
11 *Complete Works*, Vol. VI, pp. 66–67.
12 Robert Todd Lincoln Collection (6663). Also David C. Mearns, *The Lincoln Papers* (1948), Vol. II, pp. 418–419.
13 Gilbert A. Tracy, *Uncollected Letters of Abraham Lincoln* (1917), pp. 175–176.
14 Robert Todd Lincoln Collection (7249).
15 *Appleton's*, Vol. IV, p. 767.
16 *Complete Works*, Vol. VI, p. 360.
17 *Cincinnati Enquirer*, April 16, 1861. Also *Harper's*, p. 68.
18 Edward Conrad Smith, *The Borderland in the Civil War* (1927), p. 267.
19 *Cincinnati Enquirer*, April 17, 1861.
20 *Louisville Journal*. Reprinted by *Cincinnati Enquirer*, April 17, 1861.
21 *Ibid.*, May 4, 1861.
22 *Harper's*, p. 169.
23 *Frankfort* (Ky.) *Yeoman*. Reprinted by *The Crisis* (Columbus, Ohio), Oct. 24, 1861.
24 *Cincinnati Enquirer*, May 10, 1861.
25 *Cincinnati Gazette*, July 31, 1861.
26 *Ohio State Journal* (Columbus), Aug. 21, 1861.
27 Richard H. Collins, *History of Kentucky* (1874), p. 312.
28 *Cincinnati Gazette*, Sept. 26, 1861.
29 *Kentucky Statesman* (Lexington).

30 *Louisville* (Ky.) *Daily Courier*. Reprinted by *Cincinnati Gazette*, Sept. 24, 1861.
31 *Cincinnati Enquirer*, Sept. 19, 1861.
32 *Louisville Courier* (at Nashville, Tenn.), March, 1862. Quoted by *Harper's*, p. 17.
33 *Cincinnati Gazette*, Nov. 28, 1862.
34 Frank Luther Mott, *American Journalism* (1941), footnote, p. 360.
35 *Ibid.*
36 *Louisville* (Ky.) *Democrat*. Reprinted by *The Crisis*, May 28, 1862.
37 *Louisville Journal*. Reprinted by *The Crisis*, July 23, 1862.
38 *Allen County Democrat* (Lima, Ohio). Reprinted by *The Crisis*, July 23, 1862.
39 *The Crisis*, Oct. 22, 1862.
40 *Chicago Times*. Quoted by *Cincinnati Gazette*, March 10, 1863.
41 *Cincinnati Gazette*, March 10, 1863.
42 *New York Tribune*. Reprinted by *Cincinnati Gazette*, March 10, 1863.
43 *New York Times*. Reprinted by *Cincinnati Gazette*, March 18, 1863.
44 *Cincinnati Gazette*, Nov. 25, 1862.
45 *Ibid.*, May 3, 1863.
46 *Louisville Journal*. Reprinted by *Cincinnati Enquirer*, July 26, 1864.
47 *Cincinnati Enquirer*, Sept. 3, 1864.
48 *Louisville Journal*. Reprinted by *The Crisis*, Oct. 5, 1864.
49 *Cincinnati Enquirer*, Nov. 7, 1864.
50 *Cincinnati Gazette*, Nov. 11, 1864.
51 *Indianapolis* (Ind.) *Daily Journal*, Nov. 17, 24, and 28, 1864.
52 Robert Todd Lincoln Collection (29588).
53 Venable, *op. cit.*, pp. 400–401.
54 *Cincinnati Gazette*, Oct. 20, 1864. The correspondent's news letter was datelined "Louisa, Ky., October 11, 1864," and signed "Wilbur."
55 Robert Todd Lincoln Collection (37523).
56 *Ibid.* (37607).
57 *Knoxville* (Tenn.) *Whig and Rebel Ventilator*, Nov. 5, 1864. Reprinted by *Cincinnati Gazette*, Nov. 12, 1864.
58 Dispatch in *Cincinnati Gazette* and other newspapers, Dec. 5, 1864.

59  Piatt, *op. cit.*, p. xl.
60  *Cincinnati Enquirer*, Oct. 6, 1864.
61  *Ibid.*, March 4, 1863.
62  *Ibid.*, April 4, 1865.
63  *Louisville Democrat*, Nov. 10, 1864. Reprinted by *Cincinnati Enquirer*, Nov. 12, 1864.
64  *Frankfort* (Ky.) *Commonwealth.* Reprinted by *New York Times*, April 29, 1864. Also *Complete Works*, Vol. X, pp. 65–68.
65  *New York Times*, April 29, 1864.
66  *Cairo* (Ill.) *Democrat*, Nov. 22, 1864. Quoted by *Cincinnati Enquirer*, Nov. 24, 1864.
67  *Richmond* (Va.) *Enquirer*, Jan. 21, 1865. Reprinted by *Cincinnati Enquirer*, Jan 30, 1865.
68  *Cincinnati Gazette*, Sept. 3, 1864.
69  David Rankin Barbee, "President Lincoln and Doctor Gurley," *The Abraham Lincoln Quarterly*, Vol. V (March 1948), p. 16.
70  Barbee, *op. cit.*, p. 16. Letter in Robert Todd Lincoln Collection.
71  *Ibid., op. cit.*, pp. 17–18.

CHAPTER TWENTY-FIVE

1   *Illinois Daily State Journal* (Springfield), Jan. 6, 1863.
2   *The History of Sangamon County, Illinois* (1881), pp. 213–240.
3   Edward L. Pierce, *Memoir and Letters of Charles Sumner* (1877–1893), Vol. IV, p. 114.
4   *Detroit* (Mich.) *Free Press*, Jan. 29, 1861. Quoted by Wood Gray, *The Hidden Civil War* (1942), p. 47.
5   *Joliet* (Ill.) *Signal*, Jan. 29, 1861. Quoted by Gray, *op. cit.*, p. 46.
6   *Missouri Democrat* (St. Louis). Reprinted by *Daily Whig and Republican* (Quincy, Ill.), Sept. 10, 1863.
7   *Ibid.*
8   *Daily Illinois State Register* (Springfield), Aug. 7, 1864.
9   *Ibid.*, Nov. 10, 1864.
10  *The History of Sangamon County*, pp. 216–217.
11  *Ibid.*, p. 219.
12  *Ibid.*, p. 217.
13  *Illinois Daily State Journal*, March 7, 1866.

14  Gray, *op. cit.*, p. 45.
15  *Ibid.*
16  *Carlinville* (Ill.) *Spectator.* Reprinted by Gray, *op. cit.*, pp. 93–94.
17  *Cincinnati Gazette*, Oct. 18, 1861.
18  *Daily Whig and Republican*, Aug. 13, 1863.
19  *Daily Illinois State Register*, Aug. 25, 1862.
20  *Paris* (Ill.) *Beacon.* Reprinted by *Illinois State Journal*, Aug. 22, 1862.
21  *Illinois State Journal*, Aug. 11, 1862.
22  *Ibid.*
23  *Journal of Commerce* (New York). Reprinted by *Cincinnati Enquirer*, Oct. 6, 1864.
24  *Olney* (Ill.) *Journal.* Reprinted by *Illinois State Journal*, Sept. 12, 1863. Also *Missouri Republican* (St. Louis), Sept. 11, 1863.
25  *Illinois State Journal*, Dec. 20, 1862.
26  *Alton* (Ill.) *Telegraph*, Dec. 6, 1862. Reprinted by *Illinois State Journal*, Dec. 11, 1862.
27  *Illinois State Journal*, Aug. 22, 1862.
28  *Illinois State Register*, Aug. 23, 1862.
29  *Illinois State Journal*, Aug. 16 and 25, 1862.
30  *Carbondale* (Ill.) *Times.* Reprinted by *Illinois State Journal*, Sept. 4, 1862.
31  *Illinois State Journal*, Aug. 2, 1862.
32  *Shawneetown* (Ill.) *Mercury.* Reprinted by *Illinois State Journal*, Aug. 23, 1862.
33  *Missouri Republican*, March 5, 1863.
34  *Chicago Times.* Reprinted by *Ohio Statesman* (Columbus), May 28, 1864.
35  *Davenport* (Iowa) *Democrat*, Feb. 12, 1864.
36  *Chicago Times*, Feb. 17, 1864.
37  *Illinois State Journal*, July 29, 1864.
38  *Ibid.*
39  *Alton* (Ill.) *Democrat.* Reprinted by *Illinois State Journal*, July 29, 1864.
40  *Waterloo* (Ill.) *Advocate*, July 29, 1864.
41  *Ibid.*
42  *Gallatin County* (Ill.) *Democrat*, Sept. 13, 1864. Reprinted by *Cincinnati Gazette*, Sept. 15, 1864. This

story is written in the first person by the editor, and he does not give his name.

43 *Schuyler* (Ill.) *Citizen.* Reprinted by *Illinois State Journal,* Aug. 1, 1864.

44 *Appleton's,* Vol. V, p. 60.

45 *La Crosse* (Wis.) *Democrat.* Reprinted by *Cincinnati Enquirer,* July 30, 1864.

46 *Ibid.* Reprinted by *Ohio Statesman,* Aug. 29, 1864.

47 *Complete Works,* Vol. X, pp. 122–123.

48 *Detroit Free Press.* Reprinted by *The Crisis* (Columbus, Ohio), Dec. 2, 1862.

49 *Ibid.* Reprinted by *Cincinnati Enquirer,* Sept. 11, 1863.

50 *Ann Arbor* (Mich.) *Journal.* Reprinted by *Cincinnati Enquirer,* Sept. 17, 1864.

51 *Cincinnati Gazette,* Oct. 22 and 23, 1861.

52 *Illinois State Journal,* Aug. 22, 1862.

53 *Cincinnati Gazette,* Sept. 5, 1861.

54 *Indianapolis* (Ind.) *Daily State Sentinel,* Feb. 3, 1863.

55 *Cincinnati Enquirer,* Oct. 6, 1864.

56 *Indianapolis Sentinel,* March 17, 1863.

57 *Ibid.* Elder's letter to his son in Indianapolis, published by the *Sentinel.*

58 *Cincinnati Enquirer,* March 17, 1863.

59 *Chicago Times.* Reprinted by *Cincinnati Enquirer,* Feb. 25, 1864.

60 *Vincennes* (Ind.) *Gazette.* Reprinted by *Indianapolis Sentinel,* March 7, 1864.

61 *Union Democrat* (Princeton, Ind.). Reprinted by *Indianapolis Sentinel,* March 8, 1864.

62 *Cincinnati Enquirer,* March 24, 1864.

63 *Indianapolis Sentinel,* March 28, 1864.

64 U. S. Grant, *Personal Memoirs* (1886), Vol. II, p. 118.

65 *Indianapolis Sentinel,* March 28, 1864.

66 *Cincinnati Enquirer,* Feb. 13, 1864.

67 *Illinois State Journal,* Dec. 2 and 6, 1862.

68 *Appleton's,* Vol. III, pp. 19–20.

69 William B. Rice, *The Los Angeles Star* (1947), pp. 233–234.

70 *Equal Rights Expositor* (Visalia, Calif.). Quoted by Rice, *op. cit.,* p. 237.

71 Rice, *op. cit.,* p. 238.

72 *Ibid.,* pp. 238–254.

73 Hubert Howe Bancroft, *History of Oregon* (1888), Vol. II, pp. 450–451.

74 Charles Henry Carey, *History of Oregon* (1922), p. 664.

75 Bancroft, *op. cit.,* footnote, p. 492.

CHAPTER TWENTY-SIX

1 *Daily Evening Journal* (Philadelphia). Reprinted by *Philadelphia Inquirer,* Jan. 31, 1863.

2 *American Annual Cyclopaedia* (1864), Vol. III, p. 470.

3 *Philadelphia Inquirer,* Jan. 31, 1863.

4 *Ibid.,* Feb. 3, 1863.

5 *American Annual Cyclopaedia* (1864), Vol. III, pp. 470–472.

6 *The World* (New York). Reprinted by *Philadelphia Inquirer,* Feb. 3, 1863.

7 *The Age* (Philadelphia). Quoted by Ray H. Abrams, "Copperhead Newspapers and the Negro," *The Journal of Negro History* (1935), Chap. XX, pp. 131–152.

8 J. Thomas Scharf and Thompson Wescott, *History of Philadelphia* (1884), Vol. III, pp. 2032–2033.

9 *Appleton's,* Vol. III, p. 7.

10 *The Crisis* (Columbus, Ohio), Aug. 20, 1862.

11 *Ibid.,* Aug. 27, 1862.

12 John A. Marshall, *American Bastile* (1874), pp. 501–503.

13 *New York Evening Express.* Reprinted by *The Crisis,* Aug. 20, 1862.

14 *The Liberator* (Boston). Reprinted by *The Crisis,* Aug. 27, 1862.

15 *The Crisis,* Sept. 17, 1862.

16 *Cincinnati Gazette,* Aug. 20, 1861.

17 *The Crisis,* Nov. 28, 1861.

18 *New York Day Book,* Aug. 23, 1861.

19 *Philadelphia Inquirer,* Aug. 27, 1861.

20 *Cincinnati Enquirer,* Oct. 6, 1864.

21  *Mentor* (Kittaning, Pa.). Reprinted by *The Crisis*, Oct. 14, 1863.
22  *Cincinnati Enquirer.* Oct. 6, 1864.
2{  *Patriot and Union* (Harrisburg, Pa.). Reprinted by *Cincinnati Enquirer*, Feb. 6, 1864.
24  *Ibid.* Reprinted by *Ohio Statesman* (Columbus), March 23, 1864.
25  *Cincinnati Enquirer*, Oct. 6, 1864.
26  *Patriot and Union.* Reprinted by *Ohio Statesman*, Aug. 11, 1864.

CHAPTER TWENTY-SEVEN

1   *American Annual Cyclopaedia* (1864), Vol. III, p. 473.
2   The editorial, "A Great Old Sunset," appeared in the *Ohio Statesman* (Columbus), May 19, 1853.
3   This account of the arrest is from Cincinnati and Columbus newspapers, May 5 and 6, 1863.
4   *Cincinnati Gazette*, May 6, 1863. Other newspapers carried substantially the same story.
5   *Dayton* (Ohio) *Daily Journal*, May 7, 1863. Also *Dayton Newspapers and Their Editors* (1937).
6   *Cincinnati Gazette*, May 7, 1863. The *Dayton* (Ohio) *Daily Empire* published the editorial May 6, 1863.
7   *American Annual Cyclopaedia* (1864), Vol. III, p. 474. Text as published by Democratic newspapers.
8   *Ibid.*
9   *Ibid.*
10  *Ibid.*, p. 478.
11  The decision was handed down May 16, 1863, a Saturday. The *Cincinnati Gazette* carried the text the following Monday, May 18, 1863.
12  *Complete Works*, Vol. VIII, "Letter to Secretary Stanton," p. 274. Lincoln said Chase thought the case would be before either Judge Swaim or Judge Leavitt. The Judge's name was Swayne, not Swaim. Swayne was out of town, and the case was heard by Leavitt alone, although Pugh's petition was addressed to the "judges" of the United States circuit court.
13  *Appleton's*, Vol. III, p. 649. Some Lincoln scholars doubt this, but it is well authenticated. The court's ver-

dict set a pattern for handling dissenters.
14  *Cincinnati Gazette*, May 12, 1863. Also *American Annual Cyclopaedia* (1864), Vol. III, p. 481.
15  *Ibid.*, May 19, 1863.
16  *American Annual Cyclopaedia* (1864), Vol. III, p. 483.
17  *The Crisis* (Columbus, Ohio), May 20, 1863.
18  *Cincinnati Gazette*, May 19, 1863.
19  *Ibid.*, May 11, 1863.
20  *Louisville* (Ky.) *Journal.* Reprinted by *American Annual Cyclopaedia* (1864), Vol. III, p. 483.
21  *National Intelligencer* (Washington, D. C.). Reprinted by *American Annual Cyclopaedia* (1864), Vol. III, p. 483.
22  *New York Times.* Reprinted by *Cincinnati Gazette*, May 22, 1863.
23  *Cincinnati Gazette*, May 25, 1863.
24  *Complete Works*, Vol. VIII, pp. 278–279.
25  This version of the news story was carried by the *Cincinnati Gazette*, May 26, 1863.
26  *American Annual Cyclopaedia* (1864), Vol. III, p. 483.
27  *Ibid.*, pp. 799–800.
28  *Complete Works*, Vol. VIII, p. 284.
29  *American Annual Cyclopaedia* (1864), Vol. III, pp. 800–802. Also *Complete Works*, Vol. VIII, pp. 298–314.
30  *Ibid.*, p. 803.
31  *Ibid.*, pp. 803–806.
32  *Complete Works*, Vol. IX, pp. 1–10.
33  *American Annual Cyclopaedia* (1864), Vol. III, pp. 806–807.
34  *Complete Works*, Vol. VIII, p. 286.
35  *The Crisis*, June 3, 1863.
36  *Evening Post* (New York). Reprinted by *American Annual Cyclopaedia* (1864), Vol. III, p. 483.
37  *Cleveland* (Ohio) *Herald.* Reprinted by *Dayton Newspapers and Their Editors.*
38  *Dayton Newspapers and Their Editors.*
39  *The Crisis*, Dec. 23, 1863.
40  *Dayton Empire*, March 4, 1864.
41  *Cincinnati Enquirer*, March 4, 1864; *Ohio Statesman*, March 5, 1864; *Dayton Empire*, March 7, 1864.

42  Dayton, Columbus, and Cincinnati newspapers, March 4 and 5, 1864.
43  *Dayton Empire*, March 11, 1864.
44  *Ibid.*, March 9, 1864.
45  *Harper's*, II, p. 654.
46  *Ibid.* Also *Appleton's*, Vol. I, p. 391.

CHAPTER TWENTY-EIGHT

1   *The Crisis* (Columbus, Ohio), May 6, 1863.
2   *Appleton's*, Vol. III, p. 109.
3   *The Crisis*, May 27, 1863.
4   *Ibid.*
5   *Appleton's*, Vol. I, pp. 386–387.
6   *New York Evening Express*, Feb. 25, 1861.
7   Frank Luther Mott, *American Journalism* (1941), p. 356.
8   *New York Express*, March 4, 1861.
9   *Ibid.* Reprinted by *The Crisis*, May 27, 1863. The paper suppressed was the *Plymouth* (Ind.) *Democrat*, May 4, 1863.
10  *The World* (New York). Reprinted by *The Crisis*, May 27, 1863.
11  *New York Express*. Correspondence reprinted by *The Crisis*, May 27, 1863.
12  *Cincinnati Gazette*. Reprinted by *The Crisis*, June 17, 1863.
13  *Commercial Advertiser* (Buffalo, N. Y.). Reprinted by *The Crisis*, May 27, 1863.
14  *The Crisis*, July 1, 1863.
15  *Ibid.*
16  *New York Express*, Aug. 12, 1863. Reprinted by *The Crisis*, Aug. 19, 1863.
17  *Ibid.* Reprinted by *The Crisis*, Aug. 26, 1863.
18  *Ibid.*
19  *Ibid.*
20  *The Crisis*, Aug. 26, 1863.
21  *Ibid.*, Aug. 17, 1864.

CHAPTER TWENTY-NINE

1   *Chicago Tribune*, June 4, 1863.
2   L. E. Ellis, "The Chicago Times During the Civil War," *Illinois State Historical Society Transactions* (1932), p. 167. Mrs. Ellis's study of the *Times* is one of the best authorities. Files of the *Times*, incomplete, are at the Chicago Li-

brary and the Newberry Library in Chicago.
3   *Ibid.*, pp. 167–168. Cites A. C. Cole, *The Era of the Civil War* (1922), p. 303.
4   Frank Luther Mott, *American Journalism* (1941), p. 357.
5   *Dictionary of American Biography* (1936), Vol. XVIII, pp. 97–98.
6   Ellis, *op. cit.*, pp. 139–140.
7   *Ibid.*, pp. 135–138.
8   *Chicago Times*, Sept. 23, 24, and other issues, 1862.
9   *Ibid.*, Jan. 3, 1863.
10  Ellis, *op. cit.*, p. 146.
11  *American Annual Cyclopaedia* (1864), Vol. III, p. 423.
12  *Ibid.*
13  *Ibid.*, p. 424.
14  *Chicago Tribune*, June 4, 1863.
15  *Ibid.*
16  *Ibid.*
17  *American Annual Cyclopaedia* (1864), Vol. III, p. 424.
18  *Ibid.*
19  A. T. Andreas, *History of Chicago* (1885), Vol. II, p. 495.
20  *American Annual Cyclopaedia* (1864), Vol. III, p. 424.
21  *Chicago Tribune.* Cited by Philip Kinsley, *The Chicago Tribune* (1943), Vol. I, p. 274.
22  *American Annual Cyclopaedia* (1864), Vol. III, p. 424.
23  *Ibid.*, p. 425.
24  *Complete Works*, Vol. X, p. 108.
25  John T. Morse, editor, *Diary of Gideon Welles* (1911), Vol. I, p. 321.
26  James G. Randall, *Constitutional Problems Under Lincoln* (1926), pp. 494–495.
27  *Ibid.*, p. 724.
28  *Complete Works*, Vol. VIII, p. 290.
29  *Chicago Tribune*, June 5, 1863. Quoted by Kinsley, *op. cit.*, p. 275.
30  *Ibid.*, June 6, 1863.
31  *Ibid.*
32  *Ibid.*, June 7, 1863.
33  Ellis, *op. cit.*, p. 169. Cites J. M. Lee, *History of American Journalism* (1923), p. 286.
34  *Ibid.*
35  *Chicago Times.* Reprinted by *The Crisis* (Columbus, Ohio), July 29, 1863.

36  *Chicago Tribune*, Oct. 18, 1863.
    Quoted by Kinsley, *op. cit.*, p. 289.
37  *Chicago Times*, April 21, 1864.
38  *Ibid.*, March 20, 1864.
39  *Ibid.*, March 4, 1865.
40  *Ibid.*, March 6, 1865.
41  *Complete Works*, Vol. VIII, pp. 292–293.
42  Andreas, *op. cit.*, p. 494.
43  *Chicago Post*, Feb. 27, 1864.

CHAPTER THIRTY

1   *Harper's*, p. 140.
2   *Ibid.*, p. 142.
3   *Cincinnati Enquirer*, Oct. 6, 1864.
4   *Ibid.*, May 29, 1861.
5   *The Crisis* (Columbus, Ohio), June 11, 1862.
6   *Ibid.*, Aug. 6, 1862.
7   *Cincinnati Enquirer*, March 8, 1863.
8   *Ibid.*, Oct. 6, 1864.
9   *Appleton's*, Vol. III, p. 321.
10  *Harper's*, II, p. 621.
11  *New York Herald.* Reprinted by *Daily Ohio Statesman* (Columbus), July 14, 1864.
12  *Cincinnati Commercial.* Reprinted by *Ohio Statesman*, July 15, 1864.
13  *New York Tribune.* Reprinted by *Ohio Statesman*, Aug. 9, 1864.
14  *New York Daily News* and *Wheeling* (W. Va.) *Daily Register.* Reprinted by *Ohio Statesman*, July 29, 1864.
15  *Ohio Statesman*, July 10, 1864.
16  *Ibid.*, July 14, 1864.
17  *Cincinnati Enquirer*, July 21, 1864.
18  *Parkersburg* (W. Va.) *Gazette.* Reprinted by *The Crisis*, July 20, 1864.
19  *Wheeling* (W. Va.) *Daily Intelligencer.* Reprinted by *Ohio Statesman*, July 14 and Aug. 4, 1864.
20  *Cincinnati Enquirer.* Reprinted by *The Crisis*, July 20, 1864.
21  *Wheeling Intelligencer.* Reprinted by *Ohio Statesman*, July 14, 1864.
22  *Ohio Statesman*, Aug. 9, 1864.
23  *Ibid.*
24  *Wheeling Intelligencer.* Reprinted by *Ohio Statesman*, July 14, 1864.
25  *Harper's*, II, pp. 707–708.
26  *Ibid.*, p. 708.
27  *Ohio Statesman*, Aug. 12, 1864.
28  *Ibid.*, Sept. 2, 1864.

CHAPTER THIRTY-ONE

1   *Harper's*, II, pp. 646–647.
2   *Ibid.*, I, p. 218.
3   *Ibid.*, II, p. 648. Also *Appleton's*, Vol. V, p. 477.
4   *Ibid.*, pp. 505–513.
5   *Cincinnati Enquirer* and other newspapers, July 9, 1863. Also *Harper's*, II, p. 650.
6   *Appleton's*, Vol. V, pp. 676–677.
7   *Harper's*, II, p. 650.
8   *New York Daily News.* Reprinted by *The Crisis* (Columbus, Ohio), July 8, 1863.
9   *The World* (New York), July 10, 1863. Reprinted by *The Crisis*, July 22, 1863.
10  *New York Tribune*, July 13, 1863.
11  *Ibid.*
12  *The World.* Reprinted by *New York Tribune*, July 15, 1863.
13  *Journal of Commerce* (New York). Reprinted by *New York Tribune*, July 15, 1863.
14  *New York Daily News.* Reprinted by *New York Tribune*, July 15, 1863.
15  *New York Tribune*, July 14, 1863. This writer's impression of the riots and related incidents is from New York newspapers, chiefly the *Tribune.*
16  *Appleton's*, Vol. V, p. 477. Also *Harper's*, p. 654.
17  *New York Tribune*, July 14, 1863.
18  Don C. Seitz, *Horace Greeley, Founder of the New York Tribune* (1926), pp. 209–210.
19  *Newark* (N. J.) *Advertiser.* Reprinted by *New York Tribune*, July 17, 1863.
20  *New York Tribune*, July 15, 1863.
21  *The World*, July 15, 1863. Reprinted by *New York Tribune*, July 16, 1863.
22  *New York Tribune*, July 16, 1863.
23  Seitz, *op. cit.*, pp. 211–213.

CHAPTER THIRTY-TWO

1   Cincinnati news dispatch of July 27, 1863. Also *The Crisis* (Columbus, Ohio), July 29, 1863.

2 *Logan* (Ohio) *Gazette.* Reprinted by *The Crisis*, April 18, 1861.
3 Alfred E. Lee, *History of the City of Columbus* (1892), Vol. I, p. 424.
4 *Ibid.*, p. 491.
5 *The Crisis*, July 29, 1863.
6 *Cincinnati Enquirer*, Dec. 6, 1863.
7 *Ohio State Journal* (Columbus), Dec. 8, 1863.
8 *Cincinnati Gazette*, Dec. 7, 1863.
9 *The Crisis*, Dec. 30, 1863.
10 *Ibid.*, June 15, 1864.
11 *Cincinnati Commercial*, June 10, 1864.
12 *The Crisis*, July 13, 1864.
13 *Cincinnati Commercial.* Reprinted by *The Crisis*, July 13, 1864.
14 *Toledo* (Ohio) *Blade.* Reprinted by *The Crisis*, Aug. 10, 1864.
15 *Cincinnati Commercial.* Reprinted by *The Crisis*, July 27, 1864.
16 *The Crisis*, Sept. 14, 1864.
17 Allan Nevins, *The Evening Post, A Century of Journalism* (1922), p. 426.
18 *Ibid.*, p. 427.
19 John T. Morse, editor, *Diary of Gideon Welles* (1911), Vol. II, pp. 78–79.
20 *Complete Works*, Vol. X, pp. 135–136.
21 Nevins, *op. cit.*, pp. 428–429.

CHAPTER THIRTY-THREE

1 *Philadelphia Inquirer*, Nov. 21, 1863.
2 John Russell Young, *Men and Memories* (1901), Vol. I, p. 59.
3 *National Intelligencer* (Washington, D. C.), Nov. 20, 1863.
4 Young, *op. cit.*, p. 59.
5 *Ibid.*
6 Tyler Dennett, *Lincoln and the Civil War in the Diaries and Letters of John Hay* (1939), pp. 119–120.
7 Young, *op. cit.*, pp. 59 and 69.
8 Dennett, *op. cit.*, p. 120.
9 Wire news story. This from Columbus *Ohio Statesman*, Nov. 22, 1863.
10 Dennett, *op. cit.*, pp. 120–121.
11 Young, *op. cit.*, p. 60.
12 Dennett, *op cit.*, p. 121.
13 Young, *op. cit.*, pp. 61–63.
14 *Ibid.*, pp. 63–64.

15 *Ibid.*, p. 64.
16 *Ibid.*, pp. 64 and 69.
17 Wire news story. This from *Ohio Statesman*, Nov. 22, 1863.
18 Young, *op. cit.*, p. 68.
19 *Ibid.*, p. 69.
20 *Ibid.*, pp. 68 and 70.
21 The version of the Gettysburg address used here is from *Complete Works*, Vol. IX, pp. 209–210.
22 Young, *op. cit.*, p. 70.
23 *Ibid.*, p. 69.
24 *Ibid.*, p. 70.
25 *Ibid.*, pp. 70–71.
26 *Philadelphia Inquirer*, Nov. 20, 1863.
27 *Springfield* (Mass.) *Republican.* Quoted by Richard Hooker, *The Story of an Independent Newspaper* (1924), pp. 95–96.
28 *Chicago Times.* Quoted by Carl Sandburg, *Abraham Lincoln, The War Years* (1939), Vol. II, p. 472.
29 *Patriot and Union* (Harrisburg, Pa.). Quoted by Sandburg, *op. cit.*, p. 472.
30 *London Times.* Quoted by Sandburg, *op. cit.*, p. 474.
31 *Ohio State Journal* (Columbus), Nov. 23, 1863.

CHAPTER THIRTY-FOUR

1 *The World* (New York), July 10, 1863.
2 Frank Luther Mott, *American Journalism* (1941), pp. 350–351.
3 *Appleton's*, Vol. IV, p. 199.
4 *The World*, June 3, 1863.
5 *Daily Morning Chronicle* (Washington, D. C.), Oct. 10, 1864.
6 *The World*, May 18, 1864.
7 *American Annual Cyclopaedia* (1865), Vol. IV, p. 390.
8 *New York Tribune*, May 19, 1864.
9 *Ibid.*
10 David Homer Bates, *Lincoln in the Telegraph Office* (1907), p. 235.
11 *Ibid.*, p. 230.
12 *Ibid.*, pp. 232–233.
13 *The World*, May 23, 1864.
14 *Journal of Commerce* (New York), May 23, 1864.
15 *New York Tribune*, May 19, 1864.
16 *Ibid.*

17  New York Times, May 19, 1864.
18  Statement to New York Tribune, May 19, 1864.
19  American Annual Cyclopaedia (1862), Vol. I, p. 329.
20  Mott, op. cit., p. 352.
21  New York Herald and other New York newspapers, May 19, 1864.
22  Mott, op. cit., p. 352.
23  Bates, op. cit., p. 231.
24  John T. Morse, editor, Diary of Gideon Welles (1911), Vol. II, pp. 37-38.
25  Complete Works, Vol. X, pp. 103-104.
26  Ibid., p. 104.
27  Cincinnati Enquirer, Oct. 6, 1864, and Appleton's, Vol. I, p. 158.
28  Bates, op. cit., pp. 235-236.
29  Ibid., p. 237.
30  Ibid., p. 242.
31  Journal of Commerce, May 23, 1864.
32  New York Tribune, May 23, 1864.
33  Ibid.
34  The World, May 23, 1864.
35  New York Tribune, May 19, 1864. Also other New York newspapers of same date.
36  Ibid.
37  New York Daily News, May 19, 1864.
38  New York Tribune, May 20, 1864.
39  Bates, op. cit., pp. 239-240.
40  Journal of Commerce, May 23, 1864.
41  Bates, op. cit., p. 240.
42  Commercial Advertiser (New York). Reprinted by The Crisis (Columbus, Ohio), June 15, 1864.
43  New York Tribune, May 23, 1864, and other papers of date.
44  Ibid.
45  New York Herald, May 20, 1864, and Journal of Commerce, May 23, 1864.
46  Journal of Commerce, May 23, 1864.
47  The World, May 23, 1864. Marble's letter to Lincoln was privately published in book form in 1867 under the title, Letter to Abraham Lincoln. The edition was confined to ninety-nine copies. One of these is in the public library at Columbus, Ohio. It has been inscribed with pen, "William M. Brooke, with re-

gards to his friend." Over it has been written in pencil in a bold hand, "I have little sympathy for Mr. Marble and do not endorse the spirit of this letter. Wm. Brooke."
48  New York Tribune, May 23, 1864. Contemporary newspaper reports failed to agree. The government never explained the circumstances of the Howard arrest.
49  Brooklyn (N. Y.) Eagle. Reprinted by Ohio Statesman (Columbus), May 27, 1864.
50  Atlas and Argus (Albany, N. Y.). Reprinted by Journal of Commerce, May 23, 1864.
51  Cincinnati Gazette. Reprinted by The Crisis, June 1, 1864.
52  Bates, op. cit., pp. 242-243.
53  American Annual Cyclopaedia (1865), Vol. IV, p. 390.
54  Advertiser and Farmer (Bridgeport, Conn.). Reprinted by The Crisis, June 8, 1864.
55  Bates, op. cit., pp. 242-243.
56  James G. Randall, Constitutional Problems Under Lincoln (1926), pp. 497-499.
57  American Annual Cyclopaedia (1865), Vol. IV, p. 391.
58  Complete Works, Vol. X, pp. 201-202. Also Bates, op. cit., p. 241.
59  Mott, op. cit., p. 352. The writer has no further information on Mallison.
60  Journal of Commerce, May 23, 1864.

CHAPTER THIRTY-FIVE

1  Harper's, II, pp. 663-664.
2  Ibid., p. 664.
3  Cincinnati Enquirer, April 2, 1864.
4  Illinois Staats-Anzeiger (Springfield). Reprinted by The Crisis (Columbus, Ohio), May 25, 1864.
5  New York Times, May 28 and June 3, 1864.
6  Harper's, II, p. 665.
7  Philadelphia Inquirer, June 10, 1864.
8  The World (New York), June 20, 1864.
9  Ibid. Reprinted by The Crisis, Aug. 3, 1864. This writer has been unable to identify the Essex Statesman,

a search in which the New York Public Library, the New York State Library at Albany, and the Ohio State Archaeological and Historical Society joined. The Union List of Newspapers does not include it.

10 Ward Hill Lamon, *Recollections of Abraham Lincoln* (1911), p. 145.
11 *The World*, Sept. 9, 1864.
12 Lamon, *op. cit.*, pp. 145–150.
13 *New York Times*, Oct. 6, 1862.
14 John T. Morse, editor, *Diary of Gideon Welles* (1911), Vol. II, pp. 103–105.
15 *The World*, Aug. 2, 1864.
16 *Ibid.*
17 Henry Luther Stoddard, *Horace Greeley, Printer, Editor, Crusader* (1946), p. 227.
18 Allan Nevins, *The Evening Post* (1922), pp. 311–312. He cites letter of William Cullen Bryant to his wife, Sept. 7, 1864.
19 See Augustus Maverick, *Henry J. Raymond and the New York Press for Thirty Years* (1870). Also Horace Greeley, *Recollections of a Busy Life* (1868).
20 *The Sun* (New York), June 30, 1889. An article entitled, "Unwritten History, the Secret Movement to Supersede Abraham Lincoln in '64."
21 *Ibid.*
22 *Ibid.*
23 *Ibid.*
24 *Harper's*, pp. 667–668.
25 Frank M. O'Brien, *The Story of The Sun* (1928). He devotes Chapter VIII, pp. 121–147, to *The Sun* during the Civil War.

### CHAPTER THIRTY-SIX

1 *Harper's*, II, p. 666.
2 Memorandum signed by Abraham Lincoln in the Robert Todd Lincoln Collection. Cited by Lloyd A. Dunlap, "President Lincoln and Editor Greeley," *The Abraham Lincoln Quarterly*, Vol. V (June 1948), p. 101.
3 Robert Todd Lincoln Collection (35089).
4 *Complete Works*, Vol. X, p. 182.

5 Robert Todd Lincoln Collection (35139).
6 *Complete Works*, Vol. X, pp. 184–185.
7 Robert Todd Lincoln Collection (35171).
8 *Harper's*, II, p. 667; *Appleton's*, Vol. II, pp. 657–658.
9 William Starr Meyers, "Correspondence of New York Editors with Governor Bradford," *Maryland Historical Magazine*, Vol. III (June 1908), pp. 176–178.
10 *New York Tribune*, Sept. 6, 1864.
11 Don C. Seitz, *Horace Greeley, Founder of the New York Tribune* (1926), p. 268. He quotes a story written by D. S. Alexander, published in the *Republican* of Lyons, N. Y., Aug. 3, 1921.
12 *New York Tribune*, Sept. 27, 1864.
13 Allan Nevins, *The Evening Post* (1922), pp. 312–313.
14 *Ibid.*
15 *Evening Post* (New York). Reprinted by *The Crisis* (Columbus, Ohio), April 20, 1864.
16 *New York Tribune*, Sept. 19, 1860.
17 *Appleton's*, Vol. I, p. 417.
18 *Evening Post*, Sept. 20, 1864. Quoted by Nevins, *op. cit.*, p. 313.
19 *Ibid.*, p. 311.
20 *Ibid.*, p. 310.
21 Nevins, *op. cit.*, pp. 293–294.
22 *Evening Post*, March 5, 1865.
23 *Ibid.*, April 12, 1865.
24 *New York Herald*, May 20, 1864.
25 A. K. McClure, *Abraham Lincoln and Men of War Times* (1892), pp. 80–82.
26 David C. Mearns, *The Lincoln Papers* (1948), Vol. I, pp. 261–262.
27 Don C. Seitz, *The James Gordon Bennetts* (1928), pp. 177–178.
28 *New York Herald*, April 22, 1861.
29 Seitz, *op. cit.*, pp. 173–177.
30 *Ibid.*, pp. 179–181. Revealed in memoirs of Henry Villard.
31 *Ibid.*, pp. 181–182. Quotes Lincoln letter in files of Treasury Department.
32 *Ibid.*, pp. 186–187. Quotes the letters.
33 *New York Herald.* Reprinted by *The Crisis*, Oct. 29, 1862.

34  Seitz, *op. cit.*, pp. 187–188.
35  *Vanity Fair*, Aug. 16, 1862. Cited by
    Seitz, *op. cit.*, pp. 187–188.
36  McClure, *op. cit.*, pp. 80–82.
37  Robert Todd Lincoln Collection
    (41070).
38  Seitz, *op. cit.*, p. 192. Also *Appleton's*, Vol. II, pp. 113–114.
39  *New York Herald*, March 4, 1865.
40  *Ibid.*, March 5, 1865.
41  *The Crisis*, July 5, 1865.
42  *Appleton's*, Vol. VI, p. 419.
43  *Complete Works*, Vol. IX, pp. 168–
    169.
44  *Ibid.*, Vol. X, p. 56.
45  *New York Herald*. Reprinted by
    *Ohio Statesman* (Columbus), June
    1, 1864.
46  *New York Times*, Oct. 17, 1864.
47  *Ibid.*

CHAPTER THIRTY-SEVEN

1  *Harper's*, II, p. 667.
2  George Fort Milton, *Abraham Lincoln and the Fifth Column* (1942),
   p. 308.
3  *Harper's*, II, p. 667.
4  Milton, *op. cit.*, p. 245.
5  *Ibid.*, p. 244.
6  *New York Tribune*, June 23, 1863,
   and *Cincinnati Enquirer*, Oct. 6,
   1864.
7  Indianapolis newspapers and *Cincinnati Enquirer*, Oct. 28 and 29,
   1864. Bingham's sworn testimony.
8  *Indianapolis* (Ind.) *Daily State Sentinel*. Reprinted by *The Crisis*
   (Columbus, Ohio), Sept. 12, 1861.
9  *Ibid.*
10  Milton, *op. cit.*, pp. 87–88.
11  *Ibid.*, p. 295. Also Bingham's sworn
    statement. See *Cincinnati Enquirer*,
    Oct. 28 and 29, 1864.
12  *Ibid.*, pp. 295–296.
13  *Cincinnati Enquirer*, Sept. 22–30,
    1864. Also Milton, *op. cit.*, p. 312.
14  *Indianapolis Sentinel*, Oct. 3, 1864.
15  *Ibid.*, Oct. 6, 1864.
16  *Cincinnati Enquirer*, Oct. 7, 1864.
17  *Ibid.*, Oct. 9, 10, and 12, 1864.
18  *Ibid.*, Oct. 24, 1864.
19  *Ibid.*, Oct. 19, 1864.
20  Milton, *op. cit.*, p. 315.

21  Indianapolis newspapers, Oct. 21–29,
    1864.
22  *Cincinnati Enquirer*, Oct. 31, 1864.
23  Milton, *op. cit.*, p. 318.
24  *Indianapolis Sentinel*. Reprinted by
    *Cincinnati Enquirer*, Jan. 3, 1865.
25  Milton, *op. cit.*, pp. 318–322.
26  *Cincinnati Gazette*, Oct. 15, 1864.
27  *Indianapolis Sentinel*, Nov. 9, 1864.
28  *Ibid.*, Dec. 3, 1864.
29  *Indianapolis Daily Journal*, Nov. 8,
    1864.
30  James G. Randall, "The Newspaper
    Problem in its Bearing Upon Military Secrecy During the Civil
    War," *The American Historical
    Review*, Vol. XXIII (1918), pp.
    310–311.
31  *Lafayette* (Ind.) *Journal*, Nov. 15,
    1864. Reprinted by *Indianapolis
    Sentinel*, Nov. 16, 1864.
32  *Cincinnati Enquirer*, Nov. 16, 1864.
33  *Indianapolis Journal*, Nov. 17, 1864.
34  *Ibid.*, Nov. 15, 1864.
35  *Cincinnati Enquirer*, Nov. 17, 1864.
36  *Indianapolis Journal*, Nov. 23, 1864.
37  *Ibid.*, Nov. 22, 1864.

CHAPTER THIRTY-EIGHT

1  *Indianapolis* (Ind.) *Daily State Sentinel*, Nov. 9, 1864.
2  Alfred E. Lee, *History of the City
   of Columbus* (1892), Vol. I, p. 475.
3  *Appleton's*, Vol. IV, pp. 284–285.
4  Lee, *op. cit.*, p. 476.
5  *The Crisis* (Columbus, Ohio), Jan.
   31, 1861.
6  *Ibid.*
7  *Ibid.*, Feb. 7 and 14, March 28 and
   April 18, 1861.
8  *Ibid.*, Sept. 19, 1861.
9  *Fremont* (Ohio) *Messenger*. Reprinted by *The Crisis*, June 8, 1862.
10  *The Crisis*, Aug. 13, 1862.
11  *Dayton* (Ohio) *Daily Empire*. Reprinted by *The Crisis*, July 16, 1862.
12  *The Crisis*, Sept. 24, 1862.
13  *Ibid.*, Jan. 7, 1863.
14  *Ibid.*, July 30, 1862.
15  *Ibid.*, May 6, 1863.
16  *Boston Post*. Reprinted by *The
    Crisis*, May 13, 1863.
17  *Columbus* (Ga.) *Enquirer*. Re

printed by *The Crisis*, May 20, 1863.
18 *The Crisis*, Aug. 10, 1864.
19 *Cincinnati Enquirer*. Reprinted by *The Crisis*, June 29, 1864.
20 *Ohio State Journal* (Columbus), March 6, 1863.
21 *Ibid.*
22 *The Crisis*, March 11, 1863.
23 *Ohio State Journal*, March 13, 1863.
24 *Ohio Statesman* (Columbus), March 6, 1863.
25 *The Crisis*, March 11, 1863.
26 *Ibid.*, March 18, 1863.
27 *Ibid.*
28 *Ibid.*
29 *Dayton Empire* and *Chicago Times*. Reprinted by *The Crisis*, March 18, 1863.
30 *Placer* (Calif.) *Herald*. Reprinted by *The Crisis*, June 3, 1863.
31 *The Crisis*, March 25, 1863. The essay as printed by Medary.
32 *Ibid.*, April 15, 1863.
33 *Ibid.*, April 29, 1863.
34 *Ibid.*, July 29, 1863.
35 *Ibid.*, Aug. 19, 1863.
36 *Ibid.*, Jan. 6, 1864.
37 *Ibid.*, May 25, 1864.
38 *Ibid.*, June 1, 1864.
39 *Ibid.* All comment collected by Medary.
40 *Ibid.*, June 8, 1864.
41 *Ibid.*, Sept. 14, 1864.
42 *Ohio Statesman*, Nov. 8 and 12, 1864.
43 *Ohio State Journal*, Nov. 8, 1864.
44 *The Crisis*, Jan. 25, 1865. Medary's successor as editor explained that the *San Francisco Press* found the article in the *Nevada Gazette* and reprinted it with an editorial defending the late editor. [In 1932, Samuel Medary was elected to the Journalism Hall of Fame of the Ohio State University.]

CHAPTER THIRTY-NINE

1 *Harper's*, II, p. 669.
2 Allen Thorndike Rice, editor, *Reminiscences of Abraham Lincoln* (1886), pp. 371–373. Dana's own story.
3 *Harper's*, II, p. 669.
4 *Ibid.*, pp. 675–692.

5 *Ibid.*, p. 693.
6 *Ibid.*, p. 669.
7 *New York Daily News*. Reprinted by *The Crisis* (Columbus, Ohio), Feb. 22, 1865.
8 Henry Luther Stoddard, *Horace Greeley, Printer, Editor, Crusader* (1946), p. 228.
9 *New York Tribune*, March 17, 1865.
10 *Harper's*, II, pp. 751–766.
11 Noah Brooks, *Abraham Lincoln* (1888), pp. 444–446.
12 *Harper's*, II, pp. 767–772.
13 Brooks, *op. cit.*, pp. 446–448.
14 *Ibid.*, p. 449.
15 Noah Brooks, *Washington in Lincoln's Time* (1896), pp. 252–255.
16 *Complete Works*, Vol. XI, pp. 85–92. "Last Public Address." Also footnote, p. 84.
17 From Lincoln's "Mexican War Speech." *Complete Works*, Vol. I, p. 341.
18 Don C. Seitz, *Horace Greeley, Founder of the New York Tribune* (1926), p. 270.
19 Edward Everett Hale, *James Russell Lowell and his Friends* (1899), pp. 178–179.
20 *Harper's*, II, p. 783.
21 Hale, *op. cit.*, pp. 178–179.
22 *Daily Morning Chronicle* (Washington, D. C.), April 18, 1865.
23 *The Jeffersonian* (West Chester, Pa.), May 6, 1865. Cited by Ray H. Abrams, "The Jeffersonian, Copperhead Newspaper," *The Pennsylvania Magazine of History and Biography*, Vol. LVII (1933), p. 282.
24 *Boston Daily Evening Transcript*, April 18, 1865.
25 *Chicago Times*, April 17, 1865.
26 *Ibid.*
27 *Ibid.* Also *Chicago Tribune*, April 19, 1865. John Bruce, *Gaudy Century* (1948), pp. 134–139, says the *Voz de Mejico* and the *Irish News* also were destroyed.
28 *Ibid.*
29 *Cincinnati Commercial*, April 19, 1865. Story dated "April 16."
30 *Associated Press*, April 18, 1865. In *Cincinnati Commercial* and other

newspapers, April 21, 1865. For detailed account of rioting, see story "dated May 3, 1865," in *Chicago Tribune*, June 2, 1865.

31 *The World* (New York). Reprinted by *Cincinnati Enquirer*, June 7, 1865.

32 *Baltimore American*, April 21, 1865.

33 The case history and trial were published in a day-by-day account in the *Baltimore American* during the week ending June 7, 1865. J. Thomas Scharf, *History of Western Maryland* (1882), Vol. II, p. 960, ignored the Shaw murder in his history of the newspaper. Laurence Greene, *America Goes to Press* (1938), p. 180, mentions the Shaw death.

34 *New York Herald*, April 16, 1865.

CHAPTER FORTY

1 *National Intelligencer* (Washington, D. C.), April 17, 1865.

2 *Ibid.*, April 21, 1865.

3 *Harper's*, II, p. 778.

4 *The World* (New York). Reprinted by *National Intelligencer*, April 17, 1865.

5 *Journal of Commerce* (New York). Reprinted by *National Intelligencer*, April 17, 1865.

6 *New York Daily News*. Reprinted by *National Intelligencer*, April 17, 1865.

7 *Boston Courier*. Reprinted by *National Intelligencer*, April 19, 1865.

8 *Boston Journal*. Reprinted by *National Intelligencer*, April 17, 1865.

9 *Boston Transcript*, April 15, 1865.

10 *The Sun* (Baltimore), April 17, 1865.

11 *Baltimore American*, April 18, 1865.

12 *National Intelligencer*, April 15, 1865.

13 *Ibid.*, April 17, 1865.

14 *Daily Morning Chronicle* (Washington, D. C.), April 15, 1865.

15 *The Press* (Philadelphia), April 17, 1865.

16 *Philadelphia Inquirer*, April 17, 1865.

17 *New York Times*, April 17, 1865.

18 *New York Herald*, April 17, 1865.

19 *New York Tribune*, April 19, 1865.

20 Allan Nevins, *The Evening Post* (1922), p. 291.

21 *The Crisis* (Columbus, Ohio), April 19, 1865.

22 *Ibid.*, April 26, 1865.

23 *Dayton* (Ohio) *Daily Empire*, April 17, 1865.

24 *Milwaukee* (Wis.) *Sentinel*, April 17, 1865.

25 *Toledo* (Ohio) *Blade*, April 15, 1865.

26 *Cincinnati Enquirer*, April 17, 1865.

27 *Chicago Times*, April 17, 1865.

28 *Daily Illinois State Register* (Springfield), April 15, 1865.

29 *Ibid.*

30 *Ibid.*, April 18, 1865.

31 *Chicago Tribune*, April 17, 1865.

32 *Richmond* (Va.) *Whig*. Reprinted by *National Intelligencer*, April 19, 1865.

33 *Texas Republican* (Marshall), April 28, 1865. Quoted by Ralph W. Steen, "Texas Newspapers and Lincoln," *The Southwestern Historical Quarterly*, Vol. LI (January 1948), pp. 199–212.

34 *Galveston* (Texas) *News*, April 28, 1865. Quoted by Steen, *op. cit.*

35 *Dallas* (Texas) *Herald*, May 4, 1865. Quoted by Steen, *op. cit.*

36 All quotes from the foreign press are taken from a volume issued by the Government Printing Office at Washington in 1867, *Tributes of the Nations to Abraham Lincoln*. These appeared in the French press April 28 and 29, 1865.

37 *Tributes of the Nations*. These were published April 27, 28, and 29, 1865.

38 *Ibid.* These were published April 27 and May 1, 1865.

39 *Morning Star* (London), April 27, 1865.

40 *London Daily News*, April 27, 1865.

41 *London Times*, April 27, 1865.

42 *Evening Standard* (London), April 27, 1865.

43 *London Spectator*, April 29, 1865.

44 *Tributes of the Nations*. These were published April 27 and 29, 1865.

# Quoted and Source Newspapers

**ALABAMA**
Mobile Tribune
Montgomery Advertiser
Selma Sentinel

**CALIFORNIA**
Equal Rights Expositor (Visalia)
Mariposa Star
Placer Herald
San Francisco Bulletin
San Francisco Press

**CONNECTICUT**
Advertiser and Farmer (Bridgeport)
Hartford Courant
Hartford Press
New Haven Palladium

**DELAWARE**
Wilmington Journal and Statesman

**GEORGIA**
Atlanta Confederacy
Atlanta Intelligencer
Augusta Constitutionalist
Augusta Sentinel
Columbus Enquirer
Columbus Times
Savannah News
Savannah Republican

**ILLINOIS**
Alton Democrat
Alton Telegraph
Belleville Advocate
Cairo Democrat
Carbondale Times
Carlinville Spectator
Central Illinois Gazette (Champaign)
Chicago Daily Democrat
Chicago Journal
Chicago Post
Chicago Press
Chicago Press and Tribune
Chicago Times
Chicago Tribune
Daily Herald (Quincy)
Daily Illinois State Register (Springfield)

Daily Whig and Republican (Quincy). At one time called Quincy Whig.
Free West (Chicago)
Galesburg Democrat
Gallatin County Democrat
Illinois Daily State Journal (Springfield). Name changed several times, but always included word Journal. Established as Sangamon Journal and later called Sangamo Journal.
Illinois Staats-Anzeiger (Springfield)
Joliet Signal
Olney Journal
Paris Beacon
Peoria Daily Message. Was sometimes quoted as Daily Messenger.
Peoria Democratic Press
Peoria Transcript
Rockford Forum
Sangamo Journal (Springfield). See Illinois Daily State Journal.
Schuyler Citizen
Shawneetown Mercury
Vandalia Free Press
Waterloo Advocate

**INDIANA**
Evansville Daily Times
Indianapolis Daily Journal
Indianapolis Daily State Sentinel
Lafayette Journal
Union Democrat (Princeton)
Vincennes Gazette

**IOWA**
Burlington Argus
Burlington Hawkeye
Burlington State Gazette
Davenport Democrat
Dubuque Herald
Iowa Courier (probably Ottumwa)

**KANSAS**
Daily Press (Kansas City)
Kansas National Democrat (Lecompton)
Leavenworth Times

KENTUCKY
*Frankfort Commonwealth*
*Frankfort Yeoman*
*Kentucky Statesman* (Lexington)
*Louisville Daily Courier*
*Louisville Daily Journal*
*Louisville Democrat*
*Winchester National Union*

LOUISIANA
*New Orleans Crescent*
*New Orleans Delta*
*New Orleans Picayune*

MAINE
*Democrat* (Bangor)
*Portland Advertiser*
*Whig and Courier* (Bangor)

MARYLAND
*Baltimore American*
*Baltimore Patriot*
*The Clipper* (Baltimore)
*Daily Exchange* (Baltimore)
*Daily Gazette* (Baltimore)
*Daily Republican* (Baltimore)
*The South* (Baltimore)
*The Sun* (Baltimore)

MASSACHUSETTS
*Boston Advertiser*
*Boston Atlas and Bee.* Also called *Boston Atlas.*
*Boston Daily Evening Transcript*
*Boston Evening Courier*
*Boston Herald*
*Boston Journal*
*Boston Pioneer*
*Boston Post*
*Boston Traveller*
*Journal and Courier* (Lowell)
*The Liberator* (Boston)
*National Aegis* (Worcester)
*Springfield Republican*
*Worcester Spy*

MICHIGAN
*Ann Arbor Journal*
*Detroit Daily Advertiser*
*Detroit Free Press*

MISSISSIPPI
*Oxford Mercury*
*Vicksburg Whig*

MISSOURI
*Missouri Democrat* (St. Louis)
*Missouri Republican* (St. Louis)
*St. Louis News*

NEVADA
*Nevada Gazette* (probably Carson City)

NEW HAMPSHIRE
*Portsmouth Chronicle*

NEW JERSEY
*Evening Journal* (Newark)
*Newark Advertiser*
*The True American* (Trenton)

NEW YORK
*Albany Daily Union*
*Albany Evening Journal*
*Atlas and Argus* (Albany)
*Brooklyn Daily Eagle*
*Brownson's Quarterly Review* (New York)
*Buffalo Daily Courier*
*Buffalo Express*
*Commercial Advertiser* (Buffalo)
*Commercial Advertiser* (New York)
*Daily Courier and Union* (Syracuse)
*Evening Post* (New York)
*Freeman's Journal* (New York)
*Journal of Commerce* (New York)
*Metropolitan Record* (New York)
*New York Daily News*
*New York Day Book*
*New York Evening Express*
*New York Herald*
*The New York Times*
*New York Tribune*
*Rochester Advertiser*
*Rochester Democrat*
*Spirit of the Times* (New York)
*The Sun* (New York)
*Syracuse Journal*
*Syracuse Standard*
*Troy Daily Times*
*Troy Whig*
*The World* (New York)

NORTH CAROLINA
*New Bern Progress*
*Raleigh Press*
*The Standard* (Raleigh)
*Wilmington Herald*
*Wilmington Journal*

OHIO
*Allen County Democrat* (Lima)
*The Banner of Reunion* (Cincinnati)
*Cincinnati Daily Commercial*
*Cincinnati Daily Enquirer*
*Cincinnati Daily Gazette*
*Cincinnati Daily Times*
*Cincinnati Press*
*Clermont County Sun* (Batavia)
*Cleveland Herald*
*Cleveland Leader*
*Cleveland Plain Dealer*

Columbus Gazette
The Crisis (Columbus)
Daily Commercial Register (Sandusky)
Daily Ohio Statesman (Columbus)
Dayton Daily Empire
Dayton Journal
Fremont Messenger
Jackson Express
Logan Gazette
Mansfield Herald
National Democrat (Cleveland)
Ohio Eagle (Lancaster)
Ohio Patriot (Lisbon)
Ohio State Journal (Columbus)
The Patriot (Wellesville)
Stark County Democrat (Canton)
State Capital Fact (Columbus)
Toledo Blade
Toledo Commercial
True Telegraph (Hamilton)
The Union (Somerset)
Xenia News
Xenia Torch-Light

PENNSYLVANIA
The Age (Philadelphia)
Christian Observer (Philadelphia)
Daily Evening Bulletin (Philadelphia)
Daily Evening Journal (Philadelphia)
Evening Telegraph (Philadelphia)
Greensburg Argus
The Jeffersonian (West Chester)
Mentor (Kittaning)
Patriot and Union (Harrisburg)
Philadelphia Inquirer
Pittsburgh Journal
The Press (Philadelphia)
Public Ledger (Philadelphia)
Sunday Dispatch (Philadelphia)
Washington Examiner

RHODE ISLAND
Providence Journal
Providence Post

SOUTH CAROLINA
Charleston Courier
Charleston Mercury

TENNESSEE
Gallatin Courier and Enquirer
Knoxville Register
Knoxville Whig
Knoxville Whig and Rebel Ventilator
Memphis Appeal
Memphis Enquirer

Nashville Patriot
Nashville Republican Banner

TEXAS
Dallas Herald
Galveston News
Houston Telegraph
Texas Republican (Marshall)

VIRGINIA
Alexandria Sentinel
Richmond Dispatch
Richmond Enquirer
Richmond Examiner
Richmond Whig

WASHINGTON, D. C.
Daily Morning Chronicle
National Intelligencer
Washington Constitution
Washington Republican
Washington Sentinel

WEST VIRGINIA
Parkersburg Gazette
Wheeling Daily Intelligencer
Wheeling Daily Register

WISCONSIN
La Crosse Democrat
Milwaukee Sentinel

ENGLAND
Carlisle Examiner
Daily Post (Liverpool)
Evening Standard (London)
Leeds Mercury
London Daily News
London Morning Post
London Spectator
London Times
Morning Star (London)
Punch (London)

FRANCE
Constitutionnel
Époque
Journal des Débats
La Presse
Le Pays
Opinion Nationale
Siècle

IRELAND
Daily Express (Dublin)
Freeman's Journal (Dublin)
Ulster Observer (Belfast)

SCOTLAND
Caledonian Mercury (Edinburgh)
Glasgow Herald

# Bibliography

ABRAMS, RAY H. "The Jeffersonian, Copperhead Newspaper," *The Pennsylvania Magazine of History and Biography*, LVII, July 1933.
——. "Copperhead Newspapers and the Negro," *The Journal of Negro History*, XX, April 1935.
*American Annual Cyclopaedia and Register of Important Events*, 5 vols., D. Appleton & Company, Inc., New York, 1862–1866.
ANDREAS, A. T. *History of Chicago from the Earliest Period to the Present Time*, Vol. II, Chicago, 1885.
ANGLE, PAUL M. *Here I Have Lived*, Abraham Lincoln Association, Springfield, Ill., 1935.
——. *Lincoln, 1854–1861*, Abraham Lincoln Association, Springfield, Ill., 1933.
——. *New Letters and Papers of Lincoln*, Houghton Mifflin Company, Boston, 1930.
*Appleton's Cyclopaedia of American Biography*. James Grant Wilson and John Fiske, editors, 6 vols., D. Appleton & Company, Inc., New York, 1888–1889.
BANCROFT, HUBERT HOWE. *History of Oregon*, Vol. II, The History Company, San Francisco, 1888.
BARBEE, DAVID RANKIN. "President Lincoln and Doctor Gurley," *The Abraham Lincoln Quarterly*, Vol. V, March 1948.
BARTON, WILLIAM E. *The Life of Abraham Lincoln*, Vol. I, Bobbs-Merrill Company, Indianapolis, 1925.
BASLER, ROY P. "James Quay Howard's Notes on Lincoln," *The Abraham Lincoln Quarterly*, Vol. IV, December 1947.
BATES, DAVID HOMER. *Lincoln in the Telegraph Office*, D. Appleton & Company, Inc., New York, 1939.
BEVERIDGE, ALBERT J. *Abraham Lincoln*, 2 vols., Houghton Mifflin Company, Boston, 1928.
BLEYER, WILLARD GROSVENOR. *Main Currents in the History of Journalism*, Houghton Mifflin Company, Boston, 1927.
BROOKS, NOAH. *Abraham Lincoln*, Centennial Edition, G. P. Putnam's Sons, New York, 1888.
——. *Washington in Lincoln's Time*, Century Company, New York, 1896.
BROWNLOW, W. G. *Sketches of the Rise, Progress, and Decline of Secession; With a Narrative of Personal Adventures Among the Rebels*, George W. Childs, Philadelphia, Applegate and Co., Cincinnati, 1862.
BRUCE, JOHN. *Gaudy Century*, Random House, New York, 1948.
BULLARD, F. LAURISTON. *Famous War Correspondents*, Little, Brown & Company, Boston, 1914.
CAREY, CHARLES HENRY. *History of Oregon*, The Pioneer Historical Publishing Company, Chicago-Portland, 1922.
CARPENTER, FRANCIS B. *Six Months at the White House with Abraham Lincoln*, Hurd and Houghton, New York, 1867.
COLLINS, RICHARD H. *History of Kentucky*, Collins and Co., Covington, Ky., 1874.
CORTISSOZ, ROYAL. *The Life of Whitelaw Reid*, Vol. I., Charles Scribner's Sons, New York, 1921.

CURRAN, RUTH GERTRUDE. "David Kellogg Cartter," *Ohio Archaeological and Historical Publications*, XLII, 1933.

*Dayton Newspapers and Their Editors.* One hundred and fourteen pages of bound manuscript at Dayton, Ohio, Public Library. 1937.

DENNETT, TYLER. *Lincoln and the Civil War in the Letters and Diaries of John Hay*, Dodd, Mead & Company, Inc., New York, 1939.

*Dictionary of American Biography.* Vols. III (1929), VI (1931), and XVIII (1936), Charles Scribner's Sons, New York.

DUNLAP, LLOYD A. "President Lincoln and Editor Greeley," *The Abraham Lincoln Quarterly*, Vol. V., June 1948.

ELLIS, L. E. "The Chicago Times During the Civil War," *The Illinois State Historical Society Transactions*, 1932.

FAHRNEY, RALPH RAY. *Horace Greeley and the Tribune in the Civil War*, The Torch Press, Cedar Rapids, Iowa, 1936.

FORNEY, JOHN W. *Anecdotes of Public Men*, 2 vols., Harper & Brothers, New York, 1874.

FUTHEY, J. SMITH, and GILBERT COPE. *History of Chester County, Pennsylvania*, Louis H. Evarts, Philadelphia, 1881.

GILMORE, JAMES R. *Personal Recollections of Abraham Lincoln and the Civil War*, L. C. Page & Company, Boston, 1898.

GRANT, U. S. *Personal Memoirs*, Vol. II., Charles L. Webster & Company, New York, 1886.

GRAY, WOOD. *The Hidden Civil War*, The Viking Press, Inc., New York, 1942.

GREELEY, HORACE. *Recollections of a Busy Life*, Ford, New York, 1868.

GREENE, LAURENCE. *America Goes To Press*, Garden City Publishing Company, Inc., Garden City, New York, 1938.

HALE, EDWARD EVERETT. *James Russell Lowell and His Friends*, Houghton Mifflin Company, Boston, 1899.

*Harper's Pictorial History of the Civil War*, Alfred H. Guernsey and Henry M. Alden, New York, 1866.

HERNDON, WILLIAM H., and JESSE W. WEIK, *Abraham Lincoln, The True Story of a Great Life*, 2 vols., D. Appleton & Company, Inc., New York and London, 1923.

HOOKER, RICHARD. *The Story of an Independent Newspaper*, The Macmillan Company, New York, 1924.

HOOPER, OSMAN C. *History of Journalism in Ohio*, Spahr and Glenn Co., Columbus, 1933.

HOWELLS, W. D. *Years of My Youth*, Harper & Brothers, New York, 1916.

KINSLEY, PHILIP. *The Chicago Tribune*, Vol. I., Alfred A. Knopf, Inc., New York, 1943.

KOERNER, GUSTAVE. *Memoirs*, Thomas J. McCormick, editor, Vol. II, Cedar Rapids, Iowa, 1909.

LAMON, WARD HILL. *Recollections of Abraham Lincoln*, Dorothy Lamon Teillard, editor, The University Press, Cambridge, 1911.

LEE, ALFRED E. *History of the City of Columbus*, Vol. I, Munsell & Co., New York and Chicago, 1892.

LINN, WILLIAM ALEXANDER. *Horace Greeley, Founder and Editor of the New York Tribune*, D. Appleton & Company, Inc., New York, 1903.

LYFORD, JAMES O., editor. *History of Concord, New Hampshire*, Vol. II., The Rumford Press, Concord, N. H., 1903.

McCLURE, A. K. *Abraham Lincoln and Men of War Times*, The Times Publishing Company, Philadelphia, 1892.

MARBLE, MANTON. *Letter to Abraham Lincoln*, privately published, New York, 1867.

MARSHALL, JOHN A. *American Bastile*, Thomas W. Hartley, Philadelphia, 1874.

MATTHEWS, SIDNEY T. "Control of the Baltimore Press During the Civil War," *Maryland Historical Magazine*, XXXVI, June 1941.

MAVERICK, AUGUSTUS. *Henry J. Raymond and the New York Press for Thirty Years*, A. S. Hale and Company, Hartford, Conn., 1870.

MEARNS, DAVID C. *The Lincoln Papers*, 2 vols., Doubleday & Company, Inc., New York, 1948.

MERRIAM, GEORGE S. *The Life and Times of Samuel Bowles*, Vol. I., Century Company, New York, 1885.

MEYERS, WILLIAM STARR. "Correspondence of New York Editors With Governor Bradford," *Maryland Historical Magazine*, III, June 1908.

MILTON, GEORGE FORT. *Abraham Lincoln and the Fifth Column*, The Vanguard Press, New York, 1942.

MORSE, JOHN T., editor, *Diary of Gideon Welles*, Vols. I and II, Houghton Mifflin Company, Boston, 1911.

MOTT, FRANK LUTHER. *American Journalism*, The Macmillan Company, New York, 1941.

NEVINS, ALLAN. *American Press Opinion*, D. C. Heath and Company, Boston, 1928.

——. *The Evening Post, A Century of Journalism*, Boni and Liverwright, New York, 1922.

NICOLAY, JOHN G., and JOHN HAY. *Complete Works of Abraham Lincoln*, 12 vols., Sponsors' Edition, Lincoln Memorial University, Copyright 1894.

O'BRIEN, FRANK M. *The Story of The Sun*, D. Appleton & Company, Inc., New York, 1928.

OGDEN, ROLLO. *Life and Letters of Edwin Lawrence Godkin*, Vol. I, The Macmillan Company, New York, 1907.

PIATT, JOHN JAMES. *The Poems of George D. Prentice*, Robert Clarke & Co., Cincinnati, 1877.

PICKETT, THOMAS J. "Reminiscences of Abraham Lincoln," *The Lincoln Herald*, December 1943, Harrogate, Tenn.

PIERCE, EDWARD L. *Memoir and Letters of Charles Sumner*, Vol. IV, Roberts Bros., Boston, 1877–1893.

POLLARD, JAMES E. *The Presidents and The Press*, The Macmillan Company, New York, 1947.

PRENTICE, GEORGE D. *Prenticeana*, Claxton, Remsen & Heffelfinger, Philadelphia, 1871.

RANDALL, JAMES G. *Constitutional Problems Under Lincoln*, D. Appleton & Company, Inc., New York, 1926.

——. "The Newspaper Problem in its Bearing Upon Military Secrecy During the Civil War," *The American Historical Review*, Vol. XXIII, Macmillan & Co., Ltd., London, 1918.

RANKIN, HENRY B. *Intimate Character Sketches of Abraham Lincoln*, J. B. Lippincott Company, Philadelphia, 1924.

RHODES, JAMES FORD. *History of the United States from the Compromise of 1850*, Vols. II and III, The Macmillan Company, New York, 1904.

RICE, ALLEN THORNDIKE, editor, *Reminiscences of Abraham Lincoln*, North American Publishing Company, New York, 1886.

RICE, WILLIAM B. *The Los Angeles Star*, University of California Press, Berkeley, 1947.

ROBINSON, ELWIN BURNS. "The Press: President Lincoln's Philadelphia Organ," *The Pennsylvania Magazine of History and Biography*, LXV, 1941.

ROSEBOOM, EUGENE H. *The History of the State of Ohio*, Vol. IV, Ohio State Archaeological and Historical Society Publications, Columbus, 1944.

RYAN, DANIEL J. "Lincoln and Ohio," *Ohio Archaeological and Historical Publications*, XXXII, 1923.

SANDBURG, CARL. *Abraham Lincoln, The Prairie Years,* 2 vols., Harcourt, Brace and Company, Inc., New York, 1926.

——. *Abraham Lincoln, The War Years,* Vol. II, Harcourt, Brace and Company, Inc., New York, 1939.

SCHARF, J. THOMAS. *History of Western Maryland,* Vol. II, Louis H. Evarts and Company, Philadelphia, 1882.

——. *The Chronicles of Baltimore,* Turnbull Brothers, Baltimore, 1874.

——. and THOMPSON WESCOTT, *History of Philadelphia.* Vols. I and III, Louis H. Evarts and Company, Philadelphia, 1884.

SEITZ, DON C. *Horace Greeley, Founder of the New York Tribune,* Bobbs-Merrill Company, Indianapolis, 1926.

——. *Lincoln the Politician,* Coward-McCann, New York, 1931.

——. *The James Gordon Bennetts, Father and Son, Proprietors of the New York Herald,* Bobbs-Merrill Company, Indianapolis, 1928.

SHAW, ARCHER H. *The Plain Dealer,* Alfred A. Knopf, Inc., New York, 1942.

SMITH, EDWARD CONRAD. *The Borderland in the Civil War,* The Macmillan Company, New York, 1927.

SMITH, JOSEPH P. *History of the Republican Party in Ohio,* Vol. I, The Lewis Publishing Company, Chicago, 1898.

SPARKS, EDWIN ERLE. *The Lincoln-Douglas Debates of 1858,* Collections of the Illinois State Historical Library, Vol. III, Lincoln Series, Vol. I, Springfield, Ill., 1908.

SPENCER, RICHARD HENRY, editor, *Encyclopaedia of the State of Maryland,* The American Historical Society, New York, 1919.

STEEN, RALPH W. "Texas Newspapers and Abraham Lincoln," *The Southwestern Historical Quarterly,* Vol. LI, January 1948.

STODDARD, HENRY LUTHER. *Horace Greeley, Printer, Editor, Crusader,* G. P. Putnam's Sons, New York, 1946.

TARBELL, IDA M. *In the Footsteps of the Lincolns,* Harper & Brothers, New York, 1924.

TASHER, LUCY LUCILLE. "The Missouri Democrat and the Civil War," *Missouri Historical Review,* XXXI, July 1937.

TAYLOR, EDWIN C. "Whitelaw Reid in Columbus," *Ohio Archaeological and Historical Publications,* XVIII, 1909.

TEBBEL, JOHN. *An American Dynasty,* Doubleday & Company, Inc., New York, 1947.

TEMPLE, OLIVER P. *Notable Men of Tennessee 1833–1875,* Cosmopolitan Press, New York, 1912.

*The History of Sangamon County, Illinois.* Inter-State Publishing Company, Chicago, 1881.

*The Robert Todd Lincoln Collection of the Papers of Abraham Lincoln.* Library of Congress, Microfilm, Illinois State Historical Library.

TRACY, GILBERT A. *Uncollected Letters of Abraham Lincoln,* Houghton Mifflin Company, Boston, 1917.

*Tributes of the Nations to Abraham Lincoln.* Government Printing Office, Washington, 1867.

VENABLE, W. H. *Beginnings of Literary Culture in the Ohio Valley,* Robert Clarke & Co., Cincinnati, 1891.

VILLARD, HENRY. *Memoirs,* Vol. I, Houghton Mifflin Company, Boston, 1904.

WALSH, WILLIAM S. *Abraham Lincoln and the London Punch,* Moffat, Yard and Company, New York, 1909.

WEST, RICHARD S., Jr. *Gideon Welles: Lincoln's Navy Department,* Bobbs-Merrill Company, Indianapolis, 1943.

WILKIE, FRANC B. *Pen and Powder,* Ticknor and Company, Boston, 1888.

WILLIAMS, T. J. C. *History of Frederick County, Maryland,* Vol. I, L. R. Titsworth and Co., Hagerstown, Md., 1910.

WILSON, RUFUS ROCKWELL. *Lincoln in Caricature,* The Primavera Press, Inc., Elmira, N. Y., 1945.

WORKMAN, CHARLES H. "Tablet to Abraham Lincoln at Mansfield," *Ohio Archaeological and Historical Quarterly,* XXXIV, October 1925.

YOUNG, JOHN RUSSELL. *Men and Memories,* Edited by May D. Russell Young, Vol. I, F. Tennyson Neely, New York and London, 1901.

# Index

*Newspapers are listed under the names of the cities in which they appear. See also pages 393 to 395 for a list of quoted and source newspapers.*

Ives, Malcolm, reporter, *New York Herald*, arrested, 132–133

## J

Jackson, Mich., *Patriot*, 257
Jackson, Ohio, *Express*, 198
mobbed, 207
James, B. F., ed., *Tazewell* (Ill.) *Whig*, assists Lincoln's candidacy for Congress, 7–8
Jaquess, James F., 313
Jerome, Leonard W., 275
Jerseyville, Ill., *Democratic Union*, 226
Johnson, Andrew, accused of inciting newspaper mobbing, 339
condition at inauguration, 184
nominated for Vice-President, 305
Johnson, Bradley T., pub., *Maryland Union* (Frederick), becomes Confederate brigadier general, 163
Johnson, Herschel V., 62
Johnston, Maj. Gen. Joseph E., 103
Joliet, Ill., *Signal*, 223, 224
Jones, M. J., city ed., *Patriot and Union* (Harrisburg), imprisoned, 236–238
Joyce, Stephen J., assoc. ed., *Republican* (Baltimore), banished, 161
Judd, Norman B., 19, 22, 52
Junction City, *Kansas Frontier*, mobbed, 152

## K

Kansas-Nebraska Act, 13, 16, 18
Kees, John W., ed., *Circleville* (Ohio) *Watchman*, imprisoned, 199, 200, 202
Kelly, Michael J., pub., *Catholic Mirror* (Baltimore), imprisoned, 161–162
Keokuk, Iowa, *Constitution*, mobbed, 151
Kerr, Orpheus C. (Newell, R. H.), 187
Kimball, Ambrose L., ed., *Essex County Democrat* (Haverhill, Mass.), tarred and feathered, 190
King, Rufus, ed., *Milwaukee Sentinel*, 357
appointed minister to Rome by Lincoln, 76
Kinsella, Thomas, ed., *Brooklyn Daily Eagle*, 122

Kittanning, Pa., *Mentor*, mobbed, 238
Knights of Golden Circle, 260, 326, 335
Knoxville, Tenn., *Register*, 170
*Whig*, 69, 165–169
*Whig and Rebel Ventilator*, 171
Koelkenbeck, L. W., ed., *Republikaner* (Pittsburgh), warned by U.S. district attorney, 238

## L

Lacon, Ill., *Gazette*, "nominates" Lincoln for President, 27
La Crosse, Wis., *Democrat*, 228
Lafayette, Ind., *Argus*, editor beaten, 230
*Journal*, 90
Lamon, Ward Hill, 82, 87, 105–106, 307
Lancaster, Ohio, *Eagle*, mobbed, 202
*Gazette*, 201
Lane, Joseph, 62, 232
Lanphier, Charles H., ed., *Daily Illinois State Register* (Springfield), 2, 8, 13, 223
La Porte, Ind., *Democrat*, mobbed, 230
Leavenworth, Kans., *Inquirer*, mobbed, 153
*Times*, editor jailed, 152–153
*Western Sentinel*, mobbed, 152
Leavitt, Humphrey H., 243, 340–341
Lebanon, Ohio, *Citizen*, mobbed, 202
Lebanon, Pa., *Advertiser*, mobbed, 238
Lee, Gen. Robert E., 172, 176, 271, 274, 346
Leeds, Eng., *Mercury*, 362
Leonardtown, Md., *Beacon*, editor arrested, 164
Letcher, John, 264
Lewiston, Ill., *Fulton Ledger*, 224
Lexington, Ky., *Statesman*, 212
Lincoln, Abraham, appoints news men to office, 76
assassinated, 347–348
as Congressman, 7–10
debates with Douglas, 21–26
defeated for Senate by Douglas, 26
dubbed "rail splitter," 49–50
enters Washington incognito, 87–89
fears hostile press, 74–75
jokes about editors, 97–98
leaves Springfield for Washington, 79–81
letter to Bryant, 281
letters from editors, 184–186

■001910892